For John Stewart
my gratitude
Joan Crawford

FILMARAMA

Volume II

The Flaming Years,

1920-1929

compiled by

JOHN STEWART

76470

The Scarecrow Press, Inc.

Metuchen, N.J.   1977

Library of Congress Cataloging in Publication Data   (Revised)

Stewart, John, 1920-
 Filmarama.

   Includes index.
   CONTENTS: v. 1.   The formidable years, 1893-1919.
v. 2.   The flaming years, 1920-1929.
     1.   Moving-picture actors and actresses.   2.   Moving-
pictures--Indexes.   I.   Title.
PN1998. A2S67   791. 43'028'0922 [B]   75-2440
ISBN 0-8108-0802-1 (v. I)
ISBN 0-8108-1008-5 (v. II)

Manufactured in the United States of America

To

MISS JOAN CRAWFORD

whose first film, <u>Pretty Ladies</u>, started her
on a career spanning 51 years (longest in film
history) and has earned her the title of First
Lady of American Films. Miss Crawford is
a beautiful lady not only in looks, talent, and
business, but most importantly as a person.

INTRODUCTION

The decade of the twenties, which we have called The
Flaming Years, was known by many names. Frederick Lewis
Allen dubbed it the New Freedom and the New Era. To most,
it was the Roaring Twenties. F. Scott Fitzgerald named it
the Jazz Age. "It was," he wrote, "an age of miracles, it
was an age of art, it was an age of excess, and it was an
age of satire. In the real dark night of the soul it is always
three o'clock in the morning."

Horse and buggy Victorian morals drowned in a deluge
of bathtub gin. It was a time to plunge into the new American way. Flappers raised their skirts and bobbed their hair.
Joe College sported raccoon coats and hip flasks. Flaming
Youth shimmied, foxtrotted and Charlestoned from coast to
coast. Alice White portrayed Dorothy in Paramount's version
of Gentlemen Prefer Blondes. She made such films as Hot
Stuff and Naughty Baby.

Elinor Glyn wrote It, but Clara Bow, the naughty baby
of the twenties was the IT GIRL, moving from Flappers to
Flaming Youth with shocking abandon. In a 1951 interview,
Miss Bow stated: "We did as we pleased. We had individ-
uality. We stayed up late. We dressed the way we wanted.
I'd whiz down Sunset Boulevard in my open Kissel, flaming
red of course, with seven red chow dogs to match my hair.
Today they're [stars] different and end up with better health.
But we had more fun."

The Flaming Years may have been fun, but beneath
the surface were tragedies, beginning in 1920 with the poison
death of Olive Thomas. The Virginia Rappe-Fatty Arbuckle
scandal followed in 1921. William Desmond Taylor's murder
shattered the careers of Mabel Normand and Mary Miles
Minter in 1922. Drink and drugs took the lives of Art
Acord, Barbara La Marr, Wallace Reid and many others who

v

thought they were having fun.

Myths and legends of the twenties filled the motion
picture screens as a compendium of the pervading nonsense,
cynicism, speakeasy wit, and debauchery of the times.

Then, as now, there were bad films, but the industry
would have burned itself out during those flaming years if
good films had not outnumbered the bad. The scope of films
grew beyond all expectations as a medium of entertainment
and education. At the height of the flames came a depres-
sion that cooled the fire, and from its embers came crackling
sounds. Sounds that grew into the talkies.

Many performers, burned by sound, were soon lost or
forgotten. Volume II of Filmarama sifts through the ashes
to preserve their names. Without them and their enormous
zest for life, films could not have grown beyond The Flaming
Years.

I have tried to make these first two volumes of Filmarama not only a valuable reference, but a lasting tribute to
the artists. A sort of all time Who's Who of films, from
extras to stars.

During the years 1920-1929 a tendency remained to use
initials, madame, monsieur, and Mrs. for names. Princes
and Princesses, Kings and Queens made film appearances, as
did various sports figures. Many people played but a brief
moment and disappeared from the screen. Some turned to
writing, producing, or directing--others just seemed to van-
ish. When talkies replaced silents, voices killed off careers
like a plague.

In those days it was the habit of Europeans to retitle
American films and vice versa. All titles are given and
cross-referenced in the index. In Volume VI, the Explosive
Years, a section will be devoted to title changes through the
years. England seemed to enjoy changing cast names of
American films to add British flavor and identification; the
character names in this work are those given in the original
scripts.

Cartoons came into popularity, especially when a young
man from Chicago joined the Kansas City Film Ad Company.
He made animated commercials in 1920 and called them

Newman Laugh-O-Grams, each running less than a minute
duration.   In 1922 he started an animation firm of his own
called Laugh-O-Grams.   In 1923, Alice in Cartoonland, a
combination of live action and animation was born; it died in
1926.   In 1927 came Oswald, the Lucky Rabbit, followed in
1928 by the inimitable Mortimer Mouse, quickly rechristened
Mickey, along with Minnie Mouse and Peg-leg Pete.   Walt
Disney, born in 1901, reigned as King of Animation from
1922 until his death in 1966.   Laugh-O-Grams and Alice in
Cartoonland titles are listed under their name.   Oswald's
screen credits are listed only through 1928 while created under Disney; the series was then taken over by Walter Lantz
and Universal Studios.

        One unusual item in this volume should be mentioned
here.   During its early years the cinema brought Shakespeare
(in many guises) to larger audiences than ever before.   An
entry is included here, SHAKESPEARE IN SILENT FILMS,
which lists all those silents appearing from 1889 to 1929 which
were based on the Bard's works.

        Special thanks are due far too many people to list their
names, but you know who you are.   Reference sources are
so extensive that a book as large as this one would be needed
to catalogue them.   As to errors and omissions, put the
blame where it belongs--on me.   I'd greatly appreciate hear-
ing from you in this area.   Write me in care of the publisher.

                                            John Stewart

Covina, California
1975

FILMARAMA

- A -

1
AASEN, John*
Why Worry?

2
ABBAS, Hector*
Wandering Jew, The (Zapportas)

3
ABBE, Jack*
Tale of Two Worlds, A (The Worm)

4
ABBOTT, Marion*
Tol'able David (Mother Kinemon)

5
ABEL, Alfred (1880-1939)
Dr. Mabuse the Gambler (Count Tolst)
Eine Du Barry von Heute [A Modern DuBarry] (Sillon)
Die Flamme [The Flame] /aka/ Montmartre (Leduc's friend)
Gold
Der Leibgardist [The Guardsman]
Metropolis (Jon Fredersen; John Masterman in U.S.)
Phantom, The
Prinzessin Olala [Princess Olala] /aka/ Art of Love (bit)

6
ABEL, Robert*
Under the Greenwood Tree (Penny)

7
ABER, Johnny*
Boxing Gloves

8
ACADEMY AWARDS
†Indicates author's choice if different from winner.

1927/28
Best Actress: Janet Gaynor (Seventh Heaven, Street Angel, Sunrise)
Nominees: Louise Dresser (A Ship Comes In)
Gloria Swanson (Sadie Thompson)

Best Actor: Emil Jannings (The Last Command, The Way of All Flesh)
Nominees: Richard Barthelmess (The Noose, The Patent Leather Kid)
Charlie Chaplin (The Circus)

Best Picture: Wings
Nominees: The Last Command
The Racket
Seventh Heaven†
The Way of All Flesh

1928/29
Best Actress: Mary Pickford (Coquette)
Nominees: Ruth Chatterton (Mme. X)
Betty Compson (The Barker)
Jeanne Eagles (The Letter)
Bessie Love (The Broadway Melody)

Best Actor: Warner Baxter (In Old Arizona)
Nominees: George Bancroft (Thunderbolt)
Chester Morris (Alibi)†
Paul Muni (The Valiant)

---

*Indicates date is unknown.
 Stage credits represent New York Productions, unless otherwise indicated and are representative only, not complete.
 Dates of film production or release and companies are listed in the index, followed by the artist numbers.

Lewis Stone (The
Patriot)

Best Picture: The Broadway
Melody
Nominees: Alibi†
Hollywood Revue
In Old Arizona
The Patriot

1929/30
Best Actress: Norma Shearer (The
Divorcee)
Nominees: Nancy Carroll (The Dev-
il's Holiday)
Ruth Chatterton (Sarah
and Son)
Greta Garbo (Anna
Christie, Romance)†
Norma Shearer (Their
Own Desire)
Gloria Swanson (The
Trespasser)

Best Actor: George Arliss (Dis-
raeli)
Nominees: George Arliss (The
Green Goddess)
Wallace Beery (The Big
House)
Maurice Chevalier (The
Love Parade, The Big Pond)
Ronald Colman (Bulldog
Drummond, Condemned)
Lawrence Tibbett (The
Rogue Song)

Best Picture: All Quiet on the
Western Front
Nominees: The Big House
Disraeli
The Divorcee
The Love Parade

9
ACHARD, Marcel*
Entra'acte

10
ACHTERBERG, Fritz*
Hamlet (Fortinbras)

11
ACKER, Eugene*
Vanity Fair (Max)

12
ACKER, Jean*
Affairs of Anatol, The
Arabian Knight, The
Brave Heart
Brewster's Millions
Her Own Money
Round Up, The
Scarlet Shawl, The
See My Lawyer
Wealth
Woman in Chains

13
ACKROYD, Jack*
Better 'Ole, The
Isle of Lost Ships, The

14
ACORD, Art (1890-1931)
Call of Courage
Circus Cyclone
Hard Fists
His Last Battle
In the Days of Buffalo Bill [serial]
Lazy Lightning
Loco Luck
Man from the West
Moon Riders, The [serial]
Oregon Trail, The [serial]
Pursued
Riding Rascal
Rustler's Ranch
Scrappin' Kid, The
Set Free
Set Up, The
Sky High Corral
Spurs and Saddles
Three in Exile
Two Gun O'Brien
Western Pluck
Western Rover
White Horseman, The
White Outlaw
Winners of the West [serial]

15
ACOSTA, Enrique*
Don Q, Son of Zorro (Ramon)

16
ADAIR, Alice*
Private Life of Helen of Troy, The
(Aphrodite)
Saturday Night Kid, The (girl)
Wild Party, The (Maisie)

17
ADAIR, Josephine*
Third Alarm, The (Alice M'Dowell)

18
ADAIR, Tim*
Canary Murder Case, The (George
   Y. Harvey)

19
ADALBERT, Max*
Destiny /aka/ Between Worlds, The
   Tired Death, The Three Lights
Die Flamme [The Flame] /aka/
   Montmartre

20
ADAMOWSKA, Helenka /aka/ Hel-
   ena*
Grit (Annie Hart)
Second Fiddle

21
ADAMS, Claire*
Big Parade, The (Justyn Reed)
Brass Commandments
Certain Rich Man, A
Do and Dare
Dwelling Place of Light
Fast Set, The (Fay Colleen)
Great Lover, The
Helen's Babies (Helen Lawrence)
In Arabia
Just Tony
Lure of Egypt, The
Man of the Forest, The
Married Alive
Money Changers, The
Mysterious Rider, The
Oh, You Tony!
Penalty, The (Barbara)
Riders of the Dawn
Scarlet Car, The
Sea Wolf, The
Spenders, The
White Silence
Yellow Fingers

22
ADAMS, Ernie S. *
Blackbird, The (Bertie's No. 2 Man)
Lawless Legion, The
Nevada
Saturday Night Kid, The (gambler)

23
ADAMS, Harry*
Music Fiends

24
ADAMS, Jimmie*
Christie player 22, 27-28
Educational player 24-26
Hallroom Boys [series]
Triumph (a painter)

25
ADAMS, Kathryn*
Pathé player 20

26
ADAMS, Lionel*
Fantomas [serial]
Janice Meredith (Thomas Jefferson)
Success

27
ADAMS, Stella*
Me, Gangster

28
ADORÉE, Renée (Jeanne de la Fonte)
   (1898-1933)
Back to God's Country
Bandolero
Big Parade, The (Melisande)
Blackbird, The (Fifi)
Blarney
Certain Young Man, A
Cossacks, The (Maryana)
Count of Monte Cristo, The /aka/
   Monte Cristo (Eugenie Danglars)
Day Dreams
Escape /aka/ The Exquisite Sinner
Eternal Struggle, The
Flaming Forest, The
Forbidden House, The
Heaven on Earth
Hollywood Revue of 1929
Honor First
La Boheme (Musette)
Law Bringers, The
Made in Heaven
Man and Maid
Man's Mate, A
Mating Call
Michigan Kid, The
Mr. Wu (Nang Ping)
Mixed Faces
Mystic Faces
On Ze Boulevard
Pagan, The
Parisian Nights
Redemption (Masha)
Self Made Man, A
Show, The
Show People (cameo)

Six Fifty
Spieler, The
Strongest, The
Tide of the Empire
Tin Gods
West of Chicago

29
AESOP FABLES (Cartoons)
Pathé 23-28

30
AGAR-LYONS, Harry*
Henry, King of Navarre (Pierre)

31
AGNEW, Robert (1899-)
Bluebeard's Eighth Wife (Albert de
    Marceau)
Clarence
College Hero
Dancing Days
Dangerous Adventure [serial]
Down the Stretch
Frisky Mrs. Johnson
Great Love, The
Heart of Broadway
Heart of Salome, The
Highest Law, The
Kick-In
Marriage Maker, The
Metro player 23
Midnight Taxi
Only 38
Passion Flower
Prince of Headwaiters
Prodigal Daughters (Lester Hodge)
Quarantined Rivals
Racing Blood
She's My Baby
Sign on the Door, The
Sin that Was His, The
Slightly Used
Snowbound
Spanish Dancer, The (Juan)
Sporting Duchess, The
Taxi Mystery, The
Tessie
Unknown Treasures /aka/ The
    House Behind the Hedge
Valley of Doubt
Wandering Girls
Wild Oats Lane
Wine (Harry Van Alstyne)
Without Fear
Woman Proof
Wonderful Thing, The

32
AHERNE, Brian (Brian de Lacy
    Aherne) (1902-)
Eleventh Commandment, The
King of the Castle
Safety First
Shooting Stars
Squire of Long Hadley, The
Underground
Woman Redeemed, A

33
AHERNE, Lassie Lou*
Uncle Tom's Cabin (Little Harry)

34
AHERNE, Patrick (1901-1970)
Blinkeyes (the Basher)

35
AIKEN, Mary*
Charley's Aunt (Amy)

36
AINLEY, Henry (1879-1945)
Armistice (voice)
Build Thy House
Inscrutable Drew Investigator [series]
Money
Royal Oak, The
Sally Bishop (John)

37
AINSWORTH, Cupid*
Big News (Vera Wilson)

38
AINSWORTH, Phil*
Chorus Girl's Romance, A (Steve
    Reynolds)

39
AINSWORTH, Sydney /aka/ Sidney
    (1872-1922)
Branding Iron, The (Jasper Morena)
Doubling for Romeo
Madame X

40
AINSWORTH, Virginia*
Passion's Playground

41
AITKEN, Spottiswoode (-1933)
Around the World in 18 Days [serial]
At the End of the World
Count of Monte Cristo, The /aka/
    Monte Cristo (Abbe)

Dangerous Love
Merry-Go-Round (Minister of War)
Nomads of the North (Old Roland)
Reputation
Trap, The (the Factor)
Triumph (Torrini)
Unknown Wife
White Circle, The
Young Rajah, The

42
AKIN, Mary*
My Son (Rosa Pina)

43
ALBANESI, Meggie*
Skin Game, The (Jill)

44
ALBERNI, Luis (1857-1962)
Bright Shawl, The (Vincente Escobar)

45
ALBERS, Hans (1892-1960)
Eine DuBarry von Heute [A Modern DuBarry] (Darius Kerbelian)
Midsummer Night's Dream, A (Demetrius)
Prinzessin Olala [Princess Olala] /aka/ Art of Love (René)

46
ALBERTI, Fritz*
Cafe Electric /aka/ Wenn ein Weib den Weg Verliert [When a Woman Loses Her Way] (Göttlinger)

47
ALBERTSON, Coit*
Restless Wives
Why Girls Leave Home

48
ALBERTSON, Frank (1909-1964)
Blue Skies
Farmer's Daughter, The
Prep and Pep
Salute
Son of the Gods (Kicker)
Words and Music

49
ALBRIGHT, Wally, Jr.*
Thunder (Davey)
Trespasser, The (Jack Merrick)

50
ALCORN, Olive Ann*
Phantom of the Opera, The (La Sorelli)

51
ALDEN, Mary*
April Fool
Bond Boy
Brown of Harvard
Cossacks, The (Lukashka's mother)
Eagle's Feather, The
Earth Woman
Fools for Luck (Mrs. Hunter)
Girl Overboard
Goldwyn player 21
Has the World Gone Mad?
Hidden Woman, The (Mrs. Randolph)
Honest Hutch
Inferior Sex, The
Joy Girl, The
Ladies of the Mob ("Soft Annie")
Lovey Mary
Man with Two Mothers
Milestones (Rose Sibley)
Nobody's Girl
Notoriety
Old Nest, The
Parted Curtain
Plastic Age, The (Mrs. Carver)
Port of Dreams
Potters, The (Ma Potter)
Sawdust Paradise, The
Siege
Silk Husbands and Calico Wives
Someone to Love
Tents of Allah
Trust Your Wife
Witching Hour
Woman's Woman, A

52
ALDERSON, Erville*
America /aka/ Love and Sacrifice (Justice Montague)
Fazil (Iman Idris)
Isn't Life Wonderful? (Judge Henry L. Foster)
White Rose, The (Man of the World)

53
ALEE*
Nanook of the North (the Son)

54
ALEXANDER, Ben (Nicholas Benton Alexander) (1911-1969)
Boy of Mine

Divine Lady, The
Family Honor
Fighting for Fame [serial]
First National player 22
Frivolous Sal
Heart Line
Highbinders, The
In the Name of the Law
Penrod and Sam (Penrod Schofield)
River Pirate
Scotty of the Scouts [serial]
Self-Made Failure, A
Triflers

55
ALEXANDER, Dick*
Godless Girl, The (a guard)
Mysterious Lady, The

56
ALEXANDER, Georg*
Prinzessin Olala [Princess Olala]
    /aka/ Art of Love (the Chamber-
    lain)

57
ALEXANDER, Muriel*
Skin Game, The (Anna)

58
ALEXANDER, Richard*
Sin Sister (a trader)

59
ALEXANDRESCO*
Arab, The (Oulad Nile)

60
ALEXANDROV, Grigori*
Potemkin (Chief Officer Gilyarovsky)
Stachka /aka/ Strike

61
ALI, George*
Peter Pan (Nana, the dog)

62
ALICE in Cartoonland (1923-1926)
    Live action and animation. See:
    Marjorie Gay
Alice and the Dog Catcher 24
Alice and the Three Bears 24
Alice and the Toreador 24
Alice and the Wild West Show 24
Alice at the Carnival 26
Alice at the Rodeo 26
Alice Cans the Cannibals 24
Alice Charms the Fish 26

Alice Chops the Suey 25
Alice Cuts the Ice 26
Alice Foils the Pirates 26
Alice Gets Strung 25
Alice Helps the Romance 26
Alice Hunting in Africa 24
Alice in Dutch at School 24
Alice in the Alps 26
Alice in the Big League 26
Alice in the Jungle 25
Alice in the Klondike 26
Alice in the Wooly West 26
Alice Is Stage Struck 25
Alice Loses Out 25
Alice on the Farm 25
Alice Picks the Champ 25
Alice Plays Cupid 25
Alice Plays the Pipers 24
Alice Rattled by Rats 25
Alice Solves the Puzzle 25
Alice the Beach Nut 26
Alice the Collegiate 26
Alice the Fire Fighter 26
Alice the Golf Bug 26
Alice the Jail Bird 26
Alice the Lumber Jack 26
Alice the Peacemaker 24
Alice the Whaler 26
Alice Wins the Derby 26
Alice's Auto Race 26
Alice's Balloon Race 25
Alice's Brown Derby 26
Alice's Channel Swim 26
Alice's Circus Daze 26
Alice's Day at Sea 24
Alice's Egg Plant 25
Alice's Fishy Story 24
Alice's Knaughty Knight 26
Alice's Little Parade 25
Alice's Medicine Show 26
Alice's Monkey Business 26
Alice's Mysterious Mystery 25
Alice's Ornery Orphan 25
Alice's Picnic 26
Alice's Spanish Guitar 26
Alice's Spooky Adventure 24
Alice's Three Bad Eggs 26
Alice's Tin Pony 25
Alice's Wonderland 23

63
ALLAN, Hugh*
Annapolis
Beware of Married Men
Birds of Prey
Cruel Truth
Dress Parade
Good Time Charley

Hold 'Em Yale!
Object Alimony
Plastered in Paris
Sally
Sin Town
Tiger's Shadow, The [serial]
Voice of the Storm
What Happened to Father?
Wild Beauty

64
ALLAN, Marguerite*
Under the Greenwood Tree (Fancy)

65
ALLEN, Alfred*
Flying Fleet, The

66
ALLEN, C. J.*
Foolish Wives (Albert I, Prince of
  Monaco)

67
ALLEN, Diana*
Beyond the Rainbow (Frances Gard-
  ner)
Flying Fists
Get-Rich-Quick Wallingford (Ger-
  trude Dempsey)

68
ALLEN, Dorothy*
Beyond Price
If Winter Comes (High Jinks)
Over the Hill (Agulutia)

69
ALLEN, Edith*
Scaramouche (Climene Binet)

70
ALLEN, Florence*
Ace of Scotland Yard [serial] (Lady
  Diana)

71
ALLEN, Gracie (1902-1964)
Burns and Allen in Lambchops

72
ALLEN, Harry*
Two Lovers (Jean)

73
ALLEN, Hugh*
Dress Parade

74
ALLEN, Joseph*
Seven Keys to Baldpate
Stage:
Tavern, The (the hired man) Chicago
  21

75
ALLEN, Lester (1891-1949)
Pusher-in-the-Face, The
Stage:
Top Speed (Elmer Peters) 29
Ziegfeld Follies of 1921
Ziegfeld Follies of 1922
Ziegfeld Follies of 1924

76
ALLEN, Marguerite*
Widdecombe Affair, The (the squire's
  daughter)

77
ALLEN, Phyllis*
Pay Day

78
ALLEN, Ricca*
Close Harmony

79
ALLEN, Sam*
Sea Beast, The (sea captain)

80
ALLEN, Willi*
Jew of Mestri, The (Ali)

81
ALLGOOD, Sara (Sally Allgood) (1883-
  1950)
Blackmail (Mrs. White)

82
ALLISON, May (1895-)
Are All Men Alike?
Big Game
Cheater, The
City, The
Extravagance
First National player 26
Flapper Wives
Greater Glory, The
Held in Trust
I Want My Man
Marriage of William Ashe, The
Men of Steel
Mismates
One Increasing Purpose

Telephone Girl
Viennese Melody, The
Walk-Offs, The
Woman Who Fooled Herself, The

83
ALLISTER, Claude (William Claud
  Michel Palmer) (1894-1970)
Bulldog Drummond (Algy)
Charming Sinners, The
Monte Carlo
Three Live Ghosts
Trial of Mary Dugan, The (Henry
  Plaisted)

84
ALLWORTH, Frank*
Manhandled (salesman)
That Royale Girl (Oliver)

85
ALSEN, Elsa*
Rogue Song, The (Yegor's mother)

86
ALTEM, Mlle.*
Three Musketeers, The (Dona Este-
  fona)

87
ALVARADO, Don (José Paige)
  (1904-1967)
Apache
Battle of the Sexes (Babe Winsor)
Breakfast at Sunrise
Bridge of San Luis Rey, The (Manu-
  el)
Driftwood
Drums of Love (Count Leonardo de
  Alvia)
Loves of Carmen, The (Don José)
Monkey Talks
No Other Woman
Rio Rita (Roberto Ferguson)
Scarlet Lady
United Artists player 27

88
AMES, Gerald (1881-1933)
Amazing Quest of Mr. Ernest Bliss,
  The (Darrington)
Anna the Adventuress
Aylwyn
Flights Through the Ages [series]
God's Prodigal
Helen of Four Gates
John Forrest Finds Himself
King's Highway, The

Light Woman, A
Little People, The
Loves of Queen Mary of Scots, The
Mr. Justice Raffles
Mrs. Erricker's Reputation
Once Aboard the Lugger
Rising Generation, The
Royal Divorce, A
Tansy
Wild Heather
Woman Who Obeyed, The

89
AMES, Percy*
Adam and Eva

90
AMES, Robert (1889-)
Black Waters
Marianne
Nix on Dames
Rich People (Noel Nevins)
Three Faces East
Trespasser, The (Jack Merrick)
Voice of the City
Stage:
Hero, The (Oswald Lane) 21
Icebound (Ben Jordan) 23

91
AMOR, Carlos*
Ramona (a sheep herder)

92
ANDER, Charlotte*
Midsummer Night's Dream, A (Hermia)
Tragödie der Lieb [Tragedy of Love]

93
ANDERS, Glenn (1889-)
Sally of the Sawdust (Leon)
Stage:
Demi-Virgin, The (Wally Dean) 21
Dynamo (Reuben Light) 29
Hell-Bent fer Heaven (Andy Lowry) 24
Scrambled Wives (Larry McLeod) 20
Strange Interlude (Edmund Darrell) 28
They Knew What They Wanted (Joe) 24

94
ANDERSEN, John*
Witchcraft Through the Ages /aka/
  Häxan

95
ANDERSON, C. E. /aka/ Cap*
Border Cavalier
California Mail, The

Love Gambler, The
Uncle Tom's Cabin (Johnson)

96
ANDERSON, Claire*
Fatal Sign, The [serial]
Yellow Stain, The

97
ANDERSON, Gilbert M. "Bronco
Billy" (Max Aaronson) (1882-
1970)
Greater Duty

98
ANDERSON, James*
Freshman, The (college hero)

99
ANDERSON, Mary (1859-1940)
Half-Breed, The (Evelyn Huntington)

100
ANDERSON, Robert*
Once to Every Woman (Phineas
Scudder)
Temptress, The

101
ANDRA, Anny*
Blackmail

102
ANDREW, M.*
Two Little Vagabonds (the Cough
Drop)

103
ANDREWS, Frank*
Warrens of Virginia, The (General
Griffin)

104
ANDREYOR, Yvette*
Chantelouve

105
ANGELO, Jean*
Atlantide (Capt. Morhange)
La Ronde Infernale

106
ANNABELLA (Suzanne Charpentier)
(1909-)
La Bacarolle d' Amour
Napoleon

107
ANNAND, James*
Amazing Quest of Mr. Ernest Bliss,
The (Mr. Crowley)

108
ANSON, Ina*
Shooting of Dan McGrew, The (a dan-
cer)

109
ANSON, Laura*
Easy Road, The

110
ANTONOV, Alexander*
Potemkin (Vakulinchuk)
Stachka /aka/ Strike
Tanka-Trakitirschitsa /aka/ Portin
Otsa, Against Her Father, and
Tanka, the Innkeeper

111
AOKI, Tsuru (1892-1962)
Breath of the Gods
Five Days to Live
Locked Lips
Tokio Siren, A

112
APFEL, Oscar (-1938)
Brewster's Millions
Half Way to Heaven
Marianne
Not Quite Decent
Romance of the Underworld, A
Smiling Irish Eyes
True Heaven
Valley of Hunted Men

113
APOLON, Uni*
Maré Nostrum [Our Sea] (The Triton)

114
APPLEGATE, Roy*
Sally of the Sawdust (detective)
Yolanda (Sir Karl de Pitti)

115
ARBUCKLE, Andrew*
Quincy Adams Sawyer
Son of Wallingford, The (Talbot Curtis)

116
ARBUCKLE, Maclyn (1866-1931)
Gilded Highway, The
Janice Meredith (Squire Meredith)

Mr. Bingle
Mr. Potter of Texas
No Laughing Matter
Prodigal Judge, The
Squire Phin
That Old Gang of Mine   .
Welcome to Our City
Yolanda (Bishop LaBalue)

117
ARBUCKLE, Maclyn, Mrs. *
Janice Meredith (Martha Washington)

118
ARBUCKLE, Roscoe "Fatty" (Roscoe
   Conklin Arbuckle) /aka/ Will B.
   Good (1887-1933)
Brewster's Millions
Crazy to Marry
Dollar a Year Man, The
Gasoline Gus
Life of the Party, The
Out West
Paramount player 21
Red Mill, The
Round Up, The
Special Delivery
Travelling Salesman, A
Windy Riley Goes to Hollywood
Stage:
Baby Mine (Jimmy Jenks) 27

119
ARCHDALL, Mabel*
Wee MacGreegor's Sweetheart (Aunt
   Purdie)

120
ARDEN, Mildred*
Janice Meredith (Tabitha Larkin)

121
ARGUS, Edwin*
Janice Meredith (Louis XVI)
Scaramouche (Louis XVI)

122
ARLEGA, Sophie*
Sadie Thompson (Amiena)

123
ARLEN, Richard (Richard Van Mat-
   timore) (1900-1976)
Beggars of Life
Behind the Front
Blood Ship, The
Coast of Folly (bit)
Dangerous Curves (Larry Lee)

Enchanted Hill, The
Feel My Pulse
Figures Don't Lie
Four Feathers, The (Harry Feversham)
In the Name of Love
Ladies of the Mob (Red)
Man I Love, The
Manhattan Cocktail (Fred)
Padlocked
Rolled Stockings
Sally in Our Alley
She's a Sheik
Thunderbolt
Under the Tonto Rim
Vengeance of the Deep
Virginian, The (Steve)
Wings (David Armstrong)

124
ARLISS, Florence (Florence Montgomery)*
Disraeli (Lady Beaconsfield) (two versions)

125
ARLISS, George (George Agustus Andrews) (1868-1946) Born in London, April 10, son of William
   Arliss-Andrews. Grey hair,
   brown eyes, 5'9". Married Florence Montgomery Sept. 16, 1899.
   Began career in London with his
   own amateur drama society.
   First stage appearance in London
   1887. He acted with Mrs. Patrick
   Campbell. In 1901, American
   producer, George Taylor arranged
   an American tour for Mr. Arliss
   and Mrs. Campbell. His film de-
   but was in Disraeli--1922. Died
   in London Feb. 5, 1946. ACAD-
   EMY AWARD 1929/30--Disraeli.
   ACADEMY NOMINATION 1929/30--
   The Green Goddess.
Devil, The
Disraeli (Title role) (two versions)
Green Goddess, The (Rajah of Rukh)
   (two versions)
Man Who Played God, The
Ruling Passion, The
Twenty Dollars a Week
Stage:
Across Her Path - London 1890
Becky Sharp (Marquis of Steyne) 04
Darling of the Gods (Zakkuri) 02
Devil, The (Title role) 08
Disraeli (Title role) 11
Green Goddess, The (Rajah of Rukh) 21

Hedda Gabler (Judge Brack) 04
Merchant of Venice, The (Shylock) 28
Mr. and Mrs. Daventry - London
　1900
Old English (Sylvanus Heythrop) 24
Paganini (Nicolo Paganini) 16
Poldekin (Title role) 20

126
ARMAND, Margot*
First Born, The (Sylvia Finlay)

127
ARMAND-BERNARD, Monsieur*
Three Musketeers, The (Planchet)

128
ARMETTA, Henry (1888-1945)
Alias Jimmy Valentine
Homesick
In Old Arizona (Barber)
Jazz Heaven
Lady of the Pavements (Papa Pierre)
Love, Live, and Laugh
Love Song, The
Street Angel (Masetto)
Trespasser, The (Barber)

129
ARMIDA (1913-)
General Crack (Fidelia)
Show of Shows, The

130
ARMSTRONG, Margot*
Comin' Thro' the Rye (Alice Adair)

131
ARMSTRONG, Marguerite--see:
　Miss DuPont

132
ARMSTRONG, Robert (1896-1973)
Baby Cyclone
Big News (Steve Banks)
Boys Will Be Boys
Calebrity, The
Cop, The
Girl in Every Port, A (Salamie)
Honey Girl
Is Zat So?
Judy
Leatherneck, The
Leopard Lady, The
Main Event, The
Man Who Came Back, The
Ned McCobb's Daughter (Babe Cal-
　lahan)

New Brooms
Oh, Yeah!
Racketeer, The (Mahlon Keane)
Shady Lady
Shavings
Show Folks (Owens)
Silent Voice
Square Crooks
Sure Fire
War and Women
Woman from Hell
Stage:
Is Zat So? (Eddie "Chick" Cowan) 25

133
ARNHEIN, Gus and Orchestra (1897-
　1955)
Broadway (themselves)
Street Girl (themselves)

134
ARNO, Siegfried /aka/ Sig (Siegfried
　Aron) (1895-)
Diary of a Lost Girl
Loves of Jeanne Ney, The
Manon Lescaut (Lescaut)
Pandora's Box

135
ARNOLD, Gertrude*
Die Nibelungen /aka/ The Nibelungs
　(Ute)

136
ARNOLD, Jessie*
Idol of the North, The (big blonde)
Playing with Souls

137
ARNST, Bobbe*
Night Club

138
ARTAULD, Antonin*
Passion of Joan of Arc, The

139
ARTEGA, Sophia--see: Sophie Arlega

140
ARTHUR, George K. (George K. A.
　Brest) (1884-1952)
All at Sea
Almost a Lady
Baby Mine
Bardelys the Magnificient (de Saint
　Eustache)
Big Parade, The

Boob, The (Peter)
Boy Friend, The
Brotherly Love
China Bound
Circus Rookies
Dear Fool, A
Detectives
Don't Marry for Money
Escape /aka/ The Exquisite Sinner
Gingham Girl
Her Sister from Paris
Hollywood
Hollywood Revue of 1929
In Old Heidelberg
Irene
Kiki
Kipps
Lamp in the Desert
Last of Mrs. Cheyney, The (George)
Lights of Old Broadway (Andy)
Lovers
Madness of Youth
Paddy the Next Best Thing (Jack O'Hara)
Pretty Ladies
Road Show
Rookies
Salvation Hunters, The
Show People (cameo)
Spring Fever (Eustace Twekabury)
Student Prince, The (a student)
Sunny Side Up
Tillie the Toiler (Mr. Whipple)
Waning Sex, The
Wheels of Chance
When the Wife's Away
Wickedness Preferred

141
ARTHUR, Jean (Gladys Georgianna
   Greene) (1908-   )
Bigger and Better Blondes
Block Signal, The
Born to Battle
Broken Gates
Brotherly Love
Cameo Kirby
Canary Murder Case, The (Alice La-
   Fosse)
Case Dismissed
College Boob, The
Cowboy Cop, The
Drug Store Cowboy
Easy Come, Easy Go
Eight Cylinder Bull
Fast and Fearless
Fighting Cheat, The
Flying Luck
Fox player 23

Galloping On 27
Greene Murder Case, The (Ada Greene)
Half Way to Heaven
Hello, Lafayette /aka/ Lafayette,
   Where Are We?
Here Comes the Band Wagon
Horseshoes
Hurricane Horseman, The
Husband Hunters
Lightnin' Bull
Mad Racer, The
Man of Nerve, A
Masked Menace, The [serial]
Mysterious Dr. Fu Manchu, The (Lia
   Eltham)
Paramount player 27
Poor Nut, The
Powerful Eye, The
Ridin' Rivals
Roaring Rider
Saturday Night Kid, The (Janie)
Seven Chances
Sins of the Father (Mary Spengler)
Spring Fever
Stairs of Sand
Tearin' Loose
Temple of Venus, The
Thundering Through
Travelin' Fast
Twisted Triggers
Wallflowers
Warming Up
Winners of the Wilderness

142
ARTHUR, Johnny*
Aviator, The
Desert Song, The (Bennie Kidd)
Divorce Made Easy
Eligible Mr. Bangs, The
Gamblers, The
Mademoiselle Midnight
Monster, The (Under Clerk)
On Trial (Stanley Glover)
Show of Shows, The
Unknown Purple, The
Warner Brothers player 26

143
ASHBY, Johnnie*
Mademoiselle Parley-Voo (Mademoi-
   selle's son)

144
ASHBY, Ruth*
Dancin' Fool (Dorothy Harkins)

145
ASHER, Max (Max Ascher) (1880-1957)
Ladder Jinx, The
Shooting of Dan McGrew, The (Isador
    Burke)
Show Boat (utility man)
We're in the Navy Now
What Happened to Jane? [series]

146
ASHTON, Charles*
American Prisoner, The (Gunlayer
    Carberry)
Claude Duval (Tom Crisp)

147
ASHTON, Herbert*
Me, Gangster (Sucker)

148
ASHTON, Sylvia*
Bachelor's Paradise, A
Barker, The
Blushing Bride, The
Cheating Cheaters
City Sparrow, The
Conrad in Quest of His Youth (Mary
    Page)
Crash, The
Daughter of Luxury, A
Garments of Truth
Greed (Mama Sieppe)
Head Man, The (Mrs. Briggs)
Hold Your Horses
Jack Straw
Jenny Be Good
Ladies' Night in a Turkish Bath
Leopard Lady, The
Love Special
Manslaughter (prison matron)
Queen Kelly (Kelly's aunt)
Saturday Night (Mrs. O'Day)
Snob, The
Souls for Sale (Tiny Tilly)
Sweet Lavender
Thou Art the Man
While Satan Sleeps
White Flower
Why Change Your Wife? (Aunt Kate)
Wrecking Boss, The
Youth to Youth

149
ASTHER, Nils (1901-)
Adrienne Lecouvreur
Adventure Mad
Blue Danube, The
Budden Geheimnisse

Cardboard Lover, The
Cossacks, The (Prince Olenin)
Dream of Love (Prince Mauritz)
Die Drei Uhren
Gaiuner im Frack
Der Goldene Schmetterling
Hollywood Revue of 1929
Hotelratté
Laugh, Clown, Laugh (Luigi)
Loves of an Actress
Our Dancing Daughters (Norman)
Patsy, The (André)
Single Standard, The (Packy Cannon)
Sorrell and Son (Christopher Sorrell)
Sveket Nej Volontar
Topsy and Eva
Die Versunckene Flotte
When Fleet Meets Fleet (German officer)
Wiener Herzen
Wienersarnet
Wild Orchids (Prince de Gace)
Wrath of the Sea

150
ASTELL, Betty (1912-)
Lead Kindly Light

151
ASTOR, Camille*
For Those We Love (Vida)

152
ASTOR, Gertrude (1906-)
Alice Adams
Behind the Front
Beyond the Rocks (Morella Winmarleigh)
Boy Friend, The
Branding Iron, The
Burning Daylight
Butter and Egg Man, The
Cat and the Canary, The (Cecily)
Chasing Husbands
Cheerful Fraud
Cohens and the Kellys in Paris, The
Concert, The
Dame Chance
Don Juan's Three Nights
Fall of Eve, The
Family Group, The
Fascinating Widow
Five and Ten Cent Annie
Frozen Justice
Ginsberg the Great
Great Lover, The
Great Moment, The
Hit of the Show
Hurricane's Gal
Impossible Mrs. Bellew, The (Alice
    Granville)

Irresistible Lover
Kentucky Pride
Kiki
Lorna Doone
Naughty Duchess, The
Ne'er-Do-Well, The
Occasionally Yours
Old Soak, The
Pay As You Enter
Pretty Clothes
Pursued
Rose Marie
Rupert of Hentzau (Paula)
Secrets (Mrs. Mainwright)
Shanghaied
She Goes to War
Small Backelor
Spenders, The
Stage Struck (Lillian Lyons)
Stocks and Blondes
Strong Man, The (Gold Tooth)
Synthetic Sin
Taxi Dancer (Kitty)
Through the Back Door (Hortense
  Reeves)
Too Many Women
Twin Beds
Two Weeks Off
Uncle Tom's Cabin
Untamed
Wall Flower, The
Who Am I?

153
ASTOR, Mary (Lucille Vasconellos
  Langhanke) (1906-)
Beau Brummel (Lady Margery Alvan-
  ley)
Beggar Maid, The (Title role)
Bought and Paid For (bit)
Bright Shawl, The (Narcissa Esco-
  bar)
Bullets or Ballots (bit)
Don Juan (Adriana Della Varnese)
Don Q, Son of Zorro (Dolores de
  Muro)
Dressed to Kill
Dry Martini
Enticement
Fighting American, The
Fighting Coward, The
Forever After
Good Bad Girl, The
Heart to Heart
Her Primitive Mate
High Steppers
Hollywood
Hope

Inez from Hollywood
John Smith
Lost at the Front
Man Who Played God, The
Marriage Maker, The
New Year's Eve
No Place to Go
Oh, Doctor!
Pace That Thrills, The
Playing with Souls
Price of a Party, The
Puritan Passions
Racket, The
Rapids, The
Romance of the Underworld, A
Rose of the Golden West
Rough Riders, The
Sailor's Wives
Scarecrow, The
Scarlet Saint, The
Sea Tiger, The
Second Fiddle
Sentimental Tommy (bit, debut)
Success
Sunset Derby
Three Ring Marriage
To the Ladies (credited, but did not
  appear)
Two Arabian Nights
Unguarded Women
Wise Guy, The
Woman from Hell
Woman Proof
Young Painter, The

154
ATES, Roscoe (1892-1962)
South Sea Rose

155
ATHERTON, Ella*
First Born, The (Mme. Nina de Lande)

156
ATKINSON, George*
Conquering Power, The (Young Cruchot)

157
ATKINSON, Ione*
Black Oxen (a flapper)

158
ATWELL, Roy (1880-)
Souls for Sale (Arthur Tirrey)
Stage:
Americana 26

159
ATWILL, Lionel (1885-1946)
Highest Bidder, The
Indiscretion
Lionel Atwill in the Actor's Advice
    to His Son
White-Faced Fool, The
Stage:
Caesar and Cleopatra (Caesar) 25
Deburau (Jean-Gaspard Deburau) 20
Grand Duke, The (Grand Duke Feo-
    dor Michaelovitch) 21
Outside, The (Anton Ragatzy) 24

160
AUBREY, Jimmy*
Back Yard, The
Blizzard, The
Call of the Klondike
China Slaver
Comedy series 24
Dames and Dentists
Down Grade, The
Gallant Fool, The
Girl He Didn't Buy, The
Have a Heart
He Laughs Last
He Who Gets Crowned
His Jonah Day
Keep Smiling
Little Wild Girl
Look-Out Girl, The
Maid and Muslin
Nuisance, The
Out with the Tide
Pathé player 21
Pirate of the Sky
Pugs and Pats
Rah! Rah! Rah!
Simple Sap, A
Tale of the Shirt, The
Too Many Wives
Trouble Hunter, The
When Seconds Count
Wilful Youth

161
AUBURN, Jane*
Her Love Story (Clothilde)

162
AUBURN, Joy*
Mother Knows Best (Bessie)

163
AUER, Florence (1880-1962)
Beautiful City, The
That Royale Girl (Baretla's girl)

164
AUER, Mischa (Mischa Ounskowsky)
    (1905-1967)
Marquis Preferred
Something Always Happens (debut)
Universal player 28

165
AUGUST, Edwin (Philip Von der Butz)
    (1883-1964)
Idol of the North, The (Martin Bates)

166
AULT, Marie (Marie Cragg) (1870-
    1951)
Dawn (Madame Rappard)
Every Mother's Son (Miss Wimple)
Hindle Wakes (Mrs. Hawthorne)
Lodger, The
Madame Pompadour (Belotte)
Mademoiselle from Armentieres (Ma-
    demoiselle's aunt)
Monkey's Paw, The (mother)
Paddy the Next Best Thing (Mrs.
    Adair)
Rat, The (Mère Colline)
Return of the Rat, The (Mère Colline)
Roses of Picardy (Baroness D'Arche-
    ville)
Triumph of the Rat, The (Mère Col-
    line)
Wee MacGreegor's Sweetheart (Miss
    Tod)
Woman to Woman (Henrietta)

167
AUSEN, Wolfgang von Waltersh*
Menschen am Sonntag [People on Sun-
    day]

168
AUSTIN, Albert*
Circus, The
Kid, The

169
AUSTIN, Frank*
Hotter than Hot
Terror, The ("Cotton")

170
AUSTIN, George*
Monster, The (Rigo)

171
AUSTIN, Harold*
Black Lightning (Roy Chambers)
North Star, The

172
AUSTIN, Leslie*
Dr. Jekyll and Mr. Hyde

173
AUSTIN, Sam*
Fifth Form at St. Dominic's (Ben Cripps)

174
AUSTIN, William*
Drums of Love
Embarrassing Moments
Fifty-Fifty Girl, The
Flaming Forest, The
Her Big Night
Honeymoon Hate
Illusion
It (Monty)
Just Married
Marriage Playground, The (Lord Wrench)
Mysterious Dr. Fu Manchu, The (Sylvester Wadsworth)
Number Please
Paramount player 25
Pollyanna
Red Hair (Dr. Eustace Gill)
Ruggles of Red Gap
Someone to Love
Suds
Sweetie (Professor Willow)
Swim, Girl, Swim
What a Night!
What Happened to Jones?
World at Her Feet, The

174a
AVERY, Patricia*
Annie Laurie (Enid)
Night Life (maid)

175
AYRES, Agnes (Agnes Hinkle) (1896-1940)
Affairs of Anatol, The (Annie Elliott) (Elliott)
Bluff
Borderland
Bought and Paid For
Broken Hearted
Bye-Bye Buddy
Cappy Ricks
Clarence (the governess)
Daughter of Luxury, A
Donovan Affair
Eve's Love Letters
Forbidden Fruit (Mary Maddock)
Furnace, The

Go and Get It
Heart Raider, The
Held by the Enemy
Her Market Value
Inner Voice, The
Lady of Victory
Love Special
Love that Had No Turning, The
Marriage Maker, The
Modern Salome, A
Morals for Men
Napoleon and Josephine
Ordeal, The
Racing Hearts
Sheik, The (Diana Mayo)
Son of the Sheik (Sheik's wife)
Story Without a Name, The
Ten Commandments, The (the outcast)
Tomorrow's Love
Too Much Speed
When a Girl Loves

176
AYRES, Lew (Lewis Ayer) (1908-)
Big News (copy boy)
Compromised
Holiday
Kiss, The (Pierre)
Shakedown, The
Sophomore, The (bit)
Stage:
Henry Halstead's Orchestra 29
Ray West's Orchestra - Cocoanut Grove, L.A. 29

177
AYRTON, Louise*
His House in Order (nursemaid)

178
AYRTON, Randle (1869-)
Chu-Chin-Chow (Kasim Baba)
Nell Gwyn (King Charles II)

- B -

179
BABE, Angelus*
On with the Show

180
BABY PEGGY--see: Baby Peggy Montgomery

181
BÄCK*
Der Mensch am Wege [Man by the Roadside]

182
BACKUS, George*
Warrens of Virginia, The (General
  Warren)

183
BACLANOVA, Olga (1900-1974)
Avalanche
Czarina's Secrets, The
Dangerous Woman
Docks of New York, The
Dove, The
Forgotten Faces
Man I Love, The
Man Who Laughs, The (Duchess
  Josiana)
Street of Sin
Three Sinners
Wolfe of Wall Street, The (the wife)
Woman Disputed
Stage:
Carmencita and the Soldier 25
Lysistrata (Title role) 25

184
BACON, Irving (1893-1965)
Button My Back
Caught in the Kitchen
Half Way to Heaven
Head Man, The (mayor)
No One Man
Old Barn, The
Saturday Night Kid, The (McGonigle)
Side Street
Two Sisters
Union Depot

185
BACON, Irwin*
Girl from Everywhere, The

186
BADDELEY, Hermione (1908-)
Guns of Loos, The

187
BADIOLE, Charles*
Les Miserables (Gavroche)

188
BAERAUD, George*
Ned McCobb's Daughter (George Cal-
  lahan)

189
BAGGOTT, King (1880-1948)
Better Man, The
Cheated Love

Cheater, The
Cross Wires
Darling of New York, The
Down the Stretch
Dwelling Place of Light
Fighting Breed
Forbidden Thing, The
Gaiety Girl
Girl in the Taxi, The
Girl Who Knew All About Men, The
Gossip
His Last Race
Home Maker, The
House of Scandal, The
Jane and the Stranger
Kentucky Derby
Lavender Bath Lady, The
Life's Twist
Love Letter
Lovey Mary
Moonlight Follies
Nobody's Fool
Notorious Lady
Perch of the Devil
Raffles
Romance of a Rogue
Shadow of Lightning Ridge
Shadows
Snowy Baker
Thirteenth Piece of Silver
Tornado
Town Scandal

190
BAILEY, Norton*
Three O'Clock in the Morning

191
BAIRD, Hugh*
America /aka/ Love and Sacrifice
  (Major Pitcairn)

192
BAIRD, Leah (1887-1971)
Barriers Burned Away
Bride's Confession, The
Capitol, The
Cynthia of the Minute
Destroying Angel, The
Devil's Island
Don't Doubt Your Wife
Heart Line
Is Divorce a Failure?
Primrose Path, The
Return of Boston Blackie, The
Spangles
When Husbands Deceive
When the Devil Drives

193
BAKER, Belle (1895-1957)
Song of Love

194
BAKER, Betty Bly*
My Lady of Whim (Mary Severn)
Painted Angel, The

195
BAKER, Doris*
Ella Cinders

196
BAKER, Lee (1876-1948)
Fighting Blade, The (Earl of Staver-
   sham)

197
BAKER, Nellie Bly*
Kid, The
Love and the Devil
Woman of Paris, A

198
BAKER, Sam*
Isle of Lost Ships, The
Sea Beast, The (Queequeg)
Thief of Bagdad, The (the sworder)

199
BAKEWELL, William (1908-   )
Annapolis
Battle of the Sexes (Billy Judson)
Devil's Trade-Mark, The
Gold Diggers
Gold Diggers of Broadway (Wally)
Harold Teen
Hot Stuff
Iron Mask, The (dual role Louis
   XIV/ his twin
Lady of the Pavements (a pianist)
Last Edition
Latest from Paris
Mother
On with the Show (Jimmy)
Show of Shows, The
West Point (Tex McNeil)

200
BALFOUR, Augustus*
Any Wife

201
BALFOUR, Betty (1903-   )
Blinkeyes (Title role)
Champagne
Little Bit of Fluff, A

Love, Life and Laughter
Mord Em'ly
Nothing Else Matters
Paradise
Reveille
Satan's Sister
Somebody's Darling
Squibs ("Squibs" Hopkins)
Squibs' Honeymoon ("Squibs" Hopkins)
Squibs, MP ("Squibs" Hopkins)
Squibs Wins the Calcutta Sweep
   ("Squibs" Hopkins)
Vagabond Queen
Wee MacGreegor's Sweetheart (Chris-
   tina)

202
BALFOUR, Eva*
Fantomas [serial]

203
BALL, Lucille (Lucille Desirée Ball)
   (1911-   )
Bulldog Drummond (bit)

204
BALLARD, Elmer*
Alibi /aka/ The Perfect Alibi (Soft
   Malone)
Her Private Affair (Grimm)

205
BALLIN, Mabel (1885-1958)
Ave Maria
Code of the West (Mary Stockwell
East Lynne (Isabel Vane)
Hodkinson player 22
Jane Eyre
Journey's End
Married People
Other Women's Clothes
Pagan Love
Riders of the Purple Sage (Jane With-
   ersteen)
Under Crimson Skies
Vanity Fair (Rebecca Sharp)

206
BANCROFT, George (1882-1956)
Code of the West (Enoch Thurman)
Docks of New York, The
Dragnet
Driven
Enchanted Hill, The
Mighty, The (Blake Greeson)
Old Ironsides
Paying the Penalty
Pony Express

Rough Riders, The
Runaway, The (Lesher Skidmore)
Sea Horses
Showdown, The
Tell It to Sweeney
Thunderbolt
Too Many Crooks
Underworld ("Bull" Ward)
White Gold (Sam Randall)
Wolfe of Wall Street, The (Title
   role)

207
BAMLJEAD. Tallulah (1902-1968)
His House in Order (Nina Graham)
Stage:
Conchita - London 24
Dancers, The - London 23
Exciters, The ("Rufus" Rand) 22
Fallen Angels - London 25
Green Hat, The - London 25
Her Cardboard Lover 28
Nice People (Hallie Livingston) 21

208
BANKS, Estar*
John Smith
Know Your Men

209
BANKS, Monty (Mario Bianchi)
   (1897-1950)
Adam's Apple
Atlantic (Dandy)
Atta Boy!
Bride and Groom
Cocktails
Flivver Wedding, The
Flying Luck
His Dizzy Days
Honeymoon Abroad
Horseshoes
Keep Smiling
Peaceful Alley
Perfect Gentleman, A
Play Safe
Poor Simp, The
Warner player 21
Week-End Wives

210
BANKY, Vilma (Vilma Lonchit)
   (1903-)
Das Auge des Toten
Awakening, The
Case of Lena Smith, The
Dark Angel, The (Kitty Vane)
Eagle, The (Mascha Troekouroff)

Galathea
Hotel Potemkin /aka/ Die Letze
   Stinde
Im Letzen Augenblick
L'Image /aka/ Das Bildnis
Imtermezzo Einer Ehe in Sieben
   Tagen /aka/ Sollman Heiraten
Kauft Mariett-Aktien
King of the Circus
Lady from Paris, The /aka/ Das
   Schone Abenteuer
Die Lebe des Dalai Lama /aka/ Das
   Verbotene Land
Magic Flame, The (the aerial artiste)
Night of Love, The (Princess Marie)
Schattenkinder des Glücks
Son of the Sheik, The (Yasmin)
Tavaszi Zerelem
This Is Heaven
Two Lovers (Donna Lenora de Vargas)
Veszelyben a Pokol
Winning of Barbara Worth, The (Title
   role)
Der Zukuskönig /aka/ Clown aus
   Liebe

211
BANNISTER, Harry*
Her Private Affair (Judge Kessler)

212
BANTHIM, Larry*
Footlights and Fools (Bud Burke)
Hot Stuff

213
BARA, Theda (Theodosia Goodman)
   (1890-1955)
La Belle Russe (dual role)
Lure of Ambition, The
Madame Mystery (Madame Mysterieux)
Unchastened Woman (Caroline Knolys)
Stage:
Blue Flame, The (Ruth Gordon) 20

214
BARANOVSKAYA, Vera*
End of St. Petersburg, The
Mother

215
BARBAN, Harvey*
Blackmail (Chief Inspector)

216
BARBAT, Percy (1883-1965)
Peter Pan

217
BARD, Ben*
Arizona Wildcat
Come to My House
Dressed to Kill
Fleet Wings
Love and the Devil
Love Makes 'Em Wild
No Other Woman
Romance of the Underworld, A
Sandy
Secret Studio, The
Seventh Heaven (Brissac)
Two Girls Wanted (Jack Terry)

218
BARDA, Antonio*
White Sister, The (Alfredo's tutor)

219
BARING, Norah (Norah Baker)
   (1907-)
Celestial City, The
Cottage on Dartmoor, The
Runaway Princess, The
Underground

220
BARKER, Bradley*
Brown Derby, The
Crackerjack, The
Fighting Blade, The (Watt Musgrove)
Into the Net [serial]
Master Mind, The
Potters, The (Eagle)
Rubber Heels
Twenty-One

221
BARKER, Corrine*
Restless Sex, The (Helen Davis)
Why Girls Leave Home

222
BARLOW, Jeff*
Chu-Chin-Chow (Mustafa)

223
BARLOW, Kitty*
Night Life (war profiteer's wife)

224
BARLOW, Reginald*
Clothes Make the Pirate
Stage:
Queen's Husband, The (General
   Northrup) 28

224a
BARLOW, William*
Circus Days
Greed

225
BARNARD, Ivor (1887-1953)
Skin Game, The (Dawker)

226
BARNELLE, Mary Beth*
Virgin Paradise, A

227
BARNES, Binnie (Gertrude Maude
   Barnes) (1906-)
Phonofilm

228
BARNES, Frank*
General, The (Annabelle's brother)

229
BARNES, Mac M.*
Get-Rich-Quick Wallingford (Andrea
   Dempsey)

230
BARNES, Ray*
Seven Chances

231
BARNES, T. Roy (1880-1936)
Adam and Eva
Blonde for a Night
Body and Soul
Chicago
Cosmopolitan player 22
Crowded Hour, The
Dangerous Curves (Pa Spinelli)
Dangerous Friends
Gate Crasher, The
Go Getter, The
Great White Way, The
Her Face Value
Hollywood
Is Matrimony a Failure?
Kiss in Time, A
Ladies of Leisure
Leave It to Me
Lone Eagle
Old Homestead, The
Price of Pleasure, The
Sally (Otis Hooper)
Scratch My Back
See My Lawyer
Seven Chances
Smile, Brother, Smile

So Long Letty
Tender Hour
Unknown Cavalier, The

232
BARNES, V. L.*
Elmo, the Fearless [serial]

233
BARNET, Boris*
Storm over Asia

234
BARNUM, George*
Mountain Woman, The

235
BARRAUD, George (1894-)
Bellamy Trial, The (Pat Ives)
Flaming Youth
Last of Mrs. Cheyney, The (Charles)
Little Old New York (Henry Beevort)
Ned McCobb's Daughter
Strange Cargo
Woman to Woman

236
BARRIE, Nigel /aka/ Nigel Barre
  (1889-)
Amateur Gentleman, The (Sir Mor-
  timer Carnaby)
Bolted Door, The
Charge It
Claude Duval (Title role)
Climbers, The (Duke of Arrogan)
East Is West
Girl in the Web, The
Heroes and Husbands
Hogan's Alley
Home Struck
Little Fool
Little Minister, The
Lone Eagle
Notorious Miss Lisle, The
Peg o' My Heart (Christian Brent)
Prince There Was, A
Shield of Honor
Steel Preferred
Stranger's Banquet, The
Sunshine of Paradise Alley
Their Mutual Child
Traffic Cop
Turning Point, The
Under the Greenwood Tree (Shimar)
White Shoulders

237
BARRISCALE, Bessie (1884-1965)
Breaking Point, The (Ruth Marshall)

Broken Gates
Green Swamps
Kitty Kelly, M. D. (Title role)
Life's Twist
Luck of Geraldine Laird, The
Notorious Mrs. Sands, The
Show Folks (Kitty)
Skirts, The
Twin Beds
Woman Who Understood, The

238
BARROIS, Charles*
Carmen (Lillas Pastia)
Shadows of Fear

239
BARROWS, Henry*
All Aboard
Between Friends
Captain Blood (Lord Willoughby)
Cobra (Henry Madison)
Drake Case, The
Drusilla with a Million
His Majesty Bunker Bean
Little Irish Girl, The
Man on the Box, The
Oh! What a Nurse
Sea Hawk, The (Bishop)
Shock, The (John Cooper, Sr.)
Skinner's Dress Suit
Sporting Youth
Sunset Derby
Three's a Crowd

240
BARROWS, James O.*
Daddy's Gone-A-Hunting
Goose Woman, The (Jacob Riggs)
Sea Beast, The (Rev. Harper)
Sea Hunt, The
Signal Tower, The
Stephen Steps Out

241
BARRY, A.*
Mumsie (Carl Kessler)

242
BARRY, Cecil*
American Prisoner, The (Peter Nor-
  cot)
Dawn (Col. Schultz)

243
BARRY, Doris*
Sonia (Bavarian maidservant)

244
BARRY, Gerald*
Unholy Night, The (Capt. Bradley)

245
BARRY, Joan (1903-)
Atlantic (Betty Tate Hughes)
Blackmail (dubbing voice)
Card, The
Happy Ending, The
Rising Generation, The

246
BARRY, Leon /aka/ Leon Bary*
Iron Mask, The (Athos)
Kismet
Suzanna
Temple of Venus, The (Phil Grey-
son)
Three Musketeers, The (Athos)

247
BARRY, Wesley (1907-)
Battling Bunyon
Bits of Life
Bob Hampton of Placer
Country Kid, The
Dinty
Don't Ever Marry
Fighting Cub, The
George Washington, Jr.
Go and Get It
Heroes of the Streets
His Own Law
In Old Kentucky
Lotus Eater, The
Midshipman, The
Penrod
Printer's Devil, The
Rags to Riches
School Days
Stranger than Fiction
Top Sergeant Mulligan
Wild Geese

248
BARRYE, Emily*
Godless Girl, The (an inmate)
King of Kings, The (bit)

249
BARRYMORE, John (John Blythe)
(1882-1942)
Beau Brummel (George Byran
Brummel)
Beloved Rogue, The (Francois Vil-
lon)
Cardigan's Last Case

Dr. Jekyll and Mr. Hyde (Henry Jekyll
and Oscar Hyde)
Don Juan (Title role)
Eternal Love (Marcus Paltram)
Forever
General Crack (dual role, Duke of
Kurland/Prince Christian)
His Lady /aka/ When a Man Loves
(Chevalier Fabien des Grieux)
King of the Bernina
Lotus Eater, The
Paramount player 21
Sea Beast, The (Ahab Ceeley)
Sea Hunt, The
Sherlock Holmes /aka/ Moriarty
(Title role)
Show of Shows, The
Tempest, The
Third Degree, The
Warner Brothers player 25
Stage:
Claire de Lune (Gwymplane) 20
Hamlet (Title role) N.Y. 22, London
24
Richard III (Title role) 20

250
BARRYMORE, Lionel (Lionel Blythe)
(1878-1954)
Alias Jimmy Valentine (Doyle)
America (Capt. Walter Butler)
Barrier, The (Starr Bennett)
Bells, The
Body and Soul
Boomerang Bill
Brooding Eyes
Children of the Whirlwind
Cooperhead, The
Decameron Nights
Devil's Garden, The
Drums of Love (Duke Cathos de
Alvia)
Enemies of Women (Prince Lubimoff)
Eternal City, The (Baron Bonelli)
Face in the Fog, The
Fifty-Fifty
Girl Who Wouldn't Work, The
Great Adventure, The
Hollywood Revue of 1929
I Am the Man
Iron Man, The
Jim the Penman
La Granga
Lion and the Mouse, The
Love
Lucky Lady, The
Madame X
Master Mind, The

Meddling Women
Mysterious Island, The
Paris at Midnight
River Woman
Road House, The
Sadie Thompson (Rev. Davidson)
Seats of the Mighty
Show, The
Spendid Road, The
Temptress, The (Canterac)
Thirteenth Hour, The (Professor Le-
Roy)
Two Minutes to Go
Unseeing Eyes
West of Zanzibar (Crane)
Women Love Diamonds
Wrongdoers, The
Stage:
Claw, The (Achille Cortelon) 21
Laugh, Clown, Laugh (Tito Beppi)
23
Letter of the Law, The (Mouzon) 20
Macbeth (Title role) 21
Man or Devil (Nicholas Snyders) 25
Piker, The (Bernie Kaplan) 25
Taps (Sgt. Volkhardt) 25

250a
BARSAC, Madame*
Living Dead Man, The

251
BARSKY, Vladimir*
Potemkin (Capt. Golikov)

252
BARTELS, Louis John*
Broadway Nights (Baron)
Canary Murder Case, The (Louis
Mannix)
Dance Magic
Stage:
Show Off, The (Aubrey Piper) 24

253
BARTHELMESS, Richard (Richard
Semler Barthelmess) (1895-1963)
Adiss
Amateur Gentleman, The (Barnabas
Barty)
Beautiful City, The
Bond Boy, The
Bright Shawl, The (Charles Abbott)
Classmates
Drag
Drop Kick, The
Enchanted Cottage, The
Experience

Fighting Blade, The (Karl Van Ker-
stenbrock)
Fury
Head Man, The
Idol Dancer, The (the beachcomber)
Just a Song at Twilight
Just Suppose
Kentucky Courage
Little Shepherd of Kingdom Come,
The (Title role)
Love Flower, The (Bruce Sanders)
New Toys
Noose, The
Out of the Ruins
Patent Leather Kid, The (Title role)
Ranson's Folly
Scarlet Days
Scarlet Seas (Steve Donker)
Seventh Day, The
Shore Leave
Show of Shows, The
Son of the Gods (Sam Leigh)
Sonny (dual role)
Soul Fire /aka/ Golden Youth
Synthetic Sin
Tol'able David (David Bartlett)
Beary River
Wheels of Chance
White Black Sheep, The
Winning Through (Duncan Irving, Jr.)
Young Nowheres

254
BARTLETT, Elsie*
Show Boat (Ellie)

255
BARTLETT, Hetta*
Sonia (Lady Dainton)
Woman of No Importance, A (Lady
Cecelia)

256
BARTON, Buzz (1914-)
Bantam Cowboy, The
Boy Rider
Fighting Redhead, The
Freckled Rascal, The
Lariat Kid, The
Little Buckaroo, The
Little Savage, The
Orphan of the Sage
Pals of the Prairie
Pinto Kid, The
Rough Ridin' Red
Slingshot Kid, The
Vagabond Cub, The
Wizard of the Saddle

257
BARWYN, Max /aka/ Max Barwin*
Bardelys the Magnificient
Beverly of Graustark (Saranoff)
Climbers, The (King Ferdinand VII)
Fighting Eagle, The
Valencia

258
BARY, Jean*
Cock-Eyed World, The (Fanny)

259
BASQUETTE, Lina (Lina Belcher)
  (1907-)
Celebrity, The
Come Across
Godless Girl, The (Title role)
Noose, The
Ranger of the North
Serenade
Show Folks (Rita)
Trapped
Universal player 27
Wheels of Chance
Younger Generation, The

260
BASSERMAN, Albert (1867-1952)
Fraulein Else
Das Weib des Pharao [The Wife of
  the Pharao] (Sotis)

260a
BASTIAN, Jack*
Loves of Carmen

261
BASTON, J. Thornton*
Beyond Price
Down to the Sea in Ships (Samuel
  Siggs)
Mountain Woman, The
Tiger's Club, The
Virgin Paradise, A
White Moll, The

262
BASTON, John /aka/ Jack*
Circus Ace, The
Diplomats, The
Hired and Fired
Snow Bride, The

262a
BATALOF, M.*
Mother

263
BATALOV, Nikolai*
Bed and Sofa
Mother

264
BATCHELOR, Rev. Dr.*
Road to London, The (the Vicar)

265
BATEMAN, Victory*
Eternal Three, The
Tess of the D'Urbervilles (Joan Dur-
  beyfield)

266
BATES, Les*
Buck Privates
Vanity Fair (Mr. Sharp)

266a
BATES, Tom*
Huckleberry Finn
In the Palace of the King
Through the Dark

267
BATTEN, John*
Battle of the Sexes (Judson's Friend)
Under the Greenwood Tree (Dick)

268
BATTISTA, Miriam (1914-)
At the Stage Door
Boomerang Bill
Custard Cup
Good Privider
Humoresque
Just Around the Corner
King of Kings, The
Man Who Played God, The
Shining Adventure
Smiling Through (Little Mary)
Steadfast Heart, The

268a
BAUDET, Louise*
Sally

269
BAUDIN, Henri*
Pawns of Passion
Terror /aka/ The Perils of Paris
Three Musketeers, The (DeRochefort)

270
BAUER, Harry /aka/ Harry Baur
  (1881-1941)
La Voyante

271
BAXTER, George*
Careless Age, The (La Grande)
Marianne (André)

272
BAXTER, Warner (1893-1951)
  Born in Columbus, Ohio, March
  29, 1893. Dark brown hair,
  brown eyes, 5'10-3/4". Married
  Winifred Bryson. First theatre
  appearance with Dorothy Shoe-
  maker in Louisville, Kentucky.
  Film debut in 1922, The Runaway.
  Died May 7, 1951 in Beverly
  Hills. ACADEMY AWARD
  1928/29--In Old Arizona.
Air Mail, The
Alimony
Aloma of the South Seas (Nuitane)
Awful Truth, The
Behind that Curtain (John Beetham)
Best People
Blow Your Own Horn
Cheated Hearts
Christine of the Hungry Heart
Coward, The
Craig's Wife
Danger Street
Drums of the Desert
Far Call
Female, The
First Love
Garden of Weeds, The
Girl in His Room
Girl's Desire, A
Golden Bed, The (Bunny O'Neil)
Great Gatsby (Title role)
Happy Days
Her Market Value
Her Own Money
If I Were Queen
In Old Arizona (The Cisco Kid)
In Search of a Thrill
Linda
Mannequinn
Marriage Circle, The (pulled from
  cast, replaced by Monte Blue)
Mismates
Miss Brewster's Millions
Ninety and Nine, The
Paramount player 23, 26
Ramona (Alessandro)
Romance of the Rio Grande
Rugged Water
Runaway, The (Wade Murrell)
Saint Elmo
Sheltered Daughter

Singed
Son of His Father, A
Tailor Made Man, The
Telephone Girl
Those Who Dare
Three Sinners
Through Different Eyes (Jack Win-
  field)
Tragedy of Youth, The
Welcome Home
West of Zanzibar (Doc)
Woman's Way, A

273
BAYFIELD, Peggy*
Sherlock Holmes /aka/ Moriarty
  (Rose Faulkner)

274
BAYLEY, Hilda*
Carnival (Desdemona)

275
BAYNE, Beverly (1896-)
Age of Innocence, The
Her Marriage Vow
Making the Grade
Modern Marriage
Passionate Youth
Smiling All the Way
Tenth Woman, The

276
BEAL, Frank*
Best Bad Man, The (Mr. Swain)
Marriage in Transit (Burnham)
Stolen Bride, The

277
BEARD, Ray*
Taming of the Shrew, The (Lucentio)

278
BEAUDET, Louise (1861-1948)
Gold Diggers (Cissie Gray)
Her Lord and Master
Sally (Mme. Julie DuFey)
Slaves of Pride

279
BEAUMONT, Grace*
Virgin Paradise, A

280
BEAUMONT, Lucy (1873-1937)
Ashes of Vengeance (Charlotte)
Beloved Rogue, The (mother)
Bit of Heaven, A

Branded Men, The
Butter and Egg Man, The
Closed Gates
Comrades
Crowd, The (Mary's mother)
Family Secret, The
Fighting Failure, The
Girl in the Show, A
Greater Glory, The
Greyhound Limited, The
Hard Boiled Rose
Hook and Ladder No. 9
Horace Goes to Hollywood
Knights Out
Little Yellow House, The
Lucretia Lombard
Man Without a Country, The /aka/
    As No Man Has Loved
Old Soak, The
One Splendid Hour
Outcast Souls
Resurrection
Riding Demon, The
She Knew Men
Sonny Boy
Stool Pigeon, The
Stranded
Torrent, The (Dona Pepa Moreno)
Trouble with Wives, The
What Every Girl Knows
Youth Triumphant

281
BEAUMONT, Tom*
Christie Johnstone (Saunders)

282
BEAUPLAN, Marsha*
Madame Pompadour (Madame Pois-
    son)

283
BEAVERS, Louise (1889-1962)
    (Note: Was personal maid to
    Leatrice Joy prior to 1928)
Barnum Was Right
Coquette (Julia)
Glad Rag Doll
Gold Diggers of Broadway
Nix on Dames
Uncle Tom's Cabin (debut)
Wall Street
Stage:
Ladies Minstrel Troupe 26

284
BEBAN, George (1873-1928)
Greatest Love of All, The

Loves of Ricardo, The
One Man in a Million
Sign of the Rose

284a
BECHTAL, William*
Jazz Age, The

284b
BECHTEL, William*
Spite Marriage

285
BECK, J. Emmett*
Broadway Melody, The (Babe Hatrick)
Shadow of the Law, The (Martin)

286
BECK, John*
Shock, The (Bill)

287
BECK, Mabel*
Adventurous Sex, The (the girl's
    mother)

288
BECKER, F. G. *
Prisoner of Zenda, The (Detchard)

289
BECKER, Fred*
Black Pirate, The
Blood and Sand (Don Jose)
Man Without a Country, The /aka/
    As No Man Has Loved
Marriage in Transit (a conspirator)

290
BECKER, Theodor*
Midsummer Night's Dream, A (Thes-
    eus)

291
BECKERSACHE, Carl*
Waltz Dream, The (Peter Ferdinand)

292
BECKMANN, Karl*
Der Juxbaron [The Imaginary Baron]
    (landlord)

292a
BECKWITH, Bainard*
Sun Up

293
BEDFORD, Barbara*
Acquittal, The

Alias Julius Caesar
And How!
Another Man's Shoes
Arabian Love
Back Stage
Big Punch, The
Bitter Sweets
Broken Mask, The
Brothers
Cavalier, The
Cinderella of the Hills, A
City of Purple Dreams, The (Esther
    Strom)
Cradle of Courage
Deep Waters
Devil's Dice, The
Face of the World
Girl from Gay Paree, The
Gleam o' Dawn
Goldwyn player 22
Haunted House, The
Heroic Lover
Last of the Mohicans, The (Cora
    Monroe)
Mad Whirl, The
Man under Cover
Manhattan Nights
Man's Past, A
Marry the Girl
Mockery (Tatiana)
Notorious Lady
Old Loves and New /aka/ The
    Desert Healer
Out of the Silent North
Percy
Port of Missing Girls, The
Romance Land
Smoke Bellew
Spoilers, The (Helen Chester)
Sporting Lover, The
Step on It!
Sunshine of Paradise Alley
Talker, The
Tie that Binds, The
Tumbleweeds
Unfoldment
What Fools Men
Winning with Wits
Women Who Give

294
BEEBE, Marjorie (1909-)
Ankles Preferred
Hollywood Star, A
In Holland
Love Hungry
New Halfback, The
Not Quite Decent

Rich but Honest
Speakeasy
Uppercut O'Brien
Very Confidential

295
BEECHER, Sylvia*
Innocents of Paris (Louise Leval)

296
BEERBOHM, Claude*
His House in Order (Pryce Ridgeley)

297
BEERBOHN, Elizabeth*
Glorious Adventure, The (Barbara
    Castlemaine)

298
BEERY, Noah, Jr. (1913-)
Father and Son

299
BEERY, Noah, Sr. (1884-1946)
Beau Geste (Sgt. Lejaune)
Beau Sabreur (El Hamel)
Bits of Life
Bob Hampton of Placer
Call of the Canyon
Careers
Coming of Amos, The
Contraband
Cross Roads of New York
Crown of Lies, The
Dinty
Don Juan
Don Q, Son of Zorro
Dove, The
East of Suez
Ebb Tide
Enchanted Hill, The
Evening Clothes
False Feathers
Female, The
Fighting Coward, The
Fighting Shepherdess, The
Flesh and Blood (Li Fang)
Four Feathers, The (slave trader)
Go and Get It
Godless Girl, The (the brute)
Goldwyn player 23
Good Men and True
Hell-Ship Bronson
Heritage of the Desert, The
Isle of Lost Ships, The
Light of the Western Stars, The
Lily of the Dust
Linda

Lord Jim
Love in the Desert
Love Mart, The
Main Street
Mark of Zorro, The (Sgt. Pedro)
Mormon Maid, The
Mutiny of the Elsinore
Noah's Ark (dual role, King Nephi-
    lim/Nickoloff)
North of '36
Old Shoes
Omar the Tent Maker
Padlocked
Paradise
Passion Song, The
Penrod
Rough Riders, The
Sagebrusher, The
Sea Wolf, The (George Medford)
Show of Shows, The
Soldier's Plaything, A
Song of the Flame
Soul of the Beast, The
Spaniard, The
Spiker and the Rose, The
Spoilers, The (Alex McNamara)
Stephen Steps Out
Storm Swept
Thundering Herd, The (Randall Jett)
Tipped Off
To the Last Man
Tol'able David
Two Lovers (Duke of Alva)
Vanishing American, The /aka/ The
    Vanishing Race (Booker)
Wanderer of the Wasteland (Dismukes)
Wandering Daughters
Welcome Stranger, The
Wild Honey
Wild Horse Mesa
Youth to Youth

300
BEERY, Wallace (1886-1949)
Adventure
Alias Julius Caesar
Another Man's Wife
Ashes of Vengeance (Duc de Tours)
Bavu
Beggars of Life
Behind the Door
Behind the Front
Big Killing, The
Casey at the Bat (Title role)
Chinatown Nights
Coming Through
Devil's Cargo, The
Drifting
Drums of Jeopardy, The

Dynamite Smith
813
Eternal Struggle, The
Fireman, Save My Child
Flame of Life, The
Four Horsemen of the Apocalypse,
    The (Lt. Col. Von Richthoffen)
Golden Snare, The
Great Divide, The
Hurricane's Gal
I Am the Law
In the Name of Love
Last of the Mohicans, The (Magua)
Last Trail, The
Let Women Alone
Lost World, The (Prof. Challenger)
Madonna of the Streets, A
Man from Hell's River, The
Mollycoddle, The (Henry Van Holkar)
Night Club
Now We're in the Air
Old Ironsides
Only a Shop Girl
Partners in Crime
Patsy
Pony Express
Red Lily, The (Bobo)
Richard the Lion-Hearted (Title role)
Ridin' Wild
River of Romance
Robin Hood (Richard the Lion-Hearted)
Rookies Return, The
Rosary, The
Round Up, The
Rugged Water
Sagebrush Trail, The
Sea Hawk, The (Jasper Leigh)
Signal Tower, The
So Big (Klaas Pool)
Spanish Dancer, The (Philip IV)
Stairs of Sand
Storm Swept
Strangers of the Night
Tale of Two Worlds, A (Ling Jo)
Three Ages, The
Three Musketeers, The
Trouble
Unseen Hands
Virgin of Stamboul, The
Volcano (Quembo)
Wanderer, The
We're in the Navy Now
White Tiger
Wife Savers
Wild Honey

300a
BEGG, Gordon*
Bandolero

301
BEGGS, Lee*
America /aka/ Love and Sacrifice
  (Samuel Adams)
Janice Meredith (Benjamin Franklin)

301a
BEHRLE, Fred*
Big News

301b
BELA, Nicholas*
Adoration
Night Watch, The

302
BELAJEFF, Olga*
Three Way Works, The
Wachsfigurenkabinett [The Waxworks]

303
BELANGER, Juliette*
Don Q, Son of Zorro (tango dancer)

304
BELASCO, Leon (1902-)
Best People (debut)

305
BELCHER, Charles*
Ben-Hur (Balthasar)
Black Pirate, The
Blood and Sand (Jon Joselito)
Fools in the Dark
King of Kings, The (Philip)
Rosita (Prime Minister)
Thief of Bagdad, The (The Holy Man)
Three Musketeers, The (Bernajoux)

306
BELCHER, Ernest Dancing Tots
Hollywood Revue of 1929

306a
BELKIN, Bestruce*
Versailles

307
BELL, Charles*
Wyoming

308
BELL, Colin*
Dawn (Widow Deveaux)

308a
BELL, Karina*
David Copperfield
Heart of a Clown

308b
BELL, Marie (Marie Jeanne Bellon-
  Downey) (1900-)
Figaro
Innocents of Paris
Madame Recamier

309
BELL, Montana*
Kid, The
Pilgrim, The

310
BELL, Rex (George F. Beldam) (1905-
  1962)
Country Kid, The
Girl Shy Cowboy
Joy Street
Pleasure Crazed
Salute
Taking a Chance
They Had to See Paris (McGurdy)
Wild West Romance

310a
BELL, Spencer*
Midnight Taxi, The

311
BELLAMY, Madge (Margaret Philpott)
  (1903-)
Alimony
Ankles Preferred
Are You a Failure?
Bertha, the Sewing Maching Girl
Black Paradise
Blind Hearts
Colleen
Cup of Life
Dancers, The
Dixie Merchant, A
Fool and His Money, A
Fugitives
Garrison's Finish
Hail the Women
Havoc (Tess Dunton)
Hottentot, The
Iron Horse, The (Miriam Marsh)
Lightnin'
Lorna Doone
Lost
Love and Glory
Love Never Dies
Love's Whirlpool
Man in Blue, The
Mother Knows Best (Sally Quail)
No More Women
Parasite, The
Play Girl, The

Riddle Woman, The
Sandy
Silk Legs
Soft Living
Soul of the Beast, The
Sport Girl, The
Summer Bachelors
Telephone Girl
Tinsel Harvest
Tonight at Twelve
Very Confidential
White Sin
Wings of Youth

312
BELLAMY, Ralph (1904-)
Surrender

313
BELLAMY, Somers*
Taming of the Shrew, The (Grumio)

314
BELLE, Fannie*
Hallelujah

315
BELLEW, Cosmo Kyrle (1886-1948)
Bellamy Trial, The
Black Butterflies
Devil's Appletree, The
Disraeli (Mr. Terle)
French Dressing
Hit of the Show
Magic Flame, The (the husband)
Man, Woman and Sin
Midnight Life
Strange Cargo
Summer Bachelors

316
BELLEW, Dorothy*
In the Blood

316a
BELMONT, Baldy*
Young April

317
BELMONT, Gladys*
Redskin, The (Corn Blossom)

318
BELMONT, Morgan, Mrs. *
Way Down East (Diana Tremont)

318a
BELMORE, Daisy*

We Americans

319
BELMORE, Lionel (1867-1953)
Bardelys the Magnificent (Vicomte
  de Lavedan)
Barnstormer, The (manager)
Boy of Flanders, A
Circus Kid, The
Demi-Bride
Dub
Eve's Secret
Evidence
From Headquarters
Godless Men
Good-Bye Kiss, The
Great Lover, The
Guile of Women, The
Heart Trouble
Jes' Call Me Jim
Kindred of the Dust
King of Kings, The (a Roman Noble)
Love Comes Along
Love Parade, The (Prime Minister)
Madame X
Man Who Fights Alone, The (Meggs)
Man Who Had Everything, The
Matinee Idol, The
Milestones (Richard Sibley)
Moonlight Follies
My Wife's Relations
Never the Twain Shall Meet
Oliver Twist (Mr. Brownlow)
Peg o' My Heart (Hawks)
Play Girl, The
Red Lights
Redeeming Sin, The
Return of Peter Grimm, The (Rev.
  Bartholomey)
Roarin' Fires
Rogue Song, The (Ossman)
Rose-Marie (Henri Duray)
Sea Hawk, The (Justice Anthony Baine)
Shocking Night, A
Sorrell and Son
Stark Mad
Sting of the Lash, The (Ben Ames)
Strange Boarder, The
Student Prince, The
Sunset Derby
Try and Get It
Two Minutes to Go
Unholy Night, The (Major Endicott)
Winners of the Wilderness (Gov. Din-
  widdie)
Within the Law (Irwin)
World's Champion
Yellowback, The

319a
BELOT, Marthe*
Living Dead Man, The

320
BENCHLEY, Robert (1889-1945)
Furnace Trouble
Lesson No. 1
Sex Life of the Polyp, The
Spellbinder, The
Stewed, Fried and Boiled
Treasurer's Report, The

320a
BENDA, W. T.*
American Venus, The

321
BENDER, Harry*
Der Juxbaron [The Imaginary Baron]
    (Hugo Windisch)

322
BENDIX, Lissen*
Han og Hun og Hamlet

323
BENDOW, Wilhelm*
Der Kleine Napoleon [The Little Na-
    poleon] /aka/ So Sind die Männer
    [Men Are Like That]; Napoleon's
    Kleiner Bruder [Napoleon's Little
    Brother] (Jerome's valet)
Midsummer Night's Dream, A (Flute)

324
BENEDICT, Brooks*
Clear the Decks
Drop Kick, The
Freshman, The (college cad)
Gorilla, The
Lost at the Front
Moran of the Marines
Only Woman, The
Orchids and Ermine
Ranson's Folly
Sophomore, The
Speedy
Strong Man, The (bus passenger)
Tramp, Tramp, Tramp
Trespasser, The (reporter)
White Flannels
Why Girls Go Back Home

324a
BENEDICT, Kingsley*
Fast and Furious
Man of Action, A

325
BENGE, Wilson*
Bulldog Drummond (Danny)
Fast and Furious
Most Immoral Lady, A
Queen Kelly (valet)
Robin Hood (Prince John's henchman)
That's My Daddy
This Thing Called Love (Dumary)
Untamed

326
BENHAM, Harry*
Polly with a Past
Town that Forgot God, The

326a
BENNER, Priscilla*
Red Kimono, The

327
BENNETT, Alma*
Best Man, The
Brooding Eyes
Dawn of a Tomorrow, A
Face on the Barroom Floor, The
Girl Crazy
Good-Bye Kiss, The
Grail, The
Grain of Dust, A
Head of the Family, The
Light of the Western Stars, The
Lilies of the Field
Long Pants
Lost World, The (Gladys Hungerford)
Man's Size, A
Midnight Daddies
My Lady's Past
New Orleans
Orchids and Ermine
Price of Success
Silent Lover, The
Squads Right
Three Jumps Ahead
Triumph (flower girl)
Two Men and a Maid
Why Men Leave Home
Without Compromise
Woman Who Was Forgotten, The

328
BENNETT, Barbara (1902-1958)
Mother's Boy (Beatrix Townleigh)
Syncopation

329
BENNETT, Belle (1891-1932)
Aloma of the South Seas

Battle of the Sexes (Mrs. Judson)
Devil's Skipper, The
Devil's Trade-Mark, The
East Lynne (Alfy Hallijohn)
Flesh and the Spirit, The
Fourth Commandment, The
His Supreme Moment
If Marriage Fails
In Hollywood with Potash and Perl-
mutter
Iron Mask, The
Lily, The
Molly and Me
Moran of the Marines
Mother
Mother Machree
My Lady's Past
Patience
Playing with Souls
Power of Silence, The
Queen of Burlesque
Reckless Lady, The
Reputation
Sporting Age, The
Stella Dallas (Title role)
Their Own Desire
Way of All Flesh, The (Mrs. Schil-
ling)
Wild Geese
Your Best Friend
Stage:
Wandering Jew, The (Ollalia Quin-
tana) 21

330
BENNETT, Billie*
Amateur Gentleman, The (Duchess
of Camberhurst)
Claw, The (Mrs. Marriat)
Eternal Three, The
Fashions in Love
Lady Windermere's Fan (gossipy
Duchess)
Ranson's Folly
Robin Hood (Lady Marian's serving
woman)

331
BENNETT, Charles*
America /aka/ Love and Sacrifice
(William Pitt)

332
BENNETT, Constance (Constance
Campbell Bennett) (1906-1965)
Adam and Eve
Alaskan, The
Clothes

Code of the West (Georgia May Stock-
well)
Cytherea (Annette Sherwin)
Evidence (Edith)
Goose Hangs High, The (Lois Ingals)
Goose Woman, The (Hazel Woods)
Her Own Free Will
Into the Net [serial]
Married? (Marcia Livingston)
Men of the Force
My Son (Betty Smith)
My Wife and I
Pinch Hitter, The (Abby Nettleton)
Reckless Youth (a chorus girl)
Rich People (Connie Hayden)
Sally, Irene, and Mary (Sally)
Son of the Gods (Allana)
This Thing Called Love (Ann Marvin)
Universal player 25
Wandering Fires (Guerda Anthony)
What's Wrong with Woman? (Elsie
Bascom)

333
BENNETT, Enid (1894-1969)
Ambrose Applejohn's Adventure (Pop-
py Faire)
Bad Man, The
Bootlegger's Daughter, The
Courtship of Miles Standish, The
False Road, The
Good Medicine
Hairpins
Her Husband's Friend
Keeping up with Lizzie
Red Lily, The (Marise LaNoue)
Robin Hood (Lady Marian Fitzwalter)
Sea Hawk, The (Rosamund Godolphin)
Silk Hosiery
Strangers of the Night
Thousand to One, A
Virtuous Thief, The
Woman in the Suitcase, The
Woman's Heart, A
Wrong Mr. Wright, The
Your Friend and Mine

334
BENNETT, Gertrude*
Merry Widow, The (Hard-Boiled Vir-
ginia)

335
BENNETT, J. Moy*
Running Wild (Mr. Johnson)
Unguarded Hour, The

336
BENNETT, Joan (1911-)
Bulldog Drummond (Phyllis Clavering)
Disraeli (Clarissa Pevensey of Glas-
    tonbury)
Divine Lady, The (extra)
Mississippi Gambler
Pathé player 29
Power (a dame)
Three Live Ghosts
Stage:
Jarnegan (Daisy Carol) 28
Pirate, The 28

337
BENNETT, Joseph*
Ace in the Hole, An
Feud, The
Gamesters, The
God's Great Wilderness
Home Stretch, The
Lariat Kid, The
Men of Daring
Shepherd of the Hills
Somewhere in Sonora
Straight Shootin'
Their Mutual Child
Three Miles Up
Valley of Hell
Wolf's Trail
Youth's Desire

338
BENNETT, Kathryn*
Only Woman, The
Soul Mates

338a
BENNETT, May*
Price of a Party, The

339
BENNETT, Mickey*
Big Brother
Cohens and the Kellys, The
Dummy, The (Barney Cook)
Footlights and Fools (call boy)
Ghost Talks, The
It's the Old Army Game (Mickey)
Man Who Played God, The
Marriage Morals
Tillie's Punctured Romance
United States Smith

340
BENNETT, Richard (1873-1944)
Eternal City, The (Bruno)
Hell Diggers

Home Towners, The
Lying Wives
Reckless Age, The
Youth for Sale
Stage:
Beyond the Horizon (Robert Mayo) 20
He Who Gets Slapped (He) 22
Hero, The (Andrew Lane) 21
Jarnegan (Jack Jarnegan) 28
They Knew What They Wanted (Tony)
    24

341
BENNY, Jack (Joseph Benjamin
    Kubelsky) (1894-1974)
Hollywood Revue of 1929 (M. C.)
Road Show

342
BENSON, Annette*
Afterglow
Confetti
Curse of the Westscott
Daughter of Israel, A
Downhill (Mabel)
Harbor Lights
Inseparables, The
Love at the Wheel
Lovers in Araby
Man from Home, The
Money Habit, The
Nonentity, The
Ringer, The
Shooting Stars
Sir or Madame
South Sea Bubble, A
Squibs (Ivy Hopkins)
Squibs Wins the Calcutta Sweep (Ivy
    Hopkins)
Temporary Lady, The
Three Live Ghosts
Week-End Wives

342a
BENTLEY, Beatrice*
Toll of the Sea

343
BERANGER, André (George André de-
    Beranger) (1895-)
Altars of Desire
Are Parents People?
Ashes of Vengeance (King Charles IX)
Bat, The (Gideon Bell)
Beau Brummel (Lord Byron)
Beauty and the Bad Man, The
Bright Shawl, The (Andres Escobar)
Confessions of a Queen

Dulcy
Eagle of the Sea, The
Fig Leaves
Five and Ten Cent Annie
Glad Rag Doll
Grand Duchess and the Waiter, The
Grounds for Divorce
If I Were Single
Lady of the Harem
Leopardess, The
Lilies of the Field
Man in Blue, The
Miss Brewster's Millions
No Questions Asked
Paradise for Two
Pay as You Enter
Poisoned Paradise
Popular Sin, The
Powder My Back
Small Bachelor
So This Is Paris
Stark Mad (Simpson)
Strange Cargo
Tiger Rose
Woman's Faith, A

343a
BERANGER, Annie*
Powder My Back

343b
BERCZY, Gezo*
Paul Street Boys, The

343c
BEREGI, Oscar*
Butterflies in the Rain
Flaming Forest, The
Moon of Israel

344
BERESFORD, Harry (1867-1944)
Quarterback, The
Stage:
Michael and Mary (P. C. Tuff) 29
Old Soak, The (Clem Hawley) 22
Shavings (J. Edward Winslow) 20

344a
BERESFORD, Miss*
Miss Brewster's Millions

344b
BERGEN, Arthur*
Slums of Berlin

345
BERGER, Charly*
Sein Grösster Bluff [His Greatest

Bluff] (Count Koks)

345a
BERGERE, Ouida (1866-1974)
Bella Donna
Kick-In

346
BERGMAN, Henry*
Circus, The (The Merry Clown)
Gold Rush, The (Hank Curtis)
Idle Class, The
Kid, The
Pay Day
Pilgrim, The
Woman of Paris, A

347
BERGNER, Elizabeth (1900-)
Dona Juana
Der Evangeliman
Fraulein Else
Der Geiger von Florenz [Violinist of
    Florence]
Impetuous Youth
Liebe
NJU
Stage:
Constant Nymph, The (Teresa) -
    Berlin
Doll's House, A (Nora) - Berlin
Hamlet-Ophelia - Zurich 20
Hannele - Berlin
Last of Mrs. Cheyney, The - Berlin
St. Joan (Title role) - Berlin
Shrew, The (dual role, Viola/Kathe-
    rine) - Berlin
Strange Interlude (Nina) - Berlin

347a
BERHARD, Raymond*
Jeanne Dore

348
BERLE, Milton (Milton Berlinger)
    (1908-)
Divorce Coupons
Humoresque
Lena Rivers
Mark of Zorro, The
Sparrows /aka/ Human Sparrows

348a
BERLEY, André*
Passion of Joan of Arc, The

348b
BERLIN FIRE DEPARTMENT
When Duty Calls

349
BERLYN, Ivan*
Merchant of Venice, The (Shylock)

349a
BERNARD, Armand*
Miracle of the Wolves, The

350
BERNARD, Barney (1877-)
Potash and Perlmutter
Stage:
Partners Again (Abe Potash) 22

351
BERNARD, Dorothy (1890-1955)
Unfair Sex, The
Wild Goose, The

352
BERNARD, Harry*
Berth Marks
Men o' War
Perfect Day, A

353
BERNARD, Josephine*
Way Down East (Mrs. Tremont)

353a
BERNARD, Lester*
Flying Romeos
Sweet Rosie O'Grady

354
BERNARD, Sylvia*
Sparrows /aka/ Human Sparrows

355
BERNARDI, Nerio*
Shepherd King, The

355a
BERNHARDT, Curtis*
Die Frau, Nach der Man Sich Sehnt
   [The Woman One Longs For]
   /aka/ Three Loves

356
BERNHARDT, Sarah (Rosalie Ber-
   nard) (1845-1923)
Jeanne Dore
Le Voyaloe

356a
BERNIS, Blanche*
Le Tourmoi

357
BERRELL, George*
City of Masks, The
Everlasting Whisper, The
Pollyanna

357a
BERRY, Aileen*
Soul Fire /aka/ Golden Youth

357b
BERTONE, Alfredo*
Romola
White Sister, The

357c
BERTRAM, William*
Dramatic Life of Abraham Lincoln,
   The

358
BESSERER, Eugenie /aka/ Eugenia
   (-1934)
Anna Christie
Bread
Breaking Point, The (Mrs. Janeway)
Bridge of San Luis Rey, The (nun)
Captain Salvation
Circle, The
Coast of Folly (Nanny)
Confessions of a Queen
Drums of Love (Dutchess Alvia)
Fast Company
Fighting Shepherdess, The
Fire Brigade, The
Flesh and the Devil (Leo's mother)
For the Soul of Rafael
Friendly Enemies
Gift Supreme, The (Martha Vinton)
Good Women
Hands of Nara, The
His Lady /aka/ When a Man Loves
   (the landlady)
Illusion
Jazz Singer, The (Sara Rabinowitz)
June Madness
Kiki
Lady of Chance, A
Light in the Clearing, A
Lilac Time
Madame X (Rose)
Mr. Antonio
Molly-O, The
Penrod
Price She Paid, The
Rosary, The
Seven Faces
Sin of Martha Queed, The

Sitting on the World
Slightly Used
Speedway
Stranger's Banquet, The
Tess of the D'Urbervilles
Thunderbolt
Two Lovers (Madame Van Rycke)
What Happened to Rosa?
Whispering Winds
Yellow Lily, The

359
BEST, Edna (1900-1974)
Couple of Down and Outs, A
Tilly of Bloomsbury (Tilly)
Stage:
High Road, The (Elsie Hilary) 28
Michael and Mary
Swan, The - New York and London
There's Always Juliet
These Charming People (Pamela
  Crawford) 25

360
BEST, Martyn*
Chorus Girl's Romance, A (F. W.
  Jordon)

361
BETTS, William*
Sainted Devil, A

362
BETZ, Matthew L. (-1938)
Big City, The (Red)
Boomerang Bill
Broadway After Midnight
Burn 'Em Up Barnes
Crimson City, The
Exiles
Five Aces
Flame of the Yukon
Fugitives
Girl in the Glass Cage, The (Doc
  Striker)
Girls Gone Wild
Good References (Kid Whaley)
He Learned About Women
Iron Mike
Lighthouse by the Sea, The
Lights of Old Broadway (Red Hawkes)
Little Irish Girl, The
Love's Whirlpool
Luck
My Lady's Lips (Eddie Gault)
My Old Kentucky Home
Oh! What a Nurse
Only Woman, The

Patent Leather Kid, The
Shepherd of the Hills
Shipwrecked
Single Track
Sins of the Father (Gus)
Siren of Seville, The
Telling the World
Terror, The (Joe Connor)
Those Who Dare
Unholy Three, The (Regan)
Way of a Girl, The
Wedding March, The (Schani)

363
BEVAN, Billy (William Bevan Harris)
  (1887-1957)
Astray from the Steerage (a steerage
  passenger)
Be Reasonable
Beach Club, The
Best Man, The
Bicycle Flirt
Bull Fighter, The
Butter Fingers
Button My Back
By Heck
Calling Hubby's Bluff
Cannon Ball Express
Caught in the Kitchen
Circus Today
Cured in the Excitement
Divorce Dodger
Don't Get Jealous
Duck Hunter, The
Easy Pickings
Fireside Brewer, A
Flight Night
Flirty-Four-Flushers
Foolish Husbands
From Rags to Britches
Giddap!
Gold Digger of Weepah, The
Gold Nut, The
Gymnasium Jim
Hayfoot, Strawfoot!
High Voltage (Gus)
His New Steno
His Unlucky Night
Hoboken to Hollywood
Honeymoon Hardships
Hubby's Latest Alibi
Hubby's Quiet Little Game
Hubby's Weekend Trip
Ice Cold Cocos
Inbad the Sailor
Iron Nag, The
It's a Boy
Let 'Er Go

Lion's Roar, The
Lion's Whiskers, The
Lizzies of the Field
Love, Honor and Behave
Ma and Pa
Masked Mamas
Mother Knows Best
Motorboat Mamas
Motoring Mamas
Muscle Bound Music
My Goodness!
Nip and Tuck
Oh, Daddy!
On Patrol
One Spooky Night
Over There-Abouts
Peaches and Plumbers
Pink Pajamas
Quack Doctor
Riley the Cop
Sea Dog's Tale, A
Should Sleepwalkers Marry?
Skinners in Silk
Sky Hawk, The (Tom Berry)
Small Town Idol, A
Small Town Princess
Sneezing Breezers
Super-Hooper-Dyne Lizzies
Trespasser, The (reporter)
Trimmed in Gold
Wall Street Blues
Wandering Waistlines
Wandering Willies
When Summer Comes
Whispering Whiskers /aka/ Railroad
    Stowaways

364
BEVANI, Alexander*
Phantom of the Opera, The (Mephis-
    topheles)

365
BEYER, Charles*
Man Must Live, A
Pace that Thrills, The
Shock Punch, The
Unguarded Hour, The
Unseeing Eyes

366
BIANCHETTI, Suzanne*
Casanova
Loves of Casanova
Madame Sans Gene (Empress Marie
    Louise)

367
BIANCINI, Ferrucio*
Shepherd King, The
Theodora

368
BIAS, Albert*
Oppressed, The

369
BICKEL, George*
Beneath the Law
In Holland

370
BICKFORD, Charles (1889-1967)
Dynamite (Hagon Derk; debut)
Hell's Heroes
South Sea Rose

371
BIDDLE, Baldy*
Condemned (prison inmate)

372
BIDDLE, Craig*
Fashion Row
Three Wise Fools

373
BIENERT, Gerhard*
Der Mensch am Wege [Man by the
    Roadside]

374
BIENSFELDT, Paul*
Anna Boleyn /aka/ Deception
Die Bergkatze /aka/ The Mountain
    Cat; The Wild Cat (Dafko)
Destiny /aka/ The Tired Death; The
    Three Lights; Between Worlds;
    Der Mude Tod
Der Kleine Napoleon [The Little Na-
    poleon] /aka/ So Sind die Manner
    [Men Are Like That] Napoleons
    Kleiner Bruder [Napoleon's Little
    Brother] (king's court marshall)
Romeo und Julia im Schnee [Romeo
    and Juliet in the Snow] Sumurun
    /aka/ One Arabian Night (slave
    dealer)
Das Weib des Pharao [The Wife of
    the Pharao] /aka/ The Loves of
    Pharaoh (Menon)

375
BIG TREE, Chief*
Iron Horse, The (Cheyenne Chief)

Ranson's Folly
Spoilers of the West
Winners of the Wilderness (Pontiac)

375a
BILDT, Paul*
Slums of Berlin

376
BILL, Buffalo, Jr. (Jay Wilsey)
   (1902-)
Bad Man's Bluff
Ballyhoo Buster, The
Bonanza Buckaroo, The
Desert Demon
Deuce High
Fast and Fearless
Final Reckoning
Gallopin' Gobs
Hard Hittin' Hamilton
Interferin' Gent
Obligin' Buckaroo
On the Go
Pals in Peril
Pirates of Panama
Quicker 'n Lightnin'
Rarin' to Go
Rawhide
Ridin' Rowdy
Roarin' Broncos
Saddle Cyclone
Speedy Spurs
Streak of Luck, A
Trumpin' Trouble
Valley of Hunted Men

377
BILL, Maude*
Sandra

378
BILL, Teddy*
Der Juxbaron [The Imaginary Baron]
   (Hans von Grabow)

379
BILLBREW, A. C. H.*
Hearts in Dixie

380
BILLINGS, Elmo*
Locked Doors

381
BILLINGS, Florence*
Little Child Shall Lead Them, A
Marriage Morals
Miss Bluebeard
Sinners in Heaven

382
BILLINGS, George A.*
Dramatic Life of Abraham Lincoln,
   The /aka/ Abraham Lincoln
   (Title role)
Hands Up! (Abraham Lincoln)
Man Without a Country, The /aka/
   As No Man Has Loved
Woman to Woman

383
BILLOUPS, Robert*
Wildfire

384
BILTMORE QUARTETTE, The
Words and Music

385
BING, Herman (1889-1947)
Married in Hollywood
Song of Kentucky, A

386
BINNEY, Constance (1900-)
Bill of Divorcement, A
Case of Becky, The
Sleepwalker, The
Something Different
Stolen Kiss
Such a Little Queen
Three O'Clock in the Morning
39 East

387
BINNEY, Faire*
Frontier of the Stars, The (Hilda Shea)
Man's Home, A
Second Youth
Speed Spook, The
What Fools Men Are
Wonder Man, The
Stage:
He and She (Millicent) 20

388
BIRD, Betty*
Waterloo

389
BIRD, Charles*
Padlocked

390
BIRD, Charlotte*
Legion of the Condemned, The
Mannequinn
Mantrap (the stenographer)
Padlocked

391
BIRD, Getty*
Saturday Night Kid, The (Riche)

392
BIRKETT, Viva*
Prince of Lovers, The

393
BISHOP, Detective Sergeant*
Blackmail

394
BISWANGER, Erwin*
Metropolis

395
BLACK, Buck*
Durand of the Badlands (Jimmie)
Empty Hearts (Val Kimberlin)
Last Man on Earth, The
Senor Daredevil
Which Shall It Be?

396
BLACK, G. Howe*
Wizard of Oz, The

397
BLACK, Maurice*
Broadway Babies
Carnation Kid, The
Dark Streets
Leaping Love

398
BLACK, William*
Fascinating Youth
Highest Bidder, The

399
BLACKFORD, Lottie*
Tilly of Bloomsbury (Mrs. Banks)

400
BLACKMER, Sidney (1895-1973)
Love Racket, The
Most Immoral Lady, A
Stage:
Love in a Mist (Gregory Farnham)
  26
Mima (Janos) 29
Moon-Flower, The (Peter) 24
Mountain Man, The (Aaron Winter-
  field) 21
Not So Long Ago (Billy Ballard) 20
Quarantine (Tony Blunt) 24

401
BLACKTON Charles Stuart (1914-)
Gypsy Cavalier, The (Valerius, age 8)
Passers By

402
BLACKTON, Greg*
Fascinating Youth

403
BLACKTON, Marian*
Virgin Queen, The (Mary Arundel)

404
BLACKTON, Violet Virginia*
Virgin Queen, The (Lettice Knollys)

405
BLACKWELL, Carlyle (1880-1955)
Bulldog Drummond (Hugh Drummond)
Beloved Vagabond, The (dual role,
  Gaston de Merac/Paragot)
Hound of the Baskervilles, The (Sher-
  lock Holmes)
Monte Carlo
Prodigals of Monte Carlo
Restless Sex, The (Oswald Grismer)
She
Sherlock Holmes /aka/ Moriarty
Third Woman, The
Two Little Vagabonds (George Thorn-
  ton)
Virgin Queen, The (Lord Robert Dud-
  ley)
Wrecker, The

406
BLACKWELL, Jim*
Love's Wilderness

407
BLAINE, Ruby*
Two Tars

408
BLAISDELL, William*
Yankee Clipper, The

409
BLAKE, Lucius*
American Prisoner, The (Seaman Cuf-
  fee)

410
BLAKE, Tom*
Restless Wives
Wild Fire
Wonderful Chance, The

411
BLANC, Sally*
Wife Savers

412
BLANC-MAETERLINCK, Georgette*
New Enchantment, The

413
BLANCHAR, Pierre (1892-1963)
Le Capitaine Fracasse
Jocelyn
La Marche Nuptale

414
BLANCHE, Kate*
Without Limit

415
BLANDICK, Clara (1881-1962)
Men Are Like That
Poor Aubrey
Wise Girl, The (debut)
Stage:
Hell-Bent fer Heaven (Meg Hunt) 24

416
BLANE, Sally (Elizabeth Jane Young)
  (1910-)
Casey at the Bat
Dead Man's Curve
Eyes of the Underworld
Fools for Luck (Louise Hunter)
Half Marriage
Her Summer Hero
Horseman of the Plains
King Cowboy
Outlawed
Paramount player 27
Rolled Stockings
Sheik, The (extra)
Shootin' Irons
Show of Shows, The
Tanned Legs
Vagabond Lover, The
Vanishing Pioneer, The
Very Idea, The
Wife Savers
Wolves of the City

417
BLANKE, Kate*
Why Girls Leave Home

418
BLANKE, Tom*
Lunatic at Large, The

419
BLATCHER, William*
Two Girls Wanted

420
BLAYDON, Richard*
Fifty-Fifty

421
BLEIFER, John*
We Americans

422
BLENSFELD, Paul*
Destiny /aka/ The Tired Death; The
  Three Lights; Between Worlds;
  Der Mude Tod

423
BLETCHER, Billy*
Beneath the Law

424
BLINN, Genevieve*
Don't Tell Everything (Mrs. Morgan)
Queen of Sheba, The (Beth Sheba)

425
BLINN, Holbrook (1872-1928)
Bad Man, The
Janice Meredith (Lord Clawes)
Masked Woman, The
New Commandment, The
Power
Rosita (the king)
Telephone Girl
Unfair Sex, The
Yolanda (King Louis XI)
Zander the Great (Juan Fernandez)
Stage:
Bad Man, The (Pancho Lopez) 20
Dove, The (Don Jose Maria Lopez y
  Tostado) 25
Play's the Thing, The (Sandor Turai)
  26

426
BLOCK, Dorothy*
If I Marry Again

427
BLOMSTEDT, George*
Doctor's Women, The

428
BLOOMER, Raymond*
Fool, The
If Winter Comes (Lord Tybar)

Love Light, The (Giovanni)
Sensation Seekers

429
BLORE, Eric (1888-1959)
Great Gatsby, The

430
BLOSS, Schmid*
William Tell

431
BLOSSOM, Rose*
White Flannels

432
BLOSSOM, Winter*
Thief of Bagdad, The (slave of the
lute)

433
BLUE, Ben (Ben Bernstein) (1901-
1975)
Extra and bit parts 26-29

434
BLUE, Monte (1890-1963)
Across the Atlantic
Across the Pacific
Affairs of Anatol, The (Abner El-
liott)
Being Respectable
Bitter Apples
Black Diamond Express, The
Black Swan, The
Brass
Brass Knuckles
Broadway Rose
Brute, The
Bush Leaguer, The
Conquest
Cumberland Romance, A
Daughters of Pleasure (Kent Merrill)
From Headquarters
Greyhound Limited, The
Her Marriage Vow
Hogan's Alley
How to Educate a Wife
Jucklins, The
Kentuckians, The
Kiss Me Again (Gaston Fleury)
Limited Mail, The
Little Bit of Heaven
Love of Gamble
Lover of Camille, The
Loving Lies
Lucretia Lombard
Mademoiselle Midnight

Main Street
Man Upstairs, The
Marriage Circle, The (Dr. Braun)
Memory Lane
Moonlight and Honeysuckle
My Old Kentucky Home
No Defense
One Round Hogan
Orphans of the Storm (Danton)
Other Men's Wives
Other Women's Husbands
Peacock Alley (Elmer Harman)
Perfect Crime, A (Wally Griggs)
Purple Highway, The
Recompence
Red Hot Tires
Revelation
Show of Shows, The
Skin Deep
So This Is Paris (Dr. Giraud)
Something to Think About (Jim Dirk)
Tents of Allah
Thirteenth Commandment, The
Those Who Dare
Tiger Rose (Devlin)
Too Much Johnson
Undersea Kingdom [serial]
Warner Brothers player 22
White Shadows of the South Seas (Dr.
Matthew Lloyd)
Wolf's Clothing

435
BLUM, Sam*
Iron Man, The
Rio Rita (cafe owner)
Winning of Barbara Worth, The (Blan-
ton)

436
BLY, Nellie*
Salvation Hunters, The

437
BLYSTONE, Stanley*
Circus Ace, The
Through Different Eyes (3rd reporter)
Waltzing Around

438
BLYTHE, Betty (Elizabeth Blythe
Slaughter) (1893-1972)
Breath of Scandal, The
Chu-Chin-Chow (Zahrat)
Darling of the Rich
Daughter of Israel, A
Domestic Troubles
Eager Lips

Fair Lady
Folly of Vanity
Fox player 23
Girl from Gay Paree, The
Glorious Betsy
His Wife's Husband
His Wife's Relations
How Men Love
In Hollywood with Potash and Perl-
   mutter
Into No Man's Land
Jacob's Well
Million Bid, A
Nomads of the North (Nanette Roland)
Percy
Queen of Sheba, The (Title role)
Recoil, The
She
Silver Horde, The
Sinner or Saint?
Sisters of Eve
Slander
Snowbound
Southern Love
Stolen Love
Third Generation, The
Truth About Wives, The
Yellowback, The

439
BOARDMAN, Eleanor (1898-)
Auction Block, The (Lory Knight)
Bardelys the Magnificent (Roxalanne
   de Lavedan)
Circle, The
Crowd, The (Mary Simms)
Day of Faith, The
Diamond Handcuffs
Exchange of Wives
Gimme
Memory Lane
Only Thing, The (Princess of Svend-
   borg)
Proud Flesh
Redemption
Road to Mandalay, The (Norma Dale)
She Goes to War
Silent Accuser, The
Sinners in Silk
So This Is Marriage
Souls for Sale (Remember Seddon)
Stranger's Banquet, The
Tell It to the Marines
Three Wise Fools
True as Steel
Vanity Fair (Amelia Sedley)
Way of a Girl, The
Wife of the Centaur, The
Wine of Youth, The

440
BOARDMAN, Virginia True*
Blind Bargain, The (Mrs. Sandell)
Home Maker, The
Lady Lies, The (Amelia Tuttle)
Pioneer Trails
Third Alarm, The (Mother M'Dowell)

441
BOBARDS, James*
Footloose Widows

442
BOBBIE--a monkey
Hero for a Night, A

443
BOCCI, Gildo*
Last Days of Pompeii, The (Diomed)
Messalina

444
BODART, Madame*
Dawn (Madame Ada)

445
BOETLER, Wade*
Big News (O'Neil)
Man of Action, A

446
BOHLER, Fred*
Rough Riders, The

447
BOHN, Jack Lionel*
Ashamed of Parents
Inside of the Cup, The
Story Without a Name, The

448
BOHNEN, Michael*
Kopf Hoch, Charly! [Heads Up, Char-
   ly!] (John Jacob Benjes)
Sajenko, the Soviet

449
BOIS, Ilse*
Ghost Train, The (Miss Bourne)

450
BOLAND, Eddie (1885-)
Face on the Barroom Floor, The
June Madness
Kid Brother, The
Lady Raffles [series]
Last Performance, The
Little Robinson Crusoe
Long Live the King

Love Lesson, The
Making the Varsity
Mama's Boy
Nobody's Business
Nothing Matters
Oliver Twist (Toby Crackitt)
Prince Pistachio
Queens Up
Roach player 27
Star Comedies
Straight Crook, A
Sunrise (Obliging Gentleman)
Who's My Wife?
Within the Law (Darcy)

451
BOLDER, Robert*
Beyond the Rocks (Josiah Brown)
Butterflies in the Rain
Captain Blood (Admiral Van der Kuy-
len)
Christian, The (Rev. Golightly)
Sea Hawk, The
Vanity's Price
Wise Wife
Women's Wares

452
BOLES, John (1895-1969)
Bride of the Colorado
Bride of the Night
Desert Song, The (The Red Shadow)
Fazil (John Clavering)
Last Warning
Loves of Sunya, The (Paul Judson)
Man-Made Women
Rio Rita (Capt. Jim Stewart)
Romance of the Underworld, A
Scandal
She Goes to War
Shepherd of the Hills
So This Is Marriage
Song of the West (Stanton)
Virgin Lips
Water Hole, The (Bert Durland)
We Americans
What Holds Men?
Stage:
Mercenary Mary (Lyman Webster) 25

453
BOLEY, May (1882-1963)
Beneath the Law
Dance of Life, The
Dangerous Curves (Ma Spinelli)
Woman from Hell

454
BOLTON, Betty*
Balaclava (Natasha)

455
BOLTON, Helen*
Hired and Fired
Music Fiends

456
BOMER, Marjorie*
Broadway Lady

457
BONAPARTE, Napoleon*
Scaramouche (Lt. of Artillery)

458
BONAPARTE, Napoleon (a dog)
Thirteenth Hour, The

459
BOND, Brenda*
Fool, The
Rainbow Riley

460
BOND, Frank*
Hogan's Alley
Tell It to Sweeney

461
BOND, Ward (1905-1960)
Born Reckless
Salute
Words and Music

462
BONDI, Alex*
Un Chapeau de Paille d'Italie [The
Italian Straw Hat]

463
BONDIRE*
Living Image, The

464
BONDWIN, Billy*
Which Shall It Be?

465
BONGINI, Rafael*
Humming Bird, The (Bouchet)
Sainted Devil, A (Sancho)

466
BONI, Carmen*
Jolly Peasant, The

Prinzessin Olala [Princess Olala]
/aka/ Art of Love (Princess
Xenia)

467
BONILLAS, Myrta*
Claw, The (Saba Rockwood)
Gingham Girl

468
BONN, Ferdinand*
Strauss, the Waltz King

469
BONNER, Marjorie*
Ancient Highway, The
Daughters of Today
Reno

470
BONNER, Priscella*
April Showers
Bob Hampton of Placer
Broadway after Midnight
Charley's Aunt (Kitty)
Drusilla with a Million
Earth Woman
False Alarm
Fog Man
Girls Who Dare
Golden Shackles
Home Stuff
Homer Comes Home
Honest Hutch
It (Molly)
Little Church Around the Corner,
The
Long Pants
Man Who Had Everything, The
Maud Miller
Officer 666
Outcast Souls
Paying the Price
Prince of Headwaiters
Proud Flesh
Red Kimono, The
Shadows (Mary Brent)
Son of Wallingford, The (Mary Curtis)
Strong Man, The (Mary Brown)
Tarnish
Three Bad Men

471
BONOMO, Joe (1898-)
Courtin' Wildcats
Flaming Frontier, The
Great Circus Mystery, The [serial]
King of Kings, The (bit)

Noah's Ark (aide to soldier leader)
Perils of the Wild [serial] (Frederic
Robinson)
Phantoms of the North
Wamping Venus
You Never Know Women

472
BOOK-ASTA, George*
Night Bird, The

473
BOOKER, Beulah*
Saphead, The

474
BOOP, Betty
Max Fleischer cartoons began 1915
and continued through the 20's.
(Voice: Helen Kane)

475
BOOTH, Edwina (Josephine Con-
stance Woodruff) (1909-)
Manhattan Cocktail
Our Modern Maidens

476
BOOTH, Walter*
Roulette

477
BORCHERT, Brigette*
Menschen am Sonntag [People on Sun-
day]

478
BORDEN, Eddie*
Battling Butler
Dove, The

479
BORDEN, Eugene*
Gentlemen Prefer Blondes (Louis)
Hold Your Man

480
BORDEN, Martin*
Grit (Bennie Finkel)

481
BORDEN, Olive (1906-1947)
Albany Night Boat
Come to My House
Country Beyond, The
Dance Hall
Eternal Woman, The
Fig Leaves

Gang War
Half Marriage
Happy Warrior, The
Joy Girl, The
Love in the Desert
Monkey Talks, The (Olivette)
My Own Pal
Pajamas
Secret Studio, The
Sinners in Love
Stool Pigeon, The
Three Bad Men
Virgin Lips
Wedding Rings
Yankee Senor, The
Yellow Fingers

482
BORDONI, Irene (1894-1953)
Paris
Show of Shows, The
Stage:
As You Were (Gervaise) 20
French Doll, The (Georgine Mazu-
    lier) 22
Little Miss Bluebeard (Colette) 23
Naughty Cinderella (Germaine Lever-
    rier) 25
Paris (Vivienne Rolland) 28

483
BORG, Sven Hugo*
Rose-Marie

484
BORGATO, Augustino /aka/ Agos-
    tino Borgato*
Coffin Maker, The
Fashions for Women
Hula (Uncle Edwin)
Kiss in a Taxi, A
Magic Flame, The (the ringmaster)
Romance of the Rio Grande
She Goes to War

485
BORGATO, Emilo*
Private Life of Helen of Troy, The
    (Sarpedon)

486
BORGSTROM, Hilda*
Stroke of Midnight, The
Thy Soul Shall Bear Witness

487
BORIO, Josephine*
Fazil (Aicha)

488
BORISOFF, S. *
Flames on the Volga

488a
BORLAND, Barlowe*
Man Who Fights Alone, The (Mike
    O'Hara)

489
BORLIN, Jean*
Entr' Acte

490
BORODIN, Elfriede*
Atlantic (Betty Von Schroeder)

491
BORSTWICK, Edith*
Thank You

492
BOSC, Henri*
Madame Pompadour (King Louis XV)

493
BOSCO, Wallace*
Mademoiselle Parley-Voo (Bollinger)

494
BOSKY, Marquisette*
Der Kleine Napoleon [The Little Napo-
    leon] /aka/ So Sind die Manner
    [Men Are Like That]; Napoleons
    Kleiner Bruder [Napoleon's Little
    Brother] (prima ballerina)

495
BOSOCKI, Madam*
Smiling Irish Eyes

496
BOSTWICK, E. F. *
Kitty

497
BOSTWICK, Edith*
Pilgrim, The

498
BOSWORTH, Hobart (Hobart Van
    Zandt Bosworth) (1867-1943)
After the Storm
Annapolis
Annie Laurie (the MacDonald chieftan)
Behind the Door
Below the Surface
Big Parade, The (Mr. Apperson)

Blind Hearts
Blood Ship, The
Bread
Brute Master, The
Burning Daylight
Captain January
Chickie
Chinese Parrot, The
Common Law, The
Cup of Life
Eternal Love (Pastor Tass)
Eternal Three, The
Far Cry, The
Freckles
General Crack (Count Hensdorf)
Half-Way Girl, The
Hangman's House
Hearts of Oak
His Own Law
Hurricane, The
If I Marry Again
In the Palace of the King
King of the Bernina
King of the Mountain
Little Church Around the Corner, The
Man Alone
My Best Girl
My Son (Sheriff Ellery Parker)
Name the Man
Nellie, the Beautiful Cloak Model
Nervous Wreck, The
Rupert of Hentzau (Col. Sapt)
Sawdust Paradise, The
Sea Lion, The
Show of Shows, The
Silent Watcher, The
Smart Set, The
Steel Preferred
Stranger's Banquet, The
Sundown
Thousand to One, A
Three Hours
Through the Dark
Vanity Fair (Lord Steyne)
White Hands
Winds of Chance
Woman of Affairs, A (Sir Montague)
Woman on the Jury, The
Zander the Great (the sheriff)

499
BOTELER, Wade (-1945)
Alias the Night Wind
Baby Cyclone
Big News
Capital Punishment (Officer Dugan)
Close Harmony

Crash, The
Cry of Fury
Daughter of Mother McGuire, The
Deserted at the Altar
Ducks and Drakes
Ghost Patrol, The
Going Up
Gold Braid
Hard Proposition
Havoc (Sgt. Major)
High School Hero
Hold that Lion
Home Stretch, The
Introduce Me
Just Married
Lahoma
Last Edition
Leatherneck, The
Let 'em Go Gallagher
Let It Rain
Life's Like That
Marriage in Transit (a conspirator)
New Halfback, The
Old-Fashioned Boy, An
Ridin' Wild
Seven Keys to Baldpate
She Couldn't Help It
Soft Cushions
Sporting Goods
Stranger than Fiction
That's My Baby
That's My Daddy
Through the Dark
Toilers, The
Top Sergeant Mulligan
Very Good Young Man, A
Warming Up
While Satan Sleeps
Winds of Chance
Woman Against the World, A
Wrecking Boss, The

500
BOTSFORD, Richard*
Satan in Sables

501
BÖTTCHER, Herman*
Prinzessin Olala [Princess Olala] (the prince)

502
BOTTOMLEY, Roland*
Dawn of a Tomorrow, The
Devil, The
Enticement

503
BOUCHIER, Chili (Dorothy Bouchier)
  (1910-)
Chick
City of Play
Dawn
Downstream
Maria Marten
Palais de Danse
Shooting Stars
Silver King, The
Warned Off
Woman in Pawn, A
You Know What Sailors Are

504
BOUCICAULT, Nina*
Paddy the Next Best Thing (Mrs.
  Blake)

505
BOUDWIN, Jimmy*
One Woman to Another

506
BOULDER, Robert*
Dramatic Life of Abraham Lincoln,
  The /aka/ Abraham Lincoln
Marriage of William Ashe, The
  (Lord Parham)

506a
BOURDELLE, Thomy*
Sea Fever

507
BOUTON, Betty*
Cytherea (Claire Morris)
Enemies of Women (Alicia's maid)
Exiles, The
Mollycoddle, The (Molly Warren)

508
BOW, Clara (Clara Gordon Bow)
  (1904-1965)
Adventurous Sex, The (the girl)
Ancient Mariner, The (Doris)
Best Bad Man, The (Peggy Swain)
Beyond the Rainbow (Virginia Gard-
  ner; debut)
Black Lightning (Martha Larned)
Black Oxen (Janet Oglethorpe)
Capital Punishment (Delia Tate)
Children of Divorce (Kitty Flanders)
Dancing Mothers (Catherine "Kittens"
  Westcourt)
Dangerous Curves (Pat Delaney)
Daring Years, The (Mary)

Daughters of Pleasure (Lila Millas)
Down to the Sea in Ships (Dot Morgan)
Empty Hearts (Rosalie)
Enemies of Women (girl dancing on
  table)
Eve's Lover (Rena D'Arcy)
Fleet's In, The (Trixie Deane)
Free to Love (Marie Anthony)
Get Your Man (Nancy Worthington)
Grit (Orchit McGonigle)
Helen's Babies (Alice Mayton)
Huly ("Hula" Calhoun
It (Betty Lou)
Keeper of the Bees, The (Lolly Cam-
  eron)
Kid Boots (Jane Martin)
Kiss Me Again (Grizette)
Ladies of the Mob (Yvonne)
Lawful Cheaters (Molly Burns)
Mantrap (Alvena Easter)
Maytime (Alice Tremaine)
My Lady of Whim (Prudence Severn)
My Lady's Lips (Lola Lombard)
Parisian Love (Marie)
Plastic Age, The (Cynthia Day)
Poisoned Paradise (Margot LeBlanc)
Primrose Path, The (Marilyn Merrill)
Red Hair ("Bubbles" McCoy)
Rough House Rosie (Rosie O'Reilly)
Runaway, The (Cynthia Meade)
Saturday Night Kid, The (Mayme)
Scarlet West, The (Miriam)
Shadow of the Law, The (Mary Brophy)
This Woman (Aline Sturdevant)
Three Weekends (Gladys O'Brien)
Two Can Play (Dorothy Hammis)
Wild Party, The (Stella Ames)
Wine (Angela Warriner)
Wings (Mary Preston)

509
BOWERS, John (1891-1936)
Ace of Hearts (Forrest)
Affinities
Barefoot Boy, The
Bits of Life
Bonded Woman
Chickie
Code of the Wilderness, The
Confessions of a Queen
Cumberland Romance, A
Danger Girl
Desire
Dice Woman, The
Divorce
Empty Hearts (Milt Kimberlin)
First National player 26
Godless Men

Golden Gift, The
Hearts and Fists
Hearts of the Yukon
Heroes in Blue
Laddie
Lorna Doone
Madame X
Night Rose, The
Opening Night
Pals in Paradise
Poverty of Riches, The
Quincy Adams Sawyer (Title role)
Ragtime
Richard the Lion-Hearted (Sir Ken-
    neth, Knight of the Leopard)
Roads of Destiny
Rocking Moon
Say It with Songs
Silent Call, The
Skin Deep
Sky Pilot
So Big (Purvis DeJong)
South of Suva
Three Hours
Voices of the City (Graham)
What a Wife Learned
When a Man's a Man
Whispering Smith
Woman in Room 13, The
Woman of Bronze, The

509a
BOWLES, Frank*
Beloved Brute, The

510
BOWMAN, Patricia*
Versailles

511
BOYD, Betty*
Green Goddess, The (an ayah)

512
BOYD, Dorothy (1907-)
Auld Lang Syne
Ball of Fortune, The
Burglar and the Girl, The
Constant Nymph, The (Paulina)
Dream Faces
Easy Virtue (Whittaker's younger
    sister)
Knee Deep in Daisies
Love's Option
Sentence of Death, The
Somehow Good
Toni
Veteran, The

513
BOYD, Marilynn*
Temple of Venus, The (Juno)

514
BOYD, Mildred*
Gentlemen Prefer Blondes (Lulu)
Riley, the Cop

515
BOYD, William "Bill" (William Law-
    rence Boyd) (1898-1972)
Affairs of Anatol, The
Bobbed Hair
Changing Husbands
Cop, The
Dress Parade
Eve's Leaves
Feet of Clay (young society man)
Flying Fool, The
Forty Winks
Her Man o' War
High Voltage (Bill)
His First Command
Jim, the Conqueror
King of Kings, The (Simon of Cyrene)
Lady of the Night
Lady of the Pavements (Count Karl
    von Arnim)
Last Frontier, The
Leatherneck, The
Locked Door, The
Love Song, The
Midshipman, The
Moonlight and Honeysuckle
Night Flyer, The
Officer O'Brien
Power (Quirt)
Road to Yesterday, The (Jack More-
    land)
Skyscraper
Steel Preferred
Tarnish
Temple of Venus, The (Stanley Dale)
Thumbs Down
Two Arabian Nights
Volga Boatman, The (Feodor)
Why Change Your Wife?
Wolf Song
Wolves of the Air
Yankee Clipper, The
Young Rajah, The

516
BOYER, Charles (1899-)
La Bacarolle d'Amour
Le Captaine Fracasse
Chantelouve

L'Esclave
Le Grillon du Foyer
L'Homme du Large
Le Proces de Mary Dugan (The Trial of Mary Dugan)
La Ronde Infernale
Stage:
Les Jardins de Murcie - Paris 20
Mélo - Paris 28
Le Voyaguer - Paris 22

517
BOYTON, Betty*
Enemies of Women (Alicia's maid)

518
BRABAN, Harvey*
Blackmail

519
BRACY, Sidney (1882-1941)
Amateur Devil, The
Being Respectable
Bishop Murder Case, The
Blackbird, The (Bertie's No. 1 man)
Cameraman, The
Courtship of Miles Standish, The
Crazy to Marry
Dictator, The
Haunted House, The
Her Night of Romance
His Captive Woman
Home, James
Is Matrimony a Failure?
Man-Made Women
March Hare, The
Merry-Go-Round (Gisella's groom)
Merry Widow, The (Danilo's footman)
Midnight
Miser's Revenge, The
Morals
Nobody's Bride
Painting the Town
Passion Fruit
Queen Kelly (the Prince's butler)
Radio King, The [serial]
Show People
Sioux Blood
Snapshots
So This Is Marriage
Social Buccaneer, The [serial]
Wedding March, The (valet)
Why Men Leave Home
Win that Girl
Woman on Trial, The
Woman Outside, The
You Never Know Women

520
BRADBURY, James, Jr. (1894-   )
Alibi /aka/ The Perfect Alibi (Blake)
Annie Against the World
Bits of Life
Cheyenne
Classmates
Drop Kick, The
Flying Romeos
Glorious Trail, The
Hawk's Nest, The
Hell-Ship Bronson
In Old Arizona (soldier)
Let It Rain
Night Stick
Rogue Song, The (Azamat)
She's a Sheik
Smilin' Guns
Walking Back
Waterfront
Winning Through ("Silent" Clay)

521
BRADBURY, James, Sr. (1857-   )
Blockade
Blood Ship
Circus Ace, The
Fair Co-Ed, The
Fascinating Youth
Hot Heels
Leopard Lady, The
Manhattan
Scarlet Seas (Johnson)
Skinner's Big Idea
Tide of the Empire
Woman from Hell

522
BRADBURY, Kitty*
Code of the Wilderness, The
Our Hospitality
Pilgrim, The (the girl's mother)

523
BRADDELL, Maurice*
Dawn (British airman)

524
BRADFORD, Virginia*
Chicago
Country Doctor, The
Craig's Wife
Two Lovers (Grete)
Wreck of the Hesperus, The

525
BRADIN, Jean*
At the Edge of the World (the lieutenant)

Eine Du Barry von Heute [A Modern
  Du Barry] (King Sandro)
Moulin Rouge
Theatre

526
BRADLEY, Estelle*
All Steamed Up

527
BRADLEY, Malcolm*
Sentimental Tommy

528
BRADY, Alice (1893-1939)
Anna Ascends
Dawn of the East
Fear Market, The
Hush Money
Land of Hope, The
Leopardess, The
Little Italy
Missing Millions
New York Idea, The
Out of the Chorus
Sinners
Snow Bride, The
Stage:
Anna Ascends (Anna Ayjobb) 20
Bride of the Lamb, The (Ina Bow-
  man) 26
Drifting (Cassie Cook) 22
Game of Love and Death (Sophie de
  Courvoisier) 29
Karl and Anna (Anna) 29
Love Letter, The (Marie) 21
Oh, Mama (Jacqueline LaGarde) 25
Zander the Great (Mamie) 23

529
BRADY, Edward (1889-)
Alibi /aka/ The Perfect Alibi
  (George Stanislaus David)
Boy Crazy
Bush Ranger, The
Clancy's Kosher Wedding
Code of the Scarlet
Do Your Duty
Dressed to Kill
False Code, The
Harold Teen
If You Believe It, It's So
Kentucky Colonel
Light in the Clearing, A
Lost at the Front
Marry Me
Old Dad
Old Homestead, The

Over the Border
Price She Paid, The
Pride of Palomar, The
Racing Hearts
Rough Diamond
Silent Call, The
Siren Call, The
Stewed, Fried and Boiled
Three Faces West
To the Last Man
Trail of the Lonesome Pine, The
Who Pays? [serial]

530
BRADY, Edwin J. (1889-)
Broken Wing, The
Eternal Struggle, The
Fighting American, The
Flower of the Night
King of Kings, The (bit)
Old Homestead, The
Thundering Herd, The (Follanshee)
Trail of the Lonesome Pine, The
Winning of Barbara Worth, The

531
BRADY, Philip*
Valley of the Giants, The

532
BRAHAM, Lionel*
Don Juan (Duke Margoni)
Night Life (a war profiteer)
Skinner's Dress Suit

533
BRAIDON, Thomas*
Great Adventure, The

534
BRAIDWOOD, Frank*
Only Thing, The

535
BRAITHWAITE, Lillian (1873-1948)
Downhill (Lady Berwick)
Stage:
Vortex, The (Florence Lancaster) 25

536
BRAMLEY, Flora*
College
We Americans

537
BRANDER, Allen*
Making of O'Malley, The

538
BRANDON, Dickie*
Spirit of the U. S. A. , The

539
BRANDON, Mary*
Bashful Sister, The

540
BRANDT, Mathile*
Hamlet (Gertrude)

541
BRANDT, Walter*
Midsummer Night's Dream, A (Snug)

542
BRANION, Antonio*
Cabiria

543
BRANTFORD, Albert*
This Freedom

544
BRANTFORD, Mickey (1912-)
Dawn (Jacques)
Maré Nostrum [Our Sea] (Esteban)
This Freedom (Robert)

545
BRASSEUR, Pierre (1903-1972)
Claudine à l'Ecole

546
BRATHWAYT, Raymond*
Beyond the Rocks (Sir Patrick Fitz-
gerald)
Great Moment, The (Lord Crombie)

547
BRAUSEWETTER, Hans*
Jew of Mestri, The (Lanzelot Gobbo)
Jolly Peasant, The
Der Oberkellner
Der Sprung ins Leben [The Leap into
Life]

548
BREAMER, Sylvia (1896-)
Barefoot Boy, The
Bavu
Blood Barrier, The
Calvert's Valley
Dawn
Devil, The
Doubling for Romeo
Flaming Youth

Girl of the Golden West, The
Her Temporary Husband
Lightning Reporter
Lilies of the Field
Lord of Thundergate
Man Unconquerable, The
Moonshine Trail, The
My Lady's Garter
Not Guilty
Paramount player 20
Respectable by Proxy
Unseen Forces
Up in Mabel's Room
Woman on the Jury, The

549
BRECHER, Egon*
Royal Box, The

550
BRECKER, Fred*
Folly of Vanity

551
BREEDEN, John*
Movietone Follies of 1929 (George
Shelby)
Salute
Shannons of Broadway, The

552
BREESE, Edmund (1871-1935)
Back to Liberty
Beyond the Rainbow (Insp. Richardson)
Brown Derby, The
Burn 'Em Up Barnes
Burning Daylight
Conquest
Curse of Drink, The
Damaged Hearts
Fancy Baggage
Finders Keepers
From Headquarters
Gamblers, The
Girl Overboard
Girls Gone Wild
Haunted House, The
Highbinders, The
Home Made
Hottentot, The
In the Headlines
Jacqueline of the Blazing Barriers
Little Red School House, The
Live Wire, The
Luck
Man's Home, A
Marriage Morals
On Trial (Judge)

Paradise for Two
Perfect Crime, A
Port of Dreams
Restless Wives
Shooting of Dan McGrew, The
Sonny Boy
Speed Spook, The
Stepping Along
Sure-Fire Flint
Three O'Clock in the Morning
Wild Fire
Womanhandled
Wright Idea, The
Stage:
So This Is London (Hiram Draper) 22

553
BREGMER, Sylvia*
Not Guilty

554
BREITENSTRÄTER, Hans*
Sein Grösster Bluff [Her Greatest
  Bluff] (bit)

555
BRENDEL, El (Elmer G. Brendel)
  (1898-1964)
Arizona Bound
Campus Flirt, The
Cock-Eyed World, The (Olson)
Cross Pull
Fox player 27
Frozen Justice
Hot for Paris
Jubilo
Man of the Forest, The
Paramount player 26
Sunny Side Up (Eric Svenson)
Too Many Crooks
What Price Glory?
Wings (August Schmidt)
You Never Know Women

556
BRENNAN, Dennis*
Rising of the Moon, The

557
BRENNAN, Joseph*
Highest Bidder, The

558
BRENNAN, Walter (1894-1974)
Lariat Kid, The
Long, Long Trail, The
One Hysterical Night
Shannons of Broadway, The

Silks and Saddles
Smilin' Guns
Watch Your Wife (extra)

559
BRENON, Juliet*
Kiss for Cinderella, A (third customer)
Street of Forgotten Men, The

560
BRENT, Evelyn (Mary Elizabeth Riggs)
  (1899-)
Beau Sabreur (Mary vanBrugh)
Blind Alleys
Broadway (Pearl)
Broadway Lady
Dangerous Flirt
Darkened Rooms
Door that Has No Key, The
Dragnet
Fast Company
Flame of the Argentine
Forbidden Cargo
Held to Answer
His Tiger Lady
Imposter, The
Interference
Jade Cup, The
Lady Robinhood
Last Command, The (Natacha Dabrova)
Law Divine, The
Lone Chance, The
Love 'em and Leave 'em
Love's Greatest Mistake
Loving Lies
Married to a Mormon
Mating Call
Midnight Molly
Nevada
Night of Mystery, A
Queen of Diamonds
Secret Orders
Showdown, The
Shuttle of Life, The
Silk Stocking Sal
Smooth as Satin
Sonia (Sonia Dainton)
Spanish Jade
Sybil
Three Wise Crooks
Tiger Lady, The
Underworld ("Feathers" McCoy)
Why Bring that Up?
Why Men Forget
Woman Trap
Woman Who Came Back, The
Women's Wares

561
BRETT, Angela*
Knight in London, A

562
BRETTEL, Colette*
Blood Money (Felice Deschannel)
Der Juxbaron [The Imaginary Baron]
  (Hilda von Grabow)

563
BRIAN, Mary (1908-)
Air Mail, The
Alias the Deacon
Beau Geste (Isobel)
Behind the Front
Big Killing, The
Black Waters
Brown of Harvard
Children of Divorce
Enchanted Hill, The
Forgotten Faces
Harold Teen
Her Father Said No
High Hat
It Must Be Love
Kibitzer, The
Knockout Reilly
Little French Girl, The
Man I Love, The
Man Power
Marriage Playground (Judith Wheater)
More Pay, Less Work
Paris at Midnight
Partners in Crime
Peter Pan (Wendy)
Prince of Tempters, The
Regular Fellow, A
River of Romance
Running Wild (Elizabeth)
Shanghai Bound
Someone to Love
Stepping Along
Street of Forgotten Men, The
Two Flaming Youths (Mary Gilfoil)
Under the Tonto Rim
Varsity
Virginian, The (Molly Wood)

564
BRICE, Betty*
Beau Brummel (Mrs. Snodgrass)

565
BRICE, Fanny (Fanny Borach) (1891-
  1951)
My Man
Night Club

Stage:
Music Box Revue, The 24
Ziegfeld Follies of 1920
Ziegfeld Follies of 1921
Ziegfeld Follies of 1923

566
BRIESC, Gerd*
U-Boat 9

567
BRINDEAU, Jeanne*
Enemies of Women (Madame Spadoni)
Michael Strogoff (Marfa)

568
BRINK, Elga*
Quo Vadis?

569
BRINKLEY, Neil*
Great White Way, The

570
BRINKMAN, Dolores*
Mysterious Island, The

571
BRISBANE, Arthur*
Great White Way, The

572
BRISSON, Carl (Carl Brisson Peder-
  sen) (1897-1958)
American Prisoner, The (Lt. Stark)
Chelsea Nights
Manxman, The
Ring, The

573
BRITTON, Hutin*
Wandering Jew, The (Judith)

574
BROAD, Kid*
Great White Way, The

575
BROCK, Baby Dorothy*
So Big (Dirk DeJong)
Woman on Trial, The

576
BROCK, Dorothy*
Christine of the Hungry Heart
Just a Woman
Lilies of the Field
So Big

577
BROCKMANN
Der Mensch Am Wege [Man by the
  Roadside]

578
BROCKWELL, Gladys (1893-1930)
Ancient Mariner, The (Life in Death)
Argyle Case, The (Mrs. Martin)
Carnival Girl
Chickie
Continued Above
Darling of New York, The
Devil's Riddle, The
Double Stakes
Drake Case, The
From Headquarters
Hard Boiled Rose
Harold Teen (Lillums)
Her Sacrifice
Home Towners, The
Hottentot, The
Hunchback of Notre Dame, The (Sis-
  ter Godule)
La Granga
Last Frontier, The
Law and the Man, The
Lights of New York (Molly)
Long Pants
Man, Woman and Sin
Mother of His Children, The
My Home Town
Oliver Twist (Nancy Sikes)
Paid Back
Penrod and Sam (Mother Schofeld)
Rose of Nome
Sage Hen, The
Satin Woman, The
Seventh Heaven (Nana)
Sister to Salome
So Big (Marchie Poole)
Spangles
Splendid Road, The
Stella Maris
Thieves Again
Twinkletoes (Cissie)
White Lies
Woman Disputed (the Countess)

579
BRODERICK, Helen (1891-1959)
Quarterback, The
Stage:
Fifty Million Frenchmen (Violet Hil-
  degarde) 29

580
BRODIE, Buster*
All Aboard

581
BRODY, Ann (1894-)
Afraid to Love
Alias the Lone Wolf
Case of Lena Smith, The
Clancy's Kosher Wedding
Fool and His Money, A
Footlights
Headin' Home
Jake, the Plumber
Lost in a Big City
Manicure Girl, The
My Man
Sainted Devil, A
Shams of Society
So This Is College
Times Square
Turn Back the Hours
Why Girls Say No
Wolf Song (Duenna)

582
BRODY, Estelle (1904-)
Flight Commander, The
Glad Eye, The
Hindle Wakes (Fanny Hawthorne)
Kitty
Mademoiselle from Armentieres (Title
  role)
Mademoiselle Parley-Voo (Title role)
Me and the Boys
Plaything
Sailors Don't Care
This Marriage Business
Week-End Wives
White Heat

583 [No entry]

584
BRONEAU, Helen*
Merry-Go-Round (Jane)

585
BRONSON, Betty (1906-)
Are Parents People?
Bellamy Trial, The (girl reporter)
Ben-Hur (Madonna)
Brass Knuckles
Cat's Pajamas, The
Companionate Marriage, The
Everybody's Acting
Golden Princess, The (Title role)
Grand Duchess and the Waiter, The
Kiss for Cinderella, A (Cinderella)
Little French Girl, The
Locked Door, The
Modern Sappho, A
Not So Long Ago

One Stolen Night
Open Range
Paradise
Paradise for Two
Paramount player 26
Peter Pan (Title role)
Ritzy
Singing Fool, The
Sonny Boy

586
BRONTE, Jean*
Moonshine Valley (Jeane, the dog)

587
BROOK, Clive (Clifford Brook) (1891-
    1974)
Afraid to Love
Awakening, The
Barbed Wire
Charming Sinners, The (Robert Mills)
Christie Johnstone (Astral Hither)
Christine of the Hungry Heart
Compromise
Dangerous Woman, A
Daniel Deronda (Mallinger Grand-
    court)
Debt of Honor, A
Declassee
Devil Dancer, The
Enticement
Experiment, The
For Alimony Only
Forgotten Faces
Four Feathers, The (Capt. Durrance)
French Dressing
Heliotrope
Her Penalty
Home Maker, The
Hula (Anthony Haldane)
Human Desires
If Marriage Fails
Interference
Kissing Cup's Race (Lord Rattlington)
La Traviata
Laughing Lady, The
Loudwater Mystery, The
Love and a Whirlwind
Married to a Mormon
Midnight Madness
Mirage, The
Money Habit, The
Out to Win
Parson's Fight, The
Passionate Adventure, The
Perfect Crime, The
Playing with Souls
Pleasure Buyers

Popular Sin, The
Recoil, The
Return of Sherlock Holmes, The
    (Sherlock Holmes)
Reverse of the Medal, The
Rigoletto
Royal Oak, The
Seven Sinners
Sheik, The
Shirley
Sir Rupert's Wife
Slightly Scarlet
Sonia (David O'Rane)
Sportsman's Wife, A
Stable Companions
Tale of Two Cities, A
This Freedom (Harry Occlene)
Three Faces East
Through Fire and Water
Trent's Last Case
Underworld ("Rolls Royce")
Universal player 25
Vanity Fair
When Love Grows Cold
Whispering
White Shadow, The
Why Girls Go Back Home
Wine of Life, The
Woman Hater, The
Woman to Woman (David Compton/
    David Anson-Pond)
Yellow Lily, The
You Never Know Women

588
BROOK, Helen*
Woman Hater, The

589
BROOK, Hugh*
Rat, The (Paul)

590
BROOK, Olive*
This Freedom
Why Girls Go Back Home

591
BROOKE, Claude*
Classmates
Pied Pipper Malone
Winning Through (Duncan Irving, Sr.)

592
BROOKE, Tyler*
Cradle Snatchers, The
Dynamite (the life of the party)
Fazil (Jacques Debreuze)

Kiss Doctor, The
Madame Mystery (hungry artist)
Night of Daze, A
None but the Brave
Rich, but Honest
Stage Madness
Too Many Cookies
Van Bibber Comedies (8)

593
BROOKE, Van Dyke*
Crimson Cross, The
Fortune Hunter, The
Midnight Bell, A
Passionate Pilgrim, The
Son of Wallingford, The (Henry Bee-
    goode)

594
BROOKS, Alan*
Hole in the Wall, The (Jim)
King of Kings, The (Satan)
Pals in Paradise
Red Dice
Shanghaied
South Sea Love
Young April
Stage:
Expressing Willie (Taliaferro) 24

595
BROOKS, Louise (1900-)
American Venus, The
Beauty Prize
Beggars of Life
Canary Murder Case, The (Margaret
    O'Dell)
City Gone Wild, A
Diary of a Lost Girl
Evening Clothes
Girl in Every Port, A (French girl)
It's the Old Army Game (Mildred
    Marshall)
Just Another Blonde /aka/ Girl
    from Coney Island
Love 'em and Leave 'em
Now We're in the Air (dual role)
Pandora's Box
Rolled Stockings
Show-Off, The
Social Celebrity, A
Street of Forgotten Men
Too Many Women
We're in the Navy Now
Windy Riley Goes to Hollywood
Stage:
George White Scandals 24
Ruth St. Denis and Ted Shawn Co.
    21-24

Ziegfeld Follies 25

596
BROOKS, Roy*
High and Dizzy (the boy's friend)

597
BROPHY, Edward (1895-1960)
Cameraman, The
Yes or No?

598
BROSKE, Octavia*
Great Adventure, The

599
BROUGH, Mary (1863-1934)
Amazing Quest of Mr. Ernest Bliss,
    The (Gloria Mott)
Dawn (Madame Pitou)
Only Way, The (Miss Pross)
Squibs (Mrs. Lee)

600
BROWDER, Robert*
Honeymoon Express, The

601
BROWER, Otto*
All the Brothers Were Valiant (Mor-
    rell)
Excuse My Dust (Henderson)

602
BROWER, Robert (1850-)
Adam's Rib (Hugo Kermaier)
Beggars of Life
City Sparrow, The
Cumberland Romance, A
Faith Healer, The
Fifth Avenue Models
Fools First
Gay Defender, The
Harbinger of Peace
Held by the Enemy
Honeymoon Express, The
Jack Straw
Jucklins, The
Last Trail, The
Little Minister, The
Long Live the King
Lost Romance
Lying Truth, The
Singed Wings
What Every Woman Knows

603 [No entry]

604
BROWN, Charles D. *
Dance of Life, The (Lefty)
Dangerous Curves (Spider)

605
BROWN, Dorothy*
Girl from Havana, The

606
BROWN, Edwin*
Jenny Be Good

607
BROWN EYES (a cow)
Go West

608
BROWN, Halbert*
Civilian Clothes (Major General
   Girard)
Democracy, the Vision Restored

609
BROWN, Joe*
Cock-Eyed World, The (Brownie)
Dressed to Kill
Ghost Talks, The
In Old Arizona (bartender)
Me, Gangster (himself)
Sunny Side Up (Joe Vitto)

610
BROWN, Joe E. (Joseph Even
   Brown) (1892-1973)
Circus Kid, The
Crooks Can't Win
Hit of the Show
Maybe It's Love
Molly and Me
My Lady's Past
On with the Show (Beaton)
Painted Faces
Protection
Reputation
Sally (Connie, the Grand Duke)
Song of the West (Hasty)
Square Crooks
Take Me Home
Stage:
Captain Jinks (Hap Jones) 25
Jim Jam Jems (Philip Quick) 20

611
BROWN, John Edwin (1892-)
Queen of Burlesque
Scaramouche (Monsieur Benoit)

612
BROWN, Johnny Mack (1904-1974)
Angel Face
Annapolis
Bugle Call, The (debut)
Coquette (Michael Jeffery)
Divine Woman, The
Fair Co-ed, The (Bob)
Hurricane, The
Jazz Heaven
Lady of Chance, A
Little Angel, The
Metro-Goldwyn player 27
Our Dancing Daughters (Ben Black)
Play Girl, The
Single Standard, The (Tommy Hewlett)
Soft Living
Sport Girl, The
Square Crooks
Valiant, The
Varsity
Woman of Affairs, A (David)

613
BROWN, Josephine*
Strange Cargo

614
BROWN, Julia*
Abysmal Brute, The (Violet MacTavish)

615
BROWN, Nacio Herb*
Broadway Melody, The (Gleason's pi-
   anist)

616
BROWN, Peggy*
Gold Diggers, The (Trixie Andrews)

617
BROWN, Tom (1913-)
Hoosier Schoolmaster, The
Lady Lies, The (Bob Rossiter)
Sons of the Legion
That Old Gang of Mine
Wrongdoers

618
BROWN, Virginia*
Old Fashioned Boy, An

619
BROWN, W. H. *
Dancin' Fool (Gaines)

620
BROWNE, Harry C. *
Know Your Men

621
BROWNE, Irene*
Letter, The

622
BROWNE, J. Edwin--see: Brown,
    John Edwin

623
BROWNIE (a dog)
Little Johnny Jones

624
BROWNLEE, Frank*
Beggars of Life
Desert Flower, The
Riders of the Dawn
Sawdust Paradise
Shore Acres
Social Highwayman, The
Through Different Eyes (bit)

625
BROX SISTERS, The
Hollywood Revue of 1929

626
BRUCE, Billy*
Smitty

627
BRUCE, Clifford*
Devil May Care

628
BRUCE, Kate*
City of Silent Men, The
Experience
Flying Pat
I Want My Man
Idol Dancer, The (Mrs. Blythe)
Jacqueline of the Blazing Barriers
Mary Ellen Comes to Town
Orphans of the Storm (Sister Gene-
    vieve)
Star Dust
Studio Secret, The
Way Down East (Mrs. Bartlett)
White Rose, The (an aunt)

629
BRUCE, Michael*
His House in Order (the footman)

630
BRUCE, Nigel (William Nigel Bruce)
    (1895-1953)
Red Aces

Stage:
Debut in London 1920

631
BRUCE, Virginia (Helen Virginia
    Briggs) (1910-)
Blue Skies
Fugitives
Illusion
Lilies of the Field
Love Parade, The (2nd lady in waiting)
Why Bring That Up?
Woman Trap

632
BRUNDAGE, Matilde*
Ambrose Applejohn's Adventure (Mrs.
    Agatha Whatcombe)
Charmer, The
Dangerous Business (Mrs. Flavell)
Fashion Row
Front Page Story, A
Love Me and the World Is Mine
Seven Sinners
Strangers of the Night
That's My Daddy

633
BRUNEL, Adrian*
Face at the Window, The

634
BRUNETTE, Fritzi (1894-1943)
Bells of San Juan, The
Boss of Camp Four, The
Coast of Opportunity, The
Devil to Pay, The
Dream Cheater, The
Driftwood
Footlight Ranger
Give Me My Son
Green Flame, The
House of Whispers, The
Live Sparks
Lord Loves the Irish, The
Man from Lost River, The'
Number 99
Pace that Thrills, The
Sure Fire
Thirty Thousand Dollars
Tiger True

635
BRUNO, Jennie*
Street Angel (landlady)

636
BRYANT, Charles E. (1887-1948)
Billions

Doll's House, A
Heart of a Child, The
Salome
Stronger than Death

637
BRYANT, Kay*
Wild Party, The (Thelma)

638
BRYSON, Arthur*
Wild Fire

639
BRYSON, Winifred*
Adoration
Awful Truth, The
Broken Barriers
Crashing Through
Flirting with Love
Great Night, The
Her Face Value
Hunchback of Notre Dame, The
   (Fleur de Lys)
Pleasure Mad
South of Suva
Suzanna
Truxton King, The

640
BUCCOLA, Guy*
Street Girl

641
BUCHANAN, Claud*
Fascinating Youth
Running Wild (Jerry Harvey)

642
BUCHANAN, Jack (1891-1957)
Audacious Mr. Squire, The
Bulldog Drummond's Third Round
Confetti
Happy Ending, The
Paris
Settled Out of Court
Show of Shows, The
Toni
Stage:
A to Z - London 21
Wake Up and Dream 29

643
BUCHMA, Ambrose*
Arsenal

644
BUCK, Nell Roy*
Forever

645
BUCKLEY, William*
Sky High (Victor Castle)

646
BUDDY (a dog)
Devil's Circus, The

647
BUGHARDT, George*
Dancing Vienna

648
BULL, Charles Edward*
Iron Horse, The (Abraham Lincoln)

649
BULLERJAHN, Curt*
Sein Grösster Bluff [Her Greatest
   Bluff] (a gangster)

650
BULLOCK, Boris*
Border Cavalier

651
BUNKE, Ralph*
Scrambled Wives

652
BUNNY, George*
Enticement
Lights of Old Broadway (Tony Paster)
Locked Door, The
Lost World, The (Colin McArdle)
Man and the Moment, The

653
BUNSTON, Herbert*
Last of Mrs. Cheney, The (Lord El-
   ton)
Stage:
Young Woodley (Simmons) 25

654
BURANI, Michelette*
Aloma of the South Seas

655
BURCH, Helen*
Married? (7-11 Sadie)

656
BURCHARDT, Elsa*
Eva and the Grasshopper

657
BURDETTE, Jack*
Street of Sin

658
BURDICK, Rose*
Butterflies in the Rain
Kiss in a Taxi, A

659
BURG, Eugen*
Dancing Vienna
Eine Du Barry von Heute [A Modern
   Du Barry]
Sein Grösset Bluff [Her Greatest
   Bluff] (Police Superintendent)
When Fleet Meets Fleet (German
   commander's father)
Wrath of the Sea

660
BURGESS, Dorothy (1907-)
In Old Arizona (Tonia Maria)
Pleasure Crazed
Protection
Song of Kentucky

661
BURKE, Billie (Mary William Ethel-
   bert Appleton Burke (1886-1970)
Away Goes Prudence
Education of Elizabeth, The
Frisky Mrs. Johnson
Glorifying the American Girl
Let's Get a Divorce
Sadie Love
Stage:
Annie Dear (Annie Leigh) 24
Intimate Strangers, The (Isabel) 21
Marquise, The (Eloise de Kestournel)
   27

662
BURKE, Joe*
Fascinating Youth
Hangman's House
His Children's Children
Pied Piper Malone
Too Many Kisses
West of the Water Tower

663
BURKE, Johnny*
Bride's Relations, The
Good-Bye Kiss, The
Matchmaking Mamas
Old Barn, The

664
BURKE, Joseph*
Adventurous Sex, The
Lucky Devil, The

Pinch Hitter, The (Charlie)
Royal Rider
Show of Shows, The
White Rose, The (landlord)

665
BURKE, Marie R. *
Evidence (Mrs. Bascom)
Heart Raider, The
Little Miss Rebellion
Little Old New York (Mrs. Schuyler)
Three Miles Out
Without Fear

666
BURLEIGH, Bertram*
Black Spider, The

667
BURLO, Josephine*
Cossacks, The

668
BURMEISTER, Augusta /aka/ Augusta
   Burmaster*
Greene Murder Case, The (Gertrude
   Mannheim)

669
BURNABY, Davy (1881-1949)
Co-optimists, The

670
BURNHAM, Beatrice*
Riders of the Purple Sage (Millie Erne)
Siege

671
BURNHAM, Nicholas*
Uncle Sam of Freedom Ridge

672
BURNS, Bobby*
Cock-Eyed World, The
Movietone Follies of 1929

673
BURNS, Eddie /aka/ Edward, Edmund
   (1892-)
Black Cargo of the South Seas
Broadway after Dark
Children of the Ritz
Chinese Parrot, The
Country Kid, The
Dramatic Life of Abraham Lincoln
   /aka/ Abraham Lincoln (John
   McNeil)
East Is West

Forlorn River
Green Temptation
Guilty One, The
Hard to Get
Hell's High Road
Humming Bird, The (Randall Carey)
Jazzmania
Lady in the Wilderness
Love Racket, The
Made for Love
Manicure Girl, The
Million Dollar Handicap
Out of the Storm
Paris at Midnight
Phyllis of the Follies
Poor Girls
Princess from Hoboken
Ransom
Ruling Passion, The
Scars of Jealousy
Shamrock and the Rose, The
She Goes to War
Simon, the Jester
Sunny Side Up
Tanned Legs
To Please a Woman
Virgin of Stamboul, The
Whispering Wires

674
BURNS, Fred*
California Mail, The
Rio Rita (Wilkins)

675
BURNS, George (Nathan Birnbaum)
  (1896-)
Burns and Allen in Lambchops

676
BURNS, Neal (1892-1962)
Any Old Port
Christie Comedies (10)
Darn that Stocking
Dollar Down, A
Educational Comedies
He Married His Wife
Hot Scotch
Hot Water
Loose Change
Mary's Ankles
Should Scotchmen Marry?
Slick Slickers, The
That Son of a Sheik

677
BURNS, Paul*
Mollycoddle, The (a college boy)

678
BURNS, Robert "Bobby"*
Arabian Love
Cock-Eyed World, The (Connors)
Lazy Days
Movietone Follies of 1929

679
BURR, Eugene*
Son of Tarzan, The [serial] (Ivan
  Paulovich)

680
BURRELL, George*
Sea Beast, The (Perth)
Sea Hunt, The

681
BURROUGHS, James*
Broadway Melody, The (singer)

682
BURT, Margaret*
Night of Mystery, A

683
BURT, William P.*
Leopard Lady, The

684
BURTON, Clarence (1882-)
Adam's Rib (cave man)
Angel of Broadway, The
Barnum Was Right
Beautiful and Damned
Behold, My Wife!
Bluff
Chicago
Coming of Amos, The
Conrad in Quest of His Youth
Crimson Challenge, The
Dynamite (an officer)
Fighting Chance
Fighting Eagle, The
Fool's Paradise (Manuel)
Forbidden Fruit (Steve Maddock)
Garrison's Finish
Godless Girl, The (a guard)
Her Husband's Trademark (Mexican
  bandit)
Her Own Money
Impossible Mrs. Bellew, The (detec-
  tive)
Jucklins, The
King of Kings, The (Dysmas, the re-
  pentant thief)
Law and the Woman, The
Lost Romance

Love Racket, The
Love Special
Man Unconquerable, The
Midnight Madness
Miss Lulu Bett (Ninian Deacon)
Mr. Billings Spends His Dime
Navigator, The
Nervous Wreck, The
Nobody's Money
One Glorious Day
Only Way, The (Jacques Deforge)
Ordeal, The
Red Dice
Road to Yesterday, The (Hugh Arm-
strong)
Rubber Tires
Six Best Cellars, The
Square Crooks
Stand and Deliver (Commanding Of-
ficer)
Stool Pigeon, The
Submarine
Ten Commandments, The (The Task-
master
Thou Art the Man
Three Faces West
What's Your Hurry?
Yankee Clipper, The

685
BURTON, Frederick (1871-)
Bits of Life
Fighting Blade, The (Oliver Crom-
well)
Heliotrope
Rejected Woman, The
Running Wild (Mr. Harvey)
Yes or No?

686
BURTON, Langhorne (1872-)
Amateur Gentleman, The
Appearances
At the Villa Rose
Bonnie Briar Bush
By Berwen Banks
Children of Gibeon, The
Little Dorrit
Man's Shadow, A
Moth and Rust
Sexton Blake [series]
Temptress, The
Two Little Wooden Shoes
Who Is the Man?

687
BURTON, Ned*
Daughter of Two Worlds, A

688
BUSCH, Mae (1897-1946)
Alibi /aka/ The Perfect Alibi (Daisy
Thomas)
Beauty Shoppers
Black Butterflies
Bread
Bride of the Night
Broken Barriers
Brothers under the Skin
Christian, The (Glory Quayle)
Devil's Passkey, The (La Belle Odera)
Fazil (Helene Debreuze)
Flaming Love
Foolish Wives (Princess Vera Petsch-
nikoff)
Fools of Fashion
Frivolous Sal
Her Husband's Friend
Her Own Money
Kiss Me Again
Love Charm, The
Love 'em and Weep
Man's Man, A
Married Flirts
Miracle of Life, The
Name the Man
Nellie, the Beautiful Cloak Model
Night Stick
Nut Cracker /aka/ You Can't Fool
Your Wife
Only a Shop Girl
Pardon My Nerve
Parisian Scandal, A
Perch of the Devil
Racing Through
Ruthful Sex, The
San Francisco Nights
Shooting of Dan McGrew, The (Flo
Dupont)
Sisters of Eve
Souls for Sale (Robina Teele)
Time, the Comedian
Tongues of Scandal
Unaccustomed as We Are
Unholy Three, The (Rosie O'Grady)
While the City Sleeps (Bessie)

689
BUSH, Kenneth R. *
Drivin' Fool, The

690
BUSH, Pauline*
Enemy Sex, The

691
BUSH, Renee*
White Shadows of the South Seas (Lucy)

692
BUSHELL, Anthony (1904-   )
Disraeli (Lord Charles Deeford)
Green Stockings
Jealousy
Lilies of the Field
Show of Shows, The

693
BUSHMAN, Francis X. , Jr. (Ralph
  E. Bushman) (1903-   )
Brown of Harvard
Dangerous Traffic
Eyes Right
Four Sons
It's a Great Life
Marlie, the Killer
Marriage Clause, The
Masked Bride, The
Midnight Faces
MGM player 25 and 29
Our Hospitality
Scarlet Arrow, The [serial]
Thirteenth Juror, The
Understanding Heart, The (Tony Gar-
  land)

694
BUSHMAN, Francis X. , Sr. (Francis
  Xavier Bushman) (1883-1966)
According to Hoyle
Ben-Hur (Messala)
Charge of the Gauchos
Grip of the Yukon, The
Lady in Ermine, The
Making the Grade
Man Higher Up, The
Marriage Clause, The
Masked Bride, The
Midnight Life
Modern Marriage
Say It with Sables
Scarlet Arrow, The [serial]
Smiling All the Way
Thirteenth Juror, The

695
BUSHMAN, Ralph E. --see: Francis
  X. Bushman, Jr.

696
BUTLAND, William*
Q Ships

697
BUTLER, David (1894-   )
According to Hoyle
Bing, Bang, Boom!

Blue Eagle, The (Nick Galvani)
Code of the West (Bid Hatfield)
Conquering the Woman
Country Fair, The
Don't Ever Marry
Fickle Women
Havoc (Smithy)
Hero, The
His Majesty Bunker Bean
Hoodman Blind
In Hollywood with Potash and Perlmut-
  ter
Man on the Box, The
Meet the Prince
Milky Way, The
Narrow Street, The
Nobody's Widow
Noise in Newboro, A
Oh, Baby!
Plastic Age, The (Coach Henley)
Poor Men's Wives
Private Affairs
Quarterback, The
Rush Hour, The
Salute
Seventh Heaven (Gobin)
Sky Pilot
Smiling All the Way
Temple of Venus, The (Nat Harper)
Tracked in the Snow Country
Triflers
Village Blacksmith, The
Wise Kid, The
Womanpower

698
BUTLER, Frank E. *
Bluebeard's Eighth Wife (Lord Henry
  Seville)

699
BUTLER, Frank R. *
Beyond the Rocks (Lord Wensleydon)
Compromise
Great Moment, The (Eustace)
My American Wife (Horace Peresford)
Satan in Sables
Sheik, The (Sir Aubrey Mayo)
Tailor Made Man, The

700
BUTLER, Fred J. *
Bluff
In Hollywood with Potash and Perlmut-
  ter
Marriage in Transit (a conspirator)
Plastic Age, The
Welcome Stranger, The

701
BUTLER, George*
Chinese Bungalow, The (a Chinese
   servant)

702
BUTT, Johnny*
Blackmail
Every Mother's Son (Tricky)
Nell Gwyn (Samuel Pepys)

703
BUTT, Lawson (W. Lawson Butt)*
Any Woman
Barriers Burned Away
Beloved Rogue, The (Duke of Bur-
   gundy)
Dante's Inferno
Earthbound
Sting of the Lash, The (Rhodes)
Ten Commandments, The (Dathn,
   the Discontented)

704
BUTTERWORTH, Charles (1897-1946)
Life of the Party, The
Stage:
Allez-Oop 27
Americana 26
Sweet Adeline (Ruppert Day) 29

705
BUTTERWORTH, Ernest*
Deadwood Coach, The
Soul of Youth, The

706
BUTTERWORTH, Joe*
Black Lightning (dual role, Larned/
   Dick)
Born to the West
Little Annie Rooney
Narrow Street, The
Penrod and Sam (Sam Williams)

707
BUTTS, Billy*
Alias Jimmy Valentine (Bobby)
Canadian, The
Sparrows /aka/ Human Sparrows
   (a sparrow)
Two-Gun Man, The

708
BUTUMKIN, Gregory*
Rasputin, the Holy Sinner

709
BUZZELL, Eddie (Edward Buzzell)
   (1897-)
Little Johnny Jones
Stage:
Gingham Girl, The (John Cousins) 22

710
BYER, Charles*
Alex the Great
Cabaret
Clothes Make the Woman
New York
Red Hot Speed
Romance of the Rio Grande
Shanghai Bound

711
BYFORD, Roy*
John Falstaff (Title role)

712
BYRNE, Betsy*
Love's Greatest Mistake

713
BYRNE, Rosalind*
Fast Set, The (Connie Gallies)

714
BYRON, Eva*
Kreutzer Sonata, The

715
BYRON, Jack*
Air Mail, The
Fighting American, The
Four Walls
Spite Marriage

716
BYRON, Marion (Miriam Bilenkin)
   (1911-)
Broadway Babies
Forward Pass, The
His Captive Woman
Pair of Tights, A
Plastered in Paris
Show of Shows, The
So Long Letty
Song of the West (Penny)
Steamboat Bill, Jr.

717
BYRON, Peanut*
Forward Pass, The

718
BYRON, Roy*
Palm Beach Girl, The

719
BYRON, Walter (Walter Butler) (1901-)
Awakening, The
Queen Kelly (Prince Wild Wolfram)
Sacred Flame, The
Tommy Atkins

- C -

720
CABO, Louise*
Risky Business

721
CABOT, Elliott*
Puritan Passions
Stage:
Coquette (Michael Jeffery) 27
Mrs. Partridge Presents (Sydney
   Armstead) 25
Silver Cord, The (David) 26

722
CADE, Rose*
Salvage (the maid)

723
CADELL, Jean*
Anna the Adventuress
Stage:
At Mrs. Beam's (Miss Shoe) 26

724
CAGNEY, James (1904-)
Warner Brothers Stock Co. 29
Stage:
Grand Street Follies of 1928, The
Grand Street Follies of 1929, The
Maggie the Magnificent (Elwood) 29
Outside Looking In (Little Red) 25
Pitter Patter (chorus) 20
Ritz Girls (chorus) 20
Women Go on Forever (Eddie) 27

725
CAIN, Robert*
Children of Jazz
Crossroads of New York, The
Dancer of Paris, The
Drums of Fate
Everlasting Whisper, The
Golden Bed, The (Savarac)
Impossible Mrs. Bellew, The (Lance
   Bellew)

Man-Woman-Marriage
Romance of a Queen, The (Verchoff)
Three Weeks
Wilderness Woman, The
Wings of Youth

726
CAIRNS, Dallas*
Sally Bishop (Mr. Durlacher)

727
CALDWELL, Betty*
Ground Lightning

728
CALDWELL, Orville R. (1896-1967)
Cross Wires
Flamingo, The
French Doll, The
Girl's Diary, A
Harvester, The
Independent player 24
Judgment of the Hills
Little Yellow House, The
Lonesome Road, The
Patsy, The (Tony Anderson)
Ramon the Sailmaker
Sackcloth and Scarlet
Scarlet Lily, The
Wives of the Prophet
Stage:
Mecca (Al Malik Al-Nasir, The Sultan)
   20
Miracle, The (the knight) 24

729
CALHERN, Louis (Carl Henry Vogt)
   (1895-1956)
Blot, The
Last Moment, The
Too Wise Wives
What's Worth While?
Woman, Wake Up!
Stage:
Cobra (Jack Race) 24
In a Garden (Norrie Bliss) 25
Song and Dance Man, The (Joseph
   Murdock) 23
Woman Disputed, The (Lt. "Yank"
   Trinkard) 26

730
CALHOUN, Alice (1903-1966)
Angel of Crooked Street
Between Friends
Bride of the Desert
Charming Deceiver, The
Closed Doors
Code of the Wilderness, The

Down Grade, The
Everlasting Whisper, The
Flaming Gold
Flying High
Girl in His Room
Girl's Desire, A
Happy Warrior, The
Hero of the Big Snows
Hidden Aces
In the First Degree
Isle of Forgotten Women
Little Minister, The
Little Wildcat, The
Man from Brodney's, The
Man Next Door, The
Man on the Box, The
Masters of Men, The
Matrimonial Web
Midnight Alarm
One Stolen Night
Other Woman's Story, The
Pampered Youth
Peggy Puts It Over
Pioneer Trails
Power of the Weak
Princess Jones
Rainbow, The
Sea Rider
Tentacles of the North
Trunk Mystery, The
Vitagraph player 22

731
CALHOUN, Jeanne*
Officer 666

732
CALHOUN, Kathleen*
Man on the Box, The

733
CALHOUN, Pat*
Vanity Fair (Mrs. Quill)

734
CALLAHAN, Andrew J.*
Redskin, The

735
CALLIGA, George*
Bedroom Window, The

736
CALLIS, David*
Sin Sister

737
CALTHROP, Donald (1888-1940)
Atlantic (Pointer)

Blackmail (Tracy)
Shooting Stars

738
CALVERT, Catherine*
Dead Men Tell No Tales
Heart of Maryland, The (Maryland
    Calvert)
Indian Love Lyrics
Moral Fibre
That Woman
You Find It Everywhere
Stage:
Blood and Sand (Dona Sol) 21

739
CALVERT, E. H. (1890-)
Bluff
Border Legion, The
Canary Murder Case, The (D. A. John
    F. Markham)
Dark Streets
Darkened Rooms
East of Suez
First Auto, The
Girl from Montmartre, The
Greene Murder Case, The (D. A. John
    F. Markham)
Inez from Hollywood
Kibitzer, The
King Robert of Sicily
Legion of the Condemned, The (com-
    mandant)
Let 'em Go Gallagher
Love Parade, The (Sylvanian Ambas-
    sador)
Men Are Like That
Mighty, The
Moran of the Marines
Only Woman, The
Peacock Alley
Prep and Pep
Rookies
Sally (Richard Farquar)
Silent Partner, The
Studio Murder Mystery, The (Grant)
Talker, The
Thunderbolt
Virginian, The (Judge Henry)
Why Men Leave Home
Why Sailors Go Wrong
Wizard, The

740
CAMEO, the Wonder Dog
Penrod and Sam (Duke)

741
CAMERE, Manuel*
Tiger Love

742
CAMERON, Gene*
Circe the Enchantress
Excuse Me
Gay Retreat, The
Midnight Kiss, The (Spencer Atkins)

743
CAMERON, Hugh*
Cappy Ricks
For the Love of Mike (Patrick
    O'Malley)
Homeward Bound
Man Who Found Himself, The
Pied Piper Malone

744
CAMERON, Jack*
Applause (Joe King)

745
CAMERON, Rudolph*
Coney Island
For the Love of Mike (Henry Sharp)
Song of the West (Singleton)
Three-Ring Marriage

746
CAMPBELL, Betty*
Hound of the Baskervilles, The

747
CAMPBELL, Colin*
White Monkey, The

748
CAMPBELL, Daisy*
Woman of No Importance, A (Lady
    Hunstanton)

749
CAMPBELL, Margaret*
Children of Divorce (Mother Superior)
Fast Worker, The
Home Maker, The

750
CAMPBELL, Webster*
Love Racket, The

751
CAMPEAU, Frank (-1943)
Alaskan, The
Candy Kid, The

Cheating Cheaters
Coming Through
Crimson Challenge, The
False Kisses
First Auto, The
For Those We Love (Frank)
Frozen River
Gamblers, The
Golden Cocoon, The
Greater Duty
Heart of the Yukon
Hoodman Blind
In Old Arizona (cowboy)
In the Headlines
Isle of Lost Ships, The (Detective
    Jackson)
Just Tony
Kid, The
Killer, The
Lane that Has No Turning Point, The
Let It Rain
Life of the Party, The
Lightnin'
North to Hudson Bay
Points West
Quicksands
Rio Grande
Sea Fury
Sea Horses
Sin of Martha Queed, The
Skin Deep
Small Town Idol, A
Spider and the Rose, The
Those Who Dare
Three Bad Men
Three Who Paid
To the Last Man
Trap, The (police sergeant)
Yosemite Trail

752
CANNON, Maurice*
Alaskan, The
Forbidden Hours, The
Little French Girl, The
Love's Wilderness
Shadows of Paris
Side Show of Life, The
Trilby

753
CANNON, Norman*
Disraeli (Foljambe)

754
CANNON, Pomeray*
Four Horsemen of the Apocalypse,
    The (Madariaga)
Trifling Women

755
CANNON, Raymond*
Chickens

756
CANTOR, Eddie (Edward Israel Is-
    kowitz) (1892-1964)
Glorifying the American Girl
Kid Boots (Title role)
1927 Follies
Special Delivery
That Party in Person
Radio:
Eveready Hour, The (guest)
Stage:
Kid Boots (Title role) 23
Make It Snappy 22
Whoopee (Henry Williams) 28
Ziegfeld Follies of 1927

757
CANUTT, Yakima (Enos Edward
    Canutt) (1895-)
Bad Men's Money
Branded Bandit, A
Captain Cowboy
Carrying the Mail
Dark Command, The
Days of '49, The
Desert Greed
Devil Horse, The
Fighting Stallion
Greed of Gold
Hellhounds of the Plains
Human Tornado, The
Iron Rider, The
King of the Rodeo
Outlaw Breaker, The
Riders of Storm Ranch
Ridin' Mad
Riding Comet, The
Romance and Rustlers
Scar Hanan
Stunt Man
Three Outcasts
Vanishing West, The [serial]
White Thunder

758
CAPRICE, June (1899-1936)
Damsel in Distress, A
In Walked Mary
Pirate Gold [serial]
Rogues and Romance
Sky Rangers, The [serial]

759
CAREW, James*
Anna the Adventuress

Comin' thro' the Rye (Col. Adair)

760
CAREW, Ora (1893-1955)
After Your Own Heart
Beyond the Crossroads
Big Town Round-Up, The
Girl from Rocky Point, The
Ladyfingers
Little Fool
Love's Protege
Paying the Limit
Peddler of Lies, The
Sherlock Holmes /aka/ Moriarty
Smiles Are Trumps
Smudge
Three Days to Live
Voice in the Dark, A
Waterfront Wolves

761
CAREWE, Andrew*
Breath of the Gods

762
CAREWE, Arthur Edmund (1894-)
Boomerang, The
Breath of the Gods
Cat and the Canary, The (Harry)
Children of Destiny
Claw, The (Major Anthony Kinsella)
Daddy
Diplomacy
Easy Road, The
Ghost Breaker, The
Lover's Oath, A
Man's Past, A
Only Thing, The (Gigberto)
Palace of Darkened Windows
Phantom of the Opera (the Persian)
Price of a Party, The
Prodigal Judge
Refuse
Rio Grande
Sandra
Sham
Silent Lover, The
Something Money Can't Buy
Song of Love, The
Torrent, The
Trilby
Uncle Tom's Cabin (George Harris)
Volcano (Maurice Duval)

763
CAREWE, Edwin (1883-1940)
Bad Man, The
Evangeline
Girl of the Golden West, The

Isobel /aka/ The Trail's End
Joanna
Lady Who Lied, The
Madonna of the Streets, A
My Son
Playthings of Destiny
Ramona
Resurrection
Revenge
Silver Wings
Son of the Sahara
Spoilers, The

764
CAREWE, Millicent*
Dr. Jekyll and Mr. Hyde (Martha
  Mansfield)

765
CAREWE, Rita*
High Steppers
Joanna
Resurrection
Revenge
Stronger Will, The /aka/ Will of a
  Woman, The

766
CAREY, Harry (1875-1947)
Bad Lands, The
Battle of Elderbush Gulch, The
Beyond the Border
Blue Streak McCoy
Border Patrol
Bullet Proof
Burning Bridges
Canyon of the Fools
Crashing Through
Cry for Help, A
Desert Driven
Desperate Trails
Driftin' Through
Flaming '40s, The
Fox, The
Freeze-Out
Frontier Trail
Good Men and True
Hair Trigger Burke
Hearts Up
Human Stuff
If Only Jim
Kick-Back
Lightning Rider
Little Journey, A
Love's Lariat
Man from Red Gulch, The
Man from Texas, The
Man to Man

Man Who Wouldn't Shoot, The
Miracle Baby, The
Night Hawk, The
Night Riders
Outlaw and the Lady, The
Overland Red
Prairie Pirates
Roaring Rails
Satan Town
Seventh Bandit, The
Sheriff's Baby, The
Silent Sanderson
Six Shootin' Justice
Slide, Kelly, Slide
Soft Shoes
Sundown Slim
Telephone Girl and the Lady, The
Texas Trail, The
Tiger Thompson
Trail of '98, The (Jack Locasto)
Wallop, The
Wanderer, The
West Is West

767
CARILLO, Mario*
Barrier, The (Poleon Dore)
Dance Madness
Déclassée
Diplomacy
Eve's Secret
Girl from Montmartre, The
His Hour
His Tiger Lady
Hot News
Just Married
Lost, a Wife
Only Thing, The
Private Life of Helen of Troy, The
  (Ajax)
Rosita (Majordomo)
Song of Love, The
Time to Love
Torrent, The
Venus of Venice

768
CARL, M. Roger*
Jade Casket, The

769
CARL, Renée*
Les Misérables (La Thenardier)

770
CARL, Roger*
L'Homme du Large

CARLBERG, Hilbur*
Witch Woman, The

772
CARLE, Richard (1871-1941)
Coming of Amos, The
Fleet's In, The (Judge Hartley)
Habeas Corpus
His Glorious Night
It Can Be Done
Madame X (Perissard)
Soft Cushions
Understanding Heart, The
While the City Sleeps (Wally)
Zander the Great (Mr. Pepper)

773
CARLETON, William*
Inside of the Cup, The
Law and the Woman, The

774
CARLETON, William T.*
Homeward Bound

775
CARLISLE, Jack*
City of Purple Dreams, The (Kelly)

776
CARLISLE, Peggy*
Hindle Wakes /aka/ Fanny Hawthorne
    (Mary Hollins)

777
CARLISLE, Rita*
Brothers

778
CARLYE, Grace*
Fast Set, The (Jane Walton)
Notorious Lady
Wine (Mrs. Bruce Carwin)

779
CARLYLE, Richard (1879-)
Baby Cyclone
Bridge of Sighs, The
Brotherly Love
Children of the Ritz
Copperhead, The
Girl in the Show, A
Hearts in Dixie
In Old California
Inside of the Cup, The
It Can Be Done
Out of the Chorus
Purple Knight, The

Stolen Will, The
Taking a Chance
Ten Nights in a Bar Room
Those Who Toil
Valiant, The

780
CARLYLE, Sidney*
Humoresque

781
CARMAGNOLE DANCERS, The
Orphans of the Storm

782
CARMEN, Jewel*
Bat, The (Dale Ogden)
Nobody
Rossmore Case, The
Silver Lining
You Can't Get Away With It

783
CARMINATI, Tullio (1894-1971)
Bat, The (Moletti, the bat)
Duchess of Buffalo, The
Honeymoon Hate
Patriot, The
Stage Madness
Sybil
Three Sinners
Stage:
Strictly Dishonorable (Count Di Ruvo
    29)

784
CARNEY, Daniel*
America /aka/ Love and Sacrifice
    (Nancy's Servant)

785
CARNS, Roscoe*
Moran of the Marines

786
CAROL, Sue (Evelyn Lederer) (1908-)
Air Circus, The
Beau Broadway
Captain Swagger
Chasing Through Europe
Cohens and the Kellys in Paris, The
Exalted Flapper, The
Girls Gone Wild
Is Zat So?
It Can Be Done
Movietone Follies of 1929
Skyscraper
Slaves of Beauty

Soft Cushions
Walking Back
Why Leave Home?
Win That Girl

787
CARON, Irma*
Romance of Hine-Moa, The

788
CARON, Patricia*
Dance Hall
Fourflusher, The
Girl from Woolworths, The
Home Towners, The

789
CARPENTER, Betty*
Cardigan
Iron Trail, The

790
CARPENTER, Jean*
Boy of Flanders, A

791
CARPENTER, Jeanne*
Ashes of Vengeance (Anne)
Helen's Babies (Budge)

792
CARPENTER, Peter*
Silver King, The

793
CARPENTIER, Georges*
Gypsy Cavalier, The (dual role,
    Merodach/Valerius Carew)
Pathetic Symphony
Show of Shows, The
Wonder Man, The

794
CARR, Alexander*
In Hollywood with Potash and Perl-
    mutter)
Partners Again
Potash and Perlmutter
Stage:
Partners Again (Mawruss Perlmut-
    ter) 22

795
CARR, Cameron*
Beloved Vagabond, The (Bradshaw)

796
CARR, "Fatty"*
Little Johnny Jones

797
CARR, Jimmie*
Night Club

798
CARR, Louella*
Over the Hill (Susan, the woman)

799
CARR, Mary (1874-1973)
Blonde or Brunette?
Capital Punishment (Mrs. O'Connor)
Custard Cup
Dame Care
Daring Years, The (Mrs. Browning)
Drusilla with a Million
East of Broadway
False Alarm
Flaming Waters
For Sale (Mrs. Harrison Bates)
Fourth Commandment, The
Frenzied Flames
Go Straight
God's Great Wilderness
Great Adventure, The
Hidden Way
Hogan's Alley
Jesse James
King of the Turf
Lights of New York (Mrs. Morgan)
Love over Night
Midnight Message, The
Million for Love, A
Night Patrol
On the Banks of the Wabash
On Your Toes
Over the Hill (Ma Benton)
Painted People
Parasite, The
Paying the Price
Pleasures of the Rich
Red Kimono, The
Regular Scout, A
Roulette
Sailor's Holiday
Show Girl
Silver Wings
Slave of Fashion, A
Some Mother's Boy
Special Delivery
Spirit of the U. S. A.
Stop, Look and Listen
Swelled Head
Three O'Clock in the Morning
Three Women (Fred's mother)
Thunderclap
Whom Shall I Marry?
Why Men Leave Home
Wise Guy, The

Wizard of Oz, The
Woman on the Jury, The
You Are Guilty!

800
CARR, May Beth*
Madonna of the Streets, A (Judy
Smythe)
Over the Hill (Susan, the child)

801
CARR, Nat*
Her Big Night
Jazz Singer, The (Levi)
Kosher Kitty Kelly
Love Thrill, The
Private Izzy Murphy
Proud Heart, The

802
CARR, Percy*
One Exciting Night (Butler)

803
CARR, Rosemary*
Over the Hill (Rebecca, the child)

804
CARR, Stephen*
Life of Riley, The
Little Old New York (Patrick O'Day)
North of '36
Over the Hill (Thomas, the boy)
Restless Sex, The (Jim, as a boy)

805
CARR, William*
Get-Rich-Quick Wallingford (Quigg)

806
CARRADO, Gino* (see also: Gino
Corrado)
Flaming Youth
Reckless Age, The

807
CARRICKSON, S. B. *
Irish Luck

808
CARRIGAN, Thomas J. *
Making of O'Malley, The
Tiger's Club, The

809
CARRILLO, Leo (1881-1961)
Dove, The
Escape from Hong Kong
Foreigner, The

Hellgate of Soissons
Mr. Antonio

810
CARRINGTON, Evelyn C. *
In Search of a Sinner

811
CARROLL, John (Julian la Faye)
(1907-)
Devil May Care
Hearts in Exile
Marianne

812
CARROLL, Madeleine (Marie-Madeliene
Bernadette O'Carroll) (1906-)
American Prisoner, The (Grace)
Atlantic (Monica)
Crooked Billet, The
First Born (Madeleine Boycott)
Guns of Loos, The
L'Instinct
What Money Can't Buy
Young Woodley
Stage:
Lash, The - London 27
Mr. What's His Name

813
CARROLL, Moon*
Last of Mrs. Cheney, The (Joan)

814
CARROLL, Nancy (Ann Veronica La
Hiff) (1905-1965)
Abie's Irish Rose (Rosemary Murphy)
Chicken a la King (Masie Devoe)
Close Harmony (Marjorie Merwin)
Dance of Life, The (Bonny Kane)
Easy Come, Easy Go (Babs)
Illusion (Claire Jernigan)
Ladies Must Dress (Mazie)
Manhattan Cocktail (Babs)
Mr. Romeo
Shopworn Angel, The (Daisy Heath)
Sin Sister (Pearl)
Sweetie (Barbara Pell)
Water Hole, The (Judith Endicott)
Wolf of Wall Street, The (Gert)
Stage:
Hollywood Music Box Revue 27
Loose Ankles - Los Angeles and San
Francisco 27
May Flowers (Jane) 25
Nancy - Long Beach and Los Angeles
26
One Man's Woman 27

Orpheum Theatre "Amateur Night" 22
Passing Show of 1923, The 23
Passing Show of 1924, The 24
Roxy Hart - Chicago 27
Topics 24

815
CARROLL, Taylor*
Fighting American, The

816
CARROLL, William A. *
Ancient Highway, The
Born to the West
Branded Four, The [serial]
I'll Show You the Town
North of '36
Sporting Youth
Unknown, The
Wanderer of the Wasteland (Merry-
vale)

817
CARTELLIERI, Carmen*
Hands of Orlac, The

818
CARTER, Calvert*
Slave of Desire

819
CARTER, Captain*
Havoc (Adjutant)

820
CARTER, Harry*
Fatal Sign, The [serial]
Hope Diamond Mystery, The /aka/
The Romance of the Hope Diamond
[serial]

821
CARTER, Hubert*
Beloved Vagabond, The (Mr. Dubosc)
Blinkeyes (Chang)
Gypsy Cavalier, The (Bartholomew
Griggs)
Virgin Queen, The (Sir William Cecil)
Wandering Jew, The (the ruler)

822
CARTER, Richard*
Tony Runs Wild

823
CARTON, Gwen*
Woman of No Importance, A (Elsie
Farquhar)

824
CARTON, Harold*
Only Way, The (Stryver)

825
CARTON, Pauline*
Living Dead, The
Par Habitude

826
CARTWRIGHT, Peggy (1915-)
Iron Horse, The (Miriam Marsh,
age 8)
One Terrible Day

827
CARVER, Kathryn*
Beware of Widows
His Private Life
Ladies for Service
No Defense
Outcast, The
Serenade

828
CARVER, Louise (Louise Spigler Mur-
ray) (1875-1956)
Bride's Relations, The
First Hundred Years Are the Worst,
The
Fortune Hunter, The
Four Married Men
Must We Marry?
Redeeming Sin, The
Sap, The
Shameless Behavior
Tillie's Punctured Romance
Wolves of the City

829
CARVILL, Henry*
Disraeli (Duke of Glastonbury)
If I Were King

830
CARY, Jim*
Last Outlaw, The

831
CASAJUANA, Maria*
Girl in Every Port, A (Buenos Aires
girl)

832
CASHIER, Isidore*
Broken Hearts

833
CASPERSEN, Karen*
David Copperfield

834
CASSAVANT, Nina*
Dangerous Business (Genevieve)

835
CASSIDY, Ellen*
Dark Secrets (Mildred Rice)

836
CASSINELLI, Dolores*
Anne of Little Smoky
Challenge, The
Dangerous Money
Do Dreams Come True?
Forever
Greek Singer, The
Hidden Light, The
Right to Lie, The
Secrets of Paris
Stars of Glory
Tarnished Reputations
Unguarded Hour, The
Virtuous Model, The
Web of Deceit
Web of Lies, The

837
CASSITY, Ellen*
Highest Bidder, The
Passers By

838
CASSJUANA, Maria--see: Maria
Casajuana

839
CASTELLANI, Brute*
Quo Vadis? (Ursus)

840
CASTLE, Harry*
Me, Gangster (Philly Kid)

841
CASTLE, Irene (Irene Foote) (1893-
1968)
Amateur Wife
Broadway Bride, The
French Heels
No Trespassing
Slim Shoulders

842
CASTLE, Robert*
Single Standard, The

843
CASTLETON, Barbara (1896-)
Branding Iron, The (Joan Carver)
Child Thou Gavest Me, The
Dangerous Days
Fair Lady /aka/ The Net
False Fronts
My Friend the Devil
Out of the Storm
Sham
Shame of Society, The
Streets of New York
What's Wrong with Women? (Janet
Lee)
Wild Honey

844
CATELAIN, Jacques*
Apaches of Paris
Der Rosenkavalier
L' Homme du Large
Living Image, The
New Enchantment, The

845
CATLETT, Walter (1889-1960)
Married in Hollywood
Second Youth
Summer Bachelors
Why Leave Home?

846
CATTLE, Harry--see: Harry Castle

847
CAULSON, Roy*
Don Q, Son of Zorro (Duenna's ad-
mirer)

848
CAVALIERI, Lina (1874-)
Mad Love

849
CAVAN, Allan*
Million Dollar Collar
Trespasser, The (doctor)

850
CAVANAGH, Paul (1895-1959)
Devil to Pay, The
Grumpy
Runaway Princess, The
Tesha
Two Drummer Boys
Women in the Night

851
CAVANAUGH, Helene*
Ranger of the Big Trees, The

852
CAVANAUGH, Hobart*
San Francisco Nights

853
CAVANAUGH, William*
Down to the Sea in Ships (Henry
  Morgan)
Snow Bride, The

854
CAVANNA, Elsie*
Love 'em and Leave 'em

855
CAVENDER, Glenn*
General, The (Captain Anderson)

856
CAVENS, Fred*
Three Must-Get-Theres, The

857
CAVIN, Jess*
Ramona (bandit leader)
Revenge

858
CAWTHORN, Joseph (1867-1949)
At Yale
Dance Hall
Hold 'em Yale!
Jazz Heaven
Secret Studio, The
Silk Legs
Speakeasy
Street Girl
Tailor-Made Man, The
Taming of the Shrew, The (Gremio)
Two Girls Wanted (Philip Hancock)
Very Confidential
Stage:
Blue Kitten, The (Theodore Vander-
  pop) 22
Half Moon, The (Henry Hudson Hob-
  son) 20
Sunny (Siegfried Peters) 25

859
CAWTHORNE, Peter*
His Glorious Night

860
CAZENUVE, Paul*
French Doll, The

861
CECIL, Edward*
Crown of Lies, The
Phantom of the Opera, The (Faust)
Temple of Dawn, The (Rajah Govind
  Singh)
What Happened to Jones?

862
CECIL, Nora (1879-)
Baby Cyclone
Cavalier, The
Daughter Pays, The
Deadwood Coach, The
Devil Dancer, The
Driftwood
Footfalls
Fortune Hunter, The
His Majesty Bunker Bean
Passionate Quest
Piccadilly Jim
Poor Dear Margaret Kirby
Red Foam
Seven Day's Leave
Seven Footprints to Satan
Too Many Crooks
Town that Forgot God, The

863
CEDERBORG, Gucken*
Peter, the Tramp

864
CEDERSTROM, Ellen*
Story of Gösta Berling, The (Countess
  Martha Dohna)

865
CHADWICK, Clive*
Woman Hater, The

866
CHADWICK, Cyril*
Actress, The
Best Bad Man, The (Frank Dunlap)
Black Watch, The
Brass
Christian, The (Lord Robert Ure)
Clothes
Don't Marry for Money
Excess Baggage
Foreign Devils
Forty Winks
Gigolo
Happiness
His Supreme Moment
His Wife's Money
Hold that Lion
Iron Horse, The (Peter Jesson)

Is Zat So?
King of the Khyber Rifles (Major
    Twynes)
Last of Mrs. Cheyney, The (Willie
    Winton)
Little Church Around the Corner,
    The
Man Who Came Back, The
Mating Call
Men Women Marry, The
Misleading Lady
Peter Pan (Mr. Darling)
Rustle of Silk, The (Paul Chalfon)
Slander the Woman
Stranger's Banquet, The
Thank You
Thirteenth Chair, The
Thirty Days
Three Live Ghosts
Till We Meet Again
Trelawney of the Wells (Captain De-
    falnix)

867
CHADWICK, Helene (1897-1940)
Bachelor Baby
Black Swan, The
Border Legion, The
Brothers under the Skin
Confessions of a Wife
Cup of Fury, The
Cupid, Cow-Puncher
Dancing Days
Dangerous Curve Ahead
Dust Flower, The
Father and Son
First National player 24
From the Ground Up
Getaway Kate [serial]
Gimme
Glorious Fool, The
Godless Men
Golden Cocoon, The
Hard Boiled Haggerty
Her Own Free Will
Long Arm of Mannister, The
Modern Mothers
Old Nest, The
Pity the Chorus Girl
Pleasures of the Rich
Quicksands
Reno
Rose of Kildare
Say It with Sables
Scratch My Back
Sin Flood, The
Solitary Sin, The
Stage Kisses

Still Warm
Why Men Leave Home
Woman Hater, The
Women Who Dare
Yellow Men and Gold

868
CHAKOLOUNY*
Michael Strogoff (Ogareff)

869
CHALIAPIN, Fedor, Jr.*
Das Schiff der Verlorenen Menschen
    [The Ship of Lost Souls] /aka/ Le
    Navire des Hommes Perdus; The
    Ship of Lost Men (crew member)

870
CHALLENGER, Percy*
Sally (butler)
Sky Hawk, The

871
CHALMERS, Thomas*
Blind Alleys
Puritan Passions
Stage:
Wild Duck, The (Relling) 25

872
CHAMBERS, Kathleen*
That Royale Girl (Adele Ketlar)
Vanity Fair (Mrs. Sharp)

873
CHAMBERS, Margaret*
Woman to Woman

874
CHAMBERS, Marie*
That Royale Girl

875
CHANDLER, Edward*
Marriage in Transit (a conspirator)

876
CHANDLER, George (1902-)
Black Hills
Clean Sweep, A
Close Call, A
Cloud Dodger, The
Dangerous Dude, The
Go Get 'em, Kid
Jackson Comes Home
Kid's Clever, The
Light of the Western Stars, The
Red Romance, A

Riding Romeo
Saps and Saddles
Tenderfoot Hero, A
Tenderfoot Thrillers
Two Gun Morgan

877
CHANDLER, Helen (1909-1965)
Joy Girl, The
Mother's Boy (Rose Lyndon)
Music Master, The
Salute
Sky Hawk, The (Joan Allan)
Stage:
Wild Duck, The (Hedvig) 25

878
CHANDLER, Lane (1899-)
Big Killing, The
First Kiss, The
Forward Pass, The (assistant coach)
Legion of the Condemned, The (a
    Texan)
Love and Learn
Open Range
Paramount player 27
Red Hair (Robert Lennon)
Single Standard, The
Studio Murder Mystery, The (Martin)
Wolf of Wall Street, The

879
CHANEY, Lon (1883-1930)
Ace of Hearts (Farralone)
All the Brothers Were Valiant (Mark
    Shore)
Big City, The (Chuck Collins)
Bits of Life (an oriental)
Blackbird, The (dual role, Blackbird/
    Bishop)
Blind Bargain, The (Dr. Lamb)
Daredevil Jack [serial]
Flesh and Blood (David Webster)
For Those We Love (Trix Ulner)
Gift Supreme, The (Merney Stagg)
Glory of Love, The
He Who Gets Slapped ("He")
Hunchback of Notre Dame, The (Qua-
    simodo)
Laugh, Clown, Laugh (Tito)
Light in the Dark, The (Tony Pantel-
    li)
London after Midnight (Burke)
Mr. Wu (Title role)
Mockery (Sergei)
Monster, The (Dr. Ziska)
Next Corner, The (Juan Serafin)
Night Rose, The

Nomads of the North (Raoul Challoner)
Oliver Twist (Fagin)
Outside the Law (dual role, Black
    Mike Silva/Joe Wang)
Penalty, The (Blizzard)
Phantom of the Opera, The (Erik, the
    Phantom)
Quincy Adams Sawyer (Obadiah Strout)
Road to Mandalay, The (Singapore
    Joe)
Shadows (Yen Sin)
Shock, The (Wilse Dilling)
Tell It to the Marines (Sgt. O'Hara)
Thunder (Grumpy Anderson)
Tower of Lies, The (Jan)
Trap, The (Gaspard)
Treasure Island (dual role, Pew/Mer-
    ry)
Unholy Three, The (Echo)
Unknown, The (Alonzo)
Voices of the City (O'Rourke)
West of Zanzibar (Phroso)
Where East Is East (Tiger Haynes)
While Paris Sleeps (Henri Santados)
While the City Sleeps (Dan)

880
CHANEY, Norman "Chubby"*
Bouncing Babies
Boxing Gloves
Lazy Days
Moan and Groan, Inc.
Railroadin'

881
CHANG, King Hoo*
Son of the Gods (Moy)

882
CHAPIN, Alice*
Argentine Love
Crowded Hour, The
Icebound
Manhattan

883
CHAPIN, Jacques*
Beggars of Life

884
CHAPLIN, Alice--see: Alice Chapin

885
CHAPLIN, Charlie (Charles Spencer
    Chaplin) (1889-)
Ben-Hur (spectator)
Circus, The (Charlie)
Gold Rush, The (lone prospector)

Hollywood (himself)
Idle Class, The (dual role)
Kid, The
Nut, The (himself)
Pay Day
Pilgrim, The (Title role)
Show People (himself)
Woman of Paris, A (walk-on)

886
CHAPLIN, Mildred Harris--see:
    Mildred Harris

887
CHAPLIN, Syd /aka/ Sydney; Sidney
    (1885-1965)
Better 'Ole, The
Charley's Aunt (Sir Fancourt Babber-
    ley)
Fortune Hunter, The
Her Temporary Husband
King, Queen, Joker
Little Bit of Fluff, A
Man on the Box, The
Missing Link, The
Oh, What a Nurse!
Pay Day
Perfect Flapper, The
Pilgrim, The (the father)
Rendezvous, The
Skirts
Wild Waiter, The

888
CHAPMAN, Edythe (1863-1948)
American Beauty
Beyond the Rocks (Lady Bracondale)
Bits of Life
Broken Barriers
Bunty Pulls the Strings
Classified
Count of Ten, The
County Fair
Crystal Cup, The
Daddy's Gone-a-Hunting
Dangerous Curves Ahead
Daughters of Pleasure (Mrs. Hadley)
Divorce
Double-Dyed Deceiver, The
Faith
Girl I Loved, The
Happiness Ahead
Havoc (Mrs. Chappell)
Heart Troubles
Her Husband's Trademark (Mother
    Berkeley)
Huckleberry Finn
Idle Rich, The

Idols of Clay
In the Name of Love
Just out of College
Learning to Love
Lightnin'
Little Shepherd of Kingdom Come,
    The
Little Yellow House, The
Love Hungry
Man Crazy
Manslaughter (Adeline Bennett)
My American Wife (Donna Isabella
    LaTassa)
Naughty, but Nice (Mrs. Altiwood)
Navy Blues
One Minute to Play
Out of the Storm
Pinto
Runaway, The (Mrs. Murrell)
Sally's Shoulder
Saturday Night (Mrs. Prentiss)
Shepherd of the Hills
Soul Mates
Student Prince, The
Synthetic Sin
Tailor Made Man, The
Tale of Two Worlds, A (Mrs. New-
    comb)
Ten Commandments, The (Mrs. Mar-
    tha McTavish)
Three Faces West
Three Weekends (Ma O'Brien)
Twin Beds
Voices of the City (Mrs. Rodman)
Worldly Goods

889
CHAPMAN, Leonard*
Our Hospitality

890
CHAPMAN, Marcia*
Girl from Havana, The

891
CHAPMAN, William*
Elmo, the Fearless [serial]
Winter Has Come

892
CHAPPELL, Dorothy*
Handcuffs or Kisses

893
CHARLAND, Ainse*
Keeper of the Bees, The ("Fat Ole
    Bill")

894
CHARLAND, Alme*
Boy of Flanders, A

895
CHARLE, Gustav*
Dancing Vienna

896
CHARLES, Rosalind*
Love Parade, The (a Lady in Waiting)

897
CHARLESON, Mary (1885-1968)
Human Stuff

898
CHARLIA, Georges*
L'Equipage
Legion of Honor, The
Sea Fever
Soul of France, The

899
CHARLIER, Monsieur*
Three Musketeers, The (D'Artagnan's
  father)

900
CHARSKY, Boris*
Captain Lash
Red Dance, The

901
CHARTERS, Spencer (1878-1943)
April Folly (Dobbs)
Dancing Mothers (butter & egg man)
Janice Meredith (Squire Hennion)
Little Old New York (Bunny)

902
CHASE, Albert*
Beloved Vagabond, The (Asticott)

903
CHASE, Charlie (Charles Parrott)
  (1893-1940)
All Parts
Big Squawk
Booster, The
Bromo and Juliet
Call of the Cuckoo
Chasing Husbands
Crazy Feet
Crazy Like a Fox
Dog Shy
Family Group, The
Fight Pest, The

Fluttering Hearts
Great Gobs
Imagine My Embarrassment
Is Everybody Happy?
Kids and Kids
Leaping Love
Limousine Love
Loud Speakers
Midsummer Mush
Modern Love
Movie Night
One Can't Buy Love
Roach player 27
Snappy Sneezer, The
Stepping Out
Thundering Fleas

904
CHASE, Colin*
Big News
Iron Horse, The (Tony)
King of Kings, The (bit)

905
CHASE, Ilka (1905-)
Careless Age, The (Bunter)
Paris Bound (Fanny Shipman)
Red Hot Rhythm
Rich People (Margery Mears)
South Sea Rose
Why Leave Home?

906
CHATTERTON, Ruth (1893-1961)
Charming Sinners (Kathryn Mills)
Doctor's Secret, The
Dummy, The (Agnes Meredith)
High Road, The
Laughing Lady, The
Madame X (Jacqueline)
Sins of the Father (Gretta)
Stage:
Changelings, The (Kay Faber) 23
La Tendresse (Marthe Dellieres) 22
Little Minister, The (Lady Babbie) 25
Magnolia Lady, The (Lily-Lou Rave-
  nel) 24
Man with a Load of Mischief, The
  (a lady) 25
Mary Rose (Title role) 20

907
CHAUTARD, Emile (1881-1934)
Adoration
Bardelys the Magnificient
Blonde or Brunette?
Caught in the Fog
Flaming Forest, The

His Tiger Lady
House of Horror, The
Lilac Time
Love Mart, The
Marianne (Père Joseph)
My Official Wife
Now We're in the Air
Olympic Hero
Out of the Ruins
Seventh Heaven (Père Chavillon)
South Sea Rose
Tide of the Empire
Tiger Rose
Times Square
Untamed Youth
Upstream

908
CHEBAT, Georges*
Son of the Sahara

909
CHEFEE, Jack*
Marquis Preferred
Redeeming Sin, The
Reward
Runaway Girls
Tailor Made Romance
Veiled Woman, The

910
CHEKOVA, Olga*
City of Temptation
His Late Excellency
Moulin Rouge
Pawns of Passion

911
CHERON, Andre*
Diplomats, The
Evening Clothes
Four Devils
His Private Life
King of Kings, The (wealthy mer-
    chant)
Love Parade, The (Paulette's hus-
    band)
Magic Flame, The (the manager)
Marriage Clause, The
Rose of the Golden West
They Had to See Paris (valet)
True Heaven

912
CHERRINGTON, Ruth*
Caught in the Fog
Lone Wolf's Daughter, The

913
CHERRY, Kate*
Reckless Youth (Martha Whipple)

914
CHERRYMAN, Rex*
Camille
Madame Peacock
Stage:
Noose, The (Nickie Elkins) 26
Trial of Mary Dugan, The (Jimmy) 27

915
CHESEBRO, George (1890-)
Brothers
Hope Diamond Mystery, The /aka/
    The Romance of the Hope Diamond
    [serial]
Lost City, The [serial]
Should a Girl Marry?
Show Boat (Steve)

916
CHESNEY, Arthur*
Hindle Wakes /aka/ Fanny Hawthorne
    (Sir Timothy Farrar)
Lodger, The

917
CHEUNG, Louie*
Branding Iron, The (Wan Oh)
Tale of Two Worlds, A (Chinaman)

918
CHEVALIER, Maurice (Maurice Augus-
    te Chevalier) (1888-1972)
L'Affaire de la Rue de Lourcine
Bonjour New York! (himself)
Gonzague
Innocents of Paris (Maurice Marney)
Jim Bougne Boxeur
Love Parade, The (Count Alfred Ren-
    ard)
Le Match Criqui (Ledaux)
Le Mauvais Garcon
Par Habitude

919
CHEW, Frank*
Chinatown Nights
Shanghai Bound

920
CHICHESTER, Emily*
Once to Every Woman (Patience Mere-
    dith)
School for Wives
Wedding Bells

921
CHILDERS, Naomi (1892-1964)
Courage
Duds
Earthbound
Hold Your Horses
Mr. Barnes of New York
Restless Wives
Street Called Straight, A
Success
Trial Marriage
Virtuous Liars

922
CHISTYAKOV, A. *
End of St. Petersburg The
Mother

923
CHMARA, Grigory*
Die Freudlose Gasse [The Joyless
   Street] /aka/ The Street of Sor-
   row (a waiter)

924
CHRISMAN, Pat*
Sky High (Pasquale)

925
CHRISTENSEN, Benjamin (1879-1959)
Chained
Devil's Circus, The
Hawk's Nest, The
Mockery
Seive Frau die Unbekannte
Seven Footprints to Satan
Witchcraft through the Ages /aka/
   Häxan

926
CHRISTENSEN, Mary*
Bride 13 [serial]

927
CHRISTIAKOV, A. P. --see: A.
   Chistyakov

928
CHRISTIAN, Mary*
Kiss for Cinderella, A (Sally)

929
CHRISTIANS, George*
Foolish Wives (U.S. Ambassador
   Hughes)

930
CHRISTIANS, Mady (1900-1959)
   Das Weib des Pharao [The Wife

of the Pharaoh] /aka/ The Loves
   of Pharaoh
Runaway Princess, The
Slums of Berlin
Waltz Dream, The (Princess Alix)

931
CHRISTIANS, Rudolph*
Foolish Wives (Andrew J. Hughes)

932
CHRISTIANSEN, Rasmus*
David Copperfield

933
CHRISTIE, Dorothy*
That's My Wife

934
CHRISTIE, Ivan*
Son of the Gods (cafe manager)

935
CHRISTINE, Lillian*
Wee MacGregor's Sweetheart (Lizzie
   Robinson)

936
CHRISTY, Ann (1909-)
Fire Brigade
Hell Wreckers
Kid Sister, The
Love Charm, The
Seven Footprints to Satan
Speedy
Water Hole, The (Dolores)

937
CHRISTY, Lya*
Prinzessin Olala [Princess Olala]
   /aka/ Art of Love (Lady Jackson)

938
CHURCHILL, Berton (1876-1940)
Five Minutes from the Station
Nothing but the Truth
Tongues of Flame
Stage:
Alias the Deacon (the deacon) 25

939
CHURCHILL, Marguerite (1910-)
Diplomats, The
Pleasure Crazed
Seven Faces
They Had to See Paris (Opal Peters)
Valiant, The
Stage:
Skidding (Marion Hardy) 28

940
CHUVELYOV, Ivan*
End of St. Petersburg, The

941
CLAIR, René (René Chometti)
    (1898-)
Un Chapeau de Paille d'Itali [The
    Italian Straw Hat]
Entr'acte
L'Orpheline
Paris Qui Dort
Sous Les Toits de Paris

942
CLAIRE, Bernice (Bernice Jahnigan)*
First National player 29
No, No, Nanette (Nanette)
Song of the Flame

943
CLAIRE, Ethlyne (Ethlyne Williams)
    (1908-)
Battling Buckaroo
From Headquarters
Guardian of the Wild
Hero on Horseback
Hey, Rube!
Newlyweds and Their Baby [series]
    (Mrs. Newlywed)
Painted Ponies
Queen of the Northwoods [serial]
Riding for Fame
Road to Eldorado
Show of Shows, The
Vanishing Rider, The [serial]

944
CLAIRE, Gertrude*
Brothers Divides
Cradle of Courage (Mother Kelly)
Daughters of Today
Forbidden Thing, The
Goose Hangs High, The (Granny)
Hail the Woman
Her Sister from Paris
His Majesty Bunker Bean
Human Hearts
Little Irish Girl, The
Married Alive
Money Changers, The
Oliver Twist (Mrs. Maylie)
Paris Green
Sin of Martha Queed, The
Society Secrets
Tumbleweeds
We're All Gamblers
What Are Your Daughters Doing?
Wine of Youth, The

945
CLAIRE, Ina (Ema Fagan) (1892-)
Awful Truth, The
Polly with a Past
Stage:
Awful Truth, The (Lucy Warriner) 22
Bluebeard's Eighth Wife (Monna) 21
Grounds for Divorce (Denise Sorbier)
    24
Last of Mrs. Cheyney, The (Mrs.
    Cheyney) 25
Our Betters (Lady George Grayson
    [Pearl]) 28

946
CLAPHAM, Leonard--see: Tom London

947
CLARE, Mary (1894-)
Becket
Black Spider, The
Constant Nymph, The (Linda)
Gypsy Cavalier, The (Janet)
Prince of Lovers, The
Skin Game, The (Chloe)

948
CLARENDON, Hal*
Virgin Paradise, A

949
CLARK, [Mr.]*
Lost in the Arctic

950
CLARK, Andrew*
Sporting Chance, The

951
CLARK, Andy*
Beggars of Life
Shamrock Handicap, The (Chesty Mor-
    gan)

952
CLARK, Bobby (Robert Edwin Clark)
    (1888-1960)
All Steamed Up
Bath Between, The
Belle of Samoa, The
Beneath the Law
Clark and McCullough in the Honor
    System
Clark and McCullough in the Interview
Detectives Wanted
Diplomats, The
Hired and Fired
In Holland

Knights Out
Medicine Men, The
Music Fiends
Ramblers, The (debut)
Waltzing Around
Stage:
Chuckles - London 22
Music Box Revue, The 22; 24
Ramblers, The (Prof. Cunningham) 26

953
CLARK, Bridgetta*
Four Horsemen of the Apocalypse,
  The (Dona Luisa)
Greater Glory, The

954
CLARK, Charles Dow*
Confidence Man, The
Old Home Week

955
CLARK, Dowling*
America /aka/ Love and Sacrifice
  (Lord Chamberlain)

956
CLARK, Estelle*
Crowd, The (Estelle)
Denial, The
His Secretary
Merry Widow, The (French barber)
Sinners in Silk
So This Is Marriage
Tillie the Toiler (Sadie)

957
CLARK, Harry*
Understanding Heart, The

958
CLARK, Harvey*
Camille (the Baron)
Get Your Man (Marquis de Ville-
  neuve)
Havoc (Batman)
He Who Gets Slapped (Briquet)
Head Man, The (McKugg)
In Old Kentucky
In the Palace of the King
Ladies' Night in a Turkish Bath
Magic Flame, The (the aide)
Man Who Came Back, The
Man Without a Country, The /aka/
  As No Man Has Loved
Marriage in Transit (aide)
Midnight Lovers
Milestones (Sam Sibley)

Night Bird, The
Putting Pants on Philip
Rose of the Golden West
Roughneck, The
Secrets (Bob)
Seven Keys to Baldpate
Twelve Miles Out
Understanding Heart, The

959
CLARK, Herbert*
Big News (Pells)

960
CLARK, John J. *
Pajamas

961
CLARK, Marguerite (1883-1940)
All of a Sudden Peggy
Easy to Get
First National player 21
Girl Named Mary, A
Scrambled Wives

962
CLARK, Trilby*
Just Off Broadway
Lover of Camille, The
Maria Marten
Silent Sanderson

963
CLARK, Westcott* See also Wescott
  B. Clarke
Trial of Mary Dugan, The (Capt.
  Price)

964
CLARKE, Betty Ross*
Fox player 21
If I Were King
Man from Downing Street, The

965
CLARKE, C. Downing*
Know Your Men
Monsieur Beaucare (Lord Chesterfield)

966
CLARKE, Harvey--see: Harvey Clark

967
CLARKE, Mae (1910-)
Big Time, The
Nix on Dames

968
CLARKE, Redfield*
Twenty Dollars a Week

969
CLARKE, Wescott B.* See also
    Wescott Clark
Dramatic Life of Abraham Lincoln,
    The /aka/ Abraham Lincoln
Safety Last (the floorwalker)

970
CLARY, Charles*
Auction Block, The (Homer Lane)
Beverly of Graustark (Mr. Calhoun)
Blind Goddess, The
Breath of Scandal, The
Coast of Folly (bit)
Connecticut Yankee in King Arthur's
    Court, A (King Arthur)
Empty Hands
Golden Bed, The (treasurer)
His Lady /aka/ When a Man Loves
    (a Lay Brother)
In the Palace of the King
King of Kings, The (bit)
Penalty, The (doctor)
Prisoners
Prodigal Daughters (Stanley Garside)
Red Dice
Sailor's Holiday
See You in Jail
Smile, Brother, Smile

971
CLATY, Charles*
Seven Days

972
CLAUDE, Toby*
For Alimony Only
Lost, a Wife

973
CLAYTON, Arthur*
Three Live Ghosts
Whip, The

974
CLAYTON, Edward /aka/ Eddie*
College Coquette, The
Lady Be Good
Mad Hour, The
Why Be Good?

975
CLAYTON, Ethel (1884-1966)
Bar C Mystery, The [serial]
Beyond

Blessed Miracle, A
Buccaneer, The
Can a Woman Love Twice?
City Sparrow, The
Cocoanut Grove
Cradle, The
Crooked Streets
Dollars and the Woman
Exit the Vamp
For the Defense
Fortune Hunter, The
Her Own Money
His New York Wife
Hit the Deck
If I Were Queen
Inspiration
Ladder of Lies, The
Lady in Love, A
Mad Hour, The
Merry Widower, The
More Deadly than the Male
Mother Machree
Preferred player 26
Price of Possession, The
Princess Broadway
Remittance Woman
Risky Business
Sham
Sins of Rosanne, The
Sunny Side Up
Thirteenth Commandment, The
Wealth
Wings of Youth
Young Mrs. Winthrop

976
CLAYTON, Gilbert*
Below the Line
Blood and Sand (Garabata)
Partners Again

977
CLAYTON, Marguerite (1896-)
Bride 13 [serial]
Canyon of the Fools
Dangerous Love
Dawn of a Tomorrow, The
Forbidden Love /aka/ Women Who
    Wait
Go Get 'em Hutch [serial]
Inside of the Cup, The
Man of the Desert, A
Palm Beach Girl
Pleasure Seekers
Stardust

978
CLEARY, Michael*
Show of Shows, The

979
CLEGG, Cy*
Tiger Rose

980
CLEMAN, Majel*
Girl in the Glass Cage, The (Isabelle VanCourt)

981
CLEMENS, LeRoy*
Aloma of the South Seas

982
CLEMENTE, Steve*
Rainbow Trail, The

983
CLEMENTO, Steve*
Temptress, The
Trigger Fingers

984
CLERGET, Paul*
My Lady's Garter

985
CLEWING, Carl*
Sumurun /aka/ One Arabian Night
    (Sheik's son)

986
CLIFFE, H. Cooper*
His Children's Children
Monsieur Beaucare (Beau Nash)

987
CLIFFORD, Kathleen*
Excess Baggage
Richard the Lion-Hearted (Queen
    Berengaria)

988
CLIFFORD, Ruth (1900-)
Amazing Woman, An
April Showers
As Man Desires
Black Gate, The
Brooding Eyes
Dangerous Age, The
Daughters of the Rich
Devil's Appletree, The
Don Mike
Dramatic Life of Abraham Lincoln,
    The /aka/ Abraham Lincoln
    (Anne Rutledge)
Eternal Love
Eternal Woman, The

Face on the Barroom Floor, The
Fires of Youth
Her Husband's Secret
Home, James
Invisible Ray, The
Love Hour, The
My Dad
Ponjola (Gay Lypiatt)
Show of Shows, The
Thrill Seekers
Tornado
Tropical Love
Truxton King, The
Universal player 20

989
CLIFFORD, William*
Ashes of Vengeance (Andre)

990
CLIFTON, Elmer (1890-1947)
Devil's Appletree, The
Maid to Order
Six Cylinder Love
Tropical Nights
Virgin Lips
Wreck of the Hesperus, The

991
CLINE, Brady*
Fourth Commandment, The

992
CLINE, Edward (1892-1961)
Broadway Fever
Ladies' Night in a Turkish Bath
Sherlock Junior
Three Ages, The

993
CLINE, George*
Janice Meredith
Pinch Hitter, The (Coach Nolan)

994
CLINE, Robert*
Temple of Venus, The (Neptune)

995
CLINTON, Geoffrey*
Glorious Adventure, The (Charles
    Hart)

996
CLONINGER, Ralph*
Count of Monte Cristo, The /aka/
    Monte Cristo (Fernand)

997
CLOSE, Iva*
Jolly Peasant, The

998
CLOSE, Ivy (1893-   )
Expiation
Was She Justified?
Worldlings, The

999
CLOVELLY, Cecil*
Dr. Jekyll and Mr. Hyde

1000
CLUGSTON, H. M.*
Navigator, The

1001
CLYDE, Andy (1892-1967)
Barber's Daughter, The
Bee's Buzz, The
Best Man, The
Big Palooka, The
Blindfolded
Branded Men, The
Bride's Relations, The
Bulls and Bears
Case of Mary Brown, The
Circus Today
Clancy at the Bat
Constable, The
Girl Crazy
Golfers, The
Good-Bye Kiss, The   .
His New Mama
Hold 'er Cowboy
Hollywood Star, A
Ice Cold Cocos
Ladies Must Eat
Lunkhead, The
Midnight Daddies
New Halfback, The
Old Barn, The
Sea Dog's Tale, A
Ships of the Night
Should a Girl Marry?
Super-Hooper-Dyne Lizzies
Swim Princess, The
Taxi Driver [series]
Taxi Scandal, A
Uppercut O'Brien
Whirls and Girls
Whispering Whiskers /aka/ Railroad
    Stowaways

1002
CLYDE, June (1909-   )
Hit the Deck

Midnight Mystery, The
Tanned Legs

1003
COAD, Joyce Marie*
Children of Divorce (Little Kitty)
Devil's Circus, The
Drums of Love (little sister)
Mother
One Woman to Another
Scarlet Letter, The (Pearl)
Society Scandal, A

1004
COAKLEY, Marion*
Enchanted Cottage, The
Stage:
Meanest Man in the World, The   20

1005
COAKLEY, Patty*
Kiss for Cinderella, A (Marie-Terese)

1006
COALTER, Frazer*
Society Scandal, A (Schuyler Burr)

1007
COATES, Franklin*
Revenge of Tarzan, The /aka/ The
    Return of Tarzan (Paul D'Arnot)

1008
COBB, Clifford*
Fifth Form at St. Dominic's (Mr.
    Rastle, Master of the Fourth)

1009
COBB, Edmund (1892-   )
At Devil's Gorge
Bashful Whirlwind, The
Battling Bates
Beyond the Smoke
Blasted Hopes
Boundary Battle, The
California in '49
Call of the Heart
Danger Line, The
Days of '49 [serial] (Cal Calhoun)
Desert Scorpion, The
Dodging Danger
Fangs of Destiny
Fighting Redhead, The
Fighting with Buffalo Bill [serial]
Final Reckoning, A [serial]
Finders Keepers
Four-Footed Ranger
Galloping Cowboy, The
Hearts of the West

Hound of Silver Creek
Indians Are Coming, The
Just in Time
Lariat Kid, The
Law Rustlers, The
Out of the Depths
Perilous Paths
Playing It Wild
Range Blood
Rider of the Sierras
Rodeo Mixup
Sting of the Scorpion
Western Feuds
Western Yesterday
Winged Rider, The
Wolf's Trail
Wolves of the Street

1010
COBB, Joe "Fat" (1917-)
Boxing Gloves
Lazy Days
Our Gang Comedies
Railroadin'
Small Talk

1011
COBURN, Dorothy*
Flying Elephants

1012
COBURN, Gladys*
East Lynne (Barbara Hare)

1013
COCCIA, Aurelio*
Aloma of the South Seas
Argentine Love
Humming Bird, The (Bosque)

1014
CODY, Albert*
Daredevil Jack [serial]

1015
CODY, Lew (Louis Joseph Coté)
    (1884-1934)
Adam and Evil
Baby Cyclone
Beau Broadway
Butterfly Man, The
Dangerous Pastime, A
Demi-Bride
Exchange of Wives
Gay Deceiver, The
His Secretary
Husbands and Lovers
Jacqueline of the Blazing Barriers

Lawful Larceny
Man About Town
Man and Maid
MGM player 26
Monte Carlo
Nellie, the Beautiful Cloak Model
Occasionally Yours
On Ze Boulevard
Reno
Revelation
Rupert of Hentzau (Title role)
Secrets of Paris
Shooting of Dan McGrew, The (Dan-
    gerous Dan McGrew)
Sign on the Door, The
Single Man, A
Slave of Fashion, A
So This Is Marriage
Souls for Sale (Owen Scudder)
Sporting Venus, A
Tea for Three
Three Women (Edmund Lamont)
Time, the Comedian
Tower of Lies, The
Valley of Silent Men
Wickedness Preferred
Within the Law (Joe Carson)
Woman on the Jury, The

1016
CODY, William "Buffalo Bill" (1891-
    1948)
Arizona Whirlwind, The
Border Justice
Eyes of the Underworld
Galloping Cowboy, The
King of the Saddle
Laddie Be Good
Price of Fear, The
Slim Fingers
Tip Off, The
Wolves of the City

1017
COE, Rose*
Melody Lane

1018
COFFEE, Lenore*
Angel of Broadway, The

1019
COFFEY, Clark*
Days of '49 [serial] (Judge Coleman)

1020
COFFYN, Frank*
Deadwood Coach, The
Ranson's Folly

1021
COFFYN, Pauline*
Passers By

1022
COGHLAN, Junior (Frank Coghlan,
   Jr.) (1917-)
Bobbed Hair
Cause for Divorce
Country Doctor, The
Fourth Musketeer, The
Gallagher
Garrison's Finish
Her Man o' War
Last Frontier
Let 'em Go Gallagher
Marked Money
Mike
Poverty of Riches, The
Road to Yesterday, The
Rubber Tires
Skyrocket
Slide, Kelly, Slide
Square Shoulders
Yankee Clipper, The

1023
COGHLAN, Rose /aka/ Rosalind
   (1853-)
Beyond the Rainbow (Mrs. Burns)
Secrets of Paris
Under the Red Robe

1024
COGLEY, Nick (1869-)
Abie's Irish Rose (Father Whalen)
Boys Will Be Boys
Honest Hutch
In Old Kentucky
Jes' Call Me Jim
Old Nest, The
Unwilling Hero, An

1025
COHEN, Sammy*
Cradle Snatchers
Gay Retreat, The
Plastered in Paris
Return of Peter Grimm, The (clown)
Skyrocket, The
What Price Glory? (Pvt. Pipinsky)
Why Sailors Go Wrong

1026
COLAS, Monsieur*
Count of Monte Cristo, The [serial]
   (Danglars)

1027
COLBERT, Claudette (Lily Chauchoin)
   (1905-)
First National player 28
For the Love of Mike (Mary)
Hole in the Wall, The (Jean Oliver)
Lady Lies, The (Joyce Roamer)
Stage:
Barker, The - New York 27, London
   28
Cat Came Back, The   25
Dynamo (Ada Fife) 29
Fake, The (Understudy) - Washington
   25
Fast Life, The (Patricia Mason) 28
Ghost Train, The (Peggy Murdock) 26
High Stakes (Anne Cornwall) - Tour
   26
Kiss in a Taxi, A (Ginette) 25
La Gringa (Carlotta D'Astradente)
Leah Kleschna - Boston and Chicago
   25
Marionette Man, The - Washington 25
Mulberry Bush, The (Sylvia Bain-
   bridge) 27
Pearl of Great Price, The (Pilgrim)
   26
See Naples and Die 29
Tin Pan Alley (Jill O'Dare) 28
We've Got to Have Money - Chicago
   24
Wild Wescotts, The (Sybil Blake) 23

1028
COLE, Slim*
Great Circus Mystery, The [serial]

1029
COLEBURN, Catherine*
Society Scandal, A (Marjorie's friend)

1030
COLEMAN, Charles*
Good Morning, Judge
That's My Daddy

1031
COLEMAN, Don*
Black Aces

1032
COLEMAN, Jim*
Show Boat (stagehand)

1033
COLEMAN, Mabel*
Corporal Kate

King of Kings, The (bit)
Snob, The

1034
COLEMAN, Majel*
Bluebeard's Eighth Wife (bit)
Girl in the Glass Cage, The
King of Kings, The (Pilate's wife,
    Proculla)

1035
COLEMAN, Major*
Romance of the Rio Grande

1036
COLEMAN, Vincent*
Good References (William Marshall)
Has the World Gone Mad?
Paramount player 24
Partners of the Night
Purple Highway, The

1037
COLLIER, Constance (Laura Con-
    stance Hardie) (1878-1955)
Bleak House
Bohemian Girl, The (gypsy queen)
Stage:
Our Betters (Duchesse De Surennes)
    28
Serena Blandish (Countess Flor di
    Folio) 29

1038
COLLIER, William, Jr. /aka/ Bus-
    ter (1900-)
Age of Desire
At the Stage Door
Bachelor Girl
Back Stage
Beware of Bachelors
Broadway Sap, The
Broken Gates
Cardigan
College Coquette, The
College Widow, The
Convoy
Dearie
Desired Woman, The
Devil's Cargo, The
Donovan Affair, The
Enemies of Women (Gaston)
Eve's Secret
Everybody's Sweetheart
Floating College
God Gave Me Twenty Cents
Good Provider
Hard Boiled Rose

Heart of Maryland, The (Lloyd Cal-
    vert)
Just Another Blonde /aka/ Girl from
    Coney Island
Lady of the Harem
Lighthouse by the Sea, The
Lion and the Mouse, The
Loyal Wives
Lucky Lady, The
New Orleans
Night of Mystery, A
One Stolen Night
Playing with Souls
Pleasure Mad
Rainmaker, The
Red Sword, The
Sea Hawk, The (Marzak)
Secrets of Paris
Show of Shows, The
So This Is Love
Soul of Youth, The
Stranded
Sunset Derby
Tide of the Empire
Tragedy of Youth, The
Two Men and a Maid
Wanderer, The
Wine of Youth, The
Women They Talk About

1039
COLLIER, William, Sr. (1866-1944)
Servant Question, The
Stage:
Hottentot, The (Sam Harrington) 20
Merry-Go-Round 27
Music Box Revue, The 21
Nifties of 23 - 23

1040
COLLINS, C. Pat*
Racket, The

1041
COLLINS, Kathleen*
Black Cyclone
Gun Grit
Riding Demon, The
Unknown Cavalier, The

1042
COLLINS, Mae*
Red Hot Romance

1043
COLLINS, Monte, Jr. *
Why Bring That Up?

1044
COLLINS, Monte, Sr.*
Boy of Flanders, A
Desert Flower, The
King of Kings, The (rich Judaean)
Long Live the King
Loves of Ricardo, The
Men
Our Hospitality
Tiger Love
Tumbleweeds

1045
COLLYER, June (Dorothy Heermance)
(1907-1968)
Broadway Nights (bit)
East Side West Side
Four Sons
Hangman's House
Husbands Are Liars
Illusion (Hilda Schmittlap)
Let's Make Whoopee
Love Doctor, The
Me, Gangster (Mary Regan)
Not Quite Decent
Pleasant Sin, The
Red Wine
River of Romance
Woman Wise

1046
COLMAN, Ronald (1891-1958)
Anna, the Adventuress (Brendon)
Beau Geste (Michael "Beau" Geste)
Black Spider, The (Vicomte Beauvais)
Bulldog Drummond (Hugh Drummond)
Condemned (Michael Oban)
Dark Angel, The (Hilary Trent)
Eternal City, The (unbilled)
Handcuffs or Kisses (bit)
Heart Trouble
Her Night of Romance (Paul Menford)
Her Sister from Paris (Joseph W.
Seyringer)
His Supreme Moment (John Douglas)
I Have Been Faithful
Kiki (Renal)
Lady Windermere's Fan (Lord Dar-
lington)
Magic Flame, The (dual role, Tito,
the Clown/Le Count Cosati)
Night of Love (the Montero)
Rescue, The (Tom Lingrad)
Romola (Carlo Buccellini)
Son of David, A (Jewish prizefighter)
Sporting Venus, The (Donald MacAl-
lan)
Stella Dallas (Stephen Dallas)

Tarnish (Emmett Carr)
Thief in Paradise, A (Maurice Blake)
Twenty Dollars a Week
Two Lovers (Mark VanRycke)
White Sister, The (Capt. Giovanni
Severi)
Winning of Barbara Worth, The
(Willard Holmes)
Stage:
Dauntless Three, The   20
East Is West 20
La Tendresse 21

1047
COLOMBO, Russ (Ruggerio de Ru-
dolpho Columbo) (1908-1934)
Street Girl
Wolf Song (Ambrosia Guiterrez)

1048
COLOSSE, M.*
Manhandled (Bippo)

1049
COLVIN, Gilly*
Nix on Dames

1050
COLVIN, Marion*
Branding Iron, The (Mrs. Upper)

1051
COLVIN, William*
My Own Pal

1052
COMBE, Boyce*
Daddies

1053
COMBS, Jackie*
Lovey Mary
Smitty
Sweet Rosie O'Grady

1054
COMONT, M.*
Thief of Bagdad, The (Persian Prince)

1055
COMONT, Mathilde*
Enchanted Hill, The
Girl from Montmartre, The
If Marriage Fails
La Boheme (Madame Benoit)
Loves of Carmen, The
Puppets
Ramona (Marda)

Rosita (Rosita's mother)
Sea Beast, The (Mula)
Streets of Shanghai

1056
COMONT, Nattie*
His Hour

1057
COMPSON, Betty (1897-)
Always the Woman
At the End of the World
Awakening, The
Barker, The
Beggar on Horseback
Belle of Broadway, The
Big City, The (Helen)
Blaze O'Glory
Bonded Woman
Cheating Cheaters
Counsel for the Defense
Court Martial
Desert Bride
Docks of New York, The
Enemy Sex, The
Eternal Survivor, The
Eve's Secret
Fast Set, The (Margaret Sones)
Female, The
For Those We Love (Bernice Arnold)
Garden of Weeds, The
Great Gabo, The (Maria)
Green Temptation
Hollywood
Kick-In
Ladies Must Live
Lady Bird
Law and the Woman, The
Life's Mockery
Little Minister, The (Lady Babbie)
Locked Doors
Love Call, The
Love Me and the World Is Mine
Masked Angel
Miami
Midnight Mystery, The
Miracle Girl, The
New Lives for Old
On with the Show (Nita)
Over the Border
Palace of Pleasure
Paramount player 20 and 24
Paths to Paradise
Pony Express
Pride's Fall
Prisoner of Love, A
Ramshackle Hour
Royal Oak, The

Rustle of Silk, The (Lola De Breze)
Say It with Diamonds
Scarlet Seas (Rose McRay)
Show of Shows, The
Skin Deep
Stranger, The
Street Girl
Temptations of a Shop Girl
Time, the Place and the Girl, The
To Have and to Hold
Twelve Miles Out
Weary River
White Flower, The
White Shadow, The
Wise Guy, The
Woman to Woman (Deloryse--two versions)
Woman with Four Faces, The (Elizabeth West)

1058
COMPTON, Fay (1894)
Bill of Divorcement, A
Claude Duval (Frances, Duchess of Brentleigh)
Diana of the Crossways
Eleventh Commandment, The
Fashions in Love
Happy Ending, The
House of Peril
Judge Not
London Love
Loves of Mary Queen of Scots
Old Wives' Tale, The
Robinson Crusoe
Settled out of Court
Somehow Good
This Freedom (Rosalie Aubyn)
Woman of No Importance, A (Rachel)
Zero
Stage:
Olympia (Princess Olympia Orsolini)
  28

1059
COMPTON, Joyce (Eleanor Hunt)
  (1907-)
Ankles Preferred
Border Cavalier
Broadway Lady
Dangerous Curves (Jennie Silver)
Sally (Peggy Phillips)
Salute
Sky Hawk, The
Soft Living
Syncopating Sue
What Fools Men
Wild Party, The (Eva Tutt)

1060
COMPTON, Juliette*
Chinese Bungalow, The (Sadie)
Nell Gwyn (Lady Castlemaine)
Triumph of the Scarlet Pimpernel,
   The (Theresa Cabbarus)
Woman Tempted, The
Woman to Woman

1061
CONDON, Jackie (1913-   )
Hallroom Boys [series]
Little Lord Fauntleroy
Love Light, The
One Terrible Day
Our Gang Comedies
Pollyanna

1062
CONKLIN, Charles "Heinie" (1880-
   1959)
Air Circus, The
Beau Broadway
Beau Brummel
Below the Line
Beware of Widows
Clash of the Wolves, The
Day of Faith, The
Drums of the Desert
East Lynne with Variations
Feel My Pulse
Fig Leaves
Find Your Man
Ham and Eggs at the Front
High Life, The
Man About Town
Married Life
Married 'n Everythin'
Night Cry, The
Rainstorm, The
Red Hot Tires
Seven Sinners
Show of Shows, The
Side Street
Silk Stockings
Tiger Rose (Gus)
Tut Tut
Two Tough Tender Feet
Uncle Tom Without the Cabin
Up in the Air
Wet and Warmer
You Wouldn't Believe It

1063
CONKLIN, Chester (1888-   )
Behind the Front
Beware of Widows
Big Noise, The

Blue Ribbon Comedies
Bulldog Yale
Cabaret
Chicken a la Cabaret
Drums of the Desert
Duchess of Buffalo, The
Feel My Pulse
Fool's for Luck (Samuel Hunter)
Galloping Fish, The
Gentlemen Prefer Blondes (Judge)
Greed (Papa Sieppe)
Ham and Eggs at the Front
Haunted House, The
Horseman of the Plains
House of Horror, The
Kiss in a Taxi, A
McFadden's Flats
Marquis Preferred
Masked Bride, The
Midnight Lovers
Nervous Wreck, The
One Year to Live
Paramount player 26
Rubber Heels
Say It Again
Shanghai Rose
Show of Shows, The
Silk Stockings
Social Celebrity, A
Stairs of Sand
Studio Murder Mystery, The (gateman)
Sunset Pass
Sybil
Taxi Thirteen
Tell It to Sweeney
Tennek Film Corp. Comedies
Tillie's Punctured Romance (circus
   owner)
Trick of Hearts
Two Flaming Youths (Sheriff Ben Hol-
   den)
Varsity
Virginian, The (Uncle Hughey)
We're in the Navy Now
Where Was I?
Wilderness Woman, The
Woman of the World, A

1064
CONKLIN, William (1877-1935)
Brute Master
Darling of New York, The
Divine Lady, The (Romney)
Enfoldment, The
Fifth Avenue Models
Goldfish, The
Hairpins
Life's Crossroads

Love Madness
Man Without a Country, The /aka/
    As No Man Has Loved
Other Woman, The
Red Hot Dollars
Rose of the Golden West
Sex
Sweet Rosie O'Grady
When Dawn Came
Winds of Chance
Woman in the Suitcase, The

1065
CONLEY, Lige*
Educational Comedies

1066
CONLON, Francis*
New Toys

1067
CONNELLY, Bobby*
Humoresque

1068
CONNELLY, E. J. *
In Old Kentucky

1069
CONNELLY, Edward*
Across to Singapore
Bardelys the Magnificent
Brotherly Love
Cinderella's Twin
Conquering Power, The (Notary Cru-
    chot)
Denial, The
Devil, The
Forbidden Hours, The
Four Horsemen of the Apocalypse,
    The (lodgekeeper)
Goldfish, The
Lovers
Merry Widow, The (Ambassador)
Mysterious Lady, The
Only Thing, The (King of Chekia)
Prisoner of Zenda, The (Marshal von
    Strakencz)
Quincy Adams Sawyer (Deacon Petten-
    gill)
Red Hot Romance
Revelation
Saphead, The
Scaramouche (King's Minister)
Shore Acres
Show, The
Sinners in Silk
Slave of Desire

So This Is Marriage
Someone in the House
Student Prince, The (court marshal)
Sun Up
Torrent, The (Pedro Moreno)
Trifling Women
Turn to the Right
Unholy Three, The (Judge)
War in the Dark
Where the Pavement Ends (Pastor
    Spencer)
Willow Tree, The
Winners of the Wilderness (General
    Contrecoeur)

1070
CONNELLY, Edwin*
Beggar on Horseback
Blind Goddess, The

1071
CONNELLY, Erwin*
Beggar on Horseback
Cheating Cheaters
Crown of Lies, The
Fire Brigade, The
Kiki
Rubber Tires
Seven Chances
Sherlock Junior (henchman)
Son of the Sheik (the Zouave)
Winning of Barbara Worth, The (Pat)

1072
CONNELLY, Jane*
Sherlock Junior

1073
CONNELLY, One-Eye*
Barker, The

1074
CONNORS, Eddie*
Hallelujah! (singer and bit)

1075
CONOVER, Teresa Maxwell*
I Want My Man
Light in the Dark, The (Mrs. Temple-
    ton Orrin)
When Knighthood Was in Flower
    (Queen Catharine)
Yolanda (Queen Margaret)

1076
CONRAD, Con*
Cock-Eyed World, The (conductor)

1077
CONRAD, Eddie*
Blaze O'Glory

1078
CONRADI, Paul*
Hamlet (the ghost)

1079
CONSEULLA, Senorita*
Temple of Venus, The (Thetis)

1080
CONSTANTIN, Mila*
Black Oxen (a flapper)

1081
CONSTANTINI, Nino*
16-1/2 x 11

1082
CONSUELLA, Senorita--see: Senorita Conseulla

1083
CONTI, Albert (1887-1967)
Alex the Great
Average Husband
Blonde Saint, The
Camille (Henri)
Captain Lash
Chinese Parrot, The
Devil Dancer, The
Dry Martini
Eagle, The (Kuschka)
Exalted Flapper, The
Green Grass Widows
He Loved the Ladies
Jazz Heaven
Lady of the Pavements (Baron Finot)
Legion of the Condemned, The
Love Me and the World Is Mine
Love Song, The
Magnificent Flirt, The (Count D'Estranges)
Making the Grade
Merry-Go-Round (Baron Rudi von Leightsinn)
Merry Widow, The (Danilo's Adjutant)
Monte Carlo
Old Loves and New
Plastered in Paris
Romance of the Underworld, A
Saturday's Children
Show People
Slipping Wives
Stocks and Blondes
Such Men Are Dangerous

Tempest, The
Warner Brothers player 27
Wedding March, The (guard)
Woman from Moscow

1084
CONTI, Louise*
Wandering Jew, The (Maria)

1085
CONVERSE, Thelma*
Society Scandal, A (Mrs. Hamilton Pennfield)

1086
CONWAY, Booth*
Esmeralda (Quasimodo)
Nell Gwyn (King's messenger)

1087
CONWAY, Martin*
Only Way, The (citizen prosecutor)

1088
COOGAN, Jack*
Kid, The
Old Clothes (Timothy Kelly)

1089
COOGAN, Jackie (1915-)
Boy of Flanders, A
Bugle Call, The
Buttons
Circus Days
Daddy
Johnny Get Your Haircut
Kid, The (Title role)
Little Robinson Crusoe
Long Live the King
My Boy
Old Clothes
Oliver Twist (Title role)
Peck's Bad Boy
Rag Man, The
Trouble

1090
COOK, Caroline Frances*
Bells, The

1091
COOK, Clyde (1891-)
Barbed Wire
Beware of Bachelors
Beware of Married Men
Brute, The
Bush Leaguer, The
Captain Lash

Celebrity, The
Climbers, The (Pancho Mendoza)
Dangerous Woman, A
Docks of New York, The
Domestic Troubles
Don't Tickle
Eskimo, The
Five and Ten Cent Annie
Fox player 21
Good Time Charley
He Who Gets Slapped (clown)
In the Headlines
Interference
Jazz Heaven
Lucky in Love
Masquerade
Miss Nobody
No Questions Asked
Officer O'Brien
Pay as You Enter
Sailor's Sweetheart, A
Simple Sis
So This Is Marriage
Spieler, The
Strong Boy, The
Taming of the Shrew, The (Grumio)
Through the Breakers
White Gold (Homer)
Winning of Barbara Worth, The (Tex)

1092
COOK, Warren /aka/ Warren Cooke*
April Folly (Earle of Mannister)
Civilian Clothes (Mr. Lanham)
Dark Secrets (Dr. Case)
Knockout, The
Lady Rose's Daughter
Lunatic at Large, The
My Lady's Garter
Shore Leave
Silent Command, The
Wild, Wild Susan

1093
COOKE, Al*
Almost a Gentleman
Arabian Fights, The
Are Husbands People?
Broadway Ladies
Come Meal
Her Father Said No
Jessie's James
Legionaires in Paris
Mild, but She Satisfies
My Kingdom for a Horse
Naughty Forties, The
Pacemakers, The
Rah! Rah! Rexie!

Restless Bachelors
Ruth Is Stranger than Fiction
Silk Sock Harold
Six Best Fellows, The
Sweet Buy and Buy
That Wild Irish Pose
Too Many Hisses
Top Taps
Wages of Synthetic
Watch Your Pep!
You Just Know She Dares 'em

1094
COOKE, Baldwin*
Berth Marks
Hoose Gow, The
Men O' War
Perfect Day, A

1095
COOKE, Beach*
Classmates
Winning Through (Bobby Dumble)

1096
COOKE, Frank*
Three-Must-Get-Theres, The

1097
COOKE, Ray*
Broadway Melody, The (bellhop)

1098
COOKE, Stanley*
Alf's Button (Rev. Julian Gaskins)

1099
COOKSEY, Curtis*
Silver Horde, The

1100
COOLEY, Frank*
First Year, The
Honor Bound

1101
COOLEY, Hallam (1888-)
Are You a Failure?
Beauty's Worth (Henry Garrison)
Beware of the Bride
Black Waters
Fancy Baggage
First National player 24
Foolish Age, The
Forever After
Free to Love (Jack Garner)
Going Up
Helen and Warren [series]

Her Wild Oat
Ladies at Play
Ladies Must Dress (Art)
Leave It to Me
Light Woman, A
Little Wildcat, The
Long Arm of Mannister, The
Monster, The (Watson's head clerk)
Naughty, but Nice (Paul Ames)
No Place to Go
O. Henry [series]
Old Fashioned Boy, An
One Week of Love
Paris Bound (Peter)
Pinto
Playing with Fire
Seven Days
So Long Letty
Some Pun'kins
Sporting Youth
Stolen Kisses
Stop Flirting
Ten-Dollar Raise, The
Tom Boy, The
Tonight at Twelve
Trumpet Island
Up and at 'em
Wedding Bills
Wedding Rings
What Do Men Want?
White Sin

1102
COOLEY, James*
Ashes of Vengeance (Paul)
Song of Love, The

1103
COOLEY, Willard*
Enchanted Hill, The
Fog Bound
Wanderer of the Wasteland (camp
   doctor)

1104
COOMBS, Jackie*
Callahans and the Murphys, The
   (Timmy Calahan)

1105
COOPER, Bigelow*
Bad Company
Exciters, The

1106
COOPER, Edna Mae*
Folly of Vanity
Grounds for Divorce

King of Kings, The (bit)
Sally, Irene and Mary (Maggie)
Why Change Your Wife? (maid)

1107
COOPER, Frederick*
Every Mother's Son (Tony Browning)
Only Way, The (Charles Darnay)
Skin Game, The (Rolf)

1108
COOPER, Gary (Frank James Cooper)
   (1901-1961)
Arizona Bound
Beau Sabreur (Henri Beaujolais)
Betrayal, The
Children of Divorce (Ted Larrabee)
Doomsday
Eagle, The (extra)
Enchanted Hill, The (extra)
First Kiss, The
Half a Bride
It (reporter)
Last Outlaw, The
Legion of the Condemned, The (Gale
   Price)
Lightnin' Wins (extra)
Lightning Justice (extra)
Lilac Time
Lucky Horseshoe, The (extra)
Nevada
Old Ironsides (extra)
Only the Brave
Patriot, The
Poverty Row (extra)
Seven Days Leave
Shopworn Angel, The (William Tyler)
Texan, The
Three Pals (extra)
Thundering Herd, The (extra)
Tricks (extra)
Vanishing American, The /aka/ The
   Vanishing Race (extra)
Virginian, The (Title role)
Watch Your Wife (extra)
Wild Horse Mesa (extra)
Wings (Cadet White)
Winning of Barbara Worth, The (Abe
   Lee)

1109
COOPER, George (1891-)
Barker, The
Barrier, The (Sgt. Murphy)
Claude Duval
Daughter of Mother McGinn
Devil's Appletree, The
Devil's Cargo, The

Diamond Handcuffs
Eternal Three, The
For Those We Love (Bert)
Goose Woman, The (reporter)
Great Divide, The
Her Temporary Husband
Just a Woman
Lawful Cheaters (Johnny Burns)
Lilac Time
Little Church Around the Corner,
  The
Lovelorn, The
Mills of the Gods
Nth Commandment, The
Pals First
Quicksands
Red Dice
Rose Marie (Fuzzy)
Sailor's Holiday
Settled out of Court
Seven Days Leave
Shadow of the Law, The (chauffeur)
Shriek of Araby
Smouldering Fires
Suzanna
Through the Dark
Tin Hats
Trail of '98, The (Samuel Foote, the
  worm)
Turn to the Right
Unholy Night, The (orderly)
Unknown Soldier, The
Veiled Mystery, The
Widdecombe Affair (the farmer)
Wise Guy, The
Women Love Diamonds

1110
COOPER, Gladys (Gladys Constance
  Cooper) (1888-1971)
Bohemian Girl, The (Arline Arnheim)
Bonnie Prince Charles
Stage:
Second Mrs. Tanqueray, The - Lon-
  don 22

1111
COOPER, Jack*
Three Live Ghosts

1112
COOPER, Jackie (John Cooper, Jr.)
  (1922-)
Bouncing Babies
Boxing Gloves
Lloyd Hamilton Comedies
Moan and Groan, Inc.
Movietone Follies of 1929

Our Gang Comedies
Sunny Side Up

1113
COOPER, Miriam (1894-)
Broken Wing, The
Daughters of the Rich
Deep Purple, The
Her Accidental Husband
Is Money Everything?
Kindred of the Dust
Oath, The
Serenade

1114
COOPER, Rosemary*
Climbers, The (Queen)
Dressmaker from Paris, The
Drums of Love (maid)
Spirit of the U. S. A.
White Flannels

1115
COPPA, Joe*
Keeper of the Bees, The ("Angel
  Face")

1116
CORBET, Ben*
Black Aces
Royal Rider

1117
CORBETT, James J. (1867-1933)
Prince from Avenue A, The

1118
CORBETT, William D. *
Uncle Sam of Freedom Ridge

1119
CORBIN, Virginia Lee (1910-)
Bare Knees
Broken Laws
City that Never Sleeps, The
Driven from Home
Footlights and Fools (Claire Floyd)
Forbidden Room, The
Hands Up! (Alice Woodstock)
Handsome Brute, The
Head of the Family, The
Headlines
Honeymoon Express, The
Jazzland
Ladies at Play
Little Snob, The
Loose Ankles
No Place to Go

North Star, The
Perfect Sap, The
Play Safe
Sinners in Silk
Universal player 25
Whole Town's Talking, The
Wine of Youth, The

1120
CORDA, Maria*
Eine Du Barry von Heute [A Modern
   Du Barry] (Toinette)
Last Days of Pompeii, The (Nydia)
Der Leibgardest [The Guardsman]
Madame Wünscht Keine Kinder [Ma-
   dame Doesn't Want Children]
   /aka/ Madame Wants No Chil-
   dren (Elayne Parizot)
Moon of Israel
Private Life of Helen of Troy, The
   (Helen)
Samson and Daliah (Daliah)
Tesha
Woman in the Night, A

1121
CORDAY, Marcelle*
Dry Martini
Flesh and the Devil (Minna)
His Lady /aka/ When a Man Loves
   (Marie)
Into Her Kingdom
Jim, the Conqueror
Lost, a Wife
Midnight Mystery, The
Quality Street (Henrietta Turnbull)
Scarlet Letter, The (Mistress Hib-
   bins)
Spendid Crime, The
They Had to See Paris (Marquise de
   Brissac)
Trespasser, The (Blanche)
We Moderns

1122
CORDAY, Raymond (-1956)
A Nous la Liberté

1123
CORDING, Harry*
Christina (Dirk Torpe)
Isle of Lost Ships, The
Knockout, The
Patriot, The (Stefan)
Rescue, The
Sins of the Father (Hijacker)
Squall, The (Peter)

1124
COREY, Eugene*
Her Bridal Nightmare

1125
CORMON, Nelly*
Count of Monte Cristo, The [serial]
   (Mercedes)

1126
CORNELL, Melva*
Movietone Follies of 1929

1127
CORNWALL, Anne (1897-)
Ashes of Vengeance
College
Copperhead, The
Dulcy
Everything but the Truth
Eyes of the Totem
Fighting Fannie
Flaming Frontier, The
Girl in the Rain, The
Gold Diggers, The (Violet Dayne)
Halfback Hannah
Heart of the Yukon
Her Gilded Cage (Jacqueline Ornoff)
Introduce Me
La, La, Lucille
Love's Young Scream
Only 38
Paramount Comedies (12)
Path She Chose, The
Rainbow Trail, The
Roughneck, The
Seventh Day, The
Splendid Crime, The
To Have and to Hold
Under Western Skies

1128
CORRADO, Gino* (see also: Gino
   Carrado)
Adam's Rib (Lt. Braschek)
Amateur Gentleman, The (Prince Re-
   gent)
Desert Flower, The
Devil's Skipper, The
Gun Runner, The
Hot News
House of Scandal, The
Iron Mask, The (Aramis)
La Boheme (Marcel)
Men
My American Wife (Pedro DeGrossa)
One Woman Idea
Patience

Prowlers of the Sea
Rainbow, The
Senor Americano
Sunrise (bit)
Tide of the Empire
Volga Boatman, The
White Black Sheep, The
Women's Wares

1129
CORRIGAN, D'Arcy*
Last Warning
Merry Widow, The (Horatio)
Napoleon's Barber
Tarzan and the Golden Lion

1130
CORRIGAN, E.*
Partners of the Night

1131
CORRIGAN, Emmett*
Lion and the Mouse, The

1132
CORRIGAN, James*
Auction Block, The (Mr. Knight)
Brewster's Millions
Divorce
Durand of the Badlands (Joe Gore)
Front Page Story, A
Jack-Knife Man, The
Lavender and Old Lace
Peck's Bad Boy
Sky Pilot
Slave and Fashion, A

1133
CORRIGAN, Lloyd*
It (yacht cabin boy)
Splendid Crime, The

1134
CORRIGAN, Tom*
Nut Cracker /aka/ You Can't Fool
   Your Wife

1135
CORTES, Armand*
Music Master, The
Palm Beach Girl, The
Revenge of Tarzan, The /aka/ The
   Return of Tarzan (Rokoff)

1136
CORTESI, Giulio*
Loves of Ricardo, The

1137
CORTESI, Giulio, Mrs.*
Loves of Ricardo, The

1138
CORTEZ, Armand* See also Armand
   Cortes
Crowded Hour, The
Rubber Heels
Wages of Virtue

1139
CORTEZ, Ricardo (Jake Krantz)
   (1899-)
Argentine Love
Bedroom Window, The
Behind Office Doors
By Whose Hands?
Call of the Canyon
Cat's Pajamas, The
Chicago
Children of Jazz
City that Never Sleeps, The
Eagle of the Sea, The (Jean Lafitte)
Excess Baggage
Feet of Clay (Tony Channing)
Gentleman from America, The
Grain of Dust, A
Gun Runner, The
Hollywood
In the Name of Love
Ladies of the Night Club
Lost Zeppelin, The
Man's Man, A
Midstream
Mockery (Dimitri)
New Orleans
New York
Next Corner, The (Don Arturo)
Not So Long Ago
Paramount player 23
Phantom in the House
Pony Express
Private Life of Helen of Troy, The
   (Paris)
Prowlers of the Sea
Sixty Cents an Hour (debut)
Society Scandal, A
Sorrows of Satan, The (Geoffrey Tem-
   pest)
Spaniard, The
Swan, The
This Woman (Whitney Duane)
Torrent, The (Rafael Brull)
Volcano (Stephane Duval)
Woman of Destiny, A

1140
CORTHELL, Herbert*
Classmates
Second Youth
Winning Through (drummer)

1141
COSGRAVE, Jack*
Percy

1142
COSGRAVE, Luke*
Contraband
Duke Steps Out, The
Durand of the Badlands (Kingdom
   Come Knapp)
Flaming Barriers
Gentlemen Prefer Blondes (Lorelei's
   grandfather)
Light that Failed, The
Lightnin'
Mating Call
Merton of the Movies
Red Mark, The
Welcome Home

1143
COSGROVE, John*
Queen of Sheba, The (King of Tyre)

1144
COSSAR, John*
Doubling for Romeo
Hunchback of Notre Dame, The (Jus-
   tice of the Court)
My Lady of Whim (Severn)
Voices of the City (Garrison)

1145
COSTA, Miss*
Jeanne Dore

1146
COSTELLO, Carmen*
Man Who Laughs, The

1147
COSTELLO, Dolores (1905-)
Bobbed Hair
Bridge of the Storm
College Widow, The
Divine Lady, The (Lady Hamilton)
Glad Rag Doll, The
Glorious Betsy
Heart of Maryland, The
Hearts in Exile
His Lady /aka/ When a Man Loves
   (Manon Lescaut)

Lawful Larceny
Little Irish Girl, The
Madonna of Avenue A
Mannequinn
Million Bid, A
Noah's Ark (dual role, Miriam/Mary)
Old San Francisco
Redeeming Sin, The
Sea Beast, The (Esther Harper)
Sea Hunt, The
Second Choice
Show of Shows, The
Tenderloin
Third Degree, The

1148
COSTELLO, Helene (1903-1957)
Bobbed Hair
Broken Barriers
Bronco Twisters
Burning up Broadway
Circus Kid, The
Comrades
Don Juan (Rena)
Fatal Warning, The [serial]
Finger Prints
Fortune Hunter, The
Good Time Charley
Ham and Eggs at the Front
Heart of Maryland, The
Honeymoon Express, The
Husbands for Rent
In Old Kentucky
Lights of New York (Kitty Lewis)
Love Toy, The
Man on the Box, The
Midnight Taxi
Much Ado About Nothing
Phantom of the Turf
Show of Shows, The
Wet Paint
When Dreams Come True
While London Sleeps

1149
COSTELLO, John*
Married? (Judge Tracey)

1150
COSTELLO, Maurice (Herbert Blythe)
   (1877-1950)
Black Feather
Camille (Armand's father)
Conceit (bit)
Deadline at Eleven (bit)
Determination
Eagle of the Night [serial]
Fog Bound

Glimpses of the Moon
Human Collateral
Jean and the Calico Dog
Johnny Get Your Haircut
Law and the Lady, The
Let Not Man Put Asunder
Love of Woman
Mad Marriage
Man and Wife
Man Who Won, The
Melody, The
None So Blind
Roulette
Shamrock and the Rose, The
Spider Web, The
Story without a Name, The
Tower of Jewels, The
Virtuous Liars
Wagon Show, The
Weekend Husbands
What a Change of Clothes Did
Wives of the Prophet
Wolves of the Air

1151
COSTELLO, Mildred*
Great Gobs

1152
COSTELLO, William*
King of Kings, The (Babylonian
   Noble)

1153
COSTILLO, Carmen*
Loves of Carmen, The

1154
COTTON, Billy*
Old Nest, The

1155
COTTON, Lucy*
Blind Love
Cosmopolitan player 21
Devil, The
Invisible Foe, The
Misleading Lady
Sin that Was His, The

1156
COTY, Anny*
Cafe Electric /aka/ Wenn ein Weib
   den Weg Verliert (When a Woman
   Loses Her Way)

1157
COUCH, Robert*
Hallelujah! (a Johnson kid)

1158
COULSON, Roy*
Don Q, Son of Zorro (Tango dancer's
   admirer)
Flaming Forest, The
Robin Hood (King's Jester)
Scaramouche (Jean Paul Marat)
Temptress, The

1159
COULTER, Frazier*
Heart Raider, The
Prince of Tempters, The

1160
COURTENAY, William F. (1875-1933)
Evidence
Sacred Flame, The
Show of Shows, The

1161
COURTENEY, Shelia*
His House in Order (Annabel Jesson)

1162
COURTLEIGH, William (1869-1930)
Madame X
Pollyanna

1163
COURTNEY, Pat*
His House in Order (Derek Jesson)

1164
COURTOIS, Leon*
Le Capitaine Fracasse

1165
COURTOT, Juliette*
Down to the Sea in Ships (Judy Peggs)

1166
COURTOT, Marguerite (1897-)
Beyond the Rainbow (Esther)
Cradle Buster, The
Down to the Sea in Ships (Patience
   Morgan)
Jacqueline of the Blazing Barriers
Outlaws of the Sea
Pirate Gold [serial]
Rogues and Romance
Steadfast Heart, The
Velvet Fingers [serial]
Yellow Arrow, The

1167
COURTWRIGHT, William*
Are Parents People?
For Wives Only

Girl I Loved, The
Grand Duchess and the Waiter, The
Jesse James
Man of Action, A
Peaceful Valley
Thank You
Trouble with Wives, The
Two-Gun Man, The

1168
COVANS, Four, The
On with the Show

1169
COVENTRY, Tom*
Claude Duval (Innkeeper Crisp)
Gypsy Cavalier, The (Ballard)
Nell Gwyn (innkeeper)
Paddy the Next Best Thing (Mickey
    Doolan)

1170
COVINGTON, Bruce*
Fighting Coward, The
Love's Wilderness
Phantom of the Opera, The (M. Mon-
    charmin, Mgr.
Wife of the Centaur, The

1171
COVINGTON, Z. Wall*
Goose Hangs High, The (Noel Derby)
To the Ladies

1172
COWAN, Lynn*
Compromise
Social Highwayman, The

1173
COWL, George*
Secrets (John Carlton, Jr.)

1174
COWLES, Jules*
Bringing up Father
Idol of the North, The (One-Eye
    Wallace)
Leatherneck, The
Lord Jim
Lost World, The (Zambo)
Ne'er Do-Well, The
Road to Romance, The
Sal of Singapore
Scarlet Letter, The (Beadle)
Seven Chances

1175
COWLEY, Hilda*
Nell Gwyn (Maid of Honor)

1176
COX, Freddie*
Lovey Mary

1177
COXEN, Edward*
Man without a Country, The /aka/
    As No Man Has Loved
Our Hospitality
Scaramouche (Jacques)
Singer Jim McKee

1178
COZENEUVE, Paul*
Queen of Sheba, The (envoy of King
    Pharaoh)

1179
CRAIG, Blanche (1878-)
Dynamite (a neighbor)
Magic Cup, The

1180
CRAIG, Bob*
Quarterback, The

1181
CRAIG, Burton*
Luck of the Navy, The (Lord Nelson)

1182
CRAIG, Charles*
Beyond the Rainbow (Col. Henry Gart-
    wright)
My Lady's Garter

1183
CRAIG, Charles, Mrs. *
Name the Man

1183a
CRAIG, Charles G., Mrs. *
Barriers Burned Away

1184
CRAIG, Gordon*
Dawn (Phillipe Bodart)

1185
CRAIG, Hal*
Love and Learn

1186
CRAIG, Nell*
Boy of Flanders, A

Dangerous Hours
Dramatic Life of Abraham Lincoln,
   The /aka/ Abraham Lincoln
   (Mary Todd Lincoln)
Her First Elopement
Passion's Playground
Peddler of Lies, The
Queen of Sheba, The (Princess Vash-
   ti)
Triflers

1187
CRAIG, R. Gordon*
Christie Johnstone (Charles Gatty)

1188
CRAIG, Robert*
New Klondike, The

1189
CRAIG, Robert W. *
Quarterback, The

1190
CRAMER, Marguerite*
Wild Party, The (Gwen)

1191
CRAMER, Richard /aka/ Dick
   (1889-)
Big News (a hood)
Kid Gloves
Trespasser, The (reporter)

1192
CRAMPTON, Howard*
Screaming Shadow, The

1193
CRANDALL, Edward*
Glorifying the American Girl

1194
CRANE, Earl*
Queen of Sheba, The (Joab, a sol-
   dier)

1195
CRANE, Frank*
Children of the Ritz

1196
CRANE, Helen*
Hole in the Wall, The (Mrs. Lyons)

1197
CRANE, James*
Drake Case, The
Paramount player 20

1198
CRANE, Phyllis*
Forward Pass, The
So This Is College
Stolen Kisses

1199
CRANE, Violet*
Unholy Three, The (Arlington baby)

1200
CRANE, Ward (-1928)
Auctioneer, The
Beauty Shoppers
Blind Goddess, The
Boy Friend, The
Bread
Broadway Rose
Classified
Crimson Runner, The
Destiny's Isle
Down the Stretch
Empty Hands
Famous Mrs. Fair, The
Flag Maker, The
Flaming Frontier, The
French Heels
Frisky Mrs. Johnson
Harriet and the Piper
Heart of a Fool, The
Honeymoon Flats
How Baxter Buttered In
Lady in Ermine, The
Luck of the Irish, The
Mad Whirl, The
Million Dollar Handicap
No Trespassing
Pleasure Mad
Price of Pleasure, The
Risky Business
Rush Hour, The
Scoffer, The
Sherlock Junior (the villain)
Something Different
Sporting Lover, The
That Model from Paris
Under Western Skies
Upstage
Within the Law (English Eddie)

1201
CRANE, William H. *
Saphead, The
Three Wise Fools
True as Steel

1202
CRAUFORD, Kent*
Ace of Scotland Yard [serial]

Love Flowers, The (the visitor)

1203
CRAVEN, Frank (1878-1945)
Very Idea, The
Stage:
First Year, The (Thomas Tucker) 20
19th Hole, The (Vernon Chase) 27

1204
CRAWFORD, Alice*
Glorious Adventure, The (Stephanie Dangerfield)

1205
CRAWFORD, Florence*
Scarlet West, The (Mrs. Harper)

1206
CRAWFORD, Joan /aka/ Billie Cassin (Lucille LeSueur) (1908-)
Lucille LeSueur was born March 23, 1908 in San Antonio, Texas. She grew up as Billie Cassin. She worked in Kansas City waiting on tables to earn her schooling at Saint Agnes Academy. After a Academy in Kansas City. After a brief stay at Stephens College, she began appearing in dancing contests. In 1923 she appeared for one week with Katharine Emerine Revue in Kansas, then won an amateur dance contest and became a Chicago chorus girl. From there to Oriole Terrace in Detroit doing eight routines a night. It was there J. J. Shubert hired her for the chorus of Innocent Eyes on Broadway in 1924. On January 1, 1925, she was on her way to Hollywood and MGM studios. Her first job was as double for Norma Shearer in Lady of the Night.
Marriages: Douglas Fairbanks, Jr. 1929, divorced 1933; Franchot Tone 1935, divorced 1939; Phillip Terry 1942, divorced 1946; Alfred N. Steele 1955, widowed 1959.
Children, adopted: Cathy and Cynthia (Twins) and Christopher and Christina.
Hair: Auburn. Eyes: Blue.
Height: 5'4½".
Across to Singapore (Priscilla Crow-

inshield)
Boob, The (Jane)
Double for Norma Shearer in 1925
Dream of Love (Adrienne)
Duke Steps Out, The (Susie)
Four Walls (Frieda)
Hollywood Revue of 1929
Lady of the Night (dual role)
Law of the Range, The (Betty Dallas)
Old Clothes (Mary Riley)
Only Thing, The (young Lady Catherine)
Our Dancing Daughters (Dangerous Diana)
Our Modern Maidens (Billie Brown)
Paris (the girl)
Pretty Ladies (Bobby; debut, billed as Lucille LeSueur)
Proud Flesh
Rose Marie (Title role)
Sally, Irene and Mary (Irene)
Spring Fever (Allie Monte)
Taxi Dancer, The (Joselyn Poe)
Tramp, Tramp, Tramp (Betty)
Twelve Miles Out (Jane)
Understanding Heart, The (Monica Dale)
Unknown, The (Estrellita)
Untamed ("Bingo")
West Point (Betty Channing)
Winners of the Wilderness (René Contrecoeur)
Stage:
Harry Richman's Night Club 24
Innocent Eyes (chorus) 24
Katherine Emerine Revue - Kansas City 23
Oriole Terrace - Detroit
Passing Show of 1924

1207
CRAWFORD, Richard*
Night Bride, The

1208
CRAWFORD, Sam*
College

1209
CREDAN, Simone*
La Bacarolle d' Amour

1210
CRESPO, Jose*
Revenge

1211
CREWS, Laura Hope (1880-1942)
Charming Sinners (Mrs. Carr)

1212
CRIMMINS, Dan*
Midnight Express, The
Not So Long Ago
Once to Every Woman (Chichester
    Jones)
Pretty Ladies

1213
CRIPPS, Kernan*
Alibi /aka/ Perfect Alibi (Trask)

1214
CRISP, Donald (1882-1974)
Black Pirate, The (McTavish)
Bonnie Brier Bush, The
Don Q, Son of Zorro (Don Sebas-
    tian)
Navigator, The
Pagan, The
Return of Sherlock Holmes, The
River Pirate
Stand and Deliver (London club mem-
    ber)
Trent's Last Case
Viking, The

1215
CRISP, Marie*
Moonlight Follies

1216
CRITTENDEN, Dwight*
Fast Worker, The
Old Nest, The
Pioneer Trails
Tale of Two Worlds, A (Mr. Car-
    michael)

1217
CROCKER, Harry*
Circus, The (Rex, high wire king)
South Sea Love
Tillie the Toiler (Pennington Fisk)

1218
CROCKER-KING, C. H.
One Exciting Night (the neighbor)

1219
CROCKETT, Charles*
Daddy's Gone a-Hunting
Dressmaker from Paris, The
Into Her Kingdom
Sundown
Vanishing American, The /aka/ The
    Vanishing Race (Ames Holliday)
Winds of Chance

1220
CROMMIE, Liege*
Astray from the Steerage (an unim-
    portant husband)

1221
CROMWELL, John*
Dummy, The (Walter Bobbing)
Stage:
Gentlemen of the Press (Wick Snell)

1222
CROSBY, Jack*
Black Is White

1223
CROSBY, Juliette*
Charming Sinners, The (Margaret)
Paris Bound (Nora Cope)

1224
CROSLAND, Alan, Jr. *
Three Weeks

1225
CROSMAN, Henriette (1865-1944)
Wandering Fires (Mrs. Carroll)
Stage:
Children of the Moon (Madame Ather-
    ton) 23
Merry Wives of Windsor, The 28
Trelwaney of the Wells (Miss Violet
    Sylvester) 27
Two Orphans, The (Countess DeLini-
    eres) 26

1226
CROSS, Rhoda M. *
Give and Take

1227
CROSSLEY, Syd*
Fatal Warning, The [serial]
Gorilla, The
Unknown Soldier, The

1228
CROWELL, Arthur*
For Wives Only

1229
CROWELL, Bubbles*
Words and Music

1230
CROWELL, Joseph*
Ashes of Vengeance

1231
CROWELL, Josephine (-1929)
Ashes of Vengeance (Catherine de
   Medici)
Bunty Pulls the Strings
Crooked Streets
Dangerous to Men
Don't Neglect Your Wife
Fighting Love
Flowing Gold
Half a Chance
Held by the Enemy
Homespun Vamp, A
Hot Water
Man Who Laughs, The (Queen Anne)
Mantrap (McGavvity)
Merry Widow, The (Queen Milena)
New Brooms
Nobody's Money
Padlocked
Rupert of Hentzau (Mother Holf)
Six Best Cellars, The
Snob, The
Splendid Crime, The
Sporting Venus, A
Welcome Home
White Lies
Wrong Again

1232
CRUTE, Dally*
His Children's Children

1233
CULDER, Mary*
Man Next Door, The

1234
CULL, Howard*
Music Master, The

1235
CULLEN, Arthur*
Blood Money (Matthew Harper)

1236
CULLEN, James F. *
Summer Bachelors

1237
CULLINGTON, Margaret*
Son of Wallingford, The (Caroline
   Beegoode)

1238
CUMMING, Dorothy /aka/ Dorothy
   Cummings*
Applause (Mother Superior)

Butterflies in the Rain
Cheat, The
Coast of Folly, The (Constance Fay)
Dancing Mothers (Mrs. Mazzarene)
Divine Lady, The
Divine Woman, The (Queen of Naples)
Don't Tell Everything (Jessica Ram-
   sey)
Female, The
For Wives Only
Forbidden Hours
Idols of Clay (Lady Gray)
In Old Kentucky
King of Kings, The (Mother Mary)
Kiss for Cinderella, A (queen)
Kitty
Ladies Must Live
Life's Mockery
Lovelorn, The
Mademoiselle Modiste
Man from Home, The
Manicure Girl, The
Manslaughter (Eleanor Bullington)
Nellie, the Beautiful Cloak Model
New Commandment, The
Next Corner, The (Paula Vrain)
Notorious Miss Lisle, The
Notorious Mrs. Sands, The
Our Dancing Daughters (Diana's
   mother)
Sally in Our Alley
Thief, The
Twenty-One
Wind, The (Cora)
Woman and the Puppet, The
Woman Who Understood, The

1239
CUMMINGS, Irving (1888-1959)
As Man Desires
Beautifully Trimmed
Behind that Curtain
Broad Daylight
Brute, The
Cameo Kirby
Cameron of the Royal Mounties
Country Beyond, The
Dressed to Kill
East Side West Side
Environment, The
Eternal Flame, The (Count De Mar-
   say)
Flesh and Blood
Harriet and the Piper
Hell's River
In Every Woman's Life
In Old Arizona
Jilt, The

Johnstown Flood, The
Not Quite Decent
Old Dad
Paid Back
Romance of the Underworld, A
Rupert of Hentzau (Bernenstein)
Rustlin' for Cupid
Saphead, The
Scar, The

1240
CUMMINGS, Richard*
Bride's Play, The
Galloping Cowboy, The
Thank You

1241
CUNARD, Grace (1893-1967)
Ace of Scotland Yard [serial] (Queen
   of Diamonds)
Blake of Scotland Yard [serial]
Chinatown Mystery, The
Dangerous Adventure [serial]
Eyes of the Underworld
Last Man on Earth, The
Masked Angel
Price of Fear, The
Untamed

1242
CUNDALL, C. W.*
Four Feathers, The (Lt. Trench)

1243
CUNEO, Lester (1888-1925)
Are All Men Alike?
Blazing Arrows
Blue Blazes
Days of the Buffalo
Devil's Ghost, The
Eagle's Feather, The
Good for Scandal
Lone Hand Tex
Lone Hand Wilson
Masked Avenger, The
Pat o' the Range
Range Vultures
Ranger and the Law, The
Silver Spurs
Terror, The
Two-Fisted Thompson
Western Grit

1244
CUNNING, Patrick*
Very Confidential

1245
CUNNINGHAM, Cecil (-1959)
Their Own Desire

1246
CUNNINGHAM, Robert*
Luck of the Navy, The (Adm. May-
   bridge)

1247
CUNY, Joe*
Phantom Foe, The
Sky Ranger, The [serial]

1248
CURLEY, Pauline*
Power (still another Dane)
Veiled Mystery, The
Vitagraph player 21

1249
CURRIE, George*
It's the Old Army Game

1250
CURRIER, Art*
That's My Daddy

1251
CURRIER, Frank (1857-1928)
Across to Singapore
Annie Laurie /aka/ Ladies from
   Hell (Cameron of Lochill)
Being Respectable
Ben Hur (Arrius)
California
Callahans and the Murphys, The
   (Grandpa Callahan)
Cheater, The
Children of Jazz
Clay Dollars
Clothes
Darling of New York, The
Easy Come, Easy Go (Mr. Quayle)
Enemy, The
Escape /aka/ The Exquisite Sinner
Fatal Hour, The
First Year, The
Foreign Devils
Go Getter, The
Graustark (king)
Iron Mike
La Boheme (theatre manager)
Lights of Old Broadway (Lambert de
   Rhonde)
Lotus Eater, The
Men of Steel
Message from Mars

Metro player 22
Misleading Lady
My Old Kentucky Home
Pleasure Seekers
Reckless Youth (Cumberland Whipple)
Red Lily, The (Hugo Leonnec)
Revelation
Riders of the Dark
Right of Way, The
Road to Mandalay, The (General
    Wilcox)
Rookies
Rookies' Return, The
Sea Hawk, The (Asad-Ed-Dim)
Should a Woman Tell?
Stephen Steps Out
Tell It to the Marines
Telling the World
Tents of Allah
Too Many Kisses
Why Announce Your Marriage?
Winners of the Wilderness
Without Limit
Woman Who Fooled Herself, The

1252
CURRY, John*
Day of Faith, The

1253
CURTIS, Jack*
Baree, Son of Kazan
Beach of Dreams
Big Punch, The
Canyon of the Fools
Captain Blood (Wolverstone)
Caught Bluffing
Courage of Marge O'Doone, The
Day of Faith, The
Devil's Riddle, The
Flower of the North
Free and Equal
Gift Supreme, The (Rev. Ebenezer
    Crowley Boggs)
Greed (McTeague's father)
Hell Ship, The
His Back Against the Wall
Long Chance, The
Masters of Men, The
Scarlet Seas (Toomey)
Sea Lion, The
Seeds of Vengeance
Servant in the House, The
Show of Shows, The
Silent Vow, The
Spoilers, The (Bill Nolan)
Steelheart
Torrent, The

Two Kinds of Women
Western Speed

1254
CURWOOD, Bob*
Stunt Cowboy [series]

1255
CUSMICH, Mario*
Die Freudlose Gasse [The Joyless
    Street] /aka/ The Street of Sor-
    rows (Colonel Irving)
Messalina

1256
CUSTER, Bob (Raymond Anthony
    Glenn) (1898-)
Ambush Alley
Arizona Days
Beyond the Rockies
Blood Hound, The
Border Whirlwind
Bulldog Pluck
Cactus Trails
Deadline, The
Devil's Gulch
Dude Cowboy, The
Fightin' Boob, The
Fighting Hombre, The
Fighting Terror, The
Flashing Spurs
Galloping Thunder
Hair Trigger Baxter
Headin' Westward
Last Roundup, The
Law of the Mounted, The
Man of Nerve, A
Man Rustlin'
Manhattan Cowboy
No Man's Law
Oklahoma Kid, The
On the Divide
Parting of the Trails
Range Terror, The
Riders of the Rio Grande
Ridin' Streak, The
Silent Trail, The
Terror of Bar X, The
Texas Bearcat, The
Texas Ranger [series]
Texas Tommy
That Man, Jack
Trigger Fingers
Valley of Bravery
West of Santa Fe

- D -

1257
DABLE, Frances*
Constant Nymph, The

1258
DACIA, Mlle*
Chu-Chin-Chow (dancing slave)
Taming of the Shrew, The (Katherina)

1259
DAGNA, Jeanette*
Cock-Eyed World, The (Katinka)

1260
DAGOVER, Lil /aka/ Lillitts Daghofer (Marta Maria Liletta)
Across to Singapore
At the Grey House
Bara en Danserka
Beyond the Wall
Die Brüder Schellenberg
Chronicles of the Grushuus
Destiny /aka/ The Tired Death; The Three Lights; Between Worlds; Der Mude Tad
Discord
Der Geheime Kurier
Goldwyn player 22
Grand Passion, The
Hungarian Rhapsody
Kable und Liebe
Love Makes Us Blind /aka/ Liebe Macht Blind
Melodie des Herzens
Monte Cristo
Red and Black
Tartuffe
Two Brothers

1261
D'ALBROOK, Sydney /aka/ Sidney*
Across the Continent
Big Game
Bucking the Barrier
Chicago
Chump, The
Flaming Clue, The
I Can Explain
King of Kings, The (Thomas)
Little Miss Smiles
Making Good
Matinee Idol, The
Midnight Mystery, The
Mutiny of the Elsinore
Over the Border

Parlor, Bedroom and Bath
Right Way, The
So This Is Paris (cop)
Spirit of Youth, The
Son of Wallingford, The (Bertram Beegoode)
West of Chicago
Yankee Doodle, Jr.

1262
DALE, Anne*
Fool, The

1263
DALE, Charlie (Charlie Marks) (1881-1971)
Paramount player 29
Warner Brothers player 29

1264
DALE, Margaret*
Disraeli (Mrs. Travers)
One Exciting Night (Mrs. Harrington)
Second Youth
Stage:
Cradle Snatchers, The (Kitty Ladd) 25

1265
D'ALGY, Antonio*
Boob, The (Harry)
Rejected Woman, The
Sainted Devil, A (Don Luis Mendoza)

1266
D'ALGY, Helena*
Don Juan (Murderess of Jose)
Let Not Man Put Asunder
Pretty Ladies
Sainted Devil, A (Julietta Valdez)

1267
D'ALGY, Tony*
Figaro

1268
DALLEUI, Monsieur*
Count of Monte Cristo, The [serial] (Calderousse)

1269
DALTON, Dorothy (1894-1972)
Behind the Masks
Bigger than Barnum's
Crimson Challenge, The
Dark Mirror
Dark Secrets (Ruth Rutherford)
Fog Bound
Fool's Paradise (Poll Patchouli)

Guilty of Love
Half an Hour
His Wife's Friend
Idol of the North, The (Colette Bris-
    sac)
Law of the Lawless, The
Lone Wolf, The
Moral Sinner, The
Moran of the Lady Letty
On the High Seas
Romantic Adventuress, A
Vampire
Woman Who Walked Alone, The

1270
DALTON, Irene*
Bluebeard's Eighth Wife (Alice
    George)

1271
DALY, Hazel*
Stop Thief!

1272
DALY, Marcella*
Two Lovers (Marda)

1273
DALY, Robert*
Yellow Stain, The

1274
D'AMBRICOURT, Adrienne (-1946)
Footlights and Fools (Jo)
Humming Bird, The (the owl)
Trial of Mary Dugan, The (Marie
    Ducrot)
Wages of Virtue (Madama La Can-
    tinere)

1275
DAMITA, Lili (Lilliane Carré)*
Bridge of San Luis Rey, The (Cam-
    ille)
Cock-Eyed World, The (Mariana El-
    emita)
Dancer of Barcelona, The
Forbidden Love
Rescue, The
Scandal in Paris
Two Lovers
Stage:
Son's o' Guns (Yvonne) 29

1276
DANA, Viola (Violet Fulgarth)
    (1897-)
Along Came Ruth

As Man Desires
Beauty Prize
Bigger than Barnum's
Blackmail
Bred in Old Kentucky
Chorus Girl's Romance, A (Marcia
    Meadows)
Cinderella's Twin
Crinoline Romance, A
Dangerous to Men
Devil of Alaska, The
Don't Doubt Your Husband
Five Dollar Baby, The
Fourteenth Lover, The
Glass Houses
Great Love, The
Heart Bandit, The
Her Fatal Millions
Home Stretch, The
Home Stuff
Ice Flood, The
In Search of a Thrill
June Madness
Kosher Kitty Kelly
Life's Darn Funny
Love in the Dark
Lure of the Night Club, The
Match Breaker, The
Merton of the Movies
Naughty Nanette
Necessary Evil, The
Noise in Newboro, A
Off-Shore Pirate, The
Oh, Annice!
One Splendid Hour
Open All Night
Parlor, Bedroom and Bath
Puppets of Fate
Revelation
Rouged Lips
Salvation Jane
Seeing Is Believing
Show of Shows, The
Silent Lover, The
Siren Call, The
Social Code, The
Stoning, The
That Certain Thing
There Are No Villains
Two Ghosts
Two Sisters (dual role)
Wild Oats Lane
Willow Tree, The
Winds of Chance

1277
DANCY, Jeanette*
Movietone Follies of 1929

1278
DANE, Frank*
Blood Money (Sarne)
Flag Lieutenant, The (Lt. Paget)

1279
DANE, Karl (Karl Daen) (1886-1934)
Alias Jimmy Valentine (Swede)
All at Sea
Baby Mine
Bardelys the Magnificent (Rodenard)
Big Parade, The (Slim)
Brotherly Love
China Bound
Circus Rookies
Detectives
Duke Steps Out, The (Barney)
Enemy, The
Hollywood Revue of 1929, The
La Boheme (Benoit)
Navy Blues
Red Mill, The (Capt. Jacop Edam)
Rookies
Scarlet Letter, The (Giles)
Show People (cameo)
Slide, Kelly, Slide
Son of the Sheik (Ramadan)
Speedway
Trail of '98, The (Lars Petersen)
Voice of the Storm
War Paint
Wyoming

1280
DANIEL, Viora*
Life of the Party, The

1281
DANIELL, Henry (1894-1963)
Awful Truth, The
Jealousy (Clement)
Stage:
Second Mrs. Tanqueray, The (Aubrey
   Tanqueray) 24

1282
DANIELS, Bebe (Virginia Daniels)
   (1901-1971)
Affairs of Anatol, The (Satan Synne)
Argentine Love
Campus Flirt
Crowded Hour, The
Dancin' Fool, The (Junie Budd)
Dangerous Money
Daring Youth
Ducks and Drakes
Exciters, The
Feel My Pulse

Fifty-Fifty Girl, The
Fourteenth Man, The
Game Chicken, A
Glimpses of the Moon, The
Heritage of the Desert
His Children's Children
Hot News
Kiss in a Taxi, A
Lovers in Quarantine
Manicure Girl, The
March Hare, The
Miss Bluebeard
Miss Brewster's Millions
Monsieur Beaucaire (Princess Hen-
   riette)
Nancy from Nowhere
Nice People
North to the Rio Grande
Oh, Lady, Lady!
One Wild Week
Palm Beach Girl, The
Paramount player 26
Pink Gods
Rio Rita (Rita Ferguson)
Senorita
She Couldn't Help It
She's a Sheik
Sick Abed
Singed Wings
Sinners in Heaven
Speed Girl, The
Splendid Crime, The
Stranded in Paris
Swim, Girl, Swim
Take Me Home
Two Weeks with Pay (dual role)
Unguarded Women
Volcano (Zabette de Chauvalon)
What a Night
Why Change Your Wife? (Sally Clark)
Wild, Wild Susan
World's Applause, The
You Never Can Tell

1283
DANIELS, Mickey*
Big Business
Doctor Jack
Mary Queen of Tots
Our Gang Comedies
Safety Last (The Kid)

1284
DANIELS, Richard*
Girl Shy

1285
DANIELS, Thelma*
Amazing Vagabond, The

What Happened to Jane? [series]

1286
DANIELS, Violet*
Easy Road, The

1287
DANIELS, Walter*
Dove, The

1288
DANTIS, Suzanne*
Le Grillon du Foyer

1289
D'ARAGON, Lionel*
Flag Lieutenant, The (Col. McLeod)
Virgin Queen, The (Earl of Northumberland)
Wandering Jew, The (Raymond)

1290
DARBY, Nettie Bell*
Greatest Love of All, The

1291
DARCEY-ROCHE, Clara*
Les Miserables (Mlle. Bapistine)

1292
DARCIEA, Edy*
Shepherd King, The

1293
D'ARCY, Alex (Alexander Sarruf) (1908-)
Champagne
Paradise

1294
D'ARCY, Roy (Roy F. Guisti) (1894-1969)
Actress, The
Adam and Evil
Bardelys the Magnificent (Comte de Chatellerault)
Beverly of Graustark (General Marianax)
Beware of Blondes
Beyond the Sierras
Black Watch, The
Buttons
Domestic Meddlers
Family Row, The
Forbidden Hours
Frisco Sally Levy
Girls Gone Wild
Graustark (Dangloss)

Grey Hat, The
His Night
King of the Khyber Rifles (Rewa Ghunga)
La Boheme (Vicomte Paul)
Last Warning
Lovers
Masked Bride, The
Masked Stranger, The
Merry Widow, The (Crown Prince)
Monte Carlo
On Ze Boulevard
Pretty Ladies
Riders of the Dark
Road to Romance, The
Stolen Kisses
Temptress, The (Manos Duros)
Trelawney of the Wells (Gadd)
Valencia
Winners of the Wilderness (Capt. Dumas)
Woman from Hell /aka/ Woman from Hell's Paradise

1295
DARE, Phyllis*
Common Law, The

1296
DARE, Zena*
Knight in London, A

1297
DARK, Michael*
Beau Brummel (Lord Manley)
Broadway after Dark
Dove, The
Flaming Youth
Regular Fellow, A

1298
DARLEY, Brian*
Highest Bidder, The

1299
DARLING, Grace (1896-)
Amazing Lovers
Common Sin
Discarded Woman, The
Even as Eve
Every Man's Price
For Your Daughter's Sake

1300
DARLING, Helen*
Youth and Beauty

1301
DARLING, Ida*
Heart of a Siren, The
Irene
Ruling Passion, The
She Loves and Lies
Singed
Stranded in Paris
Wedding Bells

1302
DARLING, Jean (1922-)
Bouncing Babies
Boxing Gloves
Lazy Days
Our Gang Comedies
Railroadin'
Small Talk
Wiggle Your Ears

1303
DARLING, Ruth*
Hidden Woman, The (Vera MacLoid)

1304
DARMATOW, Ossip*
Sein Grösster Bluff [Her Greatest
   Bluff] (Count Apollinaris)

1305
DARMOND, Grace (1898-1963)
Alimony
Below the Surface
Blow Your Own Horn
Dangerous Adventure [serial]
Daytime Wives
Hawk's Trail, The [serial]
Hope Diamond Mystery, The /aka/
   The Romance of the Hope Diamond
   [serial]
Hour of Reckoning, The
Invisible Divorce
Man from Ten Strike City, The
Marriage Clause, The
Night Patrol
See My Lawyer
So Long Letty
Song of Life, The
Wages of Conscience
Wide Open

1306
DARR, Kathryn*
City that Never Sleeps, The

1307
DARR, Vondell*
City that Never Sleeps, The

Dummy, The (Peggy Meredith)
On Trial (Doris Strickland)
Pony Express

1308
DARRO, Frankie (Frank Johnson)
   (1917-)
Arizona Streak, The
Avenging Rider, The
Battling Buckaroo
Blaze O'Glory
Circus Kid, The
Confessions of a Queen
Cowboy Cop, The
Cyclone of the Range
Eagle's Talons, The
First National player 25
Flesh and the Devil
Flying U Ranch, The
Gun Law
Hearts and Hoofs
Hearts and Spangles
Her Father Said No
Her Husband's Secret
Idaho Red
Judgment of the Hills
Kiki
Lightning Lariats
Little Mickey Grogan
Long Pants
Masquarade Bandit, The
Memory Lane
Mike
Moulders of Men
Mystery Valley
Phantom of the Range
Pride of the Pawnees
Rainbow Man, The
Red Sword, The
Road to Eldorado
Roaring Rails
Signal Tower, The
So Big (Dirk De Jong as a boy)
Terror Mountain
Texas Tornado, The
Trail of the Horse Thieves
Tyrant of Red Gulch
When the Law Rides

1309
DARROW, John*
Argyle Case, The (Bruce Argyle)
Girls Gone Wild
High School Hero
Prep and Pep
Racket, The

1310
DARVAS, Charles*
Dove, The
Fashions for Women

1311
D'ARVIL, Yola--see: Yola D'Avril

1312
DARWELL, Jane (Patti Woodward)
  (1880-1967)
Brewster's Millions
Master Mind, The

1313
D'ATTINO, Giacomo*
White Sister, The

1314
DAUDET, Jeanette*
Lily of the Dust

1315
DAUGHERTY, Jack*
Haunted Valley [serial chapter]
Scarlet Streak, The
Universal player 25
Vanishing West, The [serial]

1316
DAUMEREY, Carey*
Young April

1317
d'AUMERY, Carrie*
Cameo Kirby
Conquering Power, The (Madame
  Grandet)
Dorothy Vernon of Hadden Hall
  (Lady Vernon)
Forbidden Paradise
Lady Windemere's Fan (gossipy
  duchess)

1318
DAUMERY, Carry*
Last Warning

1319
D'AURAY, Jacques*
Claw, The (Richard Saurin)
Four Horsemen of the Apocalypse,
  The (Capt. d'Aubrey)
Humming Bird, The (Zi-Zi)
My American Wife (Gaston Navarre)

1320
D'AURIL, Yola--see: Yola D'Avril

1321
DAUVRAY, Marise*
J'Accuse

1322
DAVEN, Andre*
Monsieur Beaucaire

1323
DAVENPORT, A. Bromley*
American Prisoner, The (Squire
  Malherb)
Roses of Picardy (Baron D'Archeville)
Sally Bishop (landlord)

1324
DAVENPORT, Blanch*
White Moll, The

1325
DAVENPORT, Dorothy (Mrs. Wallace
  Reid) (1895-)
Adam's Rib
Arms and the Gringo
Broken Laws
Every Woman's Problem
Fighting Chance
Human Wreckage
Linda
Masked Avenger, The
Quack, The
Siren, The
Test, The

1326
DAVENPORT, Harry (1866-1949)
Her Unborn Child
Stage:
Thank You (David Lee) 21

1327
DAVENPORT, Milla /aka/ Millie*
Christian, The (matron)
Dangerous Innocence
Don't Trust Your Husband
Dulcy
Faith
Forbidden Woman, The
Girl from Woolworths, The
King of Kings, The (bit)
Leave It to Me
Man from Lost River, The
Red Lily, The (Madame Poussot)
Rip Van Winkle
Road to Glory, The (Aunt Selma)
Shooting of Dan McGrew, The (Mad-
  ame Renault)
Sins of the Father
Stronger than Death

You Never Can Tell

1328
DAVES, Delmer (1904-   )
Duke Steps Out, The

1329
DAVIDSON, Cliff*
Code of the Wilderness, The

1330
DAVIDSON, Dore*
East Side, West Side
Great White Way, The
Grit (Pop Finkel)
Humoresque
Light in the Dark, The (Jerusalem
   Mike)
Success
That Royle Girl (Elman)
Welcome Stranger, The

1331
DAVIDSON, John (1886-   )
Fool's Paradise (Prince Talaat-Ni)
Great Lover, The
His Children's Children
Idle Rich, The
Kid Gloves
Monsieur Beaucaire (Richelieu)
No Woman Knows
Queen of the Nightclubs
Ramschackle Hour
Rescue, The
Saturday Night (the Count)
Skin Deep
Thirteenth Chair, The
Tiger's Club, The
Time, the Place and the Girl, The
Under Two Flags (Sheik)
Universal player 23
Woman Who Walked Alone, The

1332
DAVIDSON, Lawford*
Bright Lights
Burning Daylight
Glorious Adventure, The (Lord Fitz-
   roy)
Her Private Affair (Arnold Hartmann)
Little Journey, A
Love Doctor, The
Miami
Mysterious Dr. Fu Manchu, The
   /aka/ The Insidious Dr. Fu Man-
   chu
Patent Leather Kid, The
Three-Ring Marriage

Tony Runs Wild
Wildfire

1333
DAVIDSON, Max (1875-1950)
All Parts
Blow by Blow
Boy Friend, The
Call of the Cuckoo
Came the Dawn
Carnation Kid, The
Darling of New York, The
Do Gentlemen Snore?
Doll Shop, The
Dumb Daddies
Ghost Patrol, The
Good Morning, Judge
Hats Off
Hogan's Alley
Hotel Imperial (Elias)
Idle Rich, The
Izzy [series]
Light that Failed, The
Long Fliv the King
Moan and Groan, Inc.
No Woman Knows
Old Clothes (Max Ginsburg)
Puppets
Rememberance
Second Hand Rose
Seed 'em and Weep
Should Women Drive?
So This Is College
Sunshine of Paradise Alley
That Night

1334
DAVIDSON, William (1888-1947)
Blaze O' Glory
Cradle Snatchers
Good Morning, Judge
Last Trail, The
Nobody
Queen of the Night Clubs

1335
DAVIDSON, William B. *
Carnation Kid, The
Gentleman of Paris, A
Hearts and Spurs (Victor Dufreme)
Partners of the Night
Poor Dear Margaret Kirby
Recompense
Woman Trap

1336
DAVIES, Marion (Marion Cecilia
   Douras (1897-1961)
Adam and Eva

April Folly (April Poole)
Beauty's Worth (Prudence Cole)
Beverly of Graustark (Beverly Calhoun)
Bride's Play, The (dual role)
Buried Treasure
Cardboard Lover, The (Sally)
Cinema Murder, The
Enchantment
Fair Co-ed, The (Marion)
Hollywood Revue of 1929
Janice Meredith (Title role)
Lights of Old Broadway (dual role, Fely/Anne)
Little Old New York (dual role, Patricia O'Day/Patrick O'Day)
Marianne (Title role)
Patsy, The (Patricia Harrington)
Quality Street (Phoebe Throssel)
Red Mill, The (Tina)
Restless Sex, The (Stephanie Cleland)
Show People (dual role, Peggy Pepper/Herself)
Tillie the Toiler (Tillie Jones)
When Knighthood Was in Flower (Mary Tudor)
Yolanda (dual role, Princess Mary of Burgundy/Yolanda)
Young Diana, The
Zander the Great (Mamie Smith)

1337
DAVIES, Marion Hall*
Ring, The

1338
DAVIS, Dolly*
Cafe Electric /aka/ Wenn ein Weib den Weg Verliert [When a Woman Loses Her Way] (bit)

1339
DAVIS, Edward*
Amateur Gentleman, The (John Barty)
Best People
Butterflies in the Rain
Charmer, The
Contraband
Joanna
Life of Riley, The
Love Racket, The
Only Woman, The
Price She Paid, The
Sea Hawk, The (Chief Justice of England)
Simple Sap, A
Splendid Road, The
Tramp, Tramp, Tramp

1340
DAVIS, George*
Awakening, The
Broadway (Joe)
Circus, The (the magician)
Devil May Care
Four Devils
He Who Gets Slapped (clown)
His Private Life
Kiss, The
Magic Flame, The (the utility man)
Sherlock Junior
Sin Sister

1341
DAVIS, J. Edward*
Woman on the Jury, The

1342
DAVIS, J. Gunnis*
Lord Jim
Lucky Horseshoe, The
Notorious Lady, The
Winds of Chance

1343
DAVIS, Jackie*
Big Business
Mary Queen of Tots
Our Gang Comedies

1344
DAVIS, Mildred (1903-1969)
Among Those Present
Doctor Jack
Grandma's Boy
Haunted Spooks
High and Dizzy (the girl)
His Royal Slyness
I Do
Never Weaken
Pathé player 22
Safety Last (the girl)
Sailor-Made Man, A
Temporary Marriage
Too Many Crooks

1345
DAVIS, Owen, Jr.*
They Had to See Paris (Ross Peters)

1346
DAVIS, Rex*
Every Mother's Son (David Brent)

1347
DAVIS, Roger*
Social Celebrity, A

1348
DAVIS, Tyrrell*
Mother's Boy (Duke of Pomplum)

1349
DAVIS, William*
Indiscretion

1350
D'AVRIL, Yola (1907-)
American Beauty
Awakening, The
Hard Boiled Haggerty
Hot for Paris
House of Horror, The
Lady Be Good
Love Parade, The (Paulette)
MGM player 25
Orchids and Ermines
Shanghai Lady
She Goes to War
Three-Ring Marriage
Valley of the Giants
Vamping Venus

1351
DAW, Marjorie (1902-)
Barefoot Boy, The
Bob Hampton of Placer
Butterfly Girl, The
Call of the Canyon
Cheated Hearts
Dangerous Maid
Dinty
Don't Ever Marry
East Lynne (Barbara Hale)
Experience
Fox player 27
Going Up
Great Redeemer, The
Highbinders, The
Home Made
Human Desires
In Borrowed Plumes
Lone Hand, The
Long Chance, The
Love Is an Awful Thing
One Way Street
Outlaws of Red River
Patsy, The
Penrod
Pride of Palomar, The
Prince of Lovers, The
Redheads Preferred
Revelation
River's End, The
Rupert of Hentzau (Rosa Holf)
Spoilers of the West

Topsy and Eva
Victorious Defeat
Wandering Daughters
Warrens of Virginia, The

1352
DAWN, Dorothy*
California Mail, The
Canyon of Light
Captain's Courage
Dangerous Dude
Drifter, The
Fox player 24
Great K & A Train Robbery
Hills of Kentucky
Land Beyond the Law
McFadden Flats
Obey Your Husband
Out with the Tide
Peacock Fan, The
Perfect Clown, The
Princess of Broadway
Riders of the Dark
Sawmill, The
Silver Valley
Spuds
Square Crooks
Stop, Look and Listen
Tumbling River
Virgin Queen, The
Wizard of Oz, The (Dorothy)

1353
DAWN, Hazel (Hazel La Trout)
   (1891-)
Debutante, The
Devotion
Heart of Jennifer, The
Stage:
Demi-Virgin, The (Gloria Graham) 21
Getting Gertie's Garter (Gertie Dar-
   ling) 21
Nifties of 1923
No Foolin' 26

1354
DAWN, Janet*
Hop to It
Son of Wallingford, The (Dottie Mc-
   Cabe)

1355
DAWSON, Doris (1909-)
Broadway Scandals
Children of the Ritz
Do Your Duty
Heart Trouble
His Captive Woman

Hot Stuff
Kentucky Courage
Little Shepherd of Kingdom Come,
    The
Little Wildcat, The
Man and the Moment, The
Naughty Baby

1356
DAWSON, Ivo*
First Born, The (Derek Finlay)

1357
DAX, Jean*
Last Flight, The

1358
DAY, Alice (1905-)
Alice Be Good
Cat's Meow, The
Coast of Folly
Drag
First Hundred Years Are the Worst,
    The
Flickering Youth
Gorilla, The
Her Actor Friend
His New Mama
His New York Wife
Is Everybody Happy?
Little Johnny Jones
Love Racket, The
Luck of the Foolish, The
Night Life (Anna)
Phyllis of the Follies
Puppy Love Time
Red Hot Speed
Romeo and Juliet (Juliet)
Secrets (Blanche Carlton)
See You in Jail
Shanghaied Lovers
Show of Shows, The
Skin Deep
Smart Set, The
Spanking Breezes
Temple of Venus, The
Times Square
Waiter from the Ritz, The
Way of the Strong, The
Woman on the Jury, The

1359
DAY, Frances (1908-)
Price of Divorce, The

1360
DAY, Marceline (1907-)
Barrier, The (Necia)

Beloved Rogue, The (Charlotte de
    Vauxcelles)
Big City, The (Sunshine)
Boy Friend, The
Cameraman, The
Captain Salvation
Certain Young Man, A
College Days
Detectives
Driftwood
Fools of Fashion
Freedom of the Press
Gay Deceiver, The
Hell's Four Hundred
Jazz Age, The
London after Midnight (Lucille Bal-
    four)
Looking for Trouble
MGM player 26
One Woman Idea
Red Clay
Restless Youth
Road to Romance, The
Rookies
Show of Shows, The
Single Man, A
Snapshots
Splendid Road, The
Stolen Love
That Model from Paris
Trent's Last Case
Under the Black Eagle
White Outlaw
Wild Party, The (Faith Morgan)

1361
DAY, Marjorie*
Glorious Adventure, The (Olivia)

1362
DAY, Olga*
Casanova
Loves of Casanova, The

1363
DAY, Shannon*
Affairs of Anatol, The (chorus girl)
All the Brothers Were Valiant (the
    Brown girl)
Barrier, The
Forbidden Fruit (Nadia Craig)
Honor First
Manslaughter (Miss Santa Claus)
Marriage Morals
So This Is Marriage

1364
DAY, Tom*
Red Raiders, The

1365
DAY, Yvonne (1920-)
Don Juan (Don Juan age 5)

1366
DAYTON, Lewis*
Slander the Woman
What Fools Men

1367
DEAN, Barbara*
Forever

1368
DEAN, Basil*
Constant Nymph, The
Return of Sherlock Holmes, The

1369
DEAN, Dacia*
Dawn (widow Deveaux's daughter)
Easy Virtue (John's older sister)

1370
DEAN, Dinky*
Pilgrim, The (the boy)

1371
DEAN, Dorris*
Half-Breed, The (Nanette)

1372
DEAN, Priscilla (1896-)
Aristocrat, The
Birds of Prey
Cafe in Cario, A
Conflict
Crimson Runner, The
Danger Girl
Dice Woman, The
Drifting
Flame of Life, The
Forbidden Waters
How Do You Feel?
Jewels of Desire
Outside the Law (Molly Madden)
Reputation
Siren of Seville, The
Slipping Wives
Speeding Venus
Storm Daughter
Under Two Flags (Cigarette)
Virgin of Stamboul, The
West of Broadway
White Tiger
Wild Honey

1373
DEANE, Hazel*
Bill Jones comedies (3)
Desert Within, The
Money Talks
Soft Soap
South of the Northern Lights
That Darned Stocking

1374
DEANE, Sidney*
America /aka/ Love and Sacrifice
   (Sir Ashley Montague)
Treasure Island (Squire Trelawney)

1375
DEANE, Verna*
Lady Lies, The (Bernice Tuttle)

1376
DEARHOLT, Ashton*
Branded Four, The [serial]

1377
DEARING, Edgar*
Jazz Age, The
Should Tall Men Marry?

1377a
DEBAIN, Henri*
Michael Strogoff (Blount)

1378
DE BECK, Billy*
Great White Way, The

1379
deBERANGER, André*
Ashes of Vengeance
Bright Shawl, The (Andres Escobar)
Poisoned Paradise (Krantz)
So This Is Paris (Monsieur Lalle)

1380
De BODAMERE, Madame*
Little Lord Fauntleroy (Mrs. Higgins)
Rosita (servant)
Tess of the Storm Country (Mrs.
   Longmar)

1381
DeBOURBON, Princess Marie*
Janice Meredith (Marie Antoinette)

1382
de BRIAC, Jean*
Divine Woman, The
Duchess of Buffalo, The

Love Light, The (Antonio)
Parisian Love (Knifer)

1383
de BRIAC, Twins*
Daddies
Don't Tell Everything (Morgan Twins)

1384
DE BRULIER, Nigel (1878-1948)
Ancient Mariner, The (Skipper)
Beloved Rogue, The (astrologer)
Ben Hur (Simonides)
Boy of Flanders, A
Devil Within, The
Divine Sinner, The (Minister of Police)
Doll's House, A
Don Juan (Marquis Rinaldo)
Dwelling Place of Light
Four Horsemen of the Apocalypse, The (Tchernoff)
Gaucho, The (Padre)
Greater Glory, The
Green Goddess, The (Temple Priest)
His Pajama Girl
Hunchback of Notre Dame, The (Dom Claude)
Iron Mask, The (Richilieu)
Loves of an Actress
Mademoiselle Midnight
Me, Gangster (Danish Looie)
Mother of His Children, The
Noah's Ark (dual role, High Priest/soldier)
Omar, the Tentmaker
Patent Leather Kid, The
Redemption
Regular Fellow, A
Romance of a Queen, The (Dmitry)
Rupert of Hentzau (Herbert)
Salome (Jakanaan)
Soft Cushions
Surrender
Three Musketeers, The (Richilieu)
Three Weeks
Through Different Eyes (Maynard)
Two Lovers (Prince of Orange)
Virgin of Stamboul, The
Wheel of Life, The
Wild Oranges
Wings (French peasant)
Without Benefit of Clergy

1385
DEBUCOURT, Jean (1894-1958)
La Chute de la Maison Usher [The Fall of the House of Usher]
Le Petit Chose

1386
DE CAMPO, Guiseppe*
Arab, The (Selim)

1387
DE CANONGE, Maurice*
Fifty-Fifty

1388
DE CARLTON, George*
American Venus, The
Kopf Hoch, Charly! [Heads Up, Charly!] (Rufus Quinn)

1389
DE COEUR, A.*
Two Little Vagabonds (Dido Bunce)

1390
DE CORDOBA, Pedro (1881-1950)
Bandolero, The
Dark Mirror
Enemies of Woman (Atilio Castro)
Girl of the South
Inner Chamber, The
New Commandment, The
Purple Highway, The
Sin that Was His, The
Swords and the Woman
When Knighthood Was in Flower (Duke of Buckingham)
World and His Wife, The
Young Diana, The
Stage:
Candida (Rev. James Mavor Morell)
24

1391
DE CORDOVA, Rudolf*
Glorious Adventure, The (Thomas Unwin)

1392
de COURCY, Nanette*
Veiled Secret, The (Ethel)

1393
DE COURELLE, Rose Marie*
Temple of Dawn, The (Ayah)

1394
DEDINSTEV, A.*
Storm over Asia

1395
DEEFLOS, Huguette*
Le Process de Mary Dugan [The Trial of Mary Dugan]

1396
DEELEY, Ben*
Acquital, The

1397
DEER, Alma*
Lone Hand Tex
Two-Fisted Thompson
Western Grit

1398
DEER, Louis*
Unseeing Eyes

1399
DEERING, Patricia*
Lady Lies, The (Jo Rossiter)

1400
DEERY, Jack*
Disraeli (Bascot)

1401
DE FAS, Boris*
Madonna of the Sleeping Cars, The
Michael Strogoff (Pheophar Rhan)
Tempest, The
Volga-Volga (Iwaschaka)
Woman Disputed (passer-by)

1402
DE FAST, Boris*
Das Schiff der Verlorenen Menschen
   [The Ship of Lost Souls] /aka/
   LeNavire des Hommes Perdus
   [The Ship of Lost Men] (sailor)

1403
de FELICE, Alfredo*
Messalina

1404
de FERAUDY, Maurice
Visages d' Enfants

1405
DE FOE, Annette*
One Clear Call

1406
deGEORGE, Carleton*
American Venus, The
New Klondike, The

1407
DE GRASSE, Sam (1875-1953)
Black Pirate, The (a lieutenant)
Broken Gates, The

Captain Salvation
Circus Days
Courage
Courtship of Miles Standish, The
Cowboy Doctor
Devil's Passkey, The (Warren Good-
   wright)
Erick the Great
Farmer's Daughter, The
Fighting Eagle, The
Forsaking All Others
Her Second Chance
His Lady /aka/ When a Man Loves
   (Comte Guillot de Morfontaine)
Honor Bound
In the Palace of the King
King of Kings, The (the Pharisee)
King Tut
Last Performance, The
Love's Blindness
Man Who Laughs, The (King James)
Mike
One Year to Live
Our Dancing Daughters (Freddie's
   father)
Painted People
Racket, The
Robin Hood (Prince John)
Sally, Irene and Mary (Officer O'Dare)
Silks and Saddles
Slippy McGee
So Big (Simeon Peake)
Spoilers, The (Judge Stillman)
Sun Up
Tiger Rose
Unseen Forces
Wall Street
Wife's Awakening, A
Wreck of the Hesperus, The

1408
DE GRAVONNE, Gabriel*
Michael Strogoff (Jollivet)

1409
DE GRAY, Sydney*
Amateur Gentleman, The (Captain
   Chumby)
Blood and Sand (Dr. Ruiz)
Chorus Girl's Romance, A (Fred
   Ward)
Half-Breed, The (Leon Pardeau)
Mark of Zorro, The (Don Alejandro)
My Man
Steele of the Royal Mounted
Wings of Youth

1410
DeGUINGAND, Pierre*
Ich Küsse Ihre Hand, Madame [I Kiss Your Hand Madame] (Adolf Gerard)
Le Mauvais Garcon
Three Musketeers, The (Aramis)

1411
De HAVEN, Carter*
Beating Cheaters
Girl in the Taxi, The
Goldwin two reelers (13)
Hoodooed
Marry the Poor Girl
My Lady Friends
Paramount two reelers (10)
Ringer for Dad, A
Their First Vacation
Twin Beds

1412
De HAVEN, Carter, Mrs. (Flora Parker)*
Girl in the Taxi, The
Goldwyn two reelers (13)
Hoodooed
Marry the Poor Girl
My Lady Friends
Paramount two reelers (10)
Ringer for Dad, A
Their First Vacation
Twin Beds

1413
DE HEDEMANN, Baroness*
Her Love Story (Lady in Waiting)

1414
DEHN, Dorothy*
So This Is College

1415
de KECZER, Irma*
Second Youth

1416
DE KIRBY, Annette*
Mother Knows Best (Bessie as a child)

1417
DE KIRBY, Ivar*
Mother Knows Best (Ben as a child)

1418
de KNIGHT, Fannie Belle*
Hallelujah! (Mammy)

1418a
De LACEY, Jack*
Making of O'Malley, The

1419
DE LA CRUZE, Jimmy*
Flight

1420
deLACY, Phillipe /aka/ Philippe (1917-)
Beau Geste
Broken Mask, The
Christmas
Divorce
Doll's House, A
Don Juan (Don Juan, age 10)
Elegy, The
Four Devils (Adolphus boy)
Four Feathers, The (Harry, age 10)
General Crack (Christian as a boy)
Is Matrimony a Failure?
Is Zat So?
Love (Seresha)
Magic Garden, The
Marriage Playground, The (Terry)
Mother Machree
Napoleon's Barber
One Romantic Night
Peter Pan (Michael)
Redeeming Sin, The
Rosita (Rosita's brother)
Royal Rider
Shooting of Dan McGrew, The (Little Jim)
Square Shoulders
Student Prince, The (Prince Karl as a boy)
Thelma
Tigress, The
Wasted Lives
Way of All Flesh, The (August as a boy)
Wheel of Fortune
Why Do We Live?
Without Benefit of Clergy

1421
DE LA MOTTE, Marguerite (1903-1950)
Behold This Woman
Beloved Brute, The
Broken Gates, The
Cheaper to Marry
Children of the Whirlwind
Clean Heart, The
Desire
East of Broadway

Famous Mr. Fair, The
Fifth Avenue
Final Extra, The
Hearts and Fists
Held by the Law
Hope
Iron Mask, The (Constance)
Jilt, The
Just Like a Woman
Kid Sister, The
Last Frontier, The
Man of Action, A
Mark of Zorro, The (Lolita)
Meet the Prince
Montmartre Rose
Nut, The
Pals in Paradise
People vs Nancy Preston, The
Ragtime
Red Dice
Sagebrush Hamlet, A
Sagebrusher, The
Scars of Jealousy
Shadows (Sympathy Gibbs)
Shattered Idols
Tailsman, The
Three Musketeers, The (Constance
  Bonacieux)
Trailin' Back
Trumpet Island
U. P. Trail, The
Unknown Soldier, The
Wandering Daughters
What a Wife Learned
When a Man's a Man

1421a
DELANCY, Henriette*
Daughter of Israel, A

1422
DELANEY, Charles (1892-1959)
Adventurer, The
After the Storm
Air Circus, The
Branded Man, The
Broadway Babies
Broadway Daddies
Cohens and the Kellys, The
Cohens and the Kellys in Paris, The
College Days
Do Your Duty
Faker, The
Flaming Fury
Frisco Sally Levy
Girl from Woolworths, The
Hard to Get
Home, James

Lovelorn, The
Main Event, The
Mountains of Manhattan
Outcast Souls
River Woman
Show Girl
Silent Avenger, The
Silent Power
Sky Pirate, The
Stool Pigeon, The
Thirteenth Hour, The
Those Who Dare
Tiffany player 26
Women Who Dare

1423
DELANEY, Iria*
This Freedom

1424
DELANEY, Jere*
Lights of New York (Dan Dickson)

1425
DELANNOY, Henriette*
L'Ingenu Libertin
Java Une

1426
DELANO, Clothilde*
Scaramouche (Marie Antoinette)

1427
DE LANTI, Stella*
Don Q. Son of Zorro (Queen of Spain)
Fifty-Fifty

1428
DELARO, Hattie*
April Folly (Mrs. Stanislaw)
Janice Meredith (Mrs. Meredith)

1429
DE LEON, Don Pedro*
Dancer of Barcelona, The

1430
de LIGUORO, Countess Eugenio*
Fast Set, The (Walters)
Last Days of Pompeii (Ione)
Quo Vadis? (Eunice)

1431
de LIGUORO, Rina*
Loves of Casanova, The
Messalina
Mystic Mirror, The

1432
De LIMUR, Jean*
Arab, The (Hossein)

1433
DELMAR, Thomas*
Bad Man, The
Rainbow Trail, The
Shamrock Handicap, The (Michael)

1434
DELMAS, Suzanne*
Rasputin, the Holy Sinner

1435
DELORES, Jean*
Voice from the Sky, The

1436
DE LOREZ, Claire*
Beau Brummel (Lady Manley)
Cobra (Rosa Minardi)
Last Flight, The
Morgane, the Enchantress
My Wife and I
Queen of Sheba, The (Queen Amarath)
Romance of a Queen, The (Mitze)
Siren of Seville, The
So This Is Marriage
Three Weeks

1437
DEL RIO, Dolores (Lolita Dolores
    Ansunsolo de Martinez) (1905-)
Dove, The
Evangeline
Gateway of the Moon
High Steppers
Joanna
Loves of Carmen, The (Carmen)
No Other Woman
Pals First
Ramona (Title role)
Red Dance, The /aka/ The Red Dan-
    cer of Moscow
Resurrection
Revenge
Trail of '98, The (Berna)
What Price Glory? (Charmaine)
Whole Town's Talking, The
Recording:
Ramona (RCA-LPV538)

1438
DELSCHAFT, Mady*
Last Laugh, The /aka/ Der Letz
    Mann (the daughter)
Variété [variety]

1439
DE LUNGO, Tony*
Constant Nymph, The (Roberto)

1440
DEL VAL, Jean*
Sainted Devil, A (Casimoro)

1441
DEMAIN, Gordon*
Marriage Playground, The (Mr. Dela-
    field)

1442
de MARE, Rolf*
Entr'acte

1443
DEMAREST, Drew*
Broadway Melody, The (Turpe)

1444
DEMAREST, William (1892-)
Amateur Night
Broadway Melody, The
Bush Leaguer
Butter and Egg Man, The
Crash, The
Don't Tell the Wife
Escape, The
Finger Prints (debut)
First Auto, The
Five and Ten Cent Annie
Gay Old Birds
Girl in Every Port, A
Jazz Singer, The (Buster Billings)
Matinee Ladies
Million Bid, A
Old San Francisco
Pa's Vacation
Pay as You Enter
Reno Divorce, A
Sharp Shooters
What Happened to Father?
When the Wife's Away
Wrecking Boss, The

1445
DE MAX, Edouard*
Le Mauvais Garcon
Three Musketeers, The (Cardinal
    Richelieu)

1446
DE MENDOZA, Carlo*
Dancer of Barcelona, The

1447
DEMING, Walter*
Passionate Youth

1448
DEMPSEY, Clifford*
Ghost Talks, The
Happy Days (Sheriff Benton)
Knights Out
Salute
Valiant, The

1449
DEMPSEY, Jack (William Harrison
  Dempsey) (1895-)
Daredevil Jack [serial]
Fight and Win
Stage:
Big Fight, The (Jack Dillon, The
  Tiger) 28

1450
DEMPSTER, Carol (1902-)
America /aka/ Love and Sacrifice
  (Nancy Montague)
Black Beach
Dream Street (Gypsy Fair)
Isn't Life Wonderful? (Inga)
Love Flower, The (Stella Bevan)
One Exciting Night (Agnes Harrington)
Sally of the Sawdust (Sally)
Sherlock Holmes /aka/ Moriarty
  (Alice Faulkner)
Sorrows of Satan, The (Mavis Claire)
That Royle Girl (Joan Daisy Royle)
Way Down East (extra)
White Rose, The (Marie Carrington)

1451
D'ENNERY, Guy*
Lights of New York (Tommy)
Stage:
Show Off, The (Frank Hyland) 24

1452
DENNES, Eileen*
Comin' thro' the Rye (Sylvia Fleming)

1453
DENNIS, Eddie*
All Aboard

1454
DENNISON, Eva*
His Glorious Night

1455
DENNY, Malcolm*
Any Woman

Blonde Saint, The
Sporting Youth

1456
DENNY, Reginald (Reginald Leigh
  Daymore) (1891-1967)
Abysmal Brute, The (Pat Glendon,
  Jr.)
Beggar Maid, The
California Straight Ahead
Cheerful Fraud, The
Clear the Decks
Dark Lantern, A
Disraeli (Charles Viscount Duford)
Embarrassing Moments
Fast and Furious
Fast Worker, The
Footlights
Good Morning, Judge
His Lucky Day
I'll Show You the Town
Iron Trail, The
Jenny Lind
Kentucky Derby
Leather Pushers, The [series]
Madame Butterfly
Never Let Go
Night Bird, The
Oh, Doctor!
On Your Toes
Out All Night
Paying the Piper
Price of Possession, The
Realart player 21
Reckless Age, The
Red Hot Speed
Rolling Home
Romeo in Pajamas
Sherlock Holmes /aka/ Moriarty
  (Prince Alexis)
Skinner's Dress Suit
Sporting Youth
Take It from Me
That's My Daddy
39 East
Tropical Love
What Happened to Jones?
Where Was I?

1457
DENT, Vernon (d. 1963)
All Night Long
Barber's Daughter, The
Beach Club, The
Best Man, The
Bicycle Flirt, The
Boobs in the Wood
Broken Bubbles
Campus Carmen, The

Depot Romance, A
Dumb Waiter, A
Extra Girl, The
Eye for Figures, An
Feet of Mud
Fiddlesticks
Gas Attack, A
Girl Crazy
Gold Widows
Golf
Hank Mann comedies
Harem Hero, A
His First Flame
His Marriage Wow
His Unlucky Night
Hollywood Kid, The
Ladies Must Eat
Lucky Stars
Old Barn, The
Plain Clothes
Pride of Pikesville
Remember When?
Saturday Afternoon
There He Goes

1458
DEPEW, Joe /aka/ Joseph*
Daring Years, The (La Motte boy)
Grit (Tony O'Cohen)
Icebound
Queen of the Night Clubs
Steadfast Heart
Swan, The
Sweetie

1459
DEPP, Harry*
Inez from Hollywood
Quincy Adams Sawyer (a Cobb twin)

1460
de PUTTI, Lya (1904-1931)
Autumn Love
Buck Privates
Burning Acre, The
God Gave Me Twenty Cents
Heart Thief, The
Informer, The
Jealousy
Manon Lescaut (Title role)
Midnight Rose
Othello (Emilia)
Phantom, The
Plaything
Prince of Tempters, The
Scarlet Lady, The
Sorrows of Satan, The (Princess Ol-
    ga Godovsky)

Variété [variety]
Vaudeville

1461
De RAMEY, Pierre*
Time to Love

1462
De RAVENNE, Charles*
Love and Glory

1463
De REMER, Ruby /aka/ Rubye*
Don't Marry for Money
Glimpses of the Moon
Goldwyn player 21
His Temporary Wife
Luxury
Passionate Pilgrim
Pilgrims of the Night
Unconquered Woman, The
Way Women Love, The

1464
DERIGNEY, Louise*
My Lady's Garter

1465
De RISO, Camillo*
Othello

1466
de ROCHE, Charles (1880-1952)
Cheat, The
L'Empereur des Pauvres
L'Empire des Diamants
Gigolette
Law of the Lawless
Love and Glory
Madame Sans-Gene (Lefebvre)
Marriage Maker, The
Notre Dame D'Amour
Paramount player 24
La Princesse Aux Clowns
Le Roi du Camargue
Shadows of Paris
Spanish Jade
Ten Commandments, The (Rameses)
White Moth, The

1467
De ROSA, A.*
Sainted Devil, A

1468
deRUIZ, Nick F.*
Forbidden Paradise (rebellious gene-
    ral)

Half-Breed, The (Juan Del Rey)
His Supreme Moment
Hunchback of Notre Dame, The (M.
  le Torteru)
Mademoiselle Midnight
Man Who Laughs, The (Wapentake)
Rio Rita (Pedrone)

1469
DERVIS, Charles*
Red Mark, The

1470
DESCLOS, Jeanne*
Three Musketeers, The (the queen)

1471
deSEGUROLA, Andre (d. 1953)
Behind Closed Doors
Bringing up Father
Cardboard Lover, The (the baritone)
Diplomats, The
General Crack (Colonel Pons)
Loves of Sunya, The (Paolo de Salvo)
My Man
Red Dance, The /aka/ The Red Dan-
  cer of Moscow

1472
DESHON, Florence*
Deep Waters

1473
deSILVA, Fred*
Durand of the Badlands (Pete Garson)
Rainbow Trail, The
Sea Hawk, The (Ali)

1474
DESJARDINS, Maxine*
J'Accuse
Legion of Honor, The
Soul of France, The
Three Musketeers, The (DeTreville)

1475
DESLYS, Kay*
Case of Lena Smith, The
Perfect Day, A
Tarnish

1476
DESMOND, Dagmar*
Man and Maid

1477
DESMOND, William (1878-1949)
Ace of Spades [serial]

Around the World in 18 Days [serial]
  (Phiness Fogg III)
Beasts of Paradise [serial]
Blood and Steel
Blue Bandanna, The
Breathless Moment
Broadway Cowboy
Burning Trail, The
Child Thou Gavest Me, The
Claw, The
Deuce Duncan
Devil's Trade-Mark, The
Don't Leave Your Husband
Extra Girl, The
Fightin' Mad
Man from Make-Believe, The
McQuire of the Mounted
Measure of a Man, The
Meddler, The
Mystery Rider, The [serial]
Night Life in Hollywood
No Defense
Parish Priest, The
Pathé player 21
Perils of the Wild [serial]
Perils of the Yukon [serial]
Phantom Fortune, The [serial]
Prince and Betty, The
Red Clay
Return of the Riddle Rider [serial]
Riddle Rider, The [serial] (dual role)
Sentenced to Soft Labor
Shadows of the North
Strings of Steel [serial] (Ned)
Sunset Trail
Tongues of Scandal
Winking Idol, The [serial]
Women Men Love

1478
DESNI, Xenia*
Der Oberkillner
Der Sprung ins Leben [The Leap into
  Life] (circus acrobat)
Waltz Dream, The (Franzi)

1479
D'ESTERRE, Madame*
Dick Turpin's Ride to New York (La-
  dy Weston)
Henry, King of Navarre (Henry's
  mother)

1480
DEUTSCH, Ernst (1891-1969)
Das Alto Gesetz (Baruch)
Ancient Law, The
Der Golem

DE VALASCO, Mercedes*
Behind that Curtain (Neinah)

1482
DE VAULL, Billie*
Lights of Old Broadway

1483
de VERDIER, Anton*
Hamlet (Laertes)

1484
DEVERE, Harry*
Hunchback of Notre Dame, The
Shock, The (Olaf Wismer)

1485
deVESA, Leonardo*
His Tiger Lady

1486
DEVHRYS, Rachel*
Morgane, the Enchantress

1487
DEVI, Seeta*
Light of Asia, The
Shiraz

1488
deVILBISS, Robert*
Old Nest, The
Reno

1489
DEVINE, Andy (1905-)
Flying High [serial chapter]
Hot Stuff
Lonesome
Naughty Baby
Red Lips
We Americans

1490
DEVINE, Jerry*
Over the Hill (John, the boy)
Potash and Perlmutter
Sherlock Holmes /aka/ Moriarty
   (Billy)
Steadfast Heart, The
Tongues of Flame

1491
DEVINE, John*
Over the Hill

1492
deVOGHT, Carl*
Waterloo

1493
DEVORE, Dorothy (1901-)
All Jazzed Up
Broadway Butterfly, The
Chop Suey
Christie player 21
Cutie
First Night, The
45 Minutes from Broadway
Gilded Highway, The
His Majesty Bunker Bean
How Baxter Buttered In
Magnificent Brute, The
Man Upstairs, The
Midnight Flyer, The
Mind Your Business
Money to Burn
Mountains of Manhattan
Movie Mad
Narrow Street, The
Naughty Mary Brown
No Babies Wanted
One Stormy Night
Prairie Wife
Saving Sister Suzie
Senor Daredevil
Social Highwayman, The
Three Weeks in Paris
Who Cares?
Winter Has Come
Youth and Beauty

1494
DEWEY, Arthur*
America /aka/ Love and Sacrifice
   (George Washington)

1495
DEWHURST, George*
Helen of Four Gates
Lunatic at Large
Narrow Valley, The
Tansy
Tinted Venus, The
Wild Heather

1496
deWINTON, Albert*
Love Parade, The (a Cabinet Minister)

1497
DE WITT, Jennings*
Deadwood Coach, The

1498
de WOLFE, Elsie (1865-1950)
Democracy, The Vision Restored

1499
DE XANDOVAL, Guerrero*
Carmen (Lucas, the Picador)

1500
DEXTER, Elliott (1870-1941)
Adam's Rib (Professor Nathan Reade)
Affairs of Anatol, The (Max Runyon)
Age of Innocence, The
Behold My Wife!
Broadway Gold
Capital Punishment (Gordon Harrington)
Common Law, The
Don't Tell Everything (Harvey Gilroy)
Enter Madame
Fast Set, The (Richard Sones)
Flaming Youth
Forever
Grand Larceny
Great Moment, The
Hands of Nara, The
Her Husband's Trademark
Idols of Clay
Old Sweetheart of Mine, An
Only 38
Something to Think About (David Mar-
   kley)
Stella Maris
Witching Hour, The

1501
DEYERS, Lien*
Spione [Spies]

1502
DE YZARDUY, Madame*
Michael Strogoff (Zangara)

1503
DHEPLEY, Ruth*
When Knighthood Was in Flower

1504
DIAL, Patterson*
Get Rich Quick Wallingford (Bessie)
Happiness
Man's Mate, A
Married Flirts
Tol'able David (Rose Kinemon)
Secrets (Susan)

1505
di BENEDETTA, Marie*
Greatest Love of All, The

1506
DIBLEY, Mary*
Blinkeyes (Mrs. Banning)
His House in Order (Geraldine Ridgeley)

Sally Bishop (Mrs. Priestley)

1507
DICKERSON, Milton*
Hallelujah! (a Johnson kid)

1508
DICKEY, Paul*
Robin Hood (Sir Guy of Gisbourne)

1509
DICKINSON, Milton*
Street Angel (Bimbo)

1510
DICKSON, Dorothy (1902-)
Paramount player 21

1511
DICKSON, Lydia*
Don't Marry 28

1512
DIEGELMANN, Wilhelm*
Anna Boleyn /aka/ Deception
Die Bergkatze [The Mountain Cat/
   The Wild Cat] (Claudius)
Der Mensch am Wege [Man by the
   Roadside]

1513
DIESEL, Gustav*
Pandora's Box
That Murder in Berlin

1514
DIETERLE, Eugene*
Backstairs
Three Way Works, The

1515
DIETERLE, William (Wilhelm Dieterle)
   (1894-1973)
At the Edge of the World (John)
Behind the Altar
Dame Care
Faust (Valentine)
Der Mensch am Wege [Man by the
   Roadside] (the human angel)
Russia 1908
Das Wachsfigurenkabinet [The Wax-
   works] (starving poet)
Weavers, The

1516
DIETRICH, Antonia*
Der Kleine Napoleon [The Little Na-
   poleon] /aka/ So Sind die Männer
   [Men Are Like That]; Napoleons

Kleiner Bruder [Napoleon's Little
Brother] (Charlotte)

1517
DIETRICH, Marlene (Maria Magda-
lene vonLosch) (1900-)
Cafe Electric /aka/ Wenn ein Weib
der Weg Verliert [When a Woman
Loses Her Way] (Erni)
Eine Du Barry von Heute [A Modern
Du Barry] (a Coquette)
Die Frau, Nach der Man Sich Shent
[The Woman One Longs For]
/aka/ Three Loves (Stascha)
Die Freudlose Gasse [The Joyless
Street] /aka/ Street of Sorrow,
The (young woman in breadline)
Gefahren der Brautzeit [Dangers of
the Engagement Period] /aka/
Aus dem Tagebuch eines Ver-
führers; Eine Nocht der Liebe;
Liebesnächte [Nights of Love]
Die Glückliche Mutter [The Happy
Mother] (herself)
Great Baritone, The
Ich Küsse Ihre Hand, Madame [I
Kiss Your Hand, Madame] (Law-
rence Gerard)
Der Juxbaron [The Imaginary Baron]
(Sophie)
Der Kleine Napoleon [The Little
Napoleon] /aka/ So Sind die
Männer [Men Are Like That];
Napoleons Kleiner Bruder [Na-
poleon's Little Brother] (debut-
Kathrin)
Kopf Hoch, Charly! [Heads Up,
Charly! (Edmée Marchand)
Liebersbriefe (Evelyne)
Madame Wünscht Keine Kindu [Mad-
ame Doesn't Want Children] /aka/
Madame Wants No Children (bit)
Manon Lescaut (Micheline)
Der Mensch am Wege [Man by the
Roadside] (Osmania)
Prinzessin Olala [Princess Olala]
/aka/ Art of Love (Chicotte de
Gastoné)
Das Schiff der Verlorenen Menschen
[The Ship of Lost Souls] /aka/
Navire des Hommes Perdus [The
Ship of Lost Men] (Miss Ethel)
Sein Grösster Bluff [Her Greatest
Bluff] (Yvette)
Der Sprung ins Leben [The Leap in-
to Life] (bit)
Tragödie der Liebe [Tragedy of
Love] (Lucie)
Ween ein Weib der Wag Verliert

Stage:
Broadway - Vienna 27
Eltern und Kinder - Germany 28
Es Lieght in der Luft [It's in the
Air] - Germany 28
Der Grosse Baritone [The Great
Baritone] - Germany 22
Midsummer Night's Dream, A (Hip-
polyta) - Germany 22
Die Schule von Uznach [The School
of Uznach] - Germany 27
Taming of the Shrew, The (debut) -
Germany 22
Zartlck zu Methusalem [Back to Me-
thuselah] - Germany 28
Zwei Krawatten [Two Neckties] 29

1518
DIETRICH, Tina*
Das Wieb des Pharao [The Wife of
the Pharaoh] /aka/ The Loves of
the Pharaoh

1519
DIGGES, Dudley (1879-1947)
Condemned (Warden Jean Vidal)
Stage:
Adding Machine, The (Mr. Zero) 23
Dynamo (Ramsey Fife) 29
Goethe's Faust, Part I (Mephisto-
pheles) 28
Heartbreak House (Boss Mangan) 20
Jane Clegg (Henry Clegg) 20
Major Barbara (Andrew Undershaft) 28
Man's Estate (William P. Jordan) 29
Mr. Pim Passes By (George Marden,
J. P.) 21
Outward Bound (Rev. Thompson) 24
Volpone (Title role) 28

1520
DIGNON, Edmond*
American Prisoner, The (Leverett)

1521
di LANTI, Stella*
Don Q, Son of Zorro
Only Woman, The

1522
DILLER, Marie*
Sainted Devil, A

1523
DILLER, Phyllis*
Over the Hill (Rebecca, the Woman)

1524
DILLION, John Webb /aka/ John

Webb Dillon
Air Mail, The
Devil's Cargo, The
Exiles, The
Vanishing American, The /aka/ The
  Vanishing Race
Wolf's Clothing

1525
DILLON, Andrew*
Little Old New York (John Jacob Astor)

1526
DILLON, Eddie /aka/ Edward*
Broadway Gold
Broadway Melody, The (stage manager)
Danger Girl
Deuce Woman, The
Drums of Jeopardy, The
Heart to Let, A
Hot for Paris
Lilac Time
Parlor, Bedroom and Bath
Skyrocket, The

1527
DILLON, John T. /aka/ Jack*
Dry Martini
In Old Arizona (second soldier)
Mountain Woman, The

1528
DILLS, William*
Chechahcos, The

1529
DIME, James*
Stand and Deliver (Patch Eye)

1530
DINENSEN, Marie*
David Copperfield

1531
DINENSEN, Robert*
Tatjana

1532
DION, Hector*
Courtship of Miles Standish, The
Lost City, The /aka/ The Jungle
  Princess [serial]

1533
DIONE, Rose*
Beloved Rogue (Margot)
Blushing Bride, The
Bringing up Father
Camille (Prudence)
Drifting
Duchess of Buffalo, The
Fifth Avenue Models
French Doll, The
Great Lover, The
Hearts in Exile
His Lady /aka/ When a Man Loves
His Tiger Lady
Inez from Hollywood
Little Lord Fauntleroy (Minna)
Lover of Camille, The
Mad Hour, The
Mademoiselle Modiste
Naughty Baby
Old San Francisco
Omar the Tentmaker
One Stolen Night
One Year to Live
Out of the Ruins
Pants at Any Price
Paris
Polly of the Movies
Ragtime
Red Mark, The
Salome (Herodias)
Shadows of Paris
Silent Years
Silk Hosiery
Suds
Try and Get It
Woman and the Puppet, The

1534
DI SANGRO, Elena*
Quo Vadis? (Poppaea)

1535
DIX, Richard (Ernest Carlton Brim-
  mer) (1894-1949)
All's Fair in Love
Bonded Woman
Call of the Canyon, The
Christian, The (John Storm)
Dangerous Curves Ahead
Easy Come, Easy Go (Robert Parker)
Fools First
Gay Defender, The
Glorious Fool, The
Icebound
Knockout Reilly
Lady Who Lied, The
Let's Get Married
Love Doctor, The
Lucky Devil, The
Man Must Live, A
Manhattan
Manpower
Men and Women
Moran of the Marines

Not Guilty (dual role)
Nothing But the Truth
Paradise for Two
Poverty of Riches
Quarterback, The
Quicksands
Racing Hearts
Redskin, The (Wing Foot)
Say It Again
Seven Keys to Baldpate
Shanghai Bound
Shock Punch, The
Sin Flood, The
Sinners in Heaven
Souls for Sale (Frank Claymore)
Sporting Goods
Stranger, The
Too Many Kisses
Unguarded Women
Vanishing American, The (Nophaie)
Wall Flower, The
Warming Up
Wheel of Life, The
Woman with Four Faces (R. Templer)
Womanhandled
Yellow Men and Gold

1536
DIXIE JUBILEE SINGERS, The
Hallelujah! (themselves)

1537
DIXON, Florence*
Wife in Name Only

1538
DIXON, Jean*
Lady Lies, The

1539
DIXON, Marion*
Courtship of Miles Standish, The

1540
DOBLE, Frances*
Constant Nymph, The (Florence)
Vortex, The (Bunty Mainwaring)

1541
DODD, Joseph A. *
Skin Game, The (Jackmans)

1542
DODD, Neal (1878-1966)
Only Woman, The

1543
DODGE, Anna*
Gift Supreme, The (Mrs. Wesson)

1544
DOLOREZ, Mlle. *
Four Horsemen of the Apocalypse,
   The (Mlle. Lucette)

1545
DOMINGUEZ, Beatrice*
Four Horsemen of the Apocalypse,
   The (dancer)

1546
DOMINICI, Mario*
Movietone Follies of 1929 (Le Marie)

1547
DONALDSON, Arthur*
America /aka/ Love and Sacrifice
   (King George III)
Bandolero, The
Love 'em and Leave 'em
School for Wives
Swan, The
When Knighthood Was in Flower (Sir
   William Brandon)
Yolanda (Lord Bishop)

1548
DOLAN, Anton*
Alf's Button (bit)

1549
DONLAN, James*
Big News (Deke)
Bishop Murder Case, The

1550
DONLAN, Mike*
General, The (a Union general)
Oh, Doctor!

1551
DONLEVY, Brian (1901-1972)
Gentlemen of the Press
Mother's Boy (Harry O'Day)

1552
DONLIN, Mike*
Beggars of Life
Ella Cinders
Fifth Avenue Models
Oh, Doctor!
Primrose Path, The (Parker)
Riley, the Cop
Sea Beast, The (Flask)
Sea Hunt, The
Slide, Kelly, Slide
Thunderbolt
Unknown Purple, The

Warming Up
Woman Proof

1553
DONNELLY, Donald*
Rising of the Moon, The

1554
DONNELLY, Ruth (1896-)
Rubber Heels
Stage:
Meanest Man in the World, The
   (Kitty Crockett) 21

1555
DONNIE*
Boxing Gloves

1556
DONOHUE, Joseph*
Twenty Dollars a Week

1557
DONOVAN, Jack*
Milestones (Richard Sibley)

1558
DONOVAN, Michael*
America /aka/ Love and Sacrifice
   (Major General Warren)

1559
DONOVAN, Wilfred*
Society Scandal, A (Hamilton Penn-
   field)

1560
DONOVAN, William*
Son of the Sheik (S'rir)

1561
DOOLEY, Billy (1893-)
Christie comedies (6)

1562
DOOLEY, Gordon*
Beauty's Worth (doll in charade
   scene)

1563
DOOLEY, Johnny (1887-1928)
Beauty's Worth (soldier in charade
   scene)
East Side, West Side
When Knighthood Was in Flower
   (king's jester)
Yolanda (The Dauphin, Charles,
   Duke of Paris)

1564
DOPH, Josephine*
Our Modern Maidens

1565
D'ORA, Daisy*
Pandora's Box

1566
DORA, Josefine*
Romeo und Julia im Schnee [Romeo
   and Juliet in the Snow]

1567
DORALINDA, Mlle. *
Beatrice
Midnight Gambols
Passion Flower
Sally Bishop
Stronger Passion
Twelve-Ten
Woman Untamed, The

1568
DORAN, Mary (1907-)
Broadway Melody, The (Flo)
Girl in the Show, A
Half a Bride
Lucky Boy
New York Nights
River Woman
Their Own Desire
Tonight at Twelve
Trial of Mary Dugan, The

1569
DORE, Adrienne*
Pointed Heels
Wild Party, The (Babe)

1570
DORETY, Charley*
Ike and Mike series

1571
DORMAN, Shirley*
Honeymoon Hate
One Woman Idea

1572
DORMER, Charles*
Triumph of the Rat, The (René Duval)

1573
DORNE, Mary*
Trial of Mary Dugan, The (Pauline
   Agguero)

1574
DORO, Marie (Marie Stewart) (1882-
    1956)
Maid of Mystery
Sally Bishop (Title role)

1575
DORRAINE, Lucy*
Adoration
Christina (the woman)

1576
D'ORSAY, Fifi (1907-)
Hot for Paris
They Had to See Paris (Claudine)

1577
D'ORSAY, Lawrence*
His Children's Children
Side Show of Life, The
Sorrows of Satan, The (Earl of Elton)

1578
DORVAL, Mareal*
Son of the Sahara, A

1579
DOSSETT, Chappell*
Madame X (Judge)
Mysterious Dr. Fu Manchu, The
    /aka/ The Insidious Dr. Fu Man-
    chu

1580
DOUCET, H. Paul*
America /aka/ Love and Sacrifice
    (Marquis de Lafayette)

1581
DOUGHERTY, Jack*
Arizona Bound
Special Delivery

1582
DOUGLAS, Byron*
Beyond Price
Drake Case, The
Know Your Man
Marriage in Transit (a conspirator)
Perfect Sap, The
Silent Command, The

1583
DOUGLAS, Donald (Douglas Kinley-
    side (1905-1947)
Great Gabo, The (Frank)

1584
DOUGLAS, Leal*
Every Mother's Son (Lady Browning)

1585
DOUGLAS, Lillian*
Paddy the Next Best Thing (Eileen)

1586
DOUGLAS, Tom*
Blinkeyes (Kenneth)
Footfalls
Fox player 22

1587
DOUVAN-TORZOW, J. N.*
Taras Bulba

1588
DOVE, Billie (Lillian Bohny) (1904-)
Adoration
Affair of the Follies, An
Air Mail, The
All the Brothers Were Valiant (Priss
    Holt)
American Beauty
Ancient Highway, The
At the Stage Door
Beyond the Rainbow (Marion Taylor)
Black Pirate, The (the princess)
Careers
Fighting Heart, The
Folly of Vanity
Fox player 23-25
Get-Rich-Quick Wallingford (Dorothy
    Wells)
Heart of a Follies Girl, The
Her Private Life
Kid Boots (Polly Pendleton)
Light of the Western Stars
Long Star Ranger
Lone Wolf Returns, The
Love Mart, The
Lucky Horseshoe, The
Madness of Youth, The
Man and the Moment, The
Marriage Clause, The
Night Watch, The
One Night at Susie's
Painted Angel, The
Polly of the Follies
Roughneck, The
Sensation Seekers
Soft Boiled
Stolen Bride, The
Tender Hour, The
Thrill Chaser, The
Try and Get It

Wanderer of the Wasteland (Ruth
 Virey)
Wild Horse Mesa
Yankee Madness
Yellow Lily, The
Youth to Youth

1589
DOVER, Nancy*
Dynamite (a good mixer)
Scandal
Skirt Shy

1590
DOVORSKO, Jess*
Unknown Soldier, The

1591
DO VRIES, Harry*
Two Brothers, The

1592
DOW, Mary E. *
Sea Horses

1593
DOWLING, Eddie*
Blaze O'Glory
Rainbow Man, The
Stage:
Honeymoon Lane (Tim Murphy) 26
Sall, Irene and Mary (Jimmie Du-
 gan) 22
Ziegfeld Follies of 1921

1594
DOWLING, Joseph (1850-)
Barefoot Boy, The
Beautiful Liar, The
Breaking Point, The (Mr. Marshall)
Certain Rich Man, A
Christian, The (Father Lampleigh)
Confessions of a Queen
Courtship of Miles Standish, The
Danger Point
Dollar Devils
Devil to Pay, The
Fightin' Mad
Flower of the Night
Free and Equal
Girl Who Ran Wild, The
Golden Princess
Grim Comedian, The
Half-Breed, The (Judge Huntington)
House of Whispers, The
If You Believe It, It Is So
Infidel, The
Kentucky Colonel

Life Sparks
Little Irish Girl, The
Little Lord Fauntleroy (William L.
 Havisham)
Lord Jim
Lure of Egypt, The
New Lives for Old
One Clear Call
Other Woman, The
Pride of the Palomar, The
Quincy Adams Sawyer (Nathaniel
 Sawyer)
Rainmaker, The
Sin of Martha Queed, The
Spenders, The
Spider and the Rose, The
Temporary Marriage
Tess of the D'Ubervilles (Priest)
Tiger Rose
Trail of the Ace
Turning Point, The
Two-Gun Man, The
U. P. Trail, The
Why Girls Go Back Home
With Hoops of Steel
Women Who Give

1595
DOWN, John*
Trail of '98, The

1596
DOWNEY, Morton (1902-1961)
Lucky in Love
Mother's Boy (Tommy O'Day)
Syncopation

1597
DOWNS, Johnny (1913-)
Our Gang comedies
Trail of '98, The (the mother's boy)

1598
DOYLE, Bobby*
Sunset Derby

1599
DOYLE, James S. *
Backbone

1600
DOYLE, John T. *
Mother's Boy (Bart O'Day)

1601
DOYLE, Regina*
Beyond the Smoke
Clean Sweep, A

Danger Line, The
Just in Time
Perilous Paths
Ridin' Leather
Saps and Saddles

1602
DRAIN, Emile*
Madame Sans-Gene (Napoleon)

1603
DRAKE, Josephine*
Palm Beach Girl, The
Social Celebrity, A
Song and Dance Man, The

1604
DRAYTON, Alfred (Alfred Varick)
    (1881-1949)
Scandal in Bohemia

1605
DRESDEN, Albert "Curley"*
Cock-Eyed World, The (O'Sullivan)

1606
DRESSER, Louise (Louise Kerlin)
    (1879-1965)
Air Circus, The
Blind Goddess
Broken Hearts of Hollywood
City that Never Sleeps, The
Eagle, The (Catherine the Great)
Enter Madame
Enticement
Everybody's Acting
Fifth Avenue
Garden of Eden, The
Gigolo
Glory of Clementina
Goose Woman, The (dual role, Mary
    Holmes/Marie de Nardi)
Lone Eagle, The
Madonna of Avenue A
Mr. Wu (Mrs. Gregory)
Mother Knows Best (Ma Quail)
Next Corner, The (Nina Race)
Not Quite Decent
Padlocked
Percy
Prodigal Daughters (Mrs. Forbes)
Ruggles of Red Cap
Ship Comes In, A
Third Degree, The
To the Ladies
Universal player 24
White Flannels
Woman Proof

1607
DRESSLER, Marie (Leila Von Koer-
    ber) (1869-1934)
Breakfast at Sunrise
Bringing up Father (Maggie)
Callahans and the Murphys, The
    (Mrs. Callahan)
Dangerous Female
Devine Lady, The (Mrs. Hart)
Hollywood Revue of 1929 (Venus ri-
    sing from the sea)
Joy Girl, The
Patsy, The (Ma Harrington)
Road Show
Vagabond Lover, The
Stage:
Dancing Girl, The   23
Edward Everett Horton Stock Com-
    pany, L. A.   28

1608
DREW, Ann*
Red Riders, The

1609
DREW, Jerry*
Power (the menace)

1610
DREW, Lowell*
Greene Murder Case, The (Chester
    Greene)

1611
DREW, Philip Yale*
Hobo of Pizen City, The (Young Buf-
    falo)

1612
DREW, Roland (1903-)
Broadway Fever
Evangeline
Fascinating Youth
Lady Raffles series
Paramount player 27
Racketeer, The (Tony Vaughan)
Ramona (Felipe)

1613
DREXEL, Nancy (1910-)
Bantam Cowboy
Bronco Twisters
Escape, The
Fangs of the Wild
Four Devils (Louise)
Prep and Pep
Riding Renegade
Riley, the Cop

1614
DROLLET, David*
Versailles

1615
DROMGOLD, George*
Through the Back Door (chauffeur)
Waking up the Town

1616
DRUCE, Hubert*
Laughing Lady, The
Return of Sherlock Holmes, The

1617
DRUMIER, Jack*
Pinch Hitter, The (Obadiah Parker)

1618
DUANE, Jack*
Redskin, The

1619
DUBENCOURT, Jean*
La Chute de la Maison Usher (The
    Fall of the House of Usher)

1620
DuBOIS, Gladys*
Dance of Life, The

1621
DU BOIS, Helen*
Icebound

1622
DU BRAY, Claire*
Devil Dancer, The
Drusilla with a Million
Heart of a Child, The
Infatuation

1623
DU BREY, Clair (1893-)
Americanism
Dangerous Hours
Escape /aka/ Exquisite Sinner, The
Glass Houses
Green Flame, The
Hole in the Wall
House of Whispers, The
Life's Twist
Light Woman, A
My Lady's Latch Key
Only a Shop Girl
Ordeal, The
Ponjola (Ludhia Luff)
Sea Hawk, The

That Girl Montana
To Have and to Hold
Two Sisters
Voice from the Minaret, The (Count-
    ess La Fontaine)
Walk-Offs, The
When Love Comes

1624
DUCHAMP, Marcel*
Entr'acte

1625
DU CROW, Tate*
Don Q, Son of Zorro (Bernardo)
Little Robinson Crusoe
Mark of Zorro, The (bit)
Moon Riders, The [serial]
Pride of Palomar, The
Thief of Bagdad, The (soothsayer)

1626
DUDLEY, Bernard*
Virgin Queen, The (Arthur Pole)

1627
DUDLEY, Charles*
Purple Riders, The (Doc Breamer)

1628
DUDLEY, Florence*
Broadway

1629
DUDLEY, Robert*
Big News
Day of Faith, The
Fools for Luck (Jim Simpson)
Marriage Clause, The
Night Flyer, The
Skinner's Big Idea
Sixty Cents an Hour

1630
DUFFIELD, Harry*
For Those We Love (George Arnold)

1631
DUFFY, Jack (1879-)
Blackie's Redemption
Detectives Wanted
Farmers and Framers
Halfback Hannah
Harold Teen
Hot Scotch
Lay On, MacDuff
Long Hose
Loose Change

Love's Young Scream
Misfits and Matrimony
Peg of the Ring
Purple Mask, The
Sally (the old roué)
Say Uncle
School Days
Should Scotchmen Marry?
Stop Fighting
Wireless Lizzie

1632
DUFFY, James*
Our Hospitality

1633
DUFLOS, Huguette*
Der Rosenkavalier

1634
DUGAN, James*
Warming Up

1635
DUGAN, Mary*
River, The /aka/ La Femme au
  Corbeau

1636
DUGAN, Tom /aka/ Tommy (1889-
  1958)
Barker, The
Broadway Babies
Broadway Daddies
Deadline, The
Drag
Drake Case, The
Dressed to Kill
Hearts in Exile
Kid Gloves
Lights of New York (Sam)
Melody of Love
Midnight Taxi
Million Dollar Collar
Shadows of the Night
Sharp Shooters
She Knew Men
Soft Living
Sonny Boy

1637
DUGAN, Walter*
Heart of Salome, The

1638
DUGAN, William Francis*
Hit of the Show

1639
DUKE, Ivy (1895-)
Beauty and the Beast
Bigamist, The
Boy Woodburn
Decameron Nights
Duke's Son, The
Fox Farm
Great Prince Shan, The
Knight in London, A
Lure of Crooning Water, The
Maid of Silver Sea, The
Persistent Lovers, The
Starlit Garden, The
Testimony

1640
DULLIN, Charles*
Chess Player, The
Miracle of the Wolves, The
Three Musketeers, The (Father Jo-
  seph)

1641
DUMA, Evelyn--see: Evelyn
  Dumo

1642
DUMAR, Luis*
Salome (Tigellinus)

1643
DUMAS, Jean*
Last Man on Earth, The
Our Hospitality

1644
DUMBAR, Helen*
Fighting Coward, The

1645
DUMO, Evelyn* /aka/ Evelyn Duma
Love Light, The (Maria)

1646
DUMONT, Gene*
Dangerous Money

1647
DUMONT, J. M. *
City of Masks, The

1648
DUMONT, Margaret (1889-1965)
Cocoanuts, The (Mrs. Potter)

1649
DUNBAR, Dave*
Broncho Buster, The

1650
DUNBAR, Dorothy*
Amateur Gentleman, The (Lady Cle-
    one Meredith)
First National player 25
Tarzan and the Golden Lion (Jane)

1651
DUNBAR, Helen*
Behold My Wife!
Beyond the Rocks (Lady Ada Fitz-
    gerald)
Call of the Canyon, The
Changing Husbands
Cheat, The
City of Masks, The
Compromise
Fighting Coward, The
Fine Manners (Aunt Agatha)
Furnace, The
Great Moment, The (Lady Crombie)
Her First Elopement
Her Winning Way
His Majesty Bunker Bean
Homespun Vamp, A
House that Jazz Built, The
Impossible Mrs. Bellew, The (Aunt
    Agatha)
Lady Windermere's Fan (gossipy
    Duchess)
Little Clown, The
Man of Courage
New Lives for Old
Romance of a Queen, The (Lady
    Henrietta)
Rose of the World
Sacred and Profane Love
Siege
Stranded in Paris
Sweet Rosie O'Grady
Thirty Days
This Woman (Mrs. Sturdevant)
Three Weeks
Woman Hater, The
World's Champion
You Never Can Tell
Young Mrs. Winthrop

1652
DUNCAN, Albert "Bud" (1886-1961)
Bear Facts
Bee Cured
Can-O-Bull Chief
Casper's Week End

Clean Sweep, A
Family Meal Ticket
Fixin' Father
Flaming Youth
Gyping Gypsies
Happy Daze
Haunted Ship, The
Have a Heart
Horse Play
Mabel's Mate
Maggie Pepper
Menagerie Mixup, A
Movie Mania
Mut and Jeff
Never Say Die
Iron Magnate's Revenge, The
Plastered
Rival Romeos
Rudolph's Revenge
Seaside Romeos
Soap and Water
Sour Milk
Spooky Spooks
Too Tired
Twin Caddies
Two Bad Men

1653
DUNCAN, Mary (1905-)
Four Devils (rich lady)
Fox player 29
River, The /aka/ La Femme au
    Corbeau
Romance of the Rio Grande
Soft Living
Through Different Eyes (Viola Man-
    ning)
Very Confidential

1654
DUNCAN SISTERS, The - Rosetta
    (1896-1959), Vivian (1902-)
Imperfect Ladies
It's a Great Life (Vivian only)
Topsy and Eva (Rosette as Topsy/
    Vivian as Eva)
Stage:
Tip Top 20
Topsy and Eva 24

1655
DUNCAN, Taylor*
Below the Line
Ranson's Folly
Tumbleweeds

1656
DUNCAN, Ted Captain*
Buck Privates

1657
DUNCAN, William (1878-1961)
Fast Express, The [serial]
Fighting Fate
Fighting Guide, The
No Defense
Perils of the Yukon
Playing It Wild
Riddle Rider, The
Silent Avenger, The (Phil)
Silent Vow, The (dual role)
Smashing Barriers
Steel Trail [serial]
Steelheart
When Danger Smiles
When Men Are Men
Wolves of the North [serial]

1658
DUNHAM, Phillip*
Barnstormer, The (stage carpenter)
Dangerous Maid

1659
DUNKINSON, Harry*
Husband Hunter, The (Lilah Elkins)
Last Man on Earth, The
Smile, Brother, Smile

1660
DUNLEVY, Brian*
School for Wives

1661
DUNMAR, David*
North of '36

1662
DUNN, Bobby*
Racketeer, The (The Rat)
Royal Rider

1663
DUNN, Eddie*
Bouncing Babies
Fleet's In, The (Al Pearce)
Hoose Gow, The
Saturday Night Kid, The
Sky Boy

1664
DUNN, Emma (1875-1966)
Old Lady 31
Pied Piper Malone
Side Street

1665
DUNN, Josephine (1906-)
Air Patrol
All at Sea
Big Time, The
Black Magic
China Bound
Everybody's Acting
Excess Baggage
Fascinating Youth
Fireman, Save My Child
Get Your Man (Simon de Villeneuve)
Heart of a Follies Girl, The
Love's Greatest Mistake
Man's Man, A
Melody Lane
Million for Love, A
Most Immoral Lady, A
Our Modern Maidens
Paramount player 27
Red Hot Rhythm
She's a Sheik
Sin Sister (Ethelyn)
Singing Fool, The (Molly)
Sonny Boy
Swim, Girl, Swim
We Americans

1666
DUNN, Malcolm*
Dr. Jekyll and Mr. Hyde

1667
DUNN, William*
Devil's Island
Redeeming Sin, The

1668
DUNTON, John*
America /aka/ Love and Sacrifice
(John Hancock)

1669
DUPONT, Miss (Marguerite Arm-
strong)*
Brass
Broken Wing, The
Common Law, The
False Kisses
Foolish Wives (Helen Hughes)
Golden Gallows, The
Good and Naughty
Man from Brodney's, The
Mantrap (Mrs. Barker)
One Night in Rome
Rage of Paris, The
Shattered Dreams
Sinners in Silk

That Model from Paris
What Three Men Wanted
Wonderful Wife, A

1670
DUPREE, Minnie (1873-1947)
Night Club
Stage:
Charm School, The (Miss Curtis) 20

1671
DURAND, David*
Innocents of Paris (Jo-Jo)
Song of Love, The

1672
DURAND, Edward*
King of Main Street, The

1673
DURANT, Edouard*
Long Wolf, The

1674
DURANT, M. *
Peacock Alley (Monsieur Dubois)

1675
DURANT, Thomas*
Iron Horse, The (Jack Ganzhorn)

1676
DURANTE, Jimmy (1893-)
Roadhouse Nights
Stage:
Show Girl 29

1677
DURIEUX, Tilla*
Frau im Mond [Woman in the Moon]

1678
DURLAND, Edward*
Potash and Perlmutter

1679
DURNING, Bernard*
Gift Supreme, The (Bradford Chand-
    ler Vinton)

1680
DURYEA, George /aka/ Tom Keene
    (1904-1963)
First National player 24
Godless Girl, The (the boy)
Honky Tonk (Freddie Gilmore)
Marked Money
Thunder (Jim)

Tide of the Empire

1681
DUSE, Carl*
Last Days of Pompeii (Burbo)

1682
DUSE, Eleanora (1858-1942)
Madre
Stage:
Eleanora Duse Repertory (American
    Farewell appearance 1923): Cosi
    Sia; Ghosts; La Citta Marta; Lady
    from the Sea, The; La Porta
    Chiusa

1683
DUTERTRE, Armand*
Garden of Allah, The

1684
DUVAL, Georgette*
Broadway Nights (bit)

1685
DUVAL, Paulette*
Alias the Lone Wolf
Beverly of Graustark (Carlotta)
Beware of Widows
Breakfast at Sunrise
Cheaper to Marry
Divine Woman, The
He Who Gets Slapped (Zinida)
Lady, The
Man and Maid
Monsieur Beaucaire (Madame Pompa-
    dour)
Nero
Skyrocket
Time, the Comedian
Twelve Miles Out

1686
DUVEEN, Lorna*
Knockout, The
Unguarded Hour, The

1687
DVORAK, Ann (Ann McKim) (1912-)
Hollywood Revue of 1929 (chorus girl)

1688
DWAN, Dorothy*
Parasite, The
Sinners in Silk

1689
DWYER, John*
Over the Hill (Thomas, the man)

1690
DWYER, Leslie (1906-)
Fifth Form at St. Dominic's

1691
DWYER, Ruth*
Alex the Great
Brown Derby, The
Evil Eye, The [serial]
Hero for a Night
Reckless Age, The
Sailor's Wives
Stepping Along
Seven Chances

1692
DYALL, Franklin*
Atlantic (John Rool)
Easy Virtue (Mr. Filton)

1693
DYANANANDA*
Light of Asia, The

1694
d'YD, Jean*
Passion of Joan of Arc, The

1695
DYER, William*
Branded Four, The [serial]
Courage of Marge O'Doone, The
Pioneer Trails
Silent Call, The
Singer Jim McKee
Wild Bill Hickok

1696
DYERS, Lien*
Le Capitaine Fracasse
Spione (spies)

1697
DYNAMITE (a dog)*
Fangs of Destiny
Wolf's Trail, The

1698
DYOTT, George M.*
Hunting Tigers in India (narrator)

1699
DYRESE, Jacqueline*
Godless Girl, The (an inmate)

- E -

1700
EAGAN, Jack*
Harold Teen
Mad Hour, The

1701
EAGELS, Jeanne (1894-1929)
Jealousy (Yvonne)
Letter, The (Leslie Crosbie)
Man, Woman and Sin
Stage:
Her Cardboard Lover 27
Rain (Sadie Thompson) 22
Wonderful Thing, The (Jacqueline
  Laurentée) 20

1702
EAGLE, Dan Red*
Unseeing Eyes

1703
EAGLE, Frances Red*
Unseeing Eyes

1704
EAGLE, James*
Crooks Can't Win
Son of the Gods

1705
EAGLE EYE--see: William Eagle
  Eye

1706
EAGLE EYE, William*
Serenade
Shooting of Dan McGrew, The (Miguel)

1707
EAGLE WING, Chief*
Ranson's Folly

1708
EAMES, Clare (1896-1930)
Dorothy Vernon of Haddon Hall (Queen
  Elizabeth)
New Commandment, The
Swan, The
Stage:
Juarez and Maximilian (Carlotta) 26
Macbeth (Lady Macbeth) 24
Man of Destiny, The (Lavinia) 25
Mary Stuart (Title role) 21
Ned McCobb's Daughter (Carrie Cal-
  lahan) 26

1709
EARLE, Arthur*
Bride 13 [serial]

1710
EARLE, Dorothy*
Out All Night

1711
EARLE, Edna*
Eagle, The
Model's Confession, A

1712
EARLE, Edward (1884-)
Buried Treasure
Captain's Courage, The
East Lynne (Archibald Carlyle)
False Fronts
Greater Glory, The
Hottentot, The
Irene
Kid Gloves
Lady Who Lied, The
Law of the Yukon
Man Who Played God, The
Pals First
Passion Fruit
Smiling Irish Eyes
Spite Marriage
Splendid Road, The
Spring Fever
Twelve Miles Out (John Burton)
Wind, The (Beverly)
Woman's Heart, A

1713
EARLE, Jack*
Jack and the Bean Stalk (the giant)

1714
EARLE, Josephine*
Woman to Woman (Mrs. Anson-Pond)

1715
EARLES, Harry*
That's My Baby
Three-Ring Marriage
Unholy Three, The (Tweedledee)

1716
EASON, Lorraine*
We're in the Navy Now

1717
EASON, Reeves (1866-1956)
Around the World in 18 Days [serial]
Ben Hur

Big Adventure, The
Danger Rider
Flaming Spurs
Flying Cowboy
His Last Race
Moon Riders, The [serial]
New Champion, The
Prairie King
Sing of the Claw, The
Winged Horseman, The

1718
EASTON, Jay*
Man Made Women

1719
EASTON, Lorraine*
Temple of Venus, The (Echo)

1720
EATON, Charles*
Forever
Ghost Talks, The
Knights Out
Prodigal Judge, The
Stage:
Skidding (Andy) 28

1721
EATON, Doris*
Very Idea, The
Stage:
Excess Baggage (Betty Ford) 27
Ziegfeld Follies of 1921

1722
EATON, Jay*
Lady Be Good
Naughty Baby
Synthetic Sin

1723
EATON, Mary (1902-1948)
Cocoanuts, The (Polly Potter)
Glorifying the American Girl
His Children's Children
Stage:
Five O'Clock Girl, The (Patricia
    Brown) 27
Kid Boots (Polly Pendleton) 23
Ziegfeld Follies of 1921
Ziegfeld Follies of 1922

1724
EBERT, Carl*
Jew of Mestri, The (Antonio)

1725
EBINGER, Blandine*
Kopf Hoch, Charly! [Heads Up, Char-
ly!] (seamstress)

1726
ECKHARDT, Oliver*
Cavalier, The
Last Trail, The

1727
EDDINGER, Lawrence*
Tol'able David (Senator Gault)

1728
EDDINGTON, John P. *
Madame X (doctor)

1729
EDDY, Helen Jerome (1897-)
Blue Skies
Camille (maid)
Chicago after Midnight
City Sparrow, The
Country Kid, The
County Fair, The
Dark Angel, The (Miss Pindle)
Divine Lady, The
First Born, The
Flirt, The
Forbidden Thing, The
House of Toys
Last Lap, The
Life
Light Woman, A
Marry Me
Midstream
Old Sweetheart of Mine, An
One Man in a Million
Other Woman, The
Padlocked
Pollyanna
Quality Street (Susan Throssel)
Railroadin'
Small Talk
Speed Classic
Ten-Dollar Raise, The
13 Washington Square
To the Ladies
Trembling Hour, The
Two Lovers (Inez)
When Love Comes

1730
EDDY, Lorraine*
Carnation Kid, The
Charming Sinners (Alice)
Gentleman of Paris, A

1731
EDESON, Robert (1868-1931)
Altars of Desire
Bedroom Window, The
Beware of Blondes
Blue Eagle, The (Father Joe)
Brave Heart
Chicago
Doctor's Secret, The
Don't Call It Love
Dynamite (a wise fool)
Eve's Leaves
Feet of Clay (Dr. Fergus Lansell)
Foolish Wives
George Washington Cohen
Go Straight
Golden Bed, The (Amos Thompson)
Has the World Gone Mad?
Heart Thief, The
Hell's High Road
Her Man of War
His Dog
Home Towners, The
King of Kings, The (Matthew)
Little Johnny Jones
Little Wildcat, The
Locked Doors
Luck
Mademoiselle Midnight
Marianne (the General)
Marriage by Contract
Men
Men and Women
Most Immoral Lady, A
Night Bride, The
Power of the Press
Prisoner of Zenda, The (Colonel
   Sapt)
Rejuvenation of Aunt Mary, The
Scarlet West, The (General Kinnard)
Ship Comes In, A
Silent Partner, The
Spoilers, The (Joe Dexter)
Sure Fire Flint
Ten Commandments, The (Inspector
   Redding)
Tenth Avenue
Thy Name Is Woman
Tie that Binds, The
To the Last Man
Tomorrow
Triumph (Samuel Overton)
Volga Boatman, The (Prince Nikita)
Walking Back
Welcome Stranger, The
Whispering Smith
You Are Guilty!

1732
EDINGTON, John P. --see: John P.
  Eddington

1733
EDLIN, Tubby*
Alf's Button (Alf Higgins)

1734
EDMUNDSEN, Al*
Foolish Wives (Pavel Pavlich)
Merry-Go-Round (Neopmuck Navrital)

1735
EDOUARDE, Carl*
Soul Fire /aka/ Golden Youth

1736
EDTHOFER, Anton*
Der Leibgardist [The Guardsman]

1737
EDWARD, Nils*
Husbands or Lovers

1738
EDWARDS, Alan (1893-1954)
Virgin Paradise, A

1739
EDWARDS, Cliff /aka/ "Ukelele
  Ike" (1895-1971)
Hollywood Revue of 1929
Lord Byron of Broadway
Marianne (Soapy)
Romeo in Pajamas
So This Is College
What Price Melody?

1740
EDWARDS, Edith*
Die Frau, Nach der Man Sich Sehnt
  [The Woman One Longs For]
  /aka/ Three Loves (Angela Poit-
  rier)

1741
EDWARDS, Gus (1879-1945)
Hollywood Revue of 1929

1742
EDWARDS, Harry*
Flag Lieutenant, The (Richard Las-
  celles)

1743
EDWARDS, Henry (1883-1952)
Amazing Quest of Mr. Ernest

Bliss, The (Ernest Bliss)
Aylwin
Bargain, The
Boden's Boy
Fake, The
Fear
Flag Lieutenant, The
Further Adventures of the Flag Lieu-
  tenant, The
John Forrest Finds Himself
Lilly of the Alley
Lunatic at Large, A
Naked Man, The
Ringing the Changer
Simple Simon
Temporary Vagabond, A
Three Kings, The
Tit for Tat
World of Wonderful Reality, The

1744
EDWARDS, J. Gordon, Jr.*
Plastic Age, The (Norrie Parks)

1745
EDWARDS, Jack*
So This Is Marriage

1746
EDWARDS, Neely (1889-1975)
Brewster's Millions
Dynamite (a good mixer)
Easy to Cop
Excess Baggage
Footloose Widows
Gold Diggers of Broadway (stage mgr.)
Green Temptation
Hallroom Boys comedies
His Inheritance Taxi
I'll Show You the Town
Little Clown, The
Shaky Family Tree, A
Show Boat (Schultzy)
Society Sailors
Taking Things Easy
You Never Can Tell

1747
EDWARDS, Sarah*
Glorifying the American Girl

1748
EDWARDS, Snitz (d. 1960)
Battling Butler
Charm School, The
Cheated Love
City of Masks, The
College

Dangerous Woman, A
First National player 25
General, The
Ghost Breaker, The
Going Some
Gray Dawn
Hill Billy, The
Human Hearts
Huntress, The
Inez from Hollywood
June Madness
Ladies Must Live
Love Is an Awful Thing
Love Special, The
Lover's Oath, A
Mark of Zorro, The (bit)
Mysterious Island, The
Night Life (merry-go-round mgr.)
No Woman Knows
Old Shoes
Phantom of the Opera, The (Florine
    Papillon)
Prisoner of Zenda, The (Josef)
Rags to Riches
Red Hot Romance
Red Mill, The (Timothy)
Rosita (Little Jaibo)
Seven Chances
Souls for Sale (Komikal Kale)
Splendid Road, The
Tarnish
Thief of Bagdad, The (thief's com-
    panion)
Tiger Love
Tornado
Volcano (auctioneer)

1749
EGAN, Jack*
Big Noise, The
Broadway Scandals
Cabaret
Harold Teen
It Can Be Done
Mad Hour, The
Potters, The (Bill)

1750
EGGERT, E. W. *
Aelita: The Revolt of the Robots

1751
EGGERTON, Beryl*
First Born, The (maid)

1752
EHLERS, Christl*
Menschen am Sonntag [People on

Sunday]

1753
EHRIE, Kurt*
Queen of Sin and the Spectacle of
    Sodom and Gomorrah

1754
EIBENSCHÜTZ, Lia*
Jew of Mestri, The (Jessica)

1755
EICHNOR, Edna*
Roughneck, The

1756
EILERS, Sally (Dorothea Sally Eilers)
    (1908-)
Broadway Babies
Campus Carman, The
Campus Vamp, The
Cradle Snatchers, The
Dry Martini
Good-Bye Kiss, The
Long, Long Trail, The
Matchmaking Mamas
Nice Baby
Oh, Kay!
Paid to Love (tourist)
Romeo in Pajamas
Sailor's Holiday
Show of Shows, The
Slightly Used
Sunrise (bit)
Trial Marriage
Why Leave Home?

1757
EKMAN, Gösta (1887-1937)
Charles XII
Discord
Faust (Title role)
Heart of a Clown
Husband by Proxy
Last Night, The

1758
EKMAN, John*
Thy Soul Shall Bear Witness

1759
ELDER, Ruth*
Moran of the Marines
Winged Horseman, The

1760
ELDRIDGE, Charles*
Ashamed of Parents

Hearts and Spurs (the sheriff)

1761
ELDRIDGE, Florence (Florence Mac-
    Kechnie) (1901-   )
Charming Sinners (Helen Carr)
Divorcee, The
Elegible Mr. Bangs, The
Greene Murder Case, The (Sibella
    Greene)
Six Cylinder Love
Studio Murder Mystery, The (Blanche
    Hardell)
Stage:
Ambush (Margaret Nichols) 21
Cat and the Canary, The (Annabelle
    West) 22

1762
ELG-LUNDBERG, Otto*
Story of Gösta Berling (Major Sam-
    zelius)

1763
ELIAS, Miriam*
Broken Hearts

1764
ELIZAROFF, E. *
His Hour

1765
ELINOR, Peggy*
Sinners in Silk

1766
ELKAS, Edward*
Sainted Devil, A
West of the Water Tower

1767
ELLINGFORD, William*
Cyclone, The
Once to Every Woman (Matthew Mere-
    dith)

1768
ELLIOTT, Del*
Desert Song, The (Rebel)

1769
ELLIOTT, Frank*
Dark Angel, The (Lord Beaumont)
Easy Virtue (Mr. Whitaker)
For Sale (Sir John Geddes)
Fourth Commandment, The
Goldfish, The
Impossible Mrs. Bellew, The (Count

Radistoff)
Love's Wilderness
Marriage of William Ashe, The
    (Geoffrey Cliffe)
Once to Every Woman (Duke of De-
    vonshire)
Red Lights
Ruggles of Red Gap
Secrets (Robert Carlton)
Sinners in Silk
This Woman (Gordon Duane)

1770
ELLIOTT, Gordon "William" /aka/
    "Wild Bill" (1906-1965)
Broadway Scandals
Plastic Age, The (dancer)
Private Life of Helen of Troy, The
    (Telemachus)
Reckless Youth

1771
ELLIOTT, John*
Spoilers, The (Atty Wheaton)
What Happened to Jones?

1772
ELLIOTT, Lillian*
Ankles Preferred
Call of the Cuckoo, The
Old Clothes (Mrs. Burke)
Partners Again with Potash and Perl-
    mutter
Proud Flesh
Sally, Irene and Mary (Mrs. O'Dare)

1773
ELLIOTT, Maxine /aka/ Maxine El-
    liott Hicks) (1871-1940)
Thundering Herd, The (Sallie Hudnall)
Stage:
Trimmed in Scarlet (Cordelia) 20

1774
ELLIOTT, Robert*
Divorcee, The
Empire of Diamonds, The
Headlines
Happiness Ahead
Lights of New York (Detective Crosby)
Lone Wolf's Daughter, The
Obey Your Husband
Protection
Romance of the Underworld, A
Thunderbolt
Virgin Paradise, A
Without Fear
Stage:

Rain (Sgt. O'Hara) 22

1775
ELLIS, Diane*
Cradle Snatchers, The
Happiness Ahead
High Voltage (the kid)
Is Zat So?
Leatherneck, The

1776
ELLIS, Elaine*
Home Maker, The

1777
ELLIS, Frank*
Elmo, the Fearless [serial]

1778
ELLIS, Lillian*
Waltz King, The

1779
ELLIS, Paul*
Bridge of San Luis Rey, The (Don
    Vicente)
Dancer of Paris, The
Pace that Thrills, The
Pretty Ladies
Three Hours

1780
ELLIS, Raymond*
Silver King, The

1781
ELLIS, Robert (1892-)
Broadway (Steve Crandall)
Brooding Eyes
Cafe in Cairo, A
Capital Punishment (Harry Phillip)
Dark Secrets (Lord Wallington)
Devil's Dice, The
Flame of Life, The
For Sale (Allan Penfield)
Forbidden Cargo
Freedom of the Press
Frontier of the Stars, The (Gregory)
Girl from Montmartre, The
Handcuffs or Kisses
Hurricane's Gal
Infidel, The
Ladies Must Live
Lady Robin Hood
Law and the Man, The
Law's Lash, The
Love Trap
Lover's Lane

Lure of the Night Club, The
Marry the Girl
Metro player 20
Night Parade
Perils of the Sea
Ragtime
Restless Youth
S. O. S.
Tonight at Twelve
Varsity
Wanters, The
Whispering Canyon
Wild Honey
Woman Who Fooled Herself, The

1782
ELLSLER, Effie (1855-1942)
Actress, The
Honeymoon Hate
Trelawney of the Wells (Mrs. Mossop)
Woman Trap
Stage:
Bat, The (Miss Cornelia Van Gorder)
    20

1783
ELLSWORTH, Robert*
King of Kings, The (Simon)

1784
ELMAN, Mischa (1891-)
Humoresque (piano short)

1785
ELMER, Clarence Jay*
Joy Girl, The

1786
ELMER, William*
Condemned (Pierre)

1787
ELSOM, Isobel (Isobel Reed) (1893-)
Aunt Rachel
Dance Magic
Debt of Honor
Dick Turpin's Ride to New York (Es-
    ther Bevis)
For Her Father's Sake
Game of Life, The
Glamis Castle
Harbor Lights
Human Law
Last Witness, The
Love Story of Aliette Brunon
Nance
Sign of Four, The
Tower of London, The

Wandering Jew, The (Olalla)
Who Is the Man?
Stage:
Ghost Train, The (Julia Price) 26

1788
ELTER, Amielka*
Last Moment, The

1789
ELTINGE, Julian (William Julian
   Dalton) (1882-1941)
Adventuress, An /aka/ The Isle of
   Love
Fascinating Widow
Madame, Behave!
Widow's Might, The
Stage:
Vaudeville 25

1790
ELVIDGE, June (1893-)
Beauty's Worth (Amy Tilson)
Beyond the Rocks (Lady Anningford)
Eleventh Hour, The
Fine Feathers
Forsaking All Others
Impossible Mrs. Bellew, The (Nao-
   mi Templeton)
King Tut
Man Who Saw Tomorrow, The
Painted People
Power of a Lie, The
Quincy Adams Sawyer (Betsy Ann
   Ross)
Temptation

1791
ELZER, Karl*
Luther

1792
EMERALD, Charles*
Betrayal, The
Lost Patrol, The

1793
EMERSON, Ralph*
Dance Hall
Enemy, The
Hard Boiled Rose
In Holland
Marriage by Contract
West Point

1794
EMERY, Gilbert (Gilbert Emery
   Bensby Pottle) (1889-1945)

Any Wife
Behind that Curtain (Sir Frederic
   Bruce)
Cousin Kate
Sky Hawk, The (Major Nelson)

1795
EMLYN, Fairy*
Squibs (Mrs. Wall)

1796
EMMETT, Catherine /aka/ Katherine
   Emmet*
Hole in the Wall, The (Mrs. Cars-
   lake)
Orphans of the Storm (Countess de
   Linieus)

1797
EMORY, Gilbert--see: Gilbert Emery

1798
EMORY, Maude*
Purple Riders, The (Red Feather)

1799
ENA, Rose*
Fifth Form at St. Dominic's (Mrs.
   Greenfield)

1800
ENGEL, Billie*
Cat and the Canary, The (taxi driver)

1801
ENGEL, Olga*
Dancing Vienna
Der Sprung ins Leben [The Leap into
   Life]

1802
ENGLEMAN, Andrews*
Diary of a Lost Girl, The
Three Passions, The

1802a
ENGLISH, Colonel*
Mademoiselle from Armentieres (Al-
   bert Raynor)

1803
ENGLISH, James*
Dick Turpin's Ride to New York
   (Luke's Godfather)

1804
ENGLISH, Robert*
American Prisoner, The (Col. Gro-
    verner)
Four Feathers, The (Lt. Sutch)
Knight in London, A
This Freedom (Mr. Field)

1805
ENSTEDT, Howard*
Rolling Home

1806
ERICKSON, Knute*
Illusion
Monster, The (Daffy Dan)
Scarlet Seas (Capt. Barbour)
Squall, The (Uncle Jani)
Twin Beds
Waterfront

1807
ERROL, Leon (1881-1951)
Clothes Make the Pirate
Lunatic at Large, The
Sally (Duke of Checkergovinia)
Yolanda (innkeeper)
Stage:
Louis the 14th (Louie Ketchup) 25
Sally ("Connie") 20
Yours Truly (Truly) 27

1808
ERWIN, Stuart (1903-1967)
Cock-Eyed World, The (Buckley)
Dangerous Curves (Rotarian)
Exalted Flapper, The
Happy Days (Jig)
Mother Knows Best (Ben)
New Year's Eve
Pair of Tights, A
Speakeasy
Sophomore, The
Sweetie (Axel Bronstrup)
This Thing Called Love (Fred)
Through Different Eyes (4th reporter)
Trespasser, The (reporter)

1809
ESDALE, Charles*
Soul Fire /aka/ Golden Youth
Summer Bachelors

1810
ESMELTON, Frederick*
California Straight Ahead
Chinese Parrot, The
Dulcy

Gay Defender, The
Kid Boots (Tom's lawyer)
Lady of the Night
Michigan Kid, The
Red Hot Tires
Rustle of Silk, The (Blythe)
Shield of Honor
Smooth as Satin
Two Lovers (Meinherr Van Rycke)
Winning of Barbara Worth, The
    (George Cartwright)

1811
ESMOND, Annie*
Alf's Button (Mrs. Gaskins)

1812
ESMOND, Georgette*
Tilly of Bloomsbury (Martha Welwyn)

1813
ESTERHAZY, Agnes, Countess*
Die Freudlose Gasse [The Joyless
    Street] /aka/ The Street of Sor-
    row (Regina Rosenow)
Spy of Madame de Pompadour, The
When Fleet Meets Fleet (German
    Commander's Wife)
Wrath of the Sea

1814
ETHIER, Alphonse*
Alaskan, The
Alias the Lone Wolf
Contraband
Deadline, The
Donovan Affair, The
Fighting Eagle, The
Frontier of the Stars, The (Phil Hoyt)
Hard Boiled
In Old Arizona (sheriff)
Lone Wolf, The
Message from Mars, A
Moral Sinner, The
Say It with Sables
Shadows of the Night
Smoke Bellew
Stage:
Jest, The (Neri Chiaramentesi) 26

1815
ETTLINGER, Karl*
Die Frau, Nach der Man Sich Sehnt
    [The Woman One Longs For] /aka/
    Three Loves (Mr. Poitrier)
Die Freudlose Gasse [The Joyless
    Street] /aka/ The Street of Sor-
    rows (Director General Rosenow)

That Murder in Berlin

1816
EUGENE, Billy*
Denial, The
Son of His Father, A

1817
EUGENE, William*
Captain Blood
Girl from Montmartre, The
Shooting of Dan McGrew, The (the
    purser)
Women Who Give

1818
EVA, Evi*
Carnival Crime, The
Theatre

1819
EVALD, Johanna*
Fight for the Matterhorn, The

1820
EVANGELISTI, Victor*
Last Days of Pompeii, The (Ape-
    cides)

1821
EVANS, Cecile*
Goose Hangs High, The (Mazie)
Talker, The
Worldly Goods

1822
EVANS, Charles E. (1857-1945)
Disraeli (Potter)
Happy Days (Col. Billy Bachter)

1823
EVANS, Frank*
Backbone
Running Wild (Amos Barker)
Tiger's Club, The

1824
EVANS, Fred (1889-1951)
Pimple's Three Musketeers (Pimple)
Pimple's Topical Gazette (Pimple)

1825
EVANS, Jack*
Hidden Woman, The (derelict)

1826
EVANS, Joe (1891-1967)
Pimple's Three Musketeers

Pimple's Topical Gazette

1827
EVANS, Karin*
Trial of Donald Westhof, The

1828
EVANS, Madge (1909-)
Classmates
Hedi
On the Banks of the Wabash
Son of India
Winning Through (Sylvia Randolph)

1829
EVANS, Marguerite*
Stage Struck (Hilda Wagner)

1830
EVANS, Myddleton*
This Freedom (Mr. Sturgis)

1831
EVELYN, Baby*
Greatest Love of All, The

1832
EVELYN, Mildred*
Christie Johnstone (Lady Dunsterre)
Paddy the Next Best Thing (Doreen
    Blake)

1833
EVERS, King*
Daddies
Half-Breed, The (Dick Kennion)

1834
EVERTH, Francis*
Prince and the Pauper, The

1835
EVERTON, Paul (1869-1948)
Conquest of Canaan, The
That Royle Girl (George Baretta)

1836
EVILLE, William*
Know Your Men

1837
EYTON, Bessie (1890-)
Lady in Love, A

- F -

1838
FABER, Erwin*
At the Edge of the World (the stran-
    ger)

1839
FABRAY, Nanette (Nanette Fabares)
    (1920-   )
Our Gang comedies

1840
FABRE, Fernand*
Appassionata

1841
FAIR, Elinor (1902-   )
Bachelor Brides
Broadway and Home
Driven
Eagle's Feather, The
Fox player 21
Girl in No. 20, The
Has the World Gone Mad?
Heart Thief, The
It Can't Be Done
Jim, the Conqueror
Kismet
Let 'em Go Gallegher
Lost Princess, The
My Friend from India
Sin Town
Through the Back Door (Margaret
    Brewster)
Tin Pan Alley
Volga Boatman, The (Princess Ver-
    na)
White Hands
Wife Who Wasn't Wanted, The
Yankee Clipper, The

1842
FAIR, Florence*
Moral Sinner, The
Sally of the Sawdust (Miss Vinton)

1843
FAIRBANKS, Douglas, Jr. (Douglas
    Elton Ullman) /aka/ Elton Tho-
    mas, writer (1909-   )
Air Mail, The
American Venus, The
Barker, The
Brass Band
Broken Hearts of Hollywood
Careless Age, The (Wyn)
Dance Hall

Dead Man's Curve
Fast Life (Douglas Stratton)
Forward Pass, The (Marty Reid)
Is Zat So?
Jazz Age, The
Loose Ankles
Man Bait
Modern Mothers
Our Modern Maidens (Gil)
Padlocked
Power of the Press
Show of Shows, The (Ambrose)
Stella Dallas (Richard Grosvenor)
Stephen Steps Out (debut)
Texas Steer, A
Toilers, The
Wild Horse Mesa
Woman of Affairs, A (Geoffrey)
Women Love Diamonds
Stage:
Saturday's Children - Los Angeles 28
Young Woodley - Los Angeles 28

1844
FAIRBANKS, Douglas, Sr. (Julius
    Ullman) (1883-1939)
Black Pirate, The (Title role)
Don Q. Son of Zorro (dual role, Don
    Cesar de Vega/Zorro)
Gaucho, The (Title role)
Iron Mask, The (D'Artagnan)
Mark of Zorro, The (Don Diego Vega,
    Zorro)
Mollycoddle, The (triple role, Richard
    Marshall III, IV, V)
Nut, The
Robin Hood (Earl of Huntington, Robin
    Hood)
Stephen Steps Out
Show People (cameo)
Taming of the Shrew, The (Petruchio)
Thief of Bagdad (Title role)
Three Musketeers, The (D'Artagnan)

1845
FAIRBANKS, Flobelle*
Climbers, The (Laska)
Loves of Sunya, The (Rita Ashling)

1846
FAIRBANKS TWINS (Madeline and
    Marion*
Beauty Shop, The
Mirror, The
On with the Show (twins)
Stage:
Two Little Girls in Blue 21
    (Madeline as Dolly Sartoris/

Marion as Polly Sartoris)

1847
FAIRBANKS, William (Carl Ullman)*
Blue Washington
Border Women
Catch as Catch Can
Clean-Up, The
Devil's Door Yard, The
Do It Now
Down Grade, The
Fight to the Finish, A
Fighting Bill
Flying High
Great Sensation, The
Handsome Brute, The
Hearts of the West
Hell's Border
Independent player 22
Law Rustlers, The
Mile-a-Minute Man, The
Montana Bill
New Champion, The
One Chance in a Million
Peaceful Peters
Sheriff of Sun Dog
Spawn of the Desert
Speed Mad
Spoilers of the West
Sun Dog Trails
Tainted Money
Through Thick and Thin
Under the Black Eagle
Vanishing Millions [serial]
Vanishing West, The [serial]
Western Adventure, A
Western Demon
When Danger Calls
Winning Wallop, The
Wyoming

1848
FAIRBROTHER, Sydney (Sydney Tapping) (1873-1941)
Beloved Vagabond, The (Mrs. Smith)
Nell Gwyn (Mrs. Gwyn)
Sally Bishop (landlady)

1849
FAIRE, Betty*
Claude Duval (Lady Anna)
Only Way, The (Lucie Manette)

1850
FAIRE, Virginia Brown (1904-)
Air Phantom
Body Punch, The
Burning the Wind

Canyon of Adventure
Chip of the Flying-U
Chorus Kid, The
Cricket on the Hearth, The
Danger Patrol
Devil's Chaplain, The
Donovan Affair, The
Doubling for Romeo
Fightin' Mad
First National player 22
Frenzied Flames
Friendly Enemies
Gun Gospel
Handcuffed
Hazardous Valleys
House of Shame, The
Lost World, The (Marquette)
Man in the Saddle, The
Monte Cristo (Haidee)
Old Fashioned Boy, An
Omar the Tentmaker
Peter Pan (Tinker Bell)
Proud Heart, The
Queen of the Chorus
Race for Life, A
Racing Romance
Recompense
Romance Ranch
Runnin' Straight
Sin Town
Storm Swept
Temptress, The (Celinda)
Thundergate
Tracked by Police
Undressed
Untamed Justice
Vengeance of the Deep
Wagon Show, The
Welcome Stranger, The
White Flannels
Wings of the Storm
Without Benefit of Clergy
Wolf Hunter

1851
FAIRFAX, Thurman /aka/ Thur*
Greater Glory, The
Prisoner of Zenda, The (Bersonin)
Rose of the Golden West

1852
FAIRWEATHER, Helen*
Private Life of Helen of Troy, The (Athena)

1853
FAIT, A.*
Battleship Potemkin

1854
FALCONETTI, Maria (1902-1946)
Passion of Joan of Arc, The (her
    only film)

1855
FALERON, Jean*
Paris

1856
FALKENSTEIN, Julius*
Dancing Vienna
Meistersinger
Romeo und Julia im Schnee [Romeo
    and Juliet in the Snow] (Paris)
Spione [Spies]
Waltz Dream, The (Count Rockoff)

1857
FANE, Dorothy*
Blood Money (Marguerite Deschanel)
Daniel Deronda (Gwendolen Harleth)
Vortex, The (Helen Saville)

1858
FANG, Charles*
Backbone
Ragged Edge, The

1859
FAREBROTHER, Violet*
Downhill (poetess)
Easy Virtue (Mrs. Whittaker)

1860
FARINA--see: Allan Clayton Hos-
    kins

1861
FARLEY, Dot (Dorothy Farley)
    (1894-)
Acquittal, The
All Aboard
Astray from the Steerage (just a
    Mother-in-Law)
Bee's Buzz, The
Bicycle Flirt, The
Bird in the Hand, A
Black Feather
Boy of Mine
Celebrity, The
Climbers, The (Juana)
Code of the Scarlet
Crossroads of New York, The
Divorce Made Easy
Enemy Sex, The
Girl from Everywhere, The
Girl from Nowhere, The

Grand Duchess and the Waiter, The
Head Man, The (Mrs. Denny)
His First Flame
King of Kings, The (Caiapha's maid-
    servant)
Lady Be Good
Little Irish Girl, The
Lost Limited, The
McFadden Flats
Marquis Preferred
Memory Lane
Money Talks
My Son (Hattie Smith)
Nobody's Widow
Overland Stage, The
Shamrock and the Rose, The
Should a Girl Marry?
Signal Tower, The
So Big (Widow Poarlenberg)
Vanity's Price
Whirls and Girls
Why Leave Home?
Woman of the World, A
Young April

1862
FARLEY, James /aka/ Jim (1882-)
Challenge of the Law, The
Dance of Life, The
Dynamite (an officer)
Four Horsemen of the Apocalypse
Fourteenth Man, The
General, The (General Thatcher)
Girl in the Rain, The
Gleam O'Dawn
King of Kings, The (an executioner)
Mad Hour, The
Mating Call
One Man Trail
Perfect Crime, The

1863
FARLEY, Morgan*
Greene Murder Case, The (Rex
    Greene)
Half Marriage
Love Doctor, The
Mighty, The (Jerry Patterson)
Only the Brave
Slightly Scarlet
Stage:
American Tragedy, An (Clyde Grif-
    fiths) 26
Fata Morgana (George) 24

1864
FARNEY, Billy*
Quincy Adams Sawyer (Bob Wood)

1865
FARNEY, Milton*
Untamed

1866
FARNUM, Dustin (1874-1929)
Big Happiness
Bucking the Barrier
Buster, The
Devil Within, The
Durand of the Badlands
Flaming Frontier, The
Grail, The
Iron to Gold
Kentucky Days
Man Who Won, The
My Man
Oathbound
Primal Law
Strange Idols
Three Who Paid
Trail of the Ace
Virginian, The
While Justice Waits
Yosemite Trail

1867
FARNUM, Franklyn (William Smith)
    /aka/ "Smiling Frank" (1883-
    1961) [Birthdate is correction
    from Vol. I.]
Angel Citizen, The
Battling Brewster [serial]
Border Intrigue
Breezy Bob
Calibre .45
Canyon Film westerns (26)
Crossroads
Desperate Adventure
Drugstore Cowboy
Fighting Stranger, The
Firebrand, The
Galloping Devil, The
Gambling Fool, The
Gold Grabbers
Gun Shy
Isobel /aka/ The Trail's End
Last Chance
Raiders, The
Shackles of Gold
Smilin' Jim
So This Is Arizona
Struggle, The
Texas
Two Doyles, The
Two-Fisted Tenderfoot, A
Uphill Climb, The
Vanishing Trails [serial]

White Masks
Wolves of the Border

1868
FARNUM, Helen*
Days of the Buffalo

1869
FARNUM, William (1876-1953)
Adventurer, The
Brass Commandments
Drag Harlan
Gunfighter, The
Heart Strings
His Greatest Sacrifice
If I Were King
Joyous Troublemaker, The
Man Who Fights Alone, The (John
    Marble)
Moonshine Valley (Ned Connors)
Orphan, The
Perjury
Scuttlers, The
Shackles of Gold
Stage Romance, A
Wings of the Morning
Without Compromise
Stage:
Buccaneer, The (Capt. Henry Mor-
    gan) 25

1870
FARRAR, Geraldine (1882-1967)
Riddle Woman, The
Woman and the Puppet, The

1871
FARRELL, Charles (American)
    (1902-)
Cheat, The
City Girl
Clash of the Wolves
Fazil (Prince Fazil)
Freshman, The
Happy Days (a principal)
Love Hour, The
Lucky Star (Timothy Osborn)
Man Who Came Back, The
Merely Mary Ann
Old Ironsides
Red Dance, The /aka/ The Red
    Dancer of Moscow
River, The [La Famme au Corbeau]
Rosita (bit)
Rough Riders, The
Sandy
Seventh Heaven (Chico)
Street Angel (Gino)

Sunny Side Up (Jack Cromwell)
Ten Commandments, The (extra)
Trip to Chinatown, A
Wings of Youth

1872
FARRELL, Charles (Irish) (1901-)
British child star

1873
FARRELL, Glenda (1904-1971)
Lucky Boy

1874
FARRINGTON, Adele*
Black Beauty
Gentleman of Leisure, A
Man Next Door, The
Mollycoddle, The (Mrs. Warren)
Shadow of the Law, The (aunt)

1875
FARRINGTON, Betty*
Fall of Eve, The

1876
FARRINGTON, Frank*
Courtship of Miles Standish, The
Man Who Fights Alone, The (Struthers)

1877
FAUCHE, Miriam*
Fourflusher, The

1878
FAUST, Edward*
Enemy Sex, The
Fashions for Women
Gentlemen Prefer Blondes (Robert)
New Lives for Old

1879
FAUST, Martin*
I Am the Man
North Star, The
Silent Command, The
Under the Red Robe
Yolanda (Count Calli)

1880
FAVERSHAM, William (1868-1940)
Man Who Found Himself, The
Man Who Lost Himself, The
Sin That Was His, The
Stage:
Diplomacy (Uncle Beauclere) 28
Prince and the Pauper, The (Miles

Hendon) 20
Silver Fox, The (Major Christopher
  Stanley) 21
Squaw Man, The (Capt. James Wyn-
  negate) 21

1881
FAVIERES, Henry*
Madame Sans-Gene (Fouche)

1882
FAWCETT, George (1860-1939)
Bedroom Window, The
Beyond the Rainbow (Mr. Gardner)
Branded Woman, The
Broken Barriers
Burn 'em Up Barnes
Captain Salvation
Chivalrous Charley
Circle, The
Dangerous Business (Mr. Flavell)
Deadline at Eleven
Drums of Fate
Duty's Reward
Ebb Tide
Enemy, The
Fancy Baggage
Flaming Frontier, The
Flesh and the Devil (Pastor Voss)
Forever
Four Feathers, The (Gen. Fever-
  sham)
Gamblers, The
Go Straight
Good References
Great Divide, The
Hard Boiled Haggerty
Hearts in Exile
Her Love Story (Archduke)
His Captive Woman
His Children's Children
Home Maker, The
Honeymoon
Hot for Paris
Hush Money
Idols of Clay (Jim Merrill)
Innocents of Paris (Monsieur Marney)
Java Head
Joanna
John Smith
Lady of the Pavements (Baron Houss-
  mann)
Lessons in Love
Little Firebrand, The
Little Italy
Little Miss Rebellion
Little Wildcat, The
Lost Lady, A

Love
Love Song, The
Mad Whirl, The
Man of the Forest, The
Manslaughter (Judge Homans)
Men of Steel
Merry Widow, The (King Nikita)
Mr. Billings Spends His Dime
Moon Gold
Old Homestead, The
Only 38
Painting the Town
Paying the Piper
Pied Piper Malone
Polly of the Follies
Price of Pleasure, The
Private Life of Helen of Troy, The
  (Eleoneus)
Prowlers of the Sea
Rich Men's Shoes
Riding to Fame
Salomy Jane
See You in Jail
Sentimental Tommy
Snowbound
Some Pun'kins
Son of the Sheik (André)
Souls for Sables
Sporting Chance, The
Sporting Venus, A
Spring Fever (Mr. Waters)
Tempest, The
Tess of the D'Ubervilles (John Dur-
  beyfield)
Thank You
There You Are
Tide of the Empire
Tillie the Toiler (Mr. Simpkins)
Triumph (David Garnet)
Two Can Play (John Hammis)
Two Weeks
Under Western Skies
Up the Ladder
Valley of the Giants
Way of a Maid, The
Wedding March, The (Prince Ottokar)
West of the Water Tower
Woman with Four Faces, The (Judge
  Westcott)
Wonder of Women, The
Stage:
Mountain Man, The (Jess) 21

1883
FAWCETT, George, Mrs.*
Innocents of Paris (Madame Marney)
River of Romance

1884
FAY, Frank (1897-1961)
Show of Shows, The (Master of Cere-
  monies)
Stage:
Artists and Models 23
Jim Jam Jems (Johnny Case) 20

1885
FAY, Hugh*
Little Annie Rooney

1886
FAYE, Julia (1894-1966)
Adam's Rib (The Mischievous One)
Affairs of Anatol, The (Tibra)
Bachelor Brides
Changing Husbands
Chicago
Condemned Woman
Don't Call It Love
Dynamite (Marcia Towne)
Feet of Clay (Bertha Lansell)
Fighting Eagle, The
Fool's Paradise (Samaran)
Forbidden Fruit (maid)
Godless Girl, The (an inmate)
Golden Bed, The (Mrs. Thompson)
Great Moment, The (Sadie Bronson)
Hell's High Road
His Dog
King of Kings, The (Martha)
Life of the Party, The
Main Event, The
Manslaughter (Mrs. Drummond)
Martha
Meet the Prince
Nice People
Nobody's Money
Road to Yesterday, The (Dolly Foules)
Saturday Night (Elsie Prentiss)
Six Best Cellars
Snob, The
Something to Think About (banker's
  daughter)
Ten Commandments, The (Pharaoh's
  wife)
Triumph (Countess Rika)
Volga Boatman, The (Mariusha)
Yankee Clipper, The

1887
FAZENDA, Louise (1895-1962)
Astray from the Steerage (wife)
Babe Comes Home
Bat, The (Lizzie Allen)
Beautiful and Damned, The
Beauty Shop, The

Being Respectable
Bobbed Hair
Broadway Butterfly, The
Cheaper to Marry
Compromise
Cradle Snatchers, The
Declassee
Desert Song, The (Susan)
Domestic Troubles
Down on the Farm
Dramatic Life of Abraham Lincoln
  /aka/ Abraham Lincoln (Sally)
Faro Nell
Finger Prints
Five and Ten Cent Annie
Fog, The
Foolish Age, The
Footloose Widows
Galloping Fish, The
Gay Old Birds, The
Gold Diggers, The (Mabel Munroe)
Gold Diggers of Broadway, The
Grounds for Divorce
Hard to Get
Heart to Heart
Hearts and Flowers
Hogan's Alley
Hot Stuff
House of Horror, The
It's All Greek to Me
Ladies at Play
Lady of the Harem
Lighthouse by the Sea
Loose Ankles
Love Hour, The
Main Street
Married Life
Millionaires
Night Club, The
No, No, Nanette (Sue Smith)
Noah's Ark (dual role, maid/Hilda)
Old Soak, The
On with the Show (Sarah)
Outcast, The
Passionate Quest
Pay as You Enter
Price of Pleasure, The
Quincy Adams Sawyer (Mandy Skin-
  ner)
Red Mill, The (Gretchen)
Riley the Cop
Sailor's Sweetheart, A
Show of Shows, The
Simple Sis
Spoilers, The (Tilly Nelson)
Stark Mad
Terror, The (Mrs. Elvery)
Texas Steer, A

This Woman (Rose)
Tillie's Punctured Romance (Tillie)
True as Steel
Vamping Venus

1888
FEALY, Margaret*
Love Parade, The (1st lady in waiting)

1889
FEDUCHA, Bertha*
Next Corner, The (Julie)

1890
FEENEY, Francis*
Secrets (John Carlton, Jr.)
Unknown, The

1891
FELD, Fritz (1900-)
Black Magic
Blindfolded
Broadway (Mose Levett)
Case of Mary Brown, The
Charlatan, The
Golem, The
His Country
Stage:
Miracle, The (revolutionist) 24

1892
FELDMAN, Gladys*
West of the Water Tower

1893
FELIX THE CAT
Roameo (cartoon)

1894
FELLOWES, Rockliffe (1885-1950)
Bits of Life
Border Legion, The
Borrowed Husbands
Boy of Mine
Charlatan, The
Counsel for the Defense
Crystal Cup, The
Declassee
East of Suez
Flapper Wives
Garden of Weeds, The
Golden Princess
Honesty Is the Best Policy
In Search of a Sinner
Island Wives
Pagan Love
Penrod and Sam (Father Schofeld)
Point of View

Price of Possession, The
Road to Glory, The (Del Cole)
Rocking Moon
Rose of the World
Satin Woman, The
Signal Tower, The
Silence
Spoilers, The (Matthews)
Stranger's Banquet, The
Syncopating Sue
Taxi Dancer
Third Degree, The
Trifling with Honor
Understanding Heart, The (Bob Mason)
Yes or No?

1895
FELLOWS, Edith (1923-   )
Movie Night

1896
FELUMB, Mathilde*
Han og Hun og Hamlet

1897
FENTON, Leslie (1902-   )
Ancient Mariner, The (Joe Barlowe)
Black Paradise
Broadway ("Scar" Edwards)
Dangerous Woman, A
Dragnet, The
Dynamite (a young vulture)
East Lynne (Richard Hare)
Erick the Great
First Kiss, The
Gateway of the Moon
Girls Gone Wild
Going Crooked
Havoc (The Babe)
Last Performance, The
Man I Love, The
Office Scandal
Old Flame, An
Paris Bound (Richard Parrish)
Road to Glory, The (David Hale)
Sandy
Shamrock Handicap (Neil Ross)
Showdown, The
What Price Glory? (Lt. Moore)
Woman Trap

1898
FENTON, Marc*
Behold, My Wife!
Black Lightning (doctor)
Conquering Power, The (M. deGrassins)

Four Horsemen of the Apocalypse,
The (Senator Lacour)
Name the Man
Spirit of the U. S. A.
Thank You
Yellow Stain, The

1899
FEODOROFF, Leo*
Music Master, The

1900
FERAUDY, Jacques*
Heart of a Clown
Tillers of the Soil

1901
FERGUSON, Al*
Clean Sweep, A
Grit Wins
Headin' for Danger
Hearts and Hoofs
Hoofbeats of Vengeance
Lost City, The /aka/ The Jungle
Princess [serial]
Miracle of the Jungle
Outlaw, The
Smilin' Terror, The
Sunset Jones
Tarzan the Mighty [serial] (Black
John)
Tarzan the Tiger [serial] (Bobby Nelson)
Terror Mountain
Vagabond Cub
Wagon Master, The
Whiskey Runners
Who Wins?
Wolves of the City

1902
FERGUSON, Casson (1891-   )
At the End of the World
Borderland
Bunty Pulls the Strings
Cobra
Cotera (Jack Dorning)
Drums of Fate
For Alimony Only
Gentleman of Leisure, A
Grumpy (T. Chamberlain Jarvis)
Her Reputation
King of Kings, The (the Scribe)
Law and the Woman, The
Madame X (the son)
Manslaughter (Bobby Dorset)
Mutiny of the Elsinore
Over the Border

Prince Chap, The
Road to Yesterday, The (Adrian
  Tompkyns)
Tenth Avenue
Universal player 20
Unknown Wife, An
Virginia Courtship, A

1903
FERGUSON, Elsie (1883-1961)
Footlights
Forever
His House in Order
Lady Rose's Daughter
Outcast
Sacred and Profane Love
Such a Little Queen
Unknown Lover
Stage:
Grand Duchess and the Waiter, The
  (Grand Duchess Xenia) 25
House of Women, The (Lily Shane)
  27
Moonflower, The (Diane) 24
Sacred and Profane Love (Carlotta
  Peel) 20
Scarlet Pages (Mary Bancroft) 29
Shakesperean Pagent 21
Varying Shore, The (ghost of Madame
  Leland) 21

1904
FERGUSON, Helen (1901-)
Brass
Burning Daylight
Call of the North
Casey of the Coast Guard [serial]
Desert Blossoms
Famous Mrs. Fair, The
Fire Fighters [serial]
Flaming Hour, The
Freeze-Out
Going Some
Hungry Hearts
In Old California
Jaws of Steel
Just Pals
Miss Lulu Bett (Diana Deacon)
Romance Promoters
Scarlet West, The (Nestina)
Shod with Fire
Straight from the Shoulder
Universal player 24
Unknown Purple, The
Wild West [serial]
Within the Law (Helen Morris)

1905
FERGUSON, Myrtle*
Topsy and Eva

1906
FERGUSON, William J.*
Dream Street (Mr. Fair)
John Smith
Passers By
Peacock Alley (Alex Smith)
To Have and to Hold

1907
FERKAUF, Betty*
Broken Hearts

1908
FERNANDEZ, Bijou*
Just Suppose
New Toys

1909
FERRARI, Angelo*
Cyrano de Bergerac
Kopf Hoch, Charly! [Heads Up, Char-
  ly!] (Marquis d'Ormesson)
Richthofen: The Red Knight of the
  Air

1910
FERRIS, Audrey (1909-)
Beware of Bachelors
Beware of Married Men
Fancy Baggage
Glad Rag Doll, The
Honky Tonk (Jean Gilmore)
Little Wildcat, The
Powder My Back
Silver Slave, The
Women They Talk About

1911
FERRY, Minna*
Girls Gone Wild

1912
FETCHIT, Stepin (Lincoln Theodore
  Perry) (1902-)
Big Time, The
Ghost Talks, The
Hearts in Dixie
In Old Kentucky
Movietone Follies of '29 (Swifty)
Salute
Show Boat
Through Different Eyes (janitor)

1913
FEATHERSTON, Eddie*
Old Ironsides

1914
FIELD, Ben*
Silver King, The

1915
FIELD, Chester*
Widdecombe Affair (handy man)

1916
FIELD, Elinor*
Jungle Goddess, The
Once to Every Woman (Virginia Mere-
    dith)
Purple Riders, The (Betty Marsh)

1917
FIELD, George*
Adam's Rib (Moravian Minister)
Blood and Sand (El Nacional)
Stephen Steps Out

1918
FIELD, Gladys*
Dr. Jekyll and Mr. Hyde

1919
FIELD, Madalynne*
Campus Vamp, The
Girl from Everywhere, The
Girl from Nowhere, The
Run, Girl, Run

1920
FIELD, Percy*
Fifth Form at St. Dominic's (Horace
    Wraysford)
This Freedom (Harold)

1921
FIELD, Sylvia*
Voice of the City
Stage:
Mrs. Partridge Presents (Delight
    Partridge) 25

1922
FIELDING, Clarissa*
Isle of Lost Ships, The

1923
FIELDING, Claude*
Garden of Allah, The

1924
FIELDING, Gerald*
Garden of Allah, The

1925
FIELDING, Margaret*
Drag
Exiles, The
If Winter Comes
Isle of Lost Ships, The
Paris

1926
FIELDING, Romaine (1877-)
Rose of the Golden West
Shepherd of the Hills
Ten Modern Commandments
Woman's Man, A

1927
FIELDS, Lew (Lewis Fields) (1867-
    1941)
Friendly Enemies

1928
FIELDS, Sylvia*
Stewed, Fried and Boiled

1929
FIELDS, W. C. (William Claude Dun-
    kenfield) (1879-1946)
Fools for Luck (Richard Whitehead)
It's the Old Army Game (Elmer Pret-
    tywillie)
Janice Meredith (British Sgt.)
Potters, The (Pa Potter)
Running Wild (Elmer Finch)
Sally of the Sawdust (Prof. Eustace
    McGargle)
So's Your Old Man (Samuel Bisbee)
That Royle Girl (father)
Tillie's Punctured Romance (ringmas-
    ter)
Two Flaming Youths (Gabby Gilfoil)
Stage:
Earl Carroll's Vanities 28
George White's Scandals 22
Poppy (Prof. Eustace McGargle)
    23
Ziegfeld Follies of 1920
Ziegfeld Follies of 1921
Ziegfeld Follies of 1922

1930
FIGMAN, Max*
Old Home Week

1931
FIGMAN, Oscar Brimberton*
Manhattan

1932
FICKOVSKAYA, Lena*
Scandal

1933
FILLMORE, Clyde (1876-1948)
Alimony
City Sparrow, The
Devil's Passkey, The (Rex Strong)
Midnight Guest, The
Moonlight Follies
Nurse Marjorie
Outside Woman, The
Paramount player 21
Real Adventure
Sham
Silent Accuser, The
Soul of Youth, The
Sting of the Lash, The (Joel Gant)

1934
FILOI and HER 60 SAMOAN DAN-
  CERS
Belle of Samoa, The

1935
FILS, Baron*
Venus

1936
FILSON, Al W. *
Chickens
Homespun Folks
Monte Cristo (Morrel)
Treasure Island (Billy Bones)

1937
FINCH, Flora (1869-1940)
Adventurous Sex, The (grandmother)
Brown Derby, The
Captain Salvation
Cat and the Canary, The (Susan)
Come Across
First National player 26
Five and Ten Cent Annie
Great Adventure, The
Haunted House, The
Kiss for Cinderella, A (2nd customer)
Lessons in Love
Luck
Men and Women
Monsieur Beaucaire (Duchess de
  Montmorency)
Oh, Baby!

Orphans of the Storm (starving peas-
  ant)
Quality Street (Mary Willoughby)
Rose of the Golden West
Roulette
Scarlet Letter, The
Social Errors
When Knighthood Was in Flower
  (French lady-in-waiting)
Wife's Relations, The

1938
FINDLAY, Thomas /aka/ Tom*
Heliotrope
Let's Get Married
Little Old New York (Chancellor
  Livingston)
Lucky Devil, The
Yolanda (castleman)

1939
FINE, Bud*
Battling Butler
Racketeer, The (Bernie Weber)
Wreck of the Hesperus, The

1940
FINK, Henry*
Kibitzer, The
On with the Show

1941
FINLAY, Redmon*
Beau Geste (Cordère)

1942
FINLAYSON, James /aka/ Jimmy
  (1887-1953)
Bachelor's Paradise, A
Before the Public
Big Business
Call of the Cuckoo, The
Do Detectives Think? (Judge)
Don't Weaken
Down on the Farm
Flying Elephants
Forty Five Minutes from Hollywood
Great Scott!
Hard to Get
Hoose Gow, The
In the Grease
Ladies' Night in a Turkish Bath
Lady Be Good
Liberty
Love 'em and Weep
Madame Mystery (struggling author)
Married Life

Men O' War
Nickel Hopper, The
Second Hundred Years, The
Should Husbands Pay?
Should Tall Men Marry?
Show Girl
Small Town Idol, A
Smitty
Sold at Auction
Sugar Daddies
Two Weeks Off
Wall Street
With Love and Hisses

1943
FINNEY, Benjamin F. , Jr.*
Miami

1944
FIRPO, Luis Angel*
Will He Conquer Dempsey?

1945
FISCHER, Felix*
Cafe Electric /aka/ Wenn ein Weib
   den Wag Verliert [When a Woman
   Loses Her Way] (the editor)

1946
FISCHER, Robert*
Loves of an Actress
Oath, The
Sherlock Holmes /aka/ Moriarty
   (Otto)

1947
FISCHER-KÖPPE, Hugo*
Wie Einst im Mai

1948
FISHER, Alfred*
Fighting American, The
Home Maker, The

1949
FISHER, George*
Moonlight Follies

1950
FISHER, Larry*
Boy of Flanders, A
Into Her Kingdom
Long Live the King

1951
FISHER, Laurence*
Winds of Chance

1952
FISHER, Maisie*
Virgin Queen, The (Mary, Queen of
   Scots)

1953
FISHER, Margarita (Margarita Fis-
   cher) (1893-)
Any Woman
Butterfly Girl, The
Dangerous Talent
Gamesters, The
Hellion, The
Payment Guaranteed
Their Mutual Child
Thirtieth Piece of Silver
Uncle Tom's Cabin (Eliza)
Unknown, The
Week End, The

1954
FISHER, Millicent*
Alarm Clock Andy

1955
FITZGERALD, Aubrey*
Nell Gwyn (Tom Killigrew)
Widdecombe Affair (the Bailiff)

1956
FITZGERALD, Cissy (1874-1941)
Arizona Wildcat
Babbitt
Beauty Shoppers
Crown of Lies
Diplomats, The
Fire and Steel
Flames
Flowing Gold
Her Big Night
High Flyer, The
His Lucky Day
If Marriage Fails
I'll Show You the Town
Ladies of the Night Club
Laugh, Clown, Laugh (Giacinta)
Lilies of the Field
Love Thief, The
Matinee Ladies
McFadden Flats
No Babies Wanted
Painted Angel, The
Redheads Preferred
Seven Footsteps to Satan
Swim Princess, The
Two Flaming Youths (Madge Malarkey)
Universal player 26
Vanity's Price

Women Love Diamonds
Women's Wares

1957
FITZGIBBONS, Esme*
Rat, The (Madeleine Sornay)

1958
FITZROY, Emily (d. 1954)
Ambrose Applejohn's Adventure
  (Mrs. Horace Pengrad)
Bardelys the Magnificent (Vicomtesse
  de Lanedam)
Bat, The (Cornelius Van Gorder)
Bobbed Hair
Bridge of San Luis Rey, The (Mar-
  queca)
Case of Lena Smith, The
Cheerful Fraud, The
Deadline at Eleven
Denial, The
Don Juan
Driven
Fascination
Find the Woman
Foreign Devils
Frisky Mrs. Johnson
Fury
Gentlemen Prefer Blondes (Mrs.
  Beckman)
Hard Boiled
Her Night of Romance
High Steppers
His Hour
Lady, The
Learning to Love
Love
Love Me and the World Is Mine
Love's Wilderness
Man Who Came Back, The
Marriage License
Married Alive
Mockery (Mrs. Gaidaroff)
New York Idea
No Babies Wanted
No Trespassing
Once and Forever
One Increasing Purpose
Orchids and Ermine
Peacock Alley
Purple Highway, The
Red Lily, The (Madame Bouchard)
Sea Tiger, The
Secrets (Mrs. Marlowe)
Show Boat (Parthenia Hawks)
Straight Is the Way
Strangers of the Night
Trail of '98 (Mrs. Bulkey)

Way Down East (Maria Poole)
What Happened to Jones?
Wife Against Wife
Zander the Great (the matron)

1959
FIX, Paul (1901-   )
Burlesque
Chicago
First Kiss, The
Hoodoo Ranch
Lucky Star (Joe)
Sex
Shavings
Tavern, The
Third Night, The

1960
FJORD, Olaf*
Madonna of the Sleeping Cars, The
Monna Vanna

1961
FLAMMA, Luca*
King of Kings, The (Gallant of Gali-
  lee)

1962
FLEIGEL, Gustaf*
City Without Jews, The

1963
FLEMING, Carroll*
Milestones (Thompson, the butler)

1964
FLEMING, Claude*
Unholy Night, The (Sir James Rum-
  sey)

1965
FLEMING, Philip B., Major*
West Point

1966
FLETCHER, Bramwell (1904-   )
Chick
To What Red Hell?

1967
FLOHRS, Virginia*
Alibi /aka/ The Perfect Alibi
  (theatre singer)

1968
FLORELLE, Odette*
L'Affaire de la Rue de Lourcine
Jim Bougne Boxeur

1969
FLOREY, Robert (1900-)
L'Orpheline
Straight from the Farm (sheriff)

1970
FLOUKER, Mack*
Bath Between, The
Win That Girl

1971
FLOWER, Alice*
Home Maker, The

1972
FLOWERS, Bess (1900-)
Ghost Talks, The
Glenister of the Royal Mounted
Greater Glory, The
Hands Across the Border
Hollywood
Irene
Laddie
Ladies' Man
Lone Hand Saunders
We Faw Down
Woman of Paris, A

1973
FLOYD, Henrietta*
Lost, a Wife
Virgin Paradise, A

1974
FLUKER, Mack--see: Mack Flouker

1975
FLYNN, Edythe*
Broadway (Ruby)

1976
FLYNN, M. B. "Lefty"*
Voices of the City (Pierson)

1977
FLYNN, Maurice (1876-1959)
Breed of the Border
Bucking the Line
College Boob, The
Dangerous Curves Ahead
Drums of Fate
Glenister of the Royal Mounted
Going Some
Golden Stallion, The [serial]
Great Accident, The
High and Handsome
Just Out of College
Last Trail, The

No Gun Man, The
Officer 666
Omar the Tentmaker
Open All Night
Roads of Destiny
Salomy Jane
Silver Horde, The
Sir Lumberjack
Smiles Are Trumps
Smilin' at Trouble
Snow Bride, The
Speed Wild
Traffic Cop
Woman Who Walked Alone, The

1978
FLYNN, Rita*
Girl from Woolworths, The

1979
FOGEL, V. P.*
Yellow Ticket, The

1980
FOGEL, Vladimir*
Bed and Sofa

1981
FOLEY, George*
Grip of Iron, The (Jagon and Sim-
  monnet)
Road to London, The (Rex Rowland,
  Sr.)

1982
FOLKENSTEIN, Julius*
Romeo und Julia im Schnee [Romeo
  and Juliet in the Snow]

1983
FONTANNE, Lynn (1887-)
Man Who Found Himself, The
Second Youth
Stage:
Arms and the Man (Raina) 25
At Mrs. Beam's (Laura Pasquale) 26
Doctor's Dilemma, The (Jennifier
  Dubedat) 27
Dulcy (Dulcinea) 21
Goat Song (Stanja) 26
Guardsman, The (the actress, his
  wife) 24
Meteor (Ann Carr) 29
Pygmalion (Eliza Doolittle) 26
Strange Interlude (Nina Leeds) 28
Sweet Nell of Old Drury (Lady Castle-
  maine) 23

FOOTE, Courtenay*
Ashes of Vengeance (Comte de la
  Roche)
Bronze Bell, The
Dorothy Vernon of Haddon Hall (Earl
  of Leicester)
Little Old New York (Robert Fulton)
Madonna of the Streets, A (Dr. Col-
  beck)
Passion Flower, The
Star Rover, The
Tess of the D'Ubervilles (Dick)

1985
FORBES, Mary Elizabeth (1880-1964)
Devil to Pay, The
East Is West
Her Private Life
Sunny Side Up (Mrs. Cromwell)
Thirteenth Chair, The
Trespasser, The (Mrs. Ferguson)

1986
FORBES, Ralph (1896-1951)
Actress, The
Beau Geste (John Geste)
Comin' Thro the Rye (George Tem-
  pest)
Dogs of War
Enemy, The
Fifth Form at St. Dominic's (Oliver
  Greenfield of the Fifth)
Green Goddess, The (Dr. Traherne)
High Road, The
Latest from Paris, The
Lilies of the Field
Masks of the Devil, The
Mr. Wu (Basil Gregory)
Reckless Youth
Submarine
Trail of '98 (Larry)
Trelawney of the Wells (Arthur
  Gower)
Under the Black Eagle
Whip, The
Stage:
Little Minister, The (Rev. Gavin
  Dishart) 25
Magnolia Lady, The (Kenneth Craig)
  24
Man with a Load of Mischief, The
  (his man) 25

1987
FORD, Clarence*
Under the Lash (Kaffir Bay)

1988
FORD, Eugenie*
Christie comedies (7 years)
Road to Divorce, The
Send Him Away with a Smile
Virgin of Stamboul, The

1989
FORD, Francis (Francis Feeney)
  (1883-1953)
Action
Angel Citizens, The
Another Man's Shoes
Black Watch, The
Branded Sombrero, The
Caring, The
Chinatown Mystery, The [serial]
Crimson Shoals, The
Cruise of the Hellion
Devil's Saddle, The
Drake Case, The
Fighting Heart, The
Flower of the Range
Four-Footed Ranger
Gold Grabbers
Great Reward, The [serial]
Haunted Valley [serial chapter]
Heart of Lincoln, The
Heart of Maryland, The
Hearts of Oak
I Am the Woman
Isobel /aka/ The Trails End
Lady from Longacre, The
Lariat Kid, The
Man from Nowhere, The
Men of Daring
One Glorious Scrap
Sisters of Eve
Storm Girl, The
They're Off
Three Jumps Ahead
Upstream
Village Blacksmith, The
Wolf's Trail, The
Wreck of the Hesperus, The

1990
FORD, Harrison (1892-1959)
Advice to Husbands
Blonde for a Night
Find the Woman
Food for Scandal
Foolish Wives
Girl on the Pullman, The
Gold Widows
Heart to Let, A
Her Gilded Cage (Lawrence Pell)
Her Husband's Women

Janice Meredith (Charles Fawnes)
Just Married
Lady in Love, A
Let 'em Go Gallagher
Little Old New York (Larry Delaven)
Lovers in Quarantine
Love's Redemption
Marriage Whirl, The
Maytime (Richard Wayne)
Miss Hobbs
Nervous Wreck, The
Night Bride, The
No Control
Oh, Lady, Lady!
Old Homestead, The
Passion Flower, The
Price of a Party, The
Primitive Lover, The
Proud Flesh
Rejuvenation of Aunt Mary, The
Rubber Tires
Rush Hour, The
Sandy
Shadows (John Malden)
Smilin' Through (dual role, Kenneth
  Wayne/Jeremiah Wayne)
Song and Dance Man, The
That Royle Girl (Fred Ketlar)
Three Miles Out
Three Weekends (Turner)
Up in Mabel's Room
Vanity Fair (George Osborne)
Wedding Bells
When Love Comes
Woman Against the World, A
Wonderful Thing, The
World's Applause, The
Zander the Great (Dan Marchinson)

1991
FORD, James*
Children of the Ritz
Divine Sinner, The (Heinrich)
First National player 26
House of Horror, The
Outcast, The
Prisoners
Wedding Rings

1992
FORD, John (Sean Aloysius Feely)
  (1895-1973)
Hangman's House

1993
FORD, Philip*
Blue Eagle, The (Limpy D'Arcy)

1994
FORDE, Eugenie (1898-)
Captain Salvation
Memory Lane
That's My Baby

1995
FORDE, Hal*
Great White Way, The

1996
FORDE, Stanley*
Great White Way, The

1997
FORDE, Walter (Tom Seymour)
  (1897-)
Fishing for Trouble
Handy Man, The
Never Say Die
Silent House, The
Wait and See
Walter Finds a Father
Walter Makes a Movie
Walter the Prodigal
Walter the Sleuth
Walter Wins a Wager
Walter's Day Out
Walter's Paying Policy
Walter's Trying Frolics
Walter's Winning Ways
Walter's Worries
What Next?
Would You Believe It?

1998
FOREST, Ann--see: Ann Forrest

1999
FOREST, Jean
Two Little Vagabonds (Wally)
Visages d'Enfants

2000
FOREST, Karl*
Der Leibgardest [The Guardsman]

2001
FORGAY, Wenonnah*
Loves of Ricardo, The

2002
FORMAN, Tom (1893-1938)
Are You a Failure?
Cappy Ricks
City of Silent Men
Easy Road, The
Headin' for Danger

His Lucky Day
If You Believe It, It Is So
Jackson Comes Home
Kosher Kitty Kelly
Ladder of Lies, The
Money, Money, Money
Round-Up, The
Saps and Saddles
Sea Wolf, The (George Medford)
Sins of Rosanne
Tree of Knowledge, The
Valley Beyond the Law
White Shoulders
Yellow Contraband

2003
FORREST, Alan /aka/ Allan (1889-)
Ankles Preferred
Black Feather
Captain Blood (Lord Julian Wade)
Carnival Girl
Crinoline Romance, A
Desert Bride
Dorothy Vernon of Haddon Hall (Sir
    John Manners)
Dressmaker from Paris, The
Fifth Avenue
Great Divide, The
Long Live the King
Lovelorn, The
Man Between, The
Man from Lost River, The
Noise in Newboro
Old Clothes (Nathan Burke)
Pampered Youth
Partners Again
Phantom Bullet, The
Prince of Pilsen, The
Riding for Fame
Rose of the World
Sally of the Scandals
Summer Bachelors
Two Can Play (James Radley)
Wandering Daughters
Wild West Show
Winged Horseman, The

2004
FORREST, Allen*
Siren of Seville, The

2005
FORREST, Ann (1897-)
Behold, My Wife!
Dangerous Days
Faith Healer, The
Great Accident, The
If Winter Comes

Man Who Played God, The
Marriage Morals
Prince Chap, The
Splendid Hazard, A

2006
FORREST, Arthur (1859-1933)
When Knighthood Was in Flower (Car-
    dinal Wolsey)

2007
FORST, Willi*
Atlantic (Boldi)
Cafe Electric /aka/ Wen eim Weib
    den Weg Verliert [When a Woman
    Loses Her Way] (Ferdl)
Gefahren der Brautzeit [Dangers of
    the Engagement Period] /aka/
    Aus dem Tagebuch eines Verfüh-
    rers; Eine Nocht der Liebe;
    Liebesnächte [Nights of Love];
    Liebesbriefe (Baron van Geldern)

2008
FORSTER, Rudolf (1885-1969)
At the Grey House
Tragödie der Liebe [Tragedy of Love]

2009
FORTE, Rene*
16-1/2 x 11

2010
FOSS, Kenelm (1885-1963)
Edward Kean
Joyous Adventures of Aristide Pujol

2011
FOSSE, Bunty (1916-)
Sally Bishop (child)
This Freedom (Rosalie, age 6)
Wee Mac Greegor's Sweetheart (Dit-
    to, age 7)

2012
FOSTER, Allan K. Girls
Cocoanuts, The

2013
FOSTER, Darby*
Paddy the Next Best Thing (Lawrence
    Blake)

2014
FOSTER, Helen (1907-)
Bandit's Baby, The
Circumstantial Evidence
Gentlemen of the Press

Gold Diggers of Broadway, The (Violet)
Harvest of Hate
Hell-Ship Bronson
Hoofbeats of Vengeance
Linda
Mating Call
Naughty Nanette
Painted Faces
Road to Ruin, The
Should a Girl Marry?
Sky Skidder
So Long Letty
Sweet Sixteen
13 Washington Square (Mary Morgan)
Won in the Clouds

2015
FOSTER, May*
Crown of Lies, The
Docks of New York, The
Milestones (Nancy Sibley)
Woman of the World, A

2016
FOSTER, Norman (Norman Hoeffer)
  (1900-)
Dove, The
Gentlemen of the Press

2017
FOUNTAINE, William*
Hallelujah (Hot Shot)

2018
FOWLER, J. *
Passionate Youth
Ranson's Folly
Wolf's Clothing

2019
FOX, John, Jr. /aka/ Johnny*
Contraband
Covered Wagon, The (Jed Wingate)
Lady, The
One Glorious Day
Pony Express
When a Man's a Man

2020
FOX, Lucy*
Hurricane Hutch
Lone Wolf, The
Miami

2021
FOX, Mary--see: Mary Foy

2022
FOX, Reginald*
American Prisoner, The (Capt. Mainwaring)
Daniel Deronda (Title role)

2023
FOX, Virginia*
Blacksmith, The
Cops

2024
FOX, Wilbur*
Warrens of Virginia, The (General Grant)

2025
FOXE, Earle (1891-)
Black Magic
Black Panther's Cub, The
Blindfolded
Case of Mary Brown, The
Escape, The
Fashion Row
Four Sons
Fugitives
Ghost Talks, The
Goldwyn player 23
Hangman's House
Ladies Must Dress (George Ward, Jr.)
Lady of Quality, A
Last Man on Earth, The
Man She Brought Back, The
Man Upstairs, The
New Year's Eve
News Parade, The
None but the Brave
Prodigal Judge, The
River Pirate, The
Sailors' Wives
Slaves of Beauty
Spanish Romeo, A
Through Different Eyes (Howard Thornton)
Trip to Chinatown, A
Upstream
Vanity Fair (Capt. William Dobbin)
Stage:
Come Seven (Florian Slappey) 20

2026
FOY, Eddie, Jr. (1910-)
Queen of the Nightclubs

2027
FOY, Mary*
Ankles Preferred

Dangerous Money
Hoosier Schoolmaster, The
Icebound
Irish Luck
It's the Old Army Game (Sarah Pan-
    coast)
Lucky Devil, The
Mad Hour, The
Manicure Girl, The
Pinch Hitter, The (Aunt Martha)
Second Fiddle
Slaves of Beauty
White Rose, The (landlady)

2028
FRAGANZA, Trixie--see: Trixie
    Friganza

2029
FRANCEN, Victor (1888-   )
Crepuscule d'Epouvante

2030
FRANCESCHI, M. *
Atlantide (M. le Mesge)

2031
FRANCESCI, Paul*
Arab, The (Marmont)

2032
FRANCEY, Bill*
Out All Night

2033
FRANCIS, Alec B. (1857-1934)
Beau Brummel (Mortimer)
Beyond the Rocks (Capt. Fitzgerald)
Bishop Murder Case, The
Bridge of Sighs, The
Broadway Daddies
Camille (the Duke)
Capital Punishment (Chaplain)
Charley's Aunt (Mr. Delahay)
Children of Jazz
Circle, The
Coast of Folly, The (Count de
    Tauro)
Companionate Marriage, The
Courage
Drivin' Fool, The
Earthbound
Eternal Three, The
Evangeline
Evidence
Fast Life
Forever After
Gentleman of Leisure, A

Godless Men
Gold Diggers, The (James Blake)
Great Moment, The (Sir Edward
    Pelham)
Life's Mockery
Lion and the Mouse, The
Little Snob, The
Lucretia Lombard
Mad Whirl, The
Man and Maid
Man Who Had Everything, The
Man Who Saw Tomorrow, The
Mississippi Gambler, The
Music Master, The
North to the Rio Grande
Paliser Case, The
Pals First
Return of Peter Grimm, The (Peter
    Grimm)
Rose of the World
Sacred Flame, The
Sally in Our Alley
Shepherd of the Hills
Smilin' Through (Dr. Owen)
Tender Hour, The
Terror, The (Dr. Redmayne)
Thank You
Thief in Paradise, A
Three Bad Men
Three Wise Fools
Tramp, Tramp, Tramp (Amos)
Transcontinental Limited
Under the Lash
Vanishing Millions [serial]
Virginia Courtship, A
Voice in the Dark, A
Waking up the Town
What's a Wife Worth?
Yankee Senor, The

2034
FRANCIS, Alma*
Wolf Man, The

2035
FRANCIS, Eva*
Flood, The
Silence, The

2036
FRANCIS, Kay (Katherine Edwina
    Gibbs) (1906-1968)
Cocoanuts, The (Penelope)
Dangerous Curves (Zara Flynn)
Gentlemen of the Press (Myrna May)
Honest Finder
Illusion
Marriage Playground, The (Lady
    Wrench)

Stage:
Elmer the Great (billed as Katherine
    Francis) (Evelyn Corey) 28
Hamlet (billed as Katherine Francis)
    (Player Queen) 25

2037
FRANCIS, Martha*
Scarlet West, The (Harriet Kinnard)

2038
FRANCIS, Olin*
Kid Brother, The
Win that Girl

2039
FRANCISCO, Betty (1900-1950)
Ashes of Vengeance (Margot de Vain-
    ceoire)
Boy of the Streets, A
Broadway (Mazie)
Broadway Cowboy, A
Broadway Daddies
Darling of New York, The
Don Juan's Three Nights
Exclusive Rights
Fifth Avenue Models
Flaming Youth
Furnace, The
Gay Retreat, The
Gingham Girl
Long Pants
Man Bait
Man from Make-Believe, The
Maytime (Ermintrude)
Midsummer Madness
Poor Men's Wives
Private Affairs
Queen of the Chorus
Seven Keys to Baldpate (Chicago
    Molly)
Smiling Irish Eyes
Spirit of Youth
Too Many Crooks
Uneasy Payments
You Can't Beat the Law

2040
FRANCOIS, Charles*
Sein Grösster Bluff [Her Greatest
    Bluff] (gangster)

2041
FRANEY, Agnes*
Queen of the Nightclubs
Stolen Kisses

2042
FRANEY, William /aka/ Billy*
Bath Dub, The
Cheyenne
Quincy Adams Sawyer (Bob Wood)
Royal Rider
Senor Daredevil
She's a Sheik

2043
FRANK, Bernice*
Grumpy (Susan)

2044
FRANK, Christian J.*
Ancient Highway, The
Arizona Bound
Black Cyclone
Cavalier, The
Chicago after Midnight
Easy Come, Easy Go
Ragged Edge, The

2045
FRANK, Herbert*
April Folly (Ronald Kenna)

2046
FRANK, Jacob*
Mother's Boy (Mr. Applebaum)

2047
FRANK, Will*
Last Edition

2048
FRANKLIN, Martha*
Beloved Rogue, The (maid)
Climbers, The (Clotilda)
Don Q. Son of Zorro (The Duenna)
Duchess of Buffalo, The
Serenade
Wheels of Chance
Woman from Moscow

2049
FRANKLIN, Sidney*
Boy of Flanders, A
Fashion Row
In Hollywood with Potash and Perl-
    mutter
Three Musketeers, The (Bonacieux)
Wheels of Chance

2050
FRANKLIN, Wendell*
Four Sons
Fourth Commandment, The

2051
FRANZ, Joseph J.*
Easy Come, Easy Go

2051a
FRASER, Robert--see: Robert Frazer

2052
FRASER, Tony*
Dick Turpin's Ride to New York
(Bow Street runner)
Four Feathers, The (Abou Fatma)

2053
FRAWLEY, William (1887-1966)
Fancy That
Turkey for Two

2054
FRAZER, Robert (-1944)
As a Man Loves
Back to God's Country
Black Butterflies
Bread
Broken Barriers
Burning up Broadway
Careers
Charmer, The
City, The
City of Purple Dreams (Daniel Ran-
dolph)
Dame Chance
Desert Gold
Drake Case, The
Fascination
Frozen Justice
Isle of Retribution
Jazzmania
Keeper of the Bees, The (James Mc-
Farlane)
Lightnin'
Little Snob, The
Love Piker, The
Men
Miss Bluebeard
Not of the Past
One Hour of Love
Other Woman's Story, The
Out of the Ruins
Scarlet Dove, The
Scarlet West, The (Cardelanche)
Secret Riders
Silent Hero, The
Sin Cargo
Sioux Blood
Speeding Venus
Splendid Road, The

Universal player 24
When a Man's a Man
When the Desert Calls
White Desert, The
Why Women Love
Without Limit
Woman I Love, The
Women Who Give
Yellow Men and Gold

2055
FRAZIER, Richard*
Wizard, The

2056
FRAZIER, Robert*
Peter Pan

2057
FRAZIN, Gladys*
Let Not Man Put Asunder
Return of the Rat, The (Yvonne)

2058
FREDERIC, William*
Peacock Alley (Mayor of Hormon-
town)

2059
FREDERICI, Blanche /aka/ Blanche
Friderici (-1933)
Fleet Wings
Gentlemen Prefer Blondes
Jazz Heaven
Last of the Duanes
Sadie Thompson (Mrs. Davidson)
Stolen Love
Trespasser, The (Miss Polter)
Wonder of Women
Stage:
Cat and the Canary, The ("Mammy"
Pleasant) 22
Hero, The (Sarah Lane) 21
Processional (Mrs. Euphemia Stewart
Flimins) 25

2060
FREDERICK, Freddie Burke*
Crowd, The (Junior)
Evidence
New Year's Eve
Wall Street

2061
FREDERICK, Pauline (1883-1938)
Bella Donna
Devil's Island
Evidence

Glory of Clementina
Her Honor the Governor
Joselyn's Wife
La Tosca
Let Not Man Put Asunder
Loves of Letty
Lure of Jade, The
Madame X (Title role)
Married Flirts
Mistress of Shenstone
Mumsie (Title role)
Nest, The
On Trial (Joan Trask)
Paliser Case, The
Roads of Destiny
Sacred Flame, The
Salvage (dual role, Bernice Ridge-
   way/Kate Martin)
Slave of Vanity, A
Smouldering Fires
Sting of the Lash, The (Dorothy
   Keith)
Three Women (Mrs. Mabel Wilton)
Two Kinds of Women
Vitagraph player 24
Woman Breed
Woman in Room 13, The
Stage:
Guilty One, The (Irene Short) 23

2062
FREED, Lazar*
Salome of the Tenements

2063
FREMAULT, Anita*
Four Devils (Louise as a child)
Wonder of Women

2064
FREMONT, Alfred*
Queen of Sheba, The (Captain of
   Adonijah's army)
She's a Sheik

2065
FRENCH, Charles K.*
Abysmal Brute, The (Pat Glendon,
   Sr.)
Adventurous Soul
Alaskan, The
Being Respectable
Big Hop, The
Blanky
Cowboy Cavalier
Cruise of the Hellion
Divine Lady, The
Down Grade, The

Dramatic Life of Abraham Lincoln
   /aka/ Abraham Lincoln
Extra Girl, The
Fast and Furious
Flaming Frontier, The
Flying Buckaroo, The
Free and Equal
Girl of Gold
Good as Gold
Grumpy (Mark Stone)
Hands Up!
King of the Rodeo
Last Warning
Lost Limited, The
Man, Woman and Sin
Meddlin' Stranger
Night Watch, The
Oh, What a Night!
One Chance in a Million
Perfect Crime, The
Prairie Trails
Rainmaker, The
Ride 'em High
Runaway Express, The
Slow Down
Smudge
Stronger than Death
Texas Trail, The
Under Western Skies
Unfoldment, The
War Paint
Way of a Girl, The
Winning Wallop, The
Woman of Paris, A (John's father)
World's Applause

2066
FRENCH, Dick*
Half Way to Heaven

2067
FRENCH, Evelyn*
Million Dollar Collar

2068
FRENCH, George B. (1883-)
Black Pearl, The
Reckless Sex, The
Sawdust Paradise, The
Unfoldment, The
Winter Has Come
Women Wake Up
Won in the Clouds

2069
FRENCH, Harold (1897-)
Hypocrites

2070
FRENCH, Pauline*
Last Man on Earth, The
Little Johnny Jones

2071
FRESHMAN, William A. (1905-)
Fifth Form at St. Dominic's (Loman
    of the Sixth)
Luck of the Navy, The (Wing Eden)
Widdecombe Affair (the lover)

2072
FRESNAY, Pierre (1897-)
La Vierge Folle

2073
FRIDERICI, Blanche--see: Blanche
    Frederici

2074
FRIEND, Helene*
Love Parade, The (a lady-in-waiting)

2075
FRIES, Otto*
From Soup to Nuts
Hotel Imperial (Anton)
Riley, the Cop
Surrender
Waltzing Around

2076
FRIESS, Inge*
Entr'acte

2077
FRIGANZA, Trixie (1870-1955)
Charmer, The
Coming of Amos, The
Gentlemen Prefer Blondes (Mrs.
    Spoffard)
Mind over Matter
Motor Maniac
Proud Flesh
Road to Yesterday, The (Harriet
    Tyrell)
Thanks for the Buggy Ride
Whole Town's Talking, The

2078
FRISCO, Albert*
Love Light, The (Pietro)
Song of Love, The

2079
FRITSCH, Willy /aka/ Willi (1901-)
Frau im Mond (Woman in the Moon)

Guilty
His Late Excellency
Hungarian Rhapsody
Last Waltz, The
Schuldig
Spione [Spies]
Waltz Dream, The (Lt. Nicholas)

2080
FROELICH, Gustav*
Eva and the Grasshopper
Homecoming
Meistersinger
Metropolis (Freder Fredersen - Eric
    Masterson in U.S.)
Temptation

2081
FRONDE, Louis*
Shriek of Araby, The

2082
FRONDI, Signor*
Loves of Ricardo, The

2083
FROST, Leila*
Sentimental Tommy

2084
FRUEN, Patricia*
Way Down East (Diana's sister)

2085
FRYE, Clayton*
Old Home Week

2086
FRYLAND, Alphons*
Quo Vadis (Vinicius)

2087
FUERBURG, DeGarcia*
Scaramouche (Maximilian Robespierre)

2088
FUETTERER, Werner*
Faust
Love Commandment, The
Uneasy Money

2089
FUJINO, Hideo*
Daughter of Two Fathers, A

2090
FUJITA, Toyo*
Garden of Weeds, The

2091
FULEY, Elizabeth*
Down to the Sea in Ships (Patience
    as a child)

2092
FULLER, Dale (1897-)
Babbitt
Beauty Shoppers
Ben Hur (Amrah)
Borderland
Canadian, The
Cossacks, The (Ulitka)
Devil's Cargo, The
Fazil (Zouroya)
Foolish Wives (Maruschka)
Glad Rag Doll
Greed (Maria Macapa)
Her Second Chance
His Hour
House of Horror, The
Husbands and Lovers
King of Kings, The (bit)
Lady of the Night
Man, The
Manslaughter (a prisoner)
Marriage Circle, The (Miss
    Hoffer)
Merry-Go-Round, The (Marianka
    Huber)
Merry Widow, The (Sally's maid)
Midnight Lovers
One Wonderful Night
Only Thing, The
Reno
Romance of a Queen, The (Anna)
Sacred Flame, The
Shadow of the Law, The
Six Days
Souls for Sale (Abigal Tweedy)
Speeding Venus
Three Weeks
Tomorrow's Love
Universal player 24
Volcano (Negro servant)
Wedding March, The (Katherina)
Woman Hater

2093
FULLER, Olive Gordon (1896-)
Committee on Credentials
Tess of the Storm Country

2094
FULLER, Rosalinde*
Unwritten Law, The

2095
FULTON, James F. *
Eternal Three, The
Greed (sheriff)

2096
FULTON, Maude (1881-1950)
Gingham Girl
Nix on Dames
Silk Legs

2097
FUNG, Willie*
Two Gun Man, The

2098
FURTH, Jaro*
Die Freudlose Gasse [The Joyless
    Street] /aka/ Street of Sorrow,
    The (Josef Rumfort)

2099
FURY, Barney*
Winds of Chance

2100
FUSS, Kurt*
Der Kleine Napoleon [The Little Na-
    poleon] /aka/ So Sind die Männer
    [Men Are Like That]; Napoleons
    Kleiner Bruder [Napoleon's Little
    Brother] (Royal Ballet Director)

- G -

2101
GABLE, Clark (William Clark Gable)
    (1901-1960)
Declassee (extra)
Fighting Blood (extra)
Forbidden Paradise (debut-extra)
Merry Widow, The (extra)
North Star (extra)
Pacemakers, The [serial] (extra)
Plastic Age, The (athlete)
Strongheart (extra)
Stage:
Blind Windows 29
Chicago (reporter) L. A. 27
Copperhead, The (juvenile lead) L. A.
    26
Lady Frederick - L. A. 26
Lucky Sam McCarner - L. A. 26
Lullaby (drunk sailor) - L. A. 26
Machinal (a man) 28
Madame X (Judge) - L. A. 26
Romeo and Juliet - Touring

Company 25
What Price Glory? (Kiper, then Sgt. Quirk) - West Coast Road Company 25

2102
GABRIO, Gabriel*
Les Miserables (dual role, Jean Valjean/Madeleine Champmathieu)

2103
GADE, W.*
Royal Box, The

2104
GADSON, Jacqueline*
City of Purple Dreams, The (Kathleen Otis)
Goldfish, The
His Hour
It (dual role, Jane Daly/Adela Von-Norman)
Man and Maid
Merry Widow, The (Madonna)
Not So Long Ago
Red Hair (Minnie Luther)
Regular Fellow, A
Scarlet Lady
Thirteenth Hour, The (secretary)
West of Zanzibar (Anna)
Wife of the Centaur, The

2105
GAIDAROFF, E.*
Michael Strogoff (Alexander II of Russia)

2106
GAIDAROV, Vladimir*
Manon Lescaut (desGrieux)
Michael Strogoff
Rasputin, the Holy Sinner
Russia-1908
Scandal in Paris, A
Tragödie der Liebe [Tragedy of Love]

2107
GAINES, Ernestine*
Aloma of the South Seas

2108
GAINES, William*
Brown of Harvard

2109
GALERON, Jean*
Paris

2110
GALLAGHER, Donald*
Through Different Eyes (Spencer)

2111
GALLAGHER, Johnny*
Great White Way, The

2112
GALLAGHER, Ray (1889-1953)
Abie's Irish Rose
Argyle Case, The
Around the Town
Crooked Trails
Dust
Excess Baggage
Go Get 'em
Guardians of the North
Half a Bride
Nothing to Wear
Phantom Melody, The
Secret Eyes
Tide of the Empire
Trail of '98

2113
GALLAGHER, Richard "Skeets" (1891-1955)
Alex the Great
Close Harmony (Johnny Boy)
Dance of Life, The
Daring Years, The (college boy)
Fast Company
First National player 28
For the Love of Mike ("Coxey" Pendleton)
New York
Pointed Heels
Potters, The (Red Miller)
Racket, The
Stocks and Blondes
Three-Ring Marriage

2114
GALLAHER, Donald--see: Donald Gallagher

2115
GALLERY, Tom*
Bob Hampton of Placer
Bright Skies
Chorus Girl's Romance, A (Charlie Moon)
Daughter of Luxury, A
Dinty
Dog of the Regiment, A
Eternal Three, The

Glad Rags
Goldwyn player 21
Grand Larceny
Heart of Twenty, The
Home Struck
Limited Mail, The
One Round Hogan
Parisian Scandal, A
Son of Wallingford, The (Jimmy Wallingford)
Wall Flower, The

2116
GALVANI, Dino (1890-1960)
British films from 1908-1929

2117
GAMBLE, Fred*
Tornado, The
Tumbleweeds

2118
GAMBLE, Jerry*
13 Washington Square

2119
GAMBLE, Warburton*
Fine Feathers
Paliser Case, The

2120
GAMBOLD, Fred*
Black Oxen (Oglethorpe's butler)
Red Mill, The (innkeeper)

2121
GAMBY-HALE BALLET GIRLS
Cocoanuts, The
Hole in the Wall, The

2122
GAMUT, David*
Last of the Mohicans, The

2123
GANCE, Marguerite*
La Chute de la Maison Usher [The Fall of the House of Usher]

2124
GANTVOORI, Carl*
When Romance Rides

2125
GANZHERN, Jack*
Iron Horse, The

2125a
GARAT, Monsieur*
Count of Monte Cristo, The [serial] (Fernand Mondego)

2126
GARBINI, Aristide*
Messalina

2127
GARBO, Greta (Greta Lovisa Gustafsson) (1905-)
Divine Woman, The (Marianne)
Flesh and the Devil (Felicitas)
Die Freudlose Gasse [The Joyless Street] /aka/ The Street of Sorrow (Grete Rumfort)
Kiss, The (Irene Guarry)
Love (Anna Karenina)
Man's a Man, A (herself)
Mysterious Lady, The (Tania)
Peter the Tramp (Greta)
Single Standard, The (Arden Stuart)
Story of Gösta Berling (Countess Elizabeth Dohna)
Temptress, The (Elena)
Torrent, The (Leonora Moreno)
Wild Orchids (Lillie Sterling)
Woman of Affairs, A (Diana Merrick)

2128
GARCIA, Allan*
Circus, The (circus proprietor)
Idle Class, The
Pay Day

2129
GARDE, Betty (1905-)
Lady Lies, The

2130
GARDEN, Faith*
This Freedom (Flora)

2131
GARDENER, Buster*
Best Bad Man, The (Hank Smith)
Circus Ace, The
Deadwood Coach, The

2132
GARDNER, Betty*
This Freedom

2133
GARDNER, Helen*
Sandra

2134
GARDNER, Jack
Bluff
To the Ladies
Wild Bill Hickok

2135
GARDNER, James*
Amateur Gentleman, The (Ronald
   Barrymore)

2136
GARDNER, Shayle*
Chinese Bungalow, The (Richard
   Marquess)
Comin' Thro' the Rye (Paul Vasher)
Disraeli (Dr. Williams)
Three Live Ghosts
Wandering Jew, The (Pietro)

2137
GARON, Pauline (1901-1965)
Adam's Rib (Mathilda Ramsay)
Becky Sharp
Candy Kid, The
Children of the Dust
Christine of the Big Tops
College Hero, The
Compromise
Devil's Cage, The
Dugan of the Dugout
Eager Lips
Flaming Waters
Gamblers, The
Girl He Didn't Buy
Heart of Broadway
In the Headlines
Ladies at East
Life's Mockery
Loves of Sunya, The (Anne Hagen)
Man from Glengarry, The
Must We Marry?
Naughty
Paramount player 25
Passionate Youth
Power Within, The
Princess of Broadway
Reily of the Rainbow Division
Reported Missing
Rose of the World
Satan in Sables
Show of Shows, The
Sonny
Splendid Road, The
Temptations of a Shop Girl
Where Was I?
Wine of Youth

You Can't Fool Your Wife

2138
GARREL, S. *
Czar Ivan the Terrible

2139
GARRICK, John (1902-)
Married in Hollywood
Sky Hawk, The (Jack Bardell)

2140
GARRISON, Isabelle*
Civilian Clothes (Mrs. Arkwright)

2141
GARRISON, Robert*
Chained
Constant Nymph, The (Trigorin)
Die Freudlose Gasse [The Joyless
   Street] /aka/ The Street of Sor-
   row (Ganez)
Das Schiff der Verlorenen Menschen
   [The Ship of Lost Men] (crew
   member)

2142
GARRISON, William Allen "Slickem"*
Hallelujah! (the heavy)

2143
GARRON, Kurt*
Dancing Vienna

2144
GARSIA, Marston*
Skin Game, The (Fellows)

2145
GARVEY, Ed*
East Side, West Side

2146
GARVIN, Anita (1907-)
All Steamed Up
Battle of the Century, The (lady who
   sits on pie)
Bertha, the Sewing Machine Girl
Charlatan, The
Crazy Feet
Dynamite
From Soup to Nuts
Pair of Tights, A
Play Girl, The
Sailors Beware!
Stepping Out
Their Purple Moment

2147
GARYINE, Anita*
Night Watch, The

2148
GATTY, Scott*
Blinkeyes (Mr. Banning)

2149
GAULTIER, Henry*
Passion of Joan of Arc

2150
GAWTHORNE, Peter (1884-1962)
Behind that Curtain (Insp. of Scotland Yard)
Sunny Side Up (Lake)

2151
GAXTON, William (Arturo Antonio Gaxiola) (1893-1963)
It's the Old Army Game (George Parker)
Stage:
Connecticut Yankee, A (Martin) 27
Fifty Million Frenchmen (Peter Forbes) 29

2152
GAY, Dixie*
Leaping Love
Two Weeks Off
Why Be Good?

2153
GAY, Gregory /aka/ Gregory Gaye*
They Had to See Paris (Prince Ordinsky)

2154
GAY, Marjorie (1917-   )
Alice in Cartoonland [see: under title]
Alice's Wonderland
Fighting Marine, The
Volcano (Marie de Chauvalon)

2155
GAYE, Howard*
Dante's Inferno
Passion's Playground
Prince of Lovers, The
Scaramouche (Viscount d'Albert)

2156
GAYER, Echlin*
Her Love Story

2157
GAYNOR, Janet (Laura Gainor) (1906-   )
Born in Philadelphia, Pennsylvania, October 6, 1906. Auburn hair, brown eyes, 5'. Married Lydell Peck, September, 1929, divorced 1933. Married Adrian, Aug. 14, 1939, he died Sept. 13, 1959. Married Paul Gregory, Dec. 24, 1964. One son, Robin, born July 7, 1940. Performed in school plays and at Great Lakes Naval Station in Chicago, Illinois where she and her sister, Helen, gave readings. Prior to The Johnstown Flood, Janet and her sister did extra work for Hal Roach. Janet then had various bit parts in FBO shorts; then appeared in several Roach two-reel comedies. Moving on to Universal Studios and feminine leads in cowboy films with Peewee Holmes and Ben Corbin. She had some dress-extra parts in Laura La Plante films--all under the name of Laura Gainor. She changed her name to Janet Gaynor and screen-tested at Fox for The Johnstown Flood. She won the first Academy Award for Best Actress for three films: Seventh Heaven, Sunrise, and Street Angel.
Blue Eagle, The (Rose Cooper)
Christina (Title role)
Four Devils (Marian)
Happy Days (a principal)
Johnstown Flood, The (Anna Burger)
Lucky Star (Mary Tucker)
Midnight Kiss, The (Mildred Hastings)
Pigs
Return of Peter Grimm, The (Catherine)
Seventh Heaven (Diane)
Shamrock Handicap, The (Sheila Gaffney)
Street Angel (Angela)
Sunny Side Up (Molly Carr)
Sunrise (the wife)
Two Girls Wanted (Marianna Miller)

2158
GEAR, Luella*
Adam and Eva
Stage:
Queen High (Florence Cole) 26

2159
GEARY, Maine*
Hill Billy, The
Robin Hood (Will Scarlett)
Soft Living

2160
GEBUEHR, Otto*
Waterloo

2161
GEBUHR, Otto*
Fredericus Rex

2162
GEHRING, Viktor*
Monna Vanna

2163
GEIZEL, John*
Rainbow Riley

2164
GELCKLER, Robert*
Mother's Boy (Gus leGrand)

2165
GELDERT, Clarence (1867-1936)
Adam's Rib (James Kilkenna)
Affairs of Anatol, The
All Souls' Eve
Always Audacious
Bishop Murder Case, The
Crooked Streets
Dress Parade
Fighting American, The
Flaming Forest, The
Ghost Talks, The
Great Moment, The (Bronson)
Hell Diggers
House that Jazz Built, The
Humming Wives
Love's Whirlpool
North of '36
Oh, Doctor!
Overland Telegraph
Richard the Lion-Hearted (Sir Con-
    rad de Montserrat)
Sioux Blood
Square Shoulders
Sweetie Peach
Thirteenth Chair, The
Unholy Night, The (Insp. Lewis)
Wasted Lives
Why Change Your Wife? (doctor)
Woman of Paris, A (Marie's father)
Young April

2166
GEMIER, Firmin*
Magician, The

2167
GENDRON, Pierre (1896-1956)
Bashful Suitor, The
Dangerous Flirt, The
Just Off Broadway
Lover of Camille, The
Man Who Played God, The
Three Women (Fred Colman)
Young Painter, The

2168
GEORGE, Gladys (Gladys Anna Clare)
    (1902-1954)
Below the Surface
Chickens
Easy Road, The
Homespun Folks
House that Jazz Built, The
Ince player 21

2169
GEORGE, Heinrich*
Armored Vault, The
Bondage
Der Mensch am Wege (Man by the
    Roadside)
Metropolis (Grot Number 7)
Theatre
Wasted Love
When Fleet Meets Fleet (German
    Commander's Chief Gunner)
Whirl of Life, The
Wrath of the Sea

2170
GEORGE, John*
Big City, The (the Arab)
Condemned (prison inmate)
Don Juan (hunchback)
Night of Love, The (Jester)
Road to Mandalay, The
Scaramouche (Polichinelle)
Unknown, The (Cojo)
Where the Pavement Ends (Napuka
    Joe)

2171
GEORGE, Maud (1890-)
After the Storm
Altars of Desire
Devil's Passkey, The (Madame Malot)
Foolish Wives (Princess Olga Petsch-
    nikoff)
Garden of Eden, The

Heart Strings
Honeymoon
Isle of Lost Men, The
Love Toy, The
Madame X
Merry-Go-Round (Madame Elvira)
Monte Cristo (Madame Douglass)
Road to Destiny, The
Six Days
Universal player 23
Veiled Woman, The
Wedding March, The (Princess Ma-
    ria)
Woman from Moscow
Worldly Goods

2172
GEORGE, Paul*
Passion of Jeanne of Arc, The

2173
GEORGE, Voya*
Legion of the Condemned (gambler)

2174
GEPPERT, Carl*
Jew of Mestri, The (Rippo)

2175
GERACHTY, Carmelita (1901-1966)
Bag and Baggage
Black Oxen (Anna Goodrich)
Button My Back
Campus Carmen, The
Canyon of Light
Daughter of Mother McGinn, The
Eternal Three, The
Flying Mail, The
Good-Bye Kiss, The
Great Gatsby, The
Last Trail, The
Mississippi Gambler, The
My Best Girl
My Lady of Whim (Wayne Leigh)
Object, Alimony
Paris Bound (Noel Farley)
Pleasure Garden, The
Rosita
Selznick player 24
Slaver, The
South of Panama
This Thing Called Love (Alvarez
    Guerra)
Through the Dark
To Have and to Hold
Under the Rouge
Venus of Venice
What Every Girl Should Know

2176
GERALD, Jim (Jacques Guenod)
    (1889-1958)
Un Chapeau de Paille d'Italia [The
    Italian Straw Hat]

2177
GERARD, Carl*
Ladies of the Mob (Joe)
Uncharted Seas
Up in Mabel's Room
Voice from the Minaret, The (Stan-
    hope Barry)
Wild Bill Hickok

2177a
GERARD, Charles--see: Charles
    Gerrard

2178
GERARD, Joseph*
Fleet's In, The (commandant)

2179
GERARD, Teddie*
Cave Girl, The

2180
GERASCH, Alfred*
Carnival Crime, The
Eine Du Barry von Heute [A Modern
    Du Barry] (Count Rabbatz)
Spy of Madame de Pompadour, The

2181
GERASIMOV, Sergei*
New Babylon

2182
GERBER, Neva*
Branded Four, The [serial]
Days of '49, The [serial] (Sonora
    Cardosa)
Mystery Box, The [serial]
Officer 444 [serial] (Gloria Grey)
Power of God, The [serial]
Santa Fe Trail, The
Screaming Shadow, The [serial]

2183
GERDES, Emily*
Ella Cinders

2184
GERLACH-JACOBI*
Der Mensch am Wege [Man by the
    Roadside]

2185
GERRARD, Charles (1887-)
Anna Ascends
Argyle Case, The
Better 'Ole, The
Blackbirds
California Straight Ahead
Caught in the Fog
Cheerful Fraud, The
Circe the Enchantress
Circumstantial Evidence
Conceit
Dangerous Maid
Darling of the Rich, The
Five and Ten Cent Annie
For Wives Only
Framed
French Heels
General Crack
Gilded Lily, The (John Stewart)
Glad Rag Doll
Glimpses of the Moon
Heart Thief, The
Her Temporary Husband
Heroes and Husbands
Home Made
Ladies of the Night Club
Light Fingers
Lights of New York
Lilies of the Field
Lone Wolf's Daughter, The
Madonna of Avenue A
Man on the Box, The
Mary Ellen Comes to Town
Nervous Wreck, The
Out of the Chorus
Painting the Town
Passionate Pilgrim, The
Pawned
Play Safe
Port of Missing Girls, The
Richard the Lion-Hearted (Sultan
    Saladin)
Romance of a Rogue
Sure-Fire Flint
When Knighthood Was in Flower
    (Sir Adam Judson)
Whispers
World and His Wife, The
You Can't Kill Love

2186
GERRARD, Douglas (1888-1950)
Argyle Case, The (Finley)
College Widow, The
Dearie
Desired Woman, The
First Auto, The

Five and Ten Cent Annie
Footloose Widows
General Crack (Capt. Sweeney)
Ginsberg the Great
Glad Rag Doll
Hottentot, The
Ladies of the Night Club
Lighthouse by the Sea, The
Madonna of Avenue A
Million Bid, A
Omar the Tentmaker
Tailor Made Man, The
Wolf's Clothing

2187
GERRON, Kurt*
Berlin after Dark
Diary of a Lost Girl, The
Manege
Sein Grösster Bluff [Her Greatest
    Bluff] (Rajah of Johore)
Strange Case of Captain Ramper, The
Survival
Variété [variety]

2188
GERSON, Charles*
Pony Express

2189
GERT, Valeska*
Diary of a Lost Girl, The
Die Freudlose Gasse [The Joyless
    Street] /aka/ The Street of Sor-
    row (Mrs. Greifer)
Midsummer Night's Dream, A (Puck)
Nana

2190
GETCHELL, Summer*
College Love
Flying Fleet, The
New Year's Eve

2191
GEURIN-CATELAIN, Raymond*
Nana

2192
GEVA, Tamara*
Night Club

2193
GEYMOND, Vital*
Un Chapeau de Paille d'Italie [The
    Italian Straw Hat]

2194
GHENT, Derek*
Four Horsemen of the Apocalypse,
    The (Rene Locour)

2195
GHIONE, Emile*
Last Days of Pompeii, The (Calenus)

2196
GIBLYN, Charles /aka/ Charles
    Gibbin*
Her Wild Oat
Mysterious Dr. Fu Manchu, The
    /aka/ The Insidious Dr. Fu
    Manchu
Woman Trap

2197
GIBSON, Ethlyn*
Winnie Winkle (Title role)

2198
GIBSON, Florence*
Greed (old hag)

2199
GIBSON, Helen (Rose August Wenger)
    (1892-)
Chinatown Mystery, The [serial]
Dynamite Special, The
Frustrated Holdup, The
Ghost of the Canyon, The
Girl's Decision, A
Man of God, A
Nine Points of the Law
No Man's Woman
Run of the Yellow Mail, The
Thoroughbred, The
Vanishing West, The [serial]
Why Worry?
Wolverine, The

2200
GIBSON, Hoot (Edward Gibson) (1892-
    1962)
Action
Arizona Sweepstakes
Bearcat, The
Blinky
Broadway or Bust
Buckaroo Kid, The
Burning the Wind
Calgary Stampede
Chip of the Flying-U
Clearing the Trail
Courtin' Wildcats
Danger Rider

Dead Game
Denver Dude, The
Double Dealing
Doubling for Trouble
Fighting Fury
Fire Eater, The
Flaming Frontier, The (Bob Langdon)
Flying Cowboy
Flying Fists
Forty Horses Hawkins
Galloping Fury
Galloping Kid, The
Gentleman from America, The
Harmony Ranch
Hero on Horseback
Hey, Hey, Cowboy!
Hit and Run (Swat Anderson)
Hook and Ladder
Hurricane Kid, The
Kindled Courage
King of the Rodeo
Lariat Kid, The
Let 'Er Buck!
Locked Door, The
Lone Hand, The
Long, Long Trail, The
Man in the Saddle, The
Man with the Punch, The
Mounted Stranger, The
On Sunset Range
Out of Luck
Painted Ponies
Pair of Twins, A
Phantom Bullet, The
Points West
Prairie King, The
Ramblin' Kid, The
Rawhide Kid, The
Red Courage
Ride for Your Life
Ridin' Kid from Powder River
Ridin' Wild
Riding for Fame
Roaring Dan
Saddle Hawk, The
Saddle King, The
Sawdust Trail, The
Shamless Salvation
Sheriff's Oath, The
Shootin' for Love
Should Husbands Mind Babies?
Silent Rider, The
Silks and Saddles
Single Handed
Smilin' Guns
Smilin' Kid, The
Spook Ranch
Step on It!

Sure Fire
Taming of the West
Texas Streak, The
Thrill Chaser, The
Trimmed
West Is West
Wild West Show
Winged Horseman, The

2201
GIBSON, James*
Greed (Deputy Sheriff)

2202
GIBSON, Kenneth*
Ashes of Vengeance (Phillippe)
Idle Rich, The

2203
GIBSON, Vivian*
Scandal in Paris, A

2204
GIBSON, Wynne (1907-)
Nothing But the Truth

2205
GIDDINGS, Jack*
Man's Mate, A

2206
GIELGUD, John (1904-)
Clue of the New Pin, The
Who Is the Man?
Stage:
Patriot, The (American debut; Grand
  Duke Alexander) 28

2207
GIERE, Helen*
Loves of an Actress
Time to Love

2208
GILARDONI, Eugenio*
Retribution

2209
GILBERT, Billy (1894-1971)
Betwixt and Between
Flaming Youth
Horse Play
Movie Mania
Noisy Neighbors
Simple Sap, A
Woman from Hell /aka/ Woman
  from Hell's Paradise
Woman Tamer, The

2210
GILBERT, Eugenie*
After the Storm
By Whose Hand?
Half-Breed, The (Marianne)
King of the Kongo
Obey the Law
Phantom City
Sinners in Silk
So This Is Marriage

2211
GILBERT, Florence /aka/ Flo*
Johnstown Flood, The (Gloria)
Return of Peter Grimm, The (Anne-
  marie)
Youth and Beauty

2212
GILBERT, John (John Pringle) (1895-
  1936)
Arabian Love
Bardely's the Magnificent (Marquis
  de Bardely)
Big Parade, The (Jim Apperson)
California Romance, A
Calvert's Valley
Cameo Kirby
Cossacks, The (Lukashka)
Deep Waters
Desert Nights
Exiles, The
Flesh and the Devil (Leo von Sellen-
  thin)
Four Walls (Benny)
Gleam O'Dawn
Glory of Love, The
Great Redeemer, The
He Who Gets Slapped (Bezano)
His Glorious Night
His Hour
Hollywood Revue of 1929 (Romeo)
Honor First (dual role)
Just Off Broadway
La Boheme (Rudolphe)
Ladies Must Live
Lone Chance, The
Love (Vronsky)
Love Gambler, The
Madness of Youth, The
Man, Woman and Sin
Man's Man, A (himself)
Man's Mate, A
Masks of the Devil, The
Merry Widow, The (Prince Danilo)
Monte Cristo (Edmund Dantes)
Red Viper, The
Redemption

Romance Ranch
Saint Elmo
Servant in the House, The
Shame
Should Women Tell?
Show, The
Show People (cameo)
Smith's Pony
Snob, The
Truxton King, The
Twelve Miles Out (Jerry Fay)
While Paris Sleeps (Dennis O'Keefe)
White Circle, The
Widow by Proxy
Wife of the Centaur, The
Wolf Man, The
Woman of Affairs, A (Neville)
Yellow Stain, The

2213
GILBERT, Lewis*
Dick Turpin's Ride to New York
  (Tom King)
Wandering Jew, The (Mario)

2214
GILES, Corliss*
Mountain Woman, The

2215
GILL, Basil (1877-1955)
High Treason (President of Europe)
Julius Caesar
Santa Claus
Worldlings, The

2216
GILL, Maud*
Under the Greenwood Tree (old maid)

2217
GILLEN, Ernest*
Any Woman
Auction Block, The (Carter Lane)
His Secretary

2218
GILLESPIE, William (1894-)
Easy Street
Exit Smiling
Grandma's Boy
High and Dizzy
Horse Shy
Now or Never

2219
GILLETTE, Robert*
Stella Dallas (Helen's son, 10 years

later)

2220
GILLINGWATER, Claude (1879-1939)
Alice Adams
Barbed Wire
Chapter in Her Life, A
Cheaper to Marry
Christian, The (Lord Storm)
Crinoline Romance, A
Daddies
Dangerous Woman, A
Dulcy
Dust Flower, The
Fast and Furious
Fools First
For Wives Only
Glad Rag Doll
Gorilla, The
Great Divide, The
Ham and Eggs at the Front
How to Educate a Wife
Husbands for Rent
Idle Tongues
Into Her Kingdom
Kentucky Courage
Little Lord Fauntleroy (Earl of Do-
  rincourt)
Little Shepherd of Kingdom
  Come, The
Madonna of the Streets, A (Lord
  Patrington)
My Boy
Naughty, but Nice (Judge J. R. Ate-
  wood)
Oh, Kay!
Rememberance
Seven Sinners
Smiling Irish Eyes
So Long Letty
Stark Mad
Stolen Kisses
Stranger's Banquet, The
That's My Baby
Thief in Paradise, A
Three Wise Fools
Tiger Rose
Wages of Wives
Warner Brothers player 25
We Moderns
Winds of Chance
Women They Talk About

2221
GILLMAN, Arita*
Gold Diggers, The (Eleanor Board-
  man)

2222
GILMAN, Fred*
Texas Ranger series

2223
GILMORE, Barney*
South Sea Love

2224
GILMORE, Douglas*
Dance Madness
Kiss in a Taxi, A
Married in Hollywood
One Woman Idea
Paramount player 26
Paris (the cat)
Pleasure Crazed
Rough House Rosie (Arthur Russell)
Sally, Irene and Mary (Glen Nester)
Taxi Dancer, The (Jim Kelvin)

2225
GILMORE, Helen*
Sensation Seekers

2226
GILMORE, J. H. *
Democracy, The Vision Restored

2227
GILMORE, Lillian*
Mojave Kid, The
Straight Shootin'

2228
GILSON, Charles*
Little Johnny Jones

2229
GINSBERG, Harry*
Condemned (prison inmate)

2230
GIRACCI, May*
Miss Lulu Bett (Manona Deacon)
Son of Tarzan, The (Meriam as a
    girl) [serial]

2231
GIRACI, Mary*
Lorna Doone
Miss Lulu Bett
Secrets (Audrey Carlton as a child)

2232
GIRARD, Joseph W. (1871-1949)
Back from Shanghai
Blue Fox, The [serial]

Branded Four, The [serial]
Branded H, The [serial]
Broken Barriers
Bullet Mark, The
Courtin' Wildcats
Crimson Lash, The [serial]
Dangerous Dub, The
Dangerous Paths
Devil's Door Yard, The
Eagle's Talons, The [serial]
Fatal Sign, The [serial]
Figurehead, The
Fireman, Save My Child!
Fleet's In, The
From Headquarters
Girl from Havana, The
Girl of the Golden West
Hello, Cheyenne
In Hollywood with Potash and Perl-
    mutter
Jazz Mad
King of the Rodeo
Lady Bird
Leatherneck, The
Hysteria
Nan of the North [serial]
One Woman Idea
One Wonderful Night
Partners in Crime
Perils of the Yukon [serial]
Redskin, The
Screaming Shadow, The [serial]
Sheriff of Hope Eternal
Silent Hero, The
Step on It!
Terror, The (Inspector Hallick)
When Seconds Count
Whispering Sage
Wolves of the North [serial]

2233
GISH, Dorothy de Guiche) (1898-1968)
Beautiful City, The
Bright Shawl, The (La Clavel)
Clothes Make the Pirate
Country Flapper, The
Flying Pat
Fury
Ghost in the Garret, The
Little Miss Rebellion
London
Madame Pompadour (Title role)
Mary Ellen Comes to Town
Nell Gwyn (Title role)
Night Life in New York
Old Joe
Ole Swimmin' Hole, The
Orphans of the Storm (Louise Girard)

Out of Luck
Paramount player 20
Remodeling Her Husband
Romola (Tessa)
Tip Toes
Stage:
Young Love (Fay Hilary) 28

2234
GISH, Lillian (Lillian Diana de
   Guiche) (1896-)
Annie Laurie /aka/ Ladies from
   Hell (Title role)
Enemy, The
Greatest Question, The
La Boheme (Mimi)
Love Flower, The
Orphans of the Storm (Henriette
   Girard)
Romola (Title role)
Scarlet Letter, The (Hester Prynne)
Way Down East (Anna Moore)
White Sister, The (Angela Chiar-
   monte)
Wind, The (Letty)
World Shadows (unfinished)

2235
GLASS, Gaston (1899-1965)
After the Ball
Behind Closed Doors
Branded Woman, The
Broken Barriers
Cameron of the Royal Mounted
Daughters of the Rich
Easy Payments
Exclusive Rights
Faker, The
Foreigner, The
Geraldine
Gimme
Gorilla, The
Her Sacrifice
Her Winning Ways
Hero, The
Humoresque
I Am the Law
I Am the Man
Little Miss Smiles
Monte Cristo (Albert)
Mothers-in-Law
My Home Town
Name the Woman
Obey Your Husband
Paramount player 21
Parisian Nights
Pity the Chorus Girl
Red Mark, The

Rich Men's Wives
Romance of a Million Dollars
Scarlet West, The (Captain Howard)
Show Girl
Sinews of Steel
Song of Life, The
Spider and the Rose, The
Subway Sadie
Sweet Daddies
Tentacles of the North
There Are No Villains
Tiger Rose (Pierre)
Untamed Justice
Wife's Relations, The
Woman's Justice, A
World and His Wife, The

2236
GLASSNER, Erika*
Tragödie der Liebe [Tragedy of Love]
   (Musette)

2237
GLAUM, Louise (1894-)
Fifty-Fifty
Girl Who Dared, The
Hodkinson player 22
I Am Guilty
Leopard Woman, The
Love
Love Madness
Sex

2238
GLEASON, Ada*
College Coquette, The
How Baxter Buttered In
Man Bait

2239
GLEASON, James (1886-1959)
Broadway Melody, The (Jimmy Glea-
   son, music publisher)
Count of Ten, The
Oh Yeah!
Polly of the Follies
Shannons of Broadway, The
Stage:
Charm School, The (George Boyd) 20
Is Zat So? (A. B. "Hap" Hurley)
Shannons of Broadway, The (Mickey
   Shannon) 27

2240
GLEASON, Lucille (Lucille Webster)
   (1886-1947)
Shannons of Broadway, The

Stage:
Shannons of Broadway, The (Emma
  Shannon) 27

2241
GLEASON, Russell (1908-1945)
Flying Fool, The
Officer O'Brien
Seven Faces
Shady Lady
Sisters
Sophomore, The
Strange Cargo

2242
GLECKLER, Robert*
Mother's Boy

2243
GLEIZER, Judith*
Stachka /aka/ Strike

2244
GLENDENNING, Ernest (1884-1936)
When Knighthood Was in Flower
  (Sir Edward Caskoden)
Stage:
Little Old New York (Larry Delevan)
  20

2245
GLENDON, J. Frank (1885-   )
Hush Money
Lights of Old Broadway (Thomas A.
  Edison)
Mid-Channel
Roman Candles
Soul of Rafael
Tale of Two Worlds, A (Newcomb)
Three Pals
Tricks
Upstage
What Do Men Want?
Woman in the Web

2246
GLENN, Raymond*
Ladies at Ease

2247
GLORY, Mary*
L'Argent

2248
GLYN, Elinor (1864-1943)
Affairs of Anatol, The (bridge play-
  er)
It (herself)

2249
GLYNNE, Derke*
Only Thing, The

2250
GLYNNE, Marg (1898-1954)
Bonnie Brier Bush, The
Hundredth Chance, The

2251
GODDARD, Alf /aka/ Alfred*
Alf's Button (Bill Grant)
Balaclava (Nobby)
Downhill (Swede)
Every Mother's Son (Bully)
Hindle Wakes /aka/ Fanny Haw-
  thorne (Nobby)
Mademoiselle from Armentieres
  (Fred)
Mademoiselle Parley-Voo (Fred)

2252
GODDARD, Paulette (Marion Levy)
  (1911-   )
Berth Marks (extra)
Stage:
No Foolin' (Peaches) 26
Ziegfeld Follies 25

2253
GODFREY, George*
Old Ironsides

2254
GODOWSKY, Dagmar (1897-1975)
Altar Stairs, The
Bands of Honor
Cheat, The
Common Law, The
Forced Bride
Hitchin' Posts, The
Honor Bound
In Borrowed Plumes
Marriage Pit, The
Meddling Women
Path She Chose, The
Peddler of Lies, The
Price of a Party, The
Rear Car, The
Red Lights
Roulette
Sainted Devil, A (Dona Florencia)
Story Without a Name, The
Stranger's Banquet, The
Stronger than Death
Throwback, The
Trap, The (Thalie)
Universal player 21

Virtuous Liars

2255
GOETHALS, Stanley*
Outside the Law ("That Kid")
Trap, The (the boy)

2256
GOETZ, Carl*
Pandora's Box
That Murder in Berlin

2257
GOETZKE, Bernard /aka/ Bern-
    hardt*
Children of No Importance
Destiny /aka/ The Tired Death; The
    Three Lights; Between Worlds;
    Der Mude Tod
Die Nibelungen /aka/ The Nibelungs
    (Volker)
Dr. Mabuse, the Gambler /aka/ Dr.
    Mabuse, the Great Unknown (Po-
    lice Chief DeWitt)
Guilty
Kriemhild's Revenge
Last Days of Pompeii, The (Arbaces)
Peter the Great
Schuldig
Slums of Berlin
Vanina
When Fleet Meets Fleet (German
    Commander)
Wrath of the Sea, The

2258
GOLDFADEN, Wolf*
Broken Hearts

2259
GOLIZIN, Natalie*
Napoleon's Barber

2260
GOMAROV, Mikhail*
Battleship Potemkin
Stachka /aka/ Strike

2261
GOMBELL, Minna /aka/ Winifred
    Lee/Nancy Carter (1900-1973)
Great Power, The

2262
GOMEZ, Inez*
Temptress, The

2263
GOMOROV, G. *
Potemkin (sailor)

2264
GOMOROV, Mikhail--see: Mikhail
    Gomarov

2265
GONDER, Bill*
Woman Proof

2266
GONZALES, Mark*
Argentine Love
Great Deception, The

2267
GOODALE, Elois*
Broadway Gold

2268
GOODALL, Grace*
Easy Road, The

2269
GOODRICH, Jack*
Man Who Laughs, The (clown)

2269a
GOODSELL, Alice*
Happy Days (chorus)

2270
GOODWIN, Aline*
Desert Gold

2271
GOODWIN, Harold (1902-)
Alice Adams
Bearcat, The
Bootlegger's Daughter, The
Cameraman, The
Cheer Leader, The
College
Don't Get Excited
Family Honor
Flaming Frontier, The
Flight
Her Summer Hero
Honeymoon Express, The
Kindled Courage
Kissed
Madonna of the Streets, A (Howard
    Bowman)
Man to Man
Midshipman, The
Mighty, The

Oliver Twist, Jr.
Overland Red
Pollyanna
Riders of the Purple Sage (Bern Venters)
Road Demon, The
Rosary, The
Seeing Is Believing
Snapshots
Snowbound
Suds
Sweet Lavender
Talker, The
Tarzan and the Golden Lion (overseerer)
Tracked to Earth
You Never Can Tell

2272
GOODWIN, Tom*
Into the Net [serial]
Phantom Foe, The

2273
GOODWINS, Fred*
Blood Money (Bruce Harper)

2274
GORCEY, Bernard*
Abie's Irish Rose (Isaac Cohen)

2274a
GORDON, Betty*
Happy Days (chorus)

2275
GORDON, Bobby (1913-   )
Cohens and the Kellys, The
Jazz Singer, The (Jakie, age 13)
Main Street
Penrod and Sam (Maurice Levy)

2276
GORDON, Bruce (1919-   )
After Many Days
Battling Brewster [serial]
Blazing Days
Born to the West
Bring Him In
Bucking the Truth
Clean-Up, The
Democracy, The Vision Restored
Desert Dust
Escape /aka/ The Exquisite Sinner
First Men in the Moon
Forbidden Valley
Fortieth Door, The [serial]
Hands Off!

House of the Tolling Bell
Isle of Sunken Gold, The
Life's Mockery
Little Child Shall Lead Them, A
Love Gambler, The
Moran of the Mounted
Mystery Rider [serial]
Outlaw Dog, The
Pals in Paradise
Partners in Crime
Poor Nut, The
Private Scandal, A
Riddle on the Range
Ruth of the Range [serial]
Smooth as Satin
Sonora Kid, The
Sowing and Reaping
Timber Queen, The
Toys
Transcontinental Limited
Vanishing Americans, The /aka/ The Vanishing Race

2277
GORDON, Charles*
Connecticut Yankee in King Arthur's Court, A (Clarence)

2278
GORDON, Dorothy*
Chorus Girl's Romance, A (Miss Wilson)

2279
GORDON, Eva*
Chechahcos, The
Lost Lady, A
White Moll, The

2280
GORDON, Gavin (1901-   )
All Steamed Up
Chasing Through Europe
His First Command
Knights Out

2281
GORDON, Grace*
Butterflies in the Rain
Lone Hand Wilson
Million Bid, A
Ranger and the Law, The

2282
GORDON, Harris*
Dawn of a Tomorrow, The

2283
GORDON, Huntly (1897-1956)
At the Stage Door
Beyond the Rainbow (Bruce Forbes)
Bluebeard's Eighth Wife (John Brandon)
Certain Young Man, A
Chastity
Dark Mirror, The
Don't Tell the Wife
Enemy Sex, The
Famous Mrs. Fair, The
Frisky Mrs. Johnson
Gilded Butterfly, The
Girl from Nowhere, The
Golden Cocoon, The
Golden Web, The
Gypsy of the North, The
Her Fatal Millions
Her Second Chance
His Wife's Husband
Lost at Sea
Love Hour, The
Marriage Playground, The (Cliff Wheater)
Married Flirts
Melody Lane
My Wife and I
Name the Woman
Never the Twain Shall Meet
Other Women's Husbands
Our Dancing Daughters (Diana's father)
Out of the Snow
Outcast, The
Pleasure Mad
Reckless Youth (Harrison Thornby)
Red Foam
Sally's Shoulders
Scandal
Selznick player 23
Sensation Seekers
Shadows of Paris
Silken Shackles
Sinners in Love
Society Snobs
Their Hour
Tropical Love
True as Steel
Truthful Sex, The
What Fools Men
What's Wrong with Women? (Lloyd Watson)
When the Desert Calls
Wife Who Wasn't Wanted, The
Wine (John Warriner)
Your Friend and Mine

2284
GORDON, James*
Escape, The
Excuse My Dust (Griggs)
Iron Horse, The (David Brandon, Sr.)
Last of the Mohicans (Hawkeye)
Man Who Came Back, The
Publicity Madness
Social Highwayman, The
Tumbleweeds
Wanderer of the Wasteland (Alex MacKay)

2285
GORDON, Joan*
Queen of Sheba, The (Nomis, Sheba's sister)

2286
GORDON, Julia Swayne (-1933)
Behold My Wife
Beloved Rogue, The
Bride of the Storm
Burn 'em up Barnes
Child for Sale, A
Children of Divorce (Princess de Sfax)
Dark Secrets
Darling of the Rich, The
Diplomacy
Divine Lady, The
Eternal Woman
Far Cry, The
Girl in the Glass Cage, The (Mrs. Pomfert)
Gold Diggers of Broadway (Cissy Gray)
Greater than Fame
Handcuffs or Kisses
Hearts of Men
Heaven on Earth
Heliotrope
Is Everybody Happy?
It (Mrs. Van Norman)
King of Kings, The (bit)
Leif the Lucky
Lifting Shadows
Lights of Old Broadway (Mrs. de-Rhonde)
My Old Kentucky Home
Nut Cracker, The /aka/ You Can't Fool Your Wife
Passionate Pilgrim, The
Road to Arcady, The
Roadhouse
Scandal
Scaramouche (Countess Therese de Pougastel)

Scarlet Dove, The
Shams of Society
Silver Lining
Smart Set, The
13 Washington Square
Three Weekends (Mrs. Witherspoon)
Tie that Binds, The
Till We Meet Again
Viking, The
What's Wrong with Women? (Mrs.
    Bascom)
When the Desert Calls
Why Girls Leave Home
Wilderness of Youth, The
Wings (Mrs. Armstrong)
Younger Generation

2287a
GORDON, Kay*
Happy Days (chorus)

2287
GORDON, Mary (1881-1963)
Clancy's Kosher Wedding
Dynamite (a neighbor)
Home Maker, The
Madame X (baby's nurse)
Saturday Night Kid, The (reducing
    customer)

2288
GORDON, Maude Turner (1870-)
Beyond Price
Cheating Cheaters
Civilian Clothes (Mrs. Lanham)
Enchantment
Glad Rag Doll
Home Made
Homeward Bound
Hottentot, The
Illusion
Just Married
Kid Gloves
Last of Mrs. Cheney, The (Mrs.
    Webby)
Little French Girl, The
Marriage Playground, The (Aunt
    Julia Langley)
Price of Possession, The
Sally (Mrs. TenBrock)
Sporting Goods
Wizard, The

2289
GORDON, Pete*
Golf

2290
GORDON, Robert (1895-1971)
Dollars and the Woman
Great Menace, The
If Women Only Knew
Main Street
Paramount player 21
Rosary, The
Super Sex, The
Vice of Fools

2291
GORDON, Roy Turner*
Palm Beach Girl, The

2292
GORDON, Sadie*
Vanity Fair (Miss Firkins)

2293
GORDON, Vera (1886-1948)
Cohens and the Kellys, The
Cohens and the Kellys in Atlantic
    City, The
Cohens and the Kellys in Paris, The
Four Walls (Benny's mother)
Good Provider
Greatest Love, The
Humoresque
In Hollywood with Potash and Perl-
    mutter
Kosher Kitty Kelly
Millionaires
Nice Baby
North Wind's Malice, The
Potash and Perlmutter
Private Izzy Murphy
Sorrows of Israel, The
Sweet Daddies
Your Best Friend

2294
GORDONI, Arthur*
Beyond Price

2295
GORE, Rosa*
Head Man, The (a twin)
Lovey Mary
Madonna of the Streets, A (Mrs. El-
    yard)
Once to Every Woman (Mrs. Jones)
Seven Days
Vanity Fair (Jemima Pinkerton)

2296
GORHAM, Charles*
In the Palace of the King

2297
GORLEY, Edward*
Nell Gwyn

2298
GORMAN, Bill*
Finders Keepers

2299
GORMAN, Charles*
Gay Retreat, The

2300
GOSNELL, Evelyn*
Under the Red Robe

2301
GOSS, Walter*
Fine Manners (Buddy Murphy)
Fireman, Save My Child!

2302
GOTHAM QUARTETTE, The
Alf's Button (themselves)

2303
GOTT, Barbara*
Downhill (Madame Michel)

2304
GOTTEL, Oscar*
Greed (a Sieppe twin)

2305
GOTTEL, Otto*
Greed (a Sieppe twin)

2306
GOTTLER, Archie*
Movietone Follies of 1929 (stage
manager)

2307
GOTTOWT, John*
Nosferatu
Das Wachsfigurenkabinett [The Wax-
works]

2308
GOTTSCHALK, Christian*
Han og Hun og Hamlet

2309
GOTTSCHALK, Ferdinand (1869-1944)
Zaza (Duke deBrissac)
Stage:
Buccaneer, The (Charles II) 25

2310
GOTZ, Carl--see: Carl Goetz

2311
GOTZ, Curt*
Tragödie der Liebe [Tragedy of Love]

2312
GÖTZ, Karl*
Prinzessin Olala [Princess Olala]
/aka/ Art of Love (an old cavalier)

2313
GOUDAL, Jetta (1898-)
Bright Shawl, The (La Pilar)
Cardboard Lover, The (Simone)
Coming of Amos, The
Fighting Love
Forbidden Woman, The
Green Goddess, The (the Ayal)
Her Man O'War
Lady of the Night
Lady of the Pavements (Countess
Diane des Granges)
Love Song
Matador, The
Open All Night
Paramount player 25
Paris at Midnight
Road to Yesterday, The (Malena
Poulton)
Salome of the Tenements
Shipwrecked
Spanish Love
Three Faces West
White Gold (Dolores Carson)
Stage:
Hero, The (Martha Roche) 21

2314
GOUCH, John (1897-)
Air Legion, The
Circus Kid, The
Flaming Waters
Gleam O'Dawn
Half a Chance
Judgment of the Hills
Night Patrol
Risky Business
Smooth as Satin
Street of Sin
Three Wise Crooks

2315
GOUGH, Wilfred Captain*
His Hour

2316
GOULD, Billy*
Great White Way, The

2317
GOULD, William*
Flirting with Love

2318
GOULDING, Alf*
Lady, The
Learning to Love

2319
GOWING, Gene*
Face Value

2320
GOWLAND, Gibson (1882-   )
Behind the Door
Border Legion, The
Broken Gates
Fighting Shepherdess, The
First Auto, The
Greed (McTeague)
Harbor Lights
Hell's Harbor
Isle of Forgotten Women
Ladies Must Live
Love and Glory
Mysterious Island, The
Night of Love, The (bandit)
Phantom of the Opera, The (Simon)
Prairie Wife
Red Lily, The (LeTurc)
Right of Way, The
Rose-Marie (Black Bastien)
Sea Bat, The
Shifting Sands
Topsy and Eva

2321
GOYER, Echlen*
Her Love Story (King)

2321a
GRABLE, Betty (Ruth Elizabeth Gra-
  ble) (1916-1973)
Happy Days (debut in chorus)

2322
GRACCIA, Ugo*
Kif Tebbi

2323
GRAETZ, Paul*
Die Bergatze /aka/ The Mountain
  Cat; The Wildcat (Zorfano)

Fight for the Matterhorn, The
Monna Vanna
Sumurun /aka/ One Arabian Night
  (Puffti)

2324
GRAFTON, Louise*
Irish Luck

2325
GRAHAM, Betty Jane*
Smitty

2326
GRAHAM, Charles*
Making of O'Malley
Mountain Woman, The
Untamed Lady (Shorty)

2327
GRAHAM, Frederick H. *
Knights Out
Music Fiends
Nix on Dames
Pleasure Crazed
Sin Sister

2328
GRAHAM, Martha*
Arabian Duet
Spanish Dancer, The

2329
GRAINGER, Jimmy, Jr. *
Joy Girl, The

2330
GRALLA, Dina*
Das Kund K Balletmaedel [The Royal
  Ballet Girl]
Love Commandment, The
Madame Wunscht Keine Kinder [Mad-
  ame Doesn't Want Children] /aka/
  Madame Wants No Children (Lulu)

2331
GRAN, Albert*
Beverly of Graustark (Duke Travina)
Blue Danube, The
Breakfast at Sunrise
Children of Divorce (Mr. Seymour)
Civilian Clothes (Dodson, the butler)
Dry Martini
Four Sons
Geraldine
Glad Rag Doll
Gold Diggers of Broadway (Blake)
Graustark (Count Halfont)

Her Night of Romance
Hula (Old Bill Calhoun)
Kibitzer, The
Mother Knows Best (Sam Kingston)
Our Modern Maidens (B. Bickering
  Brown)
Seventh Heaven (Boul)
Show of Shows, The
Soft Cushions
Tanned Legs
Tarnish
We Americans
Whip, The

2332
GRANACH, Alexander (1890-1945)
Der Mensch am Wege [Man by the
  Roadside] (Schuster)
Midsummer Night's Dream, A
  (Waldschrat)
Nosferatu
Schatten eine nachtliche Halluzination
Warning Shadows

2333
GRANADO, Manuel*
Bandolero, The

2334
GRANDEE, George*
Stranded in Paris

2335
GRANDIN, Ethel (1896-   )
Tailor Made Man, The

2336
GRANDSTEDT, Greta*
Behind Closed Doors
Close Harmony
College Love
Erik the Great
Excess Baggage
Girl Troubles
Mexicali Rose

2337
GRANGE, Red (Harold Grange)
One Minute to Play
Racing Romeo, A

2338
GRANGER, Dorothy*
Dance Hall
Sophomore, The
Words and Music (unbilled)

2339
GRANT, Frances Miller*
Dancer of Paris, The
Scarlet Saint, The

2340
GRANT, Harry Allen*
Danger Street

2341
GRANT, Katherine*
Oranges and Lemons
His Wooden Wedding
Kill or Cure
Looking for Sally

2342
GRANT, Lawrence (1898-1952)
At Yale
Bulldog Drummond (Dr. Lakington)
Canary Murder Case, The (John
  Cleaver)
Case of Lena Smith, The
Chorus Girl's Romance, A (Jose
  Brasswine)
Doomsday
Duchess of Buffalo, The
Exalted Flapper, The
Extravagance
Gentleman of Paris, A
Grand Duchess and the Waiter, The
Great Impersonation, The
Happiness
Held in Trust
His Hour
Hold 'em Yale!
Is Everybody Happy?
Rainbow, The
Red Hair (Judge Rufus Lennon)
Serenade
Service for Ladies
Someone in the House
Something Always Happens
Woman from Moscow

2343
GRAPEWIN, Charley (1896-1956)
Ladies' Choice
Only Saps Work
Shannons of Broadway, The /aka/
  Goodbye Broadway
That Red-Headed Hussy

2344
GRASSBY, Bertram (1880-   )
Beloved Rogue, The (Duke of Orleans)
Borderland
Captain Blood (Don Diego)

Drums of Fate
Fifty Candles
Fighting Chance
Fools in the Dark
For the Soul of Rafael
Havoc (Alexis Botskoy)
His Hour
His Lady /aka/ When a Man Loves
    (LeDuc de Richelieu)
Hold Your Horses
Hush Money
King Tut
Man from Brodney's, The
Mid-Channel
Midnight Express, The
Pioneer Trails
Straight from Paris
Tiger's Claw, The
Weekend, The

2345
GRATTON, Stephen*
Snow Bride, The

2346
GRÄTZ, Paul*
Tragödie der Liebe [Tragedy of Love]

2347
GRAUER, Bunny*
Town that God Forgot, The

2348
GRAUMANN, Karl*
Spy of Madame de Pompadour, The
Waterloo

2349
GRAVES, Ralph (1900-)
Alias the Deacon
Bachelor's Paradise, A
Bitter Sweets
Blarney
Cheer Leader, The
Christine of the Big Tops
Come on Over
Country Beyond, The
Daughters of Today
Dream Street (Spike McFadden)
Eternal Woman, The
Extra Girl, The
Fatal Warning, The [serial]
Flight
Flying Fleet, The
Ghost Patrol, The
Glad Rag Doll
Gold Braid
Greatest Question, The

Griffith player 24
Jilt, The
Just Like a Woman
Kindred of the Dust
Little Miss Rebellion
Long Chance, The
Mary Ellen Comes to Town
Mind over Matter
Out of Luck
Polly with a Past
Prodigal Daughters (Roger Corbin)
Reno Divorce, A
Rich Men's Shoes
Side Show
Silks and Saddles
Sisters
Smilin' Guns
Song of Love, The
Submarine
Swelled Head, A
That Certain Thing
Womanpower
Yolanda (Maximilian of Styria)

2350
GRAVES, Taylor*
Men of Steel
Miss Lulu Bett (Bobby Larkin)
Oliver Twist (Charley Bates)
Quincy Adams Sawyer (a Cobb twin)

2351
GRAVINA, Caesare (1858-)
Blonde Saint, The
Burning the Wind
Charmer, The
Cheating Cheaters
Circus Days
Contraband
Daddy
Divine Woman, The
Flower of the Night
Foolish Wives (Ventucci)
God's Country and the Law
Greed (Zerkow)
Honeymoon [unreleased]
How to Handle Women
Humming Bird, The (Charlot)
Madame X
Magic Garden
Man in the Saddle, The
Man Who Laughs, The (Ursus)
Merry-Go-Round (Sylvester Urban)
Midnight Sun, The
Phantom of the Opera, The (retiring
    manager)
Road to Romance, The
Scratch My Back

Trail of '98 (Berna's grandfather)
Wedding March, The (Mitzi's father)
Woman's Faith, A

2352
GRAY, Alexander*
No, No, Nanette (Tom Trainor)
Sally (Blair Farquar)
Show of Shows, The

2353
GRAY, Arnold*
Flame of the Yukon, The

2354
GRAY, Clifford*
Carnival

2355
GRAY, Eden*
Lovers in Quarantine

2356
GRAY, Elwood*
Bath Between, The

2357
GRAY, Eve (1904-)
Daughter of the Night
Moulin Rouge
One of the Best
Poppies of Flanders
Silver Lining, The
Smashing Through
Stage:
Australian stage 22

2358
GRAY, George Arthur*
Fire Detective, The

2359
GRAY, Gilda (Marianna Michalska)
   (1899-1959)
Aloma of the South Seas (Title role)
Cabaret
Devil Dancer, The
Lawful Larceny
Passionate Island
Piccadilly (Mabel Greenfield)
Stage:
Vaudeville 25
Ziegfeld Follies of 1922

2360
GRAY, Harry*
Hallelujah! (Parson)

2361
GRAY, Iris*
Fascinating Youth
Love's Greatest Mistake
Popular Sin, The
Rat, The (Rose)

2362
GRAY, Lawrence (1898-1970)
After Midnight
American Venus, The
Ankles Preferred
Are Parents People?
Callahan's and the Murphys, The
   (Dan Murphy)
Coast of Folly, The (bather)
Convoy
Deadline, The
Diamond Handcuffs
Domestic Meddlers
Dressmaker from Paris, The
Everybody's Acting
Family Row, The
Imperfect Ladies
It's a Great Life
Kid Boots (Tom Sterling)
Ladies Must Dress (Joe)
Love 'em and Leave 'em
Love Hungry
Marianne (Stag)
Marriage by Contract
Oh, Kay!
Pajamas
Palm Beach Girl, The
Patsy, The (Billy)
Rainbow, The
Shadows of the Night
Sin Sister (Peter Van Dykeman)
Stage Struck (Orme Wilson)
Telephone Girl
Tomorrow
Trent's Last Case
Untamed Lady (Larry Gastlen)

2363
GRAY, Lilian*
Life of Beethoven, The

2364
GRAY, Madeline*
Nothing but the Truth

2365
GRAZER, Wanda*
Dramatic Life of Abraham Lincoln,
   The /aka/ Abraham Lincoln

2366
GREEAR, Geraine*
Gaucho, The (Girl of the Shrine, as
   a child)

2367
GREELY, Evelyn*
Bulldog Drummond

2368
GREEN, Charles*
Bluebeard's Eighth Wife (Robert)
Empty Hands
Three Weeks

2369
GREEN, Harry (1892-1958)
Close Harmony (Max Mindel)
Kibitzer, The
Man I Love, The
Why Bring that Up?

2370
GREEN, Judd*
Chu-Chin-Chow (Ali Baba)
Nell Gwyn (sailor)
Only Way, The (prosecuting counsel)
Widdecombe Affair (landlord)
Woman Tempted, The

2371
GREEN, Mitzi (1920-1969)
Marriage Playground

2372
GREENE, Kempton (1890-)
Man from the Sea, The
Question of Right, A
Sentimental Tommy

2373
GREENWAY, Ann*
Half Marriage

2374
GREENWOOD, Charlotte (Frances
   Charlotte Greenwood (1893-)
Baby Mine
Passing Show, The
So Long Letty
Stage:
Music Box Revue 22

2375
GREENWOOD, Winifred*
Dollar a Year Man, The
Faith Healer, The
Jerry

King of Kings, The (bit)
Life of the Party, The
Sacred and Profane Love
Sick Abed
To the Last Man

2376
GREET, Clare (1871-)
Manxman, The

2377
GREGG, Arnold*
Skyrocket

2378
GREGORY, Edna (1905-)
Desert Flower, The
Her Favorite Hubby
In the Palace of the King

2379
GREGORY, Ena*
Blazing Days
Bush Ranger, The
Clean Sweep, A
Sioux Blood

2380
GREGORY, Will*
Sensation Seekers

2381
GREINER, Fritz*
Hungarian Rhapsody
Manon Lescaut (Marquis de Bli)
Sein Grösster Bluff [Her Greatest
   Bluff] (Hennessy)

2382
GRETILLAT, Jacques*
Nero

2383
GRETLER, Heinrich*
William Tell

2384
GREY, Anne (Aileen Ewing) (1907-)
Constant Nymph, The
Master and Man
Taxi for Two
Warning, The
What Money Can Buy

2385
GREY, Ethel*
Too Much Business
What Fools Men

2386
GREY, Gloria*
Blake of Scotland Yard [serial] (Lady
  Diana Blankton)
Dante's Inferno
Little Robinson Crusoe
Spirit of the U. S. A.

2387
GREY, Jack*
So Long Letty

2388
GREY, Lita (Lolita McMurry) (1908-)
Idle Class, The (debut)
Kid, The

2389
GREY, Minna*
Wee MacGreegor's Sweetheart (Aunt
  Mary Purvis)

2390
GREY, Ray*
Shriek of Araby, The

2391
GREY, Virginia (1917-   )
Heart to Heart
Jazz Mad
Michigan Kid, The
Uncle Tom's Cabin (debut as Eva)

2392
GRIBBON, Eddie (Edward T. Grib-
  bon) (1892-1905)
Alias Julius Caeser
Among Those Present
Astray from the Steerage (official
  sneak)
Bachelor's Paradise, A
Bat, The (Det. Anderson)
Border Legion, The
Buck Privates
Call a Cop
Callahans and the Murphys, The
  (Jim Callahan)
Captain Fly-by-Night
Cheating Cheaters
Clash, The
Code of the West (Tuck Merry)
Convoy
Crossed Wires
East of Broadway
Fancy Baggage
Flaming Frontier, The
Fourth Musketeer, The
From Headquarters

Furnished Rooms
Gang War
Heartbalm
Honeymoon [unreleased]
Hoodman Blind
Limited Mail, The
Love, Honor and Behave
Man Bait
Midnight Daddies
Molly-O
Mysterious Island
Nameless Men
Night Life (Nick)
Officer Cupid
On with the Show
Poor Worm, The
Road to Mandalay, The (Capt. Mad-
  den)
Seven Days
Shakedown, The
Small Town Idol, A
Smart Set
So Long Letty
Song of the West (Sgt. Major)
Speak Easy, The
Stop that Man!
Streets of Shanghai
Tailor Made Man, The
Tell It to the Marines
Tide of the Empire
Twin Beds
Two Men and a Maid
Two Weeks Off
United States Smith
Victor, The
Village Blacksmith, The

2393
GRIBBON, Harry (1888-1960)
Bat, The
Bee's Buzz, The
Big Polooka, The
Bride's Relations, The
Buck Privates
Cameraman, The
Clancy at the Bat
Constable, The
Don't Blame the Stork
Down on the Farm
Gang War
Golfers, The
His Smothered Love
Hollywood Star, A
Honeymoon [unreleased]
Knockout Reilly
Lunkhead, The
Movie Bug, A
Mysterious Island, The

New Halfback, The
On with the Show (Joe)
Rose-Marie (trooper)
Shakedown, The
Show People
Slipping Feet
Snapshots
So Long Letty
Tide of the Empire
Uppercut O'Brien
Whirls and Girls

2394
GRIFFIN, Basil*
Luck of the Navy, The (Anna)

2395
GRIFFIN, Carlton*
Girl Shy

2396
GRIFFIN, Russell Francis*
Beyond the Rainbow (Aldine)
Man Who Found Himself, The
Marriage Morals
Three O'Clock in the Morning

2397
GRIFFITH, Carlton*
Tramp, Tramp, Tramp

2398
GRIFFITH, Corinne (1898-)
Bab's Candidate
Black Oxen (dual role, Madame
    Zatianny/Mary Ogden)
Broadway Bubble
Classified
Common Law, The
Deadline at Eleven
Declassee
Divine Lady, The (Lady Emma Ham-
    ilton)
Divorce Coupons
Garden of Eden, The
Garden of Weeds
Garter Girl, The
Human Collateral
Infatuation
Into Her Kingdom
Island Wives
It Isn't Being Done This Season
Lady in Ermine
Lilies of the Field
Love's Wilderness
Mademoiselle Modiste
Marriage Whirl, The
Moral Fibre

Outcast, The
Prisoners
Received Payment
Saturday's Children
Single Track
Single Wives
Six Days
Smiling Irish Eyes
Syncopating Sue
Three Hours
Tower of Jewels, The
Virgin's Sacrifice, A
What's Your Reputation Worth?
Whisper Market, The
Yellow Girl, The

2399
GRIFFITH, Eleanor*
Alibi /aka/ Perfect Alibi, The (Joan
    Manning)

2400
GRIFFITH, Gordon*
Huckleberry Finn (Tom Sawyer)
Little Annie Rooney
Penrod
Son of Tarzan, The [serial] (Jack,
    the boy)
Village Blacksmith, The

2401
GRIFFITH, Katherine (1858-1934)
Pollyanna

2402
GRIFFITH, Raymond (1896-1957)
Changing Husbands
Crossroads of New York, The
Dawn of a Tomorrow, The
Day of Faith, The
Eternal Three, The
Fine Clothes
Fools First
Forty Winks
Going Up
Hands Up! (Jack)
He's a Prince
Lily of the Dust
Minnie
Miss Bluebeard
Much Ado About Nothing
Night Club, The
Open All Night
Paths to Paradise
Poisoned Paradise (Martel)
Red Lights
Regular Fellow, A
Rise and Shine

Silk Hat Harry
Sorrows of Satan, The
Time to Love
Trent's Last Case
Waiter from the Ritz, The
Wedding Bills
Wet Paint
White Tiger, The
You'd Be Surprised

2403
GRIFFITH, Robert*
Night Club, The

2404
GRIGG, Ann*
Great Moment, The (Blenkensop)

2405
GRIMWOOD, Herbert*
Amateur Gentleman, The (Jasper
  Gaunt)
Romola (Savonarola)
Stage:
Clair de Lune (Phedro) 21

2406
GRIPP, Harry*
Honor Bound

2407
GRISWOLD, Grace*
Disraeli (the Duchess of Glastonbury)
One Exciting Night (Auntie Fairfax)
Smilin' Through (Ellen)

2408
GRISWOLD, Herbert Spencer*
Hogan's Ally

2409
GRITSCH, Willy*
Waltz Dream, The

2410
GROETZ, Carl--see: Carl Goetz

2411
GROGAN, Reb*
Stark Love

2412
GRONAU, Ernst*
His Late Excellency
Der Mensch am Wege [Man by the
  Roadside]
Midsummer Night's Dream, A
  (Quince)

2413
GROVE, Gerald*
Man and Maid

2414
GROVE, Sybil (Sybil Westmacott Win-
  grove) (1891-)
Angel of Broadway, The
Black Pearl, The
Gaucho, The
His Private Life
Mother
My Friend from India
Piano Next Door, The
Satan and the Woman
Someone to Love

2415
GROVES, Fred*
Squibs (P. C. Charles Lee)

2416
GRUISE, Thomas S.--see: Thomas
  Guise

2417
GRÜNBERG, Max*
Jew of Mestri, The (Graziano)

2418
GRÜNING, Ilka*
Die Freudlose Gasse [The Joyless
  Street] /aka/ The Street of Sor-
  row (Mrs. Rosenow)
Geheimnisse Seele [Secrets of the
  Soul]

2419
GRUNWALD, Harry*
Das Schiff der Verlorenen Mensch
  [The Ship of Lost Souls] /aka/
  Le Navire du Hommes Perdus
  [The Ship of Lost Men] (crew
  member)

2419a
GRUZINSKY, D.*
Khveska /aka/ Bolnichny Starozh
  Khveska (hospital guard)

2420
GUARD, Kit (1894-1961)
Beau Broadway
Dead Man's Curve
Face at the Window, The
Fighting Blood [serial]
Her Father Said No
Legionnaires in Paris

Lingerie
Man About Town
Pacemakers, The [serial]
Racketeer, The (Gus)

2421
GUBIN, S. *
Scandal

2422
GUELSTORFF, Max*
Meistersinger

2423
GUERIN, Bruce*
Country Kid, The
Drifting
Parasite, The
Revelation
Salvation Hunters, The

2424
GUERRA, Armand*
Midsummer Night's Dream, A (Wenzel)

2425
GUERTZMAN, Paul*
His Private Life
Wolf of Wall Street, The

2426
GUEST, Charlie*
Golfers, The

2427
GUETTE, Toto*
Legion of the Condemned (mechanic)

2428
GUIDE, Paul*
Les Miserables (Enjolras)
Loves of Casanova, The
Two Little Vagabonds (John Scarth)

2429
GUILBERT, Yvette*
Faust (Martha)
L'Argent
Two Little Vagabonds (Biddy Mullins)

2430
GUILER, William*
Great Gobs

2431
GUILFOYLE, James*
Speakeasy

2432
GUINAN, Texas (Mary Louise Guinan)
   (1891-1933)
Capitol Westerns (21)
I Am the Woman
Queen of the Nightclubs
Stampede, The
Stage:
Padlocks of 1927

2433
GUISE, Thomas*
Alarm Clock Andy
Black Oxen (Judge Gavin Trent)
Claw, The (Marquis of Stair)
Don't Ever Marry
Free and Equal
Wedding Bills

2434
GUISE, Wyndham*
His House in Order (Sir Daniel Ridgeley)

2435
GUITTY, Madeleine*
Madame Sans-Gene (LaRousette)

2436
GULLAN, Campbell*
Pleasure Crazed
Tilly of Bloomsbury (Percy)

2437
GULLIVER, Dorothy (1913-)
Around the Bases
Benson at Calford
Clearing the Trail
College Love
Collegians, The [series]
Dog of the Regiment, A
Good Morning, Judge
Honeymoon Flats
King of the Campus
Night Parade
One Glorious Scrap
Painted Faces
Rambling Rangers
Shield of Honor
Wild West Show

2438
GULSDORFF, Max*
Kopf Hoch, Charly! [Heads
   Up Charly! (Harry Moshenheim)

2439
GUNN, Franzi*
Folly of Vanity

2440
GÜNTHER, Paul*
Midsummer Night's Dream, A
   (Egeus)

2441
GURNEY, Edmund*
Tol'able David (Hunter Kinemon)

2442
GURNYAK, K.*
Her Way of Love

2443
GUTMAN, D.*
New Babylon, The

2444
GUTMAN, Karl*
Woman of Paris, A

2445
GUZMAB, Robert E.*
Desert Song, The (Sid el Kar)

2446
GWENN, Edmund (1875-1959)
Skin Game, The (hornblower)
Unmarried, The

2447
GYARFAS, Laszlo*
Paul Street Boys, The

- H -

2448
HAACK, Kaethe*
Der Sprung ins Leben [The Leap In-
   to Life] (scholar's friend)

2449
HABAY, Andree*
Quo Vadis (Petronius)

2450
HACKATHORNE, George (1896-1940)
Cabaret Kid, The
Capital Punishment (Dan O'Connor)
Cheaters, The
College Racketeer
Gray Dawn
Highbinders

Human Hearts
Human Wreckage
Joselyn's Wife
Lady, The
La Marseillaise
Last of the Mohicans, The
Light in the Clearing, A
Little Minister, The
Merry-Go-Round (Bartholomew Gru-
   ber)
Night Life in New York
Notoriety
Paying the Price
Sally's Shoulder
Sea Urchin, The
Sin of Martha Queed, The
Squall, The
Tip Off, The
To Please One Woman
Turmoil
Universal player 23
Village Blacksmith
Wandering Fires (Raymond Carroll)
When a Man's a Man
Worldly Madonna, The

2451
HACKETT, Albert*
Boy Who Cried Wolf, The
Dope
Four Years
Grail, The
House Party
Molly-O, The
Oh, Joe!
Poor Jimmy

2452
HACKETT, Alfred*
Country Flapper, The

2453
HACKETT, Lillian*
In Hollywood with Potash and Perl-
   mutter
Ladies at Ease

2454
HACKETT, Raymond (1903-1958)
Country Flapper, The
Footlights and Fools (Jimmie Willet)
Girl in the Show, A
Loves of Sunya, The (Kenneth Ashling)
Madame X (Raymond)
Our Blushing Brides
Trial of Mary Dugan, The (Jimmy
   Dugan)

2455
HADDON, Peter*
Alf's Button (Lt. Allen)

2456
HADLEY, Bert*
Yankee Consul, The

2457
HAENCKELS, Paul*
Trial of Donald Westhof, The

2458
HAGEN, Edna*
Kiss for Cinderella, A (Gretchen)

2459
HAGNEY, Frank*
All Aboard
Anne of Little Smokey
Backbone
Broken Barriers
Burning Daylight
Captain Lash
Fight Pest, The
Fighting Marine, The [serial]
Free Lips
Frontiersman, The
Gauntlet, The
General, The (recruiting officer)
Ghost in the Garret, The
Glorious Trail
Go Get 'em Hutch [serial]
Hogan's Alley
Ice Flood, The
Last Trail, The
Masked Emotions
Midnight Madness
Oh, Yeah!
On Your Toes
One Round Hogan
Rawhide Kid, The
Roaring Rails
Sea Beast, The (Daggoo)
Through the Breakers
Two-Gun Man, The
Vultures of the Sea [serial]

2460
HAID, Liane*
Explosion
Last Waltz, The
Lucrezia Borgia
Spy of Madame de Pompadour, The
Two Brothers, The

2461
HAIG, Douglas*
Betrayal, The
Sins of the Father (Tom, as a boy)

2462
HAIM, Harry*
Bondage

2463
HAINES, Donald*
Mary Ellen Comes to Town
Smitty

2464
HAINES, Louis*
Beyond Price

2465
HAINES, Rhea*
Always Audacious
Mary Ellen Comes to Town
Master Stroke, A
Smiling All the Way
Uncharted Seas

2466
HAINES, Robert T. (1870-1943)
Careers
Does It Pay?
Dynamite (Judge)
First Kiss, The
Foreigner, The
Girl in the Glass Cage, The (Pom-
    fret's Attorney)
Governor's Lady, The
Heart of New York, The
How to Handle Women
Ladies of the Mob
Lew Tyler's Wives
Lone Wolf, The
Noose, The
Pomander Walk
Secret Agent
Shannons of Broadway, The
Ten Minutes

2467
HAINES, William (1900-1973)
Alias Jimmy Valentine (Title role)
Brothers under the Skin (debut)
Brown of Harvard
Circe the Enchantress
Denial, The
Duke Steps Out, The (the Duke)
Excess Baggage
Girl in the Glass Cage, The
Hollywood Revue of 1929

I'll Tell the World
Iron Mike
Little Annie Rooney
Little Journey, A
Lovey Mary
Man's Man, A
Memory Lane
Midnight Express, The
Mike
Navy Blues
Pacemakers, The [serial]
Road to Mandalay, The (Pvt. Skeet
  Burns)
Sally, Irene and Mary (Jimmy Du-
  gan)
Show People (Billy Boone)
Slave of Fashion, A
Slide, Kelly, Slide
Smart Set, The
Souls for Sale (Pinky)
Speedway
Spring Fever (Jack Kelly)
Tell It to the Marines
Telling the World
Three Weeks
Three Wise Fools
Tower of Lies, The (August)
True as Steel
West Point (Bruce Wayne)
Wife of the Centaur, The
Wine of Youth

Four Horsemen of the Apocalypse,
  The (Karl von Hartrott)
Fox, The
Great Impersonation, The
Heart of a Woman, The
Hollywood
Leatherneck, The
Leopard Lady, The
Long Live the King
Main Street
Oh, Kay!
One Glorious Day
Power (Flagg)
Quicksands
Red Hot Rhythm
Risky Business
Robin Hood (Little John)
Rolling Stones
Sailor's Holiday
Sal of Singapore
Sap, The
She Got What She Wanted
Shirley of the Circus
Skyscraper
Spieler, The
Stella Dallas
Trap, The (Benson)
Up and At 'em
Vanity
Wise Fool, The
Wreck of the Hesperus, The

2468
HAISMAN, Irene*
Time, the Place and the Girl, The

2469
HAJMAN, L. *
Honor

2470
HALE, Alan, Sr. (Rufus Alan Mc-
  Kahn) (1892-1950)
Bachelor's Secret, The
Black Oxen (Prince Hohenhauer)
Cameo Kirby
Code of the Wilderness
Cop, The
Covered Wagon, The (Sam Woodhull)
Cowboy and the Lady, The
Crimson Runner, The
Dick Turpin
Dictator, The
Doll's House, A
Eleventh Hour, The
False Kisses
Fighting Reverend Watts, The
Forbidden Waters

2471
HALE, Creighton (Patrick Fitzgerald)
  (1882-1965)
Annie Laurie /aka/ Ladies from Hell
  (Donald)
Beverly of Graustark (Prince Oscar)
Black Circle, The
Bridge of Sighs, The
Broken Hearts of Broadway
Cameo Kirby
Cat and the Canary, The (Paul Jones)
Child for Sale
Circle, The
Dangerous Maid
Exchange of Wives
Fascination
Forbidden Love /aka/ Women Who
  Wait
Great Divide, The
Her Majesty
House of Shame
Idol Dancer, The (Walter Kincaid)
Marriage Circle, The (Dr. Gustave
  Meuller)
Midnight Message, The
Name the Man

Oh, Baby!
Orphans of the Storm (Picard)
Reilly of the Rainbow Division
Rose-Marie (Etienne Doray)
Seven Days
Seven Footprints to Satan
Shadow on the Wall, A
Should Men Walk Home?
Sisters of Eve
Speeding Through
Tea with a Kick
This Woman (Bobby Bleedon)
Three Wise Fools
Thumbs Down
Time, the Comedian
Trilby (Little Billee)
Way Down East (Prof. Sterling)
Wine of Youth, The

2472
HALE, Florence*
Oliver Twist (Mrs. Bedwin)

2473
HALE, Georgia (1906-)
Floating College
Gold Rush, The (Georgia)
Great Gatsby, The
Gypsy of the North
Hills of Peril
Last Moment, The (Zakoro)
Man of the Forest, The
Rainmaker, The
Rawhide Kid, The
Salvation Hunters, The
Trick of Hearts
Wheel of Chance
Woman Against the World, A

2474
HALE, Louise Closser (1872-1933)
Hole in the Wall, The (Mrs. Ram-
    say)
Paris
Stage:
Expressing Willie (Mrs. Smith) 24
Miss Lulu Bett (Mrs. Bett) 20

2475
HALE, Sonnie /aka/ Robert Munro
    (John Hale-Monro) (1902-1959)
On with the Dance
Parting of the Waves, The

2476
HALL, Ben*
Girl from Woolworths, The
Harold Teen

Hot News
Hot Stuff
Nix on Dames
Skyrocket
South Sea Rose

2477
HALL, Betty (1914-)
Sting of the Lash, The (Crissy, age
    6)

2478
HALL, Charles (1899-1959)
Bacon Grabbers
Battle of the Century, The (delivery
    man)
Berth Marks
Boxing Gloves
Crooks Can't Win
Double Whoopee
Hoose Gow, The
Love 'em and Weep
Men O' War
Skirt Sky
They Go Boom (landlord)
Two Tars /aka/ Two Tough Tars
Why Bring That Up?
You're Darn Tootin'

2479
HALL, Donald*
Her Love Story (court physician)
Unguarded Women

2480
HALL, Dorothy*
Laughing Lady, The
Nothing but the Truth

2481
HALL, Ella (1896-)
In the Name of the Law
Third Alarm, The (June Rutherford)

2482
HALL, Evelyn Walsh*
Children of the Ritz
Divine Lady, The (Duchess of Devon-
    shire)
Hello Angel
Married in Hollywood
Men of Steel
My Best Girl
Nobody's Children
Our Dancing Daughters (Freddie's
    mother)
Pace that Thrills, The
Pomander Walk

She Goes to War

2483
HALL, Henry*
Primrose Path, The (court officer)

2484
HALL, James (James Brown) (1897-1940)
Campus Flirt, The
Canary Murder Case, The (Jimmie Spotswoode)
Case of Lena Smith, The
Fifty-Fifty Girl, The
Fleet's In, The (Eddie Briggs)
Four Sons
Hotel Imperial (Lt. Almasy)
Just Married
Love's Greatest Mistake
Ritzy
Rolled Stockings
Saturday Night Kid, The (Bill)
Senorita
Silk Legs
Smiling Irish Eyes
Stranded in Paris
Swim, Girl, Swim
This Is Heaven

2485
HALL, Josephine*
Love Parade, The (a lady-in-waiting)

2486
HALL, Lillian*
Last of the Mohicans, The (Alice Monroe)
Quo Vadis?

2487
HALL, Newton*
Penrod and Sam (George Bassett)
Stella Dallas (Helen's son, as a child)

2488
HALL, Thurston (1883-1959)
Empty Arms
Iron Trail, The

2489
HALL, Willard Lee*
Conquering Power, The (the Abbe)
Scaramouche (King's lieutenant)

2490
HALL, Winter (1878-   )
Affairs of Anatol, The (Dr. Johnson)
Ashes of Vengeance (Bishop)
Behold My Wife
Ben Hur (Joseph)
Bleeders, The
Boomerang, The
Breaking Point, The (Dr. Hillyer)
Burning Sands
Cheated Hearts
Child Thou Gavest Me, The
Compromise
Day of Faith, The
East Is West
Forbidden Woman, The
Free to Love (Judge Orr)
Graustark (Ambassador)
Great Impersonation, The
Her Reputation
Her Social Value
Husbands and Lovers
Jucklins, The
Kitty
Little Church Around the Corner, The
Little Clown, The
Love Parade, The (Priest)
Name the Man
On the High Seas
Only Woman, The
Paradise
Racketeer, The (Sam Chapman)
Saturday Night (the professor)
Secrets (Dr. Arbuthnot)
Skin Deep
Tree of Knowledge, The
Voice from the Minaret, The (Bishop Ellsworth)
What Every Woman Knows
Witching Hour, The
Woman in the House, A
Woman to Woman
Wrecker, The

2491
HALL-DAVIS, Lilian (1901-1933)
Afterglow
As We Lie
Blighty
Boadicea
Eleventh Commandment, The
Ernest Maltravers
Faithful Heart, The
Farmer's Wife, The
Game of Life, The
Honeypot, The
Hotel Mouse, The
I, Pagliacci

If Four Walls Told
If Youth but Knew
Knockout, The
Let's Pretend
Love Maggy
Married Love
Passionate Adventure, The
Quo Vadis? (Lygia)
Right to Strike, The
Ring, The
Roses of Picardy (Madeleine Vander-
lynden)
Royal Divorce, A
Should a Doctor Tell?
Stable Companions
Tommy Atkins
Two Lovers (Princess Zaineb)
Unwanted
White Sheik, The
Wonderful Story

2492
HALLAM, Harry*
Tol'able David (doctor)

2493
HALLER, Ray--see: Ray Hallor

2494
HALLETT, Jim*
Swim Princess, The

2495
HALLIDAY, John (1880-1947)
Eastside Sadie
Woman Gives, The

2496
HALLIGAN, Lillian*
Waltzing Around

2497
HALLOR, Ray (1900-)
Black Butterflies
Blackbirds
Circumstantial Evidence
Clash, The
Courtship of Miles Standish,
The
Dangerous Maid
Dream Street
Driven from Home
Fast Life, The (Rodney Hall)
Green-Grass Widows
Haunted Ship, The
Inez from Hollywood
Inside Prison Walls

Learning to Love
Man Crazy
Manhattan Knights
Noisy Neighbors
Pearl Story, The
Plaything of Broadway
Quarantined Rivals
Red Dice
Sally (Jimmy Spelvin)
Thundergod
Tongues of Scandal
Trail of '98, The

2498
HALM, Harry*
It's Easy to Become a Father

2499
HALSEY, Betty*
Happy Days (chorus)

2500
HALSTON, Howard*
It's a Great Life

2501
HALT, James*
Silk Legs

2502
HAM, Harry*
Blood Money (Detective Bell)
Four Feathers, The (Harry Fever-
sham, as a man)
Skirts, The

2503
HAMER, Gladys*
Every Mother's Son (Minnie)
Magician, The
This Freedom (Gertrude)

2504
HAMERSTEIN, Oscar*
What's Wrong with Woman?

2505
HAMILL, Charlotte*
Happy Days (chorus)

2506
HAMILTON, Charles*
Strange Cargo

2507
HAMILTON, Frances*
Naughty Baby

2508
HAMILTON, Gladys*
Sonia (Lady Erckmann)
This Freedom (Aunt Belle)

2509
HAMILTON, Hale (Hale Rice Hamilton) (1883-1942)
Great Gatsby, The
His Children's Children
Manicure Girl, The
Summer Bachelors
Telephone Girl, The
Tin Gods

2510
HAMILTON, Jack "Shorty'"*
Lone Hand Tex
Two-Fisted Thompson
Western Grit

2511
HAMILTON, John T. *
Mademoiselle from Armentieres (the young soldier)
Sonny Boy

2512
HAMILTON, Lloyd V. (1891-1935)
Adviser, The
Always a Gentleman
Black Waters
Breezing Along
Duck In
Dynamite
Educator, The
Extra! Extra!
Greenhorn, The
His Darker Self
Mongrels
Moonshine
No Luck
"No Sale" Smitty
Papa's Boy
Poor Boy
Rainmaker, The
Roaring Lions and Wedding Bells
Robinson Crusoe, Ltd.
Rolling Stones
Self-Made Failure, A
Show of Shows, The (cabby)
Simp, The
Son of a Hun
Speeder, The
Twilight Baby
Uneasy Feet
Vagrant, The

2513
HAMILTON, Mahlon (1885-1960)
Aristocrat, The
Christian, The (Horatio Drake)
Deadlier Sex, The
Earthbound
Fool There Was, A
Green Temptation
Half a Chance
Heart Raider, The
Her Kingdom of Dreams
His Children's Children
Honky Tonk (Jim)
I Am Guilty!
Idaho [serial]
In Old Kentucky
Ladies Must Live
Lane that Has No Turning Point, The
Life's Crossroad
Little Old New York (Washington Irving)
Midnight Guest, The
Other Woman's Story, The
Paid Back
Peg O' My Heart (Sir Gerald Adair)
Recoil, The
Rich People (Beverly Hayden)
Single Standard, The
That Girl Montana
Third Generation, The
Truant Husband, The
Under Oath
Under the Lash (Robert Waring)
Wheel, The
What Price Love?

2514
HAMILTON, Mark*
Light of the Western Stars, The
Rainbow Trail, The
Sparrows /aka/ Human Sparrows (Hog Buyer)

2515
HAMILTON, Neil (James Neil Hamilton) (1899-)
America (Nathan Holden)
Beau Geste (Digby Geste)
Big Scoop, The
Busybody, The
Dangerous Woman, A
Darkened Rooms
Desert Gold
Diplomacy
Don't Marry
Golden Princess, The
Great Gatsby, The
Grip of the Yukon, The

Hot News
Isn't Life Wonderful? (Hans)
Joy Girl, The
Kibitzer, The
Little French Girl, The
Love Trap
Men and Women
Mother Machree
Music Master, The
Mysterious Dr. Fu Manchu, The
  /aka/ The Insidious Dr. Fu Man-
  chu (Dr. Jack Petrie)
New Brooms
Number Please
Old Ironsides
Patriot, The (Crown Prince Alexan-
  der)
Shield of Honor
Showdown, The
Side Show of Life
Something Always Happens
Splendid Crime, The
Spotlight, The
Street of Forgotten Men
Studio Murder Mystery, The (Tony
  White)
Take Me Home
Ten Modern Commandments
Three Weekends (James Gordon)
Three Weeks
What a Night!
White Rose, The (John White)
Why Be Good?
Within the Law

2516
HAMMEREN, Torsten*
Story of Gösta Berling (Count Hen-
  drik Dohna)

2517
HAMMERSTEIN, Elaine (1897-1948)
After Business Hours
Broadway Gold
Daring Love
Daughter Pays, The
Drums of Jeopardy, The
Evidence (Florette)
Foolish Virgin, The
Girl from Nowhere, The
Grand Guignol, The
Greater than Fame
Handcuffs or Kisses
Midnight Express, The
Miracle of Manhattan, The
One Week of Love
Parisian Nights
Pleasure Seekers

Point of View
Poor Dear Margaret Kirby
Reckless Youth (Alice Schuyler)
Remorseless Love
Rupert of Hentzau (Queen Flavia)
Shadow of Rosalie Byrnes, The
Under Oath
Unwritten Law, The
Way of a Maid, The
Whispers
Why Announce Your Marriage?
Woman Game, The

2518
HAMMOND, C. Norman*
Through the Back Door (Jacques Lan-
  vain)

2519
HAMMOND, Charles*
Irish Luck
Lucky Devil, The
Sally of the Sawdust (Mr. Lennox, Sr.)

2520
HAMMOND, Harriet*
Astray from the Steerage (unimpor-
  tant wife)
Bits of Life
Man and Maid
Midshipman, The

2521
HAMMOND, Kay (Kay Standing)
  (1909-)
Her Private Affair (Julia Sturm)
Trespasser, The (Catherine "Flip"
  Merrick)

2522
HAMMOND, Virginia (1894-1972)
Crash, The
Manhattan Knight, A

2523
HAMPER, Genevieve*
Under the Red Robe

2524
HAMPTON, Gladys*
Tangled Trails

2525
HAMPTON, Hope (1901-)
Bait, The
Does It Pay?
Gold Diggers, The (Jerry Lamar)
Lawful Larceny

Light in the Dark, The (Bessie Mac-
 Gregor)
Love's Penalty
Lovers' Island
Modern Salome, A
Price of a Party, The
Stardust
Unfair Sex, The

2526
HAMPTON, Margaret*
Arizona Whirlwind, The

2527
HAMPTON, Myra*
Trial of Mary Dugan, The (May Har-
 ris)

2528
HANBURY, Maie*
Sally Bishop (Mrs. Durlacher)

2529
HANCOCK, Eleanor*
Cave Girl, The

2530
HANDA, Frank*
Wedding Bells

2531
HANLEY, Leo*
Happy Days (chorus)

2532
HANLON, Jack*
Shakedown, The

2533
HANNA, Franklyn*
Democracy, The Vision Restored

2534
HANNE, Pat*
Happy Days (chorus)

2535
HANNEFORD, Poodles (Edwin Han-
 neford)
Circus Kid, The

2536
HANSEN, Juanita (1897-1961)
Broadway Madonna, A
Eternal Flame, The
Girl of the Golden West
Lost City, The /aka/ The Jungle
 Princess [serial] (Princess

Elysta)
Phantom Foe, The [serial]
Red Snow, The
Yellow Arm, The [serial]

2537
HANSEN, Karen*
Telephone Girl

2538
HANSEN, Max*
His Late Excellency

2539
HANSON, Einar (-1927)
Barbed Wire
Children of Divorce (Prince Ludovico
 de Sfax)
Fashions for Women
Die Freudlose Gasse [The Joyless
 Street] /aka/ The Street of Sor-
 row (Lt. Davy)
Gunnar Hede's Saga
Her Big Night
Into Her Kingdom
Lady in Ermine, The
Masked Woman, The
Woman on Trial, The

2540
HANSON, Erling*
Anna Boleyn /aka/ Deception

2541
HANSON, Lars (1887-1965)
Buttons
Captain Salvation
Divine Woman, The (Lucien)
Emigrants, The
Flesh and the Devil (Ulrich von Klet-
 zingk)
Homecoming
In Dalarna and Jerusalem
Informer, The
Legend of Gösta Berling, The
Scarlet Letter, The (Rev. Dimmes-
 dale)
Story of Gösta Berling, The (Title
 role)
Wind, The (Lige)

2542
HARBACHER, Karl*
Der Juxbaron [The Imaginary Baron]
 (Stotterwilhelm)
Manon Lescaut
Wie Einst im Mai

2543
HARBAUGH, Carl*
College
Silent Command, The

2544
HARBEN, Hubert*
Every Mother's Son (Sir Alfred
  Browning)

2545
HARBORD, Carl*
American Prisoner, The (Lt. Burn-
  ham)

2546
HARBURGH, Bert*
Silken Shackles

2547
HARDER, Emil, Jr.*
William Tell

2548
HARDIGAN, Patrick*
Down to the Sea in Ships

2549
HARDING, Ann (Dorothy Walton Gat-
  ley) (1902-)
Babe Comes Home
Condemned (Madame Vidal)
Girl of the Golden West
Her Private Affair (Vera Kessler)
Paris Bound (Mary Hutton)
War and Women
Stage:
Candida - Philadelphia
Horse Thief, The - Chicago 22
Inheritors, The - Provincetown Play-
  ers 21
Like a King (Phyllis Weston) 21
Master Builder, The - Philadelphia
Misalliance - Philadelphia
Stock in Buffalo and Detroit 22
Stolen Fruit (Marie Millais) 25
Strange Interlude (Lena) - on tour 29
Tarnish (Letitia Tevis) 23

2550
HARDING, Lyn (David Llewellyn Har-
  ding) (1867-1952)
Barton Mystery, The
Trilby
When Knighthood Was in Flower (Hen-
  ry VIII)
Yolanda (Charles the Bold, Duke of
  Burgundy)

Stage:
Macbeth (Title role) 28

2551
HARDWICKE, Sir Cedric (Cedric
  Webster Hardwicke) (1893-1964)
Nelson
Stage:
Show Boat (Captain Andy) - Drury
  Lane in London 28

2552
HARDY, Arthur*
Atlantic (Major Boldy)

2553
HARDY, Oliver (Oliver Norville Har-
  dy) (1892-1957) [*with Stan Laurel]
Along Came Auntie
Angora Love* (himself)
Assistant Wives
Back Yard, The
Bacon Grabbers* (himself)
Bankrupt Honeymoon, A
Barnum and Ringling, Inc.
Battle of the Century, The* (himself)
Be Your Age
Berth Marks* (himself)
Big Business* (himself)
Blizzard, The
Bromo and Juliet
Call of the Cuckoo* (one of the
  cuckoos)
Counter Jumper, The
Crazy Like a Fox
Crazy to Act
Dames and Dentists
Decorator, The
Do Detectives Think?* (Det. Sherlock
  Pinkham)
Double Whoopee* (himself)
Duck Soup* (bit)
Early to Bed* (himself)
Enough to Do*
Eve's Love Letters*
Fall Guy, The
Finishing Touch, The* (himself)
Fists and Fodder
Fluttering Hearts
Flying Elephants* (Mighty Giant)
Fortune's Mask
Forty-Five Minutes from Hollywood*
  (house detective)
From Soup to Nuts* (himself)
Galloping Ghosts
Gentle Cyclone
Girl in the Limousine, The
Golf

Habeas Corpus* (himself)
Hats Off* (himself)
He Laughs Last
Her Boy Friend
His Jonah Day
Hollywood Revue of 1929* (himself)
Honorable Mr. Buggs, The
Hoose Gow, The* (himself)
Hop to It!
Is Marriage the Bunk?
Isn't Life Terrible?
King of the Wild Horses, The
King Speed
Leave 'em Laughing* (himself)
Liberty* (himself)
Lighter that Failed, The
Little Wildcat, The
Long Fliv the King
Love 'em and Feed 'em
Love 'em and Weep* (Judge Chig-
   ger)
Madame Mystery* (Capt. Schmaltz)
Maids and Muslin
Men O' War* (himself)
Nickel Hopper, The
No Man's Law
Nuisance, The
One Stolen Night
Pals and Pugs
Perfect Clown, The
Perfect Day, A* (himself)
Putting Pants on Philip* (Piedmont
   Mumblethunder)
Rogue Song, The (Murza Bek)
Sailors Beware!* (Purser Cryder)
Sawmill, The
Say It with Babies
Sea Dog's Tale, A
Second Hundred Years, The* (him-
   self)
Should Married Men Go Home?*
   (himself)
Should Men Walk Home?
Should Sailors Marry?
Slipping Wives* (Jarvis)
Springtime
Squeaks and Squawks
Stick Around
Stop, Look and Listen
Sugar Daddies* (Finlayson's
   butler)
That's My Wife* (himself)
Their Purple Moment* (himself)
They Go Boom* (himself)
Three Ages, The
Thundering Fleas
Tourist, The

Two Tars /aka/ Two Tough Tars*
   (himself)
Unaccustomed as We Are* (himself)
Wandering Papas
We Faw Down /aka/ We Slip Up*
   (himself)
Why Girls Love Sailors* (Capt. Har-
   dy)
Why Girls Say No
With Love and Hisses* (Arrogant
   Sgt.)
Wizard of Oz, The (the Tin Man)
Wrong Again* (himself)
Yes, Yes, Nanette*
You're Darn Tootin'* (himself)

2554
HARDY, Sam (1883-1935)
Acquitted
Big News (Reno)
Big Noise, The
Bluebeard's Seven Wives
Broadway Nights (Johnny Fay)
Burning up Broadway
Butter and Egg Man, The
Dear Vivien
Diamond Handcuffs
Fast Company
First National player 28
Get-Rich-Quick Wallingford (Rufus
   Wallingford)
Give and Take
Great Deception, The
Half-Way Girl, The
High Hat
Life of Riley, The
Little Old New York (Cornelius Van-
   derbilt)
Man's Man, A
Mexicali Rose
Mighty Lak' a Rose
Night Bird, The
On with the Show (Jerry)
Orchids and Ermine
Outcast, The
Perfect Sap, The
Prince of Tempters, The
Rainbow Man, The
Savage, The
Song of the West (Davolo)
Texas Steer, A
Turn Back the Hours
When Love Grows Cold

2555
HARDY, William*
Queen of Sheba, The (Olos, Sheba's
   giant slave)

2556
HARE, Lumsden (1875-1964)
Black Watch, The
Blue Pearl, The
Education of Elizabeth, The
False Colors
Frisky Mrs. Johnson
Fugitives
Girls Gone Wild
King of the Khyber Rifles (the Colo-
  nel)
Mothers of Men
No Children Allowed
On the Banks of the Wabash
Salute
Second Youth
Sherlock Holmes /aka/ Moriarty
  (Dr. Leighton)
Sky Hawk, The (Judge Allan)

2557
HARGRAVES, William*
Happy Days (chorus)

2558
HARIAN, Kenneth*
Drusilla with a Million
Man, Woman and Wife

2559
HARIEN, Macey--see: Macey Harlam

2560
HARKER, Gordon (1885-1967)
Champagne
Crooked Billet, The
Farmer's Wife, The
Return of the Rat, The (Morel)
Ring, The (debut)
Taxi for Two
Wrecker, The

2561
HARLAM, Macey*
Bella Donna
Beyond the Rainbow (Count Julien de
  Brisac)
Right to Love, The
When Knighthood Was in Flower
  (Duc De Longueville)
Without Fear
Woman and the Puppet, The

2562
HARLAN, Cris*
Shepherd of the Hills, The

2563
HARLAN, Kenneth (1895-1967)
April Showers
Beautiful and the Damned, The
Beauty and Brains
Bobbed Hair
Broken Wing, The
Butterfly
Cheating Cheaters
Code of the Air
Crowded Hour, The
Dangerous Business (Clarence Brooks)
Dawn of the East
Down the Stretch
East Side, West Side
Easy Pickings
Fallen Angels
Fighter Ranger, The
Fighting Edge, The
Finders Keepers
First National player 22
Flame of the Yukon
For Another Woman
I Am the Law
Ice Flood, The
Learning to Love
Lessons in Love
Little Church Around the Corner, The
Love, Honor and Obey
Mama's Affair
Man, Woman and Wife
Marriage Whirl, The
Married Flapper, The
Midnight Rose
Nobody
Penality, The (Wilmot)
Poisoned Paradise (Hugh Kildair)
Polly of the Follies
Primitive Lover, The
Ranger of the Big Trees, The
Rossmore Case, The
Sap, The
Stage Kisses
Streets of Shanghai
Toll of the Sea, The
Twinkletoes (Chuck Lightfoot)
United States Smith
Virginian, The
Wedding Bells
White Man, The
Wilful Youth
Woman's Place, A
World's Stage, The

2564
HARLAN, Marion*
Thank You
Tony Runs Wild

Wings of Youth

2565
HARLAN, Otis (1865-1940)
Baby Mine
Barefoot Boy, The
Barnum Was Right
Black Sheep, A
Broadway (Porky)
Captain Blood (Corliss)
Cheerful Fraud, The
Clean Heart, The
Clear the Decks
Code of the Wilderness, The
Diamonds Adrift
Dixie Handicap, The
Don't Tell the Wife
Dramatic Life of Abraham Lincoln
  /aka/ Abraham Lincoln (Denton
  Offut)
Embarrassing Moments
Eternal Flame, The (Abbe Conrad)
Everybody Loves a Fat Man
Galloping Fury
Girl in the Taxi, The
Girl Overboard
Good Morning, Judge
Grip of the Yukon, The
His Lucky Day
How Baxter Buttered In
Keeping up with Lizzie
Ladder Jinx, The
Lightnin'
Limited Mail, The
Mademoiselle Midnight
Main Street
Midnight Message
Milk White Flag, A
Mississippi Gambler
9 3/5 Seconds
Oh, Doctor!
Perfect Clown, The
Pioneer Trails
Port of Dreams
Redeeming Sin, The
Regeneration of Sam Packard, The
Romance Promoters
Shepherd of the Hills, The
Show Boat (Captain Andy Hawks)
Silent Rider, The
Silk Stockings
Silks and Saddles
Speed Classic
Spider and the Rose, The
Stranger in New York, A
Student Prince, The (Old Ruder)
Temperance Town, A
Three Bad Men

Truxton King, The
Unknown Cavalier, The
Voice from the Minaret, The
Welcome Home
Welcome Stranger, The
What Happened to Jones?
When We Were Twenty-One
Where Was I?
Whole Town's Talking, The

2566
HARLAN, Richard*
Classmates
Winning Through (Half-Breed Leader
  of Guides)

2567
HARLOW, Jean (Harlean Carpentier)
  (1911-1937)
Bacon Grabbers (extra)
Christie comedies as extra 28
Close Harmony (extra)
Double Whoopee (bit)
Fugitives (extra)
Liberty (extra)
Love Parade, The (extra)
Moran of the Marines (bit)
New York Nights (extra)
Saturday Night Kid, The (Hazel Carroll)
This Thing Called Love (bit)
Unkissed Man, The (bit)
Weak, but Willing (bit)

2568
HARMON FOUR QUARTETTE
On with the Show

2569
HARMON, Pat (1890-)
Barrier, The
Barriers Burned Away
Berth Marks
Court Martial
Duke Steps Out, The
Eternal Struggle, The
Firebrand Trevision
Freshman, The (coach)
Haunted Ship, The
Homesick
Midnight Express, The
Nathan Hale
Sal of Singapore
Show Folks
Side Show
Silent Watcher, The
Small Talk
Sunset Pass
Synthetic Sin

Warning, The
Waterfront
Weary River
When a Man's a Man

2570
HARMONY EMPEROR'S QUARTET
On with the Show (Plantation Singers)

2571
HARRIGAN, Nedda*
Laughing Lady, The

2572
HARRIGAN, William (1887-1966)
Cabaret
Nix on Dames
Stage:
Acquittal, The (Joe Conway) 20
Dove, The (Johnny Powell) 25
Great God Brown, The (William A.
   Brown) 26
Polly Preferred 23

2573
HARRING, Hildegard*
Johan

2574
HARRINGTON, Joe*
Freshman, The (tailor)
Prince of Pep, The

2575
HARRINGTON, John*
Man Who Found Himself, The
Rubber Heels
Street of Forgotten Men, The
Tin Gods

2576
HARRIS, Buddy*
Lying Wives

2577
HARRIS, Charles K. *
After the Ball

2578
HARRIS, Elmer*
Garrison's Finish

2579
HARRIS, George /aka/ Georgie*
Johnstown Flood, The (Mandel's boy)
Lights of Old Broadway
Shamrock Handicap, The (Benny Gins-
   berg)

2580
HARRIS, Helen*
Son of Wallingford, The (Cleo Patra)

2581
HARRIS, Ivy*
Fascinating Youth
Gentleman of Paris, A
Just Married
Potters, The (Mamie)
Three Sinners

2582
HARRIS, Jenks*
Flaming Disc, The [serial]

2583
HARRIS, Marcia*
Fighting Blade, The (Joan Laycock)
Greene Murder Case, The (Hemming)
Isn't Life Wonderful? (aunt)
King on Main Street, The
Love 'em and Leave 'em
Music Master, The
On the Banks of the Wabash
Reckless Lady, The
Saturday's Children
So's Your Old Man (Mrs. Bisbee)
Sorrows of Satan, The (landlady)
Take Me Home

2584
HARRIS, Maria*
Sinners in Heaven

2585
HARRIS, Marion*
Devil May Care

2586
HARRIS, Mildred /aka/ Mildred Har-
   ris Chaplin (1905-1944)
Adventurous Souls
Cruise of the Jasper B. , The
Daring Years, The (Susie LaMotte)
Dress Maker from Paris, The
First Woman, The
Flaming Love
Fool's Paradise (Rosa Duchene)
Forbidden
Girl from Rio, The
Habit
Heart of a Follies Girl, The
Hearts of Men
Inferior Sex, The
Isle of Retribution
K-the Unknown
Last Lap, The

Lingerie
Man Who Dared God, The
Melody Man, The
Melody of Love
My Neighbor's Wife
Mystery Club, The
No, No, Nanette (Betty)
Old Dad
One Hour of Love
One Law for the Woman
Out of the Past
Polly of the Storm Country
Power of the Press
Prince There Was, A
Private Affairs
Sea Fury
Show Girl
Side Street
Social Mockery
Speed Classic
Unmarried Wives
Village Prodigal, The
Whim, The
Wolf Hunter
Wolves of the Air
Woman in His House, A

2587
HARRIS, Wadsworth*
Dragon's Net, The [serial]

2588
HARRIS, Winifred*
Daughter of Two Worlds, A
Love Doctor, The
Racketeer, The (Margaret Chapman)

2589
HARRISON, Carey*
Wedding March, The (guard)

2590
HARRISON, Irma*
Alibi /aka/ Perfect Alibi, The
    (Toots)
For Woman's Favor (Lee Bradford)
One Exciting Night (maid)

2591
HARRISON, Jimmy /aka/ James*
Barricade, The
Beyond the Rainbow (Louis Wade)
Charley's Aunt (Charlie Wykeham)
Christie comedies (23-24)
Halfback Hannah
Heart to Let, A
His Wife's Relations
Lessons in Love

Long Hose
Love's Young Scream
Nifty Numbers
Say Uncle!
Stop Flirting
Stop Kidding
Wedding Bells
Why Announce Your Marriage?

2592
HARRISON, Rex (Reginald Carey
    Harrison) (1908-)
Get Your Man

2593
HARRON, Johnny (1903-)
Below the Line
Boy Friend, The
Bride of the Storm
Closed Gates
Dulcy
False Alarm
Finders Keepers
Gilded Highway, The
Gold Diggers, The (Wally Saunders)
Green-Grass Widows
Hell Bent for Heaven
Learning to Love
Little Irish Girl, The
Love Makes 'em Wild
Man in Hobbles, The
My Wife and I
Naughty
Night Cry, The
Night Life (Max)
Old Shoes
Once and Forever
Penrod
Rose of the Tenements
Satan in Sables
Silk Stockings
Street Girl
Supreme Test, The
Their Hour
Through the Back Door (Billy Boy)
Wife Who Wasn't Wanted, The
Woman Hater, The

2594
HARRON, Robert "Bobby" (1894-1920)
Coincidence
Confidence
Greatest Question, The
Way Down East (bit)

2595
HART, Albert /aka/ Al*
Doubling for Romeo

Hidden Woman, The (Bill Donovan)
Honor Bound
Man Without a Country, The /aka/
 As No Man Has Loved
Pony Express

2596
HART, Alex*
Galloping Cowboy, The

2597
HART, Bob*
Joanna

2598
HART, Florence*
Son of Wallingford, The (Mrs. Wal-
 lingford)

2599
HART, Neal (Cornelius A. Hart,
 Jr.) (1879-1949)
Butterfly Range
Danger Valley
Deadline, The
Devil's Bowl, The
Fighting Strain, The
God's Gold
Heart of a Texan, The
Hell's Oasis
King Fisher's Roost
Knight of the Western Land
Left Hand Brand
Lure of Gold
Rangeland
Salty Saunders
Sands of the Desert
Scarlet Brand, The
Scarlet Hound, The [serial]
Secret of the Pueblo, The
Skyfire
South of the Northern Lights
Square Shooter, The
Squarin' It
Table Top Ranch
Tangled Trails
Tucker's Top Hand
West of the Pecos

2600
HART, Sunshine (1886-)
Air Pockets
Bride's Relations, The
Crazy to Act
Lovey Mary
My Best Girl
Red Mill, The
Sound Your A's

Spanking Breezes
Student Prince, The
Syncopating Sue
Tiger's Club, The
White Moll, The

2601
HART, William S. (William Surrey
 Hart) (1870-1946) [Horse: Fritz
 and Midnight]
Cradle of Courage, The ("Square"
 Kelly)
Hollywood
O'Malley of the Mounted
Sand!
Show People (cameo)
Singer Jim McKee
Testing Block, The
Three Word Brand (triple role)
Toll Gate, The (Black Deering)
Travelin' On
Tumbleweeds
Whistle, The
White Oak, The
Wild Bill Hickok

2602
HARTAU, Ludwig*
Anna Boleyn /aka/ Deception

2603
HARTIGAN, Pat /aka/ Patrick
 (1881-)
Below the Line
Bobbed Hair
Clash of the Wolves, The
Code of the West (Cal Bloom)
Dark Secrets (Biskra)
Darling of New York, The
Down to the Sea in Ships (Jake Fin-
 ner)
Dramatic Life of Abraham Lincoln,
 The /aka/ Abraham Lincoln (Jack
 Armstrong)
Far Call, The
Find Your Man
From Headquarters
In Old Arizona (cowboy)
Midnight Taxi
Oh, What a Nurse!
Ranson's Folly
State Street Sadie
Tenderloin
Thundering Herd, The (Catlee)
Welcome Stranger, The
Where the North Begins

2604
HARTLEY, Irving*
Fascinating Youth
Man and Maid

2605
HARTLEY, Pete*
Great White Way, The

2606
HARTLEY-MILBURN, Julie*
Sonia (Lady Amy Loring)
This Freedom (Laetitia)

2607
HARTMAN, Gretchen /aka/ Greta
  (1897-)
Atonement
Bride 13 [serial]
College Coquette, The
She Goes to War
Time, the Place and the Girl, The

2608
HARTMAN, Paul (1904-1973)
Anna Boleyn /aka/ Deception (Hen-
  ry Norris)
At the Grey House
Haunted Castle, The
Vanina
Stage:
Vaudeville 25

2609
HARTMANN, Sadakichi*
Thief of Bagdad, The (court magi-
  cian)

2610
HARVEY, Forrester (1890-1945)
Flag Lieutenant, The (Dusty Miller)
Nell Gwyn (Charles Hart)
Tailor Made Man, The
White Sheik, The

2611
HARVEY, George Y. *
Wife Savers

2612
HARVEY, John Martin*
Only Way, The (Sidney Carton)

2613
HARVEY, Lew*
Argyle Case, The
Broadway after Dark
Eve's Lover (the agitator)

Find Your Man
Frozen River
Greyhound Limited, The
Half-Breed, The (the snake)
Lady of the Night
Pretty Ladies
Wolf's Clothing

2614
HARVEY, Lilian (1907-1968)
Adieu Mascott
Du Sollst Nicht Stechten
Eheferien
Der Fluch
Ihr Dundler Pinkt
It's Easy to Become a Father
Die Keusche Susanne
Die Kleine Von Bummel
Knight in London, A
Leidenshaft
Leise Kommt Das Gluck Zu Dir
Liebe Gert Seltsame Wege
Die Liebschaften Der Hella Von Gil-
  sar
Love Commandment, The
Prinzessin Trulala
Die Tolle Lola
Vater Werden Ist Nicht Schwer
Wenn Die Einmal Dein Herz Verschen-
  kat

2615
HARVEY, Michael Martin*
Only Way, The (Number 46)

2616
HARVEY, Paul (1884-1955)
Awful Truth, The

2617
HARVEY, William*
White Moll, The

2618
HARVIS, Sidney*
Footlights and Fools

2619
HARWOOD, Bobbie*
Four Feathers, The (Lt. Castleton)

2620
HARYTON, George*
Moon of Israel

2621
HASBROUCK, Olive (1902-)
Border Sheriff

Charge of the Gauchos
Clear the Decks
Cohens and the Kellys, The
Cowboy Cavalier
Desperate Courage
Fighting Three, The
Flying Cowboy, The
Flying Fists
Interferin' Gent
Obligin' Buckaroo
Regular Scout, A
Ride 'em High
Ridin' Rowdy
Royal Rider
Rustler's Ranch
Set Free
Shamrock and the Rose, The
Tearin' into Trouble
Thou Shalt Not Kill
Two-Gun Man, The
Universal player 24
White Pebbles
Woman Who Did Not Care, The

2622
HASBROUCK, Vera*
Cohens and the Kellys, The

2623
HASKEL, Leonhard*
Der Sprung ins Leben [The Leap
    into Life] (ringmaster)
Explosion

2624
HASKELL, Jack Girls, The
Show of Shows, The

2625
HASKELL, Jean*
True as Steel

2626
HASLET, Jessie*
Seventh Heaven (Aunt Valentine Vul-
    mir)

2627
HASSELL, George*
La Boheme (Schaunard)

2628
HASSELQUIST, Jenny*
Aftermath
Emigrants, The
Guilty
Johan
Love's Crucible

Story of Gösta Berling, The (Mari-
    anne Sinclaire)
Sumurun /aka/ One Arabian Knight
    (Zuleika)

2629
HASSEN, Jamiel*
Behind that Curtain (Habib Hanna)

2630
HATCH, William Riley*
America /aka/ Love and Sacrifice
    (Joseph Brant)
Idol of the North, The (Ham Devlin)
If Winter Comes
Little Miss Rebellion
Little Old New York (Philip Schuyler)
West of the Water Tower
Zaza (Regault)

2631
HATHAWAY, Peggy*
Christie Johnstone (Jean)

2632
HATHAWAY, Red*
Bigger than Barnum's

2633
HATSWELL, Donald*
Madness of Youth, The
Peg O' My Heart (Alaric Chichester)

2634
HATTEN, Charles*
Lorna Doone
Stella Dallas (Helen's son, 19 years
    later)

2635
HATTON, Frances*
Confessions of a Queen
Day of Faith, The

2636
HATTON, Mercy*
Christie Johnstone (Lady Barbara
    Sinclair)

2637
HATTON, Raymond (1892-1971)
Ace of Hearts (the menace)
Adventure
Affairs of Anatol, The (Hoffmeier)
At Bay
Barefoot Boy, The
Behind the Front
Big Brother

Big Killing, The
Born to the West
Bunty Pulls the Strings
Come On, Cowboys!
Concert, The
Contraband
Cornered
Dancin' Fool (Enoch Jones)
Dear Vivien
Devil's Cargo, The
Doubling for Romeo
Ebb Tide
Fashions for Women
Fighting American, The
Fireman, Save My Child!
Forlorn River
Four Hearts
Head over Heels
Hell's Heroes
His Back Against the Wall
Hottentot, The
Hunchback of Notre Dame, The
  (Gringoire)
In the Name of Love
Janice Meredith
Java Head
Jes' Call Me Jim
Lord Jim
Lucky Devil, The
Lure of the Range, The
Man of Action, A
Manslaughter (Brown)
Midnight Mystery
Mighty, The (Dogey Frank)
Mine with the Iron Door, The
Now We're in the Air
Office Scandal
Officer 666
Partners in Crime
Peck's Bad Boy
Pilgrims of the Night
Pink Gods
Rip Snorter, The
Salvage (the cripple)
Sea Wolf, The
Silence
Son of His Father, A
Stop Thief!
Three Wise Fools
Thundering Herd, The (Jude Pil-
  chuck)
Tie that Binds, The
To Have and to Hold
Tomorrow's Love
Top of the World, The
Trent's Last Case
Trimmed in Scarlet
Triumph (a tramp)

True as Steel
We're in the Navy Now
Western Fate
When Caesar Ran a Newspaper
Whirlwind Ranger
Wife Savers
Young Mrs. Winthrop

2638
HAUBER, Billy*
Golf
Midnight Taxi, The

2639
HAUPT, Ulrich (1887-1931)
Captain Swagger
Far Call
Frozen Justice
Greene Murder Case, The (Dr. Ar-
  thur vonBlon)
Iron Mask, The (DeRochefort)
Madame X (Larocque)
Rogue Song, The (Prince Serge)
Tempest, The
Wonder of Women, The

2640
HAUSE, Newton*
Which Shall It Be?

2641
HAUSSERMANN, Reinhold*
Moon of Israel

2642
HAVER, Phyllis (1899-1960)
After Business Hours
Among Those Present
Balloonatic, The
Battle of the Sexes (Marie Skinner)
Bolted Door, The
Breath of Scandal, The
Cave Man, The
Chicago
Christian, The (Polly Love)
Common Law, The
Don Juan (Imperia)
Fig Leaves
Fighting Coward, The
Fighting Eagle, The
Foolish Age, The
Golden Princess
Hard Boiled
Hearts and Flowers
Hell's Kitchen
Her Husband's Secret
His Last False Step
I Want My Man

Lilies of the Field
Little Adventuress, The
Love, Honor and Behave
Married Life
Midnight Express, The
Nervous Wreck, The
Never Too Old
New Brooms
No Control
Nobody's Widow
Office Scandal
Other Women's Husbands
Perfect Flapper, The
Rejuvenation of Aunt Mary, The
Sal of Singapore
Salome vs. Shenandoah
Shady Lady
Singer Jim Mc Kee
Single Wives
Small Town Idol, A
Snob, The
So Big (Dallas O'Meara)
Temple of Venus, The (Constance
   Lane)
Tenth Avenue
Three Bad Men
Thunder (Zella)
Universal player 23
Up in Mabel's Room
Way of All Flesh, The (The Temp-
   tress)
What Price Glory? (Shanghai Mabel)
Wise Wife
Your Wife and Mine

2643
HAVEZ, Jean C. *
Navigator, The
Seven Chances

2644
HAWES, Mary*
Only Thing, The
Scarlet Letter, The (Patience)
Soul Mates

2645
HAWLEY, Helen*
Laughing Lady, The

2646
HAWLEY, Wanda (1897-)
Affairs of Anatol, The (Emilie Dixon)
American Pluck
Barriers Burned Away
Bobbed Hair
Bread
Burning Sands

Combat
Double Speed
Eyes of the Totem
Fires of Fate
Food for Scandal
Graustark (Dagmar)
Hearts and Spangles
Held by the Enemy
Her Beloved Villain
Her Face Value
Her First Elopement
Her Sturdy Oak
House that Jazz Built, The
Kiss in Time, A
Let Women Alone
Love Charm, The
Man from Brodney's, The
Masters of Men, The
Men of the Night
Midnight Message, The
Miss Hobbs
Mrs. Temple's Telegram
Outside Woman, The
Peg O' My Heart
Phantom of the Forest, The
Pirates of the Sky
Secret Service
Sick Abed
Six Best Cellars, The
Smoke Eaters, The
Smouldering Fires
Snob, The
Stop Flirting
Tailor-Made Man, The
Thirty Days
Too Much Wife
Tree of Knowledge, The
Truthful Liar, The
La Veglione
Whom Shall I Marry?
Woman Who Walked Alone, The
Young Rajah, The

2647
HAWTHORNE, David*
His House in Order (Filmer Jerson)
Prince of Lovers, The

2648
HAY, Charles*
Return of Sherlock Holmes, The

2649
HAY, Mary (1901-1957)
First National player 21
New Toys
Sonny
Way Down East (Kate Brewster)

Stage:
Sunny ("Weenie" Winters) 25

2650
HAYAKAWA, Sessue (1889-1973)
Arabian Knight, The
Battalion, The
Black Roses
Beggar Prince, The
Brand of Lopes, The
Danger Line, The
Daughter of the Dragon
Devil's Claim, The
First Born, The
Five Days to Live
Great Prince Shan, The
House of Intrigue, The
I Killed
Illustrious Prince, The
Li Ting Lang
Night Life in Hollywood
Sen Yan's Devotion
Street of the Flying Dragon
Swamp, The
Vermillion Pencil, The
Where Lights Are Low
Stage:
Love City, The (Chang Lo) 26

2651
HAYDEN, Nora*
Chicken a la King

2652
HAYDEN-COFFIN, Adeline*
Black Spider, The
Christie Johnstone (Mrs. Gatty)
Kissing Cup's Race (Lady Carring-
ton)
This Freedom (Mrs. Aubyn)
Triumph of the Rat, The (Duchess
de l'Orme)
Woman Tempted, The

2653
HAYE, Helen (Helen Hay) (1874-
1957)
Atlantic (Mrs. Tate Hughes)
Skin Game, The (Amy)
Tilly of Bloomsbury (Lady Adela
Mainwaring)

2654
HAYES, Daniel L. --see: Daniel L.
Haynes

2655
HAYES, Danny*
New Klondike, The

2656
HAYES, Frank (-1924)
Greed (Old Grannis)
Vanity Fair (Mr. Wenham)

2657
HAYES, George "Gabby" (George F.
Hayes) (1885-1969)
Big News (reporter)
Rainbow Man, The
Smiling Irish Eyes
Why Women Remarry

2658
HAYES, Helen (Helen Hayes Brown)
(1900-)
Babs
Stage:
Babs (Title role) 20
Caesar and Cleopatra (Cleopatra) 25
Coquette (Norma Besant) 27
Golden Days (Mary Anne) 21
Quarantine (Dinah Portlett) 24
To the Ladies (Elsie Beebe) 22
What Everywoman Knows (Maggie
Wylie) 26

2659
HAYES, William T. *
Get Rich Quick Wallingford (G. W.
Battles)

2660
HAYNES, Daniel L. *
Hallelujah! (Zeke)

2661
HAYS, Guerney*
Chechahcos, The

2662
HAYSE, Emil*
Moon of Israel

2663
HAYWARD, Helen*
Chaser, The

2664
HAZLETON, Joseph H. *
Oliver Twist (Mr. Grimwig)

2665
HEADRICK, Richard (1917-)
Chicago Sal
Child Thou Gavest Me, The
East Lynne (Willie)
Environment, The
Grail, The
Hearts Aflame
Playthings of Destiny
Retribution
Rich Men's Wives
Song of Life, The
Spider and the Rose, The
Stigma, The
Toll Gate, The (The Little Fellow)
White Shoulders
Woman in His House, A

2666
HEALY, Dan*
Glorifying the American Girl
Laughing Lady, The

2667
HEARN, Edward (1888-)
All Dolled Up
Avenging Arrow, The [serial]
Bachelor Girl
Coast of Opportunity, The
Danger Line, The
Daredevil Jack [serial]
Daughters of Today
Dog Justice
Donovan Affair, The
Down Home
Drake Case, The
Face of the World, The
Glory of Clementina, The
Harvester, The
Hook and Ladder No. 9
Keeping up with Lizzie
Lawful Cheaters (Roy Burns)
Lost Express, The
Man Without a Country, The /aka/
    As No Man Has Loved
Ned McCobb's Daughter
One Man Dog
One of the Bravest
Pathé player 21
Patsy, The
Things Men Do, The
Truthful Liar, The
When a Man's a Man
Winner Take All
Winners of the Wilderness (George
    Washington)
Yellow Cameo, The

2668
HEARN, George*
Ned McCobb's Daughter (Butter-
    worth)

2669
HEARN, Lew*
Royal Box, The

2670
HEARN, Mary*
Conquering Power, The

2671
HEARNE, James A. *
Shore Acres

2672
HEATH, Rosalie*
Glorious Adventure, The (Queen
    Catherine)

2673
HEATHERLY, Clifford*
Mademoiselle from Armentieres
    (German intelligence officer)
Roses of Picardy (Uncle)

2674
HECHY, Alice*
Der Kleine Napoleon [The Little Na-
    poleon] /aka/ So Sind die Manner
    [Men Are Like That]; Napoleons
    Kleiner Bruder [Napoleon's Little
    Brother] (Annemarie)
Der Leibgardist [The Guardsman]

2675
HECK, Stanton*
Bad Man, The
Courtship of Miles Standish, The
Her Honor the Governor
Mystic, The
Old Clothes
Perfect Crime, A (Big Bill Thaine)
Silent Sanderson
Woman on the Jury, The
Yankee Clipper, The

2676
HEDQUIST, Ivan*
Youth

2677
HEENAN, James*
Woman in Gray, A (Wilfred
    Amory)

2678
HEGEMAN, Alice*
Laughing Lady, The

2679
HEGEWALD*
Der Mensch am Wege [Man by the
Roadside]

2680
HEGGIE, O. P. (1879-1936)
Actress, The
Letter, The
Mighty, The (J. K. Patterson)
Mysterious Dr. Fu Manchu, The
/aka/ The Insidious Dr. Fu
Manchu (Nayland Smith)
One Romantic Night
Trelawney of the Wells (Sir. William
Gower)
Wheel of Life, The
Stage:
Minick (Old Man Minick) 24
She Stoops to Conquer (Diggory)
28
Truth About Blayds, The (Oliver
Blayds) 22

2681
HEIDEMANN, Paul*
Die Bergkatze [The Mountain Cat;
The Wild Cat] (Lieutenant Alexis)
Der Kleine Napoleon [The Little Na-
poleon] /aka/ So Sind die Manner
[Men Are Like That]; Napoleons
Kleiner Bruder [Napoleon's Little
Brother] (Jerome Bonaparte)
Der Sprung ins Leben [The Leap in-
to Life] (young scholar)
Wie Einst im Mai

2682
HEINK, Schuman*
Wedding March, The (guard)

2683
HEINRICH, George*
Constant Nymph, The (Sanger)
Waterloo

2684
HELBERT, Jack*
Stephen Steps Out

2685
HELLER, Frank*
Happy Days (chorus)

2686
HELLER, Gloria*
So This Is Marriage
Wine of Youth

2687
HELLER, Ray*
It Must Be Love
Last Edition

2688
HELLMAN, Miriam*
Happy Days (chorus)

2689
HELLUM, Barney*
Spanking Breezes
Swim Princess, The

2690
HELM, Brigette (Gisele Eve Schitten-
helm) (1908-)
At the Edge of the World (Magda)
Crisis
Daughter of Destiny, A /aka/ Al-
raune
L'Argent
Loves of Jeanne Ney, The
Metropolis (debut-dual role, Maria/
Robot) (Mary in U. S. A.)
Wonderful Life, The

2691
HELMS, Ruth*
Fighting Chance

2692
HELTON, Percy (1894-1971)
Silver Wings

2693
HEMMING, Violet (1893-)
Cost, The
When the Desert Calls
Stage:
Jest, The (Ginevra) 26
Rivals, The (Lydia Languish) 22
Sonya (Title role) 21
Spring Cleaning (Margaret Sones)
23
This Thing Called Love (Ann Marvin)
28

2694
HENCKELS, Paul*
Shadows of Fear

2695
HENDERSON, Bert*
Wyoming

2696
HENDERSON, Del (1877-1956)
Bad Lands, The
Blazing Barriers
Broken Silence
Condemned Woman
Crowd, The (Dick)
Dynamite Allen
Gambling Wives
Getting Gertie's Garter
Hit the Deck
Iron Mike
Is Everybody Happy?
Love Bandit, The
Patsy, The (Pa Harrington)
Pay Off, The
Power of the Press
Rambling Rangers
Riley, the Cop
Shark, The
Show People (Col. Pepper)
Three-Ring Marriage

2697
HENDERSON, Joseph*
Three Miles Out

2698
HENDERSON, Lucius*
Great Deception, The
Man Must Live, A
New Commandment, The

2699
HENDRICK, Richard*
Should a Woman Tell?

2700
HENDRICKS, Ben*
Barbed Wire
Footlights and Fools (stage doorman)
Great Divide, The
Headless Horseman, The
One Minute to Play
Out All Night
Rolling Home
Skinner's Dress Suit
Synthetic Sin
Take It from Me
Tides of Passion
Twin Beds
Waterfront
Welcome Home
What Happened to Jones?

Wild Party, The (Ed)

2701
HENDRICKS, Louis*
Conquest of Canaan, The

2702
HENIE, Sonja (1912-1969)
Syv Dager for Elisabeth (debut)
Stage:
Olympics 28, 29
Olympics at Chamonix (3rd place) 24
Norwegian skating champion 26
World's first figure skating prize 27

2703
HENNESSEY, Johnny*
Great White Way, The

2704
HENNING, Uno*
Cottage on Dartmoor, A
Die Frau, Nach der Man Sich Sehnt
  [The Woman One Longs For]
  (Henry Leblanc)
Loves of Jeanne Ney, The

2705
HENRY, Gale (1893-)
All Parts
Big Squawk, The
Darkened Rooms
Déclassée
East Is Worst
Hunch, The
Long Hose
Love Doctor, The
Merton of the Movies
New Lives for Old
Open All Night
Quincy Adams Sawyer (Samanthy)
Sheik of Hollywood, The
Universal player 24

2706
HENRY, John, Jr.*
Astray from the Steerage (passenger's
  son)

2707
HENRY, William* (1918-)
Lord Jim

2708
HENSON, Leslie (1891-1958)
Alf's Button
Broken Bottles
On with the Dance

Tons of Money

2709
HEPBURN, Barton*
Dynamite (a young vulture)

2710
HERALD, Douglas*
Q Ships

2711
HERBERT, A. J.*
Fool, The

2712
HERBERT, Gwynne*
Anna, the Adventuress
Comin' Thro' the Rye (Mrs. Adair)

2713
HERBERT, Henry J. (1879-1942)
Captain Blood (Capt. Hobart)
Cyclone, The
Day of Faith, The
Enchanted Hill, The
So Big (William Storm)
Their Own Desire

2714
HERBERT, Holmes (Edward Sanger)
   (1882-1956)
Any Wife
Black Is White
Careers
Careless Age, The (Sir John)
Charlatan, The
Charlatan Mystery, The [serial]
Daddy's Gone A-Hunting
Dead Men Tell No Tales
Divorce Coupons
East Side, West Side
Enchanted Cottage, The
Evidence (Judge Rawland)
Family Closet, The
Fire Brigade, The
Fox player 21
Gay Retreat, The
Gentlemen Prefer Blondes (Henry
   Spoffard)
Heart of Salome, The
Heedless Moths
Her Private Life
His House in Order
His Lady /aka/ When a Man Loves
   (Jean Liberge)
Honeymoon Express, The
Inner Chamber, The
Kiss, The (Lassalle)

Lady Rose's Daughter
Lovers
Love's Wilderness
Madame X (Noel)
Market of Souls
Mr. Wu (Mr. Gregory)
Moonshine Valley (Dr. Martin)
My Lady's Garter
Nest, The
On Trial (Gerald Trask)
On with the Dance
One Increasing Purpose
Passionate Quest
Right to Love, The
Say It with Songs
Silver Slave, The
Sinners in Heaven
Slaves of Beauty
Stage Romance, A
Terror, The (Henry Goodman)
Their Hour
Thirteenth Chair, The
This Sporting Age
Through the Breakers
Truth About Husbands, The
Untamed (Howard Presley)
Wild Goose, The
Wildfire
Woman of the World, A
Woman's Woman, A

2715
HERBERT, Hugh (1887-1951)
Caught in the Fog
Great Gabo, The
Lights of New York

2716
HERBERT, Jack*
Excuse My Dust (Oldham)

2717
HERBERT, Joe*
Seven Keys to Baldpate

2718
HERBERT, Sidney*
Her Love Story
If Winter Comes
Orphans of the Storm (Robespierre)
Thief, The
Under the Red Robe

2719
HERBST, Häring*
Der Mensch am Wege [Man by the
   Roadside]

2720
HERDMAN, John*
Christian, The (Parson Quayle)
Lady, The

2721
HERIAT, Philippe*
Flood, The
Miracle of the Wolves, The
Sea Fever

2722
HERIBELL, Renee*
Appassionata
Madame Sans-Gene (Princess Eliza
  Bacciocni)
Trois Masques, The (The Three
  Masques)

2723
HERLINGER, Carl*
Show Boat (the wheelsman)

2724
HERMAN, Helena*
Street Angel (Andrea)

2725
HERNANDEZ, Anna*
Extra Girl, The
Name the Man

2726
HERNANDEZ, George*
Village Sleuth, The

2727
HEROLD, Douglas*
Luck of the Navy, The (Joe Briggs)

2728
HERRICK, Jack*
Beau Broadway
Dick Turpin
Is Zat So?
Way of a Girl, The

2729
HERRICK, Joe*
Cock-Eyed World, The (brawler)

2730
HERRING, Aggie (-1938)
Any Woman
Big Happiness
Blind Bargain, The (Bessie)
Children of the Ritz
Dark Streets

Do Your Duty
Down Home
Dream Cheater, The
Dwelling Place of Light
Finnegan's Ball
Girl's Decision, A
Gorilla, The
Hairpins
Head of the Family, The
Heart's Haven, The
Heroes of the Streets
Isle of Lost Ships, The (Mother
  Joyce)
Kosher Kitty Kelly
Lady Be Good
Little Shepherd of Kingdom Come,
  The
Loco Luck
Lord Loves the Irish, The
Lure of Egypt, The
McFadden Flats
Mysterious Rider, The
Ninety and Nine, The
Oliver Twist (the Widow Corney)
Pampered Youth
Pioneer Trails
Queenie
Ragged Heiress, The
Rookie's Return, The
Sagebrusher, The
Sally, Irene and Mary (Mrs. O'Brien)
Smiling Irish Eyes
That Certain Feeling
What a Wife Learned

2731
HERRING, Jess*
Beloved Brute, The

2732
HERSHFIELD, Harry (1885-   )
Great White Way, The

2733
HERSHOLT, Jean (1886-1956)
Abie's Irish Rose (Salomon Levy)
Alias the Deacon
Battle of the Sexes (Judson)
Certain Rich Man, A
Cheap Kisses
Dangerous Innocence
Deceiver, The
Don Q, Son of Zorro (Don Fabrique)
East Is West
Fifth Avenue Models
Flames
Four Horsemen of the Apocalypse
  (Prof. von Hartott)

Girl on the Barge, The
Give and Take
Golden Dreams
Golden Trail, The
Goldfish, The
Gray Dawn, The
Greater Glory, The
Greed (Marcus Schouler)
Heart's Haven, The
Her Night of Romance
If Marriage Fails
It Must Be Love
Jazz Mad
Jazzmania
Man of the Forest
Merely Mary Ann
Modern Love
My Old Dutch
Old Soak, The
Quicksands
Red Lane, The
Red Lights
Secret Hour, The
Servant in the House, The
Sinners in Silk
So Big (August Hemple)
Stella Dallas (Ed Munn)
Stranger's Banquet, The
Student Prince, The (Dr. Juttner)
Tess of the Storm Country (Don
    Lotta)
13 Washington Square (Deacon Pye-
    croft)
Torment
United Artist player 29
Universal player 29
Woman on the Jury, The
When Romance Rides
Woman's Faith, A
Wrong Mr. Wright, The
You Can't Buy Love
Younger Generation, The

2734
HERTER, Francis*
Prince and the Pauper, The

2735
HERWICH, Mme. *
Legion of Honor, The

2736
HERZINGER, Charles*
Bat, The (man in black mask)

2737
HERZOG, Fred*
Scarlet Letter, The (the jailer)

2738
HESPERIA, Alda Mme. *
Little Corporal, The

2739
HESSE, Alice*
Christian, The (Mary)

2740
HESSE, Julia*
Dramatic Life of Abraham Lincoln,
    The /aka/ Abraham Lincoln

2741
HESSELWOOD, Tom*
Glorious Adventure, The (Solomon
    Eagle)
Virgin Queen, The (Prestal the As-
    trologer)

2742
HESSLING, Catherine*
Little Match Girl, The (Title role)
Little Red Riding Hood (Title role)
Nana
La P'tite Lillie
Sea Fever

2743
HESTERBERG, Trude*
Forbidden Love
Der Juxbaron [The Imaginary Baron]
    (Fränze)
Madame Wünscht Kline Kinder [Mad-
    ame Doesn't Want Children]
    /aka/ Madame Wants No Children
    (Elayne's mother)
Manon Lescaut (Claire)
Strauss, the Waltz King
Wie Einst im Mai

2744
HEUZE, Andre*
Legion of Honor, The

2745
HEWLAND, Philip*
Kissing Cup's Race (Vereker)

2746
HEYES, Herbert (1889-1958)
Evil Half, The
Dangerous Moment, A
Queen of Sheba, The (Tamaran)

2748
HIATT, Ruth (Ruth Redfern) (1908-)
Captain Applesauce

Chinatown Mystery, The [serial]
Extra! Extra!
For the Love of Tut
Grass Skirts
Her First Flame
Long Pants
Missing Link, The
Saturday Afternoon
Shanghai Rose
Smith Family, The
Smith's Pony

2749
HICKMAN, Alfred*
Civilian Clothes (Billy Arkwright)
Enchanted Cottage, The
Passion Flower
Rescue, The

2750
HICKMAN, Howard (1880-1949)
Alias Jimmy Valentine (Mr. Lane)
Brothers
His First Command

2751
HICKS, Maxine Elliott--see: Maxine Elliott

2752
HICKS, Sir Seymour (1871-1949)
Always Tell Your Wife
Sleeping Partners

2753
HIERS, Walter (1893-1933)
Beware of Widows
Blondes by Choice
Bought and Paid For
Christine of the Hungry Heart
City Sparrow, The
Educational comedies
Excuse Me
Fair Week
Flaming Barriers
Fourteenth Man, The
Ghost Breaker, The
Going Some
Her Gilded Cage (Charles "Bud" Walton)
Hold that Lion!
Hollywood
Hot Lemonade
Hunting Trouble
Is Matrimony a Failure?
Jimmy
Mr. Billings Spends His Dime
Mrs. Temple's Telegram

Naughty
Night Life (manager)
Oh, Lady, Lady
Paramount player 21
Racing Romeo, A
Romeo and Juliet
Sham
Simple Sap, A
Sixty Cents an Hour
Snob, The
So Long Letty
Three O'Clock in the Morning
What's Your Husband Doing?
Wireless Lizzie
Woman Against the World, A

2754
HIGBY, Wilbur*
Confessions of a Queen
Ladder Jinx, The
Lights of Old Broadway (Fowler)
Richard the Lion-Hearted (Sir Thomas DeVaux)

2755
HIGGINS, David*
Confidence Man, The

2756
HIGHTOWER, Harold*
Four Feathers, The (Ali)

2757
HILBERT, Georg*
Der Mensch am Wege [Man by the Roadside]

2758
HILDEBRAND, Rodney*
Mother Machree

2759
HILDRETH, Kathryn*
Civilian Clothes (Elizabeth Lanham)

2760
HILL, Al*
Alibi /aka/ The Perfect Alibi (Brown)
Half Way to Heaven
Me, Gangster (Danny)
Racketeer, The (Squid)

2761
HILL, Doris*
Avalanche
Beauty Shoppers
Better 'Ole, The

Casey at the Bat
Court Martial
Darkened Rooms
Figures Don't Lie
Fools for Luck
His Glorious Night
Interference
Men Are Like That
Paramount player 26
Rough House Rosie (Ruth)
Studio Murder Mystery, The (Helen
    MacDonald)
Take Me Home
Tell It to Sweeney
Thief in the Dark, A
Tillie's Punctured Romance (heroine)

2762
HILL, Josephine*
Alibi /aka/ The Perfect Alibi (bit)
Heroes of the Wild
Loser's End, The
Ridin' Fool, The

2763
HILL, Kathryn*
Wanderer, The
Yankee Senor, The

2764
HILL, Lee*
Cytherea (Groves' butler)

2765
HILL, Maude*
Puritan Passions

2766
HILL, Thelma*
Barber's Daughter, The
Bee's Buzz, The
Big Palooka, The
Bride's Relations, The
Constabule, The
Crooks Can't Win
Fair Co-Ed, The
Girl Crazy
Golfers, The
Lunkhead, The
Old Barn, The
Play Girl, The
Prodigal Bridegroom, The
Two Tars /aka/ Two Tough Tars

2767
HILLBERG, Gösta*
Gunnar Hede's Saga

2768
HILLBURN, Betty*
Married? (Mary Jane Paul)

2769
HILLER, Kurt*
Last Laugh, The /aka/ Der Letze
    Mann

2770
HILLER, Max*
Last Laugh, The /aka/ Der Letze
    Mann (the daughter's fiancé)

2771
HILLIARD, Ernest (1886-1946)
Beloved Vagabond, The (Major Wal-
    ters)
Big Diamond Robbery, The
Big Hop, The
Bowery Cinderella, A
Broadway after Midnight
Broadway Lady
Burning up Broadway
Devil Dogs
Divine Sinner, The (Prince Josef
    Miguel)
Divorce Coupons
Dugan of the Dugout
Dynamite (a good mixer)
Evidence (Walter Stanley)
Fighting Failure, The
Forest Havoc
Husbands Are Liars
Lady Raffles series
Let It Rain
Little Child Shall Lead Them, A
Man and Wife
Married People
Matinee Idol, The
Matrimonial Web
Midnight Adventure, A
Midnight Watch
Modern Daughters
Modern Marriage
Out with the Tide
Racing Fool, The
Recoil, The
Red Hot Rhythm
Red Wine
Ruling Passion, The
Silent Hero, The
Silver Wings
Sinners in Love
Smile, Brother, Smile
Tropical Love
Wall Street
When Dreams Come True

White Mice
Wide Open

2772
HILLIARD, Harry*
Dangerous Talent
Girl in No. 20, The

2773
HIND, Earl*
He Who Gets Socked

2774
HINDS, Samuel S. *
Shore Leave

2775
HINES, Johnny (1895-)
Alias Jimmy Valentine
All Aboard
Brown Derby, The
Burn 'em up Barnes
Chinatown Charley
Conductor 1492
Crackerjack, The
Early Bird, The
Home Made
Little Johnny Jones
Live Wire, The
Luck
Rainbow Riley
Scrap of Paper, A
Speed Spook, The
Stepping Along
Sure-Fire Flint
Torchy
Torchy in High
Torchy Mixes In
Torchy Turns Cupid
Torchy's Big Lead
Torchy's Double Triumph
Torchy's Night Hood
White Pants Willie
Wright Idea

2776
HISLE, Betsy Ann*
Nellie, the Beautiful Cloak Model
Sorrell and Son

2777
HITCHCOCK, Alfred (1899-)
Blackmail (man on train)
Lodger, The (his first thriller film)

2778
HITCHCOCK, Raymond (1865-1929)
Beauty Shop, The

Everybody's Acting
Monkey Talks, The
Pusher-in-the-Face, The
Redheads Preferred
Upstream
Stage:
Just Fancy (Charlie Van Bibber) 27
Ziegfeld Follies of 1921

2779
HJELDE, Hakon*
Syv Dager for Elisabeth

2780
HO, Chew*
Percy

2781
HO-CHANG, King*
Piccadilly (Jim)

2782
HOBBES, Halliwell (1877-1962)
Grumpy
Jealousy (Rigaud)
Lucky in Love
Stage:
Swan, The (Father Hyacinth)

2783
HOBBS, Hayford*
Flag Lieutenant, The (Commander
    D'Arcy Penrose)
Luck of the Navy, The (Louis Peel)

2784
HOBBS, Jack (1893-)
Call of Youth, The
Crimson Circle, The
Crooked Man, The
Eleventh Commandment, The
Face at the Window, The
Happy Ending, The
Inheritance
Lonely Lady of Grosvenor Square,
    The
Naval Treaty, The
Shuttle of Life, The
Skin Game, The

2785
HOCH, Emil*
America (Lord North)
Stage Struck (Mr. Wagner)

2786
HOFFER, Emil*
Jew of Mestri, The (Marco)

2787
HOFFMAN, Otto (1879-)
Acquitted
Ambrose Applejohn's Adventure
    (Horace Pengard)
Beware of Widows
Broadway after Dark
Bronze Bell, The
Bunty Pulls the Strings
Circle, The
Confessions of a Queen
Daddies
Desert Song, The (Hassi)
Dixie Handicap, The
Five Dollar Baby, The
Fourflusher, The
Gas, Oil and Water
Glorious Fool, The
Grain of Dust, A
Great Accident, The
Homer Comes Home
Hottentot, The
Human Wreckage
Is Everybody Happy?
It's a Great Life
Jailbird, The
Just out of College
Lucretia Lombard
Madonna of Avenue A
Mr. Barnes of New York
Noah's Ark (trader)
On with the Show
Painted Ponies
Paris Green
Price She Paid, The
Rinty of the Desert
Satan in Sables
Sin Flood, The
Siren, The
Strangers of the Night
Terror, The ("Soapy" Marks)
This Woman (Judson)
U-Boat 9
Very Truly Yours

2788
HOFFMAN, Ruby*
Tiger's Club, The

2789
HOGAN, Earl*
Haunted Ship, The

2790
HOGAN, J. P. *
Black Lightning (Frank Larned)

2791
HOLCOMB, Helen*
Wild, Wild Susan

2792
HOLDEN, Harry*
Gay Defender, The
Show Boat (Means)
Treasure Island (Capt. Smollett)
Yankee Clipper, The

2793
HOLDEN, Mary*
Singer Jim McKee

2794
HOLDEN, William*
Dynamite (a wise fool)
Fast Life (the Governor)
His Captive Woman
Three Weekends (Carter)
Trespasser, The (John Merrick)
Weary River

2795
HOLDERNESS, Fay*
Dick Turpin
Last Man on Earth, The
Lonesome
Their Purple Moment

2796
HOLDING, Thomas*
Courtship of Miles Standish, The
Honey Bee, The
In Folly's Trail
Pace that Thrills, The
Ruggles of Red Gap
Sacred and Profane Love
Stranger's Banquet, The
Three Musketeers, The (George Vil-
    liers)
White Monkey, The
Woman in His House, A

2797
HOLLAND, Cecil*
Name the Man

2798
HOLLAND, Clifford*
Rich but Honest
Secret Studio, The
Summer Bachelors

2799
HOLLAND, Edwin*
America (Major Strong)

2800
HOLLAND, Joe*
Happy Days (chorus)

2801
HOLLAND, John*
College Coquette, The
Guilty
Hell's Harbor
She Goes to War

2802
HOLLEY, Ruth*
Sherlock, Junior

2803
HOLLIS, Alan*
Vortex, The (Tom Veryan)

2804
HOLLISTER, Alice (1890-)
Dancers, The
Forgotten Law, The
Great Lover, The
Married Flirts
Milestones (Gertrude Rhead)
Voice in the Dark, A

2805
HOLLOWAY, Carol*
Chicken a la King (Effie)
Dangerous Love
Rainbow Trail, The
Saphead, The
Two Moons

2806
HOLLOWAY, Stanley (1890-)
Rotters, The (debut-bit)

2807
HOLLOWAY, Sterling (1905-)
Casey at the Bat
Girl from Nowhere, The

2808
HOLM, Astrid*
Stroke of Midnight, The
Thy Soul Shall Bear Witness

2809
HOLM, Darry*
When Fleet Meets Fleet (German
    Commander's sister)
Wrath of the Sea

2810
HOLM, Magda*
Syv Dager for Elisabeth

2811
HOLMES, Ben*
Bath Between, The

2812
HOLMES, Helen (1892-1950)
Battling Brewster [serial]
Blood and Steel
Crossed Signals
Fast Freight, The
Ghost City
Hills of Missing Men
Lone Hand, The
Lost Express, The [serial]
Medicine Bend
Million in Jewels, A
Mistaken Orders
Open Switch, The [serial chapter 26]
Stormy Seas
Tiger Brand, The [serial]
Whispering Smith

2813
HOLMES, Herbert*
Up the Ladder

2814
HOLMES, Ione*
Convoy
Hit of the Show
Jazz Age, The
Mad Hour, The

2814a
HOLMES, Leon*
Frisco Sally Levy
King of Kings, The (imbecile boy)
Poker Faces

2815
HOLMES, Milton*
Wreck of the Hesperus, The

2816
HOLMES, Phillips R. (1907-1942)
Grumpy
Pointed Heels
Return of Sherlock Holmes, The
Stairs of Sand
Varsity
Wild Party, The (Phil)

2817
HOLMES, Reed*
Singing Fool, The

2818
HOLMES, Robert*
Balaclava (Father Nikolai)

2819
HOLMES, Stuart (1887-1971)
All's Fair in Love
Beloved Brute, The
Between Friends
Beware of Married Men
Body and Soul
Burning Daylight
Cavalier, The
Dangerous Affair, A
Daughters of the Rich
Everybody's Acting
Evil Eye, The [serial]
Four Horsemen of the Apocalypse,
   The (Capt. von Hartrott)
Friendly Enemies
Good and Naughty
Hawk's Nest, The
Her Husband's Trademark (James
   Berkeley)
Heroic Lover
His Lady /aka/ When a Man Loves
   (Louis XV)
Love, Honor and Behave
Man Who Laughs, The (Lord Dirry-
   Moir)
Midnight Message, The
No Woman Knows
North Star, The
Paid Back
Passion Fruit
Polly of the Movies
Primrose Path, The (Tom Canfield)
Prisoner of Zenda, The (Duke
   "Black" Michael)
Rich Men's Daughters
Rip Tide
Romance of a Queen, The (Petro-
   vitch)
Salvation Hunters, The
Shadow of the Law, The (Linyard)
Should Tall Men Marry?
Siren of Seville, The
Steele of the Royal Mounted
Stranger's Banquet, The
Strongheart
Tess of the D'Urbervilles (Alec
   D'Urberville)
Three Weeks
Trailed by Three [serial]

Under Two Flags (Marquis de Cha-
   teuroy)
Unknown Purple, The
Vanity's Price
Your Wife and Mine

2820
HOLMES, Taylor (1872-1959)
Borrowed Finery
Crimson Runner, The
He Did His Best
He Loved the Ladies
King Harold
Nothing but Lies
Nothing but the Truth
One Hour of Love
Rainbow Chaser, The
Twenty Dollars a Week
Verdict, The
Very Idea, The

2821
HOLMQUIST, Sigrid*
Crackerjack, The
Gentleman of Leisure, A
Light that Failed, The
Paramount player 25
School for Wives
Youth for Sale

2822
HOLT, George*
Bigger than Barnum's

2823
HOLT, Gloria*
Lovey Mary

2824
HOLT, Jack (1888-1951)
After the Show
All Soul's Eve
Ancient Highway, The
Avalanche
Best of Luck, The
Blind Goddess
Border Legion
Born to the West
Bought and Paid For
Call of the North
Cheat, The
Court Martial
Crooked Streets
Donovan Affair, The
Don't Call It Love
Ducks and Drakes
Empty Hands
Enchanted Hill, The

Eve's Secret
Father and Son
Flight
Forlorn River
Gentleman of Leisure, A
Held by the Enemy
Light of the Western Stars
Lone Wolf, The
Lost Romance
Making of a Man, The
Man of the Forest
Man Unconquerable, The
Marriage Maker, The
Midsummer Madness
Mysterious Rider, The
Nobody's Money
North of the Rio Grande
North of '36
On the High Seas
Sea Horses
Smart Set, The
Submarine
Sunset Legion
Sunset Pass
Thundering Herd (Tom Doan)
Tiger's Claw, The
Tigress, The
Vanishing Pioneer, The
Vengeance
Wanderer of the Wasteland (Adam
    Larey)
Water Hole, The (Philip Randolph)
While Satan Sleeps
Wild Horse Mesa

2825
HOLTZ, Tenen*
Bringing up Father
Cardboard Lover, The (Argine)
Duke Steps Out, The (Jake)
Frisco Sally Levy
House of Horror, The
Kibitzer, The
Latest from Paris, The
Law of the Range, The
Show People (bit)
Three Live Ghosts
Trail of '98, The (Mr. Balkey)
Upstage

2826
HOLTZ, Tubea*
Show People (bit)

2827
HOMANS, Robert*
Blindfold
Case of Mary Brown, The

Fast and Furious
Fury of the Wild
Isle of Lost Ships, The
Smiling Irish Eyes
Son of the Gods (Dugan)

2828
HOMOLKA, Oscar (1901-)
Aftermath
Prince of Rogues, The
Trial of Donald Westhof, The
Uneasy Money
Women Without Men

2829
HONNETT, Mickie*
It's the Old Army Game

2830
HOOPER, Frank*
Rough Riders, The

2831
HOOSER, William S.*
Spirit of the U.S.A., The

2832
HOPE, Gloria (1901-)
Colorado
Dangerous Hero, A
Free and Equal
Goldwyn player 21
Great Lover, The
Prairie Trails
Road to Divorce, The
Seeds of Vengeance
Tess of the Storm Country (Teola
    Graves)
Texan, The
Third Woman, The
Too Much Johnson
Trouble
Untamed
Woman Who Understood, The

2833
HOPKINS, Maurice (1914-)
This Freedom (Huggo, age 8)

2834
HOPKIRK, Gordon*
Wandering Jew, The (Olalla's lover)

2835
HOPPER, Frank*
Rough Riders, The (Teddy Roose-
    velt)

2836
HOPPER, Hedda (Elda Furry) (1891-
  1966)
Adam and Evil
Black Tears
Cave Man, The
Children of Divorce (Katharine Flan-
  ders)
Chorus Kid, The
Companionate Marriage
Conceit
Cruel Truth
Dance Madness
Dangerous Innocence
Declassee
Divorcee, The
Don Juan (Marquise Rinaldo)
Drop Kick, The
Free Love
Girls Gone Wild
Green-Grass Widows
Half Marriage
Happiness
Harold Teen
Has the World Gone Mad?
Heedless Moths
His Glorious Night
Inner Chamber, The
Last of Mrs. Cheyney, The (Lady
  Marie)
Lew Tyler's Wives
Love and Learn
MGM player 25
Magic Garden, The
Man Who Lost Himself, The
Matinee Ladies
Miami
Mona Lisa
New York Idea, The
Obey the Law
One Woman to Another
Orchids and Ermine
Pleasures of the Rich
Port of Missing Girls, The
Racketeer, The (Karen Lee)
Reno
Reno Divorce
Runaway Girls
Select player 20
Sherlock Holmes /aka/ Moriarty
  (Madge Larrabee)
Silver Treasure, The
Sinners in Silk
Skinner's Dress Suit
Snob, The
Song of Kentucky, A
Teaser, The
Undressed

Venus of Venice
What's Wrong with Women? (Mrs.
  Neer)
Whip Woman, The (Countess)
Why Men Leave Home
Wings (Mrs. Powell)
Zander the Great (Mrs. Caldwell)
Stage:
Six-Cylinder Love (Margaret Rogers)
  21

2837
HOPSON, Violet*
Beating the Book
Beautiful Kitty
Case of Lady Camber, The
Daughter of Love
Great Turf Mystery, The
Her Son
Imperfect Lover, The
Kissing Cup's Race (The Hon. Con-
  stance Medley)
Lady Owner, The
Remembrance
Romance of a Movie Star, The
Scarlet Lady
Son of Kissing Cup
Sportsman's Wife, A
Stirrup Cup Sensation, The
Vi of Smith's Alley
What Price Loving Cup?
When Greek Meets Greek
White Hope, The
Widecombe Affair (the widow)

2838
HÖRBIGER, Paul*
Spione [Spies]

2839
HORN, Camilla (1906-)
Eternal Love (Ciglia)
Eva and the Grasshopper
Faust (Marguerite)
Happy Vineyard
King of the Bernia /aka/ King of
  the Mountain
Royal Box, The
Tempest, The
United Artist player 28

2840
HORTON, Clara (1904-)
Action
Blind Youth
Fighting Blade, The
Fortune Hunter, The
It's a Great Life

Little Shepherd of Kingdom Come,
  The
Nineteen and Phyllis
Prisoners of Love
Servant in the House, The

2841
HORTON, Edward Everett (1886-
  1970)
Ask Dad
Aviator, The (Robert Street)
Beggar on Horseback (Neil McRae)
Eligible Mr. Bangs, The (Title role)
Flapper Wives
Forever After
Front Page Story, A (Rodney
  Marion)
Good Medicine (Dr. Graves)
Helen's Babies (Uncle Harry)
Hottentot, The (Sam Harrington)
La Boheme (Colline)
Ladder Jinx, The (Arthur Barnes)
Leave It to Me
Man Who Fights Alone, The (Bob
  Alten)
Marry Me (John Smith)
Miss Information
Nut Cracker, The /aka/ You Can't
  Fool Your Wife (Horatio)
Poker Faces (a salesman)
Prince Gabby (Title role)
Right Bed, The
Ruggles of Red Gap (Title role)
Sap, The (Bill Small)
Sonny Boy (a detective)
Taxi! Taxi! (Peter Whitley)
Terror, The (Hugh Fane)
To the Ladies (Leonard Beebe)
Too Much Business (the salesman)
Trusting Wives (George)
Try and Get It (Glenn Collins)
Visitor, The
Whole Town's Talking, The (Chester
  Binney)
Stage:
Edward Everett Horton Stock Co. -
  L. A. 28

2842
HORTON, Walter*
Fighting Blade, The (Bob Ayskew)

2843
HOSKINS, Allan Clayton "Farina"*
Big Business
Bouncing Babies
Boxing Gloves
Lazy Days

Mary Queen of Tots
Moan and Groan, Inc.
Railroadin'
Saturday's Lesson
Shivering Shakespeare
Small Talk
Spook Spoofing

2844
HOSKINS, Jannie*
Lazy Days

2845
HOT, Pierre*
La Chute de la Maison Usher [The
  Fall of the House of Usher]

2846
HOTTON, Lucille*
Any Woman

2847
HOUCK, Leo*
Cock-Eyed World, The (brawler)

2848
HOUDINI, Harry (Erich Weiss) (1874-
  1926)
Adventures of Houdini
Deep Sea Loot
Haldane of the Secret Service
Man from Beyond, The
Terror Island
Stage:
Vaudeville 25

2849
HOUSE, Newton*
Spirit of the U. S. A.

2850
HOUSMAN, Arthur (1890-1937)
Ankles Preferred
Bat, The (Richard Fleming)
Bertha, the Sewing Maching Girl
Blooming Angel, The
Broadway (Dolph)
Clay Dollars
Coast of Folly, The (reporter)
County Fair, The
Destiny's Isle
Early to Wed
Fast Company
Fighter, The
Fools for Luck (Charles Grogan)
Girl of the Golden West
Happiness Ahead
Is Life Worth Living?

Love Makes 'em Wild
Love's Masquerade
Man Must Live, A
Man Wanted
Manhandled (Chip Thorndyke)
Midnight Kiss, The (Hector Spencer)
Nellie, the Beautiful Cloak Model
Night Life in New York
Officer O'Brien
Partners in Crime
Point of View
Prophet's Paradise
Publicity Madness
Queen of the Nightclubs
Road of Ambition, The
Rough House Rosie (Kid Farrell)
Shadows of the Sea
Side Street
Singing Fool, The (Blackie Joe)
Sins of the Father (the Count)
Snitching Hour, The
Song of Love
Spotlight, The
Sunrise (Obtrusive Gentleman)
Times Square
Under the Red Robe
Way of a Maid, The
Why Announce Your Marriage?
Wife in Name Only
Worlds Apart

2851
HOUSTON, Josephine*
On with the Show (Bert)

2852
HOWARD, Constance*
Hold that Lion!
Mother Machree
Night Bride, The
Smart Set, The
White Black Sheep, The

2853
HOWARD, Eugene*
Vitaphone
Stage:
George White Scandals 26
Passing Show of 1922, The   22

2854
HOWARD, Frances*
Shock Punch, The
Swan, The
Too Many Kisses
Stage:
Intimate Strangers, The (Florence)
   21

2855
HOWARD, Frederick*
Footlights and Fools (treasurer)

2856
HOWARD, George W. *
I Want My Man
Thief, The

2857
HOWARD, Gertrude*
Easy Pickings
Hearts in Dixie
His Captive Woman
On Your Toes
Show Boat (Queenie)
Synthetic Sin
Uncle Tom's Cabin (Aunt Chloe)

2858
HOWARD, Helen*
Captain Blood

2859
HOWARD, Jack*
Loves of Ricardo, The

2860
HOWARD, Leslie (Howard Stainer)
   (1893-1943)
Bookworms
Five Pound Reward, The
Stage:
Aren't We All? (Hon. Willie Tatham)
   23
Berkeley Square (Peter Standish) 29
Escape (Matt Denant) 27
Green Hat, The (Napier Harpenden)
   25
Her Cardboard Lover (Andre Sallicel)
   27
Just Suppose (first American appear-
   ance: Hon. Sir Calverton Shipley)
   20
Outward Bound (Henry) 24
Wren, The (Roddy) 21

2861
HOWARD, Ray*
Sally, Irene and Mary (Charles Green-
   wood)

2862
HOWARD, Richard*
Desert Gold
Vanishing American, The /aka/ The
   Vanishing Race

2863
HOWARD, Sydney (1884-1946)
Splinters

2864
HOWARD, Willie*
Vitaphone
Stage:
George White's Scandals 26
Passing Show of 1922, The   22
Sky High (Sammy Myers) 25

2865
HOWATT, William*
Greatest Love of All, The

2866
HOWE, Wallace "Wally"*
High and Dizzy (girl's father)
Twenty Dollars a Week
Why Worry?

2867
HOWELL, Alice (1892-   )
Alice of the Sawdust
Balloonatics
Cinderella Cinders
Her Horsehoe Obligation
Honor of the Sawdust
Mother-in-Law, The
Neptune's Naughty Daughter
Wandering Daughters

2868
HOWELL, Yvonne*
Fashions for Women
Take Me Home

2869
HOWES, Bobby (1895-   )
Guns of Loos, The
On with the Dance

2870
HOWES, Reed (-1964)
Bobbed Hair
Come Across
Cyclone Cavalier, The
Danger Quest, The
Dangerous Dude, The
Fashion Madness
Gentle Cyclone
Hell-Ship Bronson
High Flyer, The
High Speed Lee
Kentucky Handicap, The
Ladies' Night in a Turkish Bath
Lost Limited, The

Million for Love, A
Moran of the Mounted
Night Owl, The
Paramount player 28
Racing Fool, The
Racing Romance
Romantic Rogue
Rough House Rosie (Joe Hennessey)
Royal American, The
Russ Farrell, Aviator
Sawdust Paradise, The
Scorcher, The
Self Starter, The
Singing Fool, The (John Perry)
Sky Ranger, The
Snob Buster, The
Stolen Kisses
Terror, The
Wings of the Storm
Youth's Gamble

2871
HOWLAND, Jobyna (1880-1936)
Gold Diggers, The
Second Youth
Stage:
Kid Boots (Dr. Josephine Fitch) 23
Texas Nightingale, The (Brasa Cana-
va) 22

2872
HOWLAND, Olin /aka/ Olin Howlin
   (1896-1959)
Great White Way, The
Janice Meredith (Philemon Hennion)
Zander the Great (Elmer Lovejoy)
Stage:
Two Little Girls in Blue (Morgan
   Atwell) 21

2873
HOXIE, Jack (Jack Hartford Hoxie)
   (1885-1975)
Back Trail, The
Barbed Wire
Border Sheriff
Bustin' Through
Crow's Nest, The
Cyclone Bliss
Daring Chances
Dead or Alive
Demon, The
Desert's Crucible, The
Don Daredevil
Don Quickshot of the Rio Grande
Double-O, The
Fighting Fury
Fighting Peacemaker, The

Fighting Three, The
Forbidden Trail
Forbidden Trails
Galloping Ace
Grinning Guns
Heroes of the Wild [serial]
Hidden Loot
Last Frontier, The
Looking for Trouble
Man from Nowhere, The
Man from Wyoming, The
Man in the Raw
Men of Daring
Open Trail, The
Phantom Horseman, The
Rambling Rangers
Red Hot Leather
Red Warning
Ridgeway of the Mounted
Ridin' Thunder
Roaring Adventure
Rough and Ready
Sign of the Cactus, The
Six Shootin' Romance, A
Two-Fisted Jefferson
Two-Fisted Jones
Universal player 22
Western Wallop, The
Western Whirlwind, The
Where Is the West?
White Outlaw
Wild Horse Stampede

2874
HOY, Danny (1916-   )
Dramatic Life of Abraham Lincoln,
    The /aka/ Abraham Lincoln
    (Abraham, age 7)
Tess of the Storm Country (Ezra
    Longman)
Wedding March, The (mountain
    idiot)

2875
HOYT, Arthur*
Affair of the Follies, An
Any Woman
Bluff
Coming of Amos, The
Crown of Lies
Deadline, The
Don't Neglect Your Wife
Eve's Lover (Amos Potts)
Footloose Widows
Four Horsemen of the Apocalypse,
    The (Lt. Schnitz)
Her Private Affair (Michael Strum)
Home James

In the Heart of a Fool
Is Matrimony a Failure?
Just Married
Lost World, The (Prof. Summerlee)
Love Is an Awful Thing
Love Piker, The
Love Thrill, The
Midnight Sun, The
My Man
Nurse Marjorie
Peacock Alley
Protection
Rejuvenation of Aunt Mary, The
Seven Day's Leave
Shanghai Bound
Slave of Vanity, A
Souls for Sale (Jimmy Teland)
Sporting Venus, A
Stolen Kisses
Stranger's Banquet, The
Sundown
Ten Modern Commandments
Texas Steer, A
Tillie the Toiler (Mr. Smythe)
To the Ladies
Top of New York
Trumpet Island
Wheel of Life, The
When a Man's a Man
White Flower

2876
HOYT, Julia*
Man Who Found Himself, The
Wonderful Thing, The
Stage:
Serena Blandish (a lady of refined
    appearance) 29

2877
HUBBELL, Edwin*
Lady, The

2878
HUBER, Chad*
Pretty Ladies

2879
HUBERT, Paul*
Three Musketeers, The (Felton)

2880
HUFF, Jackie (John Huff)*
Limited Mail, The
Sackcloth and Scarlet
Zander the Great (Title role)

2881
HUFF, Louise (1896-1973)
Dangerous Paradise
Disraeli (Clarissa)
Seventh Day, The
What Women Want
Stage:
Mary the Third (Mary 1st, 2nd, 3rd)
   23

2882
HUGHES, Dorothy*
Sorrows of Satan, The (Mavis'
   friend)

2883
HUGHES, Gareth (1894-1965)
Auctioneer, The
Better Days
Broadway after Midnight
Broken Hearted
Broken Hearts
Chorus Girl's Romance, A (Horace
   Tarbox)
Christian, The (Brother Paul)
Comrades
Don't Write Letters
Enemies of Women (Spadoni)
Eyes of the Totem
Forget Me Not
Garments of Truth
Heroes in Blue
Hunch, The
I Can Explain
In the First Degree
Indiscretion
Kick In
Life's Darn Funny
Little Eva Ascends
Lure of Youth, The
Men of the Night
Midnight Girl, The
Mr. Antonio
Old Age Handicap
Penrod
Penrod and Sam (Robert Williams)
Sentimental Tommy
Shadows of Paris
Silent Sentinel, The
Sky Rider, The
Spanish Dancer, The (Lazarillo)
Stay Home
Top Sergeant Mulligan
Whirlwind of Youth, The
Woman in His House, A
Stage:
Dunce Boy, The (Tude) 25

2884
HUGHES, Lloyd (1897-1960)
Acquitted
Affair of the Follies, An
American Beauty
Are You a Failure?
Beau Revel
Below the Surface
Dangerous Hours
Declassee
Desert Flower, The
Dixie Handicap, The
Ella Cinders
False Road, The
First National player 29
Forever After
Hail the Woman
Half-Way Girl, The
Heart to Heart
Her Reputation
Heritage of the Desert
High Steppers
Homespun Folks
Huntress, The
If I Marry Again
In Everywoman's Life
Irene
Ladies at Play
Loose Ankles
Lost World, The (Edward Malone)
Love Never Dies
Mother O' Mine
Mysterious Island, The
No Place to Go
Pals First
Sailor's Wives
Sally (Blair Farquar)
Scarlet Saint, The
Scars of Jealousy
Sea Hawk, The (Master Lionel Tres-
   silian)
Stolen Bride, The
Tess of the Storm Country (Frederick
   Graves)
Three-Ring Marriage
Too Many Crooks
Valencia
Welcome Stranger, The
Where East Is East (Bobby Bailey)

2885
HUGHES, Morris*
Mollycoddle, The (college boy)
Nut, The

2886
HUGHES, Rush*
Ashes of Vengeance (soldier boy)

Reno
Souls for Sale (second cameraman)
Wall Flower, The

2887
HUGHES, Yvonne*
Monsieur Beaucaire (Duchess de
  Flauhault)
Society Scandal, A (Patricia DeVoe)
Zaza (Nathalie, Zaza's maid)

2888
HULBERT, Claude (1900-1963)
Champagne

2889
HULETTE, Gladys*
As a Man Loves
Bowery Cinderella, A
Brass Bowl, The
Enemies of Women (Vittoria)
Faithless Lover, The
First National player 22
Go Straight
Hoodman Blind
How Women Love
Iron Horse, The (Ruby)
Life's Crossroads
Making the Varsity
Mystic, The
Private Affairs
Secrets of Paris
Skyrocket
Then Came the Woman
Tol'able David (Esther Hatburn)
Unknown Treasures /aka/ The
  House Behind the Hedge
Warning Signal, The

2890
HULL, Arthur S.*
Going Up
Great Moment, The (Hopper)
Impossible Mrs. Bellew, The (At-
  torney Potter)
Man of Action, A
Prince There Was, A
Within the Law (Demarest)
Woman on the Jury, The
Yankee Consul, The

2891
HULL, Henry (1890-)
For Woman's Favor (Lee Bradford)
Hoosier School Master, The
Man Who Came Back, The
One Exciting Night (John Fairfax)
Roulette

Stage:
Cat and the Canary, The (Paul
  Jones) 22
In Love with Love (Robert Metcalf)
  23
Ivory Door, The (King Hilary/King
  Percival) 27
Lulu Belle (George Randall) 26
Michael and Mary (Michael) 29
Youngest, The (Richard Winslow) 24

2892
HUMBERT, George*
Bright Shawl, The (Jaime Quintara)
Greatest Love of All, The
Ladies of the Jury

2893
HUME, Benita (1906-1967)
Balaclava (Jean MacDonald)
Clue of the New Pin, The
Constant Nymph, The (Toni)
Easy Virtue
Happy Ending, The
Her Golden Hair Was Hanging Down
  Her Back
High Treason (Evelyn Seymour)
Lady of the Lake, The
Light Woman, A
South Sea Bubble, A
They Wouldn't Believe Me
Wrecker, The

2894
HUME, Margaret*
Triumph of the Scarlet Pimpernel
  (Lady Blakeney)

2895
HUME, Marjorie (1900-)
Prince of Lovers, The
Two Little Vagabonds (Marion Thorn-
  ton)

2896
HUMES, Fred*
Border Cavalier
Circus Rookies
One Man Game, A

2897
HUMMELL, Wilson*
Dangerous Maid
Devil's Claim, The
First Born, The
Gleam O'Dawn
Honor First
Ladies Must Dress

Woman Trap

2898
HUMPHREY, Griffith*
Dawn (Court Martial President)

2899
HUMPHREY, Orral*
Huckleberry Finn

2900
HUMPHREY, William (1874-   )
Actress, The
Beau Brummel (Lord Alvanley)
Dangerous Innocence
Devil May Care
Dramatic Life of Abraham Lincoln,
   The /aka/ Abraham Lincoln
   (Stephan A. Douglas)
Drusilla with a Million
One Night in Rome
Scaramouche (Chevalier de Chabril-
   lane)
Silent Lover, The
Trelawney of the Wells (Mr. Telfer)
Unholy Three, The (Defense Attorney)
Vanity Fair (Mr. Sedley)

2901
HUMPHREYS, Cecil*
Dick Turpin's Ride to New York
   (Luke Somers)
Glorious Adventure, The (Walter
   Roderick)
Irish Luck

2902
HUMPHRIES, Joe*
Great White Way, The

2903
HUNT, Helen*
Sawdust Paradise, The

2904
HUNT, Irene*
Dramatic Life of Abraham Lincoln,
   The /aka/ Abraham Lincoln
   (Nancy Hanks Lincoln)
Eternal Three, The
Forget Me Not

2905
HUNT, Jay*
Captain Salvation
Harvester, The
Hunchback of Notre Dame, The
Lightnin'

My Own Pal
One Minute to Play

2906
HUNT, Leslie*
Old Home Week
Uncle Sam of Freedom Ridge

2907
HUNT, Madge*
Truthful Liar, The

2908
HUNTER, Glenn (1893-1945)
Broadway Boob, The
Case of Becky, The
Country Flapper, The
Cradle Buster, The
Grit ("Kid" Hart)
His Buddy's Wife
Little Giant, The
Merton of the Movies (Merton)
Pinch Hitter, The (Joel Parker)
Puritan Passions
Romance of a Million Dollars
Scarecrow, The
Second Fiddle
Silent Watcher, The
Smilin' Through (Willie Ainley)
West of the Water Tower
Youthful Cheaters
Stage:
Behold This Dreamer (Charley Tur-
   ner) 27
Intimate Strangers, The (Johnnie
   White) 21
Merton of the Movies (Merton Gill)
   22
She Stoops to Conquer (Tony Lump-
   kin) 28
Spring Is Here (Terry Clayton) 29
Young Woodley (Woodley) 25

2909
HUNTER, Ian (1900-   )
Confessions
Downhill (Archie)
Easy Virtue (plaintiff's counsel)
Girl in London, A
His House in Order (Hilary Jesson)
Mr. Oddy
Not for Sale
Physician, The
Ring, The
Syncopation
Thoroughbred, The
Valley of the Ghosts

Stage:
Olympia (Capt. Kovacs) 28

2910
HUNTLEY, Fred*
Borderland
Call of the Canyon
Excuse My Dust (Police Magistrate)
King of Kings, The (bit)
Land of the Lawless, The
Peg O' My Heart (butler)
Prince There Was, A
To the Last Man
Where the North Begins

2911
HUNTLEY, Hugh*
Second Youth
Social Celebrity, A
Steadfast Heart, The

2912
HUNTOON, Helen*
Loves of Ricardo, The

2913
HURKA, Hans
Monna Vanna

2914
HURLEY, Julia*
Argentine Love
Little French Girl, The
Married? (Madame DuPont)

2915
HURLOCK, Madeleine*
Beach Club, The
Catalina, Here I Come
Daredevil, The
First Hundred Years Are the Worst,
   The
Flirty Four-Flushers, The
From Rags to Britches
Harem Night, A
His New Mama
Luck of the Foolish, The
Paramount player 25
Romeo and Juliet
Sea Dog's Tale, A
Water Wagons
Whispering Whiskers /aka/ Railroad
   Stowaways

2916
HURST, Brandon (1866-1947)
Amateur Gentleman, The (Peterby)
Annie Laurie /aka/ Ladies from

Hell (Campbell Chiefton)
Cytheria (Daniel Randon)
Dark Lantern, A
Dr. Jekyll and Mr. Hyde (Sir George
   Carawe)
Enchanted Hill, The
First Kiss, The
Grand Duchess and the Waiter, The
Greene Murder Case, The (Sproot)
He Who Gets Slapped (clown)
Her Private Life
High School Hero
Hunchback of Notre Dame, The (Je-
   han)
Interference
King of Kings, The (bit)
Lady, The
Love (Karenin)
Lover of Camille, The
Man Who Laughs, The (Barkilphedro)
News Parade, The
Rainmaker, The
Seventh Heaven (Uncle George Vul-
   mir)
Shamrock Handicap, The (the procur-
   er)
Thief of Bagdad, The (the Caliph)
Voice of the Storm
Volcano (André de Chauvalon)
Wolf of Wall Street, The (Sturgess)
World's Applause, The

2917
HURST, Paul C. (1889-1953)
Behind the Mask
Buttons
California Mail, The
Cossacks, The (Zorka)
Courageous Coward, The
Crow's Nest, The
Fighting Cub, The
Gold Hunters, The
Haunted Ranch, The
Heart of a Texan
His First Command
Lawless Legion, The
Midnight Message, The
Officer O'Brien
Oh, Yeah!
Passing of Wolf MacLean, The
Racketeer, The (Mehaffey)
Rainbow, The
Rattler, The
Red Raiders, The
Sailor's Holiday
Table Top Ranch
Tide of the Empire
Valley of the Giants, The

2918
HURTH, Harold*
Silver King, The

2919
HURTON, Clarence*
Navigator, The

2920
HUSTON, Walter (Walter Houghston)
(1884-1950)
Bishop's Candlesticks, The
Carnival Man, The
Gentlemen of the Press (Wickland
    Snell)
Lady Lies, The (Robert Rossiter)
Two Americans
Virginian, The (Trampas)
Stage:
Barker, The (Nifty Miller) 27
Commodore Marries, The (Commo-
    dore Trunnion) 29
Desire under the Elms (Ephriam
    Cabot) 24
Elmer the Great (Elmer Kane) 28
Kongo (Flint) 26
Mr. Pitt (Marshall Pitt) 24
Vaudeville 24

2921
HUSZAR-PUFFY, Karl*
Destiny /aka/ The Third Death; The
    Three Lights; Between Worlds;
    Der Mude Tod
Ich Küsse Ihre Hand, Madame [I
    Kiss Your Hand Madame] (Tallan-
    dier)

2922
HUTCHINS, Bobby "Wheezer"*
Bouncing Babies
Boxing Gloves
Lazy Days
Moan and Groan, Inc.
Railroadin'
Shivering Shakespeare
Small Talk
Wiggle Your Ears

2923
HUTCHINSON, Charles*
Double Adventure [serial]
Fangs of the Wolf
Fatal Plunge, The
Go Get 'em Hutch [serial]
Hidden Aces
Hurricane Hutch [serial]
Law Demands, The

On Probation
Pathé player 21
Poison
Radio Flyer, The
Speed [serial]
Surging Seas, The
Ten after Ten
Trunk Mystery, The
Turned Up
Whirlwind, The [serial]

2924
HUTH, Harold (1892-1967)
Balaclava (Capt. Nolan)
City of Play
Downstream
One of the Best
Silver King, The
Sir or Madam
South Sea Bubble, A
Triumph of the Scarlet Pimpernel,
    The (Fouquier Tinville)

2925
HUTTON, Lucille*
Dick Turpin
Ladies Must Live
Wine of Youth

2926
HUTTON, Raymond*
Three Wise Fools

2927
HYAMES, John*
Broadway Scandals

2928
HYAMS, Leila (1905-   )
Alias Jimmy Valentine (Rose)
Bishop Murder Case, The
Branded Sombrero, The
Brute, The
Bush Leaguer, The
Crimson City, The
Dancing Mothers (Birdie Courtney)
Far Call, The
Father's Day
First National player 26
Foregoing Age
Honor Bound
Hurricane, The
Idle Rich, The
Kick-Off, The
Land of the Silver Fox
Masquerade
One Round Hogan
Our Dancing Daughters

Sandra
Spite Marriage
Summer Bachelors
Thirteenth Chair, The
White Pants Willie
Wizard, The
Wonder of Women, The

2929
HYLAND, Peggy (Gladys Hutchinson)*
At the Mercy of Tiberius
Black Shadows
Faith
Forbidden Cargo
Girl in Bohemia
Honeypot, The
Love Maggy
Merry-Go-Round
Mr. Prim Passes By
Price of Silence, The
Shifting Sands
Web of Chance
With Father's Help

2930
HYMAN, Bynunsky*
Night of Love, The (bandit)
Son of the Sheik (the pincher)
Vanity Fair (Mr. Moss)

2931
HYMAN, Louis*
Broken Hearts

2932
HYMER, Warren (1906-1948)
Cock-Eyed World, The (scout)
Far Call
Frozen Justice
Girl from Havana, The
Movietone Follies of 1929
Speakeasy

2933
HYTTEN, Olaf*
Chu-Chin-Chow (Mukbill)
Kitty
Salvation Hunters, The
Sonia ("Fatty" Webster)

- I -

2934
IBANEZ, Bonaventura*
Romola (Bardo Bardi)

2935
IBANEZ, Ramon*
White Sister, The (Count deFerice)

2936
IBBERSON, H. *
Only Way, The (Judge)

2937
ILLERY, Pola*
Le Capitaine Fracasse
Sous Les Toits de Paris [Under the
    Roofs of Paris]

2938
IMADASHVILLI, A. *
Caucasian Love

2939
IMBODEN, David*
King of Kings, The (Andrew)
Souls for Sale (Caxon)

2940
IMESON, A. B. *
Claude Duval (Lord Chesterton)
Virgin Queen, The (Borghese)

2941
IMHOLZ, Joseph*
William Tell

2942
INCE, Ralph (1887-1937)
After Midnight
Better Way, The
Bigger than Barnum's
Breed of the Sea
Channing of the North
Chicago after Midnight
Danger Street
Dove, The
Highest Law, The
His Wife's Money
Hurricane, The
Justice
Land of Opportunity, The
Man's Home, A
Not for Publication
Playing with Souls
Reckless Youth
Red Foam
Referee, The
Remorseless Love
Sea Wolf, The
Shanghaied
Singapore Mutiny

Success
Tropical Love
Wall Street
Wet Gold
Wide Open Town, A
Yellow Fingers

2943
INGERSOLL, William*
Partners of the Night

2944
INGLETON, George*
Beloved Brute, The
Clean Heart, The

2945
INGRAHAM, Lloyd (-1956)
Front Page Story, A
Last of the Duanes
Night Parade
Rainbow Man, The
Scaramouche (Quintin de Kercar-
    diou)
So Long Letty
Spoilers, The
Untamed

2946
INGRAM, Amo*
Wild Party, The (Jean)

2947
INGRAM, Clifford*
Hearts in Dixie

2948
INGRAM, Rex (American-Black)
    (1896-1969)
Big Parade, The
Four Feathers, The
Hearts in Dixie
Metro player 24
Ten Commandments, The

2949
INKIZHINOV, Valerji*
Heir to Genghis Khan, The
Storm over Asia

2950
INOUYE, Masso*
Daughter of Two Fathers, A

2951
IRBE, Marie-Louise, Mlle. *
Atlantide (Tanit Zerga)

2952
IRTS, Lily*
Dick Turpin's Ride to New York
    (Sally Dutton)

2953
IRVINE, Robin*
Downhill (Tim Wakeley)
Easy Virtue (John Whittaker)
Knight in London, A
Das Schiff der Verlorenen Menschen
    [The Ship of Lost Souls] /aka/
    Le Navire des Hommes Perdus
    [The Ship of Lost Men] (T. W.
    Cheyne)

2954
IRVING, George (1874-1961)
Air Mail, The
American Father, The
Bronco Twisters
Coquette (Robert Wentworth)
Craig's Wife
Dance of Life, The
Desert Gold
Dragnet
Drums of the Desert
Eagle of the Sea, The
Erick the Great
Fangs of Justice
Feel My Pulse
For Sale (Eric Porter)
Godless Girl, The
Golden Princess, The
Goose Hangs High, The (Bernard In-
    gals)
Honor Bound
Last Performance, The
Madonna of the Streets, A (Philip
    Norman)
Man Who Fights Alone, The (Dr.
    Raymond)
Manpower
Midnight Kiss, The (Thomas H. Has-
    tings, Jr.)
Modern Mothers
Moran of the Marines
Napoleon and Josephine
North of '36
One Increasing Purpose
Only Saps Work
Paris Bound (James Hutton, Sr.)
Partners in Crime
Pigs
Port of Missing Girls, The
Primrose Path, The (John Martan)
Risky Business
Runaway Girls

Shanghai Bound
Singapore Mutiny
Son of the Gods (attorney)
Spoilers, The
Three Bad Men
Thunderbolt
Two Flaming Youths (Simon Trott)
Walking Back
Wanderer of the Wasteland (Mr.
  Virey)
Wild Horse Mesa
Wings (Mr. Powell)
Wright Idea, The

2955
IRVING, Mary Jane*
Borderland
Flaming Forest, The
Godless Girl, The (the victim)
Golden Bed, The
Light that Failed, The
Lovey Mary
Night Life (profiteer's daughter)
Splendid Road, The
Stranger, The

2956
IRVING, William*
Coney Island
From Headquarters
Hearts in Exile
Pampered Youth
Winter Has Come
Wireless Lizzie

2957
IRWIN, Boyd (1880-1963)
Ashes of Vengeance (Duc de Guise)
Captain Blood
Eyes of the Eagle
Fatal Sign, The [serial]
Gilded Dream, A
Girl from God's Country, The
Lady in Love, A
Milestones (Arthur Preece)
Silken Sinner, The
Three Musketeers, The (DeRoche-
  fort)
Youth Triumphant

2958
IRWIN, Caroline*
Tornado

2959
IRWIN, John*
Barker, The

2960
IVANOV, I. *
Stachka /aka/ Strike
Tanka-Trakitirschitsa /aka/ Protin
  Osta; Against Her Father; Tanka,
  the Innkeeper

2961
IVINS, Sidna Beth*
Peg O' My Heart (Mrs. Jim O'Con-
  nell)

2962
IZARD, Winifred*
Wandering Jew, The (Rachel)

- J -

2963
JACKSON, Bee*
Lying Wives

2964
JACKSON, Bud*
Broadway Melody, The

2965
JACKSON, Charlotte*
Prince There Was, A

2966
JACKSON, Eugene*
Hearts in Dixie
Little Annie Rooney
Penrod and Sam (Verman)

2967
JACKSON, Mary Ann (1923-)
Bouncing Babies
Boxing Gloves
Lazy Days
Moan and Groan, Inc.
Railroadin'
Saturday's Lesson
Shivering Shakespeare
Small Talk
Smith's Pony
Spanking Breezes
When Greek Meets Greek
Wiggle Your Ears

2968
JACKSON, Peaches*
Circus Days
Cytherea (a Randon child)
Eternal Three, The
Lahoma

Pied Piper Malone
Poisoned Paradise
Prince Chap, The
Rio Grande
Through the Back Door (Conrad)
When Dawn Came

2969
JACKSON, Selmer*
Through Different Eyes (Defense Atty
   King)
Why Bring That Up?

2970
JACKSON, Thomas E. (1895-1967)
Broadway (Dan McCorn)

2971
JACOB, Martin*
Midsummer Night's Dream, A
   (starveling)

2972
JACOBS, Naomi*
First Born, The (Dot)

2973
JACOBSON, H. J. *
Shanghaied

2974
JACOBSON, Lilly*
Hamlet (Ophelia)

2975
JACQUET, Gaston*
Living Image, The
Three Musketeers, The (DeWinter)

2976
JAGGER, Dean (Dean Jeffries)
   (1903-)
Handcuffed
Woman from Hell /aka/ Woman
   from Hell's Paradise (debut)

2977
JAMES, David*
Charley's Aunt (Jack Cheaney)
Stop Flirting

2978
JAMES, Eddie*
Lucky Devil, The

2979
JAMES, Forrest*
Stark Love

2980
JAMES, Gardner*
Amateur Gentleman, The
Big Killing, The
Eager Lips
Fascination
Flaming Forest, The
Flying Fleet, The
Happy Warrior, The
Headless Horseman, The
Hell Bent for Heaven
Kentucky Courage
Ladies at Ease
MGM player 28
Mating Call, The
Passionate Quest
Silent Sanderson
Singapore Mutiny
Sonny
Souls Aflame
Studio Murder Mystery, The (Ted
   MacDonald)
Stage:
Advertising of Kate, The (Sam) 22

2981
JAMES, Gladden*
Adorable Cheat, The
Broken Violin, The
Bucking the Tiger
Channing of the Northwest
Clouded Name, A
Faithless Sex, The
Footfalls
Girl from Woolworth's
His Brother's Keeper
His Captive Woman
Look-Out Girl, The
Midnight Bride, The
Peacock Fan, The
Road to Ambition, The
Silver Lining
Sweet Sixteen
Temptations of a Shop Girl
Weary River
Woman with Four Faces, The (the
   boy)
Yes or No?

2982
JAMES, Gordon*
Weary River

2983
JAMES, Horace*
Get Rich Quick Wallingford (Timothy
   Battles)

Stage:
Fan, The (Monsieur Oviedo) 21
Sonny (Henry) 21

2984
JAMES, J. Wharton*
Pollyanna

2985
JAMES, Walter*
Battling Butler
Blood Ship, The
Everlasting Whisper, The
Idol Dancer, The (Chief Wando)
Irresistible Lover
Kid Brother, The
Little Annie Rooney
Me, Gangster (Police Captain Dodds)
Monster, The (Caliban)
Stage:
Monster, The (Caliban) 22

2986
JAMES, William*
Love Flower, The (Crane's assist-
ant)

2987
JAMESON, Amable*
Romeo und Julia im Schnee [Romeo
and Juliet in the Snow]

2988
JAMISON, William "Bud" (1894-1943]
Buck Privates
Chaser, The
Dante's Inferno
Heart Trouble
His First Flame
Horse Sense
Jake the Plumber
Long Pants
One Horse Town
Taxi Scandal, A
Texas Steer, A

2989
JANA, La*
Shadows of Fear

2990
JANG, Amir*
Grass (the tribal chief)

2991
JANIS, Dorothy (1910-)
Fleet Wings
Humming Wires

Kit Carson
Pagan, The
Stage:
Passing Show of 1924, The   24

2992
JANIS, Elsie (Elsie Bierbauer) (1889-
1956)
Everybody's Sweetheart
Imp, The
Vitaphone
Record:
Fo' de Lawd's Sake, Play a Waltz
(B-12529-J) (LPV 560)
Stage:
Elsie Janis and Her Gang 22
Puzzles of 1929
Vaudeville 26-28

2993
JANNEY, Leon (Laon Ramon) (1917-)
Wind, The (Cora's son)

2994
JANNEY, William (William Preston
Janney) (1908-)
Coquette (Jimmy Besant)
Mexicali Rose
Salute
Stage:
Bridge of Distance (a hotel boy) 25
Great Music (footman) 24
Tommy (Tommy Mills) 27

2995
JANNINGS, Emil (1886-1950)
Emil Jannings was born in Brooklyn, New York on July 26, 1886.
At the age of ten his parents re-
turned to Germany. His education
was at Zürich and Gorlitz. He
studied under Max Reinhardt at the
Darmstadt Royal Theatre in Berlin.
Considered by many critics and
historians as the world's greatest
actor.   Jannings was blacklisted
by the Allies because Hitler ap-
pointed him head of UFA and for
his Goebbels' Ministry of Propa-
ganda films.   Jannings retired to
Austria where he died in 1950.
Hair: Light brown. Eyes: Brown.
Height: 6'. Married four times;
his last wife, Gussie Holl, had
previously been married to Conrad
Veidt.
Algal
Alles für Geld [All for a Woman]

Anna Boleyn /aka/ Deception (Henry VII)
Betrayal, The
Danton
Du Barry, Woman of Passion
Faust (Mephisto)
Fighting the White Slave Traffic
Fortune's Fool
Husbands and Lovers
Kölhiessel's Töchter (Peter Xavier)
Last Command, The (Sergius Alexander)
Last Laugh, The /aka/ Der Letze Mann (hotel doorman)
NJU
Othello /aka/ The Moor (Title role)
Paramount player 23
Passion
Patriot, The (Tsar Paul I)
Peter the Great
Power
Quo Vadis
Ratten
Sins of the Father (Willelm Spengler)
Street of Sin
Stürme der Leidenschaft
Tartuffe, the Hypocrite (Title role)
Three Wax Men
Three Way Works
Tragödie der Liebe [Tragedy of Love] (Ombrade)
Variété [Variety]
Vendetta
Das Wachsfigurenkabinett /aka/ Waxworks (Haroun al Raschid)
Way of All Flesh, The (August Schilling)
Das Weib des Pharao [The Wife of the Pharaoh] /aka/ The Loves of Pharaoh (Pharaoh Amenes)

2996
JANSON, Victor*
At the Edge of the World (the lieutenant)
Die Bergkatze [The Mountain Cat; The Wild Cat] (Fort Tossenstein Commander)

2997
JANSSEN, Walter*
Destiny /aka/ The Tired Death; The Three Lights; Between Worlds; Der Mude Tod
Peter the Great

2998
JARAY, Hans*
Love of Jeanne Ney, The

2999
JARDON, Edward*
Alibi /aka/ The Perfect Alibi (theatre singer)

3000
JAROSLAWZEFF, W.
Flames on the Volga

3001
JARVIS, Sidney*
Casey at the Bat
Circus Rookies
Footlights and Fools (stage manager)
Unholy Night, The (butler)

3002
JASMINA, Arthur*
Salome (a page)

3003
JASPER, Thena*
Under the Lash (Memke)

3004
JAY, Jean*
Every Mother's Son (Janet Shaw)
Only Way, The (Jeanne Defarge)
Silver King, The

3005
JEAN (dog)
Ramona (the dog)

3006
JEAN, Madame*
Enemies of Woman (Madame Spadoni)

3007
JEANS, Isabel (1891-)
Downhill (Julia)
Easy Virtue (Larita Filton)
Further Adventures of the Flag Lieutenant
Lilly of Bloomsbury (Sylvia)
Power over Men
Rat, The (Zelie de Chaumet)
Return of the Rat, The (Zelie de Chaumet)
Triumph of the Rat, The (Zelie de Chaumet)
Windsor Castle

Stage:
Cobra 25
Garey Divorce Case, The 29
Road to Rome, The

3008
JEANS, Ursula (Ursula McMinn)
    (1906-1973)
Fake, The
False Colors
Gypsy Cavalier, The
Passing of Mr. Quin, The
Quinney's
Silence
S. O. S.
Virgin Queen, The
Stage:
Play's the Thing, The 28
Second Man, The 28

3009
JEAYES, Allan*
Hound of the Baskervilles, The

3010
JEFFERIES, James J. *
Beau Broadway
One Round Hogan

3011
JEFFERSON, Thomas (1859-1923)
Beauty's Worth (Peter)
Fortune Hunter, The
My Lady's Latch Key
On with the Show (Dad)
Spenders, The
Splendid Hazard, A
Straight from Paris
White Youth

3012
JEFFRIES, James J. --see: James
    J. Jefferies

3013
JEHANNE, Edith*
Chess Player, The
Love of Jeanne Ney, The

3014
JENKINS, J. W.*
Scarlet Saint, The

3015
JENNINGS, Al (Alphonso J. Jen-
    nings) (1864-1962)
Bond of Blood, The
Prisoner of Zenda, The (De Gautet)

3016
JENNINGS, Anna*
Ghost Train, The (Peggy Murdock)

3017
JENNINGS, DeWitt (De Witt Clarke
    Jennings) (1879-1937)
Air Mail Pilot
Alibi /aka/ The Perfect Alibi
    (O'Brien)
At Bay
Beating the Game
Blinky
Circus Days
Crash, The
Deep Purple, The
Enemy Sex, The
Face Between, The
Fire Brigade, The
Flesh and Blood (Detective Doyle)
From the Ground Up
Gaiety Girl
Go Straight
Great Mail Robbery, The
Greater Claim, The
Hit and Run
Home Made
Ice Flood, The
Invisible Power, The
Ladyfingers
Light that Failed, The
McFadden Flats
Marry the Girl
Merton of the Movies
Mixed Faces
Movietone Follies of 1929 (Jay Dar-
    rell)
Mystic, The
Name the Man
Night Flyer, The
Night Ride (Capt. O'Donnell)
Nineteen and Phyllis
Out of Luck
Passionate Quest
Poverty of Riches, The
Red Hot Speed
Seven Footprints to Satan
Seven Keys to Baldpate
Sherlock Brown
Splendid Road, The
There Are No Villains
Three Sevens
Through Different Eyes (Paducah)
Trial of Mary Dugan, The (Inspector
    Hunt)
Two Arabian Nights
Unbroken Purple, The
Valiant, The

Within the Law (Burke)
Wrecking Boss, The
Stage:
Blue Flame, The (Inspector Ryan)

3018
JENNINGS, Gladys (1902-)
Back to the Trees
Becket
Bodiam Castle
Colleen Bawn, The
Constant Hot Water
Crooked Man, The
Escape
Fangs of Death
Gwynneth of the Welsh Hills
Happy Ending, The
Henry, King of Navarre (Marguerite
   de Valois)
Hindle Wakes /aka/ Fanny Haw-
   thorne (Beatrice Farrar)
In the Night
Kenilworth Castle
Lady Godiva
Lamp in the Desert
Little Miss Nobody
Man and His Kingdom
Mistletoe Bough, The
Painted Lady, The
Prey of the Dragon
Prude's Fall, The
Rob Roy
Shuttle of Life, The
Whispering Gables
Woman in Pawn, A
Woman Juror, The
Young Lochinvar

3019
JENNINGS, Hilde*
Women Without Men

3020
JENNINGS, Jane*
Case of Becky, The
Little French Girl, The
Man Must Live, A
Song and Dance Man, The

3021
JENSEN, Eugen*
Love of Jeanne Ney, The

3022
JENSEN, Eulalie*
Any Wife
Baggage Smashers
Being Respectable

Charley's Aunt (Lucy D'Alvardorez)
Circle, The
Flower of the Night
Forever After
Freckles
Havoc (Alice Deering)
Heart Thief, The
Heroes and Husbands
House of the Tolling Bell
Hunchback of Notre Dame, The (Ma-
   rie)
In the Shadow of the Dome
Iron Trail, The
Kentucky Courage
King of Kings, The (bit)
Kiss in a Taxi, A
Little Shepherd of Kingdom Come,
   The
Man and His Woman
Mother Machree
Passion Flower, The
Rags to Riches
Ranger of the Big Trees, The
Respectable by Proxy
Sap, The
She Goes to War
Slave of Desire
Strong Boy, The
Sunshine Trail
Thundering Herd, The (Randall's
   wife)
Uncle Tom's Cabin (Cassey)
Volcano (Madame de Chauvalon)
When Husbands Deceive
Whisper Market, The
Wine of Youth, The
Woman with Four Faces, The (the
   mother)
Yankee Consul, The

3023
JENSEN, Frederick*
David Copperfield

3024
JEROME, M. K.*
Show of Shows, The

3025
JESSEL, George (1898-)
At Peace with the World (monologue)
George Washington Cohen
Ghetto, The
Ginsberg the Great
Happy Days (a principal)
Love, Live and Laugh
My Mother's Eyes /aka/ Lucky Boy
Private Izzy Murphy

Sailor Izzy Murphy
Record:
My Mother's Eyes (BVE 48804-1)
  (LPV 538)
Stage:
Jazz Singer, The (Jack Robin) 25
Passing Show of 1923, The
Vaudeville 24 and 28
War Song, The (Eddie Rosen) 28

3026
JEWEL, Betty*
Arizona Bound
Last Outlaw, The
Partners Again with Potash and
  Perlmutter
Rejected Woman, The

3027
JEWELL, Austin*
Greed (August Sieppe)
Wild Geese

3028
JIMINEZ, Solidad (1874-1967)
Cock-Eyed World, The (innkeeper)
In Old Arizona (cook)
Romance of the Rio Grande

3029
JOBSON, Edward*
Chorus Girl's Romance, A (Dr. Tar-
  box)
Married Virgin, The /aka/ Frivo-
  lous Wives
City of Masks, The

3030
JOFFRE, Madame*
Three Musketeers, The (Mother Su-
  perior)

3031
JOFFRE, Monsieur*
Three Musketeers, The (Bonacieux)

3032
JOHN, Bertram*
Take It from Me

3033
JOHN, Georg*
Atlantic (Vandt)
Destiny /aka/ The Tired Death; The
  Three Lights; Between Worlds;
  Der Mude Tod
Last Laugh, The /aka/ Der Letze
  Mann (night watchman)

Die Nibelungen /aka/ The Nibelungs
  (dual role, Mime/Albrich)
Variété [Variety]
Das Wachsfigurenkabinett [The Wax-
  works]

3034
JOHNS, Bertram*
Claw, The (Mr. Marriat)
Conrad in Quest of His Youth
Declassee
Forbidden Fruit (John Craig)
Grumpy (Jarvis' valet)
Hired and Fired
Marriage Maker, The
Stephen Steps Out

3035
JOHNS, Brooke*
Manhandled (himself)
Stage:
Comic Supplement, The 25
Jack and Jill (Donald Lee) 23
Piggy (Bobby Hunter) 27
Ziegfeld Follies 23

3036
JOHNS, Florence*
Frontier of the Stars, The (Mary
  Hoyt)
Stage:
Best People, The (Millie) 24
Charlatan, The (Annie) 22
Children of the Moon (Jane Atherton)
  23
Father, The (Laura) 28
Headquarters (Lydia Dale) 29
Love 'em and Leave 'em (Mame
  Walsh) 26
Mary Stuart (Mary Beaton) 21
Up the Line (Effie) 26

3037
JOHNSON, Ann*
Durand of the Badlands (Clara Belle
  Seesel)
Sparrows /aka/ Human Sparrows
Stage:
Ghost Parade, The (Joan Beggs) 29

3038
JOHNSON, Cammilla*
Sparrows /aka/ Human Sparrows (a
  sparrow)

3039
JOHNSON, Carmencita*
Wind, The (Coro's daughter)

Wonder of Women, The

3040
JOHNSON, Dick Winslow*
Love, Live and Laugh

3041
JOHNSON, Dolores*
Strong Boy, The
Through Different Eyes (Anna)

3042
JOHNSON, Edith (1895-)
Fast Express, The [serial]
Playing It Wild [serial]
Silent Avenger, The [serial]
Steel Trail, The [serial]
When Danger Smiles [serial]
Where Men Are Men [serial]
Wolves of the North [serial]

3043
JOHNSON, Emory*
Husband Hunter, The (Kent Whitney)
In the Name of the Law
Prisoners of Love

3043a
JOHNSON, Ernest W.*
Street of Sin, The

3044
JOHNSON, Jean*
Born to the West
Last Man on Earth, The

3045
JOHNSON, Kay*
Dynamite (Cynthia Crothers)
Spoilers, The
Stage:
All Dressed Up (Eileen Stevens) 25
Beggar on Horseback (Cynthia Ma-
    son) 24
Crime (Dorothy Palmer) 27
Free Soul, A (Jan Ash) 28
Go West Young Man (Laura Har-
    per) 23
Morning After, The (Patsy Andrews)
    25
No Trespassing! (Zoe Gault) 26
One of the Family (Joyce Smith) 25

3046
JOHNSON, Lawrence*
Any Wife

3047
JOHNSON, Lorimer--see: Lorimer
    Johnston

3048
JOHNSON, Martin (1884-1937)
Camera Trails in Africa
Head Hunters of the South Seas
Simba
Trailing African Wild Animals

3049
JOHNSON, Mary*
Gunnar Hede's Saga
Manege
Strange Case of Captain Ramper,
    The
Three Who Were Doomed, The
Youth Astray

3050
JOHNSON, Noble*
Adorable Savage, The
Adventure
Black Aces
Black Waters
Burning Words
Cameo Kirby
Courtship of Miles Standish
Drums of Fate
Flaming Frontier, The
Four Feathers, The (Ahmed)
Four Horsemen of the Apocalypse,
    The (Conquest)
Gateway of the Moon
Girl He Left Behind, The
Hands Up!
His Lady /aka/ When a Man Loves
    (an Apache)
King of Kings, The (charioteer)
Leopard Woman, The
Little Robinson Crusoe
Manhattan Knights
Midnight Express, The
Mysterious Dr. Fu Manchu, The
    /aka/ The Insidious Dr. Fu Man-
    chu (Li Po)
Navigator, The
Noah's Ark (broker)
Red Clay
Redskin, The (Pueblo Jim)
Robinson Crusoe [serial] (Friday)
Sal of Singapore
Serenade
Soft Cushions
Something Always Happens
Ten Commandments, The (the bronze
    man)

Thief of Bagdad, The (Indian prince)
Topsy and Eva
Under Crimson Skies
Vanity
Wallop, The
Yellow Cameo, The [serial]
Yellow Contraband

3051
JOHNSON, Norris*
Lorna Doone

3052
JOHNSON, Pauline*
Wrecker, The

3053
JOHNSON, Sessel Ann*
Riders of the Purple Sage (Erne as
   a child)
Sparrows /aka/ Human Sparrows
   (a sparrow)

3054
JOHNSON, Tefft*
New Klondike, The

3055
JOHNSTON, Andrew*
Sea Hawk, The

3056
JOHNSTON, Gladys*
Chechahcos, The
Hunchback of Notre Dame, The

3057
JOHNSTON, J. L.*
Winds of Chance

3058
JOHNSTON, J. W.*
New Klondike, The
Sawdust Paradise, The
Take Me Home
Unseeing Eyes

3059
JOHNSTON, Julanne (1906-)
Aloma of the South Seas (Sylvia)
Black Aces
Captain Fearless
Carrangole
City of Temptation
Dame Chance
Dangerous Virtue
General Crack
Good Time Charley

Her Wild Oat
Madness of Youth, The
Miss Hobbs
Name the Woman
Oh, Kay!
Olympic Hero
Pride's Fall
Prisoners
Robin Hood
Seeing It Through
Show of Shows, The
Sitting on the World
Smiling Irish Eyes
Synthetic Sin
Thief of Bagdad, The (the princess)
Twinkletoes (Lilac)
United Artist player 23
Venus of Venice
Vision, The
Whip Woman, The (Mme. Haldane)
Younger Generation, The

3060
JOHNSTON, Lorimer*
Bells, The
Dante's Inferno
Enticement
Scaramouche (Count Dupuye)
Tarzan the Mighty [serial]
Top of the World, The

3061
JOHNSTON, Renita*
If I Were King

3062
JOHNSTONE, Justine*
Blackbirds
Heart to Let, A
Moonlight and Honeysuckle
Never the Twain Shall Meet
Nothing but Lies
Playthings of Broadway
Sheltered Daughters

3063
JOLIVET, Rita (1894-)
Bride's Confession, The
Messalina
Theodora

3064
JOLSON, Al (Asa Yoelson) (1888-
   1950)
April Showers
Jazz Singer (Jakie Rabinowitz/Jack
   Robin)
Mammy's Boy

Say It with Songs
Singing Fool, The
Sonny Boy
Vitaphone
Record:
Best of Jolson-Album (DL 9100-01)
My Yellow Jacket Girl (Col 745)
Spaniard that Blighted My Life (Col 745)
That Haunting Melody (B-11409-2) (LPV 560)
Stage:
Artists and Models 26
Big Boy (Gus) 25
Bombo 21
Lambs Gambol 25

3065
JONASSON, Frank*
Fighting Coward, The
Merton of the Movies
Top of the World, The

3066
JONES, Billy (1889-1940)
Carnival comedies
Sparrows /aka/ Human Sparrows (a sparrow)

3067
JONES, Buck (Charles Jones) (1889-1942)
Against All Odds
Arizona Romeo, The
Bar Nothin'
Bells of San Juan, The
Big Dan
Big Punch, The
Big Top, The
Black Jack
Black Paradise
Blood Will Tell
Boss of Camp Four
Branded Sombrero, The
Chain Lightning
Circus Cowboy
Cowboy and the Countess, The
Cupid's Fireman
Desert Outlaw, The
Desert Valley
Desert's Price, The
Durand of the Badlands (Dick Durand)
Eleventh Hour, The
Fast Mail, The
Fighting Buckaroo, The
Firebrand Trevision
Flying Horseman, The

Footlight Ranger
Forbidden Trails
Fox player 22
Gentle Cyclone, The
Get Your Man
Gold and the Girls
Good as Gold
Hearts and Spurs (Hal Emory)
Hell's Hole
Hills of Peril
Just Pals
Last Straw, The
Lazybones
Man Four Square, A
Man Who Played Square, The
Not a Drum Was Heard
One Man Trail
Pardon My Nerve
Rainbow Trail, The
Riders of the Purple Sage
Riding Speed
Riding with Death
Rough Shod
Second Hand Love
Skid Proof
Snowdrift
Square Shooter, The
Straight from the Shoulder
Sunset Sprague
Thirty Below Zero
Timber Wolf, The
To a Finish
Trail Rider, The
Trooper O'Neill
Two Doyles, The
War Horse, The
West of Chicago
Western Luck
Western Speed
Whispering Sage
Winner Take All

3068
JONES, Eddie*
Vanity Fair (Fritz)

3069
JONES, Fred*
Fool, The

3070
JONES, Hannah*
Blackmail (landlady)
Downhill (dresser)
Piccadilly (Bessie)

3071
JONES, Harry*
Prisoner of Zenda, The (Hans)
Soft Cushions

3072
JONES, Johnny*
Edgar and the Teacher's Pet
Edgar's Little Saw
Old Nest, The

3073
JONES, Park*
Old Nest, The

3074
JONES, Tiny*
Greed (Mrs. Heise)

3075
JONES, W. W.*
America (General Gage)

3076
JORDAN, Dorothy (1908-)
Black Magic
Devil May Care
Taming of the Shrew, The
Stage:
Funny Face (bell hop) 27
Garrick Gaieties 26
Treasure Girl (Betty) 28

3077
JORDAN, Egon V.*
Richthofhen: The Red Knight of the
   Air

3078
JORDAN, Jack*
Knights Out
Through Different Eyes (1st reporter)

3079
JORDAN, Sid*
Deadwood Coach, The
Sky High (Bates)

3080
JORDON, Domaine*
William Tell

3081
JORGE, Paul*
Les Miserables (Mgr. Myriel)
Passion of Joan of Arc, The

3082
JOSANE, Lola*
Pawns of Passion

3083
JOSAYNE*
Morgane, the Enchantress

3084
JOSE ARIAS SPANISH STRING BAND
   SERENADERS
Cock-Eyed World, The

3085
JOUBE, Romauld*
J'Accuse
Miracle of the Wolves, The

3086
JOURNÉE, Léon*
Jim Bougne Boxeur (the French Heav-
   yweight Champion)

3087
JOWITT, Anthony*
Coast of Folly, The (Larry Fay)
Little French Girl, The
Lucky Devil, The
Paramount player 27
Splendid Crime, The

3088
JOY, Beatrice--see: Leatrice Joy

3089
JOY, Ernest*
Dancin' Fool (Tom Reed)

3090
JOY, Gloria*
Old Fashioned Boy, An

3091
JOY, Leatrice (Leatrice Joy Zeidler)
   (1899-)
Ace of Hearts (Lilith)
Angel of Broadway, The
Bachelor Daddy
Bellamy Trial, The (Sue Ives)
Blue Danube, The
Bunty Pulls the Strings
Changing Husbands
Clinging Vines
Dollar Bid, A
Down Home
Dressmaker from Paris, The
Eve's Leaves
For Alimony Only

Hell's High Road
Hollywood
Invisible Divorce
Java Head
Just a Wife
Ladies Must Live
Made for Love
Man Made Woman
Man Who Saw Tomorrow, The
Manslaughter (Lydia Thorne)
Marriage Cheat, The
Minnie
Most Immoral Lady, A
Nobody's Widow
Of Human Hearts
Poverty of Riches, The
Right Way, The
Saturday Night (Iris Van Suydam)
Show People (cameo)
Silent Partner, The
Smiling All the Way
Strong Boy, The
Tale of Two Worlds, A (Sui Sen)
Ten Commandments, The (Mary
  Leigh)
Triumph (Ann Land)
Tropic Madness
Vanity
Voices of the City (Georgia Rodman)
You Can't Fool Your Wife
Stage:
Vaudeville 29

3092
JOYCE, Alice (1889-1955)
Ace of Cads, The
Affairs of Anatole, The
Beau Geste (Lady Patricia Brandon)
Cousin Kate
Daddy's Gone-a-Hunting
Dancing Mothers (Ethyl "Buddy"
  Westcourt)
Desperate Heritage, The
Dollars and the Woman
Green Goddess, The (Lucilla Cres-
  pin)
Headlines
Her Lord and Master
Inner Chamber, The
Little French Girl, The
Mannequinn
Midnight Mystery
Noose, The
Passionate Adventurer
Prey, The
Scarab Ring, The
Slaves of Pride
Sorrell and Son (Fanny Garland)

So's Your Old Man (Princess Les-
  caboura)
Sporting Duchess, The
Squall, The (Maria Lajos)
Stella Dallas (Helen Morrison)
13 Washington Square (Mrs. de Pey-
  ster)
Vengeance of Durand
Vice of Fools

3093
JOYCE, Jack*
New Lives for Old
Stage:
Vaudeville 25

3094
JOYCE, Natalie*
Circus Ace, The
Dance Hall
Girl in Every Port, A (Panama girl)
Naughty Baby

3095
JOYCE, Peggy Hopkins (1893-1957)
Skyrocket
Stage:
Earl Carroll's Vanities 23
Lady of the Orchids (Simone) 28

3096
JOYCE, Virginia*
Happy Days (chorus)

3097
JOYNER, Francis*
Cooperhead, The
Kentuckians, The

3098
JOYZELLE*
Beneath the Law
Black Watch, The
Bride of the Nile
Close Harmony
Dance Madness
Moran of the Marines
Out of the Past
Souvenir

3099
JUDELS, Charles*
Hot for Paris
Little Old New York (Delmonico)
Under the Red Robe
Stage:
For Goodness Sake (Count Spinagio)
  22

Mary (Gaston Marceau) 20
Wild Flower (Gaston La Roche)

3100
JUGO, Jenny*
Casanova
Looping the Loop
Loves of Casanova, The
Royal Scandal, A

3101
JULIAN, Rupert (1886-)
Three Faces East (the Kaiser)

3102
JULIE, Lady*
Love Master, The

3103
JUNE, Mildred*
Crazy to Act
Crossroads of New York, The

3104
JUNG, Rudolph*
William Tell

3105
JUNKERMAN, Hans*
Hamlet (Polonius)
Manon Lescaut

3106
JURADO, Elena*
Girl in Every Port, A
What Price Glory? (Carmen of the
   Philippines)

- K -

3107
KADA-ABD-EL-KADER*
Maré Nostrum [Our Sea] (Esteban's
   son)

3108
KADER-BEN-ALI, Abdel*
Atlantide (Cegheir-ben-Cheikh)

3109
KAEIRED, Katharine*
Mama's Affair

3110
KAGNO, Marcia*
Hole in the Wall, The (Marcia)

3111
KAHANAMOKA, Duke*
Adventure
Lord Jim
Rescue, The
Where East Is East (wild animal
   trapper)

3112
KAHN, Art and Orchestra
Angel of Broadway, The

3113
KAINS, Maurice*
Tell It to the Marines

3114
KAISER, Helen*
Dance Hall
Rio Rita (Mrs. Bean)

3115
KAISER-TIETZ, Erich*
Hungarian Rhapsody

3116
KAJA, Katrina*
End of St. Petersberg, The

3117
KALTZ, Armand (1892-1941) /aka/
   Armand Kaliz: [see Vol. I]
Belle of Broadway, The
Devil's Cage, The
Fast and Furious
Gold Diggers of Broadway (Barney
   Bennett)
Lingerie
Love Mart, The
Marriage Playground, The (Prince
   Matriano)
Noah's Ark (dual role, King's guard
   leader/Frenchman)
Say It with Diamonds
Stolen Bride
Temptations of a Shop Girl
Temptress, The (DeBianca)
That's My Daddy
Twin Beds
Virgin Queen, The
Wife's Relations, The
Woman's Way, A

3118
KALSER, Erwin*
Rasputin, the Holy Sinner

3119
KAMERKO BALALAIKA ORCHESTRA
Cock-Eyed World, The

3120
KAMIYAMA, Sojim*
Bat, The
East of Suez

3121
KAMMEREN, Torsten*
Story of Gösta Berling, The

3122
KAMPERS, Fritz*
Berlin after Dark
His Late Excellency
Der Juxbaron [The Imaginary Baron]
  (policeman)
Der Mensch am Wege [Man by the
  Roadside]

3123
KANE, Diana*
Bluebeard's Seven Wives
Brown Derby, The
Lovers in Quarantine
Miss Bluebeard
New Commandment, The
Perfect Sap, The

3124
KANE, Eddie*
Broadway Melody, The (Francis Zan-
  field)
Illusion
Kibitzer, The
Street Girl
Why Bring that Up?

3125
KANE, Gail /aka/ Gale Kane (1892-
  1966)
Convoy
Daredevil, The
Empty Arms
Good Woman
Idle Hands
Romeo's Dad
Someone Must Pay
White Sister, The (Marshesa di Mo-
  la)
Wise Husbands
Stage:
Breaking Point, The (Beverly) 23
Come Seven (Vistar Goins) 20
Lawful Larceny (Vivian Hepburn) 22

3126
KANE, Helen (1904-1966)
Betty Boop Cartoons (voice)
Great Gabbo, The
Nothing but the Truth
Sweetie
Record:
He's So Unusual (BVE-53563-2) (LPV
  538)
Stage:
Night in Spain, A   27

3127
KANE, Jack*
Wild, Wild Susan

3128
KANE, Margie*
Great Gabbo, The (eccentric dancer)

3129
KANE, Robert*
Too Much Money

3130
KANE, Ruth*
Bride's Relations, The
Old Barn, The
Whirls and Girls

3131
KANE, Violet*
Golden Cocoon, The

3132
KARASHVILLE, Kokhta*
Caucasian Love

3133
KARELS, Harvey*
Merry Widow, The (Jimmy Watson)

3134
KARENNE, Diana*
Casanova
Loves of Casanova, The
Marie Antoinette
Rasputin, the Holy Sinner

3135
KARL, Roger*
Living Image, The

3136
KARLIN, Bo Peep*
Happy Days (chorus)

3137
KARLOFF, Boris (William Henry
  Pratt) (1887-1969)
Altar Stairs, The (Hugo)
Annie Against the World (bit)
Behind that Curtain (Sondanese ser-
  vant)
Bells, The (a mesmerist)
Burning the Wind (ranch foreman)
Cave Girl, The (half-breed)
Cheated Hearts (Nei Hamid)
Courage of Marge O'Doone (a trap-
  per)
Deadlier Sex, The (Jules Barney)
Devil's Chaplain, The (Boris)
Dynamite Dan (villain)
Eagle of the Sea, The (a pirate)
Fatal Warning, The [serial] (bit)
Flames (railroad bandit)
Flaming Fury (Gaspard)
Forbidden Cargo (ship's mate)
Golden Web, The (a murder victim)
Greater Glory, The (bit)
Hellion, The (outlaw)
Her Honor, the Governor (Snipe Col-
  lins)
Hope Diamond Mystery, The /aka/
  The Romance of the Hope Diamond
  [serial] (Dakar)
Infidel, The (ruler of Menang)
King of the Kongo [serial] (Scarface
  Macklin)
Lady Robin Hood (Cabraza)
Last of the Mohicans, The (a ma-
  rauding Indian)
Let It Rain (villain)
Little Wild Girl (Maurice Kent)
Love Mart, The (villain)
Man from Downing Street, The (a
  Maharajah)
Man in the Saddle, The (villain)
Meddlin' Stranger (bit)
Nan of the North [serial] (bit)
Never the Twain Shall Meet (bit)
Nickel Hopper, The (a masher)
Old Ironsides (a pirate)
Omar the Tentmaker (Iman)
Parisian Nights (Parisian apache)
Perils of the Wild [serial] (bit)
Phantom Buster, The (Ramon)
Phantoms of the North (the murderer)
Prairie Wife, The (half-breed)
Prince and Betty, The (bit)
Princess from Hoboken (bit)
Prisoner, The (bit)
Riders of the Plains [serial] (bit)
Soft Cushions (principal conspirator)
Tarzan and the Golden Lion (Chief of

Waziri Tribe)
Two Arabian Nights (bit)
Two Sisters (Cecil)
Unholy Night (Abdoul)
Valencia (bit)
Vanishing Rider, The [serial] (bit)
Vultures of the Sea [serial] (bit)
Without Benefit of Clergy (Ahmed
  Khan)
Woman Conquers, A (French-Cana-
  dian trapper)
Stage:
Cinderella (Demon King) - Church
  play 1897
Devil, The (Kamloops) - Canada
Harry Street Clair Players - Canada
Hotel Imperial - California 28
Idiot, The - California 28
Kongo - California 27
Virginian, The - U.S. Road Compa-
  ny 16
Window Panes - California 27

3138
KARNELLY, Leila*
Cock-Eyed World, The (Olga)
Married in Hollywood

3139
KARNS, Maurice*
Road to Mandalay, The (Harry)

3140
KARNS, Roscoe (1893-1970) /aka/
  Roscoe Karnes: [see Vol. I]
Afraid to Fight
Beau Sabreur
Beggars of Life
Bluff
Conquering the Woman
Desert Bride
Eagles of the Fleet
Family Honor
Flying Ensign, The
Headlines
Her Own Money
Jazz Mad
Jazz Singer, The (the agent)
Life of the Party, The
Man Tamer, The
Midnight Express, The
Moran of the Marines
New York Nights
Object-Matrimony
Ritzy
Shopworn Angel, The
Something Always Happens
Ten Modern Commandments

This Thing Called Love (Harry Ber-
    trand)
Too Much Married
Trouper, The
Warming Up
Win that Girl
Wings (Lt. Cameron)

3141
KASHNER, Bruno*
Love Commandment, The

3142
KASHNER, David*
Street Angel (strong man)

3143
KASSEWITZ, Helene*
William Tell

3144
KASTNER, Bruno*
Carnival Crime, The
Luther

3145
KATCHALOF, V. L.*
Lash of the Czar, The

3146
KAUFMAN, Al*
Daredevil Jack [serial]

3147
KAY, Arthur*
Movietone Follies of 1929 (orchestra
    leader)

3148
KAYSSLER, Friedrich*
Eine DuBarry von Heute [A Modern
    DuBarry] (Cornelius Corbett)

3149
KEANE, Doris (1885-1945)
Kismet
Romance
Stage:
Romance (Mme. Margharita Caval-
    lini) 21
Starlight (Aurelie) 25
Welded (Eleanor Owen) 24

3150
KEANE, James*
I Am the Man

3151
KEANE, Raymond (1907-1973)
April Fool
How to Handle a Woman
In a Persian Market
Lone Eagle, The
Magic Garden, The
Marriage by Contract
Marriage of Tomorrow
Midnight Sun, The
Patience
Tomorrow
Universal player 26

3152
KEARNEY, John*
East Side, West Side

3153
KEARNS, Allen*
Tanned Legs
Very Idea, The

3154
KEATE, Gwen*
Happy Days (chorus)

3155
KEATON, Buster (Joseph Francis
    Keaton) (1895-1966)
Balloonatic, The
Battling Butler
Blacksmith, The
Boat, The
Cameraman, The
College
Convict Thirteen
Cops
Daydreams
Electric House [short and feature]
First National player 20
Freshman, The
Frozen North, The
Garage, The
General, The (Johnny Gray)
Go West
Goat, The
Hard Luck
Haunted House, The
High Sign, The
Hollywood Revue of 1929
Love Nest, The
My Wife's Relations
Navigator, The
Neighbors
One Week
Our Hospitality
Paleface, The

Playhouse, The
Round Up, The
Saphead, The
Scarecrow, The
Seven Chances
Sherlock Junior (the boy)
Spite Marriage
Steamboat Bill, Jr.
Stage:
Vaudeville 1898

3156
KEATON, Joe (Joseph Keaton)*
General, The (Confederate officer)
Our Hospitality
Sherlock Junior (the girl's father)
Steamboat Bill, Jr.

3157
KECKLEY, Jane*
Angel of Broadway, The
Country Doctor, The
Craig's Wife
Deadwood Coach, The
Detectives Wanted
Dynamite (Bobby's mother)
Hill Billy, The
King of Kings, The (bit)
Lady in Ermine, The

3158
KEEDWELL, Norval*
Little Old New York (Fitz Green
    Hallock)

3159
KEEFE, Cornelius (1902-)
Adorable Cheat, The
Circumstantial Evidence
Cohens and the Kellys in Atlantic
    City, The
Come to My House
Devil's Chaplain, The
Hearts of Men
Hook and Ladder No. 9
Light in the Window, A
Man from Headquarters, The
Moment of Temptation, A
Poor Nut, The
Satan and the Woman
Society Scandal, A (Marjorie's
    friend)
Thanksgiving Day
Three's a Crowd
Thundergod
Unguarded Hour, The
Universal player 26

You Can't Beat the Law

3160
KEEFE, Zeena (1896-)
After Midnight
Broken Silence
Broken Violin, The
His Wife's Money
Marooned Hearts
None So Blind
Out of the Snow
Piccadilly Jim
Prejudice
Red Foam
When Love Is Young

3161
KEELER, Willie "Sugar"*
Cock-Eyed World, The (a brawler)

3162
KEELING, Robert Lee*
Reckless Youth (Mr. Schuyler-Fos-
    ter)

3163
KEEN, Malcolm (Malcolm Knee)
    (1887-)
Lodger, The
Manxman, The
Skin Game, The (Charles)

3164
KEEN, Richard*
Happy Days (Dick)
Why Leave Home?

3165
KEENAN, Frank (1858-1929)
Brass
Brothers Divided
Defender, The
Dixie Handicap, The
Dollar for Dollar
East Lynne (Magistrate Hare)
False Code, The
Gilded Butterfly, The
Hearts Aflame
Lorna Doone
My Lady's Lips (Forbes Lombard)
Night Stage
Scars of Jealousy
Smouldering Embers
Thoroughbred, The
Women Who Give
Stage:
Peter Weston (Title role) 23

3166
KEENE, Hamilton*
Lost Patrol, The

3167
KEENE, Richard*--see: Richard
    Keen

3168
KEENE, Tom /aka/ Richard Powers
    (1904-1963) (George Duryea)
Golden Girl, The
In Old California
Night Work
Pardon My Gun
Sunset Trail

3169
KEENER, Hazel*
Empty Hands
Freshman, The (college belle)
Parisian Love (Margot)

3170
KEEPFER, Margarete*
Frau im Mond (Woman in the Moon)

3171
KEILING, Robert Lee*
Success

3172
KEITH, Donald (1905-)
Bare Knees
Baree, Son of Kazan
Boomerang, The
Comrades
Cruise of the Hellion
Dancing Mothers (Kenneth Cobb)
Devil's Cage, The
Free to Love (Rev. James Crawford)
Just Off Broadway
Lone Wolf's Daughter, The
My Lady of Whim (Bartley Greer)
Paramount player 25
Parisian Love (Armand)
Phantoms of the North
Plastic Age, The (Hugh Carver)
Secrets
Should a Girl Marry?
Special Delivery
Top Sergeant Mulligan
Way of All Flesh, The (August, Jr.)
We're in the Navy Now
Whirlwind of Youth, The
Wild Geese

3173
KEITH, Eugene*
Get Rich Quick Wallingford (Harkins)
Uncle Sam of Freedom Ridge

3174
KEITH, Ian (Keith Ross) (1899-1960)
Christine of the Hungry Heart
Convoy
Divine Lady, The (Greville)
Enticement
Great Divide, The
Greater Glory, The
Her Love Story (Capt. Kavor)
Light Fingers
Look-Out Girl, The
Loves of Sunya, The (Louis Anthony)
Love's Wilderness
Man's Past, A
Manhandled (Robert Brandt)
My Son (Felipe Vargas)
Prince of Tempters, The
Prisoners
Queen's Secret, The
Street of Illusion
Talker, The
Tower of Lies, The (Lars)
Two Arabian Knights
What Every Girl Should Know
Stage:
Laugh, Clown, Laugh (Luigi Ravelli)
    23
Silver Fox, The (Capt. Douglas Bel-
    grave) 21

3175
KEITH, Isabel /aka/ Isabelle*
Annie Against the World
Desert Flower, The
Four Horsemen of the Apocalypse,
    The (German woman)
Leaping Love
Perfect Day, A
Very Confidential

3176
KEITH-JOHNSTON, Colin*
Lucky in Love
Stage:
Journey's End (Capt. Stanhope) 28

3177
KELLAR, Leon*
West Point

3178
KELLARD, Ralph*
Master Mind, The

Restless Sex, The (Jim Cleland)
Virtuous Liars
Stage:
She Couldn't Say No (Walter Turnbull) 26

3179
KELLER, Frank*
Temple of Venus, The (Jupiter)

3180
KELLERMAN, Annette (1888-1975)
Venus of the South Sea
What Women Love

3181
KELLY, Gregory*
Manhattan
Show Off, The
Stage:
Butter and Egg Man, The (Peter Jones) 25
Dulcy (William Parker) 21

3182
KELLY, John*
Dressed to Kill
From Headquarters

3183
KELLY, Kitty*
Kiss in the Dark, A

3184
KELLY, Nancy (1921-   )
Girl on the Barge, The

3185
KELLY, Paul (Paul Michael Kelly) (1899-1956)
New Klondike, The
Old Oaken Bucket, The
Paramount player 26
Slide, Kelly, Slide
Special Delivery
Uncle Sam of Freedom Ridge
Stage:
Chains (Harry) 23
Up the Ladder (John Allen) 22
Whispering Wives (Barry McGill) 22

3186
KELLY, Peggy*
Joy Girl, The
School for Wives

3187
KELLY, Scotch*
Return of the Rat, The (Bill)

3188
KELSEY, Fred (1884-1961)
Blackmail
Donovan Affair, The
Excuse Me
Faker, The
Fall of Eve, The
Gorilla, The
Harold Teen
Ladies of the Mob
Last Warning
Lawful Cheaters (Tom Horan)
Madonna of the Streets, A (Detective Griffith)
Midnight Adventure, A
Naughty Baby
On Trial (clerk)
Only Saps Work
Paths to Paradise
Puppets of Fate
Seven Keys to Baldpate (Police Chief)
Seven Sinners
Smiling Irish Eyes
Smooth as Satin
Social Highwayman, The
Soft Cushions
Tenderloin
That's My Baby
Third Degree, The
Thirteenth Hour, The
Thirteenth Juror, The
Wright Idea, The
Wrong Again
Yankee Consul, The

3189
KELSO, Bobby*
Jack-Knife Man, The

3190
KELSO, Mayme*
Conrad in Quest of His Youth (Gina)
Drop Kick, The
Ducks and Drakes
Furnace, The
Help Wanted: Male
Hope
Jack Straw
Lost Romance
March Hare, The
Nellie, the Beautiful Cloak Model
Never Get Married
Seven Keys to Baldpate (Mrs. Rhodes)
Simple Souls

Vanity
Weekend, The
Why Change Your Wife? (Harriette)

3191
KELTON, Pert (1907-1968)
Sally (Rosie)

3192
KELVIN, Thelda*
Fascinating Youth

3193
KEMP, Margaret*
Sherlock Holmes /aka/ Moriarty
 (Therese)

3194
KEMP, Matty (1907-   )
Campus Carmen, The
Campus Vamp, The
Crazy to Act
Good-Bye Kiss, The
Magnificent Flirt (Hubert)
Matchmaking Mamas
Million Dollar Collar
Universal player 27

3195
KENDALL, Henry (1898-1962)
Mr. Pim Passes By
Tilly of Bloomsbury (Richard)
Stage:
Naughty Cinderella (Gerald Gray) 25

3196
KENNEDY, Charles*
Little Old New York (Reilly)

3197
KENNEDY, Edgar (1890-1948)
All Parts
Angora Love
Bacon Grabbers
Booster, The
Boy Friend, The
Chasing Husbands
Chinese Parrot, The
Dad's Day
Family Group, The
Fight Pest, The
Finishing Touch, The (cop)
Gay Old Birds
Golden Princess
Great Gobs
Hotter than Hot
Hurdy Gurdy
Imagine My Embarrassment

Leave 'em Laughing (cop)
Liberty
Limousine Love
Moan and Groan, Inc.
My Old Dutch
Oh, What a Nurse!
Pair of Tights, A
Paths to Paradise
Perfect Day, A (uncle)
Proud Heart
Seed 'em and Weep
Should Married Men Go Home?
Their Purple Moment
They Had to See Paris (Ed Eggers)
Trent's Last Case
Two Tars /aka/ Two Tough Tars
Unaccustomed as We Are (cop)
Wedding Bills

3198
KENNEDY, Edward*
Trouble with Wives

3199
KENNEDY, Hazel*
Snob, The

3200
KENNEDY, Jack*
Not Quite Decent

3201
KENNEDY, Madge (1892-   )
Bad Company
Blooming Angel, The
Dollars and Sense
Girl with the Jazz Heart, The
Help Yourself
Highest Bidder, The
Lying Wives
Oh, Baby!
Oh Mary, Be Careful!
Primrose Path, The
Purple Highway, The
Three Miles Out
Trimmed in Red
Truth, The
Stage:
Cornered (Margaret Waring) 20
Love in a Mist (Diana Wynne) 26
Paris Bound (Mary Hutton) 27
Poppy (Poppy McGargle) 23
Spite Corner (Elizabeth Dean) 22

3202
KENNEDY, Mary (1908-   )
Little Old New York (Betty Schuyler)
Yolanda (Antoinette Castleman)

Stage:
Not So Long Ago (Rosamond Gill)
  20

3203
KENNEDY, Merna (Merna Kahler)
  (1908-1944)
Barnum Was Right
Broadway (Billie Moore)
Circus, The (the Equestrienne)
Skinner Steps Out
United Artist player 26

3204
KENNEDY, Tom (1885-1965)
Afraid to Fight
Alias the Deacon
As Man Desires
At Yale
Back Home and Broke
Behind the Front
Best Bad Man, The (Dan Ellis)
Big News (Patrolman Ryan)
Born to the West
Cohens and the Kellys in Atlantic
  City, The
Cop, The
Fireman, Save My Child!
Flaming Hour, The
Flirt, The
Glad Rag Doll
Ham and Eggs at the Front
Hold 'em Yale!
If You Believe It, It's So
Kismet
Liberty
Love over Night
Madonna of the Streets, A ("Bull"
  Brockins)
Mantrap (Curly Evans)
Marked Money
Money Talks
None but the Brave
Our Leading Citizens
Post Mortems
Roaring Lions on Parade
Serenade
Shannons of Broadway, The /aka/
  Goodbye Broadway
Sir Lumberjack
Skirts, The
Tillie's Punctured Romance (property
  man)
We're in the Navy Now
Wife Savers
Yankee Senor, The

3205
KENNY, Colin*
Black Beauty
Dorothy Vernon of Haddon Hall (Daw-
  son)
Grumpy
Ladder Jinx, The
Little Lord Fauntleroy (Bevis Errol)

3206
KENT, Arnold*
Beau Sabreur (Raoul)
Easy Come, Easy Go
Hula (Harry Dehan)
Showdown, The
Woman Disputed, A (Nika Turgenov)
Woman on Trial, The

3207
KENT, Barbara (1906-)
Drop Kick, The
Flesh and the Devil (Hertha Proch-
  vitz)
Lone Eagle, The
Lonesome
MGM player 28
Modern Mothers
Night Ride (Ruth Kearns)
No Man's Law
Retribution
Shakedown, The
Stop that Man!
That's My Daddy
Welcome Danger

3208
KENT, Charles (1852-)
Body and Soul
Forbidden Valley
Man and His Woman

3209
KENT, Crauford (1881-1953)
Abysmal Brute, The (Dean Warner)
Ace of Scotland Yard [serial] (Insp.
  Angus)
Blindfolded
Case of Mary Brown, The
Charlatan, The
Come Across
Daddies
Devil to Pay, The
Fallen Angels
Flowing Gold
Foreign Legion, The
Forgotten Faces
Frozen Legion, The
Guilty One, The

Hidden Woman, The (Bart Andrews)
His Dog
Into No Man's Land
Lilies of the Field
Love Flower, The (the visitor)
Man and Maid
Man, Woman and Wife
Manhattan Nights
Midshipman, The
Missing Link, The
Mother
Mother-in-Law, The
Other Men's Shoes
Out with the Tide
Pirates of the Sky
Playthings of Broadway
Queen of the Chorus
See You in Jail
Seven Keys to Baldpate (Hal Bentley)
Shirley of the Circus
Show Folks (McNavy)
Show People
Silas Marner
Sinners
Vanity Fair
Wallflowers
Wolf of Wall Street, The
Youthful Folly

3210
KENT, Crauford, Mrs.*
Vanity Fair

3211
KENT, Larry*
Devil's Appletree, The
Fox player 27
Hangman's House
Haunted House, The
Head Man, The (Billy Hurd)
Heart of a Follies Girl, The
Her Wild Oat
Lovelorn, The
McFadden Flats
Mad Hour, The
Masked Menace, The [serial]
Midstream
Sea Tiger, The
Spirit of Youth, The
Whirlwind of Youth, The
Women's Wares

3212
KENT, Mrs.*
Foolish Wives (Dr. Judd's wife)

3213
KENT, William (1886-1945)
When Knighthood Was in Flower
(King's tailor)

3214
KENTUCKY JUBILEE SINGERS
Lost in the Artic

3215
KENYON, Doris (1897-)
Blonde Saint, The
Born Rich
Burning Daylight
Conquest of Canaan, The
Get Rich Quick Wallingford (Fannie Jasper)
Half-Way Girl, The
Harvest Moon, The
Hawk's Nest, The
Home Towners, The
I Want My Man
Idle Tongues
If I Marry Again
Interference
Ladies at Play
Loose Ankles
Men of Steel
Mismates
Monsieur Beaucaire (Lady Mary)
Restless Wives
Ruling Passion, The
Shadows of the Sea
Strictly Business
Sure-Fire Flint
Thief in Paradise, A
Unguarded Hour, The
You Are Guilty!
Stage:
Up the Ladder (Jane) 22

3216
KENYON, Nancye*
This Freedom

3217
KEPLER, Edward*
Woman Gives, The

3218
KERGY, Albert*
Rasputin, the Holy Sinner

3219
KERLY, L.*
Two Little Vagabonds (Joseph, the butler)

3220
KERNS, Eddie*
Broadway Melody, The

3221
KEROLENKO, Agnes*
Ghost Train, The (Elsie Winthrop)

3222
KERR, Bob*
They Had to See Paris (Tupper)

3223
KERR, Frederick (Frederick Grin-
ham Keen) (1858-1934)
Devil to Pay, The
Honor of the Family, The
Raffles

3224
KERR, Geoffrey (1895-)
Just Suppose
Man from Home, The
Stage:
Just Suppose (George) 20
You and I (Roderick White) 23

3225
KERRIGAN, J. M. (Joseph M. Ker-
rigan) (1887-1964)
Lightnin'
Little Old New York (John O'Day)
Lucky in Love
Stage:
Bells, The (Father Walter) 26
Broken Branches (Mr. McCann) 22
Ever Green Lady, The (Doody) 22
Ghosts (Jacob Engstrand) 26
Grey Fox, The (Francesco Vettori)
Gypsy Fires (Rodney Oneil) 25
Henry IV, Part I (Silence) 26
Little Minister, The (Joe Cruick-
shanks) 25
Meet the Prince (Dr. Ainslie) 29
Outward Bound (Scrubby) 24
Pinch Hitter, A (Mr. Prothers) 22
Rivals, The (Sir Lucius O'Trigger)
23
Rollo's Wild Oat (Horatio Webster)
20
Romantic Age, The (Master Susan)
22
Rosmersholm (Ulric Brendel) 25
Scaramouche (Polichinelle) 23
Shadow, The (Thomas Tuttle) 22
She Stoops to Conquer (Slang) 24
Trelawney of the Wells (O'Dwyer) 27
White Wings (Herbert) 26

3226
KERRIGAN, J. Warren (Jack Warren
Kerrigan) (1880-1947)
Captain Blood (Title role)
Coast of Opportunity, The
Coast of Six, The
Covered Wagon, The (Will Bannion)
Dream Cheater, The
Girl of the Golden West, The
Green Flame, The
House of Whispers
Joyous Liar, The
Live Sparks
Lord Loves the Irish, The
Man from Brodney's, The
Night Life in Hollywood
North of '36
Number Ninety Nine
One Week End
Roray o' the Bogs
Thirty Thousand Dollars

3227
KERRIGAN, Kathleen*
Music Master, The
Stage:
Laugh, Clown, Laugh! (Signora Del-
Monte) 23

3228
KERRY, Norman (Arnold Kaiser)
(1889-1956)
Acquittal, The
Affairs of Hannerl, The
Annie Laurie /aka/ Ladies from
Hell (Ian MacDonald)
Barrier, The (Meade Burrell)
Between Friends
Body and Soul
Bondman, The
Brothers under the Skin
Buried Treasure
Butterfly
Claw, The (Maurice Stair)
Cytherea (Peyton Morris)
Fallen Angels
Fifth Avenue Models
Find the Woman
Foreign Legion, The
Get Rich Quick Wallingford (Blackie
Dow)
Hunchback of Notre Dame, The
(Phoebus)
Irresistible Lover
Is Money Everything?
Little Italy
Love Me and the World Is Mine
Love Thief, The

Mademoiselle Modiste
Man from Home, The
Man, Woman and Wife
Merry-Go-Round (Count Franz Max-
    millian von Hohenegg)
Passion's Playground
Phantom of the Opera, The (Raoul
    deChagny)
Price of Pleasure, The
Proxies
Splendid Hazard, A
Spoilers, The
Tarnish
Three Live Ghosts
Till We Meet Again
Trial Marriage
True as Steel
Under Western Skies
Universal player 20
Unknown, The (Malabar)
Wild Goose, The
Woman from Moscow

3229
KERSHAW, Willette*
Vortex, The (Florence Lancaster)

3230
KERSTEN, Albert E. *
Cafe Electric /aka/ Wenn ein Weib
    den Weg Verliert [When a Woman
    Loses Her Way] (Mr. Zerner)

3231
KESSLER, Edith*
To Please a Woman
What Do Men Want?

3232
KEY, Kathleen (1897-1954)
Beautiful and Damned, The
Bells of San Juan, The
Ben Hur (Tirzah)
Flaming Frontier, The
Four Horsemen of the Apocalypse,
    The (Georgette)
Gold Widows
Irish Hearts
Lover's Oath, A
Midshipman, The
Money Talks
North of Hudson Bay
Reno
Revelation
Sea Hawk, The
West of Chicago
Where Is My Wandering Boy To-
    night?

3233
KEYS, Nelson*
Madame Pompadour (Duc de Cource-
    lette)
Mumsie ("Speed" Murphy)
Triumph of the Scarlet Pimpernel,
    The (Robespierre)

3234
KEYSER-HEYL, Willy*
Der Jonuskopf /aka/ Love's Mockery

3235
KID, Mary*
Rasputin
Wasted Love

3236
KIENER, Hazel*
Freshman, The

3237
KILGOUR, Joseph /aka/ Joseph Kil-
    gore (1863-1933)
At the End of the World
Broken Gates
Capital Punishment (Governor)
Hearts and Trumps
I Am Guilty
Janice Meredith (General Washing-
    ton)
King on Main Street, The
Leopard Woman, The
Let's Get Married
Love
One Year to Live
Percy
Ponjola (Conrad Lypiatt)
Top of the World, The
Try and Get It
Within the Law (Edward Gilder)
Woman with Four Faces, The (Jud-
    son Osgood)

3238
KILIAN, Victor (1891-)
Gentlemen of the Press
Valley Forge

3239
KILLER (Horse)
Black Cyclone

3240
KIMBALL, Edward M. *
Cheat, The
I'll Show You the Town
Masquerader, The

Mid-Channel

3241
KING, Allyn*
Fighting Blade, The (Charlotte Musgrove)

3242
KING, Carlotta*
Desert Song, The (Margot)

3243
KING, Charles (1898-1944)
Broadway Melody, The (Eddie Kearns)
Chasing Rainbows
Climbing the Golden Stairs
Girl in the Show, A
Hollywood Revue of 1929
Merry Go Round (Baron Nicki von Eubermut)
Phantom Fingers
Road Show
Sisters of Eve
Slim Fingers
Weary Winnie
What Happened to Jones? [series]
You Can't Beat the Law
Stage:
George White's Scandals 21
Hit the Deck (Bilge) 27
Little Nellie Kelly (Jerry Conroy) 22

3244
KING, Claude (1879-1941)
Behind that Curtain (Sir George Mannering)
Bella Donna
Black Watch, The
Blue Skies
Idols of Clay (Dr. Herbert)
Irish Luck
Judy of Rogues Harbor
Knockout, The
London after Midnight (the stranger)
Love and Learn
Madame X (Valmorin)
Making of O'Malley, The
Mr. Wu (Mr. Muir)
Mysterious Dr. Fu Manchu /aka/ The Insidious Dr. Fu Manchu (Sir John Petrie)
Night of Mystery, A
Oh, Kay!
Outcast, The
Paradise
Red Hair (Thomas L. Burke)
Scarab Ring, The

Silent Lover, The
Six Days
Son of the Gods (Bathurst)
Sporting Goods
Strange Cargo
Unguarded Hour, The
Warming Up
Why Girls Leave Home

3245
KING, Emmett (1892-)
Acquittal, The
Barbara Frietchie
Billions
Captain January
Day of Faith, The
Devil's Cargo, The
Fighting American, The
Habit
In the Heart of a Fool
Kismet
Laugh, Clown, Laugh
Little Lord Fauntleroy (Rev. Mordaunt)
Lying Lips
Man in the Saddle, The
Man Without a Country, The /aka/ As No Man Has Loved
Mistress of Shenstone
Noisy Neighbors
O'Malley of the Mounted
On Trial
Pampered Youth
Reno
Shopworn Angel, The
Trifling with Honor
When Dreams Come True

3246
KING, Fay*
Great White Way, The

3247
KING, Gerald*
Time, the Place and the Girl, The

3248
KING, Joe*
Daring Years, The (Jim Moran)
Idol of the North, The (Sgt. McNair)

3249
KING, Joseph*
Laughing Lady, The
Roadhouse Nights
Salvation Neil
Tin Gods
Twenty-One

Unguarded Women

3250
KING, Judy*
Best Bad Man, The (Molly Jones)
Bonanza Buckaroo, The
Gay Retreat, The

3251
KING, L. H. *
Sin Flood, The

3252
KING, Leslie*
Bond Boy, The
Idols of Clay (Blinky)
If Winter Comes
Orphans of the Storm (Jacques For-
    get Not)

3253
KING, Louis*
Mexicali Rose

3254
KING, Margie*
Great Gabbo, The

3255
KING, Marie*
Cafe in Cairo, A

3256
KING, Molly (1898-)
Greater than Love
Her Majesty
Suspicious Wives
Women Men Forget

3257
KING, Ruth*
Cafe in Cairo, A
Dixie Handicap, The
He Who Gets Slapped (He's wife)

3258
KINGSLEY, Albert*
Condemned (Felix)

3259
KINGSLEY, Arthur*
Esmeralda

3260
KINGSLEY, Florida (1879-)
Annabel Lee
Dangerous Business (Mrs. Brooks)
Greater than Fame

Independence, B'Gosh!
Love

3261
KINGSLEY, Frank*
Fighting American, The

3262
KINGSTON, Muriel*
Dawn of Revenge
Just Another Blonde /aka/ Girl
    from Coney Island
Masked Lover, The
On Guard [serial]
Subway Sadie
Valley of Lost Souls
White Hell

3263
KINGSTON, Natalie*
All Night Long
Daredevil, The
Feet of Mud
Figures Don't Lie
Framed
Girl in Every Port, A
Harvester, The
His First Flame
His Marriage Wow
Kid Boots (Carmen Mendoza)
Long Pants
Lost at the Front
Night of Love, The (Donna Beatriz)
Painted Post
Pirate of Panama [serial]
Port of Missing Girls, The
Remember When? (Rosemary Lee)
River of Romance
Silent Lover, The
Soldier Man
Street Angel (Lisetta)
Tarzan the Mighty [serial] (Mary
    Trevor)
Tarzan the Tiger [serial] (Jane)
Wet Paint

3264
KINGSTON, Winifred (-1967)
Beyond
Trail of the Ace
Virginian, The

3265
KINO, Goro*
First Born, The
Tale of Two Worlds, A (Windlass
    man)

3266
KINZ, Franciska*
Diary of a Lost Girl, The

3267
KIPLING, Edward*
Shadows of Paris
Spanish Dancer, The (Marquis de
   Rotundo)

3268
KIRBY, David*
In the Palace of the King
Last Edition
Lawful Cheaters (Rooney)
Man Who Came Back, The
Mask of Lopez, The
Nellie, the Beautiful Cloak Model
Shield of Honor
Spirit of the U. S. A.
Sunset Derby

3269
KIRK, Evans*
Husband Hunter, The (Bob Harkness)

3270
KIRKHAM, Correan*
Milestones (The Hon. Muriel Pym)

3271
KIRKHAM, Kathleen (1895-)
Back to Yellow Jacket
Beau Revel
Bolted Door, The
Dollar for Dollar
Her Five Foot Highness
Homespun Vamp, A
Innocent Cheat, The
Little 'Fraid Lady
Married Virgin, The /aka/ Frivo-
   lous Wives
Nobody's Kid
One-Eighth Apache
Parlor, Bedroom and Bath
Pilgrims of the Night
Regular Fellow, A
Sackcloth and Scarlet
Sky Pilot, The
When Dawn Came
White Moth, The

3272
KIRKLAND, Hardee*
Ace of Hearts (Morgridge)
Honor First
Ladies Must Live
Perfect Crime, A (President Holliday)

Woman Proof

3273
KIRKMAN, Kathleen*--see: Kathleen
   Kirkham

3274
KIRKWOOD, James R. (1883-1963)
Another Man's Wife
Black Waters
Bob Hampton of Placer
Branding Iron, The (Pierre Landis)
Broken Barriers
Butterflies in the Rain
Circe, the Enchantress
Eagle's Feather, The
Ebb Tide
Gerald Cranston's Lady
Great Impersonation (dual role)
Hearts in Exile
Human Wreckage
In the Heart of a Fool
Love
Lover's Island
Love's Whirlpool
Man from Home, The
Man-Woman-Marriage
Million Dollar Mystery, The
Paramount player 24
Pink Gods
Ponjola (Lundi Druro)
Reckless Lady, The
Scoffer, The
Sin Flood, The
Someone to Love
Spoilers, The
That Royle Girl (Calvin Clarke)
Time, the Place and the Girl, The
Top of the World, The
Under Two Flags (Corp. Victor)
Wandering Husbands
Wise Guy, The
You Are Guilty
Stage:
Edgar Allan Poe (Title role) 25
Fool, The (Daniel Gilchrist) 22
Ladies of the Evening (Jerry Strong)
   24

3275
KIRTLAND, Harden*
While Paris Sleeps (O'Keefe's father)

3276
KIS, Imre*
Paul Street Boys, The

3277
KITHNOU, Mlle. (1904-)
Careers
Maré Nostrum [Our Sea] (Dona Cin-
    ta)
L'Orpheline
Parisette
La Puissance du Pasaret

3278
KLAUS, Henry*
Four Horsemen of the Apocalypse,
    The (Heinrick von Hartrott)

3279
KLEIN, Adolf*
Wie Einst im Mai

3280
KLEIN, Josef*
Anna Boleyn /aka/ Deception

3281
KLEIN, Julius*
City of Temptation

3282
KLEIN, Robert*
Ancient Mariner, The (death)
Dante's Inferno

3283
KLEIN-ROGGE, Rudolph (1889-1955)
Destiny /aka/ The Tired Death; The
    Three Lights; Between Worlds;
    Der Mude Tod
Dr. Mabuse, the Gambler /aka/
    Dr. Mabuse, the Great Unknown
    (Title role)
Forbidden Love
Kriemhild's Revenge
Loves of Casanova, The
Metropolis (Rotwang)
Die Nibelungen /aka/ The Nibelungs
Peter the Pirate
Siegfried
Spione [Spies]
Volga-Volga (Hadschi-Ali)

3284
KLEINERT, Robert*
William Tell

3285
KLINDER, Lotte*
Tradition

3286
KLÖEPFER, Eugen*
Burning Acre, The
Explosion
Luther
Street, The

3287
KLUKVIN, I. *
Czar Ivan the Terrible
Flames on the Volga
Stachka /aka/ Strike

3288
KNAPP, Otto*
William Tell

3289
KNIGHT, Bill*
Bigger than Barnum's

3290
KNIGHT, Harlan E. *
Country Flapper, The
Dance Magic
Janice Meredith (Theodore Larkin)
Knockout, The
Rapids, The
Stage:
Bottom of the Cup, The (Sheriff Bol-
    ton) 27

3291
KNIGHT, James (1891-)
Bad Sir Brian Botany
Ball of Fortune
Beautiful Kitty
Brenda of the Barge
Claude Duval (Capt. Craddock)
Crushing the Drug Traffic
Cupid in Clover
Dear Liar, A
Education of Nicky, The
Famous Music Melodies
Great Turf Mystery, The
Happy Prisoner, The
Happy Rascals, The
Hornet's Nest, The
Houpla Spangles
Impatient Patient, The
In the Welsh Hills
Jacobs, W. W. [series]
Lady Owner, The
Last Hundred Yards, The
Legend of Tichborne Dale
Lights O'London, The
Maria Marten
Mr. Nobody

Motherland
Number 7 Brick Row
Old Actor's Story, The
Playing the Game
Pluck vs. Plot
Power over Men
Rainbow [series]
Rowing to Win
Ticket O' Leave
Trainer and Temptress
What Price Loving Cup?
When Giants Fought
Woodcroft Castle

3292
KNIGHT, Percy (Percival Knight)*
Sherlock Holmes /aka/ Moriarty
   (Sir James)
Stage:
Thin Ice (Mr. Bubridge) 22

3293
KNIGHT, W. R., Capt.*
Filming of the Golden Eagle, The
   (narrator)

3294
KNIPPER-TSCHECH, O.
Prisoners of the Sea

3295
KNOTT, Adelbert*
Percy

3296
KNOTT, Clara*
Old Lady 31

3297
KNOTT, George Marion*
Rolling Home

3298
KNOTT, Lydia (1873-)
Blackmail
Breaking Point, The (Mrs. Marshall)
Dwelling Place of Light
Dynamite Smith
East Lynne (Mrs. Hare)
Free and Equal
Garrison's Finish
Homespun Folks
King of Kings, The (bit)
Lure of Youth, The
Our Dancing Daughters
Peaceful Valley
Perfect Flapper, The
Primrose Path, The (Mrs. Arm-

   strong)
Rose of the World
Those Who Dare
Turn to the Right
Two Lovers
Woman of Paris, A (John's mother)

3299
KNOWLAND, Alice (1879-)
All Soul's Eve
Coming Through
Heart Line
Parish Priest, The
Partners of the Tide
Six Best Cellars, The
Stage:
Edgar Allan Poe (Mrs. John Allan)
   25

3300
KNOX, Teddy*
Phonofilm
Rising Generation, The

3301
KNOX, W. D. C.*
Gypsy Cavalier, The (Sir George
   Forrest)
Prince of Lovers, The

3302
KNUDSEN, David*
Syv Dager for Elisabeth

3303
KOBE, Arturo*
Condemned (prison inmate)

3304
KOCH, Georg August*
Atlantic [German] (Lersner)
Die Nibelungen /aka/ The Nibelungs

3305
KOCHITZ, Nina*
Loves of Casanova, The

3306
KOENAN, Frank*
Lorna Doone

3307
KOENE, Rogers*
Silent Command, The

3308
KOESBERG, Nicolai*
Janice Meredith (La Foyette)

3309
KOHLASE, Max*
Die Freudlose Gasse [The Joyless
  Street] /aka/ The Street of Sor-
  rows (Mr. Lechner)

3310
KOHLER, Fred (1889-1938)
Blood Ship, The
Broadway Babies
Broadway Daddies
Case of Lena Smith, The
Chinatown Charlie
City Gone Wild, A
Cyclone Bliss
Dick Turpin
Dragnet
Dummy, The (Joe Cooper)
Flame of Life
Forgotten Faces
Gay Defender, The
Hell's Heroes
His Back Against the Wall
Ice Flood, The
Iron Horse, The (Deroux)
Kentucky Colonel
Last Command, The
Leatherneck, The
Loves of Carmen, The
North of Hudson Bay
Old Ironsides
Open Range
Partners of the Tide
Quitter, The
Riders of the Purple Sage (Metzger)
River of Romance, The
Roadhouse Nights
Rough Riders, The
Sal of Singapore
Say It with Songs
Scrapper, The
Shootin' Irons
Showdown, The
Son of the Wolf
Spider, The
Spieler, The
Stairs of Sand
Thousand to One, A
Three Who Paid
Thunderbolt
Thundering Herd, The (Pruitt)
Tide of the Empire
Trimmed
Underworld (Buck Mulligan)
Vanishing Pioneer, The
Way of All Flesh, The (the Tough)
Winds of Chance
Yellow Men and Gold

3311
KÖHLER, Marga*
Die Bergkatze [The Mountain Cat;
  The Wild Cat] (Commander's wife)
Romeo und Julia im Schnee [Romeo
  and Juliet in the Snow]

3312
KOHLMAR, Lee*
Flaming Disc, The [serial]
Kibitzer, The
Potash and Perlmutter
Stage:
Brass Buttons (Herman Schultz) 27
June Days (Herman Van Zandt) 25
My Country (Nathan Blumberg) 26
Partners Again (Marks Pasinsky) 22
Tangletoes (Julius Hart) 25

3313
KOLAR, Phil*
Happy Days (chorus)

3314
KOLB, John (John Phillip Kolb)*
Knockout, The
Lost at the Front
Men of Steel
See You in Jail
Twinkletoes (Bill Carsides)

3315
KOLB, Therese*
Appassionata

3316
KOLB, Wallace*
If Winter Comes

3317
KOLIN, Nikolai*
Edmund Kean, Prince Among Lovers

3318
KOLK, Scott (Walter Scott Kolk)*
Dynamite (radio announcer)
Hold Your Man
Marianne (Lt. Frane)
Stage:
Take the Air (Lt. Dale) 27

3319
KOLKER, Henry (1874-1947)
Any Woman
Bright Skies
Bucking the Tiger
Charge of the Gauchos, The
Coquette (Jasper Carter)

Disraeli
Don't Marry
East Is West
Fighter, The
Good Intentions
Greatest Love, The
Hell's Four Hundred
I Will Repay
Kiss in a Taxi, A
Leopardess, The
Love, Live and Laugh
Man of Stone
Palace of Pleasure
Pleasure Crazed
Purple Highway, The
Red Hair
Rough House Rosie (W. S. Davids)
Sally, Irene and Mary (Marcus Morton)
Silk Stockings
Snow Bride, The
Soft Living
Third Generation, The
Valiant, The
Wet Paint

3320
KOLMER, Leo (1878-1946)
Beautifully Trimmed
Breaking Home Ties
High Heels
Kibitzer, The
Orphans of the Storm (King Louis XVI)
Secret Gift, The

3321
KOMAI, Tetsu (1893-   )
Bulldog Drummond (Chong)
Chinatown Nights
Detectives
East Is West
Moran of the Marines
Mysterious Dr. Fu Manchu, The
   /aka/ The Insidious Dr. Fu
   Manchu
Woman from Moscow, The

3322
KOPP, Erwin*
Die Bergkatze /aka/ The Mountain
   Cat; The Wildcat (Tripe)

3323
KORDA, Maria*
Last Days of Pompeii, The
Love and the Devil

3324
KORFF, Arnold*
Dancing Vienna
Tragödie der Liebe [Tragedy of Love]

3325
KORLOFF, Olga*
End of St. Petersberg, The

3326
KORMAN, Mary (1917-1973)
Big Business
Mary Queen of Tots
Our Gang Comedies

3327
KORNELIA, Irma*
Campus Flirt, The
You Never Know Women
Stage:
Man in Evening Clothes, The
   (Blanche) 24

3328
KORNER, Hermine*
Der Mensch am Wege [Man by the
   Roadside]

3329
KORTMAN, Robert*
All the Brothers Were Valiant (Varde)
Sunrise (bit)

3330
KORTNER, Fritz (1892-   )
Atlantic (Heinrich Thomas)
Backstairs
Beethoven
Dame Care
Dürfen wir Schweigen?
Die Frau Nach der Man Sich Sehnt
   [The Woman One Longs For] /aka/
   Three Loves (Dr. Karoff)
Hands of Orlac, The
Life of Beethoven, The
Maria Stuart
Mata Hari: The Red Dancer
Der Morder Dmitri Roramazoo
   (Dmitri)
Pandora's Box
Primanerlieb
Scandal in Paris, A
Das Schiff der Verborenen Menschen
   [The Ship of Lost Souls] /aka/ Le
   Navire des Hommes Perdus [The
   Ship of Lost Men] (Fernando Vela)
Spy of Madame Pompadour, The
Das Wachsfigurenkabinett [Waxworks]

(Jack the Ripper)
Warning Shadows

3331
KORTON, Robert*
Courtship of Miles Standish, The

3332
KOSER, H. *
America (Col. Prescott)

3333
KOSLOFF, Theodore (1882-1956)
Adam's Rib (King of Moravia)
Affairs of Anatol, The (Nazzer
  Singh)
Beggar on Horseback
Children of Jazz
City of Masks, The
Dictator, The
Don't Call It Love
Feet of Clay (Bendick)
Fools' Paradise (John Roderiguez)
Forbidden Fruit (Pietro Guiseppe)
Golden Bed, The (Marquis de San
  Pilar)
Green Temptation, The
Idols of Clay
King of Kings, The (Malchus)
Lane that Has No Turning Point,
  The
Law and the Lawless, The
Little Adventuress, The
New Lives for Old
Prince Chap, The
Road to Yesterday
Saturday Night
Something to Think About (a clown)
To Have and to Hold
Triumph (Varinoff)
Volga Boatman, The (Stefan)
Why Change Your Wife? (Radinoff)
Woman Wise

3334
KOTSONAROS, George*
Beggars of Life
Fifty-Fifty Girl, The
Private Life of Helen of Troy, The
  (Hector)
Shakedown, The
Street of Sin, The
Tender Hour, The
Wizard, The (the monk)

3335
KOUBITZKY, Alexandre*
Napoleon

3336
KOUGOUCHEFF, Prince N. *
Michael Strogoff (General Kisoff)

3337
KOVAL-SAMBORSKY, Ivan*
Mother

3338
KOVANKO, Nathalie*
Michael Strogoff (Nadia Fedoroff)
Tales of 1,001 Nights

3339
KRAFTSCHENKO, Valerie*
Flames on the Volga

3340
KRAMER, Edith*
Hotter than Hot

3341
KRAMER, Ida*
Abie's Irish Rose (Mrs. Isaac Cohen)

3342
KRAMER, Leopold*
Hungarian Rhapsody

3343
KRAUSS, Henry*
Pathetic Symphony

3344
KRAUSS, Werner (1884-1959)
Alles für Geld [All for a Woman]
Burning Acre, The
Decameron Nights
Die Freudlose Gasse [The Joyless
  Street] /aka/ The Street of Sor-
  row (Joseph Geiringer)
Geheimnisse Seele [Secrets of a Soul]
Jealousy
Jew of Mestri, The (Shylock)
Jolly Peasant, The
Looping the Loop
Man Who Cheated Life, The
Merchant of Venice, The (Shylock)
Midsummer Night's Dream, A (Bot-
  tom)
Nana
Othello /aka/ The Moor (Iago)
Royal Scandal, A
Shattered Dreams
Student of Prague, The (devil)
Tartuffe
Three Way Works, The
Das Wachsfigurenkabinet (Waxworks]

Stage:
Miracle, The (crippled piper) 24

3345
KRAUSSNECK, Arthur*
At the Grey House
Luther

3346
KRECH, Warren W. *
Plunder [serial]
Town that Forgot God, The
Stage:
John Hawthorne (Title role) 21
Mrs. Jimmie Thompson (Edgar
  Blodgett) 20
We Girls (Dr. Tom Brown) 21

3347
KREMBS, Felix*
Heart of Maryland, The (Fulton
  Thorpe)
Stage:
Badges (Ed Gillespie) 24
Changelings (Clyde Halstead) 23
Congai (Col. Urban Chauvet) 28
Crooked Gamblers (Turner) 20
Distant Drum, A (George Wilson) 28
Glory Hallelujah (Werty) 26
It All Depends (Ned Richmond) 25
Jimmie's Women (Dr. Richard Tur-
  ner) 27
King Can Do No Wrong, The (Baron
  Almeria) 27
Lawful Larceny (Judge Perry) 22
Lights Out (Walt Sebastian) 22
Man's Name, The (Marshall Dunn)
  21
Night Duel (Dave Dannelly) 26
Spread Eagle (Gen. Ramon Angel de
  Castro) 27
Stolen Fruit (Jacques Manovard) 25
Thin Ice (Whitney Nelson) 22
Trapped (Alex) 28

3348
KRIMER, Harry*
Napoleon

3349
KRISTER, Dorothy*
Happy Days (chorus)

3350
KRONERT, Max*
Die Bergkatze /aka/ The Mountain
  Cat; The Wildcat (Masillo)
Sumurun /aka/ One Arabian Night

(Muffti)

3351
KRU*
Chang (the man)

3352
KRUGER, Otto (1885-1974)
Under the Red Robe
Stage:
Alias Jimmy Valentine (Lee Randall)
  21
Easy Come, Easy Go (Dick Tain) 25
Game of Love and Death, The (Claude
  Vallee) 29
Karl and Anna (Karl) 29
Nervous Wreck, The (Henry Williams)
  23
Royal Family, The (Anthony Caven-
  dish) 27-28
Sonya (Prince Alexander) 21
Straw, The (Stephen Murray) 21
To the Ladies! (Leonard Beebe) 22
Trelawney of the Wells (Augustus
  Colpoys) 27
Wasp, The (James "Murray") 23
Will Shakespeare (Title role) 23

3353
KRUGER, Paul (1895-)
First Auto, The
Fortune Hunter, The
Idle Rich, The
Midnight Taxi
Non-Support
One Round Hogan
Rounders, The

3354
KÜHNE, Friedrich*
Anna Boleyn /aka/ Deception
Othello /aka/ The Moor (Brabanito)
Das Weib des Pharao [The Wife of
  the Pharaoh] /aka/ The Loves of
  Pharaoh (High Priest)

3355
KULGANEK, W. *
Flames on the Volga

3356
KUMA, Profulla*
Light of Asia, The

3357
KUNKLE, George*
Tempest, The

3358
KUPFER, Margarete*
Frau im Mond [Woman in the Moon]
Slums of Berlin
Sumurun /aka/ One Arabian Night
    (old woman)

3359
KURZ, Emile*
Last Laugh, The /aka/ Der Letze
    Mann (doorman's aunt)
Manon Lescaut (Manon's aunt)
Trial of Donald Westhof, The

3360
KUTUSOW, N.*
Prisoners of the Sea

3361
KUWA, George K.*
After the Storm
Broken Barriers
Chinese Parrot, The
Enchanted Hill, The
Eternal Struggle, The
Half-Breed, The (Kito)
House Without a Key, The [serial]
    (Charlie Chan)
Money Talks
Night Bride, The
Oh, Doctor!
Secret Hour, The
Showdown, The
Son of His Father, A
Wife Who Wasn't Wanted, The

3362
KUZMINA, Yelena /aka/ Elena Kuz-
    mina*
New Babylon

3363
KVANINE, K.*
Michael Strogoff (Basil Federoff)

3364
KYASHT, Lydia*
Black Spider, The

- L -

3365
LA BISSONIERE, Erin*
Heart of a Salome, The
Knights Out

3366
LACKAYE, Wilton (1862-1932)
Lone Wolf, The
What's Wrong with Women (James
    Bascom)
Stage:
Goldfish (Jim Wetherby) 22
High Stakes (Richard Lennon) 24
Ladies of the Jury (Judge Fish) 29
Monkey Talks, The (Lorenzo) 25
Monster, The (Dr. Gustave Ziska) 22
Trelwaney of the Wells (James Tel-
    fer) 27
Trilby (Svengali) 21
Two Orphans, The (Count De Linieres)
    26

3367
LACKTEEN, Frank (1894-)
Avenging Arrow, The
Court Martial
Desert Gold
Fortieth Door, The [serial]
Green Archer, The
Hawk of the Hills [serial]
House Without a Key [serial]
Idaho [serial]
Into the Net [serial]
Leatherstocking [serial]
Pony Express
Prowlers of the Sea
Sunken Silver [serial]
Tiger's Shadow, The [serial] (Dr.
    Sandro)
Veiled Mystery, The
Warning
White Eagle

3368
LACOSTE, M.*
Legion of Honor, The

3369
LADAH*
Chang (the girl)

3370
LADY (Horse)
Black Cyclone

3371
LAEMMELE, Beth*
Hollywood Revue of 1929 (dance
    number)

3372
LAFAYETTE, Andrée*
Trilby

3373
LAFAYETTE, Ruby (1844-)
Butterflies in the Rain
Coming of Amos, The
Day of Faith, The
Marriage by Contract
Tomorrow's Love

3374
LA FONDE, Virginia*
Gateway of the Moon

3375
LA GARDE, Henri*
Marriage Clause, The

3376
LAGRANGE, Louise*
La Marche Nuptale
Sainted Devil, A (Estrella)
Side Show of Life, The

3377
LA GUERE, George*
Mama's Affair

3378
LAIDLAW, Ethan (1900-1963)
Big Diamond Robbery, The
Bride of the Desert
Dangerous Curves (Roustabout)
Laughing at Death
Little Savage, The
Outlawed
Wolf's Clothing

3379
LAIDLAW, Roy*
Cowpuncher, The
Great Accident, The
Hunchback of Notre Dame, The
Live Sparks
Splendid Road, The
Weaker Sex, The

3380
LAIDLEY, Alice*
That Royle Girl (Clarke's fiancee)
Stage:
Small Timers, The (Frances Dewitt)
   25

3381
LAING, Tony*
This Freedom

3382
LAKE, Alice (1896-1967)
Air Circus
Angel of Broadway
Body and Soul
Broken Hearts of Broadway
Broken Homes
Circumstantial Evidence
Dangerous Blonde
Environment, The
Excitement
Fast Worker, The
Frozen Justice
Golden Gift, The
Greater Claim, The
Hate
Haunted Ship, The
Hole in the Wall
I Am the Law
Kissed
Misfit Wife, The
More to Be Pitied than Scorned
Nobody's Bride
Obey Your Husband
Over the Wire
Price of Success
Red Lights
Roarin' Fires
Runaway Girls
Shore Acres
Should Women Tell?
Spider and the Rose, The
Twin Beds
Uncharted Seas
Unknown Purple, The
Untamed Justice
Watered Stock
Young Ideas

3383
LAKE, Arthur (Arthur Silverlake)
   (1905-)
Air Circus
Count of Ten, The
Cradle Snatchers
Dance Hall
Harold Teen (Title role)
Irresistible Lover
Let George Do It [series]
Lilac Time
On with the Show (Harold)
Runaway Girls
Skinner's Dress Suit
Stop that Man!
Tanned Legs
When Love Is Young

3384
LAKE, Florence*
New Year's Eve
Rogue Song, The (Nadja)
Through Different Eyes (Myrtle)
Universal player 28
Waltzing Around

3385
LAKE, Harriette--see: Ann Sothern

3386
LAKE, Wesley*
Four Devils, The

3387
LALOR, Frank*
Clothes Make the Pirate
Red Hot Romance
Stage:
Luckee Girl (Pontaves) 28
Street Singer, The (prefect of police)
29
Suzette (Tony) 21

3388
LA MARR, Barbara (Rheatha Wat-
son) (1897-1926)
Ambrose Applejohn's Adventure
(Anna Valeska)
Arabian Love
Brass Bottle, The
Cinderella of the Hills, A
Cytherea
Desperate Trails
Domestic Relations
Eternal City, The (Donna Roma)
Eternal Struggle, The
Girl from Montmartre, The
Harriet and the Piper
Heart of a Siren, The
Hero, The
Mary of the Movies
Nut, The
Poor Men's Wives
Prisoner of Zenda, The (Antoinette
de Mauban)
Quincy Adams Sawyer (Lindy Put-
nam)
Saint Elmo
Sandra
Shooting of Dan McGrew, The (the
lady known as Lou)
Souls for Sale (Leva Limaire, a
vampire)
Strangers of the Night
Three Musketeers, The (Milady de
Winter)

Thy Name Is Woman
Trifling Women
White Monkey, The
White Moth, The

3389
LA MARR, Hedy (Hedwig Eva Marie
Kiesler) (1915-)
Ein Sturm im Wasserglas [Storm in
a Water Glass]

3390
LA MARR, Margaret*
Happy Days (chorus)

3391
LAMBERT, Irene*
Sally of the Scandals

3392
LAMMING, Frank--see: Frank Lanning

3393
LA MONT, Frank*
Movietone Follies of 1929

3394
LAMONT, George*
Through Different Eyes (Traynor)

3395
LAMONT, Harry*
Blood and Sand (El Pontellino)

3396
LAMORE, Isabel*
Last Moment, The

3397
LAMOTT, Jean*
Folly of Vanity
Hearts and Spurs (Celeste)

3398
LAMY, Charles*
La Chute de la Maison Usher [The
Fall of the House of Usher]
La Cousine Bette

3399
LANCASTER, Fred*
Golf

3400
LANCHESTER, Elsa (Elizabeth Sul-
livan) (1902-)
Bluebottles

Constant Nymph, The
Day Dreams
Mr. Smith Wakes Up
One of the Best
Tonic, The

3401
LAND, Mary*
My American Wife (maid)

3402
LANDAU, David, Mrs. *
Way Down East (Mrs. Moore)

3403
LANDAU, Frances*
Into the Net [serial]

3404
LANDI, Elissa (Elizabeth Marie
    Landi) (1904-1948)
Betrayal, The
Bolivar
Ecstacy
Inseparables, The
Parisian, The
Sin
Underground
Stage:
Dandy Dick [debut, England] 23
Storm - London 24

3405
LANDIS, Cullen (1895-)
Alibi, The
Born Rich
Broadway after Midnight
Brown Mash
Buffalo Bill on the U. P. Trail
Bunty Pulls the String
Crimson Flash, The [serial]
Davy Crockett at the Fall of the
    Alamo
Devil's Skipper, The
Dixie Flyer, The
Enemy of Men
Famous Mrs. Fair, The
Fighting Coward, The
Fighting Fathers, The
Finnigan's Ball
Fog, The
Forsaking All Others
Frenzied Flames
Going Some
Heroes of the Night
It's a Great Life
Lights of New York (Eddie Morgan)
Little Wild Girl

Masters of Men
Midnight Adventure, A
Midnight Alarm
My Old Dutch
Not Quite Decent
On Guard [serial]
On to Reno
Out with the Tide
Perils of the Coast Guard
Pinto
Pioneer, The
Say It with Flowers
Smoke Eaters, The
Snow Blind
Sweet Rosie O'Grady
Then Came the Woman
Universal player 23
Voices of the City (Jimmy)
Watch Your Step
We're All Gamblers
Where Is My Wandering Boy Tonight?
Winning Futurity
Stage:
Chippies (Tony Perrotta) 29

3406
LANDIS, Margaret*
Ladder Jinx, The
Western Wallop, The

3407
LANDIS, Winifred*
Bandit Buster, The

3408
LANDSHOFF, Ruth*
Nosferatu

3409
LANE, Allan "Rocky" (Harry Alber-
    shart) (1900-1973)
Detectives Wanted
Forward Pass, The (Ed Kirby)
Knights Out
Not Quite Decent

3410
LANE, Brenda*
Flame Fighter, The
New Klondike, The

3411
LANE, Charles (1899-)
Away Goes Prudence
Barbed Wire
Blind Goddess, The
Branded Woman, The
Broadway Rose

Canary Murder Case, The (Charles
  Spotswoode)
Dark Angel, The (Sir Hubert Vane)
Dr. Jekyll and Mr. Hyde (Dr. Lany-
  on)
Fascination
Great Adventure, The
Guilty of Love
How Women Love
I Want My Man
Man from Mexico, The
Married Alive
Mrs. Black Is Back
Music Master, The
Padlocked
Restless Sex, The (John Cleland)
Romola (Baldassarre)
Ruggles of Red Gap
Sadie Thompson (Dr. McPhail)
Saturday's Children
Second Youth
Service for Ladies
Tents of Allah
Whirlwind of Youth
White Sister, The (Prince Chiar-
  monte)
Winning of Barbara Worth, The
  (Jefferson Worth)
Without Limit

3412
LANE, Katheryn*
His Children's Children

3413
LANE, Leela*
Half-Breed, The (Isabella Pardeau)

3414
LANE, Leone*
Saturday Night Kid, The (Pearl)

3415
LANE, Lola (Dorothy Mulligan)
  (1909-)
Case of Lena Smith, The
Girl from Havana, The
Movietone Follies of 1929 (Lila
  Beaumont)
Speakeasy
Stage:
War Song, The (Sally Moss) 28

3416
LANE, Lupino (Henry George Lupino) (1892-1957) [Real name cor-
  rected from Vol. I]
Be My King

Broker, The
Educational player 29
Fighting Dude, The
Friendly Husband, A
Hello, Sailor
His Private Life
Isn't Life Wonderful? (Rudolph)
Lot About a Lottery
Love Parade, The (Jacques)
Monty of the Mounted
Night Out and a Day In, A
Only Me (24 roles)
Pirates Beware
Reporter, The
Show of Shows, The (street cleaner)
Sword Points
Universal comedies 25-29
Stage:
Afgar (Coucourli) 20
Hollywood Music Box Revue, The 29
Mikado, The (Ko-Ko) 25
Vaudeville (Palace) 28
Ziegfeld Follies 24

3417
LANE, Magda*
Do or Die

3418
LANE, Nora*
Cohens and the Kellys in Atlantic
  City, The
Cohens and the Kellys in Paris, The
Flying U Ranch
Gun Runner, The
Jesse James
Kit Carson
Lawless Legion, The
Marquis Preferred
Masked Emotions
Night of Mystery, A
One Hysterical Night
Pioneer Scout
Sally (Marcia TenBrock)
Sunset Pass
Texas Tornado, The

3419
LANG, Howard*
Peacock Alley (Abner Harmon)
Stage:
Abie's Irish Rose (Dr. Jacob Samu-
  els) 22
Dawn (Matthew Slayton) 24
East of Suez (Lee Tai Cheng) 22
Jazz Singer, The (Cantor Rabino-
  witz) 25

Lady of the Rose (Barry Trevelyan) 25
Ouija Board, The (Gabriel Mogador) 20
Silent House, The (Dr. Chan-Fu) 28
Strong Man's House, A (Sam Hamerman) 29
Thumbs Down (Emmett Sheridan) 23
Unwritten Chapter, The (David Franks) 20
Wake Up, Jonathan (Adam West) 21
Wandering Jew, The (Issacher) 21

3420
LANG, Matheson (1879-1948)
Beyond the Veil
Blue Peter
Carnival (Othello)
Chinese Bungalow, The (Yuan Sing)
Dick Turpin's Ride to New York (Title role)
Guy Fawkes
Henry, King of Navarre (Title role)
Island of Despair
King's Highway, The
Mr. Wu
Qualified Adventure, The
Romance of Old Bagdad, A
Secret Kingdom, The
Slaves of Destiny
Triumph of the Scarlet Pimpernel, The (Sir Percy Blakeney)
Wandering Jew, The (Matahias)
White Slippers
Stage:
Wandering Jew, The (Matathias/ the unknown knight/Matteo Bottadios) 27

3421
LANG, Peter*
Dangerous Money

3422
LANGAN, Marius*
Happy Days (chorus)

3423
LANGDEN, John*
Atlantic

3424
LANGDON, Harry (1884-1946)
All Night Long
Big Kick, The
Boobs in the Wood
Cat's Meow, The
Chaser, The

Ella Cinders
Feet of Mud
Fiddlesticks
Fighting Parson, The
First Hundred Years Are the Worst, The
Flickering Youth
Hanson Cabman, The
Heart Trouble
His First Flame
His Marriage Wow
His New Mama
Horace Greeley, Jr.
Hotter than Hot
Long Pants
Luck O' the Foolish
Lucky Stars
Picking Peaches (debut)
Plain Clothes
Remember When?
Saturday Afternoon
Sea Squawk, The
Shanghaied Lovers
Skirt Shy
Sky Boy
Smile Please
Soldier Man
Strong Man, The (Paul Bergot)
There He Goes
Three's a Crowd
Tramp, Tramp, Tramp (Harry)
White Wing's Bride
Stage:
Circuses
Burlesque
Jim Jam Jems 20
Medicine Shows
Minstrel Shows
Vaudeville (Palace) 29

3425
LANGDON, Lillian*
After Business Hours
Blonde Saint, The
Circe, the Enchantress
Cobra (Mrs. Palmer)
Enticement
Going Some
Going Up
Great Accident, The
Hellion, The
Highest Law, The
Hope
Joanna
Oh, Lady, Lady!
Price She Paid, The
Triflers
Water, Water, Everywhere

What's a Wife Worth?

3426
LANGDON, Rose*
Road to Mandalay, The
Stage:
Jim Jam Jems 20

3427
LANGFORD-REED, Joan*
Luck of the Navy, The (Dora, as a
  child)

3428
LANGLEN, Paula*
Movietone Follies of 1929
Stage:
Iolanthe (Fleta) 26
Pirates of Penzance (Maud) 26
Mikado, The (Mikado's Sword-Bear-
  er) 27

3429
LANGLEY, Herbert*
Chu-Chin-Chow (Abou Hassan)

3430
LANGSTON, Ruth*
Daredevil Jack [serial]

3431
LANKESTER, Eric*
Glorious Adventure, The (Malloy)

3432
LANNING, Frank*
Bad Man, The
Daredevil Jack [serial]
Huckleberry Finn
Kid Brother, The
Stand and Deliver (Pietro)
Unknown, The (Gypsy)

3433
LANOE, Jacques (Jiquel Lanoe)*
Forbidden Woman, The
Four Horsemen of the Apocalypse,
  The (German woman's husband)
Prodigal Daughters (Juda Botanya)

3434
LANOY, Andre*
Blonde or Brunette?
Stranded in Paris

3435
LANPHIER, Florence*
American Venus, The

3436
LANSING, Mary*
Happy Days (chorus)

3437
LA PLANTE, Beatrice*
Dodge Your Debts
Merely a Maid

3438
LA PLANTE, Laura (1904-)
Around the World in 18 Days [serial]
Beautiful Cheat, The
Beware of Widows
Butterflies in the Rain
Butterfly
Cat and the Canary, The (Annabelle
  West)
Dangerous Blondes
Dangerous Innocence
Dead Game
813
Excitement
Fast Worker, The
Finders Keepers
Her Big Night
His Four Fathers
Hold Your Man
Home James
Last Warning
Love Thrill, The
Love Trap, The
Midnight Sun, The
Old Swimmin' Hole, The
Perils of the Yukon [serial]
Poker Faces
Scandal
Shell Shocked
Show Boat (Magnolia)
Silk Stockings
Skinner's Dress Suit
Smouldering Fires
Sporting Youth
Spring Reunion
Teaser, The
Thanks for the Buggy Ride
Wall Flower, The
Young Ideas

3439
LA PLANTE, Violet*
Clean Heart, The

3440
LAPSLEY, Jimmie*
Confidence Man, The
Stage:

Ever Green Lady, The (Ikey Sonnen-
  schein) 22

3441
la RENO, Richard*
Border Cavalier
Sea Horses

3442
LARIVE, Leon*
Passion of Joan of Arc, The

3443
LARKIN, George (1889-)
Barriers of Folly
Bulldog Courage
Flame of Passion
Her Reputation
Man Trackers
Pell Street Mystery, The
Right Man, The
Saved by Radio
Terror Trail [serial]
Universal player 20
Way of the Transgressor, The
Wolf Face [serial]
Yankee Madness

3444
LA ROCHE, Edward /aka/ Edouard*
Soul Fire /aka/ Golden Youth
Stage:
Age of Innocence (Carlos Saramonte)
  28
Great Music (Louis) 24
Lady, The (the loafer) 23

3445
LA ROCQUE, Rod (Roderick la
  Rocque de la Rour) (1898-1969)
At Yale
Bachelor Brides
Brave Heart
Brigadier General
Captain Swagger
Challenge, The
Coming of Amos, The
Cruise of the Jasper B., The
Delightful Rogue
Discarded Woman
Easy to Get
Feet of Clay (Kerry Harlan)
Fighting Eagle, The
For Your Daughter's Sake
Forbidden Paradise (Capt. Alexis
  Czerny)
French Doll, The

Garter Girl, The
Gigolo
Golden Bed, The (Admah Holtz)
Greater than Love
Hold 'em Yale!
Jazzmania
Let Us Be Gay
Locked Door, The
Love over Night
Love Pirate, The
Man and the Moment, The
Night Life in New York
Notoriety
One Woman Idea
Our Dancing Daughters
Our Modern Maidens (Abbott)
Paying the Piper
Red Dice
Resurrection (Prince Dimitri)
Show People (cameo)
Slim Shoulders
Society Scandal, A (Harrison
  Peters)
Stand and Deliver (Roger Norman)
Stolen Kiss
Suspicious Wives
Ten Commandments, The (Dan Mc-
  Tavish)
This Is Heaven
Triumph (King Garnet)
What's Wrong with Women? (Jack
  Lee)
Wild, Wild Susan
Stage:
Anna Ascends ("Bunch" Barry) 20

3446
LA ROY, Rita (Ina Stuart) (1907-)
Children of the Ritz
Dynamite
Fashions in Love
Lilies of the Field
Love Trap, The

3447
LARRINAGA, Forster*
Dr. Mabuse the Gambler /aka/ Dr.
  Mabuse, the Great Unknown

3448
LARSSON, Helmer*
Peter the Tramp

3449
LA RUBIA, Marga*
Flirting with Love
For Sale (Parisian dance hall girl)

3450
LA RUE, Fontaine*
Blind Bargain, The (Mrs. Lamb)
Daughters of Today
Faith Healer, The
Lost Romance, The
Sins of Rosanne, The

3451
LASHLEY, Donald*
Price of a Party, The
Stage:
Cape Smoke (Umtata) 25

3452
LASSIE (Dog)
Tol'able David (Racket)

3453
LATIMER, Billy*
Spieler, The

3454
LATIMER, Florence*
Pilgrim, The

3455
LA TORRE, Charles A. (Charles A.
   Dottore) (1895-)
America (debut)
Stage:
We Never Learn (Drew) 28

3456
LAUDER, Harry, Sir (1870-1950)
Auld Lang Syne
Happy Days (chorus)
Huntingtower
Stage:
Untitled Revue 22, 24, 26
Vaudeville (Knickerbocker) 28
Vaudeville (Lexington) 21

3457
LAUGHTON, Charles (1899-1962)
Bluebottles (debut)
Daydreams
Piccadilly (continental visitor)
Wolves

3458
LAUREL, Stan (Arthur Stanley Jef-
   ferson) 1890-1965) [*with Oliver
   Hardy]
Angora Love* (himself)
Atta Boy!
Bacon Grabbers* (himself)
Battle of the Century (himself)

Berth Marks* (himself)
Big Business* (himself)
Brothers under the Chin
Call of the Cuckoo* (one of the cuck-
   oos)
Collars and Cuffs
Detained
Do Detectives Think?* (Ferdinand
   Finkleberry)
Dr. Pyckle and Mr. Price
Double Whoopee* (himself)
Duck Soup* (himself)
Early to Bed* (himself)
Egg, The
Enough to Do*
Eve's Love Letters*
Finishing Touch, The* (himself)
Flying Elephants* (Little Twinkle
   Star, the shootsman)
Forty-Five Minutes from Hollywood*
   (starving actor)
From Soup to Nuts* (himself)
Frozen Hearts
Gas and Air
Get 'em Young
Habeas Corpus* (himself)
Half a Man
Handy Man, The
Hats Off* (himself)
Hollywood Revue of 1929 (himself)
Hoose Gow, The* (himself)
Kill or Cure
Leave 'em Laughing* (himself)
Liberty* (himself)
Love 'em and Weep** (Romaine
   Ricketts)
Madam Mix-Up
Madame Mystery*
Man About Town, A
Men O'War* (himself)
Merry Widower, The
Mixed Nuts
Monsieur Don't Care
Moonlight and Noses
Mother's Joy
Mud and Sand
Navy Blue Days
Near Dublin
Never Too Old
Noon Whistle
Now I'll Tell One
On the Front Page
Oranges and Lemons
Perfect Day, A* (himself)
Pest, The
Pick and Shovel
Pie-Eyed
Postage Due

Putting Pants on Philip* (Philip)
Raggedy Rose
Rent Collector, The
Rogue Song, The (Ali Bek)
Roughest Africa
Rupert of Hee-Haw
Sailors Beware!* (Chester Chaste)
Save the Ship
Scorching Sands
Second Hundred Years, The* (Little
    Goofy)
Seeing the World
Short Kilts
Short Orders
Should Married Men Go Home? (him-
    self)
Should Tall Men Marry?
Sleuth, The
Slipping Wives* (Ferdinand Flamingo)
Smithy
Snow Hawk
Soilers, The
Somewhere in Wrong
Stan Laurel Comedies
Sugar Daddies* (lawyer)
That's My Wife* (himself)
Their Purple Moment* (himself)
They Go Boom* (himself)
Twins
Two Tars /aka/ Two Tough Tars*
    (himself)
Unaccustomed as We Are* (himself)
Under Two Jags
Unfriendly Enemies
Wandering Papas
We Faw Down /aka/ We Slip Up*
    (himself)
Weak-End Party, The
West of Hot Dog
When Knights Were Cold
Whole Truth, The
Why Girls Love Sailors* (girl's lov-
    er)
Wide Open Spaces
Wise Guys Prefer Brunettes
With Love and Hisses* (Cuthbert
    Lamb)
Wrong Again* (himself)
Yes, Yes, Nanette*
You're Darn Tootin'* (himself)
Zeb vs. Paprika

3459
LAURENT, Jeanne Marie*
Shadows of Fear
Therese Raquin

3460
LAVARNE, Laura*
Vanity Fair (Miss Crawley)

3461
LA VARRE, Myrtland*
Knockout Reilly

3462
LA VELLE, Barbara*
Happy Days (chorus)

3463
LAVENDER (Horse)
Suds

3464
LA VERNE, Jane*
Melody Lane
New Year's Eve
Show Boat (dual role, Magnolia as a
    child/Kim)
That's My Daddy

3465
LA VERNE, Lucille (1872-1945)
America /aka/ Love and Sacrifice
    (refugee mother)
Among the Missing
Bells, The
Her Darker Self
Last Moment, The
Orphans of the Storm (Mother Fro-
    chard)
Sun Up
White Rose, The (Auntie Easter)
Zaza (Aunt Rosa)

3466
LAVERTY, Jean*
Captain Lash
Fleet's In, The (Betty)
Good-Bye Kiss, The
Great Divide, The
Prisoners

3467
LAVINE, Jack*
Sparrows /aka/ Human Sparrows (a
    sparrow)

3468
LA VIOLETTE, Juliette*
Rejected Woman, The
White Sister, The (Madame Bernard)

3469
LAW, Burton*
Under Two Flags (Shiek's aide)

3470
LAW, Walter*
Clothes Make the Pirate
If I Were King
Janice Meredith (Gen. Charless Lee)
Stage:
Devil Within, The (Detective Demp-
sey) 25
Good Bad Woman, A (Tim Donovan)
25
Shipwrecked (John Calvin) 24
Solid Ivory (Anthony P. Griffin) 25

3471
LAW, Winnie*
Loose Change

3472
LAWFORD, Betty*
Gentlemen of the Press (Dorothy
Snell)
Lucky in Love
Return of Sherlock Holmes
Stage:
Lady Lies, The (Florence Rossiter)
28

3473
LAWFORD, Ernest*
Irish Luck

3474
LAWLER, Anderson*
Only Saps Work
River of Romance

3475
LAWRENCE, Edward*
Knockout, The

3476
LAWRENCE, Florence (1888-1938)
Enfoldment, The
Jane, the Stranger

3477
LAWRENCE, Gerald*
Glorious Adventure, The (Hugh Ar-
gyle)

3478
LAWRENCE, Gertrude (Alexandre
Dagmar Lawrence-Klasen) (1898-
1952)

Battle of Paris, The /aka/ The Gay
Lady
Stage:
A to Z - London 21
Candle Light (Marie) 29
Charlot Revue of 1924
Oh, Kay! (Title role) 27
Treasure Girl (Ann Wainwright) 28

3479
LAWRENCE, Lillian*
Graustark (Countess Halfont)
Three Ages, The
Voice from the Minaret, The (Lady
Gilbert)

3480
LAWRENCE, Raymond*
Careless Age, The (Tommy)

3481
LAWRENCE, William E. *
Blood and Sand (Fuentes)
Bride 13 [serial]
Front Page Story, A
Love Gambler, The
Stage:
Beau Gallant (another man) 26
Solid Ivory ("Pop" Kearney) 25

3482
LAWSON, Eleanor*
It (welfare worker)
Lights of Old Broadway (Mrs. O'Tan-
dy)
Merton of the Movies

3483
LAWSON, Elsie*
Dancing Mothers (Irma Raymond)
Social Celebrity, A
Twenty-One
Stage:
Dancing Mothers (Irma Raymond) 24
People Don't Do Such Things (Dolly
Converse) 27
Triumphant Bachelor, The (Mildred
Spence) 27
Whispering Friends (Doris Crawford)
28

3484
LAWTON, Frank (1904-1969)
Young Woodley

3485
LAYCOCK, Ada*
Down to the Sea in Ships (Henny Clark)

3486
LAYE, Evelyn (1900-)
Luck of the Navy, The (Cynthia
   Eden)
Stage:
Bitter Sweet (Marchioness of Shayne/
   Sarah Millick) 29

3487
LAZZERI, Tony*
Slide, Kelly, Slide

3488
LEAHY, Margaret*
Three Ages, The

3489
LEALAND, Princess*
Tracked in the Snow Country

3490
LEASE, Rex (1901-1966)
Broadway Daddies
Cancelled Debts
Candy Kid, The
Clancy's Kosher Wedding
College Hero, The
FBO player 28
Girls Who Dare
Last Edition
Law of the Range, The ("Solitaire
   Kid")
Making the Varsity
Moulders of Men
Not for Publication
Outlaw Dog, The
Phantom of the Turf
Queen of the Chorus
Red Riders of Canada
Riders of the Dark
Speed Classic
Stolen Love
Two Sisters
When Dreams Come True
Younger Generation, The

3491
LEBEDEFF, Ivan B. (1895-1953)
Angel of Broadway, The
Burned Fingers
Charming Prince, The
Forbidden Woman, The
Fox player 28
King Frederick
Let 'em Go Gallagher
Loves of Sunya, The (Howard Mor-
   gan)
Lucky Death, The

Midnight Mystery
One Woman Idea
Sin Town
600,000 Francs Per Month
Sorrows of Satan, The (Amiel)
Soul of an Artist, The
Street Girl
They Had to See Paris (Marquis de
   Brissac)
Veiled Woman, The
Walking Back

3492
LE BORGY*
Madame Recamier

3493
LE BRANDT, Gertrude*
Mama's Affair

3494
LE BRETON, Flora (1898-)
Cause of All the Trouble, The
Crimson Circle, The
Glorious Adventure, The (Rosemary)
God's Prodigal
Gypsy Cavalier (Dorothy Forrest)
House of Peril
I Am the Man
I Will Repay
Little Miss Nobody
Love's Influence
Mistletoe Bough, The
Poupée
Rolling Road, The
Soul's Awakening, A
Ta-ra-ra-boom-de-re
Through Fire and Water
Tons of Money
While London Sleeps
White Monkey, The
Stage:
Las O'Laughter (Lass) 24
Optimists, The 28
Present Arms (Lady Delphine) 28

3495
LE CLAIR, Blanche*
Jealousy (Renee)
Stage:
Great Day! (Kitty) 29

3496
LEDERER, Francis (Franz Lederer)
   (1906-)
Atlantic [German] (Peter)
Ihre Majestat die Liebe [Her Majesty
   of Love]

Lulu (debut)
Pandora's Box
Die Wunderbar Lüge der Nina Pet-
  rovna [Wonderful Lies of Nina
  Petrovna]
Zuflucht [Refuge]

3497
LEDERER, Otto (1886-)
Avenging Arrow, The [serial]
Bells, The
Bit of Heaven, A
Black Oxen (Ausyrian advisor)
Chicago
Cohens and the Kellys in Atlantic
  City, The
Dragon's Net, The [serial]
Forget-Me-Not
From Headquarters
Hungry Hearts
Jazz Singer, The (Moisha Yudelson)
King of Kings, The (Pharisee)
One Stolen Night
Prediction
Sailor Izzy Murphy
Shamrock and the Rose, The /aka/
  The Trunk Mystery
Smiling Irish Eyes
Sweet Rosie O'Grady
Vanity Fair (Mr. Bloom)
White Eagle [serial]
Worldly Goods
Your Friend and Mine

3498
LEDERER, Pepi*
Cardboard Lover, The

3499
LEE, Betsy*
Night Bird, The

3500
LEE, Celeste*
Temple of Venus, The (Venus)

3501
LEE, Davey (1925-)
Frozen River
Say It with Songs
Singing Fool, The (Sonny Boy)
Skin Deep
Sonny Boy (Title role)

3502
LEE, Dick*
School for Wives

3503
LEE, Dixie (Wilma Wyatt) (1911-
  1952)
Dad's Girl
Happy Days (a principal)
Knights Out
Movietone Follies of 1929
Why Leave Home?

3504
LEE, Dorothy (Marjorie Millsap)
  (1911-)
Rio Rita (Dolly)
Syncopation
Stage:
Hello, Yourself (Sue Swift) 28
Vaudeville (Palace) 29

3505
LEE, Duke R. *
Circus Ace, The
Tony Runs Wild
Vanishing Trails [serial]

3506
LEE, Etta*
Camille (Mataloti)
Chinese Parrot, The
Recompense
Tale of Two Worlds, A (Ah Fah)
Thief in Paradise, A
Thief of Bagdad (slave of the Sand
  Board)
Toll of the Sea
Trouble with Wives, The

3507
LEE, Frances (1908-)
Believe It Or Not
Bugs, My Dear
Carnation Kid, The
Chicken a la King (Babe Larraine)
Confessions of a Chorus Girl
Divorce Made Easy
Hold 'Er Cowboy
Little Snob, The
Mr. Romeo
Nifty Numbers
Picture My Astonishment
Show of Shows, The
Skating Home
Slick Slickers
Stop Kidding
Sweetie
Stage:
Hassard Short's Ritz Revue 24

3508
LEE, Francis*
Good as Gold

3509
LEE, Frankie (1912-)
Barefoot Boy, The
Borderland
Christmas Carol, A
Code of the West (Bud)
God's Crucible
His Mother's People
Judy of Rogues Harbor
Killer, The
Nurse Marjorie
Old Fashioned Boy, An
Other Woman, The
Poisoned Paradise
Shame
Sin of Martha Queed, The
Swamp, The
Third Alarm, The (Little Johnny)
Unknown Purple, The

3510
LEE, Gwen /aka/ Gwendolyn
(1904-)
Actress, The
Adam and Evil
After Midnight
Angel Face
Baby Cyclone
Diamond Handcuffs
Duke Steps Out, The
Fast Company
Ghetto, The
Heaven on Earth
Her Wild Oat
His Secretary
Hollywood Revue of 1929
Lady of Chance, A
Laugh, Clown, Laugh (Diane)
Lucky Boy /aka/ My Mother's
Eyes
MGM player 27
Man and the Moment, The
Orchids and Ermine
Plastic Age, The (Carl's girl)
Pretty Ladies (Fay)
Road Show
Sharp Shooters
Show Girl
There You Are
Thief in the Dark, A
Trelawney of the Wells (Avonia)
Twelve Miles Out
Untamed (Marjory)
Upstage

Women Love Diamonds

3511
LEE, Harry*
Men of Steel
Monsieur Beaucaire (Voltaire)

3512
LEE, Jocelyn*
Afraid to Love
Broadway Babies
Campus Flirt, The
Dry Martini
Everybody's Acting
Kiss in a Taxi, A
Love Thrill, The
Marriage Playground, The (Sybil)
Night Bird, The
No, No, Nanette (Flora)
Shanghai Bound
Ten Modern Commandments
Twin Beds
Young Nowheres

3513
LEE, Katherine*
Side Show of Life, The

3514
LEE, Lila (Augusta Appel) (1905-
1973)
Adorable Cheat, The
After the Show
Another Man's Wife
Argyle Case, The (Mary Morgan)
Back Home and Broke
Bit of Heaven, A
Black Butterflies
Black Pearl, The
Blood and Sand (Carmen)
Broken Hearts
Charm School, The
Coming Through
Dark Streets
Dictator, The
Dollar a Year Man, The
Drag
Easy Road, The
Ebb Tide
Flight
Gasoline Gus
Ghost Breaker, The
Homeward Bound
Honky Tonk (Beth)
Hurdy Gurdy
If Women Only Knew
Is Matrimony a Failure?
Just Married

Little Wild Girl
Love, Live and Laugh
Love or Money
Love's Whirlpool
Man in Hobbles, The
Midnight Girl, The
Midsummer Madness
Million Dollar Mystery, The
Ne'er-Do-Well, The
New Klondike, The
Old Home Week
One Glorious Day
One Increasing Purpose
Paramount player 26
Prince Chap, The
Queen of the Nightclubs
Rent Free
Road to Arcady, The
Sacred Flame, The
Show of Shows, The
Soul of Youth, The
Terror Island
Those Who Dare
Thundergod
Top Sergeant Mulligan
Unholy Three, The
United States Smith
Wandering Husbands
Woman Proof
You Can't Beat the Law
Stage:
Bride Retires, The (Raymonde) 25
Edgar Allan Poe (Virginia Clem) 25

3515
LEE, Lois*
Prisoner of Zenda, The (Countess
  Helga)

3516
LEE, Margaret*
Man, Woman and Sin
Stage:
Dr. David's Dad (Mrs. Malone) 24
Follow Thru (Babs Bascomb) 29
June Moon (Miss Rixey) 29

3517
LEE, Raymond (1910-   )
Bread
Kid, The
Long Live the King
Pilgrim, The

3518
LEE, Robert*
Terror /aka/ The Perils of Paris

3519
LEE, Ronald*
Woman in the Suitcase, The

3520
LEE, Sylvan*
Cocoanuts, The (bit)
Stage:
Naughty Riquette (Dean) 26

3521
LEE, Virginia*
Beyond the Rainbow (Henrietta Gree-
  ley)

3522
LEFFERTY, Jean*
Matinee Ladies

3523
LEGAL, Ernst*
Das Wachsfigurenkabinett [Waxworks]

3524
LEHAY, Eugene*
Prince of Lovers, The

3525
LEHR, Anna*
Chains of Evidence
Cheated Hearts
Child for Sale, A
Cradle, The
Mr. Barnes of New York
Ruggles of Red Gap
Truth About Husbands, The
Veiled Marriage, The

3526
LEIBER, Fritz (1883-1949)
Anthony and Cleopatra
If I Were King
Queen of Sheba, The (King Solomon)
Song of the Soul, The
Stage:
Field God, The (Hardy Gilchrist) 27
Hedda Gabler (Eilert Lovborg) 24
Two Strangers from Nowhere (Ange-
  lo Desdichado) 24

3527
LEIDTKE, Harry*
Bohemian Dancer, The

3428
LEIGH, Frank*
As Man Desires
Ashes of Vengeance (Lupi)

Below the Deadline
Bob Hampton of Placer
Breath of Scandal, The
Common Property
Cup of Fury
Dangerous Days
Devil's Skipper, The
Drums of Araby
Flaming Forest, The
Golden Dreams
Hill Billy, The
His Majesty Bunker Bean
Light in the Clearing, A
Love in the Desert
Mother of His Children, The
Night of Mystery, A
Nurse Marjorie
One Hour Before Dawn
Prowlers of the Sea
Reckless Age, The
Rosita (prison commandant)
Soft Cushions
Truxton King

3529
LEIGHTON, Lillian*
All of a Sudden Peggy
Bedroom Window, The
Beloved Villain, The
Blow by Blow
Call of the Canyon, The
Code of the West (Ma Thurman)
Contraband
Crazy to Marry
Crinoline Romance, A
Dancin' Fool (Ma Budd)
Dramatic Life of Abraham Lincoln,
   The /aka/ Abraham Lincoln
Fair and Muddy
Fair Coed, The (housekeeper)
Feet of Clay
Girl from God's Country, The
Go Straight
Grub Stake, The
House of Toys
In the Name of Love
Is Matrimony a Failure?
Jack-Knife Man, The
Joanna
Lost Romance
Lovers
Only 38
Parisian Love (Frouchard)
Peck's Bad Boy
Ruggles of Red Gap
Thirteenth Piece of Silver
Thundering Herd, The (Clark's wife)
Torrent, The

Tumbleweeds
Under the Lash (Tant Anna Vanderberg)

3530
LEITGEB, Willey*
William Tell

3531
LE MOYNE, Charles*
Riders of the Purple Sage (Richard
   Tull)

3532
LENKEFFY, Isa*
Othello /aka/ The Moor

3533
LENNOL, Roy*
Fifth Form at St. Dominic's (Simon
   Wren)

3534
LENNOX, Vera*
Tilly of Bloomsbury (Amelia)

3535
LENOY, Andre*
Venus of Venice

3536
LEONARD, Barbara*
Drake Case, The
Ladies of the Night Club
Leaping Love
Son of the Gods (Mabel)

3537
LEONARD, Benny*
Evil Eye, The [serial]
Flying Fists
Stage:
Dancing Girl, The   23

3538
LEONARD, Eddie (1870-1941)
Melody Lane
Stage:
Vaudeville (Palace) 24, 26, 27

3539
LEONARD, Gus*
Barnstormer, The (theatre owner)
Girl I Loved, The

3540
LEONARD, James*
All Aboard

3541
LEONARD, LaVerne*
Happy Days (chorus)

3542
LEONG, James*
Devil Dancer, The
Shanghai Lady
Uppercut O'Brien

3543
LEONIDOV, Leon /aka/ Leon Leonidoff*
Czar Ivan the Terrible
Seeds of Freedom

3544
LEOPOLD, Archduke of Austria*
Night Life (Chief of Detectives)

3545
LERCH, Louis*
Carmen (Don Jose)
Doctor's Women, The
Whirl of Life, The

3546
LERNER, Irma*
Salome of the Tenements

3547
LERNER, Jacques*
Monkey Talks, The (Jocko)
Stage:
Monkey Talks, The (Faho) 25-26

3548
LE ROY, Mervyn (1900-)
Broadway after Dark
Going Up
Little Johnny Jones

3549
LE ROY, Rita*
Dynamite (a good mixer)

3550
LESLIE, Gladys (1899-)
Child for Sale, A
Darling of the Rich, The
Elsie in New York
Girl from Porcupine, The
God's Country and the Law
Golden Shower
Haldane of the Secret Service
If Winter Comes
Jim the Penman
Midnight Bride, The

Mystery of Gray Towers, The
Sisters
Snitching Hour, The
Straight Is the Way
Timothy's Quest
Vitagraph player 20

3551
LESLIE, Lawrence*
Gentlemen of the Press
Why Bring That Up?
Stage:
Gentlemen of the Press (Cutler) 28
John (Andrew) 27
Marriage on Approval (Henry Wippen) 28
Meteor (Curtis Maxwell) 29
Remote Control (Sgt. Devine) 29
Shelf, The (Baldwin Custard) 26

3552
LESLIE, Lila /aka/ Lyla*
Being Respectable
Forever After
Front Page Story, A
Getting Gertie's Garter
Huntress, The
Last Edition
Secret Studio, The
Son of Wallingford, The (Mrs. Blackie Daw)
Why Men Leave Home

3553
LESLIE, Rolf*
Mumsie (Edgar Symonds)
Nell Gwyn (Evelyn)

3554
LESLIE, Lya--see: Lila Leslie

3555
LESSEY, George*
Durand of the Badlands (John Boyd)
Fool, The
Silent Command, The
Stage:
Bless You, Sister (Senator Gribble) 27
Mystery Man, The (Inspector Harrison) 28
Remote Control (W. L. Oakwood) 29
Seven (Col. Bayne) 29

3556
LESTER, Kate*
Black Oxen (Jane Oglethorpe)
Cup of Fury, The

Dangerous Curves Ahead
Don't Neglect Your Wife
Doubling for Romeo
Earthbound
Eternal Flame, The (Princess Vla-
    mont-Chauvray)
Fourth Musketeer, The
Gimme
Glorious Fool, The
Goldfish, The
Hunchback of Notre Dame, The
    (Mme. deGondelavier)
Hunted Man, The
Made in Heaven
Paliser Case, The
Price of Pleasure, The
Quincy Adams Sawyer (Mrs. Sawyer)
Rememberance
Scratch My Back
Simple Souls
Tailor Made Man, The
Wife of the Centaur, The

3557
LESTINA, Adolphe*
Love Flower, The (Bevan's old ser-
    vant)
Orphans of the Storm (doctor)

3558
L'ESTRANGE, Dick*
Border Cavalier

3559
LeSUEUR, Lucille--see: Joan
    Crawford

3560
LETTINGER*
Luther

3561
LEUX, Lori*
Midsummer Night's Dream, A (Ti-
    tania)

3562
LEVANT, Oscar (1907-1972)
Dance of Life, The
Stage:
Burlesque (Jerry Evans) 27

3563
LEVETT, Harold*
East Side, West Side

3564
LEVINE, Helen*
Frisco Sally Levy

3565
LEVINE, Jack*
Sparrows /aka/ Human Sparrows

3566
LEVINNES, Carl*
Twin Beds

3567
LEVOE, Marjorie*
Happy Days (chorus)

3568
LEVSHIN, A*
Battleship Potemkin (ship's officer)

3569
LEWIS, Dora*
Chu-Chin-Chow (Mahbush)

3570
LEWIS, Fred*
Moral Sinner, The
Tilly of Bloomsbury (Abel Mainwar-
    ing)

3571
LEWIS, George (1904-)
Around the Bases
Benson at Calford
Bookworm Hero, The
Captain Blood
College Love
Collegiates, The
Devil's Island
Flying High [serial chapter]
Fourflusher, The
Give and Take
His People
Honeymoon Flats
King of the Campus
Old Soak, The
Proud Heart
13 Washington Square (Jack de Pey-
    ster)
Tonight at Twelve
We Americans

3572
LEWIS, Henry B. *
Classmates
Winning Through (Capt. Lane)
Stage:
Frivolities of 1920

3573
LEWIS, Ida*
Mary's Ankle
Paris Green
Peaceful Valley

3574
LEWIS, Jeffrys*
Peacock Alley (Toto)
Stage:
Americans in France, The (Appolo-
nie) 20
Easy Terms (Mrs. Schenck) 25

3575
LEWIS, Jera*
Only Thing, The

3576
LEWIS, Katherine*
Recompense

3577
LEWIS, Mitchell (1880-1956)
At the End of the World
Back to God's Country
Beau Sabreur (Suleiman, the strong)
Ben Hur (Sheik Ilderim)
Black Watch, The
Bonded Woman
Bridge of San Luis Rey, The (Capt.
Alvarado)
Burning Daylight
Crimson Runner, The
Daughter of the Snows
Docks of New York, The
Eagle of the Sea, The
Faith of the Strong, The
Flaming Love
Frivolous Sal
Hard Boiled Haggerty
Hawk's Nest, The
Her Accidental Husband
King of the Khyber Rifles (Moham-
med Khan)
King Spruce
Last of His People, The
Leatherneck, The
Linda
Madame X (Col. Hanby)
Metro player 20
Miss Nobody
Mystic, The
On the High Seas
One Stolen Night
Out with the Tide
Red Lily, The (D'Agut)
Road to Mandalay, The (native)

Romance of a Queen, The (Vassili)
Rupert of Hentzau (Bauer)
Salome (Herod)
Sea Wolf, The
Silent Barrier, The
Siren Call, The
Smoke Bellew
Speed Classic
Spoilers, The
Tell It to the Marines
Tenderloin
Three Weeks
Way of the Strong, The
Woman Conquers, A

3578
LEWIS, Ralph (-1937)
Bigger than Barnum's
Block Signal, The
Bridge of Sighs, The
Casey Jones
Conquering Power, The (Pere Gran-
det)
Crooks Can't Win
Dante's Inferno
Desire
East of Broadway
False Alarm
Fascinating Youth
Five Dollar Baby, The
Flesh and Blood (Fletcher Burton)
Fog, The
Girl in the Glass Cage, The (John
Cosgrove)
Held by the Law
In the Name of the Law
Lady from Hell, The
Last Edition
Man Who Came Back, The
Man-Woman-Marriage
Million Dollar Handicap
Outcast Souls
Outside the Law (Silent Madden)
Prisoners of Love
Private Scandal, A
Salvage (Cyrus Ridgeway)
Shadow of the Law, The (Brophy)
Shield of Honor
Silent Power, The
Sin Flood, The
Sowing the Wind
Sunset Derby
Third Alarm, The (Dan M'Dowell)
Vengeance of the Deep
Westbound Limited
What Women Love
When the Clouds Roll By

3579
LEWIS, Sheldon (1868-1958)
Black Magic
Bride of the Storm
Burning Gold
Chinatown Mystery, The [serial]
Chorus Kid, The
Code of the Scarlet
Cruise of the Hellion
Dangerous Flirt
Darling of New York, The
Desperate Moment
Dr. Jekyll and Mr. Hyde (Henry
   Jekyll/Oscar Hyde)
Driven from Home
Eagle of the Sea, The
Enemy Sex, The
Exclusive Rights
Fighting the Flames
Gilded Highway, The
Hazardous Valleys
Honor Among Men
Lady Bird
Life of an Actress, The
Lightning Hutch [serial]
Little Wild Girl
Marlie, the Killer
Moran of the Marines
New Lives for Old
Orphans of the Storm (Jacques Fro-
   chard)
Overland Stage, The
Red Kimono, The
River Woman
Self Starter, The
Senor Daredevil
Seven Footprints to Satan
Silent Sanderson
Sky Pirate, The
Sky Rider, The
Sporting Chance, The
Super Speed
Top of the World, The
Top Sergeant Mulligan
Turn Back the Hours
Two-Gun Man, The
Untamed Justice
Vanishing Millions [serial]

3580
LEWIS, Ted (Theodore Lewis Fried-
   man) (1891-1971)
Is Everybody Happy?
Show of Shows, The (with band)
Stage:
Artists and Models 27
Friar's Club Frolic 22
Greenwich Village Follies 21

Vaudeville [Palace] 28, 29

3581
LEWIS, Tom*
Adam and Eva
Callahans and the Murphys, The
   (Mr. Murphy)
Go-Getter, The
Great White Way, The
Marriage Morals
Passers By
Steamboat Bill, Jr.
Stage:
Blushing Bride, The (Christopher
   Pottinger) 22
Follies 25
Helen of Troy, New York (Elias
   Yarrow) 23
Lambs Gambol 25

3582
LEWIS, Vera (-1958)
Black Swan, The
Blooming Angel, The
Broadway after Dark
Broken Gates
Dark Swan
Devil's Riddle
Ella Cinders
Enticement
Eve's Secret
Gilded Butterfly, The
Glorious Fool, The
Home Towners, The
Iron Mask, The (Madame Peronne)
King of the Pack
Long Live the King
Nancy from Nowhere
Nurse Marjorie
Only Thing, The
Passionate Quest, The
Peg O' My Heart (Mrs. Chichister)
Ramona (Senora Moreno)
Resurrection
Satan and the Woman
She Couldn't Help It
Something Always Happens
Stella Dallas (Miss Tibbits)
Take It from Me
Thumbs Down
Up in Mabel's Room
What Happened to Father?

3583
LEWIS, Walter (1871-   )
Beware of Blondes
Black Sheep, A
Daughter of Devil Dan, The

Ghost in the Garret, The
Leif the Lucky
Little Shepherd of Kingdom Come,
   The
Star Rover, The
Three Miles Out
Tol'able David (Iscar Hatburn)
Torchy in High
Two Lovers
White Moll, The
Stage:
Hole in the Wall, The (Donald Ram-
   say) 20

3584
LEWIS, Willard*
Don Juan (Pedrillo)

3585
LEY, Grita*
Berlin after Dark

3586
LICALZI, Lawrence*
Boy of Mine

3587
LICHO, Adolf Edgar*
Loves of Jeanne Ney, The /aka/
   Die Liebe der Jeanne Ney

3588
LIEDTKE, Harry*
Die Bergkatze /aka/ The Mountain
   Cat; The Wild Cat
Forbidden Love
Gypsy Blood
Ich Küsse Ihre Hand, Madame [I
   Kiss Your Hand, Madame]
   (Jacques)
Jew of Mestri, The (Bassanio)
Der Kleine Napoleon [The Little Na-
   poleon] /aka/ So Sind die Männer
   [Men Are Like That], Napoleons
   Kleiner Bruder [Napoleon's Little
   Brother] (Georg von Melsungen)
Love Is a Lie
Madame Wünscht Keine Kinder [Mad-
   ame Doesn't Want Children] /aka/
   Madame Wants No Children (Paul
   Le Barroy)
Sumurun /aka/ One Arabian Night
   (Nur-Al-Djin)
Das Weib des Pharao [The Wife of
   the Pharaoh] /aka/ The Loves of
   Pharaoh (Ramphis)

3589
LIFANOFF, B. *
In Old Siberia

3590
LIGGETT, Louis*
Street Angel (Beppo)

3591
LIGGON, Grover*
Million Dollar Collar

3592
LIGHTNER, Winnie (Winifred Hanson)
   (1901-1971)
Gold Diggers of Broadway (Mabel)
Show of Shows, The
Song a Minute, A
Stage:
Gay Paree 25
George White's Scandals 23
Harry Delmar's Revels 27
Scandals 24
Vaudeville [Palace] 27

3593
LILLIE, Beatrice (Lady Peel) (1903-)
Exit Smiling (debut)
Show of Shows, The
Stage:
A to Z - London 21
Charlot Revue of 1924
Oh, Please! (Lily Valli) 26
She's My Baby (Tilly) 28
This Year of Grace 28
Vaudeville [Palace] 29

3594
LILLMORE, Clyde*
Devil's Pass Key, The

3595
LIMBURG, Olga*
Apaches of Paris

3596
LINCOLN, Caryl*
Girl in Every Port, A

3597
LINCOLN, Elmo K. (Otto Elmo Lin-
   kenhelter) (1889-1952)
Adventures of Tarzan [serial] (Tar-
   zan)
Devotion
Elmo, the Fearless [serial] (Title
   role)

Fashion Row
Flaming Disc, The [serial] (dual
  role)
Light in the Dark, The (J. Warbur-
  ton Ashe)
Man of Courage
Quincy Adams Sawyer (Abner Stiles)
Rupert of Hentzau (Simon the Woods-
  man)
Under Crimson Skies
What Is Love?
Woman God Changed, The
Woman in Chains
Women Men Marry

3598
LINDEN, Peggy*
Blood Money (Peggy)

3599
LINDER, Max (Gabriel Levielle)
  (1883-1925)
Au Secours! [Help!]
Be My Wife
King of the Circus (Count Max)
Max, the Headwaiter
Rustic Idyll
Seven Years' Bad Luck
Three-Must-Get-Theres, The (Dar-
  in-Again)

3600
LINDLEY, Bert*
Dixie Handicap, The

3601
LINDROTH, Helen*
Confidence Man, The
Humming Bird, The (Henrietta Ruth-
  erford)
Song and Dance Man, The
Swan, The
Unguarded Women
Unseeing Eyes

3602
LINDSAY, Fred*
Rough Riders, The
Stage:
Vaudeville [Palace] 28

3603
LINDSAY, Howard (1889-1968)
Dulcy
Stage:
Dulcy (Vincent Leach) 21
49ers, The 22
Sweet Nell of Old Drury (Rollins) 23

Two by Two (Richard Graham) 25

3604
LINDSAY, James*
Claude Duval (Duke of Brentleigh)
Rat, The (Detective Caillard)

3605
LINDSEY, Ben*
Soul of Youth, The

3606
LINGHAM, Thomas*
Two Sisters

3607
LINOW, Ivan*
Black Magic
Cappy Ricks
Cock'Eyed World, The (Sanovich)
Enemies of Women (Terrorist)
Far Call
Fury
In Old Arizona (Russian immigrant)
Plastered in Paris
Red Dance, The /aka/ The Red Dan-
  cer of Moscow
River, The /aka/ La Femme au
  Corbeau
Speakeasy
Three Miles Out
Unholy Three, The
Wages of Virtue (Luigi)
Waltzing Around
Zaza (Apache dancer)

3608
LIPMAN, Harry*
Lost at the Front

3609
LISSENKO, Nathalie*
Burning Brasier, The
Edward Kean
Sea Fever

3610
LISTER, Francis*
Atlantic [English] (the Padre)
Comin' thro' the Rye (Dick Fellows)
Stage:
Mary, Mary, Quite Contrary (Geof-
  frey) 23

3611
LITEL, John (1895-1972)
Sleeping Porch, The

Stage:
Adventure (Michael O'Shane) 28
Back Seat Drivers (John Wilson) 28
Beaten Track, The (Vaughn Morgan)
Sherlock Holmes (Leary) 28
Thoroughbreds (Bob Kitchell) 24

3612
LITTLE, Ann (1891-)
Blue Fox, The [serial]
Chain Lightning
Cradle of Courage (Rose Tierney)
Eagle's Talons, The [serial]
Excuse My Dust (Dorothy Walden)
Life
Nan of the North [serial]
Paramount player 20
Secret Service Saunders [serial]
Silent Shelby

3613
LITTLEFIELD, Lucian (1895-1959)
Across the Continent
Affairs of Anatol, The (Spencer val-
    et)
All Soul's Eve
Babbit
Bachelor Brides
Big Ambition
Big Money
Blonde for a Night
Broadway Eyes
Cat and the Canary, The (Dr. Ira
    Lazar)
Charley's Aunt (Brassett)
Cheating Cheaters
Clear the Decks
Deadwood Coach, The
Do Your Duty
Double Speed
Drag
Eyes of the Heart
Feet of Clay
Fourteenth Man, The
French Doll, The
Furnace, The
Girl in the Glass Cage, The (Sheik
    Smith)
Great Divide, The
Harold Teen
Head Man, The (Ed Barnes)
Heart to Heart
Hell Diggers
Her First Elopement
Her Husband's Trademark (Slithy
    Winters)
In the Palace of the King
Jack Straw

Joan of Arc
Little Clown, The
Making the Grade
Man in Hobbles, The
Manslaughter (witness)
Miser, The
Mother Knows Best (Pa Quail)
My Best Girl
Name the Man
No, No, Nanette (Jim Smith)
Our Leading Citizens
Out for Game
Pa Gets a Vacation
Painted Lady, The
Potters at Home, The
Potters Done in Oil, The
Rainbow Trail, The
Rent Free
Round Up, The
Saturday's Children
Seven Keys to Baldpate
Sheik, The (Gaston)
Ship Comes In, A
Sick Abed
Small Bachelors
Soul Mates
Take It from Me
Taxi, Taxi!
Texas Steer, A
This Is Heaven
To Have and to Hold
Tony Runs Wild
Too Much Speed
Torrent, The (Cupido)
True as Steel
Tumbleweeds
Twinkletoes (Hank)
Uncle Tom's Cabin (lawyer Marks)
Wall Street
Why Change Your Wife? (butler)

3614
LIVESEY, Roger (1906-)
Four Feathers, The (Harry Fever-
    sham, as a boy)
Married Love
Old Curiosity Shop, The (debut)
Where the Rainbow Ends

3615
LIVESEY, Sam (1873-)
Black Spider, The
Stage:
Bulldog Drummond (Carl Petersen) 21

3616
LIVINGSTON, Bob (1908-)
Flying High [serial chapter]

3617
LIVINGSTON, Margaret (1902-)
Acquitted
After Marriage
Alimony
American Beauty
Apache
Bellamy Trial, The (Mimi Bellamy)
Best People
Beware of Bachelors
Blue Eagle, The (Mary Rohan)
Brute Master
Canary Murder Case, The (dubbed
  voice for Louise Brooks)
Capital Punishment (Mona Caldwell)
Charlatan, The
Charlatan Mystery, The [serial]
Chorus Lady
Colorado Pluck
Divorce
First Year, The
Fox player 26
Girl from Gay Paree
Havoc (Violet Deering)
Hell's Three Hundred
His Private Life
House of a Thousand Candles
I'll Show You the Town
Innocents of Paris (Madame Renard)
Last Warning
Lightning
Love's Whirlpool
Lying Lips
Mad Hour, The
Married Alive
No Questions Asked
Office Scandal
Say It with Sables
Scarlet Dove, The
Secret Studio, The
Seven Keys to Baldpate
Slaves of Beauty
Streets of Shanghai
Sunrise (woman from the city)
Through the Breakers
Tonight at Twelve
Trip to Chinatown, A
Up the Ladder
Wandering Husbands
Water, Water Everywhere
Way of the Strong, The
What's Your Husband Doing?
Wheels of Chance
Woman's Way, A
Womanpower
Yankee Senor, The

3618
LIZA, Mona*
Good References (Nell Norcross)

3619
LLEWELLYN, Eve*
Widdecombe Affair (farmer's wife)

3620
LLEWELLYN, Fewlass*
Flag Lieutenant, The (Admiral Sir
  Berkeley Wynne)
This Freedom (Rev. Harold Aubyn)

3621
LLOYD, Albert S.*
Half-Breed, The (Hops)

3622
LLOYD, Alison--see: Thelma Todd

3623
LLOYD, Doris (1900-1968)
Auctioneer, The
Blackbird, The (Limehouse Polly)
Bronco Twisters
Careless Age, The (Mabs)
Come to My House
Disraeli (Mrs. Agatha Travers)
Drake Case, The
Is Zat So?
Lady, The
Lonesome Ladies
Midnight Kiss, The (Ellen Atkins)
Secrets
Trail of '98, The
Two Girls Wanted (Miss Timoney)
Stage:
Cinderella on Broadway 20

3624
LLOYD, Gaylord*
Dodge Your Debts

3625
LLOYD, Harold (1893-1971)
Among Those Present
Doctor Jack
Eastern Westerner, An
For Heaven's Sake
Freshman, The (Harold Lamb)
Get Out and Get Under
Girl Shy
Grandma's Boy
Haunted Spooks
High and Dizzy (the boy)
His Royal Slyness
Hot Water

I Do
Kid Brother, The
Never Weaken
Now or Never
Number Please
Safety Last (the boy)
Sailor-Made Man, A
Speedy
Welcome Danger
Why Worry?
Stage:
Macbeth (Felance)

3626
LOBE, Friedrich*
Jew of Mestri, The (Elias)

3627
LOCKE, William J. *
Tragedy of the East Side, A

3628
LOCKHART, Anna*
Clean Heart, The

3629
LOCKHART, Gene (Eugene Lock-
   hart) (1891-1957)
Smilin' Through (village rector)
Stage:
Bunk of 1926
Handy Man, The (Charles Chambers)
   25
Skylark (Arthur) 21
Sure Fire (Herby Brewster) 26
Sun-up (Bud) 23

3630
LOCKHART, John*
Happy Days (chorus)

3631
LOCKNEY, John P. : [see J. P.
   Lockney in Vol. I]*
Barriers Burned Away
Dixie Handicap, The
Yellow Stain, The

3632
LODER, John (John Lowe) (1898-)
Black Waters
Doctor's Secret, The
First Born, The (Lord David Har-
   borough)
Great Unknown, The
Half an Hour
Her Private Affair (Carl Weild)
Lilies of the Field

Madame Wünscht Keine Kinder [Mad-
   ame Doesn't Want Children] /aka/
   Madame Wants No Children
Money Means Nothing
Racketeer, The (Jack Oakhurst)
Rich People (Capt. Danforth)
Sunset Pass
Unholy Night, The (Capt. Dorchester)
Wedding Rehearsal

3633
LODER, Ted*
Lilies of the Field

3634
LODI, Theodore*
General Crack (Capt. Banning)
They Had to See Paris (Grand Duke
   Makaill)

3635
LODIJENSKY, General*
Her Love Story (Minister of War)
Swan, The

3636
LOFF, Jeanette*
Annapolis
Black Aces
Collegians, The [series]
.45 Calibre War
Hold 'em Yale!
Love over Night
Man-Made Woman
My Friend from India
Racketeer, The (Millie Chapman)
Sophomore, The
Uncle Tom's Cabin
Valley Beyond the Law
Young April

3637
LOGAN, Gwendolyn*
Disraeli (Duchess of Glastonbury)

3638
LOGAN, Jacqueline (1900-)
Bachelor Girl
Blind Bargain, The (Angela)
Blood Ship, The
Broadway Daddies
Burning Sands
Charge of the Gauchos
Cop, The
Dawn of Tomorrow, The
Dynamite Smith
Ebb Tide
Faker, The

Flaming Barriers
Fools' Paradise (Girda)
Footloose Widows
For Ladies Only
Gay and Devilish
General Crack (Countess Carola)
House of Youth, The
If Marriage Fails
Java Head
King of Kings, The (Mary Magdalene)
King of the Congo [serial]
Leopard Lady, The
Light that Failed, The
Look-Out Girl, The
Man Must Live, A
Manhattan
Midnight Madness
Mr. Billings Spends His Dime
Molly-O, The
North of '36
Nothing to Wear
One Hour of Love
Out of the Storm
Outsider, The
Peacock Feathers
Perfect Crime, A (Mary Oliver)
Playing with Souls
Power (Lorraine LaRue)
River Woman
Sailor-Made Man, A
Salomy Jane
Ships of the Night
Show of Shows, The
Sixty Cents an Hour
Stark Mad
Stocks and Blondes
Thank You
Tony Runs Wild
Wages of Wives
White and Unmarried
Wise Wife

3639
LOLA and ARMIDA*
Show of Shows, The

3640
LOMBARD, Carole (Jane Alice
    Peters) (1909-1942)
Beach Club, The
Best Man, The
Bicycle Flirt, The
Big News (Margaret Banks)
Campus Carmen, The
Campus Vamp, The
Divine Sinner, The (Millie Coudert)
Durand of the Badlands (Ellen Boyd)
Dynamite (cast, then dropped)

Fox player 27
Girl from Everywhere, The
Girl from Nowhere, The
Hearts and Spurs (Sybil Estabrook)
High Voltage (Lily)
His Unlucky Night
Marriage in Transit (Cecilia Hatha-
    way)
Matchmaking Mamas
Me, Gangster (Blonde Rosie)
Ned McCobb's Daughter (Jennie)
Perfect Crime, The (Grigg's daugh-
    ter)
Power (another dame)
Racketeer, The (Rhoda Philbrooks)
Road to Glory, The (bit)
Run, Girl, Run (Norma)
Show Filks (Cleo)
Smith's Pony
Swim Princess, The

3641
LOMBARDI, Dillo*
Strange Case of Captain Ramper, The

3642
LONDON, Babe (1901-)
All Aboard
Boob, The
Day's Pleasure, A
Expert Eloper, An
Fortune Hunter, The
Golden Dreams
Hula Honeymoon, A
Laundry, The
Merely Mary Ann
Parcel Post Husband, A
Rent Diggers, The
Roll Along
Sauce and Senoritas
Second Childhood
Tillie's Punctured Romance (strong
    woman)
Too Many Burglars
When Romance Rides
When the Clouds Roll By
Winter Has Come

3643
LONDON, Tom /aka/ Leonard Clap-
    ham (1882-1963)
Alibi /aka/ The Perfect Alibi
Border Wildcat, The
Call of the Canyon, The
Devil's Twin, The
Eyes of the Underworld
Harvest of Hate
Heritage of the Desert, The

Lawless Legion, The
Long Loop on the Pecos
Loser's End, The
Mystery Rider, The [serial] (the
  claw)
Nan of the North [serial]
Our Hospitality
Ridin' Fool
Snowed
To the Last Man
Untamed Justice
Winds of Chance
Yellow Cameo, The [serial]
Yellow Contraband

3644
LONERGAN, Lester*
Seven Faces

3645
LONG, Frederick*
Lost Patrol, The

3646
LONG, Nick /aka/ Nick Long, Jr.*
Shore Leave
Stage:
Kitty's Kisses (Philip Dennison) 26
Laugh, Clown, Laugh (Bibi) 23
Lollipop (Omar K. Garrity) 24
Merchant of Venice, The (court
  clerk) 22
Oh, Please! (Jack Gates) 26
She's My Baby (dance director) 28
Shore Leave (Bimby) 22
Still Waters (Senator Gummidge) 26
Street Singer, The (Ronnie) 29

3647
LONG, Sally*
Man in the Saddle, The
Stage:
George White's Scandals 22

3648
LONG, Walter (1882-1952)
Across the Continent
Back to God's Country
Beautiful and Damned, The
Black Cargo of the South Seas
Black Watch, The
Blood and Sand (Plumitas)
Bobbed Hair
Broken Wing, The
Dictator, The
Eve's Leaves
Excuse My Dust (Ritz)
Fighting Shepherdess, The

Fire Cat, The
Forbidden Grass
Gang War
Go and Get It
Grass
Held in Trust
Huntress, The
Isle of Lost Ships (Peter Forbes)
Jim, the Conqueror
Kick-In
King of the Khyber Rifles (Harrim
  Bey)
Lady, The
Last Hour, The
Little Church Around the Corner,
  The
Me, Gangster
Moran of the Lady Letty
My American Wife (Gomez)
Omar the Tentmaker
Quicksands
Red Dice
Shadows (Daniel Gibbs)
Sheik, The (Omair)
Shock, The (the captain)
Shock Punch, The
Soul Fire /aka/ Golden Youth
South of Suva
Steel Preferred
Thundergod
To Have and to Hold
What Women Love
White and Unmarried
White Pants Willie
Wine (Count Benedict Montebello)
Yankee Clipper, The

3649
LONGDEN, John (1900-)
Arcadians, The
Atlantic (English) (Lanchester)
Ball of Fortune, The
Blackmail (Frank Webber)
Bright Young Things
Flight Commander, The
Flying Squad, The
Glad Eye, The
House of Marney, The
Juno and the Paycock
Last Post, The
Mademoiselle Parley Voo (LeBeau)
Memories
Palais de Dance
Quinneys
What Money Can Buy

3650
LONGFELLOW, Malvina*
Calvary
Celestial City, The
Gamble in Lives, A
Great Terror, The
Grip of Iron, The
Indian Love Lyrics
Last Crusade, The
Last King of Wales, The
Madame Recamier
Mary Latimer, Nun
Moth and Rust
Night Hawk, The
Story of the Rosary, The
Unmarried, The
Wandering Jew, The (Gianella)

3651
LONSDALE, Harry*
Monte Cristo (Elder Dantes)
Tempest, The

3652
LOOMIS, Margaret*
Always Audacious
Conrad in Quest of His Youth (Rosa-
    lind)
Law of the Lawless, The
Sins of St. Anthony
Three Gold Coins
What Happened to Jones?

3653
LOOMIS, Virginia*
Babbitt

3654
LOOS, Theodor*
Atlantic [German] (Der Pfarrer)
Kriemhild's Revenge
Manon Lescaut (Tiberge)
Metropolis (Josephat)
Die Nibelungen /aka/ The Nibelungs
    (Gunther)
Othello /aka/ The Moor (Cassio)
Siegfried
Weavers, The

3655
LOPEZ, Augustina*
Redskin, The
Wolf Song (Louisa)

3656
LOPEZ, Raymond*
Girl from Havana, The

3657
LORCH, Louis*
Sealed Lips

3658
LORCH, Theodore*
Grip of the Yukon, The
Man on the Box, The
Royal Rider
Sea Hawk, The
Show Boat
Tracked by the Police

3659
LORD, Grace*
Death Valley

3660
LORD, Marion*
Broadway (Lil)
Stage:
Last Warning, The (Evelynda Hen-
    don) 22
Red Geranium, The (Jane) 22
Tarnish (Apolline Stutts) 23

3661
LORD, Philip*
Silver King, The
Stage:
Lights Out ("Camera Eye" Decker) 22
Nobody's Money (Bertram Miller) 21
Persons Unknown (Nicholas Gregory)
    22
Silence (Andrew Pritchard) 24
Square Crooks (Sgt. Timothy Hogan)
    26
When You Smile (Michael Malone) 25

3662
LOREDO, Linda*
Great Gobs

3663
LORENZ, Dolly*
Der Mensch am Wege [Man by the
    Roadside]

3664
LORETTO, Alfred*
Das Schiff der Verlorenen Manschen
    [The Ship of Lost Souls] /aka/ Le
    Navire des Hommes Perdus [The
    Ship of Lost Men] (crew member)

3665
LORME, Joyce*
Happy Days (chorus)

3666
LORRAINE, Harry (Henry Herd)
  (1886-)
Last of the Mohicans, The (Major
  Heyward)
Shooting of Dan McGrew, The (an
  actor)
Siege
Slave of Desire
Stranger than Fiction
Sweeny Todd
Unto Each Other

3667
LORRAINE, Jean*
Wild Party, The (Ann)

3668
LORRAINE, Leota*
Infatuation

3669
LORRAINE, Lillian (1892-1955)
Flaming Disc, The [serial]
Stage:
Blue Kitten, The (Totoche) 22
Ziegfeld Midnight Follies 20
Ziegfeld 9 o'clock Follies 20

3670
LORRAINE, Louise (1901-)
Adventures of Tarzan [serial] (Jane)
Altar Stairs, The
Baby Mine
Champion Boy Rider [series]
Chinatown Charlie
Circus Rookies
Deadline, The
Diamond Master, The [serial]
Elmo, the Fearless [serial]
Final Reckoning, A [serial]
Fire Eater, The
Flaming Disc, The [serial]
Frontiersman, The
Great Circus Mystery, The [serial]
  (Trixie Tremaine)
Hard Fists
Headin' West [serial]
Legionaires in Paris
Oregon Trail, The [serial]
Radio King, The [serial]
Rookies
Shadows of Night
Silent Flyer, The [serial]
Up in the Air About Money
Winners of the Wilderness
With Stanley in Africa [serial]
Wright Idea, The

3671
LORRING, Lotte*
Eine Du Barry von Heute [A Modern
  Du Barry] (Mannequin)
Gefahren der Brautzeit [Dangers of
  the Engagement Period] /aka/
  Aus dem Tagebuch eines Ver-
  führers; Eine Nacht der Liebe;
  Liebesnächte [Nights of Love];
  Liebesbriefe (Yvette)
Sein Grösster Bluff [Her Greatest
  Bluff] (Tilly)

3672
LORYS, Denise*
Madame Sand-Gêne (Madame DeBulow)

3673
LOSEE, Frank (-1937)
As a Man Loves
Broadway and Home
Civilian Clothes (Carter Dumont)
Dangerous Love
Dangerous Trip
Disraeli (Hugh Myers)
Don't Leave Your Husband
False Fronts
Fear Market, The
Half an Hour
His House in Order
Kismet
Lady Rose's Daughter
Last of the Mohicans, The
Man She Brought Back, The
Man Who Came Back, The
Missing Millions
Orphans of the Storm (Count deLini-
  eres)
Right to Love, The
Seventh Day, The
Sinners
Speed Spook, The
Unguarded Women
Wild Honey

3674
LOSSEN, Lena*
Trial of Donald Westhof, The

3675
LOTINGA, Ernie /aka/ Dan Roy
  (1876-1951)
Acci-dental Treatment
Doing His Duty
Joining Up
Josser K. C.
Nap
Orderly Room, The

Raw Recruit, The
Spirits

3676
LOUIS, Viola*
Godless Girl, The (an inmate)
King of Kings, The (adultress)

3677
LOUIS, Willard (1886-1926)
Babbitt
Beau Brummel (George, Prince of
  Wales)
Broadway after Dark
Certain Young Man, A
Daddies
Don Juan (Pedrillo)
Eve's Lover (Austin Starfield)
French Doll, The
Going Some
Great Accident, The
Her Marriage Vow
Highest Bidder, The
His Secretary
Hogan's Alley
Jubilo
Kiss Me Again (Dr. Dubois)
Limited Mail, The
Love Hour, The
Lover of Camille, The
Madame X
Mademoiselle Modiste
Man Without a Conscience, The
Merry-Go-Round
Only a Shop Girl
Passionate Quest, The
Roads of Destiny
Robin Hood (Friar Tuck)
Scarlet Strain, The
Shamrock Handicap, The (Martin
  Finch)
Slave of Vanity, A
Three Women (John Howard)
Unpainted Woman
Vanity Fair (Joseph Sedley)

3678
LOUISE, Anita (Anita Louise Fre-
  mault) (1917-1970)
Four Devils (Louise, as a child)
Marriage Playground, The (Blanca)
Square Shoulders
Wonder of Women

3679
LOUISE, Viola*
Chicago

3680
LOVE, Bessie (Juanita Horton)
  (1898-)
Bonnie May
Broadway Melody, The (Hank Maho-
  ney)
Chasing Rainbows
Deserted at the Altar
Dress Parade
Dynamite Smith
Eternal Three, The
Fighting Colleen
Flag Maker, The
Forget Me Not
Gentle Julia
Ghost Patrol, The
Girl in the Show, A
Going Crooked
Harp in Hock, A
Has Anybody Seen Kelly?
Hollywood Revue of 1929
Human Wreckage
Idle Rich, The
King on Main Street, The
Living Dead, The
Lost World, The (Paula White)
Lovey Mary (Title role)
Magic Skin, The
Maginee Idol, The
Meet the Prince
Midlanders, The
New Brooms
Pegeen
Penny of Hilltop Trail
Purple Dawn, The
Road Show
Rubber Tires
Saint Elmo
Sally of the Scandals
Sea Lion, The
Silent Watcher, The
Slave of Desire
Son of His Father, A
Song and Dance Man, The
Soul Fire /aka/ Golden Youth
Spirit of the Lake
Sundown
Swamp, The
Those Who Dare
Three Men to Pay
Tongues of Flame
Torment
Vermillion Pencil, The
Village Blacksmith, The
Woman on the Jury, The
Young April

3681
LOVE, Dorothea*
That Royle Girl (Lola Nelson)

3682
LOVE, Montague (1887-1943)
Ancient Highway, The
Beauty Shop, The
Bulldog Drummond (Paterson)
Case of Becky, The
Charming Sinners (George Whitley)
Condemned Woman
Darling of the Rich, The
Devil's Skipper, The
Divine Lady, The (Capt. Hardy)
Divine Love
Don Juan (Count Donati)
Eternal City, The (Minghelli)
Forever
Good Time Charley
Hands Up! (Capt. Edward Logan)
Haunted House, The
Haunted Ship, The
Hawk's Nest, The
Her Private Life
Jesse James
King of Kings, The (Roman Centuri-
    on)
Last Warning, The
Leopardess, The
Little Old New York
Love's Redemption
Midstream
Most Immoral Lady, A
Mysterious Island
Night of Love, The (Duke de la Gar-
    da)
Noose, The
Out of the Storm
Place of the Honeymoons, The
Restless Wives
Rose of the Golden West
Roulette
Secrets of Paris
Shams of Society
Silent Lover, The
Silks and Saddles
Sinners in Heaven
Social Highwayman, The
Son of the Sahara, A
Son of the Sheik, The (Ghabah)
Synthetic Sin
Tender Hour, The
Voice Within, The
What's Wrong with Women? (Arthur
    Belden)
Wind, The (Roddy)
World and His Wife, The

Wrong Woman, The
Stage:
Survival of the Fittest, The (John
    Webster) 21

3683
LOVELY, Louise /aka/ Louise Car-
    basse (Louise Welch) (1896-)
Butterfly Man, The
Connecticut Yankee in King Arthur's
    Court, A
Heart of the North
Joyous Troublemaker, The
Life's Greatest Question
Little Grey Mouse, The
Lone Star Ranger
Old Nest, The
Orphan, The
Partners of Fate
Poverty of Riches, The
Shattered Idols
Skywayman, The
Third Woman, The
Twins of Suffering Creek
While the Devil Laughs

3684
LOWE, Edmund (1892-1971)
Baloo
Barbara Frietchie
Black Paradise
Brass Devil, The
Chicken in the Case, The
Cock-Eyed World, The (Sgt. Harry
    Quirk)
Devil, The
Dressed to Kill
East Lynne (Archibald Carlyle)
East of Suez
Fool, The
Game of Graft, A
Girl in Every Port, A
Greater than a Crown
Happiness Ahead
Happy Days (a principal)
Honor Among Men
In Old Arizona (Sgt. Mickey Dunn)
In the Palace of the King
Increasing Purpose, An
Is Zat So?
Kiss Barrier, The
Living Lies
Madonnas and Men
Making the Grade
Marriage in Transit (dual role, Hol-
    den/Cyril Gordon)
My Lady's Latchkey
Nellie, the Beautiful Cloak Model

Outcast, The
Painted Angel, The
Palace of Pleasure
Paramount player 22
Peacock Alley (Phil Garrison)
Poets of Call
Publicity Madness
Siberia
Silent Command, The
Someone in the House
Soul Mates
This Thing Called Love (Robert Col-
    lings)
Through Different Eyes (Harvey Man-
    ning)
What Price Glory? (Sgt. Harry
    Quirk)
White Flower
Wife in Name Only
Wizard, The
Woman Gives, The
Woman's Business, A
Stage:
Channel Road, The (Pvt. Rosenberg)
    29
Desert Sands (Arthur "Pickering"
    Landren) 22
In the Night Watch (Lt. d'Artelle) 21
Right to Strike, The (Dr. Wrigley) 21
War Song, The (Major Von Stock) 28

3685
LOWE, Irma*
Shanghai Lady

3686
LOWE, James B. *
Uncle Tom's Cabin (Uncle Tom)

3687
LOWELL, Helen (1866-1937)
Isn't Life Wonderful? (grandmother)
Stage:
A la Carte 27
Arabian Nightmare, The (Caroline
    Twiggam) 27
Atlas and Eva (Ma Nebblepredder) 28
Blue Bonnet (Miss Sallie Jenkins) 20
God Loves Us (Mrs. Midge) 26
It's a Wise Child (Mrs. Stanton) 29
Lady for a Night, A (Miss Wimple) 28
Montmarte (Camille) 22
Nature's Nobleman (Belle Brand) 21
Night Call, The (Martha Stuart-Scott)
    22
Nobody's Money (Mrs. Judson) 21
Show-Off, The (Mrs. Fisher) 24
Torch Bearers, The (Nelly Fell) 22

3688
LOWERY, William*
Haunted Ship, The
Nut, The
Red Hot Tires
Robin Hood (High Sheriff of Notting-
    ham)

3689
LOWNEY, Raymond*
Awful Truth, The

3690
LOY, Myrna (Myrna Williams)
    (1905-)
Across the Pacific
Ben Hur
Beware of Married Men
Bitter Apples
Black Watch, The
Cave Man, The
Climbers, The (Countess Veya)
Crimson City, The
Desert Song, The (Azuri)
Don Juan (Maia)
Escape /aka/ Exquisite Sinner, The
Evidence
Fancy Baggage
Finger Prints
Gilded Highway, The
Girl from Chicago, The
Great Divide, The
Ham and Eggs at the Front
Hard Boiled Rose
Heart of Maryland, The
His Lady /aka/ When a Man Loves
If I Were Single
Jazz Singer, The (chorus girl)
King of the Khyber Rifles (Yasmani)
Last of the Duanes
Midnight Taxi
Noah's Ark (dual role, slave girl/
    dancer)
Pay as You Enter
Pretty Ladies
Sailor's Sweetheart, A
Satan in Sables
Show of Shows, The
Simple Sis
So This Is Paris? (maid)
Squall, The (Nubi)
State Street Sadie
Ten Commandments, The
Thief of Bagdad, The
Turn Back the Hours
What Price Beauty?
Why Girls Go Back Home

Stage:
Grauman's Chinese Theatre (dance
    prologue) 20

3691
LOY, Sonny*
Mr. Wu (Little Wu)

3692
LOYAL, Dash*
Pilgrim, The (the elder)

3693
LU, Sonny--see: Sonny Loy

3694
LUBEN, Jack*
Last Outlaw, The

3695
LUBIMOFF, A.*
Sonia (Bavarian innkeeper)

3696
LUBIN, Arthur*
Afraid to Love
Bardelys the Magnificent
Proud Heart
Woman on the Jury, The
Stage:
Anything Might Happen (A. Walter)
    23

3697
LUBIN, Tibi*
Prince and the Pauper, The

3698
LUBITSCH, Ernst (1892-1947)
Souls for Sale
Sumurun /aka/ One Arabian Night
    (Yeggar)

3699
LUCAS, Nick*
Gold Diggers of Broadway (Nick)
Show of Shows, The
Stage:
Vaudeville [Palace] 29

3700
LUCAS, Paul--see: Paul Lukas

3701
LUCAS, Wilfred (-1940)
Across the Deadline
Barnstormer, The (leading man)
Barriers of Folly

Beautiful Liar, The
Better Man, The
Breaking Point, The (Mortimer David-
    son)
Burnt Fingers
Can a Woman Love Twice?
Daughters of Pleasure (Mark Hadley)
Dorothy Vernon of Haddon Hall (Earl
    of Rutland)
Fighting Breed, The
Flesh and Blood (the policeman)
Girl of the Golden West, The
Her Sacrifice
Heroes of the Streets
How Baxter Buttered In
Jazzmania
Kentucky Derby
Man Without a Country, The /aka/
    As No Man Has Loved
Nest, The
Paid Back
Price She Paid, The
Riders of the Purple Sage (Oldring)
Shadow of Lightning Ridge
Through the Back Door (Elton Reeves)
Trilby
Wife Who Wasn't Wanted, The
Stage:
Noose, The ("Come On" Conly) 26
Restless Women (John Fawcett) 27

3702
LUCCHETTI, Virginia*
Shepherd King, The

3703
LUCE, Alexis B.*
Chechahcos, The
Stage:
Princess April (Robert Ballou) 24

3704
LUCY, Arnold*
Ghost Talks, The
Good References (the Bishop)
In Search of a Sinner
One Woman Idea
Stage:
American Born (Delford) 25
As You Like It (Adam) 23
Bill of Divorcement, A (Dr. Alliot) 21
Hassan (Jafar) 24
Light of the World, The (Pastor Saun-
    ders) 20
Venus (Dr. Dickey Wakely) 27
Yes, Yes, Yvette (Bishop Doran) 27

3705
LUDDY, Barbara*
Born to Battle
Rose of the World

3706
LUDEN, Jack (1902-)
Bill Grimm's Progress
City of Shadows
Dangerous Curves (Rotarian)
Easy Payments
Faro Nell
Fascinating Youth
Flame in the Sky, A
Fools for Luck (Ray Caldwell)
Forgotten Faces
Innocents of Paris (Jules)
It's the Old Army Game
Jade Cup, The
Last Outlaw, The
Partners in Crime
Shootin' Irons
Sins of the Father (Otto)
Tell It to Sweeney
Two Flaming Youths (Tony Holden)
Under the Tonto Rim
Why Bring that Up?
Wild Party, The (George)
Wolf of Wall Street, The
Woman from Moscow
Yours to Command

3707
LUDMILLA, Anna*
Alf's Button (bit)
Stage:
Greenwich Village Follies 24
Tip-Top 20

3708
LUDWIG, Arthur*
Hoosier Schoolmaster, The
Too Many Kisses
Stage:
Anathema (Purikes the Greek)
Inspector General, The (Svistunov)
Rose Marie (Black Eagle) 24

3709
LUDWIG, Ralph*
Children of No Importance

3710
LUFF, William*
Glorious Adventure, The (King
   Charles II)
Gypsy Cavalier, The (Beydach,
   gypsy king)

Virgin Queen, The (Bishop de Quad-
   ra)

3711
LUFKIN, Sam*
Battling Orioles, The
Hoose Gow, The

3712
LUGOSI, Bela (Arisztid Olt or Bela
   Lugosie Blasko) (1882-1956)
Arabesque
Chadwick Bats
Daughters Who Pay
Diadalmas Elet
Die Frau Delphin
How to Handle Women (extra)
Der Januskopf /aka/ Love's Mockery
Johann Hopkins De Dritte
Last of the Mohicans, The
Midnight Girl, The
Prisoners
Rejected Woman, The
Silent Command, The
Szinészno
Thirteenth Chair, The (Inspector Del-
   zante)
Universal player 28
Veiled Woman, The
Viennese Nights
Stage:
Arabesque (Sheik of Hammam) 25
Devil in the Cheese, The (Father
   Petros) 26
Dracula (Count Dracula) 27
Open House (Sergius Chernoff) 25
Red Poppy, The (Fernando) 22

3713
LUKAS, Paul (Pal Lugacs) (1895-
   1971)
L'Amore Di Settecento Anni
La Dama Dal Vestito Grigio
Diadalmas Elet
Egy Finnak a Fele
Grumpy
Half Way to Heaven
Helszdzeves Szerelem
Hot News
Illusion
Lady Violette
Little Fox, The
Loves of an Actress
MGM player 28
Manhattan Cocktail (Renov)
Maria Lazar
Masamôd
Nevtelen Vár /aka/ Castle Nameless

New York Expresz Kabél
Night Watch, The
Olavi
Samson and Dalilah
Sárga Armyék
Shopworn Angel, The (Bailey)
Szinészno
Szürkeruhás Hölgy, A
Three Sinners
Two Lovers (Don Ramon de Linea)
Wolf of Wall Street, The (David Ty-
    ler)
Woman from Moscow

3714
LUND, Jorgen*
Han og Hun og Hamlet

3715
LUND, Richard*
Three Who Were Doomed, The

3716
LUNDEQUIST-DAHLSTROM, Gerda*
Story of Gösta Berling, The (Major-
    skan Samzelius)

3717
LUNDHOLM, Lisa*
Thy Soul Shall Bear Witness

3718
LUNT, Alfred (1893-)
Backbone
Lovers in Quarantine
Man Who Found Himself, The
Ragged Edge, The
Sally of the Sawdust (Payton Lennox)
Second Youth
Stage:
Arms and the Man (Capt. Bluntschli)
    25
At Mrs. Beam's (Mr. Dermott) 26
Banco (Count Alexandre de Lussac)
    22
Brothers Karamazov, The 27
Caprice (Counselor Albert Von Ech-
    ardt) 28
Doctor's Dilemma, The (Louis Dube-
    dat) 27
Goat Song (Juvan) 26
Guardsman, The (the actor) 24
Intimate Strangers, The (Ames) 21
Juarez and Maximillian (Maximillian)
    26
Marco Millions (Marco Polo) 28
Meteor (Raphael Lord) 29
Ned McCobb's Daughter (Babe

Callahan) 26
Outward Bound (Tom Prior) 24
Robert E. Lee (David Peel) 23
Second Man, The (Clark Storey) 27
Sweet Nell of Old Drury (King
    Charles II) 23
Volpone (Mosca) 28

3719
LUPINO, Wallace (1897-)
Be My King
His Private Life

3720
LUPINO, Walter*
Educational Comedies

3721
LURAY, Doris*
Grumpy

3722
LURVILLE, Armand*
Passion of Joan of Arc, The

3723
LUTHER, Ann (1894-)
Her Father's Station
Isle of Destiny, The
Neglected Wives
Sinners in Silk

3724
LUXFORD, Nola*
Prince of Pep, The

3725
LYLE, Bessie*
Illusion

3726
LYNCH, Helen (1904-)
Avenging Fangs
Cheaters, The
Eternal Three, The
Fifth Avenue Models
Fools First
Honor Bound
House that Jazz Built, The
Husbands for Rent
In Old Arizona (bit)
Ladies of the Mob (Marie)
Love and Learn
Meanest Man in the World, The
Minnie
My Own Pal
Oh, Doctor!
Other Side, The

Return of Gray Wolf, The
Romance of the Underworld
Showdown, The
Smouldering Fires
Speakeasy
Stolen Love
Thundergod
Underworld (Mulligan's girl)
What's a Wife Worth?
Why Bring That Up?

3727
LYNCH, John*
It's a Great Life

3728
LYNN, Emmy*
Living Image, The
Sheik's Wife, The
La Vierge Folle

3729
LYNN, Homer*
Let Not Man Put Asunder

3730
LYNN, Jill*
School for Wives

3731
LYNN, Ralph*
Aldwych Farces (hero)
Peace and Quiet
Tons of Money

3732
LYNN, Haron (1908-1963)
Cherokee Kid, The
Clancy's Kosher Wedding
Coward, The
Dad's Choice
Flame in the Sky, A
Fox player 28
Give and Take
Happy Days (a principal)
Husbands Are Liars
Jake the Plumber
Lightnin'
Movietone Follies of 1929 (Ann Foster)
None but the Brave
One Woman Idea
Red Wine
Son of the Golden West
Speakeasy
Sunny Side Up (Jane Worth)
Trail of the Horse Thieves

3733
LYNN, Sydney*
Atlantic [English] (Capt. of the Atlantic)

3734
LYON, Ben (1901-)
Air Legion, The
Ashes
Bluebeard's Seven Wives /aka/ Purple Passions
Conquest
Custard Cup
Dance Magic
Dancing Vienna
Flaming Youth
Flying Marine, The
For the Love of Mike (Mike)
Great Deception, The
Heart of Maryland, The (Bob Telfair)
High Hat
Lily of the Dust
Morgan's Raiders /aka/ Morgan's Last Raid
Necessary Evil, The
New Commandment, The
One Way Street
Pace that Thrills, The
Painted People
Perfect Sap, The
Potash and Perlmutter
Prince of Tempters, The
Quitter, The
Reckless Lady, The
Savage, The
So Big (Dirk DeJong)
Tender Hour, The
Transgressor, The
Wages of Virtue (Marvin)
White Moth, The
Winds of Chance
Wine of Youth
Stage:
Mary the Third (triple role, William/Robert/Lynn) 23

3735
LYON, Frank A. *
Inside of the Cup, The

3736
LYON, Wanda*
Greatest Love of All, The
Stage:
In Love with Love (Marion Sears) 23
Just Beyond (Marjorie) 25
Mike Angelo (Annabelle Carlton) 23
Piggy (Suzanne Fair) 27

Stork, The (Margot) 25

3737
LYONS, Edward (1886-)
Bad News
Déclassée
Dolls and Dollars
Everything but the Truth
Fire Escape Finish, A
Fixed by George
Hasty Hazing, A
His Wife's Relatives
How Do You Feel?
La, La, Lucille
Once a Plumber
Place and Quest
Roman Romeos
Rushin' Dancers, The
Shadow of the Law, The (crook)
Shocking Night, A
There and Back
Too Much Woman

3738
LYONS, Frances*
College Coquette, The

3739
LYONS, Harry Agar*
Coughing Horror, The (Dr. Fu Man-
    chu)
Luck of the Navy, The (Col. Dupont)

3740
LYTELL, Bert (1888-1954)
Alias Jimmy Valentine
Alias the Lone Wolf
Boomerang, The
Born Rich
Brothers
Eternal City, The (David Rossi)
Eve's Lover (Baron Geraldo Maddox)
First Night, The
Gilded Butterfly, The
Idle Rich, The
Kick In
Know Your Men
Lady Windermere's Fan (Lord Win-
    demere)
Ladyfingers
Light that Failed, The
Lombardi, Ltd.
Lone Wolf Returns, The
Man Who, The
Mayflower, The
Meanest Man in the World, The
Message from Mars, A
Metro player 21

Misleading Lady
Model from Paris, The
Never the Twain Shall Meet
Obey the Law
On Trial (Robert Strickland)
Paramount player 24
Price of Redemption
Right of Way, The
Rupert of Hentzau (dual role, Ru-
    dolph Rassendy'l/King Rudolph of
    Ruritania)
Sandra
Sherlock Holmes
Ship of Souls
Son of the Sahara, A
Steele of the Royal Mounted
Temple of Dawn, The (Leigh Dering)
To Have and to Hold
Trip to Paradise, A
Women's Wares
Stage:
Brothers (dual role, Robert Naugh-
    ton/Eddie Connelly) 28
Vaudeville [Palace] 29

3741
LYTELL, Wilfred (1892-1954)
Bluebeard's Seven Wives /aka/ Pur-
    ple Passions
Fox player 20
Heliotrope
Isle of Jewels [serial]
Kentuckians, The
Know Your Men
Man Who Paid, The
Trail of the Law, The
Trailed by Three [serial]
Warrens of Virginia, The (Ned Bur-
    ton)
Wolf's Fangs, The
Wrong Woman, The
Stage:
Goldfish, The (Jim Wetherby) 22
Peter Weston (Paul Vannard) 23
Sisters (Larry) 27

3742
LYTTON, L. Rogers*
Little Child Shall Lead Them, A
Sainted Devil, A (Don Balthazar)
Zaza (stage manager)

- M -

3743
MABERY, Mary*
Law's Lash, The

Restless Youth

3744
MAC, Baby*
Close Harmony

3745
McALLISTER, Claude*
Bulldog Drummond
Charming Sinners, The
Three Live Ghosts
Trial of Mary Dugan, The

3746
McALLISTER, Mary*
Ace of Spades [serial]
Ashes of Vengeance (Denise)
Boomerang, The
Devil's Skipper, The
Fire and Steel
Half a Chance
Into No Man's Land
Loves of an Actress
Man in the Shadow
Midnight Watch
One Minute to Play
Sap, The
Simon, the Jester
Singed
Universal player 25
Waning Sex, The
Wickedness Preferred

3747
McALLISTER, Paul (1875-)
Beau Geste (St. André)
Big Killing, The
Evangeline
Forever
Long Wolf, The
Manhandled (Paul Garretson)
Moral Sinner, The
Noah's Ark (dual role, Noah/Minister)
She's a Sheik
Sign on the Door, The
Sorrell and Son (Dr. Orange)
Stage Romance, A
What's Wrong with Women? (John
   Matthews)
Winning of Barbara Worth, The (the
   Seer)
Yolanda (Count Jules d' Hymbercourt)
You Can't Fool Your Wife
Stage:
Don Juan (Duke deNunez) 21
Grand Duchess and the Waiter, The
   (Grand Duke Paul) 25

She Stoops to Conquer (George Hastings) 24

3748
McALLISTER, Ward*
Woman of No Importance, A (Gerald
   Arbuthnot)
Stage:
Jeweled Tree, The (Mena) 26

3749
McALPIN, Donald*
Rosita (Rosita's brother)

3750
MacANDREWS, John*
Comin' Thro' the Rye (Simpkins)

3751
MacARDLE, Donald*
Mumsie (Noel Symonds)
Nell Gwyn (Duke of Monmouth)
Wee MacGreegor's Sweetheart (Mac-
   Greegor)

3752
McATEE, Clyde*
Percy

3753
McAVOY, May (1901-)
Bedroom Window, The
Ben Hur (Esther)
Caught in the Fog
Clarence (Cora)
Devil's Garden, The
Enchanted Cottage, The
Everything for Sale
Fire Brigade, The
Forbidden Valley
Grumpy (Virginia Bullivant)
Her Reputation
Hollywood
Homespun Vamp, A
House of the Tolling Bell
If I Were Single
Irish Hearts
Jazz Singer, The (Mary Dale)
Kick In
Lady Windermere's Fan (Title role)
Lion and the Mouse, The
Little Snob
Love Wins
Mad Whirl, The
Man and His Woman
Married Flirts
Matinee Ladies
May McAvoy in Sunny California

Morals
My Old Dutch
No Defense
Only 38
Passionate Quest
Private Scandal, A
Reno Divorce, A
Road to Glory, The (Judith Allen)
Savage, The
Sentimental Tommy
Slightly Used
Sporting Duchess, The
Stolen Kisses
Tarnish
Terror, The (Olga Redmayne)
Tessie
Three Women (Jeanne)
Through a Glass Window
Top of New York, The
Truth About Husbands, The
Virginia Courtship, A
West of the Water Tower

3754
McBAN, Mickey*
Father and Son
Hot Water
Return of Peter Grimm, The (William)
Sorrell and Son (Christopher, as a child)
Splendid Crime, The
Splendid Road, The
Temple of Venus, The (Micky)

3755
MacBRIDE, Lux*
My Lady of Whim (yacht captain)

3756
McCARTHY, Earl*
Red Lips

3757
McCARTHY, Myles*
Captain Blood
Day of Faith, The
Lady, The

3758
McCONNELL, Gladys (1907-)
Chaser, The
Cheyenne
Code of the Scarlet
Fire Detective [serial]
Glorious Trail, The
Midnight Kiss, The (Lenore Hastings)
Perfect Crime, The

Riding to Fame
Three's a Crowd
Tiger's Shadow, The [serial]

3759
McCORMAC, Muriel*
Dynamite (Katie Derk)
King of Kings, The (blind girl)
Sparrows /aka/ Human Sparrows (a sparrow)

3760
McCORMACK, Frank*
Case of Becky, The
Stage:
Chicken Feed (Jim Bailey) 23
Gorilla, The (Mr. Garrity) 25
Monster, The ("Red" Mackenzie) 22
Thank You (Andy Beardsley) 21
Wasp's Nest, The (Hank) 27

3761
McCORMACK, Hugh*
Nix on Dames

3762
McCORMICK, Merrill*
Robin Hood (henchman)
Romance of the Rio Grande

3763
McCOY, Clyde*
Midnight Bell, A

3764
McCOY, D'Arcy*
Flaming Forest, The

3765
McCOY, Evelyn (1913-)
Sting of the Lash (Crissy, age 10)

3766
McCOY, Gertrude (1896-1967)
Charlatan Mystery, The
Christie Johnstone (Title role)
Out of the Darkness
Winsome Winnie [serial]

3767
McCOY, Harry (1894-)
Hallroom Boys Comedies
Hearts of Men
His Wife's Friend
Skirts, The
Stage:
Racket, The (Turck) 27

3768
McCOY, Ruby*
Broadway (Grace)

3769
McCOY, Tim (Timothy John Fitz-
   gerald McCoy) (1893-   )
Adventurer, The
Beyond the Sierras
Bush Ranger, The
California
Covered Wagon, The
Desert Rider, The
Explorers of the West
Foreign Devils
Frontiersman, The
Humming Wires
Indians Are Coming, The
Law of the Range, The (Jim Lock-
   hart)
Masked Stranger, The
Morgan's Raiders /aka/ Morgan's
   Last Raid
Night on the Range, A
Overland Telegraph
Riders of the Dark
Sioux Blood
Spoilers of the West
Thundering Herd, The (Burn Hudnall)
War Paint
Winners of the Wilderness (Col.
   O'Hara)
Wyoming

3770
McCRAY, Joe--see: Joel McCrea

3771
McCREA, Joel (1905-   )
Dynamite (Marco)
Five O'Clock Girl, The
Jazz Age, The
Lightnin'
Penrod and Sam (Herman)
Single Standard, The
So This Is College

3772
McCULLOUGH, Paul (1892-1936)
All Steamed Up
Bath Between, The
Belle of Samoa, The
Beneath the Law
Clark and McCullough in the Honor
   System
Clark and McCullough in the Inter-
   view
Detectives Wanted

Diplomats, The
Hired and Fired
In Holland
Knights Out
Medicine Men, The
Music Fiends
Ramblers, The (debut)
Waltzing Around
Stage:
Chuckles - London 22
Music Box Revue 22; 24
Ramblers, The (Sparrow) 26

3773
McCULLOUGH, Philo (1893-   )
Apache
Bar C Mystery, The [serial]
Boomerang, The
Calvert's Valley
Charlatan, The
Clearing the Trail
Dangerous Adventure [serial]
Daughters of Today
Dick Turpin
Easy Pickings
Everybody's Acting
Fire and Steel
First Degree, The
Fourth Musketeer, The
Heroes of the Streets
Ladies at Play
Leatherneck, The
Light that Failed, The
Lost in the Artic
Married Flapper, The
Million Dollar Collar
Mismates
More to Be Pitied than Scorned
Night Flyer, The
On Sunset Range
Outlaw Dog, The
Painted Post
Power of the Press
Primal Law
Savage, The
Seeing Is Believing
Show of Shows, The
Silver Valley
Smile, Brother, Smile
South of Panama
Strange Idols
Stranger's Banquet, The
Trilby
Trimmed in Scarlet
Untamed Justice
Warming Up
We're All Gamblers
West of Chicago

Wife of the Centaur, The
Winds of Chance
Woman Who Did Not Care, The
Yesterday's Wife

3774
McCUTCHEON, Wallace*
Phantom Foe, The [serial]
Thief, The
Stage:
Earl Carroll's Vanities 25
Rat, The (Paul) 25

3775
McDANIEL, George*
Barefoot Boy, The

3776
MacDERMOTT, Marc (1880-1929)
Amazing Lovers
Blind Wives
California
Dorothy Vernon of Haddon Hall (Sir
   Malcolm Vernon)
Flesh and the Devil (Count vonRha-
   den)
Footlights
Glorious Betsy
Goose Woman, The (Amos Ethridge)
Graustark (Prince Gabriel)
He Who Gets Slapped (Beau Regnard)
Hoodman Blind
Kiki
Lady, The
Lights of New York, The
Love Thief, The
Lucky Lady, The
Lucretia Lombard
Man, Woman and Sin
Mysterious Island, The
Resurrection
Road to Romance, The
Sea Hawk, The (Sir John Killigrew)
Siege
Spanish Jade
Taxi Dancer, The (Henry Brierhalter)
Temptress, The (Marquis Fontenoy)
This Woman (Stratini)
Three Miles Out
Tragedy of the East Side, A
Under the Black Eagle
While New York Sleeps
Whip, The
Yellow Lily, The

3777
MacDONALD, Charles*
Lucky Devil, The

Stage:
Hot Water (Paul Harding) 29
New Brooms (Simpson) 24
19th Hole, The (the postman) 27
Sun-Up (preacher) 29

3778
McDONALD, Claire*
Big Parade, The

3779
McDONALD, Dan*
Sky Pilot

3780
MacDONALD, Donald*
If Marriage Fails
Lorna Doone
Midnight Bell, A
Sky Pilot, The
Village Sleuth
Woman in the Suitcase, The
Stage:
Beware of Widows (Bill Bradford) 25
Checkerboard, The (Boris) 20
Getting Gertie's Garter (Ken Wal-
   rick) 21
Jack and Jill (Jack Andrews) 23
Love 'em and Leave em (Billings-
   ley) 26
Paris Bound (Richard Parrish) 27
Processional (Phillpots) 25
White Wings (Kit Carni) 26

3781
McDONALD, Francis (1891-1968)
Bar C Mystery, The [serial]
Battling Butler
Blockade
Brothers
Captain Fly-By-Night
Carnation Kid, The
Clean-Up, The
Desert's Toll, The
Dragnet, The
East of Broadway
Forbidden Love
Forbidden Paradise
Forgotten Faces
Girl in Every Port, A
Girl Overboard
Go Straight
Going Up
Hearts and Masks
Kentucky Colonel
Last Trail, The
Legion of the Condemned (murderer)
Mary of the Movies

Monte Cristo (Benedette)
My Lady of Whim (Rolf)
Nomads of the North (Buck Mc-
    Dougall)
Notorious Lady
Outlaws of Red River
Palace of Pleasure
Port of Dreams
Puppets
Puppets of Fate
Satan in Sables
Show Boat
So This Is Marriage
Temptress, The
Trilby
Trooper O'Neill
Valley of Hell
Wreck, The
Yankee Senor, The

3782
McDONALD, Inez*
Do or Die

3783
MacDONALD, J. Farrell (1875-1952)
Abie's Irish Rose (Patrick Murphy)
Action
Ankles Preferred
Bertha, the Sewing Machine Girl
Bonded Woman
Brass Bowl, The
Bringing Up Father (Jiggs)
Bucking the Line
Cohens and the Kellys in Paris, The
Colleen
Come On Over
Country Beyond, The
Cradle Snatchers
Dixie Merchant, A
Drifting
East Side, West Side
Family Upstairs, The
Fighting Heart, The
First Year, The
Flesh and the Devil, The
Four Devils, The (clown)
Freeze-Out
Gerald Cranston's Lady
Glory of Love, The
Happy Days (a principal)
Headlines
Hitchin' Posts, The
In Old Arizona (Tad)
Iron Horse, The (Corp. Casey)
Jazzmania
Kentucky Fair
Kentucky Pride

Last Frontier, The
Lightnin'
Little Miss Hawkshaw
Love Makes 'em Wild
Lucky Horseshoe, The
Mademoiselle Midnight
Masked Emotions
Masquerade
Me, Gangster
None but the Brave
Outlaws of Red River
Over the Border
Paid to Love
Painted Angel, The
Quicksands
Racing Hearts
Rich but Honest
Riding with Death
Riley the Cop
Scarlet Honeymoon
Shamrock Handicap, The (Dennis
    O'Shea)
Signal Tower, The
Sky High (Jim Halloway)
South Sea Rose
Strong Boy, The
Sunrise (photographer)
Thank You
Three Bad Men
Tracks
Trail Rider, The
Trailin'
Trip to Chinatown, A
Under Sentence
Wallop, The
Western Luck
While Paris Sleeps (George Morier)
Young Rajah, The

3784
MacDONALD, Jack F.*
Burning Daylight
Deep Waters
Don Q, Son of Zorro (Gen. de
    Muro)
Great Redeemer, The
Greed (Cribbons)
Lorna Doone
Show Boat (pilot)
13 Washington Square
While Paris Sleeps (Father Marionet-
    te)
White Circle, The

3785
MacDONALD, Jeanette (1906-1965)
Innocents of Paris
Love Parade, The (Queen Louise)

Stage:
Angela (Princess Alestine Victorine
  Angela) 28
Boom Boom (Jean) 29
Demi-Tasse Revue, The (debut) 20
Magic Ring, The (Iris Bellamy) 23
Sunny Days (Ginette Bertin) 28
Tip-Toes (Sylvia Metcalf) 25
Yes, Yes, Yvette (Yvette Ralston) 27

3786
MacDONALD, Katherine (1894-1956)
Beautiful Liar, The
Beauty Market, The
Chastity
Curtain
Domestic Relations
Her Social Value
Heroes and Husbands
Infidel, The
Lonely Road, The
Money, Money, Money
My Lady's Latch Key
Notorious Miss Lisle, The
Old Loves and New /aka/ The Des-
  ert Healer)
Passion's Playground
Refuge
Scarlet Lily, The
Stranger than Fiction
Thunderbolt, The
Trust Your Wife
Turning Point, The
White Shoulders
Woman Conquers, A
Woman's Side, The

3787
MacDONALD, Kenneth*
Coast Patrol, The
Dynamite Dan

3788
McDONALD, Melbourn*
Behind the Front

3789
MacDONALD, Wallace (1891-)
Angel Face Molly
Bar C Mystery [serial]
Blockade
Breaking Through
Bright Lights
Casey of the Coast Guard [serial]
Caught Bluffing
Charmer, The
Checkered Flag, The
Dark Skies

Darkened Rooms
Day of Faith, The
Drums of the Desert
Fancy Baggage
Fool There Was, A
Free Lips
Hell's Four Hundred
His Foreign Wife
Hit the Deck
Lady, The
Learning to Love
Lightnin'
Love and Glory
Maytime (Claude VanZandt)
New Lives for Old
Pampered Youth
Pearl Story, The
Poor Relation, A
Primrose Path, The (Bruce Arm-
  strong)
Red Signals
Roaring Rails
Rogue Song, The (Hassan)
Sea Hawk, The (Master Peter Godol-
  phin)
Spoilers, The (Broncho Kid)
Sweetie
Thy Name Is Woman
Tropical Nights
Trumpet Island
Tumbling River
Two Can Play (Robert MacForth)
Under Oath
Understudy, The
Universal player 26
Wandering Fires (Normal Yeull)
Whispering Smith Rides [serial]
Who Shall Judge?
Your Wife and Mine
Youth Must Have Love

3790
McDONALD, Wilfred*
A Yankee at the Court of King Ar-
  thur (Sir Launcelot)

3791
McDONALD, William*
Twinkletoes (Inspector Territon)

3792
McDONNEL, Col. G. L.*
Illusion
White Black Sheep, The

3793
McDONOUGH, W. S.*
Those Who Dare

3794
McDOUGALL, Rex*
Gypsy Cavalier, The (Ralph Carew)
Hound of the Baskervilles, The

3795
McDOWELL, Claire (Mrs. Charles
    Mailes) (1887-1967)
Almost Human
Ashes of Vengeance (Margot's aunt)
Ben Hur (Hur's mother)
Big Parade, The (Mrs. Apperson)
Black Diamond Express, The
Black Oxen (Agnes Trevor)
Cheaters, The
Chickens
Circus Days
Devil's Circus, The
Devil's Riddle, The
Dixie Merchant, A
Don't Marry
Feud, The
Flaming Forest, The
Four Devils (the woman)
Gift Supreme, The (Lalia Graun)
Girl Who Came Back, The
Gold Braid
Gray Dawn
Heart's Haven, The
Human Wreckage
In the Name of the Law
Jack-Knife Man, The
Ladies' Man
Little Journey, A
Mark of Zorro, The (Don Carlo's
    wife)
Marriage by Contract
Midnight Flyer, The
Midsummer Madness
Mother O' Mine
Nice People
Penrod
Ponjola (Mrs. Hope)
Prisoners of Love
Quincy Adams Sawyer (Mrs. Putnam)
Quitter, The
Redemption
Rent Free
Secrets (Elizabeth Canning)
Shamrock Handicap (Molly O'Shea)
Shield of Honor
Show-Off, The
Silks and Saddles
Something to Think About (house-
    keeper)
Taxi Dancer, The
Thy Name Is Woman
Tillie the Toiler (Ma Jones)

Tomorrow
Tower of Lies, The (Katrina)
Tragedy of Youth, The
Unknown Soldier, The
Viking, The
Waking up the Town
Westbound Limited, The
What Every Woman Knows
When Dreams Come True
Whispering Winds
Winds of the Pampas
Woman in the Suitcase, The

3796
McDOWELL, Melbourne*
Behind the Front
Feel My Pulse
Gift Supreme, The (Eliot Vinton)
Golden Snare, The
Nomads of the North (Duncan Mc-
    Dougall)
Outside the Law (Morgan Spencer)
Rainmaker, The
Richard the Lion-Hearted (Bishop of
    Tyre)
What Happened to Jones?

3797
McDOWELL, Nelson*
Claw, The (Scout MacBourney)
Girl of the Golden West, The
Kentucky Courage
Last of the Mohicans, The
Oliver Twist (Mr. Sawerberry)
Outlaw Breakers, The
Pioneer Trails
Ramblin' Galoot, The
Scaramouche (Rhodomont)
Shooting of Dan McGrew, The (sea
    captain)
Vanishing Rider, The [serial]

3798
MACE, Wynn*
Sky High (Patterson)

3799
McEDWARD, Gordon*
Silent Command, The

3800
McELHERN, James*
Confessions of a Queen
Courtship of Miles Standish, The
Daddy's Gone A-Hunting
Passionate Youth

3801
McEVILLY, Burton*
Janice Meredith
Stage:
Letter, The (Geoffrey Hammond) 27

3802
McEWAN, Jack*
Q Ships

3803
McEWEN, Walter (1905-)
Sonia (David O'Rane, age 15)
Stage:
Rubicon, The (Monsieur Sevin) 22

3804
McFADDEN, Ira*
Bride of the Storm

3805
McFADDEN, Ivor*
Tides of Passion
Two-Gun Man, The

3806
McFARLANE, George*
Happy Days (interlocutor)
Nix on Dames
Painted Angel, The
South Sea Rose
Stage:
Luck Break (John Bruce) 25
Revelry (Dan Lurcock) 27
Salvation (Brady) 28
Springtime of Youth (Roger Hatha-
way) 22

3807
McGARRITY, Everett*
Hallelujah! (Spunk)

3808
McGARVEY, Cathal*
Irish Destiny

3809
McGAUGH, Wilbur*
Days of '48 [serial] (Robert Marsdan)

3810
McGEE, Patricia*
Son of Wallingford, The (Plomps)

3811
McGLYNN, Frank (1867-1951)
America /aka/ Love and Sacrifice
(Patrick Henry)

Judgment of the Hills
Stage:
Abraham Lincoln (Title role) 29
Broken Chain, The (Reb Velvele
Slomner) 29
Catskill Dutch (Case Steenkoop) 24
Free Soul, A (D. A. Nolan) 28
Steadfast (Rabbi Nathan Judah) 23
That Awful Mrs. Eaton! (Andrew
Jackson) 24

3812
McGOWAN, Bryan*
Irish Destiny

3813
McGOWAN, Dorothy*
Ghost Talks, The

3814
McGOWAN, J. P. (1880-1952)
Ace of Clubs, The
Arizona Days
Bad Man's Money
Below the Deadline
Black Aces
Blood and Steel
Chinatown Mystery, The
Clean-Up, The
Code of the Scarlet
Devil Dogs
Devil's Tower, The
Dugan of the Dugout
Fighting Sheriff, The
Fighting Terror, The
Golden Bridle
Gun Gospel
Headin' Westward
Hills of Missing Men
Invaders, The
Last Roundup, The
Law of the Mounted, The
Lawless Legion, The
Lightnin' Shot, The
Lone Horseman
Lost Express, The [serial]
Lost Limited, The
'Neath Western Skies
Oklahoma Kid, The
Old Code, The
On the Divide
Painted Trail, The
Phantom Rider
Plunging Hoofs
Red Raiders, The
Red Signals
Royal American, The
Senor Americano

Senor Daredevil
Ships of the Night
Silent Trail, The
Slaver, The
Stormy Seas
Tarzan and the Golden Lion
Texas Tommy
Two Fisted Tenderfoot, A
West of Santa Fe
Whispering Smith Rides [serial]

3815
McGRAIL, Walter (1889-1970)
Across the Pacific
Adventure
American Beauty
Bad Man, The
Beware of the Bride
Blockade
Breaking Point, The (Richard Jane-
    way)
City, The
Columbia player 27
Combat
Confessions of a Wife
Dancers, The
Eleventh Hour, The
Flaming Youth
Forbidden Waters
Greater than Fame
Habit
Havoc (Roddy Danton)
Her Husband's Secret
Her Mad Bargain
Hey Rube!
Invisible Divorce
Is Divorce a Failure?
Kentucky Derby
Last of the Duanes
Life's Twist
Lights Out
Man Crazy
Marriage License
Midnight Madness
Nobody's Money
Old Code, The
Old San Francisco
One Splendid Hour
Pilgrims of the Night
Play Girl, The
Playthings of Destiny
Prisoners of the Storm
River of Romance
Scarlet West, The (Lt. Harper)
Secret Studio, The
Smouldering Fires
Son of His Father, A
Son of the Sahara, A

Sport Girl, The
Stop that Man!
Suzanna
Teaser, The
Top of New York
Unguarded Women
Uninvited Guest, The
Veiled Woman, The
Where the North Begins
Wolf Fangs
Yosemite Trail

3816
McGRATH, Larry*
Knockout Reilly

3817
McGREGOR, Gordon*
Elmo, the Fearless [serial]

3818
McGREGOR, Harmon*
Slave of Desire
Stage:
Chains of Dew (James O'Brien) 22
Mixed Marriage (Mickey O'Hara) 20

3819
McGREGOR, Malcolm (1892-1945)
All the Brothers Were Valiant (Joel
    Shore)
Bedroom Window, The
Broken Chains
Buck Privates
Can a Woman Love Twice?
Circle, The
Danger of the Nile, The (Earle)
Don Juan's Three Nights
Flaming Waters
Freedom of the Press
Gay Deception, The
Girl from Gay Paree, The
Girl on the Barge, The
Girl Who Came Back, The
Greater Glory, The
Happy Warrior, The
Headlines
Infatuation
It Must Be Love
Kid Sister, The
King Tut
Lady Bird
Lady of the Night
Mary of the Movies
Matinee Ladies
Metro player 23
Million Bid, A
Money to Burn

Noise in Newboro, A
Pearl Story, The
Place of Honor, The
Port of Missing Girls, The
Prisoner of Zenda, The (Count Fritz
    von Tarlenheim)
Silent Flyer, The [serial]
Silver Streak, The [serial]
Stormy Waters
Tropical Nights
Vanishing American, The /aka/ The
    Vanishing Race (Capt. Earl Rams-
    dell)
Wreck, The

3820
MacGRUDER, Anna*
Three Ring Marriage

3821
McGUIRE, Kathryn (1897-   )
Big Diamond Robbery, The
Border Wildcat, The
Bucking the Line
Children of the Ritz
Crossroads of New York, The
Flame of Life
Girl on the Pullman, The
Lilac Time
Long, Long Trail, The
Naughty but Nice (Alice Altewood)
Navigator, The
Playing with Fire
Printer's Devil, The
Sherlock, Jr. (the girl)
Sheik of Araby, The
Silent Call, The
Synthetic Sin
Woman of Bronze, The

3822
McGUIRE, Mickey--see: Mickey
    Rooney

3823
McGUIRE, Tom*
Captain Blood
Cinderella of the Hills, A
Lights of New York
Missing Link, The
My Own Pal
Reckless Age, The
Red Hot Tires
Sawdust Paradise, The
Shanghai Bound
Spoilers, The
Steamboat Bill, Jr.
We Moderns

3824
McGURK, J. W.*
Great White Way, The

3825
McHUGH, Charles*
Girl of the Golden West, The
Golden Cocoon, The
Lights of Old Broadway (Shamus
    O'Tandy)
Waning Sex, The

3826
McHUGH, Frank (Francis Curray
    McHugh) (1898-   )
First National player 29
If Men Played Cards as Women Do
Stage:
Conflict (Sgt. "Chink" Burt) 29
Excess Baggage (Jimmy Dunn) 27
Fog (Scraggs) 27
Show Girl 29
Tenth Avenue (Curly Neff) 27

3827
McHUGH, Jack*
Chinatown Nights
Educational Comedies

3828
McILLWAIN, William*
Passionate Youth

3829
McINTOSH, Burr (1862-1942)
Across the Atlantic
Adorable Cheat
Breakfast at Sunrise
Buckaroo Kid, The
Dangerous Friends
Driven
Exciters, The
Fancy Baggage
Fire and Steel
Fourflusher, The
Golden Stallion, The [serial]
Green Archer, The [serial] (Bellamy)
Grip of the Yukon, The
Hazardous Valleys
Hero for a Night, A
Last Warning, The
Lilac Time
Me, Gangster (Bill Lane)
Moran of the Marines
Naughty but Nice (Uncle Seth Sum-
    mers)
On the Banks of the Wabash
Once and Forever

Racket, The
Restless Wives
Rogue Song, The (Count Peter)
Sailor's Wives
See You in Jail
Silk Stockings
Skinner Steps Out
Taxi! Taxi!
That Certain Thing
Virtuous Liars
Way Down East (Squire Bartlett)
Wilderness Woman, The
Yankee Clipper, The
Stage:
Robert E. Lee (General Scott) 23
Squaw Man, The (Big Bill) 21

3830
McINTOSH, Morris*
Girl on the Barge, The

3831
McINTYRE, Tom*
Plunder [serial]

3832
McIVOR, Mary*
Ince player 21

3833
MACK, Andrew*
Bluebeard's Seven Wives /aka/ Pur-
    ple Passions
Stage:
Friar's Club Frolic 22
Humming Bird, The (Brutus J. Finn)
    23
Lambs Gambol 25
Woof, Woof (Harry McDaniel) 29

3834
MACK, Arthur*
Return of Sherlock Holmes
Stage:
Desire under the Elms (dual role,
    farmer/deputy) 24

3835
MACK, Baby*
Close Harmony
Ghost Talks, The

3836
MACK, Bobby*
Black Beauty
Evengeline
Girl from Montmartre, The
Road to Romance, The

Son of Wallingford, The ("Onion"
    Jones)
Student Prince, The (Kellerman)
Vanity Fair

3837
MACK, Charles E. (Charles E. Sel-
    lers) (1887-1934)
Why Bring that Up?
Radio:
Eveready Hour, The   23
Majestic Hour, The   27
Two Black Crows 28
Stage:
Dancing Girl, The   23
Earl Carroll's Vanities 27
Passing Show of 1921

3838
MACK, Charles Emmett (-1927)
America /aka/ Love and Sacrifice
    (Charles Philip Edward Montague)
Bad Company
Daring Years, The (John Browning)
Devil's Circus, The
Dream Street (Billy McFadden)
Driven
First Auto, The
Old San Francisco
One Exciting Night (the guest)
Rough Riders, The
Unknown Soldier, The
White Monkey, The
White Rose, The (guest at the Inn)
Why Bring that Up?
Woman of the World, A
Youth for Sale

3839
MACK, E. J.*
It's a Great Life

3840
MACK, Helen (1913-)
Grit Wins
Success
Zaza (daughter)
Stage:
Dybbuck, The (Eike) 25
Subway Express (first flapper) 29

3841
MACK, Hughie (1887-1952)
Four Sons
Going Up
Greed (Heise)
Maré Nostrum [Our Sea] (Caragol)
Merry Widow, The (innkeeper)

Reno
Seeing It Through
Silent Flyer, The
Trifling Women
Wedding March, The (wine-garden
  keeper)
Where Trails Begin
Woman's Faith, A

3842
MACK, James T. *
Home Towners, The
Queen of the Nightclubs
Swim, Girl, Swim
Women's Wares

3843
MACK, Joe*
Finders Keepers
Stage:
Ginger (Willie Fall) 23

3844
MACK, Marion (1905-)
Alice in Movieland
Carnival Girl
Fox Sunshine Comedies
General, The (Annabelle Lee)
Mary of the Movies
Mermaid Comedies
One of the Bravest

3845
MACK, Robert*
Under Two Flags (Rake)
Vanity Fair (Sir Pitt Crawley)

3846
MACK, Wilbur (1873-1964)
Argyle Case, The (Sam)
Beauty and Bullets
Honky Tonk
Slim Fingers

3847
MACK, Willard (1873-1934)
Barbarian, The
Beauty and Bullets
Body Punch
Just in Time
Phantom Fingers
Tenderfoot Hero, A
Voice of the City
Woman on the Index, The
Your Friend and Mine
Stage:
Canary Dutch (Herman Strauss) 25
Gold (Capt. Isaiah Bartlett) 21

Honor Be Damned! (John Connell) 27
Lily Sue (Joe Holly) 26
Near Santa Barbara (Bill Trainor) 21
Scarlet Fox, The (Michael Devlin) 28
Smooth as Silk ("Silk" Mullane) 21
Vaudeville [Palace] 26; 29

3848
MACK, William B. *
American Venus, The
Backbone
Heliotrope
Song and Dance Man, The
Steadfast Heart, The
Stage:
Adorable Liar, The (Mark Roque) 26
Cobra (Rosner) 24
Crooked Gamblers (Randall) 20
Damn Your Honor (Beluche) 29
Kingdom of God, The (Liborio) 28
Man in the Making, The (Al Wayman)
  21
Revelry (Andy Gandy) 27
Rose Bernd (Bernd) 22
Savage under the Skin (Rev. Brown)
  27
Some Party 22
Square Peg, A (James T. Huckins)
  23
Zeno (Dr. Moore) 23

3849
MACKAIL, Dorothy (1905-)
Barker, The
Bits of Life
Bridge of Sighs, The
Broken Violin, The
Chickie
Children of the Ritz
Convoy
Crystal Cup, The
Dancer of Paris, The
Face at the Window, The
Fighting Blade, The (Thomasine Mus-
  grove)
Great Divide, The
Hard to Get
His Captive Woman
His Children's Children
Inner Man, The
Isle of Doubt, The
Joanna
Just Another Blonde /aka/ The Girl
  from Coney Island
Ladies Night in a Turkish Bath
Lady Be Good
Lotus Eater, The
Love Racket, The

Lunatic at Large, The
Making of O'Malley
Man Crazy
Man Who Came Back, The
Mighty Lak' a Rose
Next Corner, The (Elsie Maury)
One Year to Live
Ranson's Folly
Shore Leave
Smile, Brother, Smile
Stranded in Paradise
Streets of New York
Subway Sadie
Torchy
Torchy Mixes In
Torchy's Millions
Torchy's Promoter
Twenty-One
Two Weeks Off
Waterfront
What Shall I Do?
Whip, The
Wild Apples
Woman's Woman, A

3850
MACKATHORNE, George*
Squall, The (Niki)

3851
MacKAY, Charles*
Without Fear

3852
McKAY, Winsor*
Great White Way, The

3853
McKAY, Fred*
Charlatan, The
Last Performance, The

3854
McKEE, Bob*
Happy Days (chorus)

3855
McKEE, Frank*
Happy Days (chorus)

3856
McKEE, Lafe (1872-   )
Amazing Vagabond, The
California Mail, The
Manhattan Cowboy
On the Divide
Reily of the Rainbow Division
Saddle Mates

Trail Rider, The
Upland Rider, The

3857
McKEE, Raymond*
Babbitt
Blind Bargain, The (Robert)
Blind Hearts
Burr Comedies
Campus Knights
Compromise
Contraband
Down to the Sea in Ships (Thomas
     Allen Dexter)
Exclusive Rights
Flame of Youth, The
Fortune Teller, The
Free to Love (Tony)
Frozen River
Girl o' My Heart
Jilt, The
King of the Herd
Lamplighter, The
Lawful Cheaters (Richard Steele)
Little Mother, The
Little Wanderer, The
Love's Harvest
Oh, What a Night!
Silent Accuser, The
Smith's Pony
Speed Limit
Three Women (Harvey Craig)
Through a Glass Window
Wing Toy

3858
McKEEN, Sunny*
Newlyweds and Their Baby. The
     [series] (Snookums)

3859
MacKENNA, Kenneth (1899-1962)
American Venus, The
Love, Live and Laugh
Pleasure Crazed
South Sea Rose
Stage:
Big Pond, The (Pierre De Mirande)
     28
Catskill Dutch (Peetcha) 24
Crooked Square, The (Robert Colby)
     23
Dumb-Bell (Ted Stone) 23
Endless Chain, The (Kenneth Reeves)
     22
Far Cry, The (Dick Clayton) 24
Immodest Violet (Arthur Bodkin) 20

Mad Honeymoon, The (Wally Spencer) 23
Masque of Venice, The (Jack Cazeneuve) 26
Nerves (Jack Coates) 24
Nest, The (Max Hamelin) 22
Oh, Mama (Georges La Garde) 25
Opportunity (Jimmie Dow) 20
Play Without a Name, A (John Russell) 28
Sapphire Ring, The (Dr. Erno Nemeth) 25
We Moderns (Richard) 24
What Every Woman Knows (John Shand) 26
Windows (Johnny March) 23
World We Live In (dual role, Felix/ Commander-in-Chief of Yellow Ants) 22

3860
McKENZIE, Bob*
Fifth Avenue Models

3861
MacKENZIE, Donald*
Mysterious Dr. Fu Manchu, The /aka/ The Insidious Dr. Fu Manchu
Studio Murder Mystery, The (Capt. Coffin)
True Heaven
Stage:
Spider, The (the man) 27

3862
McKIM, Robert (1887-)
All the Brothers Were Valiant (Finch)
Ambrose Applejohn's Adventure (Brorlsky)
Bat, The (Dr. Wells)
Dead Game
Deadline, The
Devil to Pay, The
Dwelling Place of Light
Flame in the Sky, A
Flaming Barriers
Human Wreckage
Lure of Egypt, The
Mademoiselle Midnight
Man of the Forest
Mark of Zorro, The (Capt. Juan Ramon)
Maytime (Monte Mitchell)
Mr. Billings Spends His Dime
Money Changers, The
Monte Cristo (De Villefort)

Mysterious Rider, The
Pay Off, The
Percy
Regular Scout, A
Riders of the Dawn
Show Girl
Silver Horde, The
Spider and the Rose, The
Spoilers, The (Struve)
Spook Ranch
Strangers of the Night
Strong Man, The (Roy McDermitt)
Thrill Seekers
Tough Guy
U. P. Trail, The
White Hands
Winning of Barbara Worth, The
Without Compromise
Wolf Hunter
Woman in Room 13, The

3863
McKINNELL, Norman*
Downhill (Sir Thomas Berwick)
Hindle Wakes /aka/ Fanny Hawthorne (Nathaniel Jeffcots)

3864
McKINNEY, Nina May (1909-1968)
Hallelujah (Chick)

3865
McKINNON, John*
Vanity Fair (Capt. Machmurdo)

3866
MACKINTOCH, Louise*
Chickie
Stage:
Awful Truth, The (Mrs. Leeson) 28
Houseparty (Mrs. Rutherford) 29
Lost (Mrs. Lansing) 27
Phantom Lover, The (Madame Jattefaux) 28
Playing the Game (Mrs. Loring) 27
Silver Box, The (Mrs. Barthwick) 28
Some Party 22

3867
MACKS, Helen--see: Helen Mack

3868
McLAGLEN, Clifford*
Fight for the Matterhorn, The
White Sheik, The

3869
McLAGLEN, Cyril*
Alf's Button (Sgt. Major)
Balaclava (John Kennedy)
Madame Pompadour (Gogo)
Underground

3870
McLAGLEN, Victor (1886-1959)
Beau Geste (Hank)
Beloved Brute, The
Big Parade, The
Black Watch
Boatswain's Mate, The
Call of the Road, The
Captain Lash
Carnival
Chinese Bungalow, The (Abdul)
Cock-Eyed World, The (Sgt.
  Flagg)
Corinthian Jack (Title role)
Crimson Circle, The
Fighting Heart, The
Gay Corinthian, The
Girl in Every Port, A (Spike Mad-
  der)
Glorious Adventure, The (Bulfinch)
Hangman's House
Happy Days (a principal)
Heartstrings
Hot for Paris
Hunted Woman, The
In the Blood
Isle of Retribution
It's the Old Army Game
King of the Khyber Rifles (Capt.
  Donald King)
Little Brother of God
Loves of Carmen, The (Esca-
  millo)
M' Lord of the White Road
Men of Steel
Mother Machree
Passionate Adventure, The
Percy
Prey of the Dragon
River Pirate
Romance of Old Bagdad, A
Romany, The
Rough and Ready
Sailor Tramp, A
Sez You, Sez Me
Sport of Kings, The
Strong Boy, The
Unholy Three, The (Hercules)
What Price Glory (Sgt. Flagg)
Winds of Chance
Women and Diamonds

3871
McLAINE, Marilyn*
Kiss for Cinderella, A (Gladys)

3872
MacLANE, Barton (1900-1969)
Cocoanuts, The
Debut in 1924
Stage:
Gods of the Lightning (Ward) 28
Subway Express, The (Officer Mul-
  vaney) 29
Trial of Mary Dugan, The (Assistant
  D. A.) 27

3873
McLANE, Mary*
Sparrows /aka/ Human Sparrows (a
  sparrow)
Which Shall It Be?

3874
MACLAREN, Ian*
Monsieur Beaucaire (Duke of Winter-
  set)
Under the Red Robe
Yolanda (Campo Basso)
Stage:
Apothecary, The (Sempronio) 26
Critic, The (Mr. Puff) 25
Dybbuk, The (Meshulach) 25
Electra (Aegisthos) 27
Exiles (Richard Rowan) 25
Fan, The (Francois Trevaux) 21
Furies, The (Dr. Paul Hemingway)
  28
Green Beetle, The (Chang Hong) 24
Green Ring, The (Ivan Yasvein) 22
Grand Street Follies, The 25; 26
Hinder, The (Denton Morgan) 22
Kuan Yin (property man) 26
Lion Tame, The (Lord John Lons-
  dale) 26
Little Clay Cart, The (Charudatta) 24
Makers of Light (David Nellis) 22
Romantic Young Lady, The (the Ap-
  parition) 26
Saint Joan (Bishop of Beauvais) 23

3875
MacLAREN, Mary (1896-)
Across the Continent
Black Swan, The
Face in the Fog, The
Forged Bride, The
Metro player 23
Outcast, The
Road to Divorce, The

Rouge and Riches
Three Musketeers, The (Queen Anne
of Austria)
Under the Red Robe
Universal player 20
Wild Goose, The

3876
McLAUGHLIN, Gibb (1884-)
Carnival
Farmer's Wife, The
Kelly
Madame Pompadour (Comte de
Maurepas)
Nell Gwyn (Duke of York)
Only Way, The (Barsad the spy)
Road to London, The (the Viscount)
White Sheik, The

3877
McLAUGHLIN, Jeff*
Madame Pompadour

3878
McLAUGHLIN, William*
Illusion

3879
McLEAN, D. D.*
Beloved Brute, The

3880
MacLEAN, Douglas (1890-1967)
Bell Boy 13
Carnation Kid, The
Chickens
Divorce Made Easy
Going Up
Hold that Lion!
Home Stretch, The
Hottentot, The
Introduce Me
Jailbird, The
Let It Rain
Let's Be Fashionable
Man of Action, A
Mary of the Movies
Mary's Ankles
Never Say Die
One a Minute
Paramount player 22
Passing Through
Question of Honor, A
Rookie's Return, The
Seven Keys to Baldpate
Soft Cushions
Sunshine Trail, The
That's My Baby

What's Your Husband Doing?
Yankee Consul, The

3881
MacLEAN, Robert*
Seven Keys to Baldpate (William Hal-
lowell Magee)

3882
MacLENNON, Andy*
Blackbird, The (the shadow)
Show, The

3883
MacLEOD, E. E., Jr.*
Loves of Ricardo, The

3884
McLEOD, Gordon*
Only Way, The (Ernest Defarge)
Stage:
Oedipus Rex (Creon) 23

3885
MacLEOD, Janet*
Take Me Home
Win that Girl

3886
McMANUS, George
Great White Way, The

3887
McMASTER, Andrew*
Lost Patrol, The

3888
MacMURRAY, Fred (1908-)
Girls Gone Wild (extra)

3889
McMURRAY, Lillian*
Idle Class, The

3890
McNAMARA, Edward*
Lucky in Love
Stage:
Becky Sharp (Adm. Sir John Hollings-
head) 29
Strictly Dishonorable (Patrolman
Mulligan) 29

3891
McNAMARA, Ted*
Gateway of the Moon
Gay Retreat, The
Monkey Talks, The

Mother Machree
Rich but Honest
Shore Leave
What Price Glory? (Pvt. Kiper)
Why Sailors Go Wrong
Stage:
Battling Butler (Spink) 23
Glory (Alonzo) 22
Up She Goes (Louis Cook) 22

3892
McNAMES, Dorothy*
Happy Days (chorus)

3893
McNAUGHTON, Charles*
Three Live Ghosts (Jimmie Gubbins)
Stage:
Old Bill, M. P. (Bert) 26
Pickwick (Sam Weller) 27
Plain Jane (Lord Gordon Hemmings-
   worth) 24
Right Age to Marry, The (Geordie
   Noodle) 26
Silent House, The (Benson) 28
Three Live Ghosts (Jimmie Gub-
   bins) 20

3894
MACOLLUM, Barry*
Hole in the Wall, The (Dogface)
Stage:
Banshee, The (Tom Scott) 27
Caravan (Jacques O'Moil) 28
Juno and the Paycock (Johnny Boyle)
   26
Loggerheads (Padna Collins) 25
Macbeth (triple role, witch/messen-
   ger/armor-bearer)
Mandarin, The (the artist) 20
Mixed Marriage (Tom Rainey) 20
Mountain Fury (Fenicle) 29
Outside Looking In (Hopper) 25
Shadow, The (Johnny Slocombe) 22

3895
McPHAIL, Addie*
Big Palooka, The
Lunkhead, The

3896
MacPHERSON, Douglas*
Let's Get Married
Stage:
Cousin Sonia (Hubert Carter) 25
Gambling (Braddock) 29
Howdy King (Baron Felipe LaVarra)
   26

Shavings (Leander Babbitt) 20

3897
McQUADE, Edward*
Monster, The

3898
MacQUARRIE, Albert*
Don Q, Son of Zorro (Col. Matsado)
Goucho, The (victim of the black
   doom)
Hunchback of Notre Dame, The
Viking, The

3899
MacQUARRIE, George*
Hole in the Wall, The (inspector)
Idol Dancer, The (Rev. Franklin
   Blythe)
Love Flower, The (Mr. Bevan)
Rejected Woman, The
Uncle Sam of Freedom Ridge

3900
MacQUARRIE, Murdock /aka/ M. J.
   MacQuarrie*
Ashes of Vengeance (Carlotte)
Hidden Woman, The (Iron MacLord)
Only Woman, The

3901
McQUIRE, Tom*
Lights of New York (Police Chief
   Collins)
Spoilers, The (Capt. Stevens)

3902
MacRAE, Gordon*
East Side, West Side
Stage:
Exceeding Small (Lou) 28
John (second guard) 27
Our Betters (first footman) 28

3903
MACSWEENEY, John*
Road to Glory, The (butler)

3904
McWADE, Edward*
Husband Hunter, The (Charles Mack)
Monster, The (Luke Watson)

3905
McWADE, Margaret*
Alice Adams
Broken Barriers
Lost World, The (Mrs. Challenger)

Sundown
Tale of Two Worlds, A (attendant)

3906
McWADE, Robert*
Home Towners, The
New Brooms
Second Youth
Stage:
Crooked Gamblers (Fred Robertson)
  20
Deep Tangled Wildwood (Harvey Wal-
  lick) 23
Deluge, The (Frazer) 22
Devil in the Cheese, The (Mrs.
  Quigley) 26
Home Towners, The (P. H. Ban-
  croft) 26
New Brooms (Thomas Bates) 24
New Toys (George Clark) 24
Old Soak, The (Cousin Webster Par-
  sons) 22
She Stoops to Conquer (Tom Twist)
  24
We've Got to Have Money (Richard
  Walcott) 23

3907
MACY, Carleton*
Seven Keys to Baldpate
Stage:
Mountain Fury (Sheriff Harmon)
  29
Scalawag, The (Jonas Beebe) 27
Scarlet Lily, The (Ira Strong) 27
Skidding (Judge James Hardy) 28
Trouper, The (David Millett) 26
Up the Line (Big Bill) 26

3908
MACY, Cora*
Irene

3909
MADD, Pierette*
Milady
Three Musketeers, The (Constance
  Bonacieux)

3910
MADDEN, Doreen*
Rising of the Moon, The

3911
MADDEN, Golda (1894-   )
Mother of His Children, The
Woman in Room 13, The

3912
MADDEN, Jerry*
Blue Eagle, The (Baby Tom)
Haunted Ship, The

3913
MADDEN, Tom*
Running Wild (truckdriver)

3914
MADDIE, Ginette*
Flood, The

3915
MADDOX, Martha*
Keeper of the Bees, The (Mrs.
  Cameron)
Woman Proof

3916
MADISON, Cleo (1882-1964)
Dangerous Age, The
Girl from Nowhere, The
Ladies Must Live
Lure of Youth, The
Price of Redemption
Retribution
Roughneck, The
Temple of Dawn, The (Anne Steel)
True as Steel
Woman's Woman, A

3917
MADISON, Martha*
Miss Bluebeard
Stage:
Connie Goes Home (Hilda) 23
My Son (Betty Smith) 24
Set a Thief (Rosie Ray) 27

3918
MADISON, Virginia*
Blind Bargain, The (Angela's
  mother)
Everlasting Whisper, The
First Year, The
Heart of Salome, The

3919
MADSEN, Harold*
Han og Hun og Hamlet (He and She
  and Hamlet)
Stage:
Just a Minute (Dick) 28

3920
MAGARILL, Sophie*
New Babylon

3921
MAGEE, Gordon*
Tiger Rose (Hainey)

3922
MAGEE, Virginia*
Bond Boy, The

3923
MAGELIS, Charles*
Merry Widow, The (Flo Epstein)

3924
MAGNESS, Annabelle /aka/ Anna-
belle Magnus*
His Dog
Lovey Mary

3925
MAGNIER, Pierre*
Cyrano de Bergerac

3926
MAGRILL, George*
Enchanted Hill, The
Lord Jim
Vanishing American, The /aka/ The
Vanishing Race
Wild Horse Mesa

3927
MAHONEY, Will*
Lost in the Artic
Stage:
Take the Air ("Happy" Hokum) 27
Vaudeville [Hippodrome] 26
Vaudeville [Palace] 25, 26, 27, 28,
29

3928
MAIA, Marise*
Un Chapeau de Paille d'Italie [The
Italian Straw Hat]

3929
MAIATIAN, Barbara*
Power of Evil, The

3930
MAILES, Charles Hill (1870-
1937)
Bellamy Trial, The (Defense
Atty)
Big Scoop, The
Bitter Apples
Bond Boy, The
Carnation Kid, The
Charge of the Gauchos, The

Chickens
City Gone Wild, A
College Widow, The
Courage
Crimson Runner, The
Drums of Love (Duke of Granada)
Faker, The
Find Your Man
Free to Love (Kenton Crawford)
Give and Take
Go and Get It
Homespun Folks
Home Stretch, The
Lighthouse by the Sea, The
Man in the Saddle, The
Manpower
Mark of Zorro, The (Don Carlos
Pulido)
Name the Man
Number, Please
Old Ironsides
One Stolen Night
Phantom City
Play Safe
Playing with Souls
Queen of the Chorus
Red Hot Dollars
Social Highwayman, The
Ten Dollar Raise, The
Treasure Island (Dr. Livesey)
Unchartered Seas
What a Night!

3931
MAILLARD, Henry*
Passion of Joan of Arc, The

3932
MAILLARD, Monsieur*
Les Miserables (Gillenormand)

3933
MAILLY, Fernand*
Marê Nostrum [Our Sea] (Count Kale-
dine)

3934
MAITLAND, Lauerdale*
Taming of the Shrew, The (Petruchio)

3935
MAITLAND, Richard*
Come to My House
Is Zat So?

3936
MAJA, Zelma*
Affairs of Anatol, The (nurse)

3937
MAJERONI, Mario*
Argentine Love
Enemies of Women (Duke De Delille)
Her Love Story (Prime Minister)
Humming Bird, The (LaRoche)
King on Main Street, The
Little French Girl, The
Partners of the Night
Rubber Heels
Snow Bride, The
Stage:
Casanova (Capt. Michael Echedy) 23
Kongo (Zoombie) 26
Mandarin, The (the stranger) 20
Stripped (M'sieu Orlando) 29

3938
MAKARENKO, Daniel*
Surrender
Stage:
Relations (Mortimer Boasberg) 28

3939
MAKAROFF, V.*
Czar Ivan the Terrible 28

3940
MAKOWSKA, Helen*
Taras Bulba

3941
MALAN, William*
One Man Game, A

3942
MALATESTA, Fred (1889-)
Bardelys the Magnificent (Castel-
    broux)
Best of Luck, The
Big Happiness
Challenge of the Law, The
Forbidden Paradise (French Ambas-
    sador)
Little Lord Fauntleroy (Dick)
Madame Mystery (Man of a Thousand
    Eyes)
Mask, The
Peacock Fan, The
Reckless Age, The
Risky Business
Sins of Rosanne, The

3943
MALIKOFF, H.*
Spy of Madame de Pompadour, The

3944
MALIKOFF, Nikolai*
Apaches of Paris
Kopf Hoch, Charly! [Heads Up,
    Charly!] (Prince Plantonoff)
President, The

3945
MALINOVSKYA, V. S.*
Station Master, The

3946
MALLON, Bobby*
Bouncing Babies
Boxing Gloves
Moan and Groan, Inc.

3947
MALMERFELT, Sixten*
Story of Gösta Berling, The

3948
MALONE, Molly (1895-)
Across the Deadline
Back Stage
Bad Man's Bluff
Bandit Buster
Battling Bunyan
Birds of a Feather
Blazing Away
Bucking the Line
Come in the Kitchen
Freshie, The
Golden Stallion, The [serial]
Her Doctor's Dilemma
It's a Great Life
Just out of College
Little Johnny Jones
Made in Heaven
Mr. Parol and Company
Molly's Millions
Molly's Mumps
Not Guilty
Picture My Astonishment
Poor Relation, A
Rawhide
Red Courage
Round Up, The
Stop Thief!
Sure Fire
Trail of Fate
Universal player 21

3949
MALONEY, Leo D. (1888-1929)
Across the Deadline
Apache Raider

Bar Cross War, The
Border Blackbirds
Boss of Rustler's Roost
Bronc Stomper
Come and Get Me
Deputized
Devil's Twin, The
Don Desperado
Drifter, The
Fatal Sign, The [serial]
Fire Detectives [serial]
.45 Calibre War
Ghost City
Headin' Through
High Hand, The
His Own Law
Huntin' Trouble
King's Creek Law
Long Loop on the Pecos
Loser's End, The
Lost, Strayed or Stolen
Luck and Sand
Man from Hardpan, The
No Man's Woman
Not Built for Running
Outlaw Express, The
Overland Bound
Payable on Demand
Perfect Alibi, The
Ranchers and Rascals
Ridin' Fool, The
Riding Double
Two Guns of Tumbleweed
Vanishing West, The [serial]
Win, Lose or Draw
Yellow Contraband

3950
MALTON, Felicitas*
Mystic Mirror, The

3951
MALTOX, Martha*
Cat and the Canary, The

3952
MAMPORIA, I.*
Caucasian Love

3953
MAN O' WAR (Horse) (1917-
    1947)
Race of the Age, The

3954
MANCE, Gina*
Napoleon

3955
MANDER, Miles /aka/ Luther Miles
    (Lionel Mander) (1888-1946)
As Luther Miles:
Children of Gibeon
Old Arm Chair, The
Palace of Honor
Rank Outsider, A
Road to London, The
As Miles Mander:
Balaclava (Capt. Gardner)
Crooked Billet, The
Doctor's Women, The
Fake, The
First Born, The (Sir Hugo Boycott)
Half a Truth
Lady in Furs, The
London Love
Lovers in Araby
Open Country
Painted Lady, The
Phonofilms
Physician, The
Pleasure Garden, The
Prude's Fall, The
Riding for a King
Temporary Lady, The
Tiptoes

3956
MANDER, Theodore*
First Born, The (Stephen, the first
    born)

3956
MANDY, Jerry*
At Yale
Gay Defender, The
Love and Learn
Love, Live and Laugh
Sap, The
Underworld (Paloma)

3958
MANES, Gina*
Therese Raquin

3959
MANETTI, Lido*
Evening Clothes

3960
MANN, Alice*
West of the Water Tower

3961
MANN, Delbert*
Iron Horse, The (Charles Crocker)

MANN, Frances*
Trailed by Three [serial] (Jane
  Creighton)

3963
MANN, Frankie*
Barriers Burned Away
John Smith
Passionate Pilgrim, The

3964
MANN, Hank (1888-)
Bon Bon Riot
Boob, The
Broadway after Midnight
Dr. Jekyll and Mr. Hyde
Donovan Affair, The
Don't Marry for Money
Empty Hands
Eye for Figures, An
Fall of Eve, The
Fazil (Ali)
Fighting Heart, The
Fox player 25
Garden of Eden, The
Harem Hero
His Bread and Butter
His First Blow Out
Lady Bird
Messenger, The
Morgan's Raiders /aka/ Morgan's
  Last Raid
Nice Baby
Paid to Love (servant)
Pants at Any Price
Patent Leather Kid, The
Quincy Adams Sawyer (Ben Bates)
Should Women Drive?
Skyrocket, The
Smile, Brother, Smile
Sporting Venus, A
Tennek Film Corp. Comedies
Village Blacksmith, The
When Danger Calls
Wings of the Storm

3965
MANN, Harry*
Abysmal Brute, The (Abe Levinsky)
Three Must-Get-Theres, The

3966
MANN, Helen*
Happy Days (chorus)

3967
MANN, Louis*
Father's Day (the father)

Stage:
Milgrim's Progress (David Milgrim)
  24
Nature's Nobleman (Carl Schnitzler)
  21
That French Lady (Karl Kraft) 27
Unwritten Chapter, The (Haym Salo-
  mon) 20
Vaudeville [Hippodrome] 26
Vaudeville [Palace] 26

3968
MANN, Margaret (1868-)
Black Beauty
Call of Home, The
Disraeli (Queen Victoria)
Four Sons
Girl and the Goose, The
Her Sister from Paris
Man, Woman, Marriage
New Disciple, The
Once to Every Woman (Mother Mere-
  dith)
River, The /aka/ La Femme au
  Corbeau

3969
MANNEL, Olga*
Madame Wünscht Keine Kinder [Mad-
  ame Doesn't Want Children] /aka/
  Madame Wants No Children
  (Louise's cook)

3970
MANNERING, Lewin*
Triumph of the Rat, The (Comte
  Henri Mercereau)

3971
MANNERS, David (Rauff de Ryther
  Duan Acklom) (1900-)
Journey's End

3972
MANNERS, John*
Ghost Train, The (Charles Murdock)

3973
MANNERS, Lady Diana*
Glorious Adventure, The (Lady Bea-
  trice Fair)
Virgin Queen, The (Title role)

3974
MANNHEIM, Lucie*
Atlantic [German] (Monica)

3975
MANNING, Aileen*
Beauty's Worth (Aunt Cynthia Whit-
ney)
Bridge of Sighs, The
Enticement
Heart to Heart
Home James
Man, Woman and Sin
Snob, The
Sweetie
Uncle Tom's Cabin (Aunt Ophelia)
Wedding Rings

3976
MANNING, Ambrose*
Squibs (ex-Inspector Robert Lee)

3977
MANNING, Hallie*
New Klondike, The
Stage:
Broadway Whirl, The 21
Ladies on the Jury (Mayme Mixter)
29
Paradise Alley (Little Annie Rooney)
24

3978
MANNING, Jack*
Love Flower, The (Crane's assist-
ant)

3979
MANNING, Mildred*
Fox player 21
Glory of Love, The
While Paris Sleeps (Bébé Larvache)

3980
MANNING, Phillipp*
Atlantic [German] (Kapitaen)

3981
MANON, Marcia (Camille Anke-
wich)*
Greater Glory, The
Ladies Must Live
Love, Live and Laugh
Masquerader, The
Skin Deep
They Had to See Paris (Miss Mason)
Vanishing Pioneer, The (the apron
woman)

3982
MANSFIELD, Duncan*
White Sister, The

3983
MANSFIELD, Martha (1899-1923)
Civilian Clothes (Florence Lan-
ham)
Dr. Jekyll and Mr. Hyde
First National player 23
Fog Bound
Gilded Lies
His Brother's Keeper
Is Money Everything?
Man of Stone
Mothers of Men
Potash and Perlmutter
Queen of the Moulin Rouge
Society Snobs
Till We Meet Again
Warrens of Virginia, The (Agatha
Warren)
Woman in Chains
Women Men Love, The
Wonderful Chance, The

3984
MANSTADT, Margit*
Doctor's Women, The

3985
MANTELL, Robert Bruce (1854-
1928)
Under the Red Robe (Cardinal Riche-
lieu)
Stage:
School for Scandal, The (Snake) 23

3896
MARR, Henry*
Moon of Israel

3987
MARA, Kya*
Bohemian Dancer
Crimson Circle, The
Dancing Vienna

3988
MARATINI, Rosita*
Proud Flesh
Shadows of Paris

3989
MARBA, Fred*
Bardely's the Magnificent

3990
MARBA, Joseph*
Beneath the Law
Diplomats, The

3991
MARBURGH, Bertram*
Affair of the Follies, An
Proud Heart
Stage:
Lancelot and Elaine (the servitor) 21
Squaw Man, The (Andy) 21
Your Woman and Mine (Hon. Amos
    T. Glossup) 22

3992
MARCELLE, Dancer*
Show of Shows, The

3993
MARCH, Frederic (Ernest Frederick
    McIntyre Bickel) (1897-1975)
Dummy, The (Trumbell Meredith)
Footlights and Fools (Gregory Pyne)
Jealousy (Pierre)
Marriage Playground, The (Martin
    Boyne)
Paris Bound (Jim Hutton)
Paying the Piper (debut-extra)
Studio Murder Mystery, The (Richard
    Hardell)
Wild Party, The (Gil Gilmore)
Stage:
Deburau (Victor Hugo) 20
Devil in the Cheese, The (Jimmie
    Chard) 26
Halfcaste, The (Dick Chester) 26
Harvest (Richard Knight) 25
Melody Man, The (Donald Clemens)
    24
Member, Harefoot Theatrical Club
    20
Puppets (Bruno Monte) 25
Shavings (Road Company) 21
Tarnish (Road Company) 23
Zeno 22

3994
MARCHAL, Arlette*
Blonde or Brunette?
Born to the West
Diplomacy
Figaro
Gentleman of Paris, A
Hula (Mrs. Bane)
Madame Sans-Gène (Queen of
    Naples)
MGM player 25
Moon of Israel
Spotlight, The
Terror /aka/ The Perils of Paris
Wings (Celeste)

3995
MARCOUX, Vanni*
Miracle of the Wolves, The

3996
MARCUS, James A. *
Beau Brummel (Snodgrass)
Buck Privates
Captain Salvation
Dick Turpin
Eagle, The (Kyrilla Troekouroff)
Eagle of the Sea, The
Evangeline
Goose Hangs High, The (Elliott Kim-
    berly)
Hell-Bent for Heaven
In Holland
In Old Arizona (blacksmith)
Iron Horse, The (Judge Haller)
Little Lord Fauntleroy (Hobbs)
Oliver Twist (Mr. Bumble)
Revenge
Sadie Thompson (Joe Horn)
Scaramouche (Challfau Binet)
Scarlet Letter, The (French sea cap-
    tain)
Serenade
Vanity Fair (Old Osborne)

3997
MARE ISLAND NAVY BAND
Cock-Eyed World, The

3998
MARENA, Emma*
Trial of Donald Westhof, The

3999
MARETINI, Rosita--see: Rosita
    Maratini

4000
MARGARILL, Dofie*
New Babylon, The

4001
MARGELIS, Charles*
Merry Widow, The

4002
MARGIE, Baby*
Chechahcos, The

4003
MARI, Joseph*
Cossacks, The (Turkish spy)

4004
MARIEVSKY, Josef*
Loves of Zero, The

4005
MARION, Don (1917-)
Children of Divorce (Little Ted)
Golden Bed, The
Golden Princess
Percy
Playing with Souls
Sennett player 20

4006
MARION, Edna (1908-)
Christie Comedies
Family Group, The
Fight Pest, The
Flying Elephants
From Soup to Nuts (maid)
Limousine Love
Loud Speakers
Should Married Men Go Home?
Sinner's Paradise
Stern Brothers Comedies
Still Alarm, The
Sugar Daddies

4007
MARION, Frances (1887-1973)
Little Lord Fauntleroy (Minna's son)

4008
MARION, Frank*
Country Doctor, The
Wreck of the Hesperus, The

4009
MARION, George (1860-1945)
Anna Christie
Bishop Murder Case, The
Clothes Make the Pirate
Evangeline
Girl I Loved, The
King of Kings, The (bit)
Loco Luck
Reckless Lady, The
Sea Bat, The
Texas Steer, A
Tumbleweeds
White Monkey, The
Wise Guy, The

4010
MARION, Oscar*
Taras Bulba

4011
MARION, William*
Hope Diamond Mystery, The /aka/
   The Romance of the Hope Diamond
   [serial]

4012
MARIOTTI, Frederick*
Marê Nostrum [Our Sea] (Toni)

4013
MARIS, Livia*
Last Days of Pompeii, The (Julie)

4014
MARIS, Mona (Maria Capdevielle)
   (1903-)
Bondage
La Bonne Botesse
Die Drei Frauen von Urban Hell
Die Leibenen
Der Marquis D'Eon
Romance of the Rio Grande
Spy of Madame de Pompadour, The
Under a Texas Moon

4015
MARKS, Willis*
Chickens
Dancin' Fool (Meeks)
Dramatic Life of Abraham Lincoln,
   The /aka/ Abraham Lincoln (Sec-
   retary Seward)
Unknown Soldier, The
Which Shall It Be?

4016
MARKSTEIN, Mrs.*
Die Freudlose Gasse [The Joyless
   Street] /aka/ The Street of Sor-
   row (Mrs. Merkl)

4017
MARLOW, Tony*
Racket, The

4018
MARLOWE, Alona*
Argyle Case, The (Kitty)

4019
MARLOWE, James*
Back Home and Broke
Stage:
Clinging Vine, The (Francis Milton)
   22
Go Easy Mabel (Edward Drenton) 22
Mary (Mr. Goddard) 20

4020
MARLOWE, June (1907-)
Alias the Deacon
Below the Line
Branded Men, The
Clash of the Wolves, The
Code of the Air
Don Juan (Trusia)
Fangs of Justice
Fighting Blood [serial] (bit)
Find Your Man
Foreign Legion, The
Fourth Commandment, The
Free Lips
Grip of the Yukon, The
Life of Reily, The
Man Without a Conscience, The
Night Cry, The
On the Stroke of Twelve
Pleasure Buyers, The
Their Hour
Tracked in the Snow Country
When a Man's a Man
Wife Who Wasn't Wanted, The
Wild Beauty

4021
MARMONT, Percy (1883-)
Aloma of the South Seas (Bob Holden)
Branded Woman, The
Broken Laws
Clean Heart, The
Daddy's Gone A-Hunting
Dead Men Tell No Tales
Enemy Sex, The
Fine Clothes
First Woman, The
Idle Tongues
If Winter Comes
Infatuation
Introspection
Just a Woman
K-the Unknown
Lady of the Lake, The
Legend of Hollywood, The
Light that Failed, The
Lord Jim
Mantrap (Ralph Prescott)
Marriage Cheat, The
Married People
Miracle of Life, The
Price, The
Rich and Strange
San Francisco Nights
Shooting of Dan McGrew, The (Jim)
Silver King, The
Sir or Madam
Sporting Duchess, The

Street of Forgotten Men, The
Stronger Will, The /aka/ The Will
  of a Woman
Warning, The
What's Your Reputation Worth?
Wife Against Wife
Without Benefit of Clergy
Woman's Faith, A
Yellow Stockings

4022
MARNEY, Jacques*
Madame Sans-Gene (Savary)

4023
MAROKOFF, M.*
Yellow Ticket, The

4024
MARRIOTT, Moore (George Thomas
  Moore-Marriott) (1885-1949)
Every Mother's Son (Nobby)
Flying Scotsman, The (Bob White)
Lady from the Sea, The (Old Roberts)
Monkey's Paw, The (father)
Sweeny Todd
Widdecombe Affair (Uncle Tom Cob-
  leigh)

4025
MARS, Severin*
J'Accuse

4026
MARSH, Mae (Mary Warne Marsh)
  (1895-1968)
Arabella
Daddies
Flames of Passion
Little 'fraid Lady
Little Liar, The
Nobody's Kid
Paddy the Next Best Thing (Paddy)
Racing Through
Rat, The (Odile Etrange)
Tides of Passion
Till We Meet Again
White Rose, The (Bessie Williams)
Woman's Secret, A

4027
MARSH, Marguerite (1892-)
Boomerang Bill
Face to Face
Idol of the North (Gloria Waldron)
Iron to Gold
Lion's Mouse, The
Oh, Mary, Be Careful

Phantom Honeymoon
Wits vs. Wits
Women Men Love

4028
MARSH, Mildred*
Country Flapper, The

4029
MARSHALL, Clark*
Voice of the City
Stage:
Scarlet Fox, The (Tommy McGuire)
  28
Weather Clear-Track Fast (Johnny
  Careleson) 27

4030
MARSHALL, Herbert (1890-1966)
Dawn
Letter, The
Mumsie (Col. Armytage)
Stage:
Fedora (Count Loris Ipanoff) 22
High Road, The (Duke of Warrington)
  28
Queen Was in the Parlor, The -
  London 26
These Charming People (Geoffrey
  Allen) 25
Voice from the Minaret, The (An-
  drew Fabian) 22

4031
MARSHALL, Madeleine*
April Folly (Lady Diana Mannister)
Stage:
Cave Girl, The (Elsie Case) 20

4032
MARSHALL, Perle*
Wizard, The

4032a
MARSHALL, Terry*
Too Much Business

4033
MARSHALL, Tully (Tully M. Phil-
  lips) 1864-1943)
Alias Jimmy Valentine (Avery)
Along Came Ruth
Barefoot Boy, The
Beautiful and Damned, The
Beware of Widows
Brass Bottle, The
Bridge of San Luis Rey, The (towns-
  man)

Broken Hearts of Broadway
Cat and the Canary, The (Roger
  Crosby)
Clothes Make the Pirate
Conquest
Covered Wagon, The (Jim Bridges)
Cup of Life, The
Dancin' Fool, The (Harkins)
Dangerous Maid
Dangerous Trails
Defying Destiny
Deserted at the Alter
Double Speed
Dream of Love
Drums of Love (Bopi)
Excuse My Dust (Pres. Mutchler)
Fools and Riches
Fools of Fortune
For Sale (Harrison Bates)
Gift Supreme, The (Irving Stagg)
Good Men and True
Gorilla, The
Hail the Woman
Half-Way Girl, The
He Who Gets Slapped (Count Mancini)
Her Beloved Villain
Her Big Night
Her Temporary Husband
Hold Your Breath
Honest Hutch
Hunchback of Notre Dame, The (Lou-
  is XI)
Is Matrimony a Failure?
Jim, the Conqueror
Ladder Jinx, The
Law of the Lawless, The
Let's Go!
Little 'fraid Lady
Lotus Blossom, The
Lying Truth
Mad Hour, The
Mam'selle Jo
Marriage Chance, The
Merry Widow, The (Baron Sadoja)
Mysterious Dr. Fu Manchu, The
  /aka/ The Insidious Dr. Fu Man-
  chu
Old Loves and New /aka/ The Desert
  Healer
Only a Shop Girl
Pace that Thrills, The
Pagan Passions
Penrod
Perfect Crime, The
Ponjola (Count Blauhimal)
Queen Kelly (Jan Vryheid)
Reckless Romance
Redskin, The (Navajo Jim)

Richard, the Lion-Hearted (the her-
  mit)
Ridin' Kid from Powder River
Right of the Strongest, The
Show of Shows, The
Sick Abed
Silent Years
Skin Deep   /
Slim Princess, The
Smouldering Fires
Stranger, The
Super Sex
Talker, The
Temporary Marriage
Three Musketeers, The
Thunderbolt
Thundergate
Tiger Rose (Hector McCollins)
Too Much Business
Torrent, The (Don Andres)
Trail of '98, The (Salvation Jim)
Twinkletoes (Dad Minasi)
Under a Texas Moon
Village Blacksmith, The
What Happened to Rosa?
Without Compromise

4034
MARSHALL, Virginia*
Daddy's Gone A-Hunting
East Lynne (Little Isabel)
How Baxter Buttered In
My Own Pal

4035
MARSTINI, Marie*
Blood and Sand (El Carnacione)
Hot for Paris
Lover of Camille, The
Redeeming Sin, The
We Americans

4036
MARSTINI, Rosita*
Big Parade, The (French mother)
Evil Eye, The [serial]
Serenade

4037
MARTAN, Manilla*
Son of Tarzan, The [serial] (Meriem,
  the woman)

4038
MARTAN, Nita*
Chasing Rainbows
Lady Be Good
Twin Beds

Stage:
When You Smile (Elaine LeMar) 25

4039
MARTELL, Alphonse*
Divine Sinner, The (Paul Coudert)
Dream of Love
Night Bird, The
Paid to Love (Michael's valet)

4040
MARTENSON, Mona*
Sealed Lips
Story of Gösta Berling, The (Count-
  ess Ebba Dohna)

4041
MARTIN, Buddy*
David Copperfield

4042
MARTIN, Christopher*
Rescue, The

4043
MARTIN, Duke*
Across to Singapore
City Gone Wild, A
Danger Street
Flying Romeos
Fortune Hunter, The
In Old Arizona (cowboy)
Marriage By Contract
Moran of the Marines
True Heaven
We're in the Air Now

4044
MARTIN, Hiram*
Luck of the Navy, The (the bruiser)

4045
MARTIN, Joe (Ape)
Adventures of Tarzan [serial]
Revenge of Tarzan, The /aka/ The
  Return of Tarzan

4046
MARTIN, Townsend*
Cradle Buster, The
Grit (Flashy Joe)
Second Fiddle

4047
MARTIN, Vivian (1893-)
His Official Wife
Husbands and Wives
Mother Eternal

Pardon My French
Song of the Soul
Stage:
Castle (Jean Farquhar) 27
Half a Widow (Antoinette) 27
Hearts Are Trumps! (Arlette Mil-
  lois) 27
Just Married (Roberta Adams) 21
Marry the Man (Mollie Jeffries) 29
Mrs. Dave's Defense (Janet Col-
  quhoun) 28
Puppy Love (Jean Brent) 26
Wild Westcotts, The (Agatha West-
  cott) 23

4048
MARTINDEL, Edward (1876-1955)
Athalie
Aviator, The
Call of the North
Captain Swift
Children of Divorce (Tom Larrabee)
Clarence
Companionate Marriage
Compromise
Daughter of Luxury, A
Day of Faith, The
Desert Bride
Desert Song, The (Gen. Birabeau)
Devil's Appletree, The
Dixie Handicap, The
Dixie Merchant, A
Duchess of Buffalo, The
Ducks and Drakes
Everybody's Acting
Fashions for Women
Footlights and Fools (Chandler Cun-
  ningham)
Forbidden Fruit
Furnace, The
Garden of Eden, The
Glory of Clementina, The
Hail the Woman
Hard Boiled Rose
In Old Kentucky
Lady Windemere's Fan (Lord Augus-
  tus)
Little Eva Ascends
Lonesome Ladies
Lovers
Love's Whirlpool
Man Without a Country, The /aka/
  As No Man Has Loved
Manslaughter (Wiley)
Midnight
Misfit Wife, The
Modern Love
Nice People

On Trial (Dr. Morgan)
Singing Fool, The (Marcus)
Song of the West (Colonel)
Sporting Venus, A
Taxi! Taxi!
Tony Runs Wild
Venus of Venice
Very Idea, The
We Americans
White Flower
Why Be Good?
Woman Who Did Not Care, The
You Never Can Tell
You'd Be Surprised

4049
MARTINELLI, Alfredo*
Romola (bit)
White Sister, The (Alfredo de Ferice)

4050
MARTINELLI, Giovanni*
Three Musketeers, The (Porthos)
Vesti la giubba

4051
MARUS, Gina*
Shadows of Fear

4052
MARUSON*
Battleship Potemkin

4053
MARVIN, Grace*
Phantom of the Opera, The (Martha)

4054
MARX, Chico (Leonard Marx) (1891-
  1961)
Cocoanuts, The (Willie the Wop)
Stage:
Animal Crackers (Emanuel Ravelli) 28
Cocoanuts, The (Willie the Wop)

4055
MARX, Groucho (Julius Henry Marx)
  (1895-)
Cocoanuts, The (Henry W. Schlem-
  mer)
Stage:
Animal Crackers (Capt. Spalding) 28
Cocoanuts, The (Henry W. Schlem-
  mer) 25

4056
MARX, Harpo (Adolph Arthur Marx)
  (1893-1964)

Cocoanuts, The (Silent Sam)
Too Many Kisses (the village Peter
    Pan)
Stage:
Animal Crackers (the professor) 28
Cocoanuts, The (Silent Sam) 25

4057
MARX, Zeppo (Herbert Marx)
    (1901-   )
Cocoanuts, The (Jamison)
Stage:
Animal Crackers (Jamison) 28
Cocoanuts, The (Jamison) 25

4058
MASOKHA, Pyotr*
Arsenal

4059
MASON, Buddy*
College

4060
MASON, Dan*
Chinese Parrot, The
Fire Brigade, The
Out All Night
Sally (Pops Shendorf)

4061
MASON, Haddon (1898-   )
Dawn (German A. P. M.)
Every Mother's Son (Jonathan Brent)
Triumph of the Scarlet Pimpernel,
    The (Tallien)

4062
MASON, James*
Across to Singapore (Finch)
Alias the Lone Wolf
Back to God's Country
Barriers Burned Away
Beggars on Horseback
Big Killing, The
Black Lightning (Jim Howard)
Chicago after Midnight
Dark Skies
Dead Man's Curve
Flying Marine, The
For Heaven's Sake
Godless Men
Heritage of the Desert, The
King of Kings, The (Gestas)
Last of the Duanes
Let It Rain
Long, Long Trail, The
Mysterious Rider, The

Old Clothes (Dapper Dan)
Old Homestead, The
Penalty, The (Peter)
Phantom City
Sage Hen, The
Sally's Shoulder
Scars of Jealousy
Show of Shows, The
Two Weeks with Pay
Under the Rouge
Wanderer of the Wasteland, The
    (Guerd Larey)
Why Worry?

4063
MASON, LeRoy (1903-1947)
Avenging Shadow, The
Closed Gates
Golden Shackles
Hit of the Show
Inside Prison Walls
Law's Lash, The
PDC player 27
Revenge
Viking, The

4064
MASON, Myrna*
Happy Days (chorus)

4065
MASON, Reginald*
Highest Bidder, The
Two Weeks
Stage:
Caste (Col. Erskine Dalbeatie Far-
    quhar) 27
Changelings, The (Fenwick Faber) 23
Creaking Chair, The (Edwin Latter)
    26
Dark Angel, The (Hilary Trent) 25
Dover Road, The (Leonard) 21
Fall of Eve, The (Larry Webb) 25
Heavy Traffic (Malcolm West) 28
Immoral Isabella (King Ferdinand of
    Aragon) 27
Locked Door, The (Frank Babbington)
    24
Man in Evening Clothes (D'Allouville)
    24
Mirage, The (Wallace Stuart) 20
Pygmalion (Henry Higgins) 26
Right You Are (If You Think You
    Are) (Lamberto Laudisi) 27
Security (Ronnie Newton) 29
Tiger Cats (Count Bernard De-
    Vauzelle) 24
You and I (Geoffrey Nichols) 23

4066
MASON, Shirley (Leona Fulgarth)
   (1900-)
Annie Against the World
Curly Top
Dark Skies
Desert Gold (Mercedes Castanada)
Don Juan's Three Nights
Eleventh Hour, The
Ever Since Eve
Flame of Youth, The
Flying Marine, The
Fox player 23
Girl o' My Heart
Great Diamond Mystery, The
Her Elephant Man
Jackie
Lamplighter, The
Let It Rain
Lights of the Desert
Little Miss Smiles
Little Wanderer, The
Lord Jim
Love Bound
Love Letter
Love Time
Love's Harvest
Merely Mary Ann
Molly and I
Mother Heart, The
My Husband's Wives
New Teacher, The
Pawn Ticket No. 210
Queenie
Ragged Heiress, The
Rich Men's Shoes
Rose of the Tenements
Runaway Girls
Sally in Our Alley
Scandal Proof
Scarlet Honeymoon
Shirley of the Circus
Show of Shows, The
Sin Cargo
So This Is Love
So This Is Paris
South Sea Love
Star Dust Trail
Stranded
Sweet Rosie O'Grady
Talker, The
That French Lady
Treasure Island (Jim Hawkins)
Very Truly Yours
Vultures of the Sea [serial]
What Fools Men
Wife's Relations, The
Wing Toy

Wreck, The
Youth Must Have Love

4067
MASSART, Mary*
Four Feathers, The (Ethne Eustace)

4068
MASSINE, Leonide*
Versailles

4069
MASTRIPIETRI, Augusto*
Messalina

4070
MATA, Yama*
River's End, The

4071
MATCHI*
Moana

4072
MATHE, Ed*
Two Little Vagabonds (Robert Dar-
   ville)

4073
MATHER, Aubrey (1885-1958)
Young Woodley

4074
MATHEWS, Dorothy*
Girl in Every Port, A

4075
MATHOT, Leon*
Appassionata
Count of Monte Cristo, The (Edmond
   Dantes)
Daughter of Israel, A

4076
MATIESEN, Otto (1893-)
Behind Closed Doors
Beloved Rogue, The (Olivier)
Bride of the Storm
Captain Blood (Judge Jeffries)
Dangerous Maid
Dawn of Tomorrow, The
Desert Bride
Folly of Vanity
General Crack (Col. Gaber)
Happy Warrior, The
Last Moment, The
Missing Man, The
Money to Burn

Napoleon and Josephine
Napoleon's Barber
Parisian Love (Apache leader)
Prisoners
Revelation
Road to Romance, The
Sackcloth and Scarlet
Saint Elmo
Salvation Hunters, The
Scaramouche (Phillipe de Vilmorin)
Scarlet Lady
Sheriff of San Juan, The
Show of Shows, The
Strange Cargo
Surrender
Tell-Tale Heart, The
Too Many Crooks
Vanity Fair (Napoleon)
Water Cross, The
West of Chicago
While London Sleeps
Woman from Moscow

4077
MATTHEWS, A. E. (1869-1960)
British films in the 20s
Stage:
Bulldog Drummond (Capt. Hugh
   Drummond) 21
First Mrs. Fraser, The (James
   Fraser) 29
Happy Husband, The (Harvey Town-
   send) 27
Heavy Traffic (Ralph Corbin) 28
Interference (Philip Voaze) 27
Last of Mrs. Cheyney, The (Charles)
   25
Peg o' My Heart (Jerry) 21
Serena Blandish (Martin) 29
This Was a Man (Edward Churt) 26

4078
MATTHEWS, Dorcas*
Blood and Sand (Senora Nacional)
Vanity Fair (Lady Jane)
Woman in the Suitcase, The

4079
MATTHEWS, Dorothy*
Son of the Gods (Alice Hart)

4080
MATTHEWS, Jessie (1907-)
Beloved Vagabond, The (bit)
Straws in the Wind (bit)
Stage:
Charlot Revue, The 26
Earl Carroll's Vanities 27

Music Box Revue (chorus and Ger-
   trude Lawrence's understudy) 23
This Year of Grace 28
Wake Up and Dream 29

4081
MATTHEWS, William*
Squibs (Peters)

4082
MATTIMORE, Van--see: Richard
   Arlen

4083
MATTONI, André*
Midsummer Night's Dream, A (Ly-
   sander)
Youth Astray

4084
MATTOX, Martha (-1938)
Angel of Crooked Street
Beauty's Worth (Aunt Elizabeth Whit-
   ney)
Big Diamond Robbery, The
Bit of Heaven, A
Butterfly Man, The
Cat and the Canary, The (Mammy
   Pleasant)
Christine of the Big Tops
Conflict
Cumberland Romance, A
Dangerous Innocence
East Lynne (Cornelia Carlyle)
Everybody's Sweetheart
Fast Worker, The
Finger Prints
Firebrand Trevision
Fools for Luck (Mrs. Simpson)
Forest Havoc
Girl O' My Heart
Hands of Nara
Head Man, The (a twin)
Hearts Aflame
Her Wild Oat
Hero, The
Home Maker, The
Huckleberry Finn
I'll Show You the Town
Infatuation
Keeper of the Bees, The
Kentucky Courage
Little Shepherd of Kingdom Come, The
Look Your Best
Love Me and the World Is Mine
Lovey Mary
Married Flapper, The
Maytime (Mathilda)

Montmartre Rose
Naughty Duchess, The
Nut Cracker /aka/ You Can't Fool
  Your Wife
Oh, Doctor!
Old Lady 31
Penrod and Sam
Restless Souls
Rich Men's Wives
Singapore Mutiny
Shameless Behavior
Snowbound
Son of Wallingford, The (Mrs. Cur-
  tis)
Thirteenth Juror, The
Three Wise Fools
Top O' the Morn
Torrent, The (Bernarda Brull)
Waning Sex, The
Wolf Hunter
Yankee Senor, The

4085
MATTRAW, Scott*
Thief of Bagdad, The (Eunnuch)
Two Lovers (Dandermonde innkeeper)

4086
MATTYASOVSKY, I.*
Paul Street Boys, The

4087
MATURIN, Eric*
His House in Order (Major Maure-
  warde)

4088
MAUDE, Cyril (1862-1951)
Grumpy
Iron Horse, The
Stage:
Aren't We All (Lord Grenham) 23
If Winter Comes (Mark Sabre) 23
These Charming People (Sir George
  Crawford Bart, M.P.) 25

4089
MAUDE, Joan*
This Freedom (Hilda)

4090
MAULE, Vee*
Happy Days (chorus)

4091
MAUPIN, Ernest*
Daughter of Israel, A

4092
MAUPIN, Georges*
Miracle of the Wolves, The

4093
MAURUS, Gerda*
Frau im Mond [Woman in the Moon]
Spione [Spies]

4094
MAXAM, Lola*
Two Doyles, The

4095
MAXAM, Louella*
Short Westerns (26)
Vanishing Trails [serial]

4096
MAXIMILIAN, Max*
Das Schiff der Verlorenen Menschen
  [The Ship of Lost Souls] /aka/ Le
  Navire des Hommes Perdus [The
  Ship of Lost Men] (Second Mate)

4097
MAXIMOVA, E.*
Village of Sin, The

4098
MAXUDIAN*
Arab, The (the Governor)
Venus

4099
MAXWELL*
I Want My Man

4100
MAXWELL, Edwin (1890-1948)
Doctor's Dilemma, The
Doctor's Secret, The
Donovan Affair, The
Easy Come, Easy Go
Gorilla, The
Jazz Singer, The
John Ferguson
Taming of the Shrew, The (Baptista)
Stage:
Cherry Orchard, The (Lopakhin) 28
Dr. David's Dad (Moritz Koppler) 24
Donovan Affair, The (Prof. Donovan)
  26
Easy Come, Easy Go (Dr. Jasper) 25
Lady of the Lamp, The (Lao Tzu
  Chung) 20
Merton of the Movies (Sigmund Rosen-
  blatt) 22

Taps (Capt. von Bannewitz) 25

(Villefort)

4101
MAY, Ann*
Dangerous Maid
Half-Breed, The (Doll Pardeau)
Paramount player 21
Peaceful Valley
Thundering Hoofs
Waking up the Town

4102
MAY, Doris*
Boy Crazy
Common Law, The
Deadwood Coach, The
Eden and Return
Foolish Age, The
Foolish Matrons
Gay and Devilish
Gunfighter, The
Jailbird, The
Let's Be Fashionable
Mary's Ankles
Paramount player 21
Peck's Bad Boy
Rookie's Return, The
Tea with a Kick
Understudy, The
Why Do We Live?

4103
MAY, Gustav*
Jew of Mestri, The (Salanio)

4104
MAY, Mia*
Dragon's Claw, The
Tragödie der Liebe [Tragedy of
    Love] (Countess Manon de Moreau)

4105
MAYALL, Herschel*
Arabian Love
Calvert's Valley
Daredevil Jack [serial]
Great Power, The
Isle of Lost Ships, The (Capt. Clark)
Queen of Sheba, The
Thirty Days
Wild Bill Hickok
Stage:
Great Power, The (Committee Chair-
    man) 28

4106
MAYER, Albert*
Count of Monte Cristo, The [serial]

4107
MAYHEW, Kate*
Tongues of Flame
Stage:
Beaux' Stratagem, The (a country-
    woman) 28
Billeted (Mrs. Brace) 22
Caravan (Concha) 28
Checkerboard, The (Mrs. Taylor) 20
Father, The (Margaret) 28
Jonesy (Katie) 29
Light of Asia (outcast woman) 28
Mecca (Zarka) 20
Only 38 (Mrs. Newcomb) 21
Small Timers, The (Mrs. Duggan) 25
Vermont (Jane Seldon) 29
Wisdom Tooth, The (Mrs. Poole) 26
Wonderful Visit, The (Mrs. Hinijer)
    24

4108
MAYNARD, Ken (1895-1973)
[Horse: Tarzan]
Between Fighting Men
California Mail, The
Canyon of Adventure, The
Cheyenne
Code of the Scarlet
Demon Rider, The (Davis)
Devil's Saddle
$50,000 Reward (Davis)
Fighting Courage
Glorious Trail
Grey Vulture, The (Davis)
Gun Gospel
Haunted Range, The (Davis)
Janice Meredith (Paul Revere)
Land Beyond the Law
Lawless Legion, The
Lucky Larkin
North Star
Overland Stage, The
Phantom City
Red Raiders, The
Royal Rider
Senor Americano
Senor Daredevil
Somewhere in Sonora
Unknown Cavalier, The
Upland Rider
Wagon Master, The
Wagon Show, The

4109
MAYNARD, Kermit*
Prince of the Plains, A

Trem Carr series

4110
MAYNARD, Tex*
Gun-Hand Garrison
Prince of the Plains, A
Ranger Fighter, The [serial]
Ridin' Luck
Wanderer of the West
Wild Born

4111
MAYNE, Eric*
Barriers Burned Away
Black Oxen (Chancellor)
Blackbird, The (a sightseer)
Cameo Kirby
Christian, The (doctor)
Conquering Power, The (Victor Gran-
  det)
East Lynne (Earl of Mount Severn)
Extra Girl, The
Goldfish, The
Hangman's House
Human Wreckage
My American Wife (Carlos De Gros-
  sa)
Prodigal Daughters (Dr. Marco
  Strong)
Suzanna
Yankee Consul, The

4112
MAYO, Christine*
Don't Marry for Money
For Sale (Mrs. Winslow)
Shock, The (Anne Vincent)

4113
MAYO, Frank (1856-1963)
Across the Deadline
Afraid to Fight
Altar Stairs, The
Barriers Burned Away
Blazing Trail, The
Bolted Door, The
Burnt Wings
Caught Bluffing
Colorado
Doctor Jim
Doughboys, The
Fighting Lover
First Degree, The
Flaming Hour, The
Girl in 29, The
Go Straight
Hitchin' Posts, The
Honor Bound

If I Marry Again
Legally Dead
Lew Tyler's Wives
Magnificent Brute, The
Man Who Married His Own Wife, The
Marriage Pit, The
Out of the Silent North
Passionate Youth
Peddler of Lies, The
Perfect Flapper, The
Price She Paid, The
Red Lane, The
Shark Master, The
Six Days
Slippery Tongue
Souls for Sale (Tom Holby)
Then Came the Woman
Through the Eyes of Men
Tiger True
Tracked to Earth
Unknown Lover
Wild Oranges
Wolf Law, The
Woman on the Jury, The

4114
MAZETTI, Georgia*
Tiger Rose

4115
MEADOWS, George*
Midnight Express, The

4116
MEAKIN, Charles*
Marriage Clause, The
Upstage

4117
MEDCROFT, Russell*
Wild, Wild Susan
Stage:
Golden Days 21
Sonny 21

4118
MEEHAN, Lew*
Blazing Arrows
Should Tall Men Marry?
West of Hot Dog

4119
MEEK, Donald (1880-1946)
Hole in the Wall, The (Goofy)
Six Cylinder Love
Stage:
Broken Dishes (Cyrus Bumpstead) 29
Easy Terms (Ed) 25

Fool's Bells (Mr. Gillicuddy) 25
Hottentot, The (Swift) 20
Ivory Door, The (Old Beppo) 27
Jonesy (Henry Jones) 29
Little Old New York (Bunny Waters) 20
Love 'em and Leave 'em (Lem Woodruff) 26
Mr. Moneypenny (John Jones) 28
Potters, The (Pa Potter) 23
Shelf, The (Rev. Herbert Chetswold) 26
Six Cylinder Love (Richard Burton) 21
Spread Eagle (Mike Riordan) 27
Tweedles (Philemon) 23

4120
MEEKER, George (1904-)
Chicken a la King
Escape, The
Four Sons
Girl Shy Cowboy
Mr. Romeo
Thief in the Dark, A
Stage:
Back Here (Peter Linden) 28
Conflict (Chet Touteen) 29
Judy (Tom Stanton) 27
Judy Drops In (Tom Danforth) 24
Lady's Virtue, A (Ralph Lucas) 25

4121
MEEKER, John*
Four Sons

4122
MEERY, Ila*
Prinzessin Olala [Princess Olala] /aka/ Art of Love (Hedy)

4123
MEHAFFEY, Blanche*
Battling Orioles, The
Princess from Hoboken
Proud Heart
Take It from Me
White Sheep, The
Woman of the World, A

4124
MEIGHAN, Thomas (1879-1936)
Admirable Crichton, The
Alaskan, The
Argyle Case, The (Alexander Kayton)
Bachelor Daddy
Back Home and Broke
Blind Alleys
Canadian, The

Cappy Ricks
City Gone Wild, A
City of Silent Men, The
Civilian Clothes (Capt. Sam McGinnis)
Coming Through
Confidence Man, The
Conquest of Canaan
Conrad in Quest of His Youth (Capt. Conrad Werrener)
Easy Road, The
Frontier of the Stars (Buck Leslie)
Hollywood
Homeward Bound
If You Believe It, It's So
Irish Luck
Man Who Found Himself, The
Man Who Saw Tomorrow, The
Manslaughter (Daniel O'Bannon)
Mating Call, The
Ne'er-Do-Well, The
New Klondike, The
Old Home Week
Our Leading Citizen
Pied Piper Malone
Prince There Was, A
Racket, The
Tin Gods (Roger Drake)
Tongues of Flame
Two Arabian Nights
We're All Gamblers
White and Unmarried
Why Change Your Wife? (Robert Gordon)
Woman Proof

4125
MEINERT, Rudolf*
Eleven Who Were Royal

4126
MEINHARD, Edith*
Diary of a Lost Girl

4127
MELCHIOR, Georges*
Atlantide (Lt. Saint Avit)

4128
MELESH, Alex*
His Private Life
Marquis Preferred

4129
MELISH, Fuller, Jr.*
Applause (Hitch Nelson)

4130
MELLER, Edith*
Die Bargkatze /aka/ The Mountain
  Cat; The Wildcat (Lilli)

4131
MELLER, Raquel*
Carmen (Title role)
Imperial Violets
Oppressed, The
La Venenosa
Violette Imperiale
Stage:
Untitled One-Woman show 26

4132
MELMERFELT, Sixten*
Story of Gösta Berling (Melchior Sin-
  claire)

4133
MELVILLE, Emelie*
Illusion

4134
MELVILLE, Josie*
Treasure Island (Mrs. Hawkins)

4135
MENDEZ, Lola*
Chicago after Midnight
Headin' for Danger

4136
MENDEZ, Lucila /aka/ Lucille*
Bigger than Barnum's
Coney Island
Stage:
Little Jessie James (Lucila) 24
Merry Merry (Conchita Murphy) 25
My Girl Friday (Frances Mordaunt)
  29

4137
MENJOU, Adolphe (Adolph Jean Men-
  jou) (1890-1963)
Ace of Cads, The
Are Parents People?
Bachelor Girl
Bella Donna
Blonde or Brunette?
Broadway after Dark
Broken Barriers
Clarence
Courage
Eternal Flame, The (Duc de Lange-
  ais)
Evening Clothes

Faith Healer, The
Fashions in Love
Fast Mail, The
Fast Set, The (Ernest Steele)
For Sale (Joseph Hudley)
Forbidden Paradise (Lord Chamber-
  lain)
Gentleman of Paris, A
Grand Duchess and the Waiter, The
Head over Heels
His Private Life
Is Matrimony a Failure?
King on Main Street, The
Kiss, The
Kiss in the Dark, A
L'Enigmatique (Mr. Parker)
Lost, a Wife
Marquis Preferred
Marriage Cheat, The
Marriage Circle, The (Prof. Joseph
  Stock)
Night of Mystery, A
Open All Night
Paramount player 1927
Pink Gods
Rupert of Hentzau (Count Rischen-
  heim)
Serenade
Service for Ladies
Shadows of Paris
Sheik, The (Raoul de St. Hubert)
Singed Wings
Sinners in Silk
Social Celebrity, A
Sorrows of Satan, The (Prince Lucio
  de Rimarez)
Spanish Dancer, The (Don Sallustre)
Swan, The
Ten Months
Three Musketeers, The (King Louis
  XIII)
Through the Back Door (James Brew-
  ster)
Tiger Lady, The
Woman of Paris, A (Pierre Revel)
World's Applause, The

4138
MENJOU, Henri*
Blonde or Brunette?
Paramount player 26

4139
MERCANTOR, Jean*
Two Little Vagabonds (Master Gerald
  Thornton)
Venus

4140
MERCER, Beryl (1882-1939)
Christian, The (Liza)
Mother's Boy (Mrs. O'Day)
Seven Day's Leave
Three Live Ghosts (Mrs. Gubbins)
We Americans
Stage:
Bit O'Love, A (Mrs. Burlacombe) 25
Brass Buttons (Mrs. Flynn) 27
Ever Green Lady, The (Madame O'-
   Halloran) 22
Fool's Bells (Mrs. Carey) 25
49ers, The 22
Outward Bound (Mrs. Midget) 24
Pygmalion (Mrs. Pearce) 26
Queen Victoria (Alexandrina Victoria)
   23
Right You Are (If You Think You
   Are) (Signora Frola) 27
Three Live Ghosts (Mrs. Gubbins) 20

4141
MERCIER, Louis*
Tiger Rose (Frenchie)

4142
MEREDITH, Charles (1890-1964)
Beautiful Liar, The
Beyond
Cave Girl, The
Cradle, The
Hail the Woman
In Hollywood with Potash and Perl-
   mutter
Judy of Rogue's Harbor
Ladder of Lies
Little 'Fraid Lady
Paramount player 21
Perfect Woman, The
Romantic Adventuress, An
Simple Souls
That Something
Woman, Wake Up!
Stage:
Starlight (Lucien) 25

4143
MEREDITH, Lois*
Headless Horseman, The
Stage:
Czarina, The (Annie Jaschikova) 22
Number 7 (Rose Ackroyd) 26

4144
MERELLE, Claude*
Milady

4145
MERKEL, Una (1903-)
Double for Lillian Gish
Fifth Horseman, The (MacMahon)
Love's Old Sweet Song
Way Down East (extra)
White Rose, The (extra)
Stage:
Coquette (Betty Lee Reynolds) 27
Gossipy Sex, The (Anna Sterling)
   27
Salt Water (Marion Potter) 29

4146
MERKYL, John*
Captain January
Fine Clothes
Unholy Three, The (jeweler)
Stage:
Our Nell (Mortimer Bayne) 22
Six-Fifty, The (Mark Rutherford)
   21

4147
MERLO, Anthony*
Thief, The

4148
MERRALL, Mary (Mary Lloyd)
   (1890-)
Duke's Son, The

4149
MERRELLI, C.*
Three Musketeers, The (Milady de
   Winter)

4150
MERRIAM, Charlotte*
Brass Bottle, The
Captain Blood (Mary Traill)
Code of the Wilderness
Nth Commandment, The
Painted People
Pampered Youth
Pleasure Crazed
Queen of the Nightclubs
So Big (Julie Hemple)
Steele of the Royal Mounted

4151
MERRILL, Frank (1892-1966)
Double for Elmo Lincoln
Little Wild Girl
Perils of the Jungle [serial]
Tarzan the Mighty [serial] (Tarzan)
Tarzan the Tiger [serial] (Tarzan)

4152
MERSCH, Mary*
Top of the World, The

4153
MERSEREAU, Violet (1894-)
Finders Keepers
Love Wins
Luck
Nero
Shepherd King, The
Thunderclap

4154
MERSON, Billy (William Thompson)
  (1881-1947)
Phonofilm

4155
MERTON, Colette*
Clear the Decks
Why Be Good?

4156
MESSINGER, Buddy (1909-)
Abysmal Brute, The (Buddy Sangster)
Angel Face
Flirt, The
Front Page Story, A
Hot Stuff
Jazz Age, The
Lady of Chance, A
Old Nest, The
Penrod and Sam (Rodney Bitts)
Shadows (Mr. Bad Boy)
Trifling with Honor
Undressed

4157
MESSINGER, Gertrude (1911-)
Barefoot Boy, The
Civilization's Back Yard
Duke Steps Out, The
Jazz Age, The
Penrod and Sam (Marjorie Jones)
Two Weeks Off

4158
MESTAYER, Harry*
Acquittal, The
Black Oxen (James Oglethorpe)
Flapper Wives
Locked Door, The
Millionaire Baby, The
Pathé player 21
Stop Thief!
Unguarded Women

Stage:
Ariadne (Horace Heldru) 25
Gypsy Jim (Worthing) 24
Madeleine and the Movies (Tony Burgess) 22
Monkey Talks, The (Dada) 25
Poppy God, The (Gin Long) 21
Right to Strike, The (Gordon Montague) 21
Vaudeville [Palace] 28

4159
METCALF, Arthur*
If Winter Comes
Seven Day's Leave
Shore Leave
Soul Fire
Stage:
Dancing Mothers (Davis) 24
Red Poppy (Prince Sergius Saratoff) 22
Three Live Ghosts (Bensen) 20

4160
METCALF, Earl (1889-1928)
Air Mail Pilot
Atta Boy!
Back to Yellow Jacket
Boomerang Justice
Devil's Saddle, The
Eagle of the Night [serial]
Eden and Return
Face at the Window, The
Flaming Forest, The
Fortune Hunter, The
Great Mystery, The
High Flyer, The
Look Your Best
Man Without a Country, The /aka/
  As No Man Has Loved
Midnight Sun, The
Mother Eternal
New Teacher, The
Night Life (Amorous Swain)
Notorious Lady, The
Partners Again /aka/ Partners
  Again with Potash and Perlmutter
Power of a Lie, The
Remember
Ship of Souls
Silent Accuser, The
Sin Cargo
Tragedy of the East Side, A
What Women Will Do
While Justice Waits
While New York Sleeps
White Eagle [serial]

4161
METEVIER, Matilda*
Evidence (Louise)

4162
MEUNIER-SURCOUF*
Magic Flame, The (sword swallower)

4163
MEUSEL, Bob*
Slide, Kelly, Slide

4164
MEUSEL, Irish*
Slide, Kelly, Slide

4165
MEXICAN MARIMBA BAND OF
AGUA CALIENTE
Cock-Eyed World, The

4166
MEYER, Greta*
Royal Box, The

4167
MEYER, Hyman*
Saturday Night Kid, The (Ginsberg)
Stage:
Johannes Kreisher (Othmar) 22

4168
MEYER, Johannes*
Master of the House

4169
MEYER, Torben*
Last Warning, The
Viking, The

4170
MEYERKHOLD, V. *
Lash of the Czar, The

4171
MEYERS, Kathleen*
Dick Turpin
Go West
His Supreme Moment

4172
MEZETTI, Charles*
Three Must-Get-Theres, The

4173
MICHAILOW, Boris*
Sein Grösster Bluff [Her Greatest
  Bluff] (Sherry)

4174
MIDDLETON, Charles B. (1879-1949)
Bellamy Trial, The (District Attor-
  ney)
Far Call
Welcome Danger

4175
MIDDLETON, Eleanor*
Bride's Play, The

4176
MIDGLEY, Fannie*
Bridge of Sighs, The
Greed (Miss Baker)
Harvester, The
Marry Me
Stephen Steps Out

4177
MIDGLEY, Florence*
Sadie Thompson (Mrs. McPhail)

4178
MIERENDORFF, Hans*
U-Boat 9

4179
MILAIDY, James*
America /aka/ Love and Sacrifice
  (James Parker)

4180
MILAINE, Amille*
Loves of Ricardo, The

4181
MILAR, Adolph*
Back to God's Country
Bulldog Drummond (Marcovitch)
Clothes Make the Woman
Devil's Skipper, The
Gateway of the Moon
Kiss Doctor, The
Love's Wilderness
Marriage in Transit (Haynes)
Michigan Kid, The
Road of Ambition
Silent Barrier, The
Something Different
Uncle Tom's Cabin (Mr. Haley)

4182
MILASCH, Robert*
Captain Blood
Thank You

4183
MILASH, Bib*
Hero for a Night, A

4184
MILERTA, John*
Night Flyer, The

4185
MILES, Bob*
Water Hole, The

4186
MILES, H. *
Chechahcos, The

4187
MILES, Luther--see: Miles Mander

4188
MILEY, Jerry*
Broken Hearts of Hollywood
Easy Pickings
Fox player 26
Joy Girl, The
Pajamas
Sally of the Scandals
Taxi Thirteen
Understanding Heart, The
Wild Oats Lane

4189
MILHALESCO*
Passion of Joan of Arc, The

4190
MILJAN, John (1899-1960)
Almost a Lady
Amateur Gentleman, The (Viscount
   Devenham)
Brooding Eyes
Crimson City, The
Desert Song, The (Capt. Fontaine)
Desired Woman, The
Devil May Care
Devil's Circus, The
Devil's Island
Empty Hearts (Frank Gorman)
Eternal Woman, The
Fashions in Love
Fashions of Paris
Final Extra, The
Flaming Waters
Footloose Widows
Framed
Glorious Betsy
Ham and Eggs at the Front
Hard Boiled Rose

Home Towners, The
Husbands for Rent
Innocents of Paris (Monsieur Renard)
Lady Be Good
Lady Bird
Land of the Silver Fox
Little Snob, The
Lone Chance, The
Lone Wolf, The
Love Letter
Lovers
My Official Wife
Old San Francisco
On the Stroke of Three
Painted Lady, The
Paying the Price
Phantom of the Opera, The (Valentine)
Quarantined Rivals
Queen of the Nightclubs
Race Wild
Romance Ranch
Rough House Rosie (Lew McKay)
Sackcloth and Scarlet
Sailor Izzy Murphy
Sailor's Sweetheart, A
Satin Woman, The
Sea Bat, The
Silent Sanderson
Silver Slave, The
Slaver, The
Speedway
Stark Mad
Stranded
Tenderloin
Terror, The (Alfred Kalman)
Times Square
Unchastened Woman (Lawrence San-
   bury)
Unholy Night, The (Major Mallory)
Unholy Three, The
Unknown Treasures /aka/ The
   House Behind the Hedge
Untamed (Bennock)
Voice of the City
What Happened to Father?
Within the Law
Wolf's Clothing
Women They Talk About
Yankee Clipper, The

4191
MILLAND, Ray /aka/ Spike Milland
   (Reginald Truscott-Jones) (1907-)
As Spike Milland:
Flying Scotsman, The (Jim Edwards)
Goodwin Sands
Informer, The (bit)
Plaything (Ian)

As Ray Milland:
Lady from the Sea, The (Tom Rob-
    erts, debut)
Passion Flower, The

4192
MILLAR, Adelqui*
Arab, The (Abdullah)
Moon of Israel

4193
MILLARD, Helene*
Their Own Desire (Beth)

4194
MILLER, Carl*
Black Swan, The
Cinderella of the Hills
Kid, The
Red Kimono, The
Redeeming Sin, The
We Moderns
Why Sailors Go Wrong

4195
MILLER, Carlton*
Bride's Play, The

4196
MILLER, Ella*
Fog Bound
North of '36

4197
MILLER, Ethel*
Broadway after Dark

4198
MILLER, Hugh*
Blind Alleys
Claude Duval (Lord Lionel Malyn)
Loves of Sunya, The (the outcast)
Stage:
Lolly (Daniel Gaylord) 29
Merchant of Venice, The (Gratiano)
    28
Novice and the Duke, The (Lucio) 29
Pickwick (Alfred Jingle) 27
When Crummles Played (Master
    Crummles) 28
Whispering Gallery, The (Martin
    Condell) 29

4199
MILLER, Joe*
Days of the Buffalo

4200
MILLER, Louis*
Chinese Bungalow, The (Chinese ser-
    vant)
Stage:
Bitter Sweet (Lt. Tranisch) 29

4201
MILLER, Marilyn (1898-1936)
Sally (Title role)
Stage:
Peter Pan (Title role) 24
Rosalie (Princess Rosalie) 28
Sally (Title role) 20
Sunny ("Sunny" Peters) 25

4202
MILLER, Mary Louise*
Bandit's Baby, The (the baby)
Jaws of Steel
Night Cry, The
Sparrows /aka/ Human Sparrows
    (Doris Wayne)
Third Degree, The
Three Hours

4203
MILLER, Patsy Ruth (1905-)
Affairs of Anatol, The
Aviator, The
Beautiful, but Dumb
Broken Hearts of Hollywood
Camille (Title role)
Daughters of Today
Drivin' Fool, The
Fall of Eve, The
Fighting Edge, The
First Auto, The
Fools in the Dark
For Big Stakes
Fortune's Mask
Gate Crasher, The
Girl I Loved, The
Girl Who Came Back, The
Handle with Care
Head Winds
Hell Bent for Heaven
Her Husband's Secret
Hero for a Night, A
Hogan's Alley
Hot Heels
Hottentot, The
Hunchback of Notre Dame, The (Es-
    meralda)
Hypocrites, The
King of Turf
Leave It to Me
Lorraine of the Lions

Marriage by Contract
My Man
Night Beat
Oh, What a Nurse!
Omar the Tentmaker
Once and Forever
Painting the Town
Pearl Story, The
Private Izzy Murphy
Red Hot Tires
Red Riders of Canada
Rememberance
Rose of the World
Sap, The
Self-Made Failure, A
Seven Sinners
Shanghaied
Sheik, The (slave girl)
Show of Shows, The
So Long Letty
So This Is Paris (Suzanne Giraud)
South Sea Love
Tomorrow
Tragedy of Youth
Tropical Nights
Twin Beds
Watch Your Step
We Americans
What Every Girl Should Know
Where Is My Wandering Boy Tonight?
Whispering Winds
White Black Sheep, The
Why Girls Go Back Home
Wolf's Clothing
Yankee Consul, The

4204
MILLER, Ruth*
Affairs of Anatol, The (Spencer maid)
Name the Man
Singer Jim McKee

4205
MILLER, Walter (1892-1940)
Beyond the Rainbow (Robert Judson)
Black Book, The [serial]
Bootlegger, The
Fighting Marine, The [serial]
Green Archer, The [serial]
Hawk of the Hills [serial]
House Without a Key, The [serial]
King of the Congo, The [serial]
Leatherstocking [serial]
Luxury
Man Without a Face, The [serial]
Melting Millions [serial]
Mysterious Airman, The [serial]
Parting of the Trails

Perilous Mission [serial]
Play Ball [serial]
Police Reporter [serial]
Prisoners of Love
Queen of the North Woods [serial]
Rapids, The
Revenge of Tarzan, The /aka/ The
    Return of Tarzan (Rokoff's hench-
    man)
Snowed In [serial]
Stealers, The
Sunken Silver [serial]
Ten Scars Make a Man [serial]
Terrible People [serial]
Tie that Binds, The
Till We Meet Again
Unconquered Woman, The
Unfair Sex, The
Unseeing Eyes
Way of a Man, The [serial]
Way Women Love, The

4206
MILLER, Winston*
Iron Horse, The (Davy as a child)
Light that Failed, The
Love Piker, The
Man and Maid
Secrets
Stella Dallas (Helen's son 10 years
    later)
Stolen Bride, The

4207
MILLETT, Arthur*
Crimson Runner, The
Man of Action, A
Open Switch, The [serial chapter 26]
Two Gun Man, The
Wolf's Clothing

4208
MILLNER, Marietta*
City Gone Wild, A
Magnificent Flirt, The (Fifi)
We're All Gamblers

4209
MILLS, Alyce*
Faint Perfume (Ledda Perrin)
Keeper of the Bees, The (Molly
    Cameron)
My Lady's Lips (Dora Blake)
Say It Again
School for Wives
Too Many Kisses (flapper)
Two Girls Wanted (Edna Delafield)
Whirlwind of Youth, The

4210
MILLS, Evelyn*
Alias Jimmy Valentine (little sister)

4211
MILLS, Frank*
Chicago after Midnight
Danger Street
Hit of the Show

4212
MILLS, Joe*
Love's Whirlpool

4213
MILLS, Marilyn*
Riders of the Plains [serial]
Three Pals

4214
MILLS, Thomas R.*
Guilty One, The
Man's Mate, A
Tides of Passion
Wolf Man, The

4215
MILOVITCH, Cordy*
Peter the Great

4216
MILOWANOFF, Sandra*
Iceland Fisherman, The
Les Miserables (dual role, Fantine/
  Cosette)

4217
MILTERN, John
Coming Through
East Side, West Side
Fine Manners (Courtney Adams)
Loves of Sunya, The (Asa Ashling)
Manslaughter (Gov. Stephen Albee)
On with the Dance
Tongues of Flame
Stage:
Canary Dutch (John Weldon) 25
Merry Wives of Gotham ("Fanshas-
  tics") (Major Fowler) 24
Persons Unknown (Harry Sheridan) 22
Ruined Lady, The (Bill Bruce) 20
Sherlock Holmes (Prof. Moriarty) 29
Trapped (Inspector Manning) 28

4218
MILTON, Georges /aka/ George*
Jim Bougne Boxeur
Par Habitude

4219
MILTON, Royce*
Fifth Form at St. Dominic's, The
  (Jellicott, Master of the Fifth)

4220
MILWARD, Dawson*
Skin Game, The (Hillcrist)

4221
MINEAU, Charlotte*
Extra Girl, The
Forty-Five Minutes from Hollywood
Happiness
Love 'em and Weep
Sparrows /aka/ Human Sparrows
  (Mrs. Grimes)
Sugar Daddies

4222
MINNEHAHA*
Four Horsemen of the Apocalypse
  (old nurse)

4223
MINTER, Mary Miles (Juliet Shelby)
  (1902-)
All Souls Eve
Cowboy and the Lady, The
Cumberland Romance, A
Don't Call Me Little Girl
Drums of Fate
Eyes of the Heart
Heart Specialist, The
Her Husband's Secret
Her Winning Ways
Jenny Be Good
Jerry
Judy of Rogues Harbor
Little Clown, The
Moonlight and Honeysuckle
Nurse Marjorie
South of Suva
Sweet Lavender
Tillie
Trail of the Lonesome Pine, The

4224
MIR, David*
Breakfast at Sunrise
Bringing up Father
Cavalier, The
Dearie
Diplomacy
His Hour
La Boheme (Alexis)
Man and Maid
Matinee Idol, The

Only Thing, The
Time, the Comedian

4225
MIRACLE, Silas*
Stark Love

4226
MISCH, Margot*
Children of No Importance

4227
MISSEN, Oud Egede*
Dr. Mabuse the Gambler /aka/ Dr.
    Mabuse, the Great Unknown (Cara
    Carozza)

4228
MISSIRIO, Cenica*
Figaro

4229
MITA, Ura*
Devil Dancer, The

4230
MITCHELL, Belle*
Flying Romeos

4231
MITCHELL, Dodson*
Deadline at Eleven
Stage:
Beau Gallant (Tom Beale) 26
Behold This Dreamer (John Strick-
    ler) 27
First Mortgage (Elmer's Father)
    29
Home Fires (Dana Roberts) 23
Izzy (David Schussel) 24
Like a King (George W. Grubble)
    21
Listening In (Johnathan Cumberland)
    22
National Anthem (John K. Carlton)
    22
Night Call, The (George Dodge) 22
Personality (John C. Kent) 21
Red Falcon, The (Grifonetto) 24
Tavern, The (tavern keeper) 20
Wild Birds (John Slag) 25

4232
MITCHELL, Irving*: [see Vol. III]

4233
MITCHELL, Martin*
Terror /aka/ The Perils of Paris

4233
MITCHELL, Martin*
Terror /aka/ The Perils of Paris

4234
MITCHELL, Rhea (1894-1957)
Danger Patrol
Devil's Claim, The
Good Women
Great Menace, The
Hawk's Trail, The [serial]
Ponjola
Ridin' Romeo, A
Scoffer, The

4235
MITCHELL, Thomas (1892-1962)
Six Cylinder Love
Stage:
Blood Money (James Bolton) 27
Kiki (Adolphe) 21
Little Accident (Norman Overbeck) 28
Nightstick (Tommy Glennon) 27
Not So Long Ago (Sam Robinson) 20
Wisdom Tooth, The (Bemis) 26

4236
MITRY, Jean*
Romeo und Julia im Schnee /aka/
    Romeo and Juliet in the Snow

4237
MITZI, Little*
Marriage Playground, The (Zinnie)

4238
MIX, Ruth (1913-)
Four Sons
Series of cowgirl films with Rex
    Lease
That Girl Oklahoma
Stage:
Vaudeville [Palace] 29

4239
MIX, Tom (Thomas Hallen Mix)
    (1880-1940)
[Horse: Old Blue (1897-1919); Tony,
    the Wonder Horse from 1917]
After Your Own Heart
Arizona Wildcat
Best Bad Man, The (Hugh Nichols)
Big Diamond Robbery, The
Big Town Roundup, The
Bronco Twisters
Canyon of Light
Catch My Smoke
Chasing the Moon

Circus Ace, The
Cyclone, The
Daredevil, The
Daredevil's Reward
Deadwood Coach, The
Desert Love
Destry Rides Again
Dick Turpin
Do and Dare
Drifter, The
Drums of Araby
Dude Ranch, The
Everlasting Whisper, The
Eyes of the Forest
Feud, The
Fighting Streak, The
Four Big Streaks
Great K and A Robbery, The
Hands Off
Hardboiled
Heartbuster, The
Hello, Cheyenne
Horseman of the Plains
Just Tony
King Cowboy
Ladies to Board
Last of the Duanes
Last Trail, The
Lone Star Ranger
Lucky Horseshoe, The
Mile a Minute Romeo
Mr. Logan, U.S.A.
My Own Pal
Night Horseman, The
No Man's Gold
North of Hudson Bay
Oh, You Tony
Outlawed
Outlaws of Red River
Painted Post
Prairie Trails
Queen of Sheba, The
Rainbow Trail, The
Riders of the Purple Sage (Jim Las-
    siter)
Riding Romeo, A
Road Demon, The
Romance Land
Rough Diamond
Rough Riding Romance
Silver Valley
Sky High (Grant Newberg)
Soft Boiled
Son of the Golden West
Stepping Fast
Teeth
Terror, The
Texan, The

Three Gold Coins
Three Jumps Ahead
Tom Mix in Arabia
Tony Runs Wild
Trailin'
Treat 'em Rough
Troubleshooter, The
Tumbling River
Untamed, The
Up and Going
Yankee Senor, The
Yes, We Have No Temper
Stage:
Vaudeville [Palace] 28

4240
MOATT, Christine*
Sea Hawk, The

4241
MODOT, Gaston*
Carmen (Garci of "The Borgne")
Miracle of the Wolves, The
Das Schiff der Verlorenen Menschen
    [The Ship of Lost Souls] /aka/
    Le Navire des Hommes Perdue
    [The Ship of Lost Men] (Morian)
Sous Les Toits de Paris [Under the
    Roofs of Paris]

4242
MOFFITT, Jefferson*
Campus Vamp, The

4243
MOHAMMED-BEN-NONI*
Atlantide (Bon-Djeina)

4244
MOISSI, Alexander*
Royal Box, The
Stage:
Everyman - Chicago 26; San Francis-
    co 29
Jedermann [Everyman] (Title role) 27
Midsummer Night's Dream, A - Chi-
    cago 27
Redemption (Fyodor Protasnoff) 28

4245
MOJA, Hella*
U-Boat 9

4246
MOLESKA, Paul*
Sein Grösster Bluff [Her Greatest
    Bluff] (gangster)

4247
MOLLANDIN, Henry M. *
Movietone Follies of 1929

4248
MOLNAR, Julius, Jr. *
Last Moment, The
Man Who Laughs, The (Gwynplaine
  as a boy)

4249
MOMAI, Tetsu*
Bulldog Drummond

4250
MONG, William V. (1875-1940)
Alias the Lone Wolf
All the Brothers Were Valiant (cook)
Barriers Burned Away
Brooding Eyes
Broken Mask, The
Burning Daylight
Chorus Girl's Romance, A (Prof.
  Dillinger)
Clown, The
Code of the Air
Connecticut Yankee in King Arthur's
  Court, A
County Fair, The
Dark Skies
Devil's Trade-Mark, The
Drifting
Excuse Me
Fifth Avenue
Fine Clothes
Flapper Wives
Fool There Was, A
Haunted House, The
House of Horror, The
In the Palace of the King
Iron Mike
Ladies Must Live
Lights of Old Broadway
Lost and Found
Luck of Geraldine Laird, The
Maker of Dreams, The
Monte Cristo (Caderousse)
Mutiny of the Elsinore
No Babies Wanted
Noah's Ark (dual role, guard/inn-
  keeper)
Off the Highway
Oh, Doctor!
Old Soak, The
Penrod and Sam (Deacon Bitts)
Pilgrims of the Night
Playthings of Destiny
Price of Honor, The

Ransom
Seven Footprints to Satan
Shadow of the Law, The (Egan)
Shadow on the Wall, A
Shame
Shattered Idols
Should a Girl Marry?
Silent Lover, The
Sowing the Wind
Stain, The
Steel Preferred
Strong Man, The (Parson Brown)
Taxi! Taxi!
Telling the World
Ten Dollar Raise, The
Thy Name Is Woman
Too Many Crooks
Travelling Salesman, A
Wandering Daughters
Welcome Stranger, The
What Price Glory? ("Cognac Pete")
Why Girls Leave Home
Why Men Leave Home
Woman He Loved, The

4251
MONGBERG, George*
Hall Room Boys, The (Ferdy)

4252
MONKEYS (Animals)
Dippy-Doo-Dads, The

4253
MONKMAN, Phyllis*
Blackmail

4254
MONNIER, Jackie*
Le Bled
Le Tourmoi

4255
MONT, Christina*
Rose of the Golden West

4256
MONTAGUE, Monty*
Ace of Scotland Yard [serial] (Jarvis)
Flaming Disc, The [serial]
Spurs and Saddles

4257
MONTANA, Bull (1887-1950)
Breaking into Society
Dick Turpin
Fight Pest, The
First National player 21

Foolish Age, The
Four Horsemen of the Apocalypse,
The (French butcher)
Gay and Devilish
Girl in Number 29, The
Glad Rags
Go and Get It
Good Morning, Judge
Hearts Are Trumps
Hollywood
How to Handle Women
Ladies' Man, A
Limousine Love
Lost World, The (ape man)
One Wild Week
Painted People
Punctured Prince, The
Rob 'em Good
Show of Shows, The
Skyrocket
Snowed Under
Son of the Sheik, The (Albi)
Three-Must-Get-Theres, The (Cardinal Richelieu)
Tiger Rose (Joe)
Timber Queen [serial]
Treasure Island (Morgan)
Two Twins, The (dual role)
Vanishing Millions [serial]
What Women Love

4258
MONTEL, Blanche*
La Ronde Infernale

4259
MONTEREY, Carlotta*
King on Main Street, The
Soul Fire

4260
MONTGOMERY, Earl*
Air Pockets

4261
MONTGOMERY, Frank*
Aloma of the South Seas (Hongi)
Sainted Devil, A
So's Your Old Man (Jeff)

4262
MONTGOMERY, Peggy /aka/ Baby
Peggy (1918-)
April Fool
Arizona Days
Baby and Dog Comedies (6)
Bad Man's Money
Captain January

Carmen, Jr.
Century Comedies (40)
Dangerous Dub, The
Darling of New York, The
Desert of the Lost
Edith's Burglar
Family Secret, The
Fighting Failure
Flower Girl, The
Grandma's Girl
Hansel and Gretel (Hansel)
Helen's Babies (Toddie)
Hollywood
Jack and the Beanstalk
Law Forbids, The
Lesser player 24
Little Red Riding Hood (Title role)
On the Divide
Peggy Behave
Playmates (debut)
Prisoners of the Storm
Saddle Mates
Saturday Afternoon
Senorita, The
Sensation Seekers
Silent Trail, The
Sonora Kid, The
There He Goes
Two Guns of Tumbleweed
West of Santa Fe
Whose Baby Are You?

4263
MONTGOMERY, Robert (Henry Montgomery, Jr.) (1904-)
College Days
Divorcee, The
Father's Day
On the Set
Single Standard, The
So This Is College (debut as Biff)
Their Own Desire (Jack)
Three Live Ghosts (William Foster)
Untamed (Andy McAllister)
Stage:
Bad Habits of 1926
Carolinian, The (Capt. Shenstone) 25
Complex, The (Blink)
Dawn (Louis Rhodes) 24
High Hatters, The (Dick Halloway) 28
Mask and the Face, The (Tito) 24
Possession (Edward Whiteman) 28
Repertory in Rochester N.Y. (70
plays in 18 months)

4264
MONTROSE, Helen*
Mighty Lak' a Rose

4265
MONTT, Christine*
Sea Hawk, The (Infanta of Spain)

4266
MOOERS, DeSacia*
Any Woman
Potash and Perlmutter
Restless Wives

4267
MOORE, Charles*
Trial of Mary Dugan, The (James
  Madison)
Stage:
Meek Mose (Mose) 28
New York Exchange (Dr. Scratch) 26

4268
MOORE, Claude*
Nana

4269
MOORE, Cleve*
It Must Be Love
Lilac Time
Stolen Bride, The
We Moderns

4270
MOORE, Clive*
Footlights and Fools (press agent)
Her Summer Hero

4271
MOORE, Colleen (Kathleen Morri-
  son) (1900-)
Affinities
April Showers
Broken Chains
Broken Hearts of Broadway
Burning Daylight
Come on Over
Common Property
Cyclone, The
Desert Flower, The
Devil's Claim, The
Dinty
Ella Cinders (Title role)
Flaming Youth
Flirting with Love
Footlights and Fools (dual role, Bet-
  ty Murphy/Fifi D'Auray)
Forsaking All Others
Gym, The
Happiness Ahead
Her Bridal Nightmare
Her Wild Oat

His Nibs
Huntress, The
Irene
It Must Be Love
Lilac Time
Look Your Best
Lotus Eater, The
Naughty but Nice (Bernice Summers)
Ninety and Nine, The
Nth Commandment, The
Oh, Kay!
Orchids and Ermine
Painted People
Perfect Flapper, The
Roman Scandal, A
Sally (Title role)
Sky Pilot
Slippy McGee
Small Bachelor
Smiling Irish Eyes
So Big (Selina DeJong)
So Long Letty
Synthetic Sin
That's a Bad Girl
Through the Dark
Twinkletoes (Title role)
Wall Flower, The
We Moderns
When Dawn Came
Why Be Good?

4271a
MOORE, Dickie (John Richard
  Moore) (1925-)
Beloved Rogue, The (debut)
Object, Alimony
Son of the Gods (boy)
Timothy's Quest

4271b
MOORE, Eva (1870-)
Chu-Chin-Chow (Alcolm)

4272
MOORE, Hilda*
Jealousy (Charlotte)

4273
MOORE, Ida*
Merry Widow, The (innkeeper's
  wife)
Thank You

4274
MOORE, Joe*
Wages of Virtue (Le Bro-way)

4275
MOORE, Matt (1888-1960)
Ambrose Applejohn's Adventure
  (Title role)
Back Pay
Beware of Blondes
Cave Man
Coquette (Stanley Wantworth)
Diplomacy
Don't Ever Marry
Drifting
Dry Martini
Early to Wed
Everybody's Sweetheart
First Year, The
Fools in the Dark
Grounds for Divorce
Hairpins
His Jazz Bride
His Majesty Bunker Bean
How Baxter Buttered In
Jilt, The
King of Kings, The (Mark)
Lost Lady, A
Love Madness
Madness of Manhattan
Man's Home, A
Married Alive
Minnie
Mystery Club, The
Narrow Street, The
No More Women
Passionate Pilgrim, The
Phyllis of the Follies
Self-Made Failure, A
Side Street
Sisters
Storm, The
Straight Is the Way
Strangers of the Night
Summer Bachelors
Three Weeks in Paris
Tillie the Toiler (Mac)
Unholy Three, The (Hector McDon-
  ald)
Way of a Girl, The
White Tiger, The

4276
MOORE, Mickey (1917-)
Cytherea (Randon child)
Impossible Mrs. Bellew, The (Lance
  Bellew, Jr., age 4)
Manslaughter (Dicky Evans)
Shame
Something to Think About (Bobby)
Temple of Dawn, The (Billy Deering)
Truxton King

4277
MOORE, Mildred*
Moon Riders, The [serial]

4278
MOORE, Owen (1886-1939)
Actress, The
Becky
Blackbird, The (West End Bertie)
Camille of the Barbary Coast
Chicken in the Case, The
Code of the West (Cal Thurman)
Condemned Woman
Dangerous Hero, A
Desperate Hero, The
Divorce of Convenience, A
East of Broadway
False Price
Go Straight
Her Temporary Husband
High Voltage (Det. Dan Eagan)
Hollywood
Husbands for Rent
Love Is an Awful Thing
Married? (Dennis Shawn)
Modern Matrimony
Money Talks
Oh, Mabel, Behave
Parasite, The
Piccadilly Jim
Poor Simp, The
Red Mill, The (Dennis)
Reported Missing
Road to Mandalay, The
Selznic player 20
Side Street
Silent Partner, The
Skyrocket
Sooner or Later
Stolen Love
Stop that Man!
Taxi Dancer, The (Lee Rogers)
Tea for Three
Thundergate
Torment
Trelawney of the Wells (Tom Wrench)
Who's Who?
Women Love Diamonds

4279
MOORE, Pat (1917-)
Broken Laws
Impossible Mrs. Bellew, The (Lance
  Bellew, Jr., age 6)
Primrose Path, The (Jimmie Arm-
  strong)
Queen of Sheba, The (Sheba's son,
  age 4)

Stephen Steps Out
Ten Commandments, The
Village Blacksmith, The
Young Rajah, The

4280
MOORE, Percy*
Shock Punch, The

4281
MOORE, Terrence*
Lover of Camille, The
Ten Commandments, The (Pharaoh's
  son)

4282
MOORE, Tom (1884-1955)
Adventure
Anybody Here Seen Kelly?
Beating the Game
Big Brother
Cabaret
Clinging Vine
Cowboy and the Lady, The
Cyclone Hickey
Dangerous Money (Tim Sullivan)
Dub
From the Ground Up
Good and Naughty
Great Accident, The
Harbor Lights
His Last Haul
Hold Your Horses
Kiss for Cinderella, A (Policeman)
Love Thrill, The
Made in Heaven
Manhandled (Jim Hogan)
Marriage Morals
Mary of the Movies
Mr. Barnes of New York
Officer 666
On Thin Ice
One Night in Rome
Over the Border
Pawned
Pretty Ladies (Al Cassidy)
Rouged Lips
Side Street
Siren, The
Song and Dance Man, The
Stop Thief!
Syncopating Sue
Trouble with Wives, The
Under the Rouge
Wise Wife
Yellowback, The
Stage:
Cup, The (Eddie) 23

4283
MOORE, Victor (1876-1962)
Man Who Found Himself, The
One reelers through the 20s
Stage:
Allez Oop! 27
Easy Come, Easy Go (Jim Bailey)
Funny Face (Herbert) 27
Heads Up! ("Skippy" Dugan) 29
Hold Everything ("Nosey" Bartlett) 28
Oh, Kay! ("Shorty" McGee) 26

4284
MOORE, Vin*
Lazy Lightning

4285
MOOREHOUSE, Bert*
Girl from Woolworths, The

4286
MOOREHOUSE, Marie*
Old Nest, The

4287
MOORHEAD, Natalie*
Girl from Havana
Through Different Eyes (Frances
  Thornton)
Trusting Wives
Unholy Night, The (Lady Vi)
Stage:
Baby Cyclone, The (Lydia Webster)
  27

4288
MORAN, Baby*
Toll of the Sea

4288a
MORAN, George (George Searcy)
  (-1949)
Why Bring that Up?
Radio:
Eveready Hour, The 23
Majestic Hour, The 27
Two Black Crows 28
Stage:
Earl Carroll's Vanities 27
Passing Show of 1921

4289
MORAN, Lee (1899-1960)
Actress, The
After Business Hours
Alimony Annie
Aviator, The
Bad News

Children of the Ritz
Dance Hall
Dolls and Dollars
Everything but the Truth
Fast and Furious
Fast Worker, The
Fifth Avenue Models
Fire Escape Finish, A
Fixed by George
Glad Rag Doll, The
Gold Diggers of Broadway (dance
  director)
Hasty Hazing, A
Her Big Night
His Wife's Relations
How Do You Feel?
Irresistible Lover
Ladies of the Night Club
La, La, Lucille
Little Irish Girl, The
Look-out Girl, The
Madonna of Avenue A
My Lady of Whim (Dick Flynn)
No Defense
On with the Show (Pete)
Once a Plumber
Outcast, The
Place and Guest
Racket, The
Roman Romeos
Rose of Kildare
Rushin' Dancers, The
Shocking Night, A
Show Girl
Show of Shows, The
Spring Fever
Syncopating Sue
Take It from Me
Tessie
Thanks for the Buggy Ride
There and Back
Thrill Seekers
Too Much Woman
Trelawney of the Wells (Colpoys)
Where Was I?
Wolf's Clothing
Woman Against the World, A

4290
MORAN, Lois (Lois Darlington Dow-
  ling) (1909-)
Behind that Curtain (Eve Mannering)
Belle of Samoa, The
Beyond the Sierras
Blindfolded
Case of Mary Brown, The
Don't Marry
False Colors

Feu-Mathies Pascal
La Galerie des Monstres
God Gave Me Twenty Cents
Irresistible Lover
Joy Street
Just Suppose
Living Dead Man, The
Love Hungry
Making the Grade
Music Master, The
Padlocked
Prince of Tempters, The
Publicity Madness
Reckless Lady, The
River Pirate
Road to Mandalay, The
Sharp Shooters
Song of Kentucky, A
Soul Fire /aka/ Golden Youth
Stella Dallas (Laurel Dallas)
True Heaven
Whirlwind of Youth
Words and Music

4291
MORAN, Percy (1886-1952)
Field of Honor, The
Lt. Daring R. N. and the Water Rats

4292
MORAN, Polly (Pauline Theresa
  Moran) (1885-1952)
Affairs of Anatol, The (orchestra
  leader)
Beyond the Sierras
Bishop Murder Case, The
Bringing up Father
Buttons
Callahans and the Murphys, The
  (Mrs. Murphy)
Came the Dawn
Carnival comedies
Caught Short
Chasing Rainbows
China Bound
Dangerous Female
Deadline, The
Divine Woman, The (Mme. Pigonier)
Enemy, The
Hollywood Revue of 1929
Honeymoon
Hot for Paris
Iron Mike
It's a Wise Child
London after Midnight (Miss Smith-
  son)
Luck
Margin Mugs

Masked Stranger, The
Road Show
Rose-Marie (Lady Jane)
Saucy Madelene
Scarlet Letter, The (townswoman)
Shadows of the Night
Show People (cameo)
Skirts, The
So This Is College (Polly)
Speedway
Telling the World
That Night
Thirteenth Hour, The
Trail of '98, The
Unholy Night, The (maid)
While the City Sleeps (Mrs. McGin-
    nis)

4293
MORAN, Priscilla*
Daddies
Love and Glory
Up the Ladder

4294
MORAN, William*
Beloved Brute, The
Dramatic Life of Abraham Lincoln,
    The /aka/ Abraham Lincoln
Drifting

4295
MORANTE, Milburn (1888-1964)
Freckled Rascal, The
Little Savage, The

4296
MORELL, Sybil*
Richthofhen: The Red Knight of the
    Air

4297
MORENA, Erna*
Peak of Fate

4298
MORENO, Antonio (1886-1967)
Adoration
Air Legion, The
Beverly of Graustark (Danton)
Bluff
Border Legion
Careers
Clash, The
Come to My House
Exciters, The
Flaming Barriers
Flaming Forest, The

Guilty Conscience, A
Her Husband's Secret
In the Land of the Sun
Invisible Hand, The [serial]
It (Cyrus Waltham)
Learning to Love
Look Your Best
Lost and Found
Love's Blindness
Madame Pompadour (Rene Loval)
Marê Nostrum [Our Sea] (Ulysses
    Ferragut)
Midnight Taxi
My American Wife (Manuel La Tassa)
Nameless Men
One Year to Live
Paramount player 25
Romance of the Rio Grande
Secret of the Hills
Spanish Dancer, The (Don Cesar de
    Bazan)
Story Without a Name, The
Synthetic Sin
Temptress, The (Manuel Robledo)
Tiger Love
Trail of the Lonesome Pine, The
Veiled Mystery, The [serial]
Venus of Venice
Whip Woman (Michael)

4299
MORENO, Marguerite*
Gonzague
Le Mauvais Garcon

4300
MOREY, Harry T. (1879-1936)
Adventurous Sex, The (girl's father)
Aloma of the South Seas (Red Mal-
    lory)
Barriers Burned Away
Beyond the Rainbow (Edward Mallory)
Birth of a Soul, The
Captain January
Curse of Drink, The
Darkest Hour, The
Fifty-Fifty Girl, The
Flaming Clue, The
Forgotten Faces
Gauntlet, The
Green Goddess, The (Major Crespin)
Headlines
Heart of a Siren, The
In Honor's Web
Man's Home, A
Marriage Morals
None but the Brave
Rapids, The

Return of Sherlock Holmes (Prof.
  Moriarty)
Roughneck, The
Sea Rider, The
Under the Tonto Rim
Where the Pavement Ends (Capt. Hull
  Gregson)
Wildness of Youth, The

4301
MORGAN, Frank (Francis Philip
  Wupperman) (1890-1949)
Belle of the Night
Born Rich
Crowded Hour, The
Love's Greatest Mistake (William
  Ogden)
Man Who Found Himself, The
Manhandled (Arno Riccardi)
Queen High
Scarlet Saint, The
Vitagraph player 24
Stage:
Among the Married (Jack Mills) 29
Amorus Antic, The (Harlow Balsam)
  29
Dream Maker, The (Geoffrey Cliffe)
  21
Firebrand, The (Alesandro, Duke of
  Florence) 24
Gentlemen Prefer Blondes (Henry
  Spoffard) 26
Hearts Are Trumps! (Raoul de
  Trembly-Matour) 27
Her Family Tree 20
Lullaby, The (Count Carlo Boretti) 23
Puppets of Passion (gentleman in
  grey) 27
Rosalie (King Cyril) 28
Seventh Heaven (Brissac)
Tenth Avenue (Guy Peters) 27
Triumph of X, The (Robert Knowles)
  21
Weak Woman, A (Henri Fournier) 26
White Villa, The (Jorgen Malthe) 21

4302
MORGAN, George*
Souls for Sale (Spoffard)
Stage:
Great Way, The (first waiter) 21

4303
MORGAN, H. A. *
Beggars of Life
Rogue Song, The (Frolov)

4304
MORGAN, Helen (1900-1941)
Applause (Kitty Darling)
Glorifying the American Girl
Roadhouse Nights
Stage:
George White's Scandals 25
Show Boat (Julie) 27
Sweet Adeline (Addie) 29
Vaudeville [Palace] 27
Ziegfeld's Midnight Follies 29

4305
MORGAN, Horace*
Sherlock, Jr.
Three Ages, The

4306
MORGAN, Jackie*
Gumps, The [series] (Chester Gump)
Tornado

4307
MORGAN, Jeanne*
Great Mail Robbery, The

4308
MORGAN, Joan /aka/ Joan Went-
  worth /aka/ Iris North (1905-)
Children of Gibeon, The
Crimson Circle, The
Curfew Must Not Ring Tonight
Dicky Monteith
Fires of Innocence
Great Well, The
Lady Noggs
Lilac Sunbonnet, The
Little Dorrit
Lowland Cinderella, A
Road to London, The (Lady Emily)
Scarlet Wooing, The
Shadow of Egypt
Three Men in a Cart
Truants
Two Little Wooden Shoes
Window in Piccadilly, A
Woman Tempted, The

4309
MORGAN, Kewpie*
Spieler, The
Whispering Whiskers /aka/ Railroad
  Stowaways

4310
MORGAN, Lee*
Universal player 25

4311
MORGAN, Leon*
Fifth Form at St. Dominic's (Bramble, Bully of the Fourth)

4312
MORGAN, Margaret*
Snow Bride, The

4313
MORGAN, Phalba*
Girl in Every Port, A

4314
MORGAN, Ralph (Ralph Wupperman)
    (1882-1956)
Man Who Found Himself, The
Stage:
Clutching Claw, The (Gordon) 28
Cobra (Tony Dorning) 24
Dagger, The (Pierre the Dagger) 25
Damn the Tears (Buckland Steele) 27
Joker, The (Dick Hamill) 25
National Anthem, The (Arthur Carlton) 22
Poppy God, The (Stanley Bennett) 21
Romancin' 'Round (Henry Conboy) 27
Take My Advice (Bradley Clement) 27
Weak Woman, A (Serge Paveneyge) 26
Woman of Bronze, The (Paddy Griggs) 27

4315
MORGAN, Sidney /aka/ Sydney*
Juno and the Paycock
Stage:
Juno and the Paycock ("Joker" Daly) 27
Plough and the Stars, The (the Covey) 27
White-Headed Boy, The (George) 21

4316
MORGAN, Thelma*
So This Is Marriage

4317
Morgan, Wallace*
Sandra

4318
MORGAN, William*
Dramatic Life of Abraham Lincoln, The /aka/ Abraham Lincoln (John Wilkes Booth)

Stage:
Dawn (Ely Robbins) 24

4319
MORISSEY, Betty*
Gold Rush, The (chum of the girl)

4320
MORITZ, Max*
Monkey Romeo

4321
MORLAY, Gaby (Blanche Fumoleau)
    (1897-1964)
Les Nouveaux Messieurs [The New Gentleman]

4322
MORLEY, Karen (Mabel Linton)
    (1905-)
Through Different Eyes (extra)
Stage:
L. A. Civic Repertory Theatre

4323
MOROSCO, Walter*
For Those We Love (Johnny Fletcher)

4324
MORRIE, Margaret*
Welcome Home

4325
MORRIS, Chester (John Chester Brooks Morris) (1901-1970)
Alibi /aka/ The Perfect Alibi (Chick Williams No. 1605)
Divorcee, The
Fast Life (Paul Palmer)
Second Choice
Show of Shows, The
Woman Trap
Stage:
Crime (Rocky Morse) 27
Exciters, The (Lexington Dalrymple) 22
Extra (Wallace King) 23
Fast Life (Chester Palmer) 28
Home Towners, The ("Waly" Calhoon) 26
Mountain Man, The (Carey) 21
Whispering Friends (Al Wheeler) 28
Yellow ("Val" Parker) 26

4326
MORRIS, Dave*
Juno and the Paycock

Old Barn, The
Tracked by the Police

4327
MORRIS, Dick*
Gift Supreme, The (Dopey Dan)

4328
MORRIS, Frances*
Thunder (Molly)

4329
MORRIS, Johnnie*
Beggars of Life
Fifty-Fifty Girl, The
Innocents of Paris (musician)
Street of Sin

4330
MORRIS, Margaret*
Best People
Born to the West
Iron Man, The (Arlene Graham)
That's My Baby
Wild Horse Mesa
Womanhandled
Stage:
Yankee Princess, The (Princess
   Rao) 22

4331
MORRIS, Richard*
Third Alarm, The (Dr. Rutherford)

4332
MORRIS, Tom*
Squibs (Gus Holly)

4333
MORRISON, Arthur*
Lazy Lightning
Riders of the Purple Sage (Frank
   Erne)
Temple of Dawn, The (Col. Des-
   mond)
Tony Runs Wild

4334
MORRISON, Clifford*
Balaclava (prisoner's friend)

4335
MORRISON, Dorothy*
Hearts in Dixie

4336
MORRISON, Ernie "Sunshine Sammy"*
One Terrible Day

Our Gang Comedies
Penrod

4337
MORRISON, Florence*
Penrod
Stage:
Circus Princess (Frau Schumberger)
   27
Fashions of 1924 (a principal) 23
Her Family Tree 20
Last Waltz, The (Countess Alexan-
   drowna Corpulinski) 21
Queen O' Hearts (Isabella Budd) 22
Student Prince, The (Grand Duchess
   Anastasia) 24

4338
MORRISON, James (1888-   )
Black Beauty
Captain Blood (Jeremy Pitt)
Dangerous Age, The
Little Minister, The
Love Without Question
Man Next Door, The
Nth Commandment, The
On the Banks of the Wabash
Only a Shop Girl
Seepore Rebellion
Sowing the Wind
Ten Commandments, The
Unknown Purple, The
Vitagraph player 20
When We Were Twenty-One
Wine of Youth
Stage:
Queen's Husband, The (Petley) 28
Two Orphans, The (Martin) 26

4339
MORRISON, Joseph*
Dixie Handicap, The
Sowing the Wind

4340
MORRISON, Louis*
Dangerous Maid
Rescue, The
Sea Hawk, The
Unholy Three, The (police commis-
   sioner)
Village sleuth

4341
MORRISON, Peter*
Blue Blazes
Bucking the Truth
Chasing Trouble

Chinatown Nights
Crossing Trails
Desperate Game, The
Escape /aka/ The Exquisite Sinner
Ghost City
Long Trail, The
Making Good
Return of Texas Pat, The
Triple Action
Two Reelers (5)

4342
MORRISON, Sunshine Sammy--see:
  Ernie Morrison

4343
MORRISSEY, Betty*
Circus, The (the vanishing lady)
Fast Worker, The
Gold Rush, The
Lady of the Night
Skinner's Dress Suit
Woman of Paris, A (Fifi)

4344
MORSE, Grace*
Old Fashioned Boy, An

4345
MORSE, Karl*
Underworld

4346
MORSQUINI, Marie (1899-) [See
  also: Marie Mosquini]
Black Book, The [serial]
Seventh Heaven (Mrs. Gobin)
Two Girls Wanted (Sarah Miller)

4347
MORTON, Charles (1904-)
Cameo Kirby
Christina (Jan)
Colleen
Far Call
Four Devils (Charles)
Four Sons
Fox player 27
New Year's Eve
None but the Brave
Rich but Honest
Street Fair

4348
MORTON, Edna*
Three Miles Out
Wildfire

4349
MORTON, Marjorie*
Unholy Three, The (Mrs. Arlington)

4350
MOSES, Raymond G., Major
West Point

4351
MOSHEIM, Grete*
Dame Care
Primanerliebe

4352
MOSJOUKINE, Ivan /aka/ Ivan Mos-
  kine (1889-1939)
Burning Brasier, The
Casanova
Edmund Keane, Prince Among Lovers
Late Matthew Pascal, The
Living Dead Man, The
Loves of Casanova, The
Michael Strogoff (Title role)
Polikushka
President, The
Satan Triumphant
Shadows that Mass
Station Master, The
Surrender
Tempest

4353
MOSKOWITZ, Jennie*
Mother's Boy (Mrs. Applebaum)

4354
MOSQUINI, Marie (1899-) [See also:
  Marie Morsquini]
Before the Public
Cowboy Sheik, The
Dumb-Bell, The
Floor Below, The
Good and Naughty
His Best Girl
His Royal Shyness
It's a Hard Life
Looking for Trouble
Make It Snappy
No Children
Pathé player 21
Rush Orders
Save the Ship
Seventh Heaven (Mrs. Gobin)
Sold at Auction
Two Girls Wanted

4355
MOULTON, Edward*
Double Cross, A
Big Killing, The
Grit Wins

4356
MOUSE, Mickey (Cartoons) (1928-)
Barn Dance
Barnyard Battle
El Terrible Toreador
Gallopin' Gaucho
Haunted House
Jazz Fool, The
Jungle Rhythm
Karnival Kid, The
Mickey's Choo Choo
Mickey's Follies
Opry House, The
Plane Crazy
Plow Boy, The
Steamboat Willie
When the Cat's Away
Wild Waves

4357
MOWER, Jack (1890-1965)
Air Patrol
Annie Against the World
Beautiful Gambler, The
Bubbles
Cotton and Cattle
Cowboy Ace, A
Face Value
False Friends
Ghetto Shamrock, The
Her Own Story
In the Days of Daniel Boone [serial]
Lost Express, The [serial]
Manslaughter (Officer Drummond)
Melodies
Officer 444 [serial]
Perils of the Wild [serial]
Pretty Clothes
Radio Detective, The [serial]
Sailor's Wives
Saturday Night (Tom McGuire)
Ships of the Night
Shock, The (Jack Cooper)
Sinners' Paradise
Ten Scars Make a Man [serial]
Third Eye, The [serial]
Tiger Brand, The [serial]
Trail of the Tiger [serial]
Uncle Tom's Cabin (Mr. Shelby)
Water Hole, The

4358
MUCCI, Eduliho*
Romola (Nello)

4359
MUELLER, H. K.*
Luther

4360
MUHSSIN, Ertugrul*
Ankara Postassi (Courier of Angora)

4361
MUKHINA, Tanya*
Tanka-Trakitirschitsa /aka/ Protin
    Otsi; Tanka Against Her Father;
    Tanka the Innkeeper

4361a
MULCASTER, G. H.*
Man in the Iron Mask, The

4362
MULHALL, Jack (1891-)
All of a Sudden Peggy
Bad Man, The
Boss of Powerville
Breath of Scandal, The
Broad Daylight
Butter and Egg Man, The
Call of the Wild
Children of the Ritz
Classified
Cold Cash
Crystal Cup, The
Dark Streets (dual role)
Dixie Merchant, A
Dulcy
Dusk to Dawn
Far Cry, The
Flesh and Blood (Ted Burton)
Folly of Vanity
Forgotten Law, The
Fourteenth Lover, The
Friendly Enemies
God Gave Me Twenty Cents
Goldfish, The
Hearts of Men
Heroes of the Streets
High Speed
Hope
Into the Net [serial]
Joanna
Just Another Blonde /aka/ Girl from
    Coney Island
Ladies' Night in a Turkish Bath
Lady Be Good
Little Clown, The

Mad Whirl, The
Man Crazy
Midnight
Molly-O
Naughty Baby
Ne'er to Return Road, The
Off Shore Pirate, The
Orchids and Ermine
Pleasures of the Rich
Poor Nut, The
Second Choice
See You in Jail
Show of Shows, The
Silence
Sleep Walker, The
Smile, Brother, Smile
Social Buccaneer, The [serial]
Subway Sadie
Sunset Legion
Sweet Daddies
Three Women of France
Turn to the Right
Twin Beds
Two Weeks Off
Two Weeks with Pay
Waterfront
We Moderns
White and Yellow
Wild West [serial]
Within the Law (Dick Gilder)
You Never Can Tell

4363
MULLEN, Sadie*
Moonshine Valley (Mrs. Connors)

4364
MULLER, Ellen*
Madame Wünscht Keine Kinder [Madame Doesn't Want Children] /aka/ Madame Wants No Children (Elyane's maid)

4365
MULLER, Hilde*
Anna Boleyn /aka/ Deception

4366
MUNDIN, Herbert (1898-1939)
British films 20's
Stage:
Charlot Revue 24-25

4367
MUNDY, Helen*
Stark Love

4368
MUNI, Paul (Muni Weisenfreund) (1895-1967)
Seven Faces
Valiant, The (debut)
We Americans (replaced by George Sidney)
Stage:
Jewish Art Theatre
London Appearance 24
We Americans [London] 26

4369
MUNIER, Ferdinand*
Broken Wing, The

4370
MUNRO, Douglas*
Amazing Quest of Mr. Ernest Bliss, The (John Masters)

4371
MUNRO, Robert--see: Sonnie Hale

4372
MUNSON, Byron*
Folly of Vanity
Learning to Love
Publicity Madness
Teaser, The

4373
MUNSON, Ona (Ona Wolcott) (1908-1955)
Head of the Family
Stage:
Hold Everything (Sue Burke) 28
Manhattan Mary (Marry Brennan) 27

4374
MÜNZ, Heinz-Rolf*
Jew of Mestri, The (Salarino)

4375
MURAT, Jean*
Carmen (the lieutenant)
L'Eau du Nil
Escaped from Hell
Legion of Honor, The
Soul of France, The
Venus

4376
MURIEL, Roel*
Rose of the Golden West

4377
MURPHY, Catherine*
Within the Law (Gilder's secretary)

4378
MURPHY, Charles Bernard*
Red Lights

4379
MURPHY, Charles Bernard, Jr.*
Price of Pleasure, The

4380
MURPHY, Edna (1904-)
Across the Atlantic
All Aboard
Bachelor's Club, The
Branded Woman, The
Burnt Fingers
Caught Bluffing
Clothes Make the Pirate
Cruise of the Hellion
Daughters of Today
Dearie
Don't Shoot
Dynamite Allen
Ermine and Rhinestones
Extra! Extra!
Fantomas [serial]
Galloping Kid, The
Going Up
Greyhound Limited, The
Her Dangerous Path
His Foreign Wife
Into the Net [serial]
Jilt, The
Kid Gloves
King of the Wild Horses
Leatherstocking [serial]
Little Johnny Jones
Lying Wives
McFadden Flats
Man Must Live, A
Midnight Adventure, A
My Man
Nobody's Bride
North Wind's Malice, The
Obey the Law
Oh, What a Night!
Ordeal, The
Our Modern Daughter
Over the Hill (Lucy)
Play Square
Ridin' Wild
Sap, The
Show of Shows, The
Silent Hero, The
Silver Comes Through

Stolen Kisses
Sunset Legion
Tarzan and the Golden Lion (Flora
    Hawks)
Valley of Hell
What Love Will Do
White Moth, The
Wildfire
Wilful Youth

4381
MURPHY, Jack (1915-)
Name the Man
Peter Pan (John)
Stella Dallas (Helen's son as a child)
Tumbleweeds

4382
MURPHY, Joe*
Cat and the Canary, The (milkman)
Gumps, The [series] (Andy Gump)

4383
MURPHY, John Daly*
Icebound
Polly of the Follies (Julius Caesar)
You Can't Fool Your Wife
Stage:
Beaux' Stratagem, The (Foigard) 28
Bonehead, The (Ethelbert St. Claire)
    20
Dumb-Bell (Jones) 23
Four Flusher, The (Horace Riggs) 25
Free Soul, A (Abe Sloan) 28
It's a Boy (Judson Blake) 22
Julie (Ezra) 27
Lady from the Sea, The (Ballested)
    29
Nightcap, The (Jerry Hammond) 21
She Stoops to Conquer (Dick) 24
Storm Center (Peter Mitchell) 27
Top Hole (Aloysious Blunt) 24
Virgin, The (Seth Brown) 26
Virginia Runs Away (Forbidden) (Has-
    tings Westover) 23
Wild Duck, The (Old Ekdal) 28

4384
MURPHY, Maurice*
Alias the Deacon
Beau Geste (Beau, as a child)
Home Maker, The
Last Man on Earth, The
Michigan Kid, The
Shepherd of the Hills, The
Thank You

4385
MURPHY, Morris*
College Coquette, The

4386
MURPHY, Steve*
Circus, The (dual role, prizefighter/
pickpocket)

4387
MURRAY, Anita*
Hot for Paris

4388
MURRAY, Charlie (1872-1941)
Boob, The (Cactus Jim)
Classified
Cohen and the Kellys, The
Cross Roads of New York, The
Dentist, The
Do Your Duty
Don't Weaken
Faint Hearts
Fatal Photo, The
Flying Romeos
Gorilla, The
Great Scott!
Head Man, The (Watts)
Her Blighted Love
Her Second Chance
Hollywood Kid, The
Irene
It's All Greek to Me
Life of Riley, The
Lilies of the Field
Lost at the Front
Love, Honor and Behave
Luck
Masked Woman, The
McFadden Flats
Mike
Mismates
My Son (Capt. Joe Bamby)
Nuisance, The
Painted People
Paradise
Percy
Pilgrim, The
Pill Pusher, The
Poor Nut, The
Reckless Lady, The
Silent Love, The
Small Town Idol, A
Social Errors
Steel Preferred
Subway Sadie
Sundown
Sweet Daddies

Unhappy Finish, The
Vamping Venus
Wizard of Oz, The
Stage:
Vaudeville [Palace] 29

4389
MURRAY, Elizabeth*
Little Old New York (Rachel Brew-
ster)
Stage:
Love Birds (Jennie O'Hara) 21
Sidewalks of New York (Mrs. O'-
Brien) 27

4390
MURRAY, Gray*
Four Feathers, The (Dermond Eus-
tace)
Taming of the Shrew, The (Baptista)

4391
MURRAY, J. Harold*
Cameo Kirby
Happy Days (a principal)
Married in Hollywood
Stage:
Captain Jinks (Title role) 25
Caroline (Capt. Robert Langdon) 23
Castles in the Air (John Brown) 26
China Rose (Cha Ming) 25
Make It Snappy 22
Passing Show of 1921, The   20
Rio Rita (Jim) 27
Springtime of Youth (Richard Stokes)
22
Vogues of 1924
Whirl of New York, The (Harry Bron-
son) 21

4392
MURRAY, James (1901-1937)
Big City, The (Curly)
Crowd, The (John Simms)
In Old Kentucky
Little Wildcat
Lovelorn, The
M.G.M. player 27
Percy
Rose-Marie (Jim Kenyon)
Shakedown, The
Shanghai Lady
Thunder (Tommy)
Stage:
Naughty Marietta (Rudolfo) 29
Three Cheers (Capt. Meurice)

4393
MURRAY, John T. *
Bardelys the Magnificent
Fazil (Gondolier)
Honky Tonk (cafe manager)
Joanna
Madonna of the Streets, A ("Slip-
pery" Eddie Foster)
Sally (Otis Hooper)
Sonny Boy
Stop Flirting
Winds of Chance
Stage:
Cinderella on Broadway 20
Floradora (Cyrus Gilfain) 20
Matrimonial Bed, The (Adolph Nob-
let) 27
Vaudeville [Palace] 27; 29
Whirl of New York, The (Icabod
Bronson) 21
Yankee Princess, The (Napoleon
St. Cloche) 22

4394
MURRAY, Ken (Don Court) (1907-   )
Half Marriage
Ladies of the Jury
Stage:
Vaudeville [Palace] 28; 29

4395
MURRAY, M. Gray*
Sonia (Sir Roger Dainton)
Woman of No Importance, A (Sir
Thomas Harford)

4396
MURRAY, Mae (Marie Adrienne
Koenig) (1889-1965)
ABCs of Love, The
Altars of Desire
Bachelor Apartment
Broadway Rose
Circe, the Enchantress
Fascination
Fashion Row (dual role)
French Doll, The
Gilded Lily (Lillian Drake)
Idols of Clay (Faith Merrill)
Jazzmania
Mademoiselle Midnight
Masked Bride, The
Merry Widow, The (Sonia)
Mormon Maid, The
On with the Dance
Peacock Alley (Cleo of Paris)
Right to Love, The
Show People (cameo)

Valencia
Stage:
Untitled Benefit 22

4397
MURRAY, Tom*
Gold Rush, The (Black Larson)
Into Her Kingdom
Pilgrim, The
Private Izzy Murphy
Tramp, Tramp, Tramp

4398
MURRELL, Alys*
Temptress, The (Josephine)

4399
MURREY, Charles*
Empty Hearts (Joe Delane)

4400
MURSKY, Alexander*
Doctor's Women, The
Die Freudlose Gasse [The Joyless
Street] /aka/ The Street of Sor-
row (Dr. Leid, attorney)
Luther

4401
MURTAGH, Cynthia*
Taming of the Shrew, The (Bianca)

4402
MUSE, Clarence (1889-   )
Hearts in Dixie (debut)

4403
MUSSETT, Charles*
Light in the Dark, The (Detective
Braenders)

4404
MÜTHEL, Lothar*
Der Golem

4405
MUZZI, Edulilo--see: Eduliho Mucci

4406
MYER, Torben*
Man Who Laughs, The (the spy)

4407
MYERS, Carmel (1899-1966)
Babbitt
Bath Between, The
Beau Brummel (Lady Hestor Stan-
hope)

Beautifully Trimmed
Ben Hur (Iras)
Breaking Through [serial]
Broadway after Dark
Broadway Scandals
Careers
Careless Age, The (Ray)
Certain Young Man, A
Cheated Love
Dancer of the Nile, The
Dangerous Moment, A
Daughter of the Law
Demi-Bride
Devil's Circus, The
Dream of Love (Countess)
Famous Mrs. Fair, The
Four Walls (Bertha)
Ghost Talks, The
Gilded Dream
Girl from Rio, The
Goodbye Girls
He Did His Best
In Folly's Trail
King Tut
Kiss, The
Last Hour
Law Against the Law, The
Little Girl Next Door, The
Love Gambler, The
Mad Marriage, The
Mary of the Movies
Metro player 24
Poisoned Paradise (Mrs. Belmire)
Prowlers of the Sea
Red Sword
Reno
Road to Mandalay, The (Zaya)
Show of Shows, The
Slave of Desire
Song of Love, The
Sorrell and Son (Florence Palfrey)
Tell It to the Marines
Understanding Heart, The (Kelcy
    Dale)
You Are in Danger
Stage:
Vaudeville [Palace] 29

4408
MYERS, Harry C. (1882-1938)
Bachelor Baby
Bad Man, The
Beautiful and Damned, The
Beautiful Cheat, The
Behold This Woman
Boy Crazy
Brass
Brass Bottle, The

Clean-Up, The
Common Law, The
Connecticut Yankee in King Arthur's
    Court, A (Title role)
Daddies
Dove, The
Dream of Love (Baron)
Exit Smiling
First Night, The
Forty-Five Minutes from Broadway
Fox player 22
Getting Gertie's Garter
Girl on the Pullman, The
Grounds for Divorce
Handle with Care
Kisses
Main Street
March Hare, The
Marriage Circle, The (detective)
Montmatre Rose
Nobody's Fool
Notorious Mrs. Sands, The
Nut Cracker, The /aka/ You Can't
    Fool Your Wife
Oh, Mary, Be Careful!
On the High Card
Peaceful Valley
R. S. V. P.
Robinson Crusoe [serial] (Title role)
Stephen Steps Out
Street of Illusion
Tarnish
Top O' the Morn'
Turn to the Right
Up in Mabel's Room
Wonder of Women, The
Zander the Great (Texas)

4409
MYERS, Kathleen*
Babbitt
Dick Turpin
Fourth Commandment, The
Go West
His Supreme Moment
Kosher Kitty Kelly

4410
MYERS, Ray*
Hunchback of Notre Dame, The (Char-
    molu's assistant)

4411
MYLES, Norbert*
One Man Game, A

4412
MYRGE, Mlle.*
Jade Casket, The

- N -

4413
NACHBAUER, Ernest*
Berlin after Dark

4414
NADEL, Eli*
Womanhandled

4415
NADEMSKY, Mikola*
Arsenal

4416
NADI, Aldo*
Le Tourmoi

4417
NADLER, Alexander*
Doctor's Women, The

4418
NAGEL, Conrad (1896-1970)
Bella Donna
Caught in the Fog
Cheaper to Marry
Dance Madness
Diamond Handcuffs
Divorce, The
Dynamite (Roger Towne)
Escape /aka/ The Exquisite Sinner
Eternal Three, The
Excuse Me
Fighting Chance
Fools' Paradise (Arthur Phelps)
Girl from Chicago, The
Glorious Betsy
Grumpy (Ernest Heron)
Heaven on Earth
Hollywood Revue of 1929
Husbands Are Liars
Hypnotist, The
Idle Rich, The
If I Were Single
Impossible Mrs. Bellew, The (John
   Helstan)
Kid Gloves
Kiss, The (André)
Lawful Larceny
Lights of Old Broadway (Dirk de
   Rhonde)
Lion and the Mouse, The

London after Midnight (Arthur Hibbs)
Lost Romance
Married Flirts
Memory Lane
Metro player 24
Michigan Kid, The
Midsummer Madness
Mysterious Lady, The /aka/ War in
   the Dark (Capt. Karl von Heiners-
   dorf)
Name the Man
Nice People
Only Thing, The (Duke of Chevenix)
Pink Gods
Pretty Ladies (Maggie's dream lover)
Quality Street (Dr. Valentine Brown)
Red Wine
Redeeming Sin, The
Redemption
Rejected Woman, The
Rendezvous, The
Romance of a Queen, The (Paul Ver-
   dayne)
Sacred and Profane Love
Sacred Flame, The
Saturday Night (Richard Prentiss)
Singed Wings
Sinners in Silk
Slightly Used
Snob, The
So This Is Marriage
State Street Sadie
Sun Up
Tenderloin
Terror, The (spoke title and credits)
Tess of the D'Urbervilles (Angel
   Claire)
There You Are
Thirteenth Chair, The
Tin Hats
Unseen Forces
Waning Sex, The
What Every Woman Knows

4419
NAH*
Chang (the boy)

4420
NAKARENKO, Dan*
Bigger than Barnum's

4421
NALDI, Nita (Anita Donna Dooley)
   (1889-1961)
Anna Ascends
Blood and Sand (Donna Sol)
Channing of the Northwest

383   Nally

Clothes Make the Pirate
Cobra (Elsie Van Zile)
Die Pratermizzi
Dr. Jekyll and Mr. Hyde (Miss Gina)
Don't Call It Love
Experience
For Your Daughter's Sake
Glimpses of the Moon
Hollywood
Lady Who Lied, The
La Femme Mie
Lawful Larceny
Life
Man from Beyond, The
Marriage Whirl, The
Miracle of Life, The
Model from Montmartre, The
Mountain Eagle, The
Nth Commandment, The
Pleasure Garden, The
Reported Missing
Sainted Devil, A (Carlotta)
Snitching Hour, The
Ten Commandments, The (Sally Lung)
Unfair Sex, The
What Price Beauty?
You Can't Fool Your Wife
Stage:
Bonehead, The (Mrs. Violet Bacon-
    Boyle) 20
Opportunity (Nellie Ross) 20

4422
NALLY, William*
Plunder [serial]
Stage:
Tin Pan Alley (Bull) 28

4423
NAMBU, K. *
Thief of Bagdad, The (Prince's coun-
    sellor)
Stage:
Commodore Marries, The (Cookie) 29

4424
NAMARA, Marguerite*
Stolen Moments
Stage:
Mikado, The (Yum-Yum) 25
Vaudeville [Hippodrome] 25

4425
NANOOK*
Nanook of the North (Title role)

4426
NAPIERKOWSKA, Stacia Mlle. *
Atlantide (Antinea)

4427
NAPOLEON (Dog)
Thirteenth Hour, The

4428
NARBEKOVA, O. *
Village of Sin, The

4429
NARES, Owen (Owen N. Ramsay)
    (1888-1943)
All the Winners
Brown Sugar
Faithful Heart, The
For Her Father's Sake
Indian Love Lyrics
Last Rose of Summer, The
Milestones
Miriam Rozella
Sentence of Death, The
Sorrows of Satan, The
Temporary Gentleman, A
This Marriage Business
Young Lochinvar

4430
NARLAY, R. *
Passion of Joan of Arc, The

4431
NASH, George (1865-1945)
Confidence Man, The
Great Gatsby, The (Charles Wolf)
Janice Meredith (Lord Howe)
Man Must Live, A
Song and Dance Man, The
Under the Red Robe (Jules, the inn-
    keeper)
When Knighthood Was in Flower
    (Capt. Bradhurst)
Stage:
Creoles (Monsieur Merluche) 27
La Gringa (Capt. Aaron Bowditch) 28
Merchants of Glory (Pigal) 25
Noose, The (Buck Gordon) 26
Trilby (Talbot Wynne) 21

4432
NASH, John E. *
Illusion

4433
NASH, June*
Dynamite (a good mixer)

Strange Cargo
Their Own Desire

4434
NASH, Nancy*
Loves of Carmen, The
Rich but Honest

4435
NASJA*
Vanishing American, The /aka/ The
Vanishing Race (Indian boy)

4436
NATHANSON, Charles*
Broken Hearts

4437
NATHEAUX, Louis*
Broadway Babies
Cop, The
Dress Parade
Fast Set, The (Billy Sommers)
Fighting Love
Four Walls (Monk)
Girls Gone Wild
King of Kings, The (bit)
Man Bait
Mexicali Rose
Ned McCobb's Daughter (Kelly)
Risky Business
Stand and Deliver (Capt. Dargis)
Tenth Avenue
Weary River
Why Be Good?

4438
NATOVA, Natacha and Company
Hollywood Revue of 1929

4439
NAVARRO, Catherine*
Happy Days (chorus)

4440
NAVARRO, Joan*
Happy Days (chorus)

4441
NAWM, Tom*
General, The (a Union general)

4442
NAZIMOVA, Alla (1879-1945)
Billions
Camille (Title role)
Doll's House, A (Nora)
Heart of a Child, The

Madame Peacock
Madonna of the Streets, A (dual role,
   Mary Carlson/Mary Ainsleigh)
Metro player 21
My Son (Ana Silva)
Redeeming Sin, The
Salome (Title role)
Stronger than Death
Stage:
Cherry Orchard, The (Madame Ranev-
   sky) 28
Dagmar (Countess Dagmar) 23
Katerina (Katerina Ivanovna) 29
Vaudeville [Palace] 23; 26; 27; 28

4443
NEAL, Richard*
Fighting Coward, The [serial]

4444
NEDELL, Bernard (1898-1972)
Knight in London, A
Return of the Rat, The (Henri)
Silver King, The

4445
NEELY, Neil*
West Point
Stage:
First Flight (Hairy Lake) 25

4446
NEFF, Pauline*
Claw, The (Nonie Valetta)
Let Not Man Put Asunder
Man Without a Country, The /aka/
   As No Man Has Loved
Midshipman, The
Masked Bride, The
Ranson's Folly
Two Girls Wanted

4447
NEGRI, Pola (Appolonia Chalupec)
   (1894-   )
Arme Viletta /aka/ The Red Peacock
Barbed Wire
Bella Donna
Die Bergkatze /aka/ The Mountain
   Cat; The Wildcat (Rischka)
Camille
Charmer, The
Cheat, The
Crown of Lies, The
Die Dame im Glashave
Devil's Pawn, The
East of Suez
Die Flamme [The Flame] (Yvette)

Flower of the Night
Forbidden Paradise (Catherine the
    Great)
Die Geschlossene Kette
Good and Naughty
Gypsy Blood (Carmen)
Hotel Imperial (Anna)
Intrigue
Last Payment, The
Lily of the Dust
Loves of an Actress (Rachel)
Mad Love /aka/ Sappho
Manja
Die Marchesa D'Arminiani
Das Martyrium
Men
Passion (Madame du Barry)
Passionate Journey, The
Secret Hour, The
Shadows of Paris
Spanish Dancer, The (Maritana)
Sumurun /aka/ One Arabian Night
    (Yannaia)
Three Sinners
Vendetta
Way of Lost Souls, The
Woman Commands, A
Woman from Moscow
Woman He Scorned, The
Woman of the World, A
Woman on Trial, The

4448
NEILAN, Marshall (1891-1958)
First National player 20

4449
NEILL, James*
Any Woman
Bits of Life
Crimson Runner, The
Double-Dyed Deceiver, The
Her Husband's Trademark (Henry
    Strom)
Idle Rich, The
King of Kings, The (James)
Little Shepherd of Kingdom Come,
    The
Love Hungry
Man's Mate, A
Manslaughter (butler)
New Brooms
Paliser Case, The
Saturday Night (Tompkins)
Ten Commandments, The (Aaron)
Thank You

4450
NEILL, Richard R. *
Born to the West
Heritage of the Desert, The
Percy
Tumbleweeds
Wanderer of the Wasteland (Collishaw)
Where East Is East (Rangho the Go-
    rilla)

4451
NEILSON, Asta (1883-)
Die Freudlose Gasse [The Joyless
    Street] /aka/ The Street of Sor-
    row (Maria Lechner)
Hamlet (Title role)
Hedda Gabler
Pandora's Box
Small Town Sinners
Vanina
Women Without Men

4452
NEISEL, Edmund*
Peaks of Destiny

4453
NELSON, Bobby*
Tarzan the Mighty (Bobby Trevor)
    [serial]

4454
NELSON, Edgar*
Get Rich Quick Wallingford (Eddie
    Lamb)
Sandra
Way Down East (Hi Holler)
Womanhandled
Stage:
Blue Bonnet (Jep Clayton) 20
Humming Bird, The (Henry Smith) 23
Just Because (Leonard Wall) 22
Katy Did (Eddie Carson) 27
Lucky Break, A (Benny Ketchum) 25
Nightstick (Soft Malone) 27
Tin Pan Alley (Johnny Dolan) 28
Yours Truly (Mike) 27

4455
NELSON, Florence*
His House in Order (housekeeper)

4456
NELSON, Frank*
Gentleman of Leisure, A
Great Mail Robbery, The
In Old Arizona (cowboy)
Sea Beast, The (Stubbs)

Sea Hunt, The
Shadows of Paris
Stephen Steps Out
Stranger, The

4457
NELSON, J. *
Down Hill (Hibbert)

4458
NELSON, Jack (1882-   )
Chickens
Home Stretch, The
I Am Guilty
Love Madness
Rookie's Return, The

4459
NELSON, Otto*
Black Oxen (Dr. Steinach)

4460
NELSON, Sam*
Circus Kid, The
Crooks Can't Win
Rio Rita (McGinn)

4461
NEMETZ, Max*
Der Mensch am Wege [Man by the
  Roadside]

4462
NENASHEVA, L. *
Tanks-Trakitirschitsa /aka/ Protin
  Otsa; Against Her Father; Tanka,
  the Innkeeper

4463
NEOLA, Princess*
Barrier, The (Alluma)

4464
NERI, Donatelle*
Kif Tebbi

4465
NERO, Curtis*
West of Zanzíbar (Bumbu)

4466
NERVO and KNOX (Jimmy and Ted-
  dy Knox)*
Alf's Button (bit)
Phonofilm
Rising Generation, The
Stage:
Vaudeville [Palace] 26

Ziegfeld Follies 22

4467
NES, Ole M. *
Chicago after Midnight
Danger Street
Hit of the Show
Jazz Heaven
Skinner's Big Idea

4468
NESBIT, Evelyn (1885-1967)
Fallen Idol, A
Hidden Woman, The (Ann Wesley)

4469
NESBIT, Pinna*
Partners of the Night

4470
NESMITH, Ottola*
Beyond Price
Girl Shy Cowboy

4471
NESS, Ole M. --see: Ole M. Nes

4472
NEST, Loni*
Die Freudlose Gasse [The Joyless
  Street] /aka/ The Street of Sor-
  row) (Rosa Rumfort)
Der Kleine Napoleon [The Little
  Napoleon] /aka/ So Sind Die Män-
  ner [Men are Like That]; Napole-
  ons Kleiner Bruder [Napoleon's
  Little Brother] (Liselotte)
Tragödie der Liebe [Tragedy of Love]

4473
NEUFOLD, Max*
Rasputin, the Holy Sinner

4474
NEUMANN, Lotte*
Romeo und Julia im Schnee [Romeo
  and Juliet in the Snow] (Julia)

4475
NEVILLE, George*
Dream Street (Tom Chudder)
Scarlet Saint, The
Way Down East (Constable Reuben
  Whipple)
Stage:
Across the Street (Calvin Abbott) 24
Babbling Brookes (Uncle Bihl) 27
Decision (John Grey) 29

Move On (Cecil Dumphy) 26
Squealer, The (Hi Loo) 28

4476
NEWALL, Guy (1885-1937)
Beauty and the Beast
Bigamist, The
Boy Woodburn
Duke's Son, The
Ghost Train, The (Teddie Deakin)
Lure of Crooning Waters, The
Maid of Silver Sea, The
Mirage, The
Number 17
Starlit Garden, The
Testimony
What the Butler Saw

4477
NEWBERG, Frank*
Home Maker, The
Married Virgin, The /aka/ Frivo-
    lous Wives

4478
NEWELL, David (1905-)
Dangerous Curves (Tony Barretti)
Hole in the Wall, The (Gordon Grant)
Kibitzer, The
Marriage Playground, The (Gerald)
Stage:
Phantom Lover, The (Lt. Jean-Mare
    Marrien) 28

4479
NEWLAND, Mary--see: Lilian Oldland

4480
NEWMAN, John K. *
Greatest Love of All, The
Stage:
Woman Disputed, The (dual role, a
    blind man/a father) 26

4481
NEWTON, A. , Mrs. *
Vanity Fair (Miss Pinkerton)

4482
NEWTON, Charles*
In the Palace of the King
Iron Horse, The (Collis P. Hunting-
ton)
Riders of the Purple Sage (Herd)
Vanity's Price

4483
NEX, Andre*
Daughter of Israel, A
Jolly Peasant, The

4484
NICHOL, Emilie*
Beloved Vagabond (Mrs. Rushwood)

4485
NICHOLLS, Fred J. *
Disraeli (butler)
Stage:
Deep Tangled Wildwood, The (Bates)
    23

4486
NICHOLS, George (1864-)
Barnstormer, The (Joel's father)
Capital Punishment (warden)
Country Kid, The
Daughters of Today
Deep Waters
Don't Marry for Money
Eagle, The (judge)
East of Broadway
Extra Girl, The
Flirt, The
Ghost Patrol, The
Gigolo
Goose Woman, The (Det. Lopez)
His Majesty Bunker Bean
Iron Rider, The
Light of the Western Stars, The
Live and Let Live
Midnight Express, The
Nineteen and Phyllis
Oliver Twist, Jr.
Pinto
Pride of Palomar, The
Proud Flesh
Queen of Sheba, The (King David)
Red Lily, The (Concierge)
Ritzy
Rolling Home
Sea Horses (Marx)
Secrets (William Marlowe)
Senor Daredevil
Shame
Suzanna
Wedding March, The (Schweisser)
White Flannels
White Gold (Alice's father)

4487
NICHOLS-BATES, H. *
Fifth Form at St. Dominic's (Jeff
    Cripps)

4488
NICHOLSON, Paul*
As Man Desires
Bertha, the Sewing Machine Girl
Bronco Twisters
Brute, The
Chickie
I Want My Man
Joanna
Johnstown Flood, The (Joe Hamilton)
Married Flirts
Nervous Wreck, The
Not Quite Decent
Port of Missing Girls, The
Smart Set, The
Up in Mabel's Room
Stage:
Red Light Annie (Robert Dugan) 23

4489
NIELSEN, Asta--see: Asta Neilson

4490
NIELSEN, Mathilde*
Master of the House

4491
NIGH, William*
Democracy, the Vision Restored

4492
NIKANDROV*
October

4493
NILSSON, Anna Q. (1893-1974)
Adam's Rib (Mrs. Michael Ramsay)
Babe Comes Home
Between Friends
Blockade
Broadway after Dark
Easy Pickings
Fighting Chance, The
Flowing Gold
Good Bad Girl, The
Greater Glory, The
Half a Dollar Bill
Hearts Aflame
Her Kingdom of Dreams
Her Second Chance
Hollywood
If I Marry Again
In the Heart of a Fool
Inez from Hollywood
Isle of Lost Ships, The (Dorothy
  Fairfax)
Lonesome Ladies
Lotus Eater, The

Luck of the Irish, The
Man from Home, The
Man Who Came Back, The
Masked Woman, The
Midnight Lovers
Miss Nobody
Oath, The
One Hour Before Dawn
One Way Street
Painted People
Pink Gods
Ponjola (Desmond)
Rustle of Silk, The (Lady Feo)
Side Show of Life, The
Sorrell and Son (Dora Sorrell)
Splendid Road, The
Spoilers, The (Cherry Malotte)
Talker, The
Thirteenth Juror, The
Three Live Ghosts
Toll Gate, The (Mary Brown)
Too Much Money
Top of the World, The
Vanity's Price
Viennese Melody, The
What Women Will Do
Whip, The
Why Girls Leave Home
Winds of Chance
Without Limit

4494
NISSEN, Aud Egede*
Anna Boleyn /aka/ Deception (Jane
  Seymour)
Dr. Mabuse the Gambler /aka/ Dr.
  Mabuse, the Great Unknown
Peter the Pirate
Slums of Berlin
Sumurun /aka/ One Arabian Night
  (Haidee)

4495
NISSEN, Greta (Grethe Ruzt-Nissen)
  (1906-   )
Beggar on Horseback
Blind Alleys
Blonde or Brunette?
Butter and Egg Man, The
Daarskat Dyd Og Driverter
Fazil (Fabienne)
In the Name of Love
King on Main Street, The
Lady of the Harem
Lost, a Wife
Love Thief, The
Lucky Lady, The
Popular Sin, The

Swan, The
Tempest, The
Wanderer, The
Stage:
No Foolin' 26

4496
NIXON, Marian (1904-)
Auctioneer, The
Big Dan
Cheerful Fraud, The
Chinese Parrot, The
Courtship of Miles Standish, The
Cupid's Fireman
Devil's Island
Down the Stretch
Durand of the Badlands (Molly Gore)
Fallen Angels
Fourflusher, The
General Crack (Archduchess Maria
   Louisa)
Geraldine
Hallroom Boys comedies
Hands Up! (Mae Woodstock)
Heroes of the Night
Honeymoon Flats
How to Handle Women
Hurricane Kid, The
I'll Show You the Town
In the Headlines
Jazz Mad
Just Off Broadway
Kentucky Days
Last of the Duanes
Little Pal
Man, Woman and Wife
Out All Night
Out of the Ruins
Rainbow Man, The
Red Lips
Red Sword
Riders of the Purple Sage (Bess
   Erne)
Rolling Home
Rosita
Saddle Hawk, The
Say It with Songs
Show of Shows, The
Silks and Saddles
Spangles
Symphony, The
Taxi! Taxi!
Temple of Venus, The
Vagabond Trail
What Happened to Jones?
Where Was I?
Young Nowheres

4497
NOBLE, Milton*
America /aka/ Love and Sacrifice
   (an old patriot)

4498
NODALSKY, Sonia*
East Side, West Side

4499
NODELL, Sonya*
Salome of the Tenements

4500
NOEL*
Over the Hill (Issac, the man)

4501
NOLAN, Bill*
Cat cartoons

4502
NOLAN, Gypo*
Informer, The

4503
NOLAN, Mary (Mary Imogen Robert-
   son) (1905-1948)
Charming Sinners (Anne-Marie Whit-
   ley)
Desert Nights
Eleven Who Were Loyal
Die Feuertanzerin
Foreign Legion
Good Morning Judge
Die Madchen Von Paris
Die Panzergewalbe
Shanghai Lady
Silks and Saddles
Sorrell and Son (Molly Roland)
Taglich
Die Unberuhrte Frau
Uneasy Money
Viennese Lover
West of Zanzibar (Maizie)
Wiener Herzen

4504
NOMIS, Leo*
California Straight Ahead

4505
NORDYKE, Kenneth*
Happy Days (chorus)

4506
NORMAN, Amber*
Love and the Devil

4507
NORMAN, Gertrude*
Greene Murder Case, The (Mrs.
  Tobias Greene)

4508
NORMAN, Josephine*
Forbidden Woman, The
King of Kings, The (Mary of Bethany)
Road to Yesterday, The (Anne Vener)
Wreck of the Hesperus, The

4509
NORMAND, Mabel (Mabel Fortescue)
  (1894-1930)
Anything Once
Extra Girl, The
Head over Heels
Jinx
Molly O'
Nickel Hopper, The
Oh, Mabel, Behave!
One Hour Married
Peck's Bad Girl
Pinto
Raggedy Rose
Should Men Walk Home?
Slim Princess, The
Suzanna
What Happened to Rosa?

4510
NORRIS, William*
Adam and Eva
Eternal Three, The
Go Getter, The
Joy Girl, The
Love Piker, The
Maytime (Matthew)
My Man
When Knighthood Was in Flower
  (Louis XII)
Stage:
Connecticut Yankee, A (dual role,
  Marvin/Merlin) 27
Dove, The (Little Bill) 25
Kissing Time (Polydore Cliquot) 20
White Wings (Ernest Inch) 26

4511
NORTH, Wilfred*
Beloved Brute, The
Captain Blood (Col. Bishop)
Drivin' Fool, The
Fourflusher, The
Happy Warrior, The
Hell Bent for Heaven
Man's Mate, A

On Thin Ice
Son of Wallingford, The (Rufus Wal-
  lingford)
Tracked by the Police
Trial of Mary Dugan, The (Judge
  Nash)

4512
NORTHRUP, Harry S. *
Burning Daylight
Devil's Island
Divine Sinner, The (Ambassador
  D'Ray)
Four Horsemen of the Apocalypse,
  The (the Count)
Last Warning, The
Prisoners
White Circle, The
Woman of Paris, A

4513
NORTON, Barry (1905-1956)
Ankles Preferred
Exalted Flapper
Fleet Wings
Four Devils (Adolph)
Heart of Salome, The
Legion of the Condemned (drunkard)
Lily, The
Mother Knows Best (the boy)
Sins of the Father (Tom Spengler)
Sunrise (bit)
What Price Glory? (Pvt. Lewisohn)
Wizard, The

4514
NORTON, Edgar*
Broadway after Dark
Enticement
Fast and Furious
Fast Set, The (Archie Wells)
King on Main Street, The
Learning to Love
Light in the Dark, The (Peters)
Lost, a Wife
Love Parade, The (Master of Cere-
  monies)
Man Who Laughs, The (High Chancel-
  lor)
Men
Oh, Kay!
Regular Fellow, A
Singed
Student Prince, The (Lutz)
Tiger Love
Woman Proof
Stage:
As You Like It (LeBeau) 23

World We Live In, The (Ichneumon
   Fly) 22

4515
NORTON, Fletcher*
Dream of Love
Stage:
Roger Bloomer (a ragged man) 23

4516
NORTON, Frederic*
Chu-Chin-Chow

4517
NORTON, William*
Three O'Clock in the Morning

4518
NORWOOD, Ellie (1841-1948)
Adventures of Sherlock Holmes [ser-
   ies] (Title role)
Crimson Circle, The
Further Adventures of Sherlock Hol-
   mes [series] (Title role)
Gentleman of France, A
Gwyneth of the Welsh Hills
Hound of the Baskervilles, The
   (Sherlock Holmes)
Hundredth Chance, The
Last Adventures of Sherlock Holmes,
   The [series] (Title role)
Recoil, The
Sign of the Four, The (Sherlock
   Holmes)
Tavern Knight, The

4519
NORWORTH, Jack*
Queen of the Nightclubs
Stage:
Vaudeville [Palace] 26; 27

4520
NOURSE, Dorothy*
Fascinating Youth

4521
NOVA, Alex*
Marê Nostrum [Our Sea] (Don Este-
   ban Ferragut)

4522
NOVA, Hedda*
Jungle Tragedy, A
My Own Pal
Shadows of the West

4523
NOVAK, Eva (1899-)
Barriers of Folly
Chasing the Moon
Daredevil, The
Desert Love
Dixie Flyer, The
Dollar Devils
Duty's Reward
For the Term of His Natural Life
Hell's River
Irene
Making of a Man, The
Man Life Passed By, The
Man Who Saw Tomorrow, The
Millionaire Policeman, The
No Man's Gold
Noise in Newboro, A
O'Malley of the Mounted
Red Signals
Romance of Runnibede, The
Rough Diamond
Sally (Rosie Lafferty)
Silk Husbands and Calico Wives
Sky High (Estella)
Smart Set, The
Society Secrets
Temptation
Testing Block, The
Thirty Below Zero
Tiger's Claw, The
Torrent, The
Trailin'
Universal player 21
Up and Going
Up in Mary's Attic
Wanted at Headquarters
Wolves of the North [serial]

4524
NOVAK, Jane (1896-)
Barbarian, The
Behind the Door
Belle of Alaska, The
Blackguard
Closed Gates
Colleen of the Pines
Dangerous Virtue
Divorce
Free Lips
Golden Trial
Great Accident, The
Isobel, or the Trails End
Jealous Husbands
Kazan
Lost at Sea
Lullaby
Lure of the Wild

Man Who Life Passed By, The
One Increasing Purpose
Other Woman, The
Pride's Fall
Redskin, The (Judith Stearns)
River's End, The
Roads of Destiny
Rosary, The
Snowshoe Trail
Soul of a Woman
Substitute Wife
Thelma
Three Word Brand
What Price Love?
Whispering Canyon

4525
NOVARRO, Ramon (Ramon Samanyagos) (1899-1968)
Across to Singapore (Joel Shore)
Arab, The (Jamil)
Ben Hur (Title role)
Certain Young Man, A
Devil May Care
Flying Fleet, The
Forbidden House
Four Horsemen of the Apocalypse (bit)
Gold Braid
Lovers
Lover's Oath, A /aka/ Rubaiyat of Omar Khayyam)
Midshipman
Mr. Barnes of New York
Pagan, The
Prisoner of Zenda, The (Rupert of Hentzau)
Red Lily, The (Jean Leonnec)
Road to Romance
Scaramouche (Andre Louis Moreau)
Small Town Idol, A
Student Prince, The (Prince Karl Heinrich)
Thy Name Is Woman
Trifling Women
Where the Rainbow Ends (Motauri)

4526
NOVELLI, Anthony*
Julius Caesar

4527
NOVELLO, Ivor (Ivor Davies) (1893-1951)
Bohemian Girl, The (Thaddeus)
Bonnie Prince Charles
Carnival (Count Maria de Bernaldo)
Case of Jonathan Drew, The

Constant Nymph, The (Lewis)
Down Hill (Roddy Berwick)
Lodger, The
Man Without Desire, The (Count Vittorio Donaldo)
Rat, The (Pierre Boucheron)
Return of the Rat, The (Pierre Boucheron)
South Sea Bubble, A
Triumph of the Rat, The (Pierre Boucheron)
Vortex, The (Nicky Lancaster)
When Boys Leave Home
White Rose, The (Joseph Beaugarde)

4528
NOWELL, Wedgwood (1878-1957)
Adam's Rib (secretary to Moravian Minister)
Ben Hur
Doll's House, A (Nils Krogstad)
Don't Marry for Money
813
Enter Madame
Eternal Flame, The (Marquis de Ronquerolles)
Little Heroes of the Street
Quo Vadis
Thelma
When Knighthood Was in Flower
Wife's Romance, A

4529
NOX, Andre--see: Andre Nex

4530
NOY, Wilfred*
Careless Age, The (Lord Durhugh)
Doctor's Secret, The
Interference (Dr. Gray)
Janice Meredith (Dr. Joseph Warren)
Stage:
Dancers, The (Duke of Winfield) 23

4531
NUGENT, Eddie (Edward J. Nugent) (1904-)
Bellamy Trial, The (boy reporter)
Duke Steps Out, The
First Kiss, The
Flying Fleet, The
Girl in the Show, A
Gold Braid
Headlines
Loose Ankles
Man in Hobbles, The
Our Dancing Daughters (Freddie)
Our Modern Maidens

Single Man, A
Untamed
Vagabond Lover, The

4532
NUGENT, Elliott (1899-)
Not So Dumb
Our Modern Maidens
Single Standard, The
So This Is College
Wise Girl, The
Stage:
Breaks, The (Jim Dolf) 28
By Request (William Abbott) 28
Dulcy (Tom Sterrett) 21
Kempy (Kempy James) 22; 27
Poor Nut, The (John Miller) 25
Rising Son, The (Ted Alamayne) 24
Wild Westcotts, The (Eddie Hudson)
  23

4533
NYE, Carroll (1901-1974)
Bishop Murder Case, The
Brute, The
Classified
Confession
Craig's Wife
Death Valley
Flying Fleet, The
Girl from Chicago, The
Girl in the Glass Cage, The (Terry
  Pomfert)
Gold Braid
Heart of Maryland, The
Her Honor the Governor
Imposter, The
Jazzland
Kosher Kitty Kelly
Land of the Silver Fox
Light Fingers
Little Mickey Grogan
Madame X (Darrell)
Perfect Crime, The
Powder My Back
Race for Life, A
Rinty of the Desert
Rose of Kildare
Silver Slave, The
Sporting Age
Squall, The (Paul Lajos)
What Every Girl Should Know
While the City Sleeps (Marty)

4534
NYE, G. Raymond*
Fighting Coward, The [serial]
Queen of Sheba, The (Adonijah)

Tenderloin
Tiger Love

4535
NYLA*
Nanook of the North (wife)

- O -

4536
OAKIE, Jack (Lewis Delaney Offield)
  (1903-)
Chinatown Nights
Close Harmony (Ben Barney)
Dummy, The (Dopey Hart)
Fast Company (Elmer Kane)
Finders Keepers (debut)
Fleet's In, The (Searchlight Doyle)
Hard to Get
Hit the Deck
Man I Love, The
Paramount extra 27
Sin Town
Someone to Love
Street Girl
Sweetie (Tap-Tap Thompson)
Wild Party, The (Al)

4537
OAKLAND, Vivien (Vivian Anderson)
  (1895-1958)
Imagine My Embarrassment
Love 'em and Weep
Madonna of the Streets (Lady Sarah
  Joyce)
Man in Hobbles, The
Rainbow Trail, The
Teaser, The
Tell 'em Nothing
Time, the Place and the Girl, The
Tony Runs Wild
Uncle Tom's Cabin (Mrs. Shelby)
Wedding Bills
Stage:
Betty Be Good (Marion Love) 20
Bombo (a principal) 21
Century Revue (a principal) 20
Midnight Rounders, The (a principal)
  20
Vaudeville [Palace] 27; 29

4538
OAKLEY, Florence*
Most Immoral Lady, A

4539
OAKMAN, Wheeler (1890-1949)
Big Scoop, The
Black Feather
Broken Mask, The
Danger Patrol
Devil's Chaplain, The
Donovan Affair, The
Fangs of Justice
Father and Son
Girl from Woolworth's, The
Good-Bye Kiss, The
Half Breed, The (Delmer Spavinaw)
Handcuffed
Heart of Broadway
Heroes of the Night
Hey, Hey, Cowboy!
Hurricane, The
In Borrowed Plumes
Lights of New York (Hawk Miller)
Little Johnny Jones
Masked Angel, The
Miracle Girl, The
Morgan's Raiders /aka/ Morgan's
  Last Raid
Number Please
On with the Show (Durant)
Out of the Night
Outside the Law (Dapper Bill Bal-
  lard)
Peck's Bad Boy
Power of the Press
Shakedown, The
Shanghai Lady
Show of Shows, The
Slippy McGee
Snarl of Hate, The
Top Sergeant Mulligan
Virgin of Stamboul, The
What a Night!
What Women Love
While the City Sleeps (Skeeter)

4540
O'BECK, Fred*
Oh, Kay!
Patent Leather Kid, The

4541
OBELENSKY, W.*
End of St. Petersberg, The

4542
OBER, Robert*
Big Parade, The (Harry)
Butterflies in the Rain
Idle Rich, The
Introduce Me

King of Kings, The (bit)
Mystic, The
Souls for Sables
Time, the Comedian
Whole Town's Talking, The
Stage:
Humming Bird, The (Phillip Carey)
  23

4543
OBERG, Gustav*
Peak of Fate

4544
OBERLE, Florence*
Barnstormer, The (leading lady)

4545
O'BRIEN, Bill*
Trespasser, The (butler)

4546
O'BRIEN, Eugene (1882-1966)
Broadway and Home
Channing of the Northwest
Chivalrous Charlie
Clay Dollars
Dangerous Innocence
Faithless Lover, The
Figurehead, The
Fine Manners (Brian Alden)
Flames
Flaming Love
Fool and His Money, A
Frivolous Sal
Gilded Lies
Graustark (Grenfall Lorry)
His Wife's Money
Is Life Worth Living?
John Smith
Last Door, The
Only the Brave
Only Woman, The
Prophet's Paradise
Romantic Age, The
Secrets (John Carlton)
Siege
Simon the Jester
Souls for Sables
Thief, The
Voice from the Minaret, The (Andrew
  Fabian)
Wonderful Chance (dual role)
Worlds Apart

4547
O'BRIEN, George (1900-   )
[Horse: Bullet]

Blindfolded
Blue Eagle, The (George D'Arcy)
Case of Mary Brown, The
Dancers, The
East Side, West Side
False Colors
Fig Leaves
Fighting Heart, The
Havoc (Dick Chappell)
Honor Bound
Iron Horse, The (Davy Brandon)
Is Zat So?
Johnstown Flood, The (Tom O'Day)
Last of the Duanes
Man Who Came Back, The
Masked Emotions
Moran of the Lady Letty
Ne'er Do-Well, The
Noah's Ark (dual role, Japeth/Travis)
Paid to Love (Crown Prince Michael)
Painted Lady, The
Riders of the Purple Sage
Romantic Age, The
Roughneck, The
Rustlin' for Cupid
Salute
Shadows of Paris
Sharp Shooters, The
Silver Treasure, The
Sunrise (the man)
Thank You
Three Bad Men
True Heaven
White Hands
Woman Proof

4548
O'BRIEN, Gypsy*
Little Old New York (Ariana De
    Puyster)
Master Mind, The
Salvation Nell
Young Diana, The
Stage:
Beau Gallant (Clare Hoyt) 26
Casanova (beautiful governess) 23
East of Suez (Sylvia Knox) 22
Easy Virtue (Nina Vansittart) 25
Ghost Train, The (Elsie Winthrop)
    26
Happy-Go-Lucky (Constance Damer)
    20
Morning After, The (Mrs. Lamb)
My Aunt from Ypsilanti (Elizabeth
    Hammond) 23
Parasites (Lady Nina Chandos) 24

4549
O'BRIEN, Hortense*
Black Oxen (a flapper)

4550
O'BRIEN, Jack*
Bride's Play, The
Iron Horse, The (Dinny)

4551
O'BRIEN, John*
Bride 13 [serial]

4552
O'BRIEN, Mary*
It Must Be Love
Stage:
Sweetheart Shop, The (Timandra) 20

4553
O'BRIEN, Pat (William O'Brien)
    (1899-)
Determination
Freckled Rascal, The
Fury of the Wild
Happy Landing
Married in Haste
Stage:
Gertie (Steve) 26
Henry Behave (Anthony Alexander) 26

4554
O'BRIEN, Tom (1898-)
Abysmal Brute, The
Annie Laurie
Anybody Here Seen Kelly?
Big Parade, The (Bull)
Bugle Call, The
Chorus Kid, The
Dance Hall
Dark Skies
Fire Brigade, The
Flaming Forest, The
Flying Fool, The
Frontiersman, The
Gentleman from America, The
His Lucky Day
Is Zat So?
It Can Be Done
Last Warning
Peacock Fan, The
Poker Faces
Private Life of Helen of Troy, The
    (Ulysses)
Rookies
Runaway Express
Sagebrusher, The
San Francisco Nights

Scarlet Car, The
Scrap Iron
Smiling Irish Eyes
So This Is Marriage
Take It from Me
That's My Daddy
Tin Hats
Twelve Miles Out
Untamed
Winners of the Wilderness

4555
O'BYRNE, Patsy*
Outcast, The

4556
O'CONNOR, Edward*
Dangerous Money (Sheamus Sullivan)
Stage:
Guest of Honor, The (Mr. Wartle)
    20
My Country (Patrick Mulcahy) 26
Sally, Irene and Mary (Mr. Mulca-
    hey) 22
Silver Tassie, The (Simon Norton)
    29
Street Wolf, The (Chick Lollipop) 29
Ten Per Cent (the character man) 27

4557
O'CONNOR, Kathleen*
Old Homestead, The
Prairie Trails
Wild Bill Hickok

4558
O'CONNOR, L. J.*
Sporting Youth

4559
O'CONNOR, Robert Emmett (1885-
    1962)
Booster, The
Broadway
Dressed to Kill
Four Walls
Freedom of the Press
Isle of Lost Ships, The
Singing Fool, The (cafe manager)
Smiling Irish Eyes
Tin Gods (a foreman)
Weary River

4560
O'CONNOR, Una (1893-1959)
Cavalcade (the housekeeper)
Dark Red Roses

Stage:
Autumn Fire (Eileen Keegan) 26
Fake, The (waitress) 24

4561
O'DARE, Eileen*
Where the River Shannon Flows

4562
O'DARE, Peggy*
Blind Chance
For Life
Kentuck's Ward
Vanishing Dagger, The [serial]

4563
O'DAY, Dawn--see: Anne Shirley

4564
O'DAY, Molly (1911-)
Hard Boiled Haggerty
Kentucky Courage
Lovelorn, The
Patent Leather Kid, The
Shepherd of the Hills
Show of Shows, The
Sisters

4565
O'DAY, Peggy*
Chinatown Mystery, The

4566
O'DELL, Garry*
Astray from the Steerage (intelligence
    department)

4567
O'DENISHAWN, Florence*
Monsieur Beaucaire (Columbine)
Stage:
Hitchy-Koo 1920 (a principal) 20
Honeymoon Lane (herself) 26
Ziegfeld Follies (a principal) 21

4568
ODETTE, Mary (Odette Goimbault)
    (1901-)
All Roads Lead to Calvary
As God Made Her
Breed of the Treshams, The
Cherry Ripe
Crimson Circle, The
De Vrouw van den Minister
Diamond Man, The
Double Event, The
Edmund Kean, Prince Among Lovers
Emerald of the East

Enchantment
Eugene Aram
Hypocrites
If Youth but Knew
Inheritance
Lion's Mouse, The
Mr. Gilfil's Love Story
Nets of Destiny
Not for Sale
Number 15 John Street
She
Street of Adventure
Torn Sails
Traitor, The
With All Her Heart
Wonderful Year, The

4569
O'DONNELL Spec (1911-)
Call of the Cuckoo, The
Casey at the Bat
Country Kid, The
Danger Street
Darling of New York, The
Devil's Cargo, The
Do Gentlemen Snore?
Dressmaker from Paris, The
Dumb Daddies
Grand Parade, The
Headlines
Hot News
It's All Greek to Me
Little Annie Rooney
Little Johnny Jones
Main Street
Movie Night
Private Izzy Murphy
Sophomore, The
Sparrows /aka/ Human Sparrows
  (Ambrose Grimes)
Tomorrow's Love
Vamping Venus
We're All Gamblers

4570
OETTEL, Wally*
Plunder [serial]

4571
O'FARRELL, Broderick*
What Happened to Jones?

4572
OFFERMAN, George*
Girl on the Barge, The
Stage:
Enemy of the People, An (Mortem)
  27

Little Poor Man, The (one of the
  children) 25
Music in May (Alois) 29
Subway Express (Thomas Delaney) 29

4573
OFFORD, Bert*
Barnstormer, The (the nut)

4574
OGDEN, Vivia*
Denial, The
Fire Brigade, The
John Smith
Lovey Mary
Slave of Fashion, A
Thank You
Unguarded Hour, The
Way Down East (Martha Perkins)

4575
OGLE, Charles (1875-)
Affairs of Anatol, The (Dr. Bowles)
Alaskan, The
Bedroom Window, The
Border Legion, The
Brewster's Millions
Code of the West (Henry Thurman)
Conrad in Quest of His Youth (Dobson)
Contraband
Covered Wagon, The (Jesse Wingate)
Flaming Barriers
Flaming Forest, The
Garden of Weeds, The
Garrison's Finish
Golden Bed, The
Grumpy (Ruddock)
Her Husband's Trademark (Father
  Berkeley)
Is Matrimony a Failure?
Jack Straw
Jucklins, The
Kick In
Manslaughter (doctor)
Merton of the Movies
Miss Lulu Bett (station agent)
One Minute to Play
Our Leading Citizens
Prince Chap, The
Rebecca of Sunnybrook Farm
Ruggles of Red Gap
Salomy Jane
Secrets (Dr. McGovern)
Sixty Cents an Hour
Stage Door, The
Ten Commandments, The (doctor)
Thirty Days
Thundering Herd, The (Clark Hudnall)

Travelling Salesman, A
Treasure Island (Long John Silver)
Triumph (James Martin)
What's Your Hurry?
When Knighthood Was in Flower (bit)
Wise Fool, The
Young Rajah, The

4576
O'GRADY, Monty*
Callahans and the Murphys, The
   (Michael Callahan)
Sparrows /aka/ Human Sparrows
   (Splutters)

4577
O'HARA, George*
Bigger than Barnum's
Cross Roads of New York
Fighting Blood
Pacemakers, The [serial]
Sea Beast, The (Derek Ceeley)
Sea Hunt, The
Why Girls Go Back Home

4578
O'HARA, Shirley*
Gentleman of Paris, A
Wild Party, The (Helen Owens)
Stage:
Button, Button (Josei) 29
Meteor (Phyllis Pennell) 29

4579
OLAND, Warner (1880-1938)
Chinatown Nights
Curly Top
Don Juan (Caesar Borgia)
Don Q, Son of Zorro (Archduke Paul)
Dream of Love (the Duke)
East Is West
Faker, The
Fighting American, The
Flower of the Night
Good Time Charley
His Children's Children
His Lady /aka/ When a Man Loves
   (Andre)
Hurricane Hutch [serial]
Infatuation
Jazz Singer, The (Cantor Rabinowitz)
Marriage Clause, The
Mighty, The ("Shiv" Sterky)
Million Bid, A
Mysterious Dr. Fu Manchu /aka/
   The Insidious Dr. Fu Manchu
   (Title role)
Mystery Club, The

Old San Francisco
One Night in Rome
Phantom Foe, The [serial]
Pride of Palomar, The
Riders of the Purple Sage (dual role,
   Lew Walters/Judge Dyer)
Road to Mandalay, The (Chinese ban-
   dit leader)
Scarlet Lady, The
So This Is Marriage
Stand and Deliver (Chika)
Studio Murder Mystery The (Rupert
   Borka)
Tell It to the Marines
Third Eye, The [serial]
Throwback, The
Tong War
Twinkletoes (Roseleaf)
What Happened to Father?
Wheel of Chance
Winding Stair, The
Yellow Arm, The [serial]

4580
OLCHANSKY, Adolf*
Gunnar Hede's Sage

4581
OLDFIELD, Barney (1877-1946)
First Auto, The

4582
OLDLAND, Lilian /aka/ Mary New-
   land (1905-   )
Bindle [series]
City of Youth, The
Daughter of Revolt, A
Flag Lieutenant, The (Sybil Wynn)
Further Adventures of the Flag Lieu-
   tenant, The
Passion Island
Secret Kingdom, The
Troublesome Wives
Virginia's Husband

4583
O'LEARY, Patsy*
Clancy at the Bat
Golfers, The
Hollywood Star, A
Lunkhead, The
New Halfback, The

4584
OLGINA, Y.*
Tanka-Trakitirschitsa /aka/ Protin
   Otsa; Against Her Father; Tanka,
   the Innkeeper

4585
OLIVER, Edna May (Edna May Cox-
Oliver Nutter) (1884-1942)
American Venus, The
Icebound
Lady Who Lied, The
Let's Get Married
Lovers in Quarantine
Lucky Devil, The
Manhattan
Paramount player 23
Restless Wives
Saturday Night Kid, The (Miss
Streeter)
Three O'Clock in the Morning
Wife in Name Only
Stage:
Cradle Snatchers (Ethel Drake) 25
Half-Moon, The (Mrs. Francis
Adams Jarvis) 20
Her Salary Man (Mrs. Sophie Per-
kins) 21
Icebound (Hannah) 23
In His Arms (Mrs. John Clarendon)
24
Isabel (Aunt Olivia) 25
My Golden Girl (Mrs. Judson Mit-
chell) 20
Show Boat (Parthy Ann Hawks) 27
Wait 'Til We're Married (Aunt
Meridan) 21
Wild Oats Jane (June) 22

4586
OLIVER, Fenwick*
Enticement
Merry-Go Round (Prince Eitel Hoge-
met)

4587
OLIVER, Guy (1875-)
Across the Continent
Affairs of Anatol, The (Spencer But-
ler)
Air Mail, The
Always Audacious
Avalanche
Bedroom Window, The
Beggars of Life
Blind Goddess, The
Cheat, The
City of Silent Men
Covered Wagon, The (Kit Carson)
Cowboy and the Lady, The
Dawn of Tomorrow, The
Docks of New York, The
Double Speed
Drums of the Desert

Eagle of the Sea, The
Easy Come, Easy Go
Excuse My Dust (Darby)
Far Western Trails
Fighting Terror, The
Fool's Paradise (Briggs)
Half a Bride
Half Way to Heaven
Homespun Vamp, A
Hot News
Jucklins, The
Kibitzer, The
Light of the Western Stars, The
Little Minister, The
Manslaughter (musician)
Mr. Billings Spends His Dime
Moonlight and Honeysuckle
Mysterious Rider, The
Nevada (Sheriff of Lineville)
North of '36
Old Ironsides
Open Range
Our Leading Citizens
Pink Gods
Prince There Was, A
Round Up, The
Shootin' Irons
Sins of Rosanne, The
Stairs of Sand
Studio Murder Mystery, The (Mac-
Donald)
Sunset Pass
Texas Tommy
Three Weekends (Pa O'Brien)
To the Last Man
Too Much Speed
Vanishing American, The /aka/ The
Vanishing Race (Kit Carson)
Vanishing Pioneer, The (Mr. Shelby)
Virginia Courtship, A
What Every Woman Knows
Woman Trap
Woman with Four Faces, The (Warden
Cassidy)
World's Champion

4588
OLLIVIER, Paul*
Un Chapeau de Paille d'Italie [The
Italian Straw Hat]
Sous Les Toits de Paris [Under the
Roofs of Paris]

4589
OLMSTEAD, Gertrude (1897-1975)
Babbitt
Becky
Big Adventure, The

Boob, The (May)
Bringing Up Father
Buttons
California Straight Ahead
Callahans and the Murphys, The
  (Monica Murphy)
Cameo Kirby
Cheer Leader, The
Cheerful Fraud, The
Cobra (Mary Drake)
Driftin' Kid, The
Empty Hands
Fighting Fury
George Washington, Jr.
Green Grass Widows
Hey, Rube!
Hit of the Show
Key Too Many, A
Kickaroo
Lone Hand, The
Lone Wolf's Daughter, The
Lover's Lane
Midnight Life
Mr. Wu (Hilda Gregory)
Monster, The (Betty Watson)
Monte Carlo
Passion Song, The
Puppets
Robinson Crusoe [serial]
Show of Shows, The
Sonny Boy
Sporting Goods
Sweet Adeline
Sweet Revenge
Sweet Sixteen
Three in a Thousand
Time, the Comedian
Time, the Place and the Girl, The
Tipped Off
Torrent, The (Remedios)
Trilby
Universal player 23
Woman Against the World, A

4590
OLSEN, George Orchestra
Happy Days (themselves)
Stage:
City Chap, The 25
Good News 27
Kid Boots 24
Lambs Gambol 25
Sunny 25
Ziegfeld Follies 24

4591
OLSEN, Lauritz*
Han og Hun og Hamlet [He and She

and Hamlet]

4592
OLSSON, Fredrik*
Peter the Tramp

4593
O'MAILLE, Kit*
Irish Destiny

4594
O'MALLEY, Aileen*
Peg O' My Heart (Peg, as a child)

4595
O'MALLEY, Charles*
Iron Horse, The (Major North)
Only Woman, The

4596
O'MALLEY, J. Patrick (Patrick H.
  O'Malley) (1891-1966)
Alibi /aka/ The Perfect Alibi (Tom-
  my Glennon)
Blooming Angel, The
Bob Hampton of Placer
Bowery Cinderella, A
Brass
Bread
Breaking Point, The (Philip Bradley)
Breath of the Gods
Brothers under the Skin
Cheaters, The
Dinty
Eternal Struggle, The
False Kisses
Fighting American, The
First National player 21
Game Chicken, A
Go and Get It
Happiness
House of Scandal, The
Last Hour, The
Man from Brodney's The
Man I Love, The
Midnight Sun, The
My Old Dutch
My Irish Rose
Night Stick
Perch of the Devil
Proud Flesh
Rose of Kildare
Sherry
Slaver, The
Spangles
Teaser, The
Ten Dollar Raise, The
Tomorrow's Love

Wandering Daughters
Watch Your Wife
White Desert, The
Woman's Law, A
Worldly Goods

4597
O'MALLEY, James*
Winds of Chance

4598
OMITSU*
Daughter of Two Fathers, A

4599
ONDRA, Anny (1903-   )
Blackmail (Alice White)
Chorus Girls
Manxman, The

4600
ONE, Benny*
Get Rich Quick Wallingford (Walling-
    ford's valet)

4601
O'NEIL, James*
Blazing Arrows

4602
O'NEIL, Nance (1875-1965)
His Glorious Night
Loves of Carmen, The
Rogue Song, The (Princess Alexan-
    dra)
Stage:
Fogbound (Hester Penny) 27
House of Women, The (Julia Shane)
    27
Passion Flower, The (Raimunda) 20
Stronger than Love (Anna de Bernois,
    Duchess de Nievres) 25
Untitled Benefit 21
Vaudeville [Palace] 28

4603
O'NEIL, Sally (Virginia Louise
    Noonan) (1910-1968)
Auction Block, The (Bernice Lane)
Bachelor's Paradise, A
Battle of the Sexes (Ruth Judson)
Battling Butler
Becky
Broadway Fever
Broadway Scandals
Callahans and the Murphys, The
    (Ellen Callahan)
Certain Young Man, A

Don't
Floating College
Frisco Sally Levy
Girl on the Barge, The
Hardboiled
Jazz Heaven
Lovelorn, The
Mad Hour, The
Mike
On with the Show (Kitty)
Sally, Irene and Mary (Mary)
Show of Shows, The
Sisters
Slide, Kelly, Slide
Sophomore, The

4604
O'NEIL, Sue*
45 Minutes from Hollywood
Wandering Papas

4605
O'NEILL, Edward*
Dawn (Lutheran Priest)

4606
O'NEILL, Harry*
America /aka/ Love and Sacrifice

4607
O'NEILL, Henry (1891-1964)
America /aka/ Love and Sacrifice
    (Paul Revere)
Stage:
Chains of Dew (Dean Davis) 22
Dream Play (the voice of Indra) 26
Hairy Ape, The (Paddy) 22
Hawk Island (Paul Cooper) 29
Jarnegan (Patsy Brady) 28
Last Night of Don Juan, The (the
    statue of the Commander) 25
Mr. Faust (the Holy One) 22
Squall, The (Don Diego) 26
Taboo (Charles) 22
Verge, The (Tom Edgeworthy) 21

4608
O'NEILL, Marie*
Juno and the Paycock
Stage:
Juno and the Paycock (Mrs. Masie
    Madigan) 27
Plough and the Stars, The (Mrs.
    Grogan) 27
White Headed Boy, The (Aunt Ellen)
    21

4609
ONIONS, Eileen*
Prince of Lovers

4610
ONNA, Ferdinand*
Moon of Israel

4611
O'REGAN, Katherine (Kathleen Melville) (1904-)
Juno and the Paycock

4612
ORELL, Felix*
William Tell

4613
ORLAMOND, William /aka/ William Orlamund) (1867-)
All the Brothers Were Valiant (Aaron Burnham)
Awakening, The
Blue Skies
Body and Soul
Camille
Dixie Handicap, The
Eternal Three, The
Fashions for Woman
Flesh and the Devil (Uncle Kutowski)
Getting Gertie's Garter
Girl from Woolworth's, The
Great Divide, The
Her Private Affair (Dr. Zeigler)
House of Horror, The
Kiki
Little Yellow House
Madame Peacock
Mantrap (McGarity)
Name the Man
Nellie, the Beautiful Cloak Model
Red Mill, The (Governor)
Reno
Rose-Marie (Emile la Flamme)
See You in Jail
Seven Keys to Baldpate (the hermit)
Skinner's Big Idea
Slave of Desire
Souls for Sale (Lord Fryingham)
Stronger than Death
Taxi Dancer, The
Texas Steer, A
That's My Baby
True as Steel
Up in Mabel's Room
While the City Sleeps (Dwiggins)
White Moth, The
Wife of the Centaur, The

Wind, The (Sourdough)
Words and Music

4614
ORLAND, William*
Skinner's Big Idea

4615
O'RORKE, Peggy*
Irish Destiny

4616
ORTEGA, Sophie*
Revenge

4617
OSBORNE, Baby Marie (1911-)
Baby Marie's Roundup
Miss Gingersnap

4618
OSBORNE, Billy*
Keeper of the Bees, The (nice child)

4619
OSBORNE, Miles "Bud" (1888-)
Bad Men's Money
Bronc Stomper
Cheyenne Trails
Days of Daring
Far Western Trails
Fighting Tenderfoot, A
Fighting Terror, The
Forbidden Trails
His Lucky Day
Invaders, The
Lariat Kid, The
Last Roundup, The
Law of the Mounted, The
Mystery Rider, The [serial]
On the Divide
Prairie Mystery
Riding Leather
Secrets of the Range
Smilin' Terror, The
Texas Flash, The
Texas Tommy
Thrill Chaser, The
Valley Beyond the Law
Vanishing Rider, The [serial]
West of Santa Fe
Where the West Begins
Yellow Contraband

4620
OSBORNE, Vivienne (1900-)
Cameron of the Royal Mounties
Foreigner, The

Good Provider, A
In Walked Mary
Love's Flame
Mother Eternal
Over the Hill (Isabella Stronk)
Restless Sex, The (Marie Cliff)
Right Way, The
Stage:
Aloma of the South Seas (Aloma) 25
Blue Bandanna, The (the girl) 24
Bonehead, The (Jean Brent) 20
Fog (Eunice) 27
Houses of Sand (Miss Kane) 25
Love Child, The (Aline De Mar) 22
New Toys (Ruth Webb) 24
One Glorious Hour (Maria) 27
Scaramouche (Climine) 23
Silver Fox, The (Frankie Turner) 21
Three Musketeers, The (Lady De
    Winter) 28
Week-End (Morga Chapman) 29

4621
OSCAR (Elephant)
Soul of the Beast, The

4622
O'SHEA, Danny*
FBO player 28
Manhattan Cocktail (Bob)
Vagabond Lover, The

4623
O'SHEA, Dennis*
Irish Destiny

4624
OSWALD the Lucky Rabbit (Cartoons)
    (1927-1928)
Africa Before Dark
All Wet
Banker's Daughter, The
Bright Lights
Empty Socks
Fox Chase, The
Great Guns
Harem Scarem
Hot Dog
Hungry Hoboes
Mechanical Cow, The
Neck 'n' Neck
Ocean Hop, The
Oh, Teacher
Oh, What a Knight
Ole Swimmin' Hole, The
Ozzie of the Mounted
Poor Papa
Rickety Gin

Ride 'em Plowboy
Rival Romeos
Sagebrush Sadie
Sky Scrappers
Sleigh Bells
Tall Timber
Trolley Troubles

4625
OSWALDA, Ossi*
Die Wohnungsnot [The Housing Short-
    age]

4626
OTIS, William R., Jr.*
Goose Hangs High, The (Hugh Ingals)

4627
OTTIANO, Rafaela*
Married? (maid)

4628
OTTINGER, Leonora*
Gilded Lily, The (Mrs. Thompson)
Stage:
Genius and the Crowd (Mrs. Lanham)
    20

4629
OTTO, Henry*
Iron Mask, The (King's valet)

4630
OTTO, Paul*
Sajenko the Soviet
Shattered Dreams
Tradition
Trial of Donald Westhof, The

4631
OUR GANG COMEDIES
Ask Grandma 25
Baby Brother 27
Baby Clothes 26
Back Stage 23
Barnum & Ringling, Inc. 28
Better Movies 25
Big Business 24
Big Show, The 23
Big Town, The 25
Bouncing Babies 29
Boxing Gloves 29
Boys to Board 23
Boys Will Be Joys 25
Bring Home the Turkey 27
Buccaneers, The 24
Buried Treasure 26
Cat, Dog and Co. 29

4632

OUR GANG KIDS [number after name
    indicates number of films]

Aber, Johnny (2)
Albright, Wally (6)
Anderson, Bobby (1)
Ayres, Maria (1)
Bailey, Sherwood "Spud" (8)
Beard, Bobby "Cotton" (5)
Beard, Carolina "Marmalade" (4)
Beard, Mathew "Stymie" (33)
Beckett, Scotty (17)
Billings, George "Derby" (6)
Bond, Tommy (24)
Breckell, Mary Ann (1)
Brown, Sheila (1)
Browning, Bobby "Gerald" (1)
Buckelew, Alvin (16)
Bupp, Sonny (1)
Bupp, Tommy (1)
Burns, Bobby (1)
Burston, Janet (16)
Chaney, Norman "Chubby" (18)
Chapman, Freddie "Bully" (6)
Chapman, Hugh (3)
Coates, Shirley "Mugsy" (8)
Cobb, Joe (7)
Comerford, Janet (1)
Cooper, Jackie (15)
Currier, Patsy (3)
Daniels, Mickey (1)
Darling, Jean (5)
deBorba, Dorothy (22)
DeNuet, Dickie (7)
Di Hemore, Patsy (1)
Downing, Barry "Ken" (2)

Downing, Rex (8)
Edwards, Marianna (7)
Ernest, George (2)
Fellows, Edith (3)
Ferrero, Robert (2)
Finnegan, Billy (1)
Five Cabin Kids, The (2)
Five Meglin Kiddies, The (2)
Folz, Artye (2)
Gay, Betsy (11)
Geil, Joe "Corky" (4)
Glass, Teresa Mae (1)
Goodrich, Barbara (1)
Greer, Douglas (5)
Gubitosi, Mickey (Later Robert
   "Bobby" Blake) (40)
Gumm, Maria Lisa (1)
Haines, Donald (15)
Hall, Dickie (5)
Harvey, Harry, Jr. (1)
Hickman, Cordell (1)
Hickman, Darryl (1)
Hill Twins (1)
Hood, Darla (48)
Hoskins, Allan Clayton "Farina" (20)
Hoskins, Jannie (2)
Hudson, Beverly "Aurelia" (1)
Hurlic, Philip (2)
Hutchins, Bobby "Wheezer" (31)
Jackson, Mary Ann (19)
Janney, Leon (1)
Jasgar, Gary "Junior" (13)
Johnson, Cullen (1)
Johnston, Dorian (5)
Jones, Dickie (4)
Kales, Tony (1)
Karol, Joline (1)
Kaye, Darwood (20)
Kibrick, Leonard "Woim" (9)
Kibrick, Sidney (23)
Kornman, Mary (10)
Kornman, Mildred (1)
Kuney, Eva Lee (1)
LaRue, Georgia Jean (2)
Laughlin, Billy "Froggy" (29)
Laughlin, Mickey (4)
Lee, Billy (1)
Lee, Eugene "Porky" (40)
Lee, Valerie (5)
Logan, Annabella (1)
Lynn, Jackie (1)
Lyons, Philbrook (3)
McComas, Kendall "Breezy/Bris-
   band" (6)
MacDonald, Budd (3)
McFarland, George "Spanky" (89)
McFarland, Tommy (5)
McHugh, Jack (1)

MacMahon, Philip (1)
Mains, Marlene (1)
Mallon, Bobby (7)
Mann, Gloria (1)
May, Baby Patsy (1)
Mindy, Billy (1)
Moore, Dickie (6)
Murray, Cecelia (2)
Polonsky, David (1)
Powell, Raymond Rayhill (1)
Proffitt, Donald (14)
Quigley, Juanita "Sally" (2)
Rickert, Shirley Jean (5)
Roberts, Josephine (1)
Salling, Jackie (2)
Scott, Betty (1)
Smith, Billy "Ray" (6)
Smith, Ray "Boxcar" (3)
Spear, Harry (5)
Switzer, Carl "Alfalfa" (60)
Switzer, Harold (22)
Taylor, Jackie "Jane" (5)
Taylor, Willie Mae "Buckwheat" (5)
Thomas, Billie "Buckwheat" (89)
Trin, Marvin "Bubbles" (6)
Tucker, Jerry (18)
Tyler, Leon (3)
Walburn, Freddie "Slicker" (6)
Watson, Bobs (2)
Watson, Delmar (2)
Wertz, Harold "Bouncy" (2)
White, Jackie (5)
Wilson, Clyde (1)
Wilson, Kenneth (1)
Winderlout, Billy (1)
Winkler, Robert (5)
Wong, Yen (1)
Young, Bobby "Bonedust" (Later
   Clifton Young) (4)

4633
OUSPENSKAYA, Maria (1876-1949)
Khveska /aka/ Bolnickny Starozh
   Khveska (hospital guard)
Tanka-Trakitirschitsa /aka/ Protin
   Otsa; Against Her Father; Tanka,
   the Innkeeper
Stage:
Jest, The (Fiametta) 26
Taming of the Shrew, The (Curtis)
   27

4634
OVEY, George*
Fight and Win
Hit the Deck
Night Ride (Ed)
Strings of Steel [serial]

Yankee Clipper, The

4635
OWEN, Catherine Dale (1903-1965)
His Glorious Night
Rogue Song, The (Princess Vera)
Stage:
Bootleggers, The (Nina Rossmore)
22
Canary Dutch (Mrs. John Weldon) 25
Love City, The (Tze-shi) 26
Love Set, The (Gertrude Lamont) 23
Mr. Moneypenny (Glory) 28
Mountain Man, The (Delaney Mc-
Cloud, "Dell") 21
Play's the Thing, The (Ilona Szabo)
26
Trelawney of the Wells (Clara De
Foenix) 25
Whole Town's Talking, The (Letty
Lythe) 23

4636
OWEN, Reginald (John Reginald
Owen) (1887-1972)
Grass Orphan, The
Letter, The
Phroso
Stage:
Candle Light (Prince Rudolf Hasel-
forf-Schlobitten) 29
Carolinian, The (Capt. Manderville)
25
Importance of Being Earnest, The
(Algernon Mancrieff) 26
Little Eyolf (Alfred Allmers) 26
Marquise, The (Esteban, El Duce De
Santaguano) 27
Play's the Thing, The (Almady) 26
Skin Deep (Parrish Weston) 27
Three Musketeers, The (Cardinal
Richelieu) 28

4637
OWEN, Seena (Signe Auen) (1895-
1966)
At the Crossroads
Back Pay
Blue Danube, The
Cheater Reformed, The
Faint Perfume (Richmiel Crumb)
Flame of the Yukon
Gift Supreme, The (Sylvia Alden)
Go-Getter, The
His Last Haul
House of Toys
Hunted Woman, The
I Am the Man

Lavender and Old Lace
Man-Made Woman
Marriage Playground, The (Rose Sel-
lers)
Paramount player 24
Price of Redemption
Queen Kelly (the Queen)
Rush Hour, The
Shipwrecked
Sinners in Love
Sisters
Sooner or Later
Temple of Dawn, The (Jean Deering)
Unseeing Eyes
Woman God Changed, The

4638
OWEN, Tudor*
Bride of the Storm

4639
OWSLEY, Monroe*
First Kiss, The
Stage:
Holiday (Ned Seton) 28
Young Blood (Sammy Bissell) 25

- P -

4640
PACK, Norman*
Publicity Madness

4641
PACKARD, Clayton*
King of Kings, The (Bartholomew)

4642
PADDEN, Sarah*
Sophomore, The
Wonder of Women, The

4643
PADDOCK, Charles*
Campus Flirt, The
College Hero, The
High School Hero, The
9 3/5 Seconds
Olympic Hero

4644
PADGEN, Jack*
King of Kings, The (Capt. of Roman
Guard)

4645
PADJAN, John*
Iron Horse, The (dual role, Wild
   Bill Hickok/General Stanford)
Tony Runs Wild

4646
PADULA, Marguerita*
Hit the Deck
Stage:
Vaudeville [Palace] 27

4647
PAGANI, Ernesto
Cabria

4648
PAGAY, Sophie*
Anna Boleyn /aka/ Deception
Der Mensch am Wege [Man by the
   Roadside]

4649
PADGEN, Leonard*
Tilly of Bloomsbury (Lucius Welwyn)

4650
PAGE, Anita (1910-)
Broadway Melody, The (Queenie
   Mahoney)
Flying Ensign, The
Flying Fleet, The
Gold Braid
He Learned About Women
Hollywood Revue of 1929
Navy Blues
Our Dancing Daughters (Anne)
Our Modern Maidens (Kentucky)
Protection
Speedway
Telling the World
While the City Sleeps (Myrtle)

4651
PAGE, Helen*
Playing with Souls

4652
PAGE, James*
Charley's Aunt (Spettigue)

4653
PAGE, Norman*
Dick Turpin's Ride to New York
   ("Ferret" Bevis)

4654
PAGE, Paul*
Girl from Havana, The
Happy Days (a principal)
Speakeasy

4655
PAGET, Alfred*
When a Girl Loves

4656
PAIGE, Jean*
Black Beauty
Captain Blood (Arabella Bishop)
Fortune Hunter, The
Hidden Dangers
Prodigal Judge, The

4657
PAIGE, Robert*
Battling Orioles, The

4658
PALASTHY, A. *
Stand and Deliver (Muja)

4659
PALASTY, Irene*
Married in Hollywood

4660
PALERME, Gina*
Au Secours! [Help!]

4661
PALLETTE, Eugene (1889-1954)
Alias Jimmy Valentine
Battle of the Century, The
Call of the Cuckoo
Canary Murder Case, The (Sgt. Er-
   nest Heath)
Chicago
Dummy, The (Madison)
Fighting Edge, The
Fine Feathers
Fools for Luck
Good-bye Kiss, The
Greene Murder Case, The (Sgt. Er-
   nest Heath)
Hell's Heroes
His Private Life
Kibitzer, The
Light of the Western Stars, The
Light that Failed, The
Lights of New York (Gene)
Loud Speakers
Love Parade, The (Minister of War)
Mantrap (Woodbury)

Men About Town
North of Hudson Bay
Out of the Ruins
Parlor, Bedroom and Bath
Pointed Heels (Joe Clark)
Ranger of the Big Trees
Red Mask, The
Rocking Moon
Santa Fe Trail
Second Hundred Years, The
Should Men Walk Home?
Should Women Drive?
Studio Murder Mystery, The (Detective Dirk)
Sugar Daddies
Terror Island
Three Musketeers, The (Aramis)
To the Last Man
Twin Beds
Two Kinds of Women
Virginian, The (Honey Wiggin)
Wandering Husbands
Without Compromise
Wolf Man, The
Yankee Senor

4662
PALM, Walter*
Hoosier Schoolmaster, The

4663
PALMA, Mona*
Cabaret
Canadian, The
Fascinating Youth
Quarterback, The

4664
PALMER, Corliss*
Clothes Make the Woman
Honeymoon Hate
Man's Past, A
Night Bird, The

4665
PALMER, Patricia*
Tempest, The
To the Ladies

4666
PALMER, Shirley*
Magic Flame, The (the wife)
Marriage by Contract

4667
PALMER, Violet*
Dearie
My Man

Night Life (beer garden waitress)

4668
PALMER, Zoe*
Luck of the Navy, The (Dora Green)

4669
PALMERI, Mimi*
Ragged Edge, The
Second Youth

4670
PANGBORN, Franklin (1896-1958)
Blonde for a Night
Cradle Snatchers
Crazy Nut, The
Getting Gertie's Garter
Girl on the Pullman, The
Lady of the Pavements (M'sieu Dubrey)
MGM player 28
Masquerade
My Friend from India
Night Bride, The
Not So Dumb
On Trial (Turnbull)
Rejuvenation of Aunt Mary, The
Sap, The
Watch Out
Stage:
Parasites (Felix Waterhouse) 24

4671
PANZER, Paul W. (1872-1948)
Ancient Mariner, The (Title role)
Best Bad Man, The (sheriff)
Black Book, The [serial]
Brass Knuckles
Candy Kid, The
City of Purple Dreams, The (Slug Nikolay)
East Lynne (Mr. Hallijohn)
Enemies of Women (Cossack)
Fool, The
George Washington Cohen
Girl from Chicago, The
Glorious Betsy
Hawk of the Hills [serial]
Jacqueline of the Blazing Barriers
Johnstown Flood, The (Joe Burger)
Mighty Lak' a Rose
Mohican's Daughter, The
Mystery Mind, The [serial]
Redskin, The
Rinty of the Desert
Romance of a Rogue
Sally in Our Alley
Shock Punch, The

Siberia
Son of the Sarhara, A
Thirty Below Zero
Thunder Mountain
Too Many Kisses (Pedro)
Under the Red Robe (French Lieu-
   tenant)
Unseeing Eyes
Wages of Virtue (Sgt. LeGros)
When Knighthood Was in Flower
   (Capt. of the guard)
Wolf's Clothing

4672
PAOLI, Raoul*
Beau Sabreur (Djfour)
Magic Flame, The (weight thrower)
Night of Mystery, A

4673
PAQUERETTE, Madame*
Garden of Allah, The
Maré Nostrum [Our Sea] (Dr. Feld-
   mann)

4674
PAQUETTE, Pauline*
Bluff

4675
PARIOS, Gus*
Close Harmony

4676
PARK, E. L.--see: E. L. Parks

4677
PARKE, William, Sr.*
Hunchback of Notre Dame, The
   (Josephus)
Stage:
Creoles (Monsieur André) 27

4678
PARKER, Charlie*
Drag

4679
PARKER, Flora--see: Mrs. Carter
   De Haven

4680
PARKER, Jack*
Four Devils (Charley as a boy)

4681
PARKER, Katherine*
Drag

4682
PARKER, Lady*
Affairs of Anatol, The (bridge play-
   er)

4683
PARKS, E. L.*
Behind that Curtain (Charlie Chan)

4683a
PARLO, Dita*
Homecoming
Hungarian Rhapsody

4684
PARRISH, Helen (1922-1959)
Movietone Follies of 1929
His First Command
When the Babe Comes Home

4685
PARROTT, Jimmie*
Are Parents Pickles?

4686
PARROTT, Paul*
His First Flat Tire
Uncovered Wagon, The

4687
PARRY, Harvey (1901-)
Stunt man 20's through 60's.
   Played James Cagney's fight
   partner in many of Cagney's
   films.

4688
PARRY, Lee*
L'Eau di Nil
Love Is a Lie
Monna Vanna

4689
PARSLEY, Ruby*
Marriage Playground, The (Beatrice)

4690
PARSONS, Louella O. (Louella Oet-
   tinger) (1881-1972)
Show People (cameo)

4691
PARTOS, Gus*
Close Harmony
Last Performance, The
Lonesome
Night Watch, The

4692
PASHA, Kalla*
Bella Donna
Cat's Meow, The
Chasing Husbands
Children of Jazz
Devil Dancer, The
Dictator, The
Dove, The
Grand Duchess and the Waiter, The
Hollywood
Love, Honor and Behave
Making of a Man, The
Mantrap
Married Life
Midnight on the Barbary Coast
Racing Hearts
Seven Footprints to Satan
Shanghaied Lovers
Show of Shows, The
Silken Shackles
Small Town Idol, A
Thirty Days
Tillie's Punctured Romance
West of Zanzibar (Babe)
Yukon Jake (Title role)

4693
PASSARGE, Paul*
Romeo und Julia im Schnee [Romeo
  and Juliet in the Snow]

4694
PATCH, Wally (Walter Vinicombe)
  (1888-)
Balaclava (Trooper Strang)
Luck of the Navy, The (Stoker
  Clarke)

4695
PATERSON, Jerry*
Janice Meredith (Cato)

4696
PATON, Charles*
Blackmail (Mr. White)

4697
PATRICK, Jerome*
Officer 666
Stage:
Nightcap, The (Robert Andrews) 21
Zander the Great (Dan Murchison) 23

4698
PATRICK, John*
After Business Hours
Black Swan, The

Cave Man, The
First Year, The
Flaming Youth
Flirting with Love
For Sale (Cabot Stanton)
Goldfish, The
Her Temporary Husband
His Jazz Bride
Honeymoon Express, The
Ladies at Play
Love Hungry
Other Women's Husbands
Palm Beach Girl, The
Prince of Head-Waiters
Recompense
Rubber Tires
Seven Sinners
Sherlock Junior
Single Wives
Sinners in Silk
So This Is Marriage
Social Highwayman, The
Thief in Paradise, A
What Fools Men

4699
PATRICK, Lee (Lee Salome Patrick)
  (1911-)
Strange Cargo (debut)
Stage:
Baby Mine (Zoie) 27
Bachelors' Brides (Mary Bowing) 25
Backslapper, The (Mrs. Kennedy) 25
Common Sin, The ("Bobo" Aster) 28
Green Beetle, The (debut as Elsie
  Chandos) 24
It All Depends (Maida Spencer) 25
June Moon (Eileen) 29
Matrimonial Bed, The (Juliette Cor-
  ton) 27
Nightstick (Joan Manning) 27
Shelf, The (Caroline Wendham) 26
Undercurrents, The (Helen Mills) 25

4700
PATRICOLA, Tom*
Frozen Justice
Happy Days (a principal)
Married in Hollywood
South Sea Rose
Words and Music
Stage:
George White's Scandals 23; 25; 26;
  28
Vaudeville [Palace] 23

4701
PATRY, Albert*
Tragödie der Liebe [Tragedy of Love]

4702
PATTERSON, Colonel*
Janice Meredith

4703
PATTERSON, Elizabeth (Mary Eli-
  zabeth Patterson) (1876-1966)
Book of Charm, The (debut)
Boy Friend, The
Minister's Wife, The
Mrs. Harper
Return of Peter Grimm, The (Mrs.
  Bartholomey)
South Sea Rose
Timothy's Quest
Words and Music
Stage:
Book of Charm, The (Mrs. Harper)
  25
Carry On (Aunt Mary) 28
Gypsy Jim (Mary Blake) 24
Intimate Strangers (Aunt Ellen) 21
Lady Cristlinda, The (Groggy) 22
Lazybones (Rebecca Fanning) 24
Magnolia (Madame Rumford) 23
Man's Estate (Minnie Jordan) 29
Marriage Bed, The (Caroline Reed)
  29
Paradise (Mrs. Margaret Elder) 27
Piper, The (Old Ursula) 20

4704
PATTERSON, Strake /aka/ Stark
  Patterson*
Tempest, The
Stage:
Chee-Chee (Prince Tao-Tee) 28
Merry World, The (a principal) 26
Sweetheart Time (Jeffries) 26

4705
PATTON, Bill*
Below the Deadline
Beyond the Trail
Freckled Rascal, The
In the Line of Duty
Lariat Kid, The
Last Chance, The
Lucky Spurs
One Man Dog
Orphan of the Sage
Outlawed
Sand!
Two Gun Morgan
Under Fire
Vagabond Cub, The
Western Trails
Winning of Barbara Worth, The

(Little Rosebud)
Yellow Contraband, The

4706
PAUDLER, Maria*
Madame Wünscht Keine Kinder [Mad-
  ame Doesn't Want Children] /aka/
  Madame Wants No Children
  (Louise Bonvin)

4707
PAUL, Fred*
Recoil, The

4708
PAULI-WINTERSTEIN, Hedwig*
Anna Boleyn /aka/ Deception
Tragödie der Liebe [Tragedy of
  Love]

4709
PAULIG, Albert*
Dancing Vienna
Eine Du Barry von Heute [A Modern
  Du Barry] (Clairet)
It's Easy to Become a Father
Der Juxbaron [The Imaginary Baron]
  (Baron von Kimmel)
Kopf Hoch, Charley! [Heads Up,
  Charley!]
Manon Lescaut
Sein Grösster Bluff [His Greatest
  Bluff] (Mimikry)

4710
PAULINE, J. Robert*
Mystery Mind, The [serial]

4711
PAULL, Alan*
Sunny Side Up (Raoul)

4712
PAULL, Muriel*
Captain Blood

4713
PAUNCEFORT, George*
White Moll, The
Stage:
Bride, The (James) 24
Honeymoon Lane (John Brown) 26
Joker, The (Henry Carson) 25
Just Suppose (Kingsley Stafford) 20
Mad Honeymoon, The (Rufus Colgate)
  23
Ups-a-Daisy (Ambrose Wattle) 28
What's Your Wife Doing? (Samuel
  Peabody Skinner) 23

4714
PAVANELLI, Livio*
Luther

4715
PAVONI, Giuseppe*
White Sister, The (Archbishop)

4716
PAWLE, Lennox (1872-1936)
Glorious Adventure, The (Samuel
    Pepys)
Great Adventure, The
Hot for Paris
Married in Hollywood
Sally (Lord Bardell)
Sky Hawk, The
Stage:
Harem, The (Petri) 24
Jack and Jill (Duke of Dippington) 23
Marjolaine (Jerome Brooke-Hoskyn,
    Esq.) 22
Mary, Mary, Quite Contrary (Mr.
    Beeby) 23
Matrimonial Bed, The (Auguste
    Chabbonais) 27
Mima (the Adjutant) 28
Mountebank, The (Horatio Bakkus) 23
Werewolf, The (Eliphos Leone) 24

4717
PAWLOVA, Vera*
Diary of a Lost Girl, The

4718
PAWLOW, Pawel*
Geheimnisse einer Seele [Secrets of
    the Soul]

4719
PAWN, Doris (1896-   )
Guile of Women
Li Ting Lang
Midnight Bell, A
Out of the Storm
Shame
Strange Boarder, The
Tower of Ivory
What Happened to Rosa?

4720
PAXTON, Sydney /aka/ Sidney*
Old Home Week
Stage:
Constant Nymph, The (Sir Bartlemy
    Pugh) 26
Loves of Lulu, The (Schigolch) 25
School for Scandal, The (Sir Oliver
    Surface) 25
Werewolf, The (the Priest) 24

4721
PAYNE, Douglas*
Triumph of the Scarlet Pimpernel,
    The (Rateau)

4722
PAYNE, Louis*
As Man Desires
Big News (Hansel)
Blind Goddess
Evangeline
For Sale (Mr. Twombly-Smith)
In Hollywood with Potash and Perl-
    mutter
Interference
King of Kings, The (bit)
Last Edition
Only Thing, The
Shamrock Handicap, The (Sir Miles
    Gaffney)
True as Steel
Vanity
Whip, The
Yankee Clipper, The

4723
PAYSON, Blanche*
Half a Man
Oh, Doctor!
We Moderns

4724
PAYTON, Gloria*
When Lights Are Low

4725
PEARCE, George*
Country Kid, The
Drop Kick, The
Hold that Lion
Home James
Irresistible Lover
Narrow Street, The
Social Highwayman, The
Valiant, The
Wife Who Wasn't Wanted, The

4726
PEARSON, Virginia (1888-1958)
Actress, The
Atta Boy!
Big City, The (Tennessee)
Impossible Catherine
Lightning Hutch [serial]
Patience

Phantom of the Opera, The (Carlotta)
Power of Silence, The
Red Kimono, The
Silence
Silks and Saddles
Sister Against Sister
Smilin' Guns
Taxi Mystery, The
Trelawney of the Wells (Mrs. Telfer)
What Price Beauty?
Wildness of Youth
Wizard of Oz, The

4727
PECK, Norman*
Vagabond Lover, The

4728
PECK, Robert*
Prep and Pep

4729
PEDLER, Gertrude*
Courtship of Miles Standish, The
Lawful Cheaters (Mrs. Perry Steele)

4730
PEDERSEN, Maren*
Witchcraft Through the Ages /aka/
   Häxan

4731
PEERS, Joan*
Applause (April Darling)
Stage:
Marry the Man! (Lillian Jeffries) 29

4732
PEGAY, Sophie*
Last Waltz, The

4733
PEGG, Vester*
Two Doyles, The

4734
PEIL, Edward (1888-1958)
Broken Chains
College Coquette, The
Don't Doubt Your Wife
Dream Street (Sway Won)
Dust Flower, The
Fighting Heart, The
Framed
Girl from Montmartre, The
In Old Arizona (bit)
Iron Horse, The (old Chinaman

Isobel or the Trail's End
King of Kings, The (bit)
Little Yellow House, The
Man Who Came Back, The
Man Without a Country, The /aka/
   As No Man Has Loved
Masked Emotions
Money Changers, The
Purple Dawn, The
Road to Divorce, The
Sein Grösster Bluff [Her Greatest
   Bluff] (dual role, Henry/Harry
   Duval)
Servant in the House, The
Song of Life, The
That Girl Montana
Wife Who Wasn't Wanted, The

4735
PEIL, Edward, Jr.*
College Coquette, The
Goose Hangs High, The (Bradley Ingals)
Rose of the World

4736
PEILE, Kinsey*
Vortex, The (Pauncefort Quentin)

4737
PELLETIER, Yvonne*
Children of Divorce (little Jean)

4738
PELZER, George*
Hoosier School Master, The
If Winter Comes

4739
PEMBLETON, Georgia*
Happy Days (chorus)

4740
PEMBROKE, Percy*
Adventures of Tarzan [serial] (Clayton)

4741
PENBROKE, Clifford*
Irish Destiny

4742
PENDLETON, Gaylord /aka/ Gay*
Manslaughter
Success
Stage:
Cold Feet (Jack Prentice) 23
Coquette (Joe Reynolds) 27

Helena's Boys (Harold "Beansy") 24

4743
PENDLETON, Nat (Nathaniel Green
  Pendleton) (1899-1967)
Hoosier Schoolmaster, The
Last of the Duanes
Laughing Lady, The
Let's Get Married
Stage:
Grey Fox, The (Don Michelotto) 28
My Girl Friday (Marcel the Great)
  29
Naughty Cinderella (K. O. Bill
  Smith) 25

4744
PENNELL, Daniel /aka/ Dan*
Bluebeard's Seven Wives /aka/
  Purple Passions
Price of a Party, The
You Can't Fool Your Wife
Stage:
Yellow (Donaldson) 26
Your Woman and Mine (Speaker of
  the House) 22

4745
PENNELL, Richard O. *
Clothes Make the Woman
Dressed to Kill
Truthful Liar, The

4746
PENNICK, Jack (1895-1964)
Four Sons
Lone Eagle, The
Mighty, The
Navy Blues
Paid to Love (a guard)
Plastered in Paris
Strong Boy, The
Virginian, The
What Price Glory? (a private)
Why Sailors Go Wrong

4747
PENNINGTON, Ann (1895-)
Gold Diggers of Broadway (Ann Col-
  lins)
Golden Strain, The
Happy Days (a principal)
Hello Baby
Is Everybody Happy?
Kiss in the Dark, A
Lucky Horseshoe, The
Mad Dancer, The
Madame, Behave!

Manhandled (herself)
Rainbow Man, The
Tanned Legs
Stage:
Follies 23; 25
George White's Scandals 21; 26; 28
Jack and Jill (Gloria Wayne) 23
Ziegfeld Follies 24

4748
PENWARDEN, Duncan*
Gentleman of the Press (Mr. Higgin-
  bottom)
Lady Lies, The
Stage:
Broken Dishes (a stranger) 29
Clutching Claw, The (Johannis Ber-
  lau) 28
Gentlemen of the Press (Abner Pen-
  nyfather) 28
Is Zat So? (Fred Hobart) 25
Now-A-Days (Mr. Huntington) 29
Scalawag, The (Judge Westcott) 27
Scarlet Lily, The (Rev. Mr. Simp-
  son) 27

4749
PERCIVAL, Cyril*
Four Feathers, The (Jack Durance)
Wee MacGreegor's Sweetheart (Uncle
  Baldwin)

4750
PERCIVAL, Walter*
Big City, The (Grogan)
Lights of New York (Jake Jackson)
Moral Sinner, The

4751
PERCY, David*
King of the Khyber Rifles (Highland
  Officer)
Movietone Follies of 1929
Words and Music

4752
PERCY, Eileen*
Back Stage
Beware of the Bride
Big Town Ideas
Blushing Bride, The
Burnt Fingers
Children of Jazz
Cobra (Sophie Binner)
East Side, West Side
Elope If You Must
Fast Mail, The
Fine Clothes

Flirt, The
Fourth Musketeer, The
Fox player 20
Her Honor, the Mayor
Hickville Broadway
Husband Hunter, The
Iron Mike
Land of Jazz, The
Little Miss Hawkshaw
Lovey Mary
Maid of the West
Man Who Dared, The
Pardon My Nerve
Phantom Bullet, The
Prisoner, The
Race Wild
Shadow on the Wall, A
Souls for Sables
Spring Fever
Telling the World
That Model from Paris
Third Eye, The [serial]
Tom Boy, The
Tongues of Flame
Twelve Miles Out
Unchastened Woman, The (Susan
   Ambie)
Under the Rouge
Whatever She Wants
Why Trust Your Husband?
Within the Law (Aggie Lynch)

4753
PERDUE, Derlys*
FBO player 23
Forbidden Range
Last Man on Earth, The
Mystery Rider, The [serial]
Small Town Idol, A
Smilin' Terror, The

4754
PERESTIANI, Ivan*
Khveska /aka/ Bolnichny Starozh
   Khveska (hospital guard)

4755
PERIOLAT, George (-1960)
Any Woman
Barefoot Boy, The
Black Butterflies
Blood and Sand (Marquise de Gueve-
   ra)
Butterflies in the Rain
Fangs of Destiny
Fatal Warning, The [serial]
Hellion, The

Life's Twist
Mark of Zorro, The (Gov. Alvar-
   ado)
Night Watch, The
One Splendid Hour
Parlor, Bedroom and Bath
Prairie King, The
Red Lily, The (Monsieur Bouchard)
Rosita (Rosita's father)
Secret Hour, The
Slave of Desire
To Have and to Hold
Two Weeks with Play
When Dreams Come True
Yankee Consul, The
Young Rajah, The

4756
PERKINS, Osgood (1893-1937)
Cradle Buster, The
Grit (Boris Giovanni Smith)
Knockout Reilly
Love 'em and Leave 'em
Mother's Boy (Jake Sturmberg)
Puritan Passions
Syncopation
Wild, Wild Susan
Stage:
Beggar on Horseback (Homer Cady)
   24
Front Page, The (Walter Burns)
   28
Loose Ankles (Andy Barton) 26
Masque of Venice, The (Joshua Cox)
   26
Pomeroy's Past (Trebus Heminway,
   D. D.) 26
Salvation (Whittaker) 28
Say It with Flowers (Prof. Paolino)
   26
Spread Eagle (Joe Cobb) 27
Weak Sisters (Siegfried Strong) 25
Women Go on Forever (Pete) 27

4757
PERKINS, Ray*
Show of Shows, The

4758
PERKINS, Walter*
Peaceful Valley

4759
PERRIN, Jack (Jack Perrin Rayart)
   (1896-1968)
Adorable Savage, The
Battle of Wits

Big Bob
Border Vengeance
Cactus Trails (Efrus)
Code of the Range
Coward of Covelo
Dangerous Little Demon
Double Fisted
Fighting Skipper, The [serial]
Fire and Steel
Grey Devil, The
Guardians of the Wild
Guttersnipe, The
Harvest of Hate
Hi-Jacking Rustlers
Hoofbeats of Vengeance
Jade Box, The
King of Hearts
Knockout Kid, The
Laffin' Fool
Lahoma
Lion Man, The
Madden of the Mounted
Man from Oklahoma, The
Match Breaker, The
Northwest Mounted Police [series]
Open Switch, The [serial chapter 26]
Outlaw, The
Overland Bound
Partners of the Tide
Phantom Terror, The
Pink Tights
Plunging Hoofs
Riders of the Plains [serial]
Ridin' Gent, A
Ridin' Law
Santa Fe Trail, The
Starlight's Revenge
Those Who Dare
Thunderbolt Strikes
Thunderbolt's Tracks
Torrent, The
Trigger Trail, The
Trouper, The
Two Outlaws
Under Secret Orders
Vanishing West, The [serial]
Water Hole, The
West of Rainbow's End
Where the North Holds Sway
Wild Blood
Yukon Gold

4760
PERROT, Irma*
Living Dead Man, The

4761
PERRY, Bob*
Beggars of Life
Deadline, The
Dressed to Kill
Fortune Hunter, The
Light of the Western Stars, The
Me, Gangster (Tuxedo George)
No Picnic
Noisy Neighbors
River Pirate
Skin Deep
Volcano (Father Benedict)
White Gold (Bucky O'Neil)

4762
PERRY, Esthryn*
Why Girls Leave Home

4763
PERRY, Kathryn*
First Year, The
Is Zat So?
Selznick player 21
Side Street
Wings of Youth

4764
PERRY, Robert--see: Bob Perry

4765
PERRY, Walter*
Foreign Legion, The
Love Master, The
Unholy Three, The (announcer)

4766
PERSSE, Tom*
It's a Great Life

4767
PETE (Circle-eyed dog)
Dog Heaven
Little Mother
Our Gang Comedies

4768
PETELLE, Martha*
Clean Heart, The
Let Not Man Put Asunder

4769
PETER, M. *
Woman to Woman (Little Davy)

4770
PETER THE GREAT (Police Dog)
Silent Accuser, The

Wild Justice

4771
PETERS, Fred /aka/ Frederick*
Salome (Naaman, the executioner)
Tarzan and the Golden Lion (Este-
    ban Miranda)

4772
PETERS, House (1888-1967)
Bishop's Carriage, The
Clothes
Combat
Counsel for the Defense
Don't Marry for Money
Great Divide, The
Great Redeemer, The
Head Winds
Held to Answer
Human Hearts
Invisible Power, The
Isobel or the Trail's End
Leopard Woman, The
Lost and Found
Lying Lips
Man from Lost River, The
Mignon
Prisoners of the Storm
Raffles
Rich Men's Wives
Rose-Marie (Sgt. Terence Malone)
Salomy Jane
Silk Husbands and Calico Wives
Storm, The
Storm Breaker, The
Tornado
Universal player 24

4773
PETERS, John S. *
Amateur Gentleman, The (Capt.
    Slingsby)
Divine Sinner, The (Lugue Bern-
    storff)
Enemy, The
Ranson's Folly
Scarlet Lady
Student Prince, The (student)

4774
PETERS, Mammy*
Lilies of the Field

4775
PETERS, Mattie*
Day of Faith, The
Helen's Babies (Mandy, the house-
    keeper)

4776
PETERSEN, Ernst*
Peaks of Destiny

4777
PETROVITCH, Ivan*
Daughter of Destiny, A /aka/ Alraune
Garden of Allah, The
Magician, The
Morgane, the Enchantress

4778
PETROVITCH, Jans*
Kreutzer Sonata, The

4779
PETROVITCH, Peter*
End of St. Petersberg, The

4780
PETROVSKY, A. *
Lash of the Czar, The

4781
PETSCHLER, Erik A. *
Peter the Tramp (Title role)

4782
PEUKERT, Leo*
Jolly Peasant, The

4783
PEYTON, Charles*
April Fool (butler)
Stage:
L'Aiglon (Dr. Malfatti) 27
Miracle, The (Sexton) 24
Racket, The (Glick) 27
Red Dust (triple role, supervisor/
    2nd passerby/secretary) 29
Springtime of Youth (Augustus Sharp)
    22

4784
PHAIR, Douglas*
Fifth Form at St. Dominic's (Tony
    Pembury, Fifth Form Cynic)

4785
PHELPS, Buster*
Last Warning, The

4786
PHELPS, Vonda*
Jungle Goddess, The

4787
PHILBIN, Mary (1903-)
Affairs of Hannerl, The
Blazing Trail, The
Danger Ahead
Drums of Love (Princess Emanuella)
Erich the Great
False Kisses
Fifth Avenue Models
Fool's Highway
Footprints
Gaiety Girl
Human Hearts
Last Performance, The
Love Me and the World Is Mine
Man Who Laughs, The (Dea)
Merry-Go-Round, The (Agnes Urban)
Morality
No Clothes to Guide Her
Once to Every Boy
Penrod
Penrod and Sam (Margaret Schofeld)
Phantom of the Opera, The (Christ-
   ine Daae)
Port of Dreams
Red Courage
Rose of Paris, The
Shannons of Broadway, The /aka/
   Goodbye Broadway
Stella Maris
Sure Fire
Surrender
Temple of Venus, The (Moira)
Trouper, The

4788
PHILIPPE, Pierre*
Nana

4789
PHILLIPS, Carmen (1895-)
All Soul's Eve
Always Audacious
Ashes of Vengeance (Marie)
Cabaret Girl, The
Fighting Coward, The
Fire Eater, The
For a Woman's Honor
Forbidden Paths
Gentleman from America, The
Great Air Robbery, The
Heart Specialist, The
Mrs. Temple's Telegram
Pagan God, The
Right of Way, The
Sheik of Araby, The
There's Many a Fool
Thirty Days

Too Much Married

4790
PHILLIPS, Dorothy (1892-)
Bar-C Mystery, The [serial]
Broken Gates
Cradle Snatchers
Gay Deceiver, The
Hurricane's Gal
Jazz Cinderella
MGM player 27
Man, Woman-Marriage
Once to Every Woman (Aurora Mere-
   dith)
Paid in Advance
Remember
Slander the Woman
Sporting Chance, The
Unknown Purple, The (Carlos)
Upstage
Women Love Diamonds
World's a Stage, The

4791
PHILLIPS, Eddie*
Bells, The
Benson at Calford
Black Lightning (Ez Howard)
Capital Punishment (condemned boy)
College Love
Collegians, The [series]
Finders Keepers
Fourflusher, The
His Lucky Day
King of the Campus
Lonesome
Love Light, The (Mario)
Nth Commandment, The
Scandal
Through the Dark
Universal player 25
We Americans
Women Who Give

4792
PHILLIPS, Helena*
Greene Murder Case, The (Miss
   O'Brien)

4793
PHILLIPS, James*
Queen of the Nightclubs
Sally of the Scandals

4794
PHILLIPS, Nancy*
City Gone Wild, A

4795
PHILLIPS, Noreen*
Secret Studio, The

4796
PHIPPS, Sally*
Bertha, the Sewing Machine Girl
Detectives Wanted
High School Hero
News Parade, The
One Woman Idea
Why Sailors Go Wrong

4797
PIACENTI, Enrico*
Retribution

4798
PICABIA, Francis*
Entr'acte

4799
PICHA, Hermann*
Dancing Vienna
Der Juxbaron [The Imaginary Baron]
   (a tramp)
Romeo und Julia im Schnee [Romeo
   and Juliet in the Snow]
Small Town Sinners
Weavers, The
Women Without Men

4800
PICK, Lupu*
Spione [Spies]

4801
PICKFORD, Jack (Jack Smith) (1896-
   1933)
Bat, The (Brooks)
Brown of Harvard
Double-Dyed Deceiver, The
End of the World, The
Exit Smiling
Gang War
Garrison's Finish
Goose Woman, The (Gerald Holmes)
Hill Billy, The
Huckleberry Finn
In Wrong
Just out of College
Little Shepherd of Kingdom Come,
   The
Man Who Had Everything, The
My Son (Tony Silva)
Through the Back Door
Valley of the Wolf
Waking up the Town

4802
PICKFORD, Lottie (Lottie Smith)
   (1895-1936)
Don Q, Son of Zorro (Lola)
Dorothy Vernon of Haddon Hall (Jen-
   nie Faxton)
Independent player 22
They Shall Pay

4803
PICKFORD, Mary (Gladys Smith)
   (1893-   ) [see Vol. I for Bio-
   graphy]
Black Pirate, The (In black wig,
   stood in for Billie Dove)
Coquette (Norma Besant)
Dorothy Vernon of Haddon Hall (Title
   role)
Gaucho, The (Our Lady of the Shrine)
Going Straight
Little Annie Rooney (Title role)
Little Lord Fauntleroy (dual role,
   Cedric Errol/Dearest)
Love Light, The (Angela)
My Best Girl
Pollyanna (Title role)
Rosita (Title role)
Sparrows /aka/ Human Sparrows
   (Mama Molly)
Suds
Taming of the Shrew, The (Katherine)
Tess of the Storm Country (Tessibel
   Skinner)
Through the Back Door (Jeanne Boda-
   mere)

4804
PIDGEON, Walter (Walter David Pid-
   geon) (1897-   )
Clothes Make the Woman
Gateway of the Moon
Girl from Rio, The
Gorilla, The (the gorilla)
Heart of Salome, The
Her Private Life
Mannequinn (debut)
Marriage License
Melody of Love
Mademoiselle Modeste
Miss Nobody
Most Immoral Lady, A
Old Loves and New /aka/ The Desert
   Healer
Outsider, The
Thirteenth Juror, The
Turn Back the Hours
Viennese Nights
Voice Within, The

Woman Wise
Records:
Remember
What'll I Do? (First artist to record
   it) Victor Records
Stage:
Puzzles of 1925 (a principal)

4805
PIEL, Edward--see: Edward Peil

4806
PIEL, Edward, Jr.--see: Edward
   Peil, Jr.

4807
PIERCE, Barbara*
Grand Duchess and the Waiter, The
Stage:
Love Set, The (Maggie) 23

4808
PIERCE, Charlotte*
Barnstormer, The (Emily)
Courtship of Miles Standish, The
Peaceful Valley

4809
PIERCE, Curtis*
Down to the Sea in Ships (town
   crier)

4810
PIERCE, Evelyn*
Border Cavalier
Tenderloin

4811
PIERCE, George*
Nerve Tonic

4812
PIERCE, James H. (1900-)
Jesse James
Ladies of the Mob (officer)
Tarzan and the Golden Lion (Tarzan)
Wings (an MP)

4813
PIERSON, Suzy /aka/ Susanne*
6-1/2 x 11

4814
PIGGOT, Tempe (1884-1962)
Black Pirate, The (Duenna)
Dawn of Tomorrow, The
Greed (Mother McTeague)
Midnight Kiss, The (Grandma Spencer)

Narrow Street, The
None but the Brave
Rustle of Silk, The (Mrs. DeBreze)
Seven Days' Leave
Vanity Fair (Mrs. Sedley)

4815
PILOT, Bernice*
Hearts in Dixie

4816
PINE, Linda*
Love's Labor Won

4817
PINGREE, Earl*
Dark Streets

4818
PIO, Elith*
Witchcraft Through the Ages /aka/
   Häxan

4819
PITCAIRN, Jack*
In the Palace of the King

4820
PITTS, ZaSu (1898-1963)
Argyle Case, The (Mrs. Wyatt)
Behind the Footlights
Bright Skies
Buck Privates
Casey at the Bat
Changing Husbands
Daughters of Today
Dummy, The (Rose Gleason)
Early to Wed
Fast Set, The (Mona)
Girl Who Came Back, The
Goldfish
Great Divide, The
Greed (Trina)
Heart of Twenty, The
Her Big Night
Her Private Life
Honeymoon
Is Matrimony a Failure?
Locked Door, The
Mannequinn
Monte Carlo
No, No, Nanette (Pauline)
Oh, Yeah!
Old Shoes
Paris
Patsy, The
Poor Men's Wives
Pretty Ladies (Maggie Keenan)

Risky Business
Seeing It Through
Sins of the Father (Mother Spengler)
Squall, The (Lena)
Sunlight of Paris
Sunny Side Up
13 Washington Square (Mathilde)
This Thing Called Love (Clara Bertrand)
Three Wise Fools
Triumph (factory girl)
Twin Beds
Universal player 22
Wedding March, The (Cecelia)
West of the Water Tower
What Happened to Jones?
Why They Left Home
Wife Savers
Wine of Youth, The
Woman's Faith, A

4821
PITTSCHAU, Warner*
Women Without Men

4822
PLANT, Joe*
Kissing Cup's Race (Bob Doon)

4823
PLATEN, Karl*
Anna Boleyn /aka/ Deception
Destiny /aka/ The Tired Death;
   The Three Lights; Between
   Worlds; Der Mude Tod
Eine Du Barry von Heute [A Modern
   Du Barry] (servant)
Luther

4824
PLATT, Billy /aka/ William*
Mother Machree
Simon the Jester
Tillie's Punctured Romance (Midget)

4825
PLAYTER, Wellington*
Golden Snare, The

4826
PLEDATH, Werner*
Der Mensch am Wege [Man by the
   Roadside]

4827
PLESCHKOFF, Michael*
Into Her Kingdom
Only Thing, The

4828
PLIMMER, Walter, Jr.*
Isn't Life Wonderful? (an American)
Stage:
Hometowners, The (Joe Roberts) 26

4829
PLUMMER, Lincoln*
Alias the Deacon
Barnstormer, The (druggist)
Dangerous Maid
Regular Fellow, A
Ten Dollar Raise, The
Within the Law (Cassidy)

4830
POFF, Lon (1870-   )
Bonnie May
Broken Gates, The
Bunty Pulls the Strings
Dante's Inferno
Dulcy
Faker, The
Girl I Loved, The
Greased Lightning
Greed (lottery agent)
Iron Mask, The (Father Joseph)
Last Straw, The
Main Street
Man Who Laughs, The
Mantrap
Merry Widow, The (Sadoja's Lackey)
Night Horseman, The
Ole Swimmin' Hole, The
Sand!
Thief in Paradise, A
Three Musketeers, The (Father
   Joseph)
Two Lovers
Village Blacksmith, The
Virginian, The

4831
POFF, Louis*
Thief in Paradise, A

4832
POHL, Claus*
Frau im Mond [Woman in the Moon]

4833
POHL, Max*
Der Mensch am Wege [Man by the
   Roadside]

4834
POINTNER, Anton*
Kopf Hoch, Charly! [Heads Up,

Charly!] (Frank Ditman)
That Murder in Berlin

4835
POLLAR, Gene (Joseph C. Pohler)
   (1892-)
Revenge of Tarzan, The /aka/ The
   Return of Tarzan (Tarzan)

4836
POLLARD, Daphne (1894-)
Big Time, The
Campus Vamp, The
Cleo to Cleopatra
Girl from Everywhere, The
Hit of the Show
Ladies Must Eat
Loose Ankles
Old Barn, The
Run, Girl, Run
Sally (Minnie)
Sinners in Love
Sky Hawk, The
South Sea Rose
Swim Princess, The
Stage:
Greenwich Village Follies 23
Vaudeville [Palace] 26; 27

4837
POLLARD, Laura*
Vanity Fair (Mrs. Tinker)

4838
POLLARD, "Snub" (Harold Fraser)
   (1886-1962)
All Dressed Up
All in a Day
All Lit Up
All Wet
Anvil Chorus, The
Any Old Port
Are Husbands Human?
At the Ringside
Bed of Roses
Before the Public
Big Game
Big Idea, The
Bike Bug, The
Blow 'em Up
Blue Sunday
Bow Wows, The
Bubbling Over
Bum's Rush, The
California or Bust
Call a Taxi!
Call the Witness
Cash Customers

Corner Pocket
Courtship of Miles Standwich, The
Cracked Wedding Bells
Cut the Cards
Days of Old
Dear Ol' Pal
Dearly Departed, The
Dig Up
Dining Hour, The
Dippy Dentist, The
Do Me a Favor
Do Your Duty
Doing Time
Don't Rock the Boat
Don't Weaken
Doughboys, The
Down and Out
Drink Hearty
Dumb-Bell, The
Fellow Citizens
Fellow Romans
Fifteen Minutes
Find the Girl
Fire, The
Flat Broke
Fresh Paint
Full O' Pep
Fully Insured
Get Busy
Getting Her Goat
Go As You Please
Gone to the Country
Grab the Ghost
Hale and Hearty
High Rollers, The
His Best Girl
His Royal Slyness
Hocus-Pocus
Home Stretch, The
Hook, Line and Sinker
Hot Off the Press
Hustler, The
In the Grease
In the Movies
Insulting the Sultan
It's a Boy
It's a Gift
Jack Frost
Jailbird, The
Join the Circus
Joy Rider, The
Jump Your Job
Kill the Nerve
Late Lodgers
Law and Order
Light Showers
Live and Learn
London Bobby, A

Lose No Time
Make It Snappy
Money to Burn
Morning After, The
Mystery Man, The
Name the Day
Nearly Rich
No Children
No Stop-Over
Old Sea Dog, The
Old Warhorse, The
On Location
Once Over
Open Another Bottle
Our Gang
Own Your Own Home
Pardon Me
Park Your Car
Penny-in-the Slot
Punch the Clock
Raise the Rent
Red Hot Hottentots
Rock-a-Bye-Baby
Rough Winter, A
Run 'em Ragged
Rush Orders
Save Your Money
Shake 'em Up
Shoot on Sight
Sink or Swim
Slippery Slices
Sold at Auction
Some Baby!
Speed to Spare
Spot Cash
Stage Struck
Start Something
Stone Age, The
Strictly Modern
Teaching the Teacher
365 Days
Trotting Through Turkey
Walkout, The
Waltz Me Around
What a Whopper
When the Wind Blows
Where Am I?
Where's the Fire?
Whirl O' the West
Why Go Home?
Why Marry
Years to Come
Yokel, The
You're Next

4839
POLLET, Albert*
Mysterious Lady, The /aka/ War

in the Dark (Karl's uncle)
Under Two Flags (Capt. Tollaire)

4840
POLO, Eddie (1875-1961)
Battle Against Odds, A
Captain Kid
Do or Die [serial]
King of the Circus [serial]
Knock on the Door, A
Return of Cyclone Smith, The
Secret Four, The [serial]
Square Deal Cyclone
Vanishing Dagger, The [serial]
With Stanley in Africa [serial]

4841
POLO, Malvine*
Foolish Wives (Marietta)
Woman of Paris, A (Pauletta)

4842
POLO, Sam*
Great Circus Mystery, The [serial]

4843
PONTOPPIDAN, Clara*
Witchcraft Through the Ages /aka/
    Häxan

4844
POOL, Elwood J.*
Plunder [serial]

4845
POPOV, N.*
October

4846
POPOV, V.*
In Old Siberia

4847
PORCASI, Paul (1880-)
Broadway (Nick Verdis)
Say It Again
Stage:
Broadway (Nick Verdis) 26
Jimmie (Vincenzo Carlotti) 20
National Anthem, The (Dr. Virande)
    22
Oh! Mama! (Maitre de Hotel) 25
Texas Nightingale, The (Count
    Houdonyi-Black) 22

4848
PORTEN, Henny (1888-)
Das Alte Gesetz (Archduchess

Elizabeth Theresa)
Ancient Law, The
Anna Boleyn /aka/ Deception (Title
    role)
Backstairs
Jew of Mestri, The (Porzia)
Kölhiessel's Töchter (dual role,
    Gretl/Lissl)

4849
PORTER, Pansy*
Branded Four, The [serial]

4850
PORTER, Paul*
Into the Net [serial]
Stage:
Burlesque (Jimmy) 27
Close Harmony (Bill Saunders) 24
Half Gods (Dennis) 29
Kosher Kitty Kelly (Wang Lee) 25
Little Old New York (Bully Boy
    Brewster) 20
Port O' London (Charlie Fix) 26
She Couldn't Say No (Ezra Pine) 26

4851
POST, Buddy*
Tender Hour, The

4852
POST, Charles A. *
Behold This Woman
Crown of Lies, The
Diplomacy
Lover's Oath, A /aka/ Rubaiyat of
    Omar Khayyam
Top of the World, The
Wild Oranges

4853
POST, Guy Bates (1876-1968)
Gold Madness
Masquerader, The (dual role)
Omar the Tentmaker

4854
POTECHINA, Lydia*
Manon Lescaut (Susanne)
Waltz Dream, The

4855
POTEL, Victor (1889-1947)
Below the Line
Billions
Bob Hampton of Placer
Captain Swagger
Contraband

Heart of a Child, The
Lavender and Old Lace
Lingerie
Little Shepherd of Kingdom Come,
    The
Lost Lady, A
Marianne
Mary's Ankles
Meanest Man in the World, The
Melody of Love
Quincy Adams Sawyer (Hiram Max-
    well)
Refuge
Sheik of Hollywood, The
Special Delivery (Nip)
Tailor-Made Man, A
Virginian, The (Nebrasky)
What Price Beauty?
Women Who Give

4856
POULTON, Mabel (1903-)
Alley Cat, The
Ball of Fortune, The
Constant Nymph, The (Tessa)
Daughter of Revolt, A
Glad Eye, The
God in the Garden, The
Hellcat
Knights and Ladies
Moonbeam Magic
Not Quite a Lady
Nothing Else Matters
Old Curiosity Shop, The
Oscillation
Palais de Dance
Return of the Rat, The (Lisette)
Silent House, The
Taxi for Two
Troublesome Wives
Virginia's Husband

4857
POUYET, Eugene*
La Boheme (Bernard)
Merry Widow, The

4858
POWELL, Bellendom*
Prince of Lovers, The

4859
POWELL, David (1887-1923)
Anna Ascends
Fog Bound
Glimpses of the Moon
Green Goddess, The (Dr. Basil
    Traherne)

Her Gilded Cage (Arnold Pell)
Hero, The
Idols of Clay (Dion Holme)
Lady Rose's Daughter
Love's Boomerang
Missing Millions
Mystery Road, The
On with the Dance
Outcast (Geoffrey Sherwood)
Princess of New York, The
Right to Love, The
Siren Call, The
Virtuous Liars

4860
POWELL, Michael*
Garden of Allah, The
Magician, The

4861
POWELL, Russell*
Boy of Flanders, A
Dangerous Curves (counterman)
Fashions in Love
Love Parade, The (Afghan Ambassador)
No Place to Go
Red Mill, The (Burgomaster)
Reiley, the Cop
Soft Cushions

4862
POWELL, Templar*
His Children's Children
Monsieur Beaucaire (Molyneux)
Stage:
Dancers, The (John Carruthers) 23

4863
POWELL, William (William Horatio Powell) (1892-)
Aloma of the South Seas (Van Templeton)
Beau Geste (Baldini)
Beau Sabreur (Becque)
Beautiful City, The (Nick DiSilva)
Bright Shawl, The (Capt. Caspar DeVaca)
Canary Murder Case, The (Philo Vance)
Charming Sinners (Karl Kraley)
Dangerous Money (Prince Arnolfo daPescia)
Desert Gold (Landree)
Dragnet (Frank Trent)
Faint Perfume (Barnaby Powers)
Feel My Pulse (Rumrunner)
Forgotten Faces (Froggy)

Four Feathers, The (Lt. Trench)
Great Gatsby, The (George Wilson)
Greene Murder Case, The (Philo Vance)
Interference (Philip Voaze)
Last Command, The (Leo Andreiev)
Love's Greatest Mistake (Don Kendall)
My Lady's Lips (Scott Seddon)
Nevada (Clan Dillon)
New York (Trent Regan)
Outcast (DeValle)
Paid to Love (Prince Eric)
Partners in Crime (Smith)
Pointed Heels (Robert Courtland)
Romola (Tito Melema)
Runaway, The (Jack Harrison)
Sea Horses (Lorenzo Salvis)
Senorita (Ramon Oliveras)
She's a Sheik (Kada)
Sherlock Holmes /aka/ Moriarity (Forman Wells)
Special Delivery (Harold Jones)
Time for Love (Prince Alado)
Tin Gods (Tony Santelli)
Too Many Kisses (Police Chief)
Under the Red Robe (Duke of Orleans)
Vanishing Pioneer, The (John Murdock)
When Knighthood Was in Flower (Francis Duc d'Angoulême)
White Mice (Roddy Forrester)
Stage:
Bavu (Michka) 22
Spanish Love (Javier) 20
Woman Who Laughed, The (John Neilson) 22

4864
POWER, Jules*
For Sale (Mrs. Twombly-Smith)

4865
POWER, Tyrone, Sr. (F. Tyrone Power) (1869-1931)
Black Panther's Cub, The
Brave Heart
Bride of the Storm
Daring Years, The (James LaMotte)
Day of Faith, The
Dream Street (street preacher)
Footfalls
Fury
Great Shadow, The
Janice Meredith (Lord Cornwallis)
Lone Wolf, The
Out of the Storm
Red Kimono, The

Regular Fellow, A
Story Without a Name, The
Test of Donald Norton, The
Truth About Wives, The
Wanderer, The
Where Was I?
Wife in Name Only
Stage:
Diplomacy (Markham) 28
Hamlet (Claudius) 22
Rivals, The (Sir Anthony Absolute)
  22
Venus (Herbert Beveridge) 27
Wandering Jew, The (Mathathias) 21

4866
POWERS, Francis*
Iron Horse, The (Sgt. Slattery)
Man Without a Country /aka/ As
  No Man Has Loved

4867
POWERS, Lucille*
Marquis Preferred
Three Weekends (Miss Witherspoon)

4868
POWERS, Maurine*
Democracy, the Vision Restored
Why Girls Leave Home

4869
POWLEY, Bryan*
Wee MacGreegor's Sweetheart (Uncle
  Purdie)

4870
POZZI, Mrs. *
Side Show of Life, The

4871
PRADE, Marie*
Gold Diggers, The (Sadie)

4872
PRADOT, Marcelle*
L'Homme du Large
Late Matthew Pascal, The
Living Dead Man, The

4873
PRASCH, Auguste*
Waterloo

4874
PRATT, Jack*
Desert Song, The (Pasha)

4875
PRATT, Lynn*
Virgin Paradise, A
Stage:
Flame of Love (Fong-lee) 24
Merton of the Movies (mysterious
  visitor) 22
Romance (Fred Livingston) 21

4876
PRATT, Purnell B. (1882-1941)
Alibi /aka/ The Perfect Alibi (Pete
  Manning)
Fast Life
Gorilla, The
Is Everybody Happy?
Locked Door, The
Midnight Lovers
Night Stick
On with the Show
Through Different Eyes (D. A. Mars-
  ton)
Trespasser, The (Hector Ferguson)
Stage:
Charlaton, The (Herbert Deering) 22
Cock O' the Roost (Henry Barron) 24
Crooked Gamblers (Bob Dryden) 20
Goose Hangs High, The (Leo Day) 24
Her Way Out (Hannibal Williams) 24
Just Married (Percy Jones) 21
Tenth Avenue (Ed Burton) 27
Thumbs Down (James Cantwell) 23

4877
PREJEAN, Albert (1898-)
Un Chapeau de Paille d' Italie [The
  Italian Straw Hat]
Gonzague
Sous les Toits de Paris [Under the
  Roofs of Paris]
Le Voyage Imaginaire

4878
PRELIA, Claire*
Living Image, The

4879
PRETAL, Camillus*
Abie's Irish Rose (Rabbi Jacob
  Samuels)

4880
PRETTY, Arline (1893-)
Barriers Burned Away
Bucking the Barrier
Life
Love in the Dark
Primrose Path, The (Helen)

Storm Swept
Valley of Doubt
Virgin Lips
Woman in Grey, A (Ruth Hope)

4881
PREVOST, Marie (Marie Bickford
  Dunn) (1898-1937)
Almost a Lady
Beautiful and the Damned, The
Being Respectable
Black Swan, The
Blonde for the Night
Bobbed Hair
Brass
Butterfly
Cave Man, The
Cornered
Dangerous Little Demon
Daughters of Pleasure (Marjory Hed-
  ley)
Divorce Made Easy
Don't Get Personal
Down on the Farm
Exodus of the New World
Flying Fool, The
For Wives Only
Girl on the Pullman, The
Godless Girl, The (the other girl)
Her Night of Nights
Heroes of the Streets
His Jazz Bride
How to Educate a Wife
Kiss Me Again (Loulou Fleury)
Kissed
Lady of Leisure, A
Love, Honor and Behave
Lover of Camille, The
Man Bait
Marriage Circle, The (Mizzie Stock)
Married Flapper, The
Moonlight Follies
Night Bride, The
Nobody's Fool
Ole Swimmin' Hole, The
On to Reno
Other Men's Wives
Other Women's Husbands
Racket, The
Recompense
Red Lights
Rush Hour, The
Seven Sinners
Side Show, The
Small Town Idol, A
Tarnish
Three Women (Harriet)
Up in Mabel's Room

Wanters, The
Within the Law

4882
PRICE, Hal*
Night Ride (Mac)

4883
PRICE, Kate (1873-1943)
Anybody Here Seen Kelly?
Artists and Models
Bright Skies
Broken Hearts of Broadway
Casey Jones
Charley's Aunt
Cohens and the Kellys, The
Cohens and the Kellys in Atlantic
  City, The
Cohens and the Kellys in Paris, The
Come on Over
Dangerous Maid
Desert Flower, The
Devil's Riddle, The
Dinty
Figurehead, The
Flesh and Blood (landlady)
Frisco Sally Levy
Girl of Gold, The
Godless Girl, The (a matron)
Guttersnipe
Her Fatal Millions
His Wife's Relations
Irene
Lady of Shalott, The
Linda
Little Lord Fauntleroy (Mrs. Mc-
  Ginty)
Mad Hour, The
Memory Lane
Mother Knows Best
Mountains of Manhattan
New Teacher, The
Orchids and Ermine
Other Woman, The
Paradise
Perfect Clown, The
Proud Heart, The
Quality Street (Patty)
Rainbow, The
Rogue Song, The (Petrovna)
Sally, Irene and Mary (Mrs. Dugan)
Sea Hawk, The
Sea Tiger, The
Show Girl
Spoilers, The (landlady)
Sporting Venus, A
Thanks for the Buggy Ride
That Girl Montana

Third Degree, The
Tornado, The
Two Weeks Off
Universal player 27
Way of a Girl, The
Wife of the Centaur

4884
PRICE, Nancy*
American Prisoner, The (Lovey
    Lee, the witch)
Comin' Thro' the Rye (Mrs. Tit-
    mouse)
Doctor's Secret, The
His House in Order (Lady Ridgeley)
Three Live Ghosts

4885
PRIMM, Frances*
Merry Widow, The (a Hansen sister)

4886
PRINCE, Jessie*
Broadway Melody, The

4887
PRINCE, John T. *
Battling Orioles, The
Black Lightning (city doctor)
Capital Punishment (doctor)
King of Kings, The (Thadeus)
Lawful Cheaters (Silent Sam Riley)
Radio Detective, The [serial]
Ramona (Father Salvierderra)

4888
PRING, Gerald*
Betrayal, The
Milestones (triple role, Ned Pym/
    Young Lord Monkhurst/Lord
    Monkhurst)
Nut, The

4889
PRINGLE, Aileen (Alieen Bisbee)
    (1895-   )
Adam and Evil
Baby Cyclone
Beau Broadway
Body and Soul
Christian, The (Lady Robert Ure)
Dance Madness
Don't Marry for Money
Dream of Love (the Duke's wife)
Earthbound
Great Deception, The
His Hour
In the Palace of the King

Kiss in the Dark, A
Man About Town
My American Wife (Hortensia de
    Vareta)
Mystic, The
Name the Man
Night Parade
One Year to Live
Romance of a Queen, The (queen)
Show People (cameo)
Single Man, A
Souls for Sale (Lady Jane)
Stranger's Banquet, The
Tea for Three
Thief in Paradise, A
Three Weeks
Tiger's Claw, The
Tin Gods (Janet Stone)
True as Steel
Wall Street
Wickedness Preferred
Wife of the Centaur, The
Wilderness Woman, The
Wildfire

4890
PRIOR, Beatrix--see: Beatrix Pryor

4891
PRIOR, Herbert*
Ace of Scotland Yard, The [serial]
    (Lord Blanton)
All at Sea
Dangerous Little Demon
Duke Steps Out, The
Garments of Truth
Garrison's Finish
Half Breed, The
House of Whispers, The
Last Outlaw, The
Little 'Fraid Lady
Made in Heaven
Madonna of the Streets, A (Nathan
    Norris)
Man from Downing Street, The
Midnight Kiss, The (Smith Hastings)
Not Guilty
Pollyanna
Slave of Desire
Snowshoe Trail
Stronger than Death
Waking up the Town
Why Girls Go Back Home

4892
PRIOR, Robert*
Little Johnny Jones

4893
PRISCOE, Albert /aka/ Al Prisco*
Ace of Scotland Yard, The [serial]
  (Prince Darius)
Great Circus Mystery, The [serial]
Midnight Sun, The
Monte Cristo (Danglars)
Sea Hawk, The (Yusef)
Soft Cushions
Song of Love, The
Voice from the Minaret, The (Seleim)
White Black Sheep, The

4894
PRIVAL, Lucien (1900-)
Adoration
American Beauty
Great Deception, The
High Hat
Hummingbird, The
Just Another Blonde
Man of Quality, A
Next Room, The
Patent Leather Kid, The
Peacock Fan, The
Puppets

4895
PROBERT, George*
Madame Peacock
Stage:
Houses of Sand (Yumato) 25
Mad Honeymoon, The (Bill Cripps)
  23
Murder on the Second Floor (Jam
  Singh) 29
New York (Sanchez) 27

4896
PROCTOR, Catherine*
Society Scandal, A (Mrs. Burr)
Stage:
Ambush (Mrs. Jennison) 21
Ariadne (Hester Chadwick) 25
East of Suez (Amah) 22
Ghost Parade, The (Lizzie) 29
Importance of Being Earnest, The
  (Miss Prism) 26
L'Aiglon (Archduchess Sophia) 27
Macbeth (gentlewoman) 24
Mirage, The (Mrs. Martin) 20
Royal Box, The (Lady Robert) 28
Sakura (O'Susume) 28
Steam Roller, The (Mrs. Worthing-
  ton) 24
Wife with a Smile, The (Marguerite
  Prévot) 21

4897
PROUTY, Jed (1879-1956)
Broadway Melody, The (Uncle Jed)
Coast of Folly, The (Cholly Knicker-
  bocker)
Ella Cinders
Everybody's Acting
Fall of Eve, The
Girl in the Show, A
Gold Diggers (Barney Barnett)
Grain of Dust, A
His Captive Woman
Imperfect Ladies
It's a Great Life
Knockout, The
Name the Woman
No Place to Go
Orchids and Ermine
Scarlet Saint, The
Sea Beast, The
Second Chance
Siren, The
Smile, Brother, Smile
Sonny Boy
Two Weeks Off
Unguarded Hour, The
Unknown Treasures /aka/ The House
  Behind the Hedge
Why Leave Home?
Stage:
Girl from Home, The (Simpson
  Alias "Jim Dodd") 20
Some Party (a principal) 22

4898
PRUSSING, Louise*
Reckless Youth (Mrs. Dahlgren)
Stage:
Berkeley Square (Duchess of Devon-
  shire) 29

4899
PRYOR, Beatrix*
Stella Dallas (Mrs. Grosvenor)

4900
PUDOFFSTIN, J.*
Aelita: The Revolt of the Robots

4901
PUFFY, Charles*
Love Me and the World Is Mine
Man Who Laughs, The (innkeeper)
Man's Past, A
Mockery (Ivan)
Open All Night
Private Life of Helen of Troy, The
  (Malapokitoratoreadetos)

4902
PUGLIA, Frank (1894-1962)
Beautiful City, The (Carlo Gillardi)
Fascination
Isn't Life Wonderful? (the brother)
Man Who Laughs, The (clown)
Orphans of the Storm (Pierre Fro-
    chard)
Romola (Adolpo Spini)
Stage:
Stock Company at Olympic Theatre,
    New York 21

4903
PURVIANCE, Edna (1894-1958)
Education of Prince
Idle Class, The
Kid, The
Pay Day
Pilgrim, The (the girl)
Seagull, The
United Artists player 23
Woman of Paris, A (Marie St. Clair)

4904
PUSEY, Arthur*
Scandal in Paris, A

4905
PUTTER, Alice Mildred*
Crowd, The (daughter)

4906
PUZHNAYA, R.*
Village of Sin, The

- Q -

4907
QUALITY, Gertrude*
Godless Girl, The (a matron)

4908
QUARTARO, Nina (1911-)
All Parts
Big Squawk
Eternal Woman, The
Frozen River
One Stolen Night
Red Mark, The
Redeeming Sin, The
Under a Texas Moon
Virginian, The

4909
QUEDENS, Eunice*
Song of Love

4910
QUILLAN, Eddie (1907-)
Catalina, Here I Come
Geraldine
Godless Girl, The (the ghost)
Hot and Bothered
Noisy Neighbors
Our Dancing Daughters
Show Folks (Eddie)
Sophomore, The
Up and at 'em (debut)
Stage:
Orpheum Theatre, Los Angeles 25

4911
QUIMBY, Margerie*
Kopf Hoch, Charly! [Heads Up,
    Charly!] (Margie Quinn)

4912
QUIMBY, Margaret*
Ghetto, The
Lucky Boy /aka/ My Mother's Eyes
New York (Helena Matthews)
Perils of the Wild [serial]
Sally of the Scandals
Squads Right
Teaser, The
Tragedy of Youth, The
Two Men and a Maid
Western Whirlwind, The
What Happened to Jones?
Whole Town's Talking, The

4913
QUINN, Charles*
Broncho Buster, The

4914
QUINN, Jimmie (James T. Quinn)*
Argyle Case, The (Skidd)
Broadway after Dark
Dance of Life, The
Dixie Handicap, The
On Thin Ice
Pretty Ladies
Red Hot Tires
Spieler, The
Two Flaming Youths (Slippery Saw-
    telle)
Wife Who Wasn't Wanted, The

4915
QUINN, Regina*
Humming Bird, The (Beatrice)

4916
QUINN, William*
Chorus Girl's Romance, A (P. P.
  Anderson)
Darling of New York, The
Stage:
Crooked Friday (Micky) 25
Little Minister, The (Micha Dow) 25
"Merry Wives of Gotham" (Fanshas-
  tics) (dual role, Patsy/a small
  German) 24
Offence, The (Martin Stapleton) 25

4917
QUIRK, Billy /aka/ William Quirk
  (1888-)
At the Stage Door
Broadway Broke
Dixie Handicap, The
My Old Kentucky Home
Salomy Jane
Success

4918
QUIVEY, Marvel*
New Lives for Old

- R -

4919
RABAGLIATI, Alberto*
Street Angel (policeman)

4920
RADAY, Imre*
At the Edge of the World (Michael)
Strauss, the Waltz King
Trial of Donald Westhof, The

4921
RADCLIFFE, E. J.--see: Edward
  J. Ratcliffe

4922
RADFORD, Basil (1897-1952)
Barnum Was Right

4923
RADNAY, Hilda*
Eine du Barry von Heute [A Modern
  DuBarry] (Juliette)

4924
RADZINA, Medea*
Bedroom Window, The
Midnight Sun, The
Sea Hawk, The (Fenzileh)

4925
RADZINA, Remea*
Next Corner, The (Countess Longue-
  val)

4926
RAE, Raida*
Craig's Wife
Death Valley
Wild Geese

4927
RAFETTO, Mike*
Tillie's Punctured Romance

4928
RAFT, George (George Ranft) (1903-)
Queen of the Nightclubs

4929
RAGABLIATI, Alberto--see: Alberto
  Rabagliati

4930
RAI, Himansu*
Light of Asia, The
Shiraz

4931
RAINS, Fred*
Nell Gwyn (Earl of Shaftesbury)
Only Way, The (Tribunal President)

4932
RAKER, Lorin*
Mother's Boy (Joe Bush)
Stage:
Arabian Nightmare, The (Bobbie
  Mudge) 27
Getting Gertie's Garter (Billy Fellon)
  21
Lights Out (Butts McAllister) 22
Mama Loves Papa (Joe Turner) 26
Queen O' Hearts (Alfred Armstrong)
  22

4933
RALE, M. W. *
Three Miles Out

4934
RALEIGH, Joe*
Janice Meredith (Arthur Lee)

4935
RALEIGH, Saba*
Prince of Lovers, The
Road to London, The (the Duchess)

4936
RALLI, Paul*
Married in Hollywood
Show People (cameo)
Water Hole, The

4937
RALPH, Hanna*
Faust
Die Nibelungen /aka/ The Nibelungs
  (Brunhilda)
Power
Siegfried

4938
RALPH, Julia*
So's Your Old Man (Mrs. Murchison)
Stage:
Arabesque (Sheik's mother) 25
Bride of the Lamb (Minnie Herrick)
  26
Ladies' Night (a policewoman) 20
Roger Bloomer (landlady) 23
Veils (Annie Hughes) 28

4939
RALPH, Louis*
Ghost Train, The (Saul Hodgkin)
Russia 1908
Spione [Spies]

4940
RALSTON, Esther (1902-   )
American Venus, The
Beggar on Horseback
Best People
Betrayal, The
Blind Goddess, The
Case of Lena Smith, The
Children of Divorce (Jean Wadding-
  ton)
Fashions for Women
$50,000 Reward
Figures Don't Lie
Goose Hangs High, The (Dagmar
  Carroll)
Half a Bride
Kiss for Cinderella, A (Fairy God-
  mother)
Lady Who Lied, The
Little French Girl, The
Love and Learn
Lucky Devil, The
Marriage Circle, The
Mighty, The (Louise Patterson)
Old Ironsides
Oliver Twist (Rose Maylie)
Peter Pan (Mrs. Darling)

Phantom Fortune, The [serial]
Power of the Press
Quarterback, The
Rememberance
Sawdust Paradise, The
Something Always Happens
Spotlight, The
Tall Timber
Ten Modern Commandments
Timberland Treachery
Trouble with Wives, The
Under Secret Orders
Wheel of Life, The
Whispering Devils
Wolves of the North [serial]
Womanhandled
Stage:
Vaudeville [Palace] 29

4941
RALSTON, Howard*
Daughter of Luxury, A
Pollyanna

4942
RALSTON, Jobyna (1902-1967)
Are Parents Pickles?
Big Hop, The
Black Butterflies
College Coquette
Count of Ten, The
For Heaven's Sake
Freshman, The (Peggy)
Gigolo
Girl Shy
Hot Water
Kid Brother, The
Lightning
Little Mickey Grogan
Night Flyer, The
Power of the Press
Pretty Clothes
Racing Romeo, A
Some Mother's Boy
Special Delivery (Madge)
Sweet Daddies
Three-Must-Get-Theirs, The
Toilers, The
Why Worry?
Wings (Sylvia Lewis)

4943
RAMA, Rau E.*
Shriaz

4944
RAMBEAU, Marjorie (1889-1970)
Fortune Teller, The

On Her Honor
Syncopating Sue
Stage:
Antonia (Title role) 25
As You Like It (Rosalind) 23
Daddy's Gone A-Hunting (Edith) 21
Goldfish, The (Jenny) 22
Just Life (Madame Bernice Chase)
Night Duel (Betty Ramsey) 26
Road Together, The (Dora Kent) 24
Untitled Benefit 22
Valley of Content, The (Marjorie
   Benton) 23

4945
RAMBOVA, Natacha (1897-1966)
When Love Grows Cold
Stage:
Creoles (Golondrina) 27
Set a Thief (Anne Dowling) 27

4946
RAMEAU, Emil*
Monna Vanna

4947
RAMIREZ, Rosita*
Maré Nostrum [Our Sea]

4948
RAMON*
Wind, The

4949
RAMON, Laon--see: Leon Janney

4950
RANCOURT, Jules*
His Tiger Lady

4951
RAND, John*
Astray from the Steerage (Intelligence
   Department)
Circus, The (property man)
Idle Class, The
Pay Day

4952
RAND, Sally (1903-   )
Black Feather
Clash, The
Crashing Through
Czarina's Secrets, The
Dressmaker from Paris
Fighting Eagle, The
Galloping Fury
Getting Gertie's Garter

Girl in Every Port, A
Gold Widows
Grounds for Divorce
Heroes in Blue
His Dog
King of Kings, The (Mary Magdalene's
   slave girl)
Main Bait
Nameless Men
Night of Love, The (Gypsy dancer)
Paris at Midnight
Road to Yesterday, The
Woman Against the World, A
Stage:
Vaudeville [Palace] 28

4953
RANDALL, Bernard*
Classified
Evil Eye, The [serial]
French Doll, The
Master Mind, The
Panjola (Eric Luff)
Pretty Ladies (Aaron Savage)
Say It Again
Show Girl
Skyrocket
Subway Sadie
Stage:
Honeymoon Lane (the boss) 26
My Girl Friday (Paul Manger) 29

4954
RANDOLF, Anders /aka/ Anders
   Randolph (1875-1930)
Behold This Woman
Big Killing, The
Black Pirate, The (pirate leader)
Bright Shawl, The (Capt. Cesar y
   Santacilla)
Buried Treasure
Climbers, The (Hans Nelson)
College Widow, The
Dangerous Curves (G. P. Brock)
Dearie
Dorothy Vernon of Haddon Hall (Sir
   George Vernon)
Erick the Great
Eternal Struggle, The
Five Aces
Four Devils, The (Cocchi)
413
Gateway of the Moon
Idol Dancer, The (the blackbirder)
In Hollywood with Potash and Perl-
   mutter
Jazz Singer, The (Dillings)
Jim, the Penman

Johnstown Flood, The (lumber camp
  boss)
Kiss, The (Irene's husband)
Last Performance, The
Love Flower, The (Matthew Crane)
Loves of Sunya, The (Robert Goring)
Madonnas and Men
Me, Gangster (Russ Williams)
Mighty Lak' a Rose
Noah's Ark (dual role, soldier lead-
  er/the German)
Old San Francisco
Patience
Peacock Alley (Hugo Fenton)
Powder My Back
Power of Silence
Ranson's Folly
Reno Divorce, A
Seven Keys to Baldpate (Thomas
  Norton)
Shanghai Lady
Sherlock Holmes /aka/ Moriarty
  (James Larrabee)
Show of Shows, The
Silent Flyer, The [serial]
Sin Sister (Joseph T. Horn)
Sinews of Steel
Slightly Used
Snappy Sneezer, The
Son of the Gods (Wagner)
Souls for Sables
Tender Hour, The
Three Sinners
Viking, The
When Knighthood Was in Flower
Womanpower
Women They Talk About
Wrong Again
Young Nowheres

4955
RANEVSKY, Boris*
Mademoiselle from Armentieres
  (liaison)

4956
RANI, Paul*
Show People

4957
RANKIN, Arthur (1900-)
Adventurous Souls
Amateur Wife
Below the Deadline
Black Swan, The
Blood Ship, The
Broken Laws
Call of the Canyon, The

Code of the Air
Companionate Marriage, The
Copperhead, The
Dearie
Fall of Eve, The
Finders Keepers
Glad Rag Doll
Great Adventure
Jim, the Penman
Love and the Law
Making the Varsity
Metro player 22
Mexicali Rose
Old Loves and New /aka/ The Desert
  Healer
Riding to Fame
Romance
Runaway Girls
Say It with Sables
Ships of the Night
Slightly Used
Submarine
Sun Up
Truth About Husbands, The
Vanity's Price
Volga Boatman, The
Wild Party, The
Wolf of Wall Street, The (Frank)
Woman Who Did Not Care, The

4958
RANKIN, Caroline*
Village Blacksmith, The

4959
RANKIN, Catherine*
Three Must-Get-Theirs, The

4960
RANKIN, Doris*
Copperhead, The
Devil's Garden, The
Great Adventure
Jim, the Penman
Stage:
Big Pond, The (Mrs. Livermore) 28
Chivalry (Kathleen Taggert) 25
Claw, The (Anne Cortelon) 21
Garden of Eden, The (Aunt Matilde)
  27
Letter of the Law, The (Yanetta) 20
Rose Bernd (Mrs. Flamm) 22
Seed of the Brute (Anne Emerson
  Roberts) 26
Vaudeville [Palace] 26

4961
RANSOM, Edith*
Lilies of the Field

4962
RAO, Enakshi Rama*
Shiraz

4963
RAPLEY, Rose--see: Rose Tapley

4964
RAPPE, Virginia (-1921)
Adventuress, An /aka/ The Isle of
  Love

4965
RAQUA, Charles*
East of Suez
King of Kings, The (James, the
  Less)
Son of the Sheik (Pierre)

4966
RASCH, Albertina Ballet
Hollywood Revue of 1929
Stage:
Vaudeville [Hippodrome] 24; 26
Vaudeville [Palace] 25; 26; 29

4967
RASCHIG, Kraft*
Die Freudlose Gasse [The Joyless
  Street] /aka/ The Street of Sor-
  rows (American soldier)

4968
RASKATOFF*
Die Freudlose Gasse [The Joyless
  Street] /aka/ The Street of Sor-
  rows

4969
RASKIE, Barney*
Running Wild (Junior)

4970
RASP, Fritz*
Diary of a Lost Girl
Frau im Mond [Woman in the Moon]
Last Waltz, The
Loves of Jeanne Ney, The
Der Mensch am Wege [Man by the
  Roadside]
Metropolis (Slim)
Midsummer Night's Dream, A (Snout)
Mystic Mirror, The
Prince of Rogues, The

Schatten eine Nachtliche Halluzination
Spione [Spies]

4971
RATCLIFFE, Edward J. (1893-)
Amazing Lovers
Black Pirate, The
Cheating Cheaters
Daughter of Two Worlds, A
Discarded Woman, The
Disraeli (Sir Michael Probert)
Every Man's Price
Fighting Cuckaroo, The
Floating College
Four Feathers, The (Col. Eustace)
Framed
Great Adventure, The
Head Man, The (Wareham)
Held by the Law
Idol of the North (Lucky Folsom)
Introduce Me
Jazz Age, The
Love, Honor and Obey
Man on the Box, The
Miss 139
No Control
Notorious Lady
Prince of Headwaiters
Publicity Madness
Rolling Home
Sally (John Farquar)
Show of Shows, The
Skinner Steps Out
Smile, Brother, Smile
Sundown
Thrill Hunter, The
Wine of Youth, The
Winning of Barbara Worth, The
  (James Greenfield)
Woman Who Walked Alone, The

4972
RATHBONE, Basil (Philip St. John
  Basil Rathbone) (1892-1967)
Barnum Was Right
Bishop Murder Case, The
Fruitful Vine, The (debut)
Great Deception, The
Innocent
Last of Mrs. Cheyney, The (Lord
  Arthur Dilling)
Loves of Mary Queen of Scots
Loves of Sunya
Masked Bride, The
PDC player 26
Pity the Chorus Girl
School for Scandal, The
This Mad World

Stage:
Assumption of Hannele, The (dual
    role, Gottwald/the stranger) 24
Captive, The (Jacques Virieu) 26
Command to Love, The (Gaston,
    Marquis du Saint-Lae) 27
Czarina, The (Count Alexei Czerny)
    22
East of Suez in London 22
Grand Duchess and the Waiter, The
    (Albert) 25
Henry IV (Hal) in London 21
Judas (Title role) 29
Julius Caesar (Cassius) 27
Love Is Like That (Vladimir Dub-
    rikei) 27
Peter Ibbetson in London 20
Port O' London (Anthony Pook) 26
R. U. R. in London 22
Swan, The (Dr. Nicholas Agi) 23

4973
RATON, Doris*
Broadway Peacock, The

4974
RAUCOURT, Jules (1890-   )
Glorious Betsy
His Tiger Lady
Ranger of the North

4975
RAUET*
Passion of Joan of Arc, The

4976
RAUSCH*
Der Mensch am Wege [Man by the
    Roadside]

4977
RAUSCHER, Hans*
City Without Jews, The

4978
RAWLINSON, Herbert (1885-1953)
Adventurous Sex, The (girl's sweet-
    heart)
Another Man's Shoes
Belle of Broadway, The
Black Bag, The
Bugle Call, The
Burning Gold
Charge It
Cheated Hearts
Clean-Up
Coming Through
Confidence

Conflict
Dancing Cheat, The
Dancing Stairways
Flame Fighter, The [serial]
Fools and Riches
Gilded Butterfly, The
Her Sacrifice
High Speed
His Mystery Girl
Hour of Reckoning, The
Jack O'Clubs, The
Man and His Woman, A
Men of the Night
Millionaire, The
Millionaire Policeman, The
Millions to Burn
My Neighbor's Wife
Nobody's Bride
One Wonderful Night
Passers By
Playthings of Destiny
Prairie Wife, The
Prisoner, The
Railroaded
Scarlet Car, The
Scrapper, The
Slipping Wives
Stolen Secrets
Trooper 77 [serial]
Victor, The
Wages of Conscience
Wakefield Case, The
Wealth
You Find It Everywhere
Stage:
City Haul (Mayor Timothy MacHugh)
    29

4979
RAY, Albert*
Fox player 21

4980
RAY, Allene (1901-   )
Black Book, The [serial]
Fortieth Door, The [serial]
Galloping Hoofs [serial]
Hawk of the Hills [serial]
High Car, The
Honeymoon Ranch
House Without a Key, The [serial]
Man Without a Face, The [serial]
Melting Millions [serial]
Overland Bound
Partners O' the Sunset
Perilous Mission [serial]
Play Ball [serial]
Snowed In [serial]

Sunken Silver [serial]
Ten Scars Make a Man [serial]
Terrible People [serial]
Tex O'Reilly
Times Have Changed
Way of a Man, The [serial]
West of the Rio Grande
Yellow Cameo, The [serial]
Your Friend and Mine

4981
RAY, Bobby*
Hop to It!
Stick Around

4982
RAY, Charles (1891-1943)
Alarm Clock Andy
Alias Julius Caesar
Auction Block, The (Bob Wharton)
Barnstormer, The (Joel)
Betty's a Lady
Bright Lights
Count of Ten, The
Courtship of Miles Standish, The
   (Miles Standish)
Deuce of Spades, The
Dynamite Smith
Fire Brigade, The
Flag Maker, The
45 Minutes from Broadway
Garden of Eden, The
Gas Oil and Water
Getting Gertie's Garter
Girl I Loved, The
Gym, The
Homer Comes Home
Midnight Bell, A
Nineteen and Phyllis
Nobody's Widow
Old-Fashioned Boy, An
Ole Swimmin' Hole, The
Paris (Jerry)
Paris Green
Peaceful Valley
Percy (Title role)
R. S. V. P.
Scrap Iron
Smudge
Some Pun'kins
Sweet Adeline
Tailor Made Man, A
Two Minutes to Go
Vanity
Village Sleuth, The
Wedding Song
Winner, The

4983
RAY, Man*
Entr'acte

4984
RAY, Mona*
Uncle Tom's Cabin (Topsy)

4985
RAY, Rene (Irene Creese) (1912-)
High Treason
Palais de Dance
Young Woodley

4986
RAY, Wallace*
Over the Hill (Charles the man)

4987
RAYFIELD, Curt*
General Crack (Lt. Dennis)

4988
RAYFORD, Alma*
Phantom Buster, The

4989
RAYMOND, Cyril*
Sonia (Tom Dainton)
Stage:
Mandarin, The (man with the dog) 20
Red Blinds (Ned Burton) 26

4990
RAYMOND, Frances*
Behind the Front
Flirting with Love
Gay Defender, The
Get Your Man (Mrs. Worthington)
Illusion
Satan in Sables
Shadows
Three's a Crowd
What Happened to Jones?

4991
RAYMOND, Frankie*
Seven Chances
Stage:
Macbeth (second messenger) 28

4992
RAYMOND, Helen*
Through the Back Door (Marie)
Twin Beds

4993
RAYMOND, Jack*
Dangerous Business (Mr. Braille)

Last Command, The (assistant
     director)
Lunatic at Large, The
Only Way, The (Firth Jacques)
Sally of the Scandals
Scarlet Saint, The
Thanks for the Buggy Ride
Three Weekends (Turner's secretary)
Wild Party, The (Balaam)
Stage:
Dr. David's Dad (Bill) 24

4994
RAYNER, Christine*
Anna, the Adventuress
Comin' Thro' the Rye (Jane Peach)

4995
RAYNHAM, Frederick*
Flag Lieutenant, The (Major William
     Thesiger)
Hound of the Baskervilles, The
Romance of a Wastdale, A (Austin
     Hawks)
Wandering Jew, The (Grand Inquisi-
     tor)

4996
RAYO, Mirra*
Woman from Moscow, The

4997
REARDON, Mildred*
Experience

4998
RECKLAW, Betty*
Win That Girl

4999
REDFORD, Barbara*
Alias Julius Caesar

5000
REDMAN, Frank*
Sky Rangers, The [serial]

5001
REED, Donald*
Convoy
Evangeline
Little Johnny Jones
Mad Hour, The
Most Immoral Lady, A
Naughty, but Nice (Paul Carroll)
Night Watch, The
Show Girl

5002
REED, Florence (1883-1967)
[Note: Birth year correct; Vol. I
     shows 1863 in error]
Black Panther's Cub, The
Eternal Mother, The
Her Game
Indiscretion
Stage:
Ashes (Marjorie Lane) 24
East of Suez (Daisy) 22
Hail and Farewell (Isabella Echeva-
     ria) 23
Lullaby, The (the old woman) 23
Macbeth (Lady Macbeth) 28
Mirage, The (Irene Moreland) 20
Shanghai Gesture, The (Mother God-
     dam) 26
Untitled Benefit 22
Vaudeville [Palace] 28

5003
REED, George H. *
All Aboard
Helen's Babies (Rastus, the coach-
     man)
Huckleberry Finn (Jim)
River of Romance
Three-Ring Marriage

5004
REED, Jane*
Roaring Guns

5005
REED, Nora*
Beyond Price

5006
REEHM, George*
Heart Thief, The

5007
REEVES, Billie*
Ready-Made Maid, A

5008
REEVES, J. Harold*
Happy Days (chorus)

5009
REEVES, Robert*
Great Radium Mystery, The [serial]

5010
REEVES, Steve*
Ridin' Wild

5011
REEVES-SMITH, H. *
Return of Sherlock Holmes, The
Romance of a Queen, The (Sir Char-
    les Verdayne)
Three Weeks
Stage:
Grounds for Divorce (Felix Roget) 24
High Road, The (Lord Crayle) 28
Just Fancy! (Marquis of Karnaby) 27
Road Together, The (Tom Porter) 24
We All Do (Allan Conover) 27

5012
REGAS, George*
Beau Geste (Maris)
Desert Gold (Verd)
Wolf Song (black wolf)

5013
REGNART, Florence*
East of Suez

5014
REGUA, Charles*
Son of the Sheik, The

5015
REHFELD, Curt*
All the Brothers Were Valiant
    (Hooper)
Four Horsemen of the Apocalypse,
    The (Major Blumhardt)

5016
REHKOPF, Paul*
Berlin after Dark
Isn't Life Wonderful? (hungry worker)

5017
REICHER, Ernest*
Armored Vault, The
Lady from Paris, The /aka/ Das
    Schone Abenteur

5018
REICHER, Frank (1875-1965)
Beau Sabreur (General de Beaujolais)
Black Waters
Blue Danube
Changeling, The
Four Sons
Her Man O' War
Her Private Affair (state's attorney)
His Captive Woman
Masks of the Devil, The
Mr. Antonio
Napoleon's Barber

Sins of the Father (the eye specialist)
Someone to Love
Strange Cargo
Sweet Sixteen
Stage:
Ambush (Walter Nichols) 21
From Morn Till Midnight (cashier) 22
Goat Song (Bogoboj) 26
Mary Stuart (David Riccio) 21

5019
REICHER, Hedwiga /aka/ Hedurga*
Godless Girl, The (a matron)
King of Kings, The (bit)
Leopard Lady, The
Lover's Oath, A /aka/ Rubaiyat of
    Omar Khayyam
Lucky Star (Mrs. Tucker)
True Heaven

5020
REICHERT, Kittens*
So's Your Old Man (Alice Bisbee)

5021
REID, Wallace (1890-1923)
Adam's Rib
Affairs of Anatol, The (Anatol DeWitt
    Spencer)
Always Audacious
Charm School, The
Clarence (Title role)
Dancin' Fool (Sylvester Tribble)
Dictator, The
Don't Tell Everything (Cullan Dale)
Double Speed
Excuse My Dust (Toodles Walden)
Forever
Ghost Breaker, The
Hell Diggers
Love Special, The
Nice People
Rent Free
Sick Abed
Thirty Days
Too Much Speed
What's Your Hurry?
World's Champion, The

5022
REIMER, Johannes*
City Without Jews, The
Scandal in Paris, A

5023
REIMHERR, George*
Queen of Sin and the Spectacle of
    Sodom and Gomorrah

Stage:
Natja (Prince Potemkin) 25

5024
REINACH, Edward*
Foolish Wives (Sect'y of State of
  Monaco)
Man's Past, A

5025
REINHARD, John*
Love, Live and Laugh

5026
REINHARDT, Harry*
Dream of Love

5027
REINIGER, Lotte (1899-)
Adventures of Prince Achmed
Cinderella
Dr. Dolittle [series]

5028
REINWALD, Greta*
Eleven Who Were Loyal
Whirl of Life, The

5029
REINWALD, Otto*
Die Freudlose Gasse [The Joyless
  Street] /aka/ The Street of Sor-
  rows (Else's husband)

5030
REISENHOFER, Maria*
Anna Boleyn /aka/ Deception

5031
REISNER, Charles*
Pilgrim, The (the crook)

5032
REJANE, Gabrielle (1857-1920)
Gypsy Passion
Miarka, the Daughter of the Bear

5033
RELLEY, Gina*
Two Little Vagabonds (Barbara
  Scarth)

5034
RELNIGER, Lotte--see: Lotte Reiniger

5035
RENALDO, Duncan (Basil Vasilecon-
  yanos) (1904-)
Bridge of San Luis Rey, The (Esta-
  ban)
Clothes Make the Woman
Devil's Skipper, The
Gun Runner, The
Marcheta
Naughty Duchess, The
Pals of the Prairie
Romany Love

5036
RENAR, Helmuth*
Waterloo

5037
RENARD, Ervin*
Eagle of the Sea, The

5038
RENARD, Kaye*
Glorifying the American Girl

5039
RENAULT, Jack*
Knockout Reilly

5040
RENAVENT, George /aka/ Georges*
Rio Rita (General Ravenoff)
Stage:
Antonia (Capt. Pierre Marceau) 25
Crooked Square, The (Prince Stefano
  Salenski) 23
Diplomacy (Antoine) 28
Genius and the Crowd (Philippe Tra-
  va) 20
Goin' Home (Commandant Juneste) 28
Grounds for Divorce (Marquis Guido
  Longoni) 24
Pigeon, The (Ferrand) 22
Texas Nightingale, The (Sascha Bloch)
  22

5041
RENDELL, Robert*
Babbitt
Her Night of Romance
Stage:
Circle, The (Arnold Chapion-Cheney,
  M. P.)
Ghost Train, The (Richard Winthrop)
Right to Kill, The (Herrick Jameson)
  26
Wings over Europe (Vere) 28

5042
RENEE, Renate*
Rasputin, the Holy Sinner

5043
RENELA, Rita*
Greed (Mrs. Ryer)

5044
RENFRO, Rennie*
And How!
Two of a Kind

5045
RENI*
Moana

5046
RENICK, Ruth*
Ask Dad
Conrad in Quest of His Youth (Tot-
    tie)
From Rags to Riches
Golden Snare, The
Jucklins, The
Molycoddle, The (Virginia Hale)
Parish Priest, The
She Couldn't Help It
What's a Wife Worth?
White Dove, The
Witching Hour, The

5047
RENNIE, James (1889-1965)
Argentine Love
Clothes Make the Pirate
Dust Flower, The
Flying Pat
His Children's Children
Mighty Lak' a Rose
Moonlight and Honeysuckle
Moral Sinner, The
Paramount player 21
Remodeling Her Husband
Restless Wives
Stardust
Stage:
Best People, The (Henry) 24
Cape Smoke (John Ormsby) 25
Crime Wave, The (Eugene Fenmore)
    27
Great Gatsby, The (Jay Gatsby) 26
Julius Caesar (Marcus Antonius) 27
Love Habit, The (the young man) 23
Madeleine and the Movies (Garrison
    Paige) 22
Mulberry Bush, The (Harry Bain-
    bridge) 27

Pot Luck (Stephen McCauley) 21
Shore Leave ("Bilge" Smith, U. S. N.)
    22
Spanish Love (Pencho) 20
Spring Fever (Jack Kelly) 25
Vaudeville [Palace] 27
Young Love (Peter Bird) 28

5048
RENWICK, Ruth*
Long Live the King

5049
REPNIKOVA*
Battleship Potemkin

5050
REQUA, Charles--see: Charles
    Raqua

5051
RETIES, Jill*
His Hour

5052
REUFER-EICHBERG, Adele*
Explosion

5053
REVALLES, Flora*
Earthbound

5054
REVELA, Rita*
Greed

5055
REVELLE, Hamilton (1872-)
Telephone Girl
Stage:
Captain Applejack (Ivan Borolsky) 21

5056
REVIER, Dorothy (Doris Velegra)
    (1904-)
Better Way, The
Beware of Blondes
Broadway Madonna, A
Clown, The
Dance of Life, The (Sylvia Marco)
Donovan Affair, The
Drop Kick, The
Enemy of Men
False Alarm
Fate of a Flirt, The
Father and Son
First National player 27
Iron Mask, The (Milady de Winter)

Just a Woman
Light Fingers
Man from God's Country, The
Mighty, The (Mayme)
Poker Faces
Poor Girls
Price of Honor, The
Quitter, The
Red Dance, The /aka/ The Red
    Dancer of Moscow
Sinner's Paradise
Siren, The
Stolen Pleasures
Submarine
Tanned Legs
Tigress, The
Wandering Girls
Warning, The
When the Wife's Away

5057
REX*
Death Falley

5058
REX (Dog)*
Running Wild (himself)

5059
REX (Horse)*
Black Cyclone
Girl on the Barge, The
Guardians of the Wild
Harvest of Hate
Hoofbeats of Vengeance
No Man's Law
Plunging Hoofs
Two Outlaws
Wild Beauty
Wild Blood

5060
REX, Eugen*
Tragödie der Liebe [Tragedy of
    Love]

5061
REX, Ludwig*
Der Mensch am Wege [Man by the
    Roadside]

5062
REY, Kathleen*
Man from Brodney's, The

5063
REYNOLDS, Ely*
Shamrock Handicap, The (Puss)

5064
REYNOLDS, Randall*
Happy Days (chorus)

5065
REYNOLDS, Tom*
Tilly of Bloomsbury (Samuel Still-
    battle)
Stage:
Bachelor Father, The (Roberts) 28
Ladies of the Evening (Daddy Pal-
    mer) 24
Laugh, Clown, Laugh! (Signora Del
    Papa)
Menace (Seth Jackson) 27

5066
REYNOLDS, Vera (1905-1962)
Almost Human
Back from Shanghai
Bedlam
Broken Barriers
Corporal Kate
Divine Sinner, The (Lillia Ludwig)
Dry and Thirsty
Feet of Clay (Amy Loring)
Flapper Wives
For Sale (Betty Twombly-Smith)
Gold Widows
Golden Bed, The (Margaret Peake)
Hearts of Oak
Icebound
Jazzland
Limited Mail, The
Little Adventuress, The
Main Event, The
Million Dollar Handicap, The
Night Club, The
Paramount player 26
Parked in the Park
Prodigal Daughters (Marjory Forbes)
Risky Business
Road to Yesterday, The (Beth Tyrell)
Saphead's Sacrifice, A
Shadows of Paris
Silence
Steel Preferred
Sunny Side Up
Tonight at Twelve
Woman Proof

5067
REYNOLDS, Wilson*
Janice Meredith (Parson McClare)
Stage:
Bad Man, The (Jasper Hardy) 20
Dove, The (John Boise) 25
Honor of the Family, The (General
    Carpentier) 26

Pasteur (Dr. Poggiale) 23
Woman on the Jury, The (Garrity)
23

5068
RHAUMA, Gypsy*
Alf's Button (Lucy)

5069
RHEKOPF, Paul*
Isn't Life Wonderful?

5070
RHODA, Sybil*
Downhill (Sybil Wakeley)

5071
RHODES, Billy (1906-)
Bluffing Father
For Sweet Charity
Star Reporter, The
Two Cylinder Courtship, A
Stage:
Tangerine (Lee Loring) 21

5072
RHODES, Elizabeth*
When a Man's a Man

5073
RICCIARDI, William*
Heart of a Siren, The
Humming Bird, The (Papa Jacques)
Man Must Live, A
Puppets
Say It Again
Side Show of Life, The
Stage:
Big Fight, The (Berrelli) 28
Mister Malatesta (Joe Malatesta) 23
Money Business (Igor) 26
Strictly Dishonorable (Tomaso Antio-
vi) 29
Treat 'em Rough (Tomasso Salvatore)
26

5074
RICE, Andy, Jr.*
Footlights and Fools (song plugger)

5075
RICE, Frank (-1936)
Dynamite Dan
Headin' for Danger
Humming Wires
Lariat Kid, The
Lawless Legion, The
Orphan of the Sage

Overland Telegraph
Rough Ridin' Red
Royal Rider
Vagabond Cub, The
Young Whirlwind, The

5076
RICH, Irene (Irene Luther) (1894-)
Beau Brummel (Frederica Charlotte,
    Duchess of York)
Behold This Woman
Being Respectable
Beware of Married Men
Boy of Mine
Brass
Brawn of the North
Captain January
Climbers, The (Duchess of Aragon)
Compromise
Condemned Woman
Craig's Wife
Cytherea (Fanny Randon)
Daughters of Desire
Dearie
Desired Woman, The
Desperate Trails
Don't Tell the Wife
Eve's Lover (Eva Burnside)
Exalted Flapper, The
Fool There Was, A
Fruits of Faith
Godless Men
Gold Diggers
Honeymoon Express, The
Invisible Power, The
Jes' Call Me Jim
Just Out of College
Lady Windermer's Fan (Mrs. Erlynne)
Lone Star Ranger
Lost Lady, A
Lucretia Lombard
Main Street
Man Without a Conscience, The
Marriage Chance, The
My Official Wife
My Wife and I
Ned McCobb's Daughter (Carrie Mc-
    Cobb)
One Clear Call
One Man in a Million
Pathé player 21
Perfect Crime, The
Pleasure Buyers
Powder My Back
Rosita (the Queen)
Shanghai Rose
Silken Shackles
Silver Slave, The

So This Is Paris
Strange Boarder, The
Strength of the Pines
Sunset Jones
Tale of Two Worlds, A (Mrs. Car-
   michael)
They Had to See Paris (Mrs. Peters)
This Woman (Carol Drayton)
Tough Proposition
Trap, The (the teacher)
Voice in the Dark, A
Wife Who Wasn't Wanted, The
Women They Talk About
Yosemite Trail
Stage:
Vaudeville [Palace] 29

5077
RICH, Lillian (1902-1954)
Afraid to Fight
Bearcat, The
Blazing Trail, The
Brave Heart
Catch My Smoke
Dancing Days
Dice of Destiny
Empty Hearts (Madeline)
Eternal Triangle, The
Exclusive Rights
Felix O'Day
Forger, The
Go Straight
God's Great Wilderness
Golden Bed, The (Flora Lee Peake)
Golden Web, The
Half a Chance
Her Social Value
High Seas
Isle of Retribution
Kentucky Derby, The
Kiss in the Dark, A
Love Master, The
Man to Man
Millionaire, The
Murdock Affair, The
Never Say Die
Old Code, The
On the Front Page
One Hour Before Dawn
One Wonderful Night
Red Lane, The
Sage Hen, The
Seven Days
Ship of Souls
Silver Rosary, A
Simon, the Jester
Snowbound
Stage Whispers

That's My Daddy
Web of Fate
Whispering Smith
Woman's Law

5078
RICHARD, Frida*
Faust (Marguerita's mother)
Die Flamme [The Flame] /aka/
   Montmartre
Die Frau, Nach der Man Sich Sehnt
   [The Woman One Longs For]
   (Mrs. Leblanc)
Jew of Mestri, The (Shylock's
   mother)
Manon Lescaut (Manon's aunt)
Peak of Fate
Der Sprung ins Leben [The Leap in-
   to Life] (scholar's aunt)
Two Brothers, The
Wie Einst im Mai

5079
RICHARD, Fritz*
Prince of Rogues, The

5080
RICHARD, Viola*
Blow by Blow
Came the Dawn
Dumb Daddies
Limousine Love
Should Married Men Go Home?

5081
RICHARDS, Rosa*
Forbidden Love

5082
RICHARDSON, Baury Bradford*
West Point

5083
RICHARDSON, Edward*
West Point

5084
RICHARDSON, Florence*
Price of a Party, The

5085
RICHARDSON, Frank*
Happy Days (a principal)
Movietone Follies of 1929
Sunny Side Up (Eddie Rafferty)

5086
RICHARDSON, Jack (1883-)
Across the Plains

Avenging Fangs
Ballyhoo Buster, The
Beau Brummell
Chinatown Mystery, The [serial]
Dangerous Adventure [serial]
Daring Years, The (Flaglier)
Eager Lips
Fighter Mad
Fog Bound
Free and Equal
Greater Love, The
Last Lap, The
Love Master, The
Marked Money
Midnight Adventure, A
Midnight Express, The
Midnight on the Barbary Coast
One Splendid Hour
Only Saps Work
Partners in Crime (Jake)
Polly of the Movies
Rainmaker, The
Sailor's Holiday
Silent Shelby
Snarl of Hate, The
Sonora Kid, The
Souls for Sale (Evarts)
Speed Classic
Sting of the Lash (Seeley)
Three-Must-Get-Theirs, The
Toll Gate, The (sheriff)
Too Much Speed
Trial Marriage
Wilful Youth
Women Who Dare

5087
RICHARDSON, John*
Beau Brummel ("Poodle" Bying)

5088
RICHMAN, Charles (1879-1940)
Curtain
Half an Hour
Harriet and the Piper
Has the World Gone Mad?
My Friend the Devil
Sign on the Door, The
Trust Your Wife
Stage:
Best People, The (Bronson Lenox) 24
Dagger, The (Rene Michelet) 25
Home Fires (Henry Bedford) 23
Ink (Franklin W. Jerome) 27
Ladies Don't Lie (Philip) 29
Love Is Like That (Michael Irslov) 27
School for Scandal, The (Charles
   Surface) 23

We All Do (Geoffrey Chester) 27

5089
RICHMOND, Al*
Courtship of Miles Standish, The

5090
RICHMOND, Edna*
Price of a Party, The
Stage:
Get Me in the Movies (secretary) 28

5091
RICHMOND, Warner R. (1895-1948)
Apache
Beast Within, The
Big Brother
Big News (Phelps)
Challenge, The
Chicago
Crowd, The
Crowded Hour, The
Deadline, The
Fifty-Fifty
Finger Prints
Fire Brigade, The
Good and Naughty
Heart of Maryland, The
Hearts of Men
Irish Hearts
Luck
Making of O'Malley, The
Man from Glengarry, The
Manhattan Madness
Missing Man, The
Mountain Woman, The
My Lady's Garter
Pace That Thrills, The
Redeeming Sin, The
Shadows of the Night
Slide, Kelly, Slide
Speed Spook, The
Stark Mad
Stop That Man
Strange Cargo
Tol'able David (Allen Kinemon)
Trail of the Lonesome Pine, The
Voice of the Storm
White Flannels
Woman's Business, A
You Can't Beat the Law

5092
RICHTER, Ellen*
Carnival Crime, The
Kopf Hoch, Charly! [Heads Up, Char-
   ly!] (Charlotte 'Charly' Ditman)
Wie Einst im Mai

5093
RICHTER, George*
Kriemhild's Revenge

5094
RICHTER, John*
Kriemhild's Revenge

5095
RICHTER, Paul*
Dr. Mabuse the Gambler /aka/ Dr.
   Mabuse, the Great Unknown
Forbidden Love
Kriemhild's Revenge
Die Nibelungen /aka/ The Nibelungs
   (Siegfried)
Peter, the Pirate
Siegfried

5096
RICKARD, Tex*
Great White Way, The

5097
RICKETTS, Tom (-1939)
Ambrose Applejohn's Adventure
   (Lush)
Black Oxen (Charles Dinwiddie)
Bobbed Hair
Buzzard's Shadow, The
Children of Divorce
Circe, the Enchantress
Counterfeit Soul, The
Crime of the Hour, The
Dangerous Maid
Dry Martini
Eternal Flame, The (Vidame the
   Pamier)
Five and Ten Cent Annie
Forbidden
Freedom of the Press
Glad Rag Doll
Great Lover, The
Great Question, The
Interference (Charles Smith)
Just Married
Killer, The
Law and the Man, The
Light Fingers
Magnificent Flirt, The
My Friend from India
My Wife and I
Oh, Doctor!
Poker Faces
Puppets of Fate
Red Hot Speed
Sham
Sins of the World

Skirt Shy
Spenders, The
Stranded in Paris
Strangers of the Night
Tailor Made Man, The
Too Many Crooks
Trifling Women
Venus of Venice
Within the Law (General Hastings)
Wives of Men

5098
RICKS, Archie*
Long, Long Trail, The

5099
RICKSEN, Lucille*
Denial, The
Hill Billy, The
MGM player 25
Old Nest, The
Rendezvous, The
Those Who Dare
Vanity's Price

5100
RICKSON, Joe*
Baree, Son of Kazan
Captain Blood
Code of the Wilderness, The
Pioneer Trails
Purple Riders, The (Rudolph Myers)
Rawhide
Riders of the Purple Sage (Slack)

5101
RICO, Mona*
Eternal Love (Pia)
Shanghai Lady

5102
RIDGELY, Cleo (1893-1962)
Beautiful and Damned, The
Dangerous Pastime, A
Forgotten Law, The
Law and the Woman, The
Sleep Walker, The

5103
RIDGES, Stanley (1891-   )
Success
Stage:
Boom Boom (Tony Smith) 29
Bride Retires, The (Claude Herbel) 25
Bye Bye Barbara (Phillip Graham) 24
Elsie (Fred Blakely) 23
Her Way Out (Sidney Carfax) 24
Mary Jane McKane (Andrew Dunn,
   Jr.) 23

Sally (Jimmie Hooper) 20

5104
RIDGEWAY, Fritz*
Flying Romeos
Getting Gertie's Garter
Hell's Heroes
Judy of Rogues Harbor
Nobody's Widow
Old Homestead, The
This Is Heaven

5105
RIDGEWAY, Fritzie (1898-1960)
Boomerang Justice
Bring Him In
Enemy, The
Face Value
Fatal Thirty, The [serial]
Hate Trail, The
Lonesome Ladies
Man Bait
Red Hot Speed
Rescue, The
Ruggles of Red Gap
Son of the Golden West
Trifling with Honor

5106
RIEFENSTAHL, Leni*
Big Jump, The
Peaks of Destiny
Sacred Mountain, The
White Hell of Pitz Palu

5107
RIEFFLER, Monsieur*
Three Musketeers, The (King Louis
   XIII)

5108
RIEGAL, Charles*
Heart Raider, The

5109
RIEKELT, Gustave*
That Murder in Berlin

5110
RIEMAN, Johannes*
Armored Vault, The

5111
RIESNER, Charles F. *
Her Temporary Husband
Kid, The
Man on the Box, The
Pilgrim, The

5112
RIGAS, George*
Beau Geste (Maris)
Desert Gold
Love Light, The (Tony)
Redskin, The (Chief Notani)
Rescue, The
That Royle Girl (henchman)
Wanderer, The
Wolf Song

5113
RIGNOLD, Harry*
Coughing Horror, The (Title role)

5114
RILCHARD, Frida*
Peaks of Destiny

5115
RILETY, Anna*
City Without Jews, The

5116
RILEY, William*
North Star

5117
RILLA, Walter (1895-)
Der Geiger von Florenz [violinist of
   Florence]
Prinzessin Olala [Princess Olala]
   /aka/ The Art of Love (Prince
   Boris)
Sajenko, the Soviet
Der Sprung ins Leben [The Leap in-
   to Life] (circus acrobat)
Wie Einst im Mai

5118
RILLON, John T. *
Dry Martini

5119
RIMSKY, Nicholas*
Tale of 1,001 Nights

5120
RIN-TIN-TIN (Dog) (1916-1930)
Below the Line
Clash of the Wolves
Dog of the Regiment, A
Find Your Man
Frozen River
Hero of the Big Snows
Hills of Kentucky
Jaws of Steel
Land of the Silver Fox

Lighthouse by the Sea
Million Dollar Collar
Night Cry, The
Race for Life, A
Rinty of the Desert
Show of Shows, The
Tiger Rose (Scotty)
Tracked by the Police
Tracked in the Snow Country
Where the North Begins
While London Sleeps
Wizard, The

5121
RINALDI, Tina C. *
Romola (Monna Ghita)

5122
RINALDI, William*
Thank You

5123
RINALDO, Duncan--see: Duncan
Renaldo

5124
RINALDO, Rinaldini*
Das Wachsfigurenkabinet /aka/ The
Waxworks (deleted from the film)

5125
RINCH-SMILES, Frank*
Doctor's Secret, The

5126
RINEHARDT, Harry*
Wedding March, The (guard)

5127
RING, Blanche (1872-1961)
It's the Old Army Game (Tessie
Overholt)
Record:
I've Got Rings on My Fingers
(B-8074-2) (LPV)560
Stage:
Alarm Clock, The (Mrs. Susie Kent)
23
Broadway Whirl, The (a principal) 21
Henry IV, Part I (Mistress Quickly)
26
Houseboat on the Styx, The (Queen
Elizabeth) 28
Untitled Benefit 22
Vaudeville [Hippodrome] 24
Vaudeville [Palace] 24

5128
RING, Cyril*
Cocoanuts, The (Harvey Yates)
Exciters, The
Guilty One, The
Homeward Bound
In Hollywood with Potash and Perl-
mutter
News Parade, The
Pied Piper Malone
Tongues of Flame
Stage:
Back Seat Drivers (Austin Spence) 28

5129
RISING, W. *
America /aka/ Love and Sacrifice
(Edmund Burke)

5130
RITCHARD, Cyril (1896-)
Blackmail (the artist)
Piccadilly (Victor Smiles)
Stage:
Puzzles of 1925 (a principal) 25

5131
RITCHARD, Viola*
Flying Elephants
Sailors Beware
Should Married Men Go Home?

5132
RITTNER, Rudolf*
At the Grey House
Meistersinger
When Duty Calls

5133
RIVALI, Tina--see: Tina C. Rinaldi

5134
RIVERO, Lorraine*
Ladies of the Mob (Little Yvonne)
Redskin, The

5135
ROACH, Bert (1891-)
Argyle Case, The (Joe)
Aviator, The
Black Bag, The
Certain Young Man, A
Crowd, The (Bert)
Denial, The
Desert Rider, The
Don't Tell the Wife
Excuse Me
Flaming Forest, The

Flirt, The
Honeymoon
Iron Mike
Lady of Quality, A
Last Warning, The
Latest from Paris, The
Marry the Poor Girl
Millionaire, The
Money Talks
No, No Nanette (Bill Early)
Riders of the Dark
Show of Shows, The (father)
Small Town Idol, A
Smouldering Fires
So Long Letty
Taxi Dancer, The
Telling the World
Tillie the Toiler (Bill)
Time, the Place and the Girl, The
Tin Hats
Twelve Miles Out
Twin Beds
Under the Black Eagle
Viennese Nights
Wickedness Preferred
Young Nowheres

5136
ROACH, Marjorie*
First Born, The (Phoebe Chivers)

5137
ROANNE, André*
Diary of a Lost Girl, The
Oppressed, The
Venus

5138
ROBARDS, Jason, Sr. (1893-1963)
Bird in the Hand, A
Casey Jones
Cohens and the Kellys, The
Flying Marine, The
Gamblers, The
Gilded Lily, The (Frank Thompson)
Heart of Maryland, The
Hills of Kentucky
Honeymoon Express, The
Irish Hearts
Isle of Lost Ships, The
Jaws of Steel
Lightnin'
On Trial (Mr. Arbuckle)
Paris
Peacock Alley
Polly of the Movies
Sisters
Some Mother's Boy

Stella Maris
Streets of Shanghai
Third Degree, The
Tracked by the Police
Trial Marriage
White Flannels
Wild Geese

5139
ROBARDS, Willis*
Three Musketeers, The (Capt. de
  Treville)

5140
ROBBINS, Marc*
Alias Jimmy Valentine

5151
ROBBINS, Walt*
Hearts and Spurs (Terry Clark)
Shanghaied

5142
ROBERS, Edith--see: Edith Roberts

5143
ROBERTS, Alice*
Pandora's Box

5144
ROBERTS, Beryl*
Soda Water Cowboy, The

5145
ROBERTS, Edith (1901-1935)
Adorable Savage, The
Age of Innocence
Alias Miss Dodd
Backbone
Big Brother
Black Cargo of the South Seas
Dangerous Age, The
Dreary House
Fire Cat, The
Flesh and Blood (the angel lady)
Front Page Story, A
Great Sensation, The
Her Five Foot Highness
In Society
Jazz Girl, The
Loving Lips
Man from Headquarters, The
Mystery Club, The
New Champion, The
On Thin Ice
Open Shutters
Pawned
Phantoms of the North

Road to Broadway, The
Roaring Rails
Roulette
Saturday Night (Shamrock O'Day)
Seven Keys to Baldpate (Mary Norton)
Shameful Behavior
Son of the Wolf
Speed Mad
Taxi Mystery, The
There You Are
Thorns and Orange Blossoms
Thunder Island
Thy Name Is Woman
Triflers
Twenty Dollars a Week
Unknown Wife, An
Wagon Master, The
White Youth

5146
ROBERTS, George*
William Tell
Stage:
Triumphant Bachelor, The (Calvert's
  butler) 27

5147
ROBERTS, J. H. (1884-)
Constant Nymph, The (Dr. Churchill)
Daughters of Today
Skin Game, The (auctioneer)

5148
ROBERTS, Joseph*
Our Hospitality
Three Ages, The

5149
ROBERTS, Ralph*
Der Oberkellner
Tradition
Stage:
Candle-Light (a waiter) 29
Kingdom of God, The (Gabriel) 28

5150
ROBERTS, Theodore (1861-1928)
Across the Continent
Affairs of Anatol, The (Gordon Bron-
  son)
Cat's Pajamas, The
Double Speed
Excuse My Dust (J. D. Ward)
Exit the Vamp
Forbidden Fruit (James Harrington
  Mallory)
Forty Winks
Furnace, The

Grumpy (Andrew "Grumpy" Bullivant)
Hail the Woman
Idols of Clay
If You Believe It, It's So
Judy of Rogues Harbor
Locked Doors
Love Special, The
Man Who Saw Tomorrow, The
Masks of the Devil, The
Miss Lulu Bett (Dwight Deacon)
Ned McCobb's Daughter (Ned McCobb)
Night Life in Hollywood
Noisy Neighbors
Old Homestead, The
Our Leading Citizens
Pollyanna
Prodigal Daughters (J. D. Forbes)
Saturday Night (uncle)
Sham
Something to Think About (Luke An-
  derson)
Stephen Steps Out
Suds
Sweet Lavender
Ten Commandments, The (Moses)
To the Ladies
Too Much Speed
Stage:
Vaudeville [Palace] 26

5151
ROBERTSHAW, Jerrold (1866-1941)
Arab, The (Dr. Hilbert)
Betrayal, The
Don Quixote
Down Hill (Rev. Henry Wakeley)
Kitty
She
Wandering Jew, The (Texada)

5152
ROBERTSON, Imogene*
Armored Vault

5153
ROBERTSON, J. Francis (James
  Francis Robertson)*
Girl on the Barge, The
Stage:
Bride of the Lamb (doctor) 26
Legend of Leonora, The (jury fore-
  man) 27
Quicksand (Parker) 28

5154
ROBERTSON, John*
Alaskan Adventures

5155
ROBEY, Sir. George (Sir George
Wade) (1869-1954)
Barrister, The
Bride, The
Don Quixote (Sancho Panza)
Her Prehistoric Man
Mrs. Mephistopheles
One Arabian Night
Rest Cure, The
Safety First

5156
ROBINSON, Earl*
Air Circus, The

5157
ROBINSON, Edward G. (Emanuel
Goldenberg) (1893-1973)
Bright Shawl, The (Domingo Escobar)
East Is West
Hole in the Wall, The (the fox)
Night Ride (Tony Garotta)
Stage:
Adding Machine, The (Shrdlu) 23
Androcles and the Lion (Caesar) 25
Banco (Louis) 22
Brothers Karamazov, The (Smerdia-
kov) 27
Chief Thing, The (the stage director)
26
Deluge, The (Nordling) 22
Firebrand, The (Octavius) 24
Goat Song, (Reb Feiwell) 26
Henry-Behave (Wescott P. Benneth)
26
Idle Inn, The (Mendel) 21
Juarez and Maximillian (Porfirio
Diaz) 26
Kibitzer (Lazarus) 29
Launzi (Louis) 23
Man of Destiny, The (Giuseppe) 25
Man with Red Hair, A (Mr. Crispin)
28
Ned McCobb's Daughter (lawyer Gro-
ver) 26
Peer Gynt (3 roles, The Button/
Moulder/Von Eberkopf) 23
Poldekin (Pinsky) 20
Racket, The (Nick Scarsi) 27
Right You Are If You Think You Are
(Ponza) 27
Royal Fandango, A (Pascual) 23
Samson and Delilah (the director) 20

5158
ROBINSON, Forrest*
Adam's Rib (Kramer)

Ashes of Vengeance (Father Paul)
Souls for Sale (Rev. John Steddon)
Tess of the Storm Country (Daddy
Skinner)
Tol'able David (Grandpa Hatburn)
When a Man's a Man
Stage:
Mad Dog, The (Padre Francolon) 21
Tarzan of the Apes (Charles Porter)
21
Transplanting Jean (Abbe Jocas) 21

5159
ROBINSON, "Spike"*
Daredevil Jack [serial]

5159a
ROBSON, Andrew*
Alarm Clock Andy
Cupid, Cow-puncher
Scratch My Back

5160
ROBSON, May (Mary Robison) (1865-
1942)
Angel of Broadway, The
Blue Danube, The
Chicago
Harp in Hock, A
King of Kings, The (Gesta's mother)
Mother's Millions
Pals in Paradise
Pathé player 29
Rejuvenation of Aunt Mary, The
Rubber Tires
Turkish Delight, A
Stage:
Two Orphans, The (La Frochard) 26

5161
ROBYNS, William*
Get Rich Quick Wallingford (Abe
Gunther)

5162
ROCCARDI, Albert*
Inside of the Cup, The
Love Parade, The (Foreign Minister)
Partners in Crime (Kanelli)
Romance of the Rio Grande
Stage:
Molly Darling (Henri Ricardo) 22
Wheel, The (Monty) 21

5163
ROCHAY, Joe*
Cock-Eyed World, The (Jacobs)

5164
ROCHE, Clara Darley*
Les Miserables

5165
ROCHE, John (1896-1952)
Awful Truth, The
Bag and Baggage
Bobbed Hair
Diamond Handcuffs
Don Juan (Leandro)
Donovan Affair, The
Dream Melody, The
First National player 24
Flowing Gold
Good Provider
Her Big Night
K-the Unknown
Kiss Me Again (Maurice Ferriere)
Lost Lady, A
Love Hour, The
Lucretia Lombard
Man Upstairs, The
Marry Me
Midnight Lovers
Monte Carlo
My Wife and I
Rainbow, The
Recompense
Return of Peter Grimm, The (Fred-
    erick Grimm)
Their Hour
This Thing Called Love (DeWitt)
Truthful Sex, The
Uncle Tom's Cabin (Augustine St.
    Clare)
Unholy Night, The (Lt. Savor)
Stage:
Deburau (the young man) 20
Madras House, The (Mr. Brigstock)
    21
Nature's Nobleman (Don Schnizler) 21
R.U.R. (Primus) 22

5166
ROCKWELL, Ed*
Happy Days (chorus)

5167
ROCKWELL, Jack*
Guardians of the Trail

5168
ROCKWOOD, Roy*
Happy Days (chorus)

5169
ROD, Einar*
Witch Woman, The

5170
RODGERS, Jimmie*
Jes' Call Me Jim

5171
RODGERS, Walter*
Purple Riders, The (Stephen
    Marsh)
Son of Wallingford, The (Petrograd
    Pete)

5172
RODMAN, Victor*
Winter Has Come

5173
RODNEY, Earl*
Campus Vamp, The
Roman Scandal, A
Winter Has Come

5174
ROESBORG, Nikolai*
Janice Meredith

5175
ROGAN, Florence*
Sparrows /aka/ Human Sparrows
    (a sparrow)

5176
ROGERS, Charles "Buddy"
    (1904-)
Abie's Irish Rose (Abie Levy)
Close Harmony (Al West)
Fascinating Youth
Get Your Man (Robert de Belle-
    contre)
Half Way to Heaven
Heads Up
Here Comes the Bandwagon
Illusion (Carlee Thorpe)
Man Must Fight, A
More Pay Less Work
My Best Girl
Paramount player 25
Potters, The
Red Lips
River of Romance
So's Your Old Man (Kenneth Murchi-
    son)
Someone to Love
Varsity
Wings (John Powell)

5177
ROGERS, Charley*
Perfect Day, A

5178
ROGERS, Ginger (Virginia Katherine
    McMath) (1911-)
Campus Sweethearts 29
Stage:
Paul Ash Orchestra (singer) 28
Texas, Oklahoma Vaudeville Tour 27
Top Speed (Babs Green) 29

5179
ROGERS, John*
Behind that Curtain (Alf Pornick)
Stage:
Blood and Sand (Garabato) 21
Dolly Jordan (Mr. Hobbes) 22
Fashions for Men (Mate) 22
Patience (Major Murgatroyd) 24
Pickwick (Mr. Perker) 27
Spider, The (Officer Simpson) 27

5180
ROGERS, Molly*
Livingstone in Africa

5180a
ROGERS, Walter*
Dramatic Life of Abraham Lincoln,
    The /aka/ Abraham Lincoln
    (General U. S. Grant)
Flaming Frontier, The
Iron Horse, The (General Grenville
    M. Dodge)
Seven Faces
Wolf's Clothing

5181
ROGERS, Warren*
Dawn of a Tomorrow, The
Flaming Barriers

5182
ROGERS, Will (William Penn Adair
    Rogers) (1879-1935)
Big Moments from Little Pictures
Boys Will Be Boys
Cake Eater, The
Cowboy Sheik, The
Cupid, Cowpuncher
Doubling for Romeo
Fruits of Faith
Going to Congress
Guile of Women
Happy Days (a principal)
Headless Horseman, The
High Brow Stuff
Honest Hutch
Hustlin' Hank
Jes' Call Me Jim

Jubilo
Jus' Passin' Through
Lightnin'
No Parking Here /aka/ Don't Park
    There!
One Day in 365
One Glorious Day
Our Congressman
Poor Relation, A
Roach comedies (12)
Ropin' Fool, The
Scratch My Back
Strange Boarder, The
Texas Steer, A
They Had to See Paris (Pike Peters)
Tip Toes
Truthful Liar, The
Two Wagons--Both Covered (dual role,
    trail scout/Dude)
Uncensored Movies
Unwilling Hero, An
Water, Water Everywhere
Stage:
Follies 24; 25
Lambs Gambol 25
Midnight Frolic 21
Three Cheers (King Pompanola) 28
Untitled One-Man Show 26
Vaudeville [Palace] 27
Ziegfeld Follies 22; 23; 24

5183
ROGERS, Will, Jr. (1912-)
Jack Riders, The

5184
ROLAND, Gilbert (Luis Antonio Da-
    maso de Alonso) (1905-)
Blonde Saint, The
Camille (Armand)
Campus Flirt, The
Cardboard Lover, The
Dove, The
Lady Who Lied, The
Love Mart, The
Midshipman, The
Monsieur La Fox
New York Nights
Plastic Age, The (debut as Carl
    Peters)
Rose of the Golden West
Woman Disputed (Paul Hartman)

5185
ROLAND, Ruth (1893-1937)
Avenging Arrow, The [serial]
Broadway Bob
Haunted Valley [serial]

Love and the Law
Masked Woman, The
Riddle of the Range, The [serial]
Ruth of the Range [serial] (Title
    role)
Ruth of the Rockies [serial] (Title
    role)
Timber Queen, The [serial]
What Would You Do? [serial]
White Eagle [serial]

5186
ROLANE, Andree*
Les Miserables (Cossette as a child)
Two Little Vagabonds (Biddy's
    nephew)

5187
ROLLAN, Henri*
Three Musketeers, The (Athos)

5188
ROLLE, Liselotte*
Der Mensch am Wege [Man by the
    Roadside]

5189
ROLLENS, Jacques*
Mother Machree
My Own Pal

5190
ROLLETTE, Jane*
Two Little Vagabonds (the maid)

5191
ROLLINS, David (1909-)
Air Circus, The
Black Watch, The
Happy Days (a principal)
High School Hero
King of the Khyber Rifles (Lt. Mal-
    colm King)
Love, Live and Laugh
Movietone Follies of 1929
Prep and Pep
Riley the Cop
Thanks for the Buggy Ride
Why Leave Home?
Win That Girl

5192
ROMAIN, George E. *
Revenge of Tarzan, The /aka/ The
    Return of Tarzan (the Count de
    Caude)
Sea Hawk, The (Spanish commander)

5193
ROMAN, Hugh*
Show Girl

5194
ROMANO, Nina*
Lost at the Front
Midnight Sun, The
What Happened to Jones?

5195
ROMANOFF, Constance*
Tender Hour, The

5196
ROMANOFF, Constantine*
Condemned (brute convict)
Kid Brother, The
Private Life of Helen of Troy, The
    (Aenear)
Wolf Song (Rube Thatcher)

5197
ROME, Bert*
Forward Pass, The (Coach Wilson)

5198
ROME, Stuart (Septimus Wernham
    Ryott) (1886-1965)
Case of Lady Camber, The
Christie Johnstone (Vicount Ipsden)
Colleen Bawn, The
Crimson Circle, The
Dark Red Roses
Dicky Monteith
Eleventh Commandment, The
Fires of Fate
Gentleman Rider, The
Great Gay Road, The
Her Son
His Penalty
Imperfect Lover, The
Man Who Changed His Name, The
Nets of Destiny
Passing of Mr. Quinn, The
Penniless Millionaire, The
Prodigal Son, The
Romance of a Movie Star, The
Somehow Good
Son of Kissing Cup
Stirrup Cup Sensation, The
Sweet Lavender
Thou Fool
Uninvited Guest, The
Ware Case, The
When Greek Meets Greek
White Hope, The
Woman Who Obeyed, The
Zero

5199
ROMMER, Cläre*
Jew of Mestri, The (Nerissa)

5200
ROOKE, Irene*
Hindle Wakes (Mrs. Jeffcote)
Romance of a Wastdale, A (Mrs. Jackson)

5201
ROONEY, Gilbert*
Daughter of Two Worlds, A
East Lynne (Richard Hare)
Stage:
Fair Circassian, The (John) 21

5202
ROONEY, Mickey (Joe Yule, Jr.)
/aka/ Mickey McGuire (1920-)
Mickey, I Love You (Mickey McGuire)
Mickey in Love (Mickey McGuire)
Mickey, the Detective (Mickey McGuire)
Mickey McGuire series (40)
Mickey, the Romeo (Mickey McGuire)
Mickey's Big Game Hunt (Mickey McGuire)
Mickey's Midnight Frolic (Mickey McGuire)
Mickey's Mixup (Mickey McGuire)
Mickey's Movies (Mickey McGuire)
Mickey's Rivals (Mickey McGuire)
Mickey's Triumph (Mickey McGuire)
Mickey's Wild West (Mickey McGuire)
Not to Be Trusted (debut as a midget)
Orchids and Ermine
Stage:
Sid Gold's Dance Act (Tour) 25

5203
ROONEY, Pat*
Night Club
Stage:
Friars Club Frolic 21
Lambs Gambol 25
Love Birds (Pat) 21
Vaudeville [Palace] 23; 28; 29

5204
ROOSEVELT, Buddy (Kent Sanderson) (1898-)
Action Galore
Bandit Buster, The

Battling Buddy
Between Dangers
Code of the Cow Country
Cowboy Cavalier
Dangerous Dub, The
Dawn in Texas
Devil's Tower, The
Easy Going
Fightin' Comeback, The
Galloping Jinx, The
Gold and Grit
Hoodoo Ranch
Lightning Shot
Lure of the Yukon, The
Mystery Valley
Painted Trail, The
Phantom Buster, The
Ramblin' Galoot, The
Reckless Courage
Ride 'em High
Rip-Roaring Roberts
Rough Ridin'
Tangled Herds
Thundering Through
Trail Riders, The
Trailin' Back
Twin Triggers
Walloping Wallace

5205
ROPER, Jack*
Duke Steps Out, The
Red Mark, The

5206
ROQUEMORE, Henry*
City of Purple Dreams, The (Quigg)
Open Switch, The [serial chapter]

5207
RORK, Al*
Notorious Lady

5208
RORK, Anne*
Blonde Saint, The
Old Loves and New /aka/ The Desert Healer
Prince of Headwaiters
Texas Steer, A

5209
ROSANOVA, Rosa (1883-)
Abie's Irish Rose (Sarah)
Blood and Sand (Senora Augustus)
Cobra (Maria)
Fashion Row
Hungry Hearts

Lover of Camille, The
Lucky Boy /aka/ My Mother's Eyes
Proud Heart, The
Sonia
Ten Commandments, The (extra)
Trilby

5210
ROSAY, Francoise (1891-)
Gribiche
Magnificent Lie, The
One Woman Idea
Le Proces de Mary Dugan [The Trial
    of Mary Dugan]
Spite Marriage

5211
ROSCA, Gabriel*
Mademoiselle from Armentieres
    (Monsieur Branz)
Triumph of the Rat, The (the Apache)

5212
ROSCOE, Albert (1887-1931)
Branding Iron, The (Rev. Frank Hol-
    liwell)
Burning Sands
Duty's Reward
Flight
Flirting with Love
Her Unwilling Husband
Java Head
Last of the Mohicans, The (Uncas)
Long Pants
Madame X
Man Who Saw Tomorrow, The
Mating Call
No Trespassing
Sawdust Paradise, The
Seven Keys to Baldpate
Spoilers, The (Mexico Mullins)
Tentacles of the North
Vagabond Lover, The

5213
ROSE, Robert*
My Lady of Whim (Sneath)

5214
ROSEMAN, Edward F. *
America /aka/ Love and Sacrifice
    (Capt. Montour)
Fantomas [serial]
On the Banks of the Wabash
Running Wild (Arvo)
Stage:
Street Wolf, The (Chief Edwards) 29

5215
ROSENBLATT, Josef*
Jazz Singer, The (himself)
Stage:
Vaudeville [Palace] 25

5216
ROSING, Bodil (-1942)
Betrayal, The
Big Noise, The
Bishop Murder Case, The
Broadway Babies
Eternal Love (housekeeper)
Fleet's In, The (Mrs. Deane)
Forgotten Faces
It Must Be Love
King of the Rodeo
Ladies of the Mob (mother)
Law of the Range, The (Mrs. Lock-
    hart)
Lights of Old Broadway
Midnight Kiss, The (Swedish maid)
Out of the Ruins
Pretty Lady
Return of Peter Grimm, The (Marta)
Sunrise (the maid)
Wheels of Chance
Why Be Good?
Woman from Moscow
Stage:
Fools Errant (maid) 22

5217
ROSITA, Eva*
Rio Rita (Carmen)

5218
ROSMER, Milton (Arthur Milton Lunt)
    (1881-)
Amazing Partnership, The
Belphegor, the Mountebank
Colonel Newcome
David Garrick
Demos
Diamond Necklace, The
Gamble with Hearts, A
General John Regan
Golden Web, The
High Treason
Passionate Friends, The
Pointing Finger, The
Romance of a Wastdale, A (David
    Gordon)
Shadow of Egypt
Torn Sails
Twelve Pound Look, The
Will, The
With All Her Heart

Woman Juror, The
Woman of No Importance, A (George
  Harford, Lord Illingsworth)
Wuthering Heights
Stage:
Twelve Miles Out 27

5219
ROSS, Betty*
If I Were King

5220
ROSS, Burt*
Sunset Derby

5221
ROSS, Churchill*
College Hero, The
College Love
Collegians, The [series]
Flying High [serial chapter]
Fourflusher, The
Plastic Age, The (boy with glasses)

5222
ROSS, Etna*
Restless Sex, The (Stephanie as a
  child)

5223
ROSS, Frances*
Gold Diggers (Gypsy Montrose)

5224
ROSS, Frank*
Saturday Night Kid, The (Ken)
Stage:
Genius and the Crowd (Parker) 20

5225
ROSS, Milton*
Dixie Handicap, The
Penalty, The (Lichtenstein)
Voice of the City (Courey)

5226
ROSS, Thomas W. (1875-)
Fine Feathers
Without Limit
Stage:
Gossipy Sex, The (John Bowen) 27
Wheel, The (Edward Baker) 21

5227
ROSSELLE, William*
Wedding Bells

5228
ROSSI, Rita*
Bandolero, The
Soul Fire /aka/ Golden Youth

5229
ROSSINTO, Angelo*
Beloved Rogue, The
Old San Francisco
One Stolen Night
Seven Footprints to Satan

5230
ROSSON, Richard*
Four Those We Love (Jimmy Arnold)

5231
ROTH, Elliott*
Merton of the Movies
Stage:
Love Letter, The (waiter) 21
Mendel, Inc. (Oscar Gassenheim) 29
Revolt (Sol Rosenbloom) 28

5232
ROTH, Lillian (1911-)
Illusion
Love Parade, The (Lulu)
Stage:
Padlocks of 1927 (a principal) 27
Shavings (Barbara Armstrong) 20

5233
ROTHAUSER, Eduard*
Manon Lescaut (Marshall des Grieux)

5234
ROUBERT, Matty*
Close Harmony

5235
ROUDENKO, Vladimir*
Napoleon

5236
ROUER, Germaine*
La Cousine Bette
Stage:
L'Homme Qui Assassina 24

5237
ROUGHWOOD, Owen*
Beloved Vagabond, The (Comte Al-
  phonse de Vernevil)

5238
ROUNDERS, The
Hollywood Revue of 1929

5239
ROUNITCH, Joseph*
Taras Bulba

5240
ROVE, Billie*
Adoration

5241
ROVELLE, Camille*
Nix on Dames

5242
ROVENSKY, Joseph*
Diary of a Lost Girl, The

5243
ROWAL, Jack*
Hindle Wakes (George Ramsbottom)

5244
ROWE, George*
Dodge Your Debts
Looking for Sally
Oranges and Lemons
Smithy

5245
ROWLAND, Adele*
Vanity Fair
Stage:
Vaudeville [Palace] 21; 28

5246
ROWLAND, Helen*
Daring Years, The (La Motte girl)
Making of O'Malley, The
What's Wrong with Women? (Baby
   Helen Lee)

5247
ROY, Charu*
Shiraz

5248
ROY, Dan--see: Ernie Lotinga

5249
ROYCE, E. W., Mrs.*
Fifth Form at St. Dominic's (Mrs.
   O'Grady)

5250
ROYCE, Ruth*
Days of '49, The [serial] (Arabella
   Ryan)
In the Days of Daniel Boone [serial]
Officer 444 [serial]
Riders of the Plains [serial]

Stage:
Vaudeville [Palace] 21; 23

5251
ROYED, Beverly*
Happy Days (chorus)

5252
ROZET, Monsieur*
Les Miserables (Marius)
Stage:
Firmin Gemier (Bassanio) 24
Le Procureur Hallers 24
L'Homme Qui Assassina 24
Taming of the Shrew, The 24

5253
RUBEN, Jose (1886-)
Dark Secrets (Dr. Mohammed Ali)
Salome of the Tenements
Stage:
Bewitched (the Marquis) 24
Checkerboard, The (Feodor Masimoff)
   20
Exile, The (Jacques Cortot) 23
Ghosts (Oswald Alving) 26
Gringo (Tito, el Tuerto) 22
Leah Kleschna (Schram) 24
Merchants of Glory (Monsieur Denis)
   25
Red Robe, The (Cardinal Bichelieu) 28
Sacred and Profane Love (Emilio
   Diaz) 20
Swords (Cannetto) 21
Thy Name Is Woman (a man) 20
Two Orphans, The (Pierre Frochard)
   26
Untitled Benefit 20

5254
RUBENS, Alma (Alma Smith) (1897-
   1931)
Cosmopolitan player 24
Cytherea (Savina Grove)
Dancers, The
East Lynne (Lady Isabel)
Enemies of Women (Alicia)
Find the Woman
Fine Clothes
Gilded Butterfly, The
Heart of Salome, The
Humoresque
Marriage License
Masks of the Devil, The
One Increasing Purpose
Passion Flower
Pelican, The
Price She Paid, The
Rejected Woman, The

She Goes to War
Show Boat (Julie)
Siberia
Thoughtless Women
Under the Red Robe (Renée de
    Cocheforet)
Unseeing Eyes
Valley of Silent Men
Woman's Faith, A
World and His Wife

5255
RUBENSTEIN, Ida*
Ship, The

5256
RUBIN, Benny (1899-   )
Casino Gardens
Daises Won't Tell
Football
Imperfect Ladies
Leathernecking
Marianne (Sam)
Naughty Baby
Thanksgiving
Stage:
Half a Widow (Izzy Preiss) 27
Vaudeville [Palace] 27

5257
RUBY, Ellalee*
Soul Fire /aka/ Golden Youth
Stage:
First Flight (Rachel Donaldson) 25
Footlights (Hazel Deane) 27

5258
RUCKERT, Ernest*
Romeo und Julia im Schnee [Romeo
    and Juliet in the Snow]

5259
RUDHYAR, Dane*
Three Weeks

5260
RUDOLPH, Oscar*
Little Annie Rooney
So This Is College

5261
RUECKERT, Ernst* (see also: Er-
    nest Ruckert)
Eleven Who Were Loyal
Rasputin, the Holy Sinner

5262
RUEDA, Jose*
Bandolero, The

5263
RUGGLES, Charles (Charles Sher-
    man Ruggles (1890-1970)
Battle of Paris, The /aka/ The Gay
    Lady
Gentlemen of the Press (Charlie
    Haven)
Heart Raider, The
Her Wedding Night
Lady Lies, The (Charlie Tyler)
Stage:
Battling Buttler (Alfred Buttler) 23
Demi-Virgin, The (Chicky Belden) 21
Ladies' Night (Fred Bonner) 20
Queen High (T. Boggs Johns) 26
Rainbow ('Nasty' Howell) 28
Spring Is Here (Peter Braley) 29
Vaudeville [Palace] 29

5264
RUMAN, Sig (Siegfried Rumann)
    (1885-1967)
Royal Box, The
Stage:
Channel Road, The (Lt. Engel) 29
Half Gods (Dr. Wolheim) 29

5265
RUMMEISTER, Augusta*
Greene Murder Case, The

5266
RUNYON, Damon (1884-1946)
Great White Way, The

5267
RUSH, Dick*
Village Sleuth, The

5268
RUSHTON, Russell*
Beau Brummel (Mr. Abrahams)

5269
RUSKIN, Shimen*
Beau Brummel

5270
RUSSELL, Byron*
Janice Meredith
World and His Wife, The
Stage:
Devil's Disciple, The (Mr. Brude-
    nell) 23
Red Poppy, The (Pierre) 22
Right to Strike, The (Sir Roger Pil-
    kington) 21
SS Glencairn (Driscoll) 29

Scotland Yard (Superintendent Drewe)
29
Sherlock Holmes (Sir Edward Leigh-
ton) 29
When Crummies Played (Snittle
Timberry) 28

5271
RUSSELL, Evangeline*
Married? (Kate Pinte)

5272
RUSSELL, Irene*
Mumsie (Louise Symonds)

5273
RUSSELL, J. Gordon*
Claw, The (wagon driver)
Hearts and Spurs (Sid Thomas)
Singer Jim McKee
Spoilers, The (Burke)
Tumbleweeds
Uncle Tom's Cabin (Loker)

5274
RUSSELL, James*
Parisian Love (D'Avril)

5275
RUSSELL, Robert*
Tess of the Storm Country (Dan
Jordon)
Stage:
Jazz Singer, The (Clarence Kahn) 25

5276
RUSSELL, William (1884-1929)
Alias the Night Wind
Anna Christie
Bare Knuckles
Before Midnight
Blue Eagle, The (Big Tim Ryan)
Boston Blackie
Brass Knuckles
Challenge of the Law, The
Cheater Reformed, The
Children of the Night
Colorado Pluck
Crusader, The
Danger Patrol
Desert Blossoms
Desired Woman, The
Eastward Ho!
Escape
Girl from Chicago, The
Girls Gone Wild
Goodbye Girls
Great Night, The

Head of the Family, The
Iron Rider, The
Lady from Longacre
Leave It to Me
Lincoln Highwayman, The
Live Wire Hicks
Madonna of Avenue A
Man Who Dared, The
Man's Size, A
Men of Zanzibar, The
Midnight Taxi
Mixed Faces
Money to Burn
On Thin Ice
Roof Tree, The
Sacred Silence
Self-Made Man, A
Shod with Fire
Singing River, The
Slam Bang Jim
Slam the Law
State Street Sadie
Still Alarm, The
Strength of the Pines
Times Have Changed
Twins of Suffering Creek
Valley of Tomorrow, The
Way of a Girl, The
When Odds Are Even
Wings of the Storm
Woman Size

5277
RUTH, Babe (George Herman Ruth)
(1895-1948)
Babe Comes Home
Headin' Home

5278
RUTH, Marshall*
Broadway Melody, The (Stew)
Nix on Dames

5278a
RUTH, Patsy*
Name the Man

5279
RUYSDAEL, Basil (-1959)
Cocoanuts, The (Hennessey)
Stage:
Cocoanuts, The (Hennessey) 25
Enchanted Isle (Stewart Haverhill-
Smith) 27
Topsy and Eva (Uncle Tom) 24

5280
RYAN, Annie*
Claw, The (Mrs. MacBourney)

5281
RYAN, Don*
Merry Widow, The (Crown Prince's
  Adjutant)
Wedding March, The (guard)

5282
RYAN, Joe*
Hidden Dangers
Purple Riders, The (Sheriff Dick
  Ranger)
Vitagraph player 21

5283
RYAN, Maurice*
Dress Parade
K-the Unknown
Midshipman, The
Poor Nut, The

5284
RYAN, Mildred*
Little French Girl, The
Live Wire, The
Man Who Found Himself, The
Wild, Wild Susan

5285
RYAN, Nancy*
Nothing but the Truth
Stage:
Happy Husband, The (Sylvia Fuller-
  ton) 28
High Road, The (Alex) 28
Last of Mrs. Cheyney, The (Lady
  Joan Houghton) 25

5286
RYAN, Robert (1910-1973)
College Widow, The
Strong Boy

5287
RYAN, Sam*
Leather Pushers, The [series]

5288
RYMAN, Tyra*
Peter the Tramp

            - S -

5289
SABATO, Alfredo*
Time to Love (Hindu Mystic)

5290
SABINI, Frank*
Blaze O'Glory

5291
SACKVILLE, Gordon*
Snob, The

5292
SADOUR, Ben*
Garden of Allah, The

5293
SAGE, Byron*
Clothes Make the Woman
Into Her Kingdom

5294
SAGE, Stuart*
Fighting Blade, The (Viscount Caris-
  ford)
Stage:
Bat, The (Brooks) 20
Elton Case, The (Charles Ramsey) 21
Hospitality (Clyde Thompson) 22

5295
SAILLARD, M. G. *
Les Miserables (Thenardies)

5296
SAILLARD, Ninette*
Les Miserables (Eponine)

5297
SAINPOLIS, John /aka/ John St.
  Polis (1887-1942)
Alaskan, The
Cappy Ricks
Coquette (Dr. John Besant)
Diplomats, The
Dixie Handicap, The
Far Cry, The
Fast Life (Mr. Hall)
Folly of Vanity
Four Horsemen of the Apocalypse,
  The (Laurier)
Grain of Dust, A
Great Lover, The
Greater Love, The
Green Grass Widows
Gun Runner, The
Held to Answer
Hero, The
Lily, The
Mademoiselle Midnight
Marriage by Contract
My Lady's Lips (inspector)

Old Dad
Patience
Phantom of the Opera, The (Phillippe
  de Chagny)
Power of Silence, The
Return of Peter Grimm, The (Andrew
  McPherson)
Romance of a Queen, The (King Con-
  stantine)
Shadows (Nate Snow)
Those Who Dare
Three Weeks
Three Wise Fools
Tomorrow
Too Many Crooks
Untamable, The
Why Be Good?
Woman Proof
Woman's Way, A
Stage:
Return of Peter Grimm, The (Fred-
  erick) 21

5298
ST. ANGELO, Robert*
King of Kings, The (bit)

5299
ST. AUDRIE, Stella*
Claude Duval (Mrs. Crisp)
Henry, King of Navarre (Catherine
  de Medici)
Sally Bishop (Mrs. Bishop)

5300
ST. CLAIR, Eric*
Find Your Man

5301
ST. JOHN, Al "Fuzzy" (1893-1963)
Ain't Love Grand?
Alarm, The
All Wet
American Beauty
Author, The
Big Secret, The
Call Your Shots
Casey Jones
City Chap, The
Cleaning Up
Dance of Life, The
Dynamite Doggie
Fair Warning
Fares, Please!
Fast and Furious
Fire Away
Flaming Romance
Full Speed

Garden of Weeds, The
Happy Pest, The
Hayseed, The
Hello, Cheyene
High Sea Blues
High Spots
Hold Your Hat
Hot or Cold
Hot Times
Iron Mule, The
Jungle Heat
Listen, Lena
Live Cowards
Lovemania
Mojave Kid, The
Out of Place
Painted Post
Paper Hangers, The
Pink Elephants
Racing Mad
Red Pepper
Roped In
Salesman, The
She Goes to War
Simp, The
Slow and Sure
Small Town Stuff
Special Delivery
Speed [serial]
Studio Rube, The
Stupid but Brave
Tailor, The
Tropical Romeo
Village Sheik, The
Who Hit Me?
Young and Dumb

5302
ST. JOHN, John*
First Born, The (Dickie)

5303
ST. JOHN, Marguerite*
Laughing Lady, The
Stage:
Aren't We All? (Hon. Mrs. Ernest
  Lynton) 23
Beau-Strings (Mrs. Bolland) 26
Becky Sharp (Lady Bareacres) 29
La Tendresse (Mademoiselle Louise)
  22

5304
ST. LEONARD, Florence*
Idol of the North, The (A. Soubrelle)

5305
SAIS, Marin (1888-)
American Girl, The

Barbed Wire
Come and Get It
Dead or Alive
Devil Dog Dawson
Girl from Frisco, The
Golden Hope, The
Hellion, The
Son of the Desert, A
Stingaree
Thunderbolt Jack [serial]

5306
SAKALL, S. Z. "Cuddles" (Eugene
  Gero Szakall) (1884-1955)
Films in Europe 1927-29

5307
SALAH, Rehba Ben*
Garden of Allah, The

5308
SALE, "Chic" Charles*
His Nibs
Marching On
Stage:
Gay Paree (a principal) 25

5309
SALE, Virginia*
Below the Deadline
Cohens and the Kellys in Atlantic
  City, The
Crowd, The
Fancy Baggage
Harold Teen
Kid's Clever, The
Legionnaires in Paris
Say Uncle
Stewed, Fried and Boiled

5310
SALISBURY, Monroe (1879-1935)
Barbarian, The
Great Alone, The
His Divorced Wife
Phantom Melody, The

5311
SALMANOVA, Lyda*
Der Golem
Lost Shadow, The
Monna Vanna
Das Weib des Pharao [The Wife of
  the Pharaoh] /aka/ The Loves of
  the Pharaoh (Makeda)

5312
SALTER, Harold /aka/ Hal*
Red Raiders, The

Stage:
Hail and Farewell (John Hart) 23
Mismates (Culbertson) 25
Square Crooks (Harry Welch) 26
Whole Town's Talking (Donald Swift)
  23

5313
SALTER, Thelma*
Huckleberry Finn (Becky)

5314
SALVER, Lianna*
Bluebeard's Eighth Wife (Lucienne)

5315
SALVI, Lola*
In Old Arizona (Italian girl)
Plastered in Paris
Through Different Eyes (maid)

5316
SALVINI, Alessandro*
Nero

5317
SALVOR, Lianne--see: Lianna Salver

5318
SALVOTTI, Vera*
Cafe Electric (Paula)

5319
SAMBORSKI, I. I. Koval*
Prince of Rogues, The
Yellow Ticket, The

5320
SAMPSON, Teddy (1895-)
Are Honeymoons Happy?
Bad Man, The
Big Jim's Heart
Bits of Life
Chicken in the Case, The
Child of the Surf, A
Don't Blame the Stork
Fencing Master, The
Fox Woman, The
Good Morning, Judge
Outcast (Nellie Essex)
Sympathetic Sal

5321
SAMUELS, Jacob*
Abie's Irish Rose (Rabbi)

5322
SANDE, Earle*
Great White Way, The

5323
SAN DIEGO MARINE BASE BAND
Cock-Eyed World, The

5324
SAN MARTIN, Carlos*
Dancin' Fool (Elkus)

5325
SANCHEZ, Marguerite*
Heart of Maryland, The (Phoebe
    Yancy)

5326
SANDERS, George (1906-1972)
Dishonor Bright
Find the Lady
Shape of Things to Come, The
Strange Cargo (debut)

5327
SANDERSON, Joey*
Woman of No Importance, A (nurse)

5328
SANDERSON, Kent*
Strong Boy

5329
SANDERSON, Lora*
Chickie

5330
SANFORD, Stanley*
Circus, The (tent maker)
Iron Mask, The (Porthos)

5331
SANFORD, Tiny*
Big Business
Flying Elephants
From Soup to Nuts
Hoose Gow, The
Movie Night
Rio Rita (Davalos)
Sailors Beware!
Second Hundred Years, The
Their Purple Moment

5332
SANTELTON, Frederick*
Darling of New York, The

5333
SANTORA, Jack*
One Stolen Night

5334
SANTSCHI, Thomas /aka/ Tom
    (1882-1931)
Adventurous Souls
Barriers Burned Away
Brass Commandments
Cradle of Courage, The (Tierney)
Crashing Through
Cruise of the Hellion
Desert's Toll, The
Eyes of the Totem
Flaming Love
Forlorn River
Hands Across the Border
Haunted Ship, The
Her Honor, the Governor
Her Kingdom of Dreams
Hills of Kentucky
His Lady /aka/ When a Man Loves
    (convict boat captain)
Honor Bound
In Old Arizona (cowboy)
Into No Man's Land
Is Divorce a Failure?
Isle of Lost Men, The
Jim, the Conqueror
Land Beyond the Law
Land of the Silver Fox
Law and the Man
Life's Greatest Game
Little Robinson Crusoe
My Own Pal
No Man's Gold
North Wind's Malice, The
Old San Francisco
Overland Stage, The
Paths to Paradise
Primrose Path, The (Big Joe Snead)
Right of the Strongest
Shanghaied
Shannons of Broadway /aka/ Goodbye
    Broadway
Siberia
Street of Tears
Tempest, The
Third Degree, The
Three Bad Men
Tipped Off
Tracked by the Police
Two Kinds of Women
Vultures of the Sea [serial]
Wagon Master, The
Yellowback, The

5335
SARGENT, Lewis (1904-)
Arabian Fights, The
Broadway Ladies
Godless Girl, The
Huckleberry Finn (Title role)
Jessie's James
Just Around the Corner
Mighty Four Hundred, The
Mild but She Satisfies
Million for Love, A
Oliver Twist (Noah Claypool)
One Splendid Hour
Racing Blood
Racing Blood [series]
River Pirate
Roadhouse
Ruth Is Stranger than Fiction
Soul of Youth, The
South of Panama
Sweet Buy and Buy
That Wild Irish Pose
Universal Pictures [14 one-reelers]
Watch Your Pep!
You Just Know She Dares 'em

5336
SARNO, Hector*
Ashes of Vengeance (Gallon)
Climbers, The (Miguel)
Cobra (Victor Minardi)
King of Kings, The (Galilean carpen-
    ter)
Lucky Star (Pop Fry)
Red Hot Speed
Sea Hawk, The (Tsamanni)
Song of Love, The /aka/ Dust of
    Desire
Temptress, The

5337
SARNO, Tom*
As Man Desires

5338
SARTA, Mary*
Madonna of the Sleeping Cars, The

5339
SARTI, Andre*
Woman on Trial, The

5340
SAUM, Cliff*
Bridge of Sighs, The

5341
SAUNDERS, Florence*
Wandering Jew, The (Joanne)

5342
SAUNDERS, Jackie (1893-)
Alimony
Broken Laws
Dad's Girl
Drag Harlan
Faint Perfume (Tweet Crumb)
Flirting Bride, The
Infamous Miss Revel, The
Man Behind, The
Puppets of Fate
Scuttlers, The

5343
SAVAGE, Nelly /aka/ Nellie*
Hole in the Wall, The (Madame Mys-
    tera)
Mismates
Sorrows of Satan, The (dancer)

5344
SAVAGE, Turner*
Callahans and the Murphys, The
    (Timmy Callahan)
Frisco Sally Levy
How Baxter Buttered In
Tumbleweeds

5345
SAVEIIEV, I.*
Village of Sin, The

5346
SAVILLE, De Sacia*
Mystery Mind, The [serial]

5347
SAVILLE, Gus*
Tess of the Storm Country (Old Man
    Longman)

5348
SAVITSKY, Viacheslav*
Last Command, The (private)

5349
SAXE, Temple*
Beau Brummel (Desmond Wertham)
Bucking the Tiger
Captain Blood (Governor Steed)
Dancers, The
Her Night of Romance
His Lady /aka/ When a Man Loves
    (Baron Chevral)
Liquid Gold
Polly with a Past
Primrose Path, The (Dude Talbot)
Time, the Comedian
White Black Sheep, The

5350
SAXON, Hugh*
Cytherea (Randon's butler)

5351
SAXON-SNELL, H. *
Luck of the Navy, The (Francois)

5352
SAYLOR, Syd*
Newlyweds, The
Stern Brothers Comedies
Universal Comedies

5353
SCAMMON, P. R. *
America /aka/ Love and Sacrifice
Stage:
Humbug, The (Prof. Justin Forbes)
  29

5354
SCANLON, E. *
America /aka/ Love and Sacrifice
  (servant at Ashley Court)

5355
SCATIGNA, Angelo*
Romola (Bratti)

5356
SCHABLE, Robert*
Bella Donna
Cheat, The
Loves of Sunya, The (Henri Picard)
Man and the Moment, The
On with the Dance
Partners Again /aka/ Partners
  Again with Potash and Perlmutter
Sailors' Wives
Sherlock Holmes /aka/ Moriarty
  (Alf Bassick)
Silent Partner, The
Silken Shackles
Stranger, The
Without Limit

5357
SCHACKELFORD, Floyd*
Forward Pass, The
Stark Mad

5358
SCHADE, Betty*
Flame of Youth
Prisoners of Love
Shod with Fire
Soul of Youth

Village Sleuth, The
Voices of the City (Sally)
Wing Toy

5359
SCHAEFER, Anne*
City of Masks, The
Goose Hangs High, The (Rhoda)
Heritage of the Desert, The
Love's Wilderness
Main Street
Night Flyer, The
Prisoners
Saturday's Children
Smiling Irish Eyes
Sparrows /aka/ Human Sparrows
Three Hours
West of the Water Tower
Wheels of Chance

5360
SCHAEFER, Billy Kent*
Enemy, The
Hills of Kentucky
Home Maker, The
Ice Flood, The
Warming Up
Wind, The (Cora's son)

5361
SCHAEFFER, A. L. *
Sparrows /aka/ Human Sparrows
  (Bailey's Confederate)

5362
SCHAFFER, Peggy*
Light That Failed, The

5363
SCHARFF, Lester*
New York (dual role, Sharpe/Izzy
  Blumenstein)

5364
SCHEFFEL, Oswald*
Sein Grösster Bluff [Her Greatest
  Bluff] (gangster)

5365
SCHELLER, George*
Happy Days (chorus)

5366
SCHENCK, Earl*
Ashes of Vengeance (Blair)
Mademoiselle Midnight
Salome (young Syrian)
Song of Love, The /aka/ Dust of
  Desire

Tides of Passion

5367
SCHENSTROM, Carl*
Han og Hun og Hamlet [He and She
   and Hamlet]

5368
SCHILDKRAUT, Joseph (1895-1964)
Blue Danube, The
Carnival
Country Doctor, The
Forbidden Woman, The
Harp in Hock, A
Heart Thief, The
His Dog
King of Kings, The (Judas)
Main Event, The
Meet the Prince
Mississippi Gambler
Night Ride (Joe Rooker)
Orphans of the Storm (Chevalier de
   Vaudrey)
Paramount player 24
Road to Yesterday, The (Kenneth
   Paulton)
Der Roman und Der Kromtesse
Shipwrecked
Show Boat (Ravenal)
Song of Love /aka/ Dust of Desire
Tenth Avenue
Young April
Stage:
Firebrand, The (Bevenuto Cellini) 24
Liliom ("Liliom") 21
Pagans (Richard Northcote) 21
Peer Gynt (Peer) 23

5369
SCHILDKRAUT, Rudolph (1862-1930)
Christina (Niklass)
Country Doctor, The
Der Fluch
Harp in Hock, A
His Country
His People
King of Kings, The (Caiaphas)
Main Event, The
Pals in Paradise
Proud Heart, The
Schlemiehl
Ship Comes In, A
Turkish Delight, A
Young April
Stage:
Miracle, The (a blind peasant) 24
Mongrel, The (Mathias) 24

5370
SCHIPA, Carlo*
Little Annie Rooney
Sally (Sascha Commuski)

5371
SCHLEGEL, Margarete*
Der Jonuskoff /aka/ Love's Mockery

5372
SCHLETTOW, Hans Adelbert*
Kriemhild's Revenge
Die Nibelungen /aka/ The Nibelungs
   (Hagen)
Shadows of Fear
Siegfried
Small Town Sinners

5373
SCHMIDT, Alexandra*
Fight for the Matterhorn, The

5374
SCHMIDT, Kai*
Mockery (butler)

5375
SCHMIEDER, Willy*
Life of Beethoven, The

5376
SCHMITZER, Henrietta*
Broken Hearts

5377
SCHNEIDER, Friedrich*
Peaks of Destiny

5378
SCHNEIDER, Hannes*
Fight for the Matterhorn, The
Peak of Fate

5379
SCHNELL, G. H.*
Nosfertau
Stage:
Redemption (musician) 28

5380
SCHODLER, Dave*
Dreams of Hawaii

5381
SCHOEN, Margaret*
Kriemhild's Revenge
Die Nibelungen /aka/ The Nibelungs
   (Kriemhild)
Siegfried

5382
SCHOENE, Mary*
Golden Princess

5383
SCHOLLER, William*
Royal Box, The

5384
SCHOLZ, Robert*
Alles für Geld [All for Money]
Isn't Life Wonderful? (hungry worker)
Kopf Hoch, Charly! [Heads Up, Char-
ly] (Duke of Sanzedilla)
Rat, The (Herman Stetz)

5385
SCHÖN, Margarete*--see: Margaret
Schoen

5386
SCHRAM, Violet (1898-)
Big Happiness
Gray Wolf's Ghost, The
Out of the Darkness
Riders of the Dawn
Walk-Offs, The
White Lies
Woman with the Parakeets, The

5387
SCHRAMM, Karla*
Hearts and Masks
Revenge of Tarzan, The /aka/ The
Return of Tarzan (Jane)
Son of Tarzan, The [serial] (Jane)

5388
SCHRECK, Max (Alfred Abel)*
At the Edge of the World (the Ped-
lar)
Jew of Mestri, The (Doge of Venice)
Nosferatu (Graf Orlok)
Rasputin: The Holy Sinner
Strange Case of Captain Rampu, The

5389
SCHREIBER, Alfred*
Prince and the Pauper, The

5390
SCHREYER, Annie*
Menschen am Sonntag [People on
Sunday]

5391
SCHROEDER, Anne*
West of the Water Tower

5392
SCHROEDER, Arthur*
Tradition

5393
SCHROELL, N.*
Copperhead, The

5394
SCHRON, Cania*
Coffin Maker, The

5395
SCHROOTH, Heinrich*
Atlantic [German] (Harry von Schroe-
der)
Carnival Crime, The
President, The

5396
SCHUKOW, A.*
Flames on the Volga

5397
SCHULER, Billy*
Boxing Gloves

5398
SCHULTZ, Harry*
Riley, the Cop

5399
SCHULTZ, Maurice*
Oppressed, The
Passion of Joan of Arc, The

5400
SCHUMANN-HEINK, Ferdinand
(1893-1955)
Awakening
Blaze O' Glory
Broadway Sap, The
Four Sons
Gallant Fool, The
Gold
Riley, the Cop

5401
SCHUNZEL, Reinhold*
Fortune's Fool
Der Juxbaron [The Imaginary Baron]
(Title role)
Last Payment, The

5402
SCHUTZ, Maurice--see: Maurice
Schultz

5403
SCHWARTZ, Emile*
Condemned (prison inmate)

5404
SCHWARTZ, John*
Condemned (prison inmate)

5405
SCHWARTZ, Maurice*
Broken Hearts
Stage:
Inspector General, The (Ivan Alexan-
  drovich Khlestakov)

5406
SCKRÖDER, Greta*
Nosferatu

5407
SCOTT, Carrie*
Manhandled (boarding house keeper)
Stage Struck (Mrs. Wagner)

5408
SCOTT, Douglas Frazer*
Dynamite (Bobby)
Strong Boy

5409
SCOTT, Fred*
Bride of the Storm

5410
SCOTT, Gregory*
Kissing Cup's Race (Lord Hillhoxton)

5411
SCOTT, Mabel Juliene (1898-)
Abysmal Brute, The (Marion Sang-
  ster)
Behold, My Wife
Concert, The
Don't Neglect Your Wife
Dream Melody, The
Fanny Herself
Jucklins, The
Mother
No Woman Knows
Power of a Lie
Round Up, The
Sea Wolf, The
Seven Days
So This Is Marriage
Steele of the Royal Mounted
Stranded in Paris
Times Have Changed
Wallflowers

5412
SCOTT, Randolph (Randolph Crane)
  (1903-)
Far Call

5413
SCOTT, William*
After Business Hours
Dante's Inferno
Light of the Western Stars, The
Voice in the Dark, A

5414
SEABURY, Forest*
Auction Block, The (Edward Blake)
Ranson's Folly

5415
SEABURY, Ynez*
Dynamite (a neighbor)

5416
SEACOMBE, Dorothy*
Blinkeyes (Bella)
Flag Lieutenant, The (Widow Dorothy
  Cameron)

5417
SEARL, Jackie (1920-)
Daughters of Desire
Radio:
The Children's Hour (Los Angeles)
  1923

5418
SEARLE, Kamuela (-1920)
Fools' Paradise (Kay)
Son of Tarzan, The [serial] (Korak,
  the man)

5419
SEARLEY, Bill*
Best Man, The

5420
SEARS, Allan /aka/ Allen*
Judy of Rogues Harbor
Long Live the King
Miss Information
Rio Grande

5421
SEARS, Zelda (1873-)
Bishop Murder Case, The
Highest Bidder, The
Stage:
Lollipop (Mrs. Garrity) 24
Untitled Benefit 20

5422
SEASTROM, Dorothy*
It Must Be Love
Pretty Ladies

5423
SEASTROM, Victor--see: Victor
Sjöstrom

5424
SEAY, Billy*
Marriage Playground, The (Bun)
My Man

5425
SEBASTIAN, Dorothy (1904-1957)
Adventurer, The
Arizona Wildcat
Bluebeard's Seven Wives
Brothers
California
Demi-Bride, The
Devil's Appletree, The
Gallant Gringo, The
Haunted Ship, The
His First Command
House of Scandal, The
Isle of Forgotten Women
Love
Morgan's Raiders /aka/ Morgan's
    Last Raid
On Ze Boulevard
Our Dancing Daughters (Beatrice)
Rainbow, The
Sackcloth and Scarlet
Show, The
Show People (cameo)
Single Standard, The
Spirit of Youth, The
Spite Marriage
Tea for Three
Their Hour
Twelve Miles Out
Unholy Night, The (Lady Efra)
Winds of Chance
Woman of Affairs, A (Constance)
Wyoming
You'd Be Surprised

5426
SEDAN, Rolfe (1896-)
Chinatown Charley
Iron Mask, The (Louis XIII)
Making the Grade
My Old Dutch
One Hysterical Night
Ritzie Rosie
Sporting Youth

5427
SEDDON, Margaret*
Actress, The
Bellamy Trial, The (Mrs. Ives)
Bright Shawl, The (Carmencita Esco-
    bar)
Case of Becky, The
Confidence Man, The
Dance Hall
Gentlemen Prefer Blondes (Lorelei's
    mother)
Gold Diggers (Mrs. Lamar)
Golden Cocoon, The
His Jazz Bride
Home Made
Inside of the Cup, The
Lady, The
Little Johnny Jones
Man Who Played God, The
Matinee Ladies
Midshipman, The
New Lives for Old
Nickel Hopper, The
Proud Flesh
Quality Street (Nancy Willoughby)
Rolling Home
She Goes to War
Silk Legs
Snob, The
Through the Dark
Trelawney of the Wells (Trafalgar
    Gower)
Women Who Give

5428
SEDGWICK, Eileen (1897-)
Beasts of Paradise [serial]
Beyond All Odds
Days of Daniel Boone [serial]
Diamond Queen, The [serial]
False Brands
Fighting Ranger, The [serial]
Love's Battle
Lure of the West
Making Good
Poverty Row
Riddle Rider, The [serial]
Strings of Steel [serial] (Miss Van-
    Norton)
Terror Trial [serial]
Thundering Speed
Vanishing West, The [serial]
When Danger Calls
White Rider, The
Winking Idol, The [serial]

5429
SEDGWICK, Josie (1900-)
Beyond the Shadow

Daddy
Daredevil Jack [serial]
Double Adventure [serial]
Duke of Chimney Butte
Paying His Debt
Sunshine Trail
White Moth, The

5430
SEDGWICK, Russell*
If Winter Comes

5431
SEDILLO, Juan*
Girl from Havana, The

5432
SEDLEY, Henry*
Blonde or Brunette
Fool, The
Ghost Talks, The
Racket, The

5433
SEEBERG*
Der Mensch am Wege [Man by the
    Roadside]

5434
SEEGAR, Miriam (1909-)
Fashions in Love
Love Doctor, The
Seven Keys to Baldpate

5435
SEELEY, Lewis*
Virgin Paradise, A

5436
SEGAL, Vivienne (1897-)
Song of the West (Virginia)
Stage:
Adrienne (Adrienne Grey) 23
Castles in the Air (Evelyn Devine) 26
Desert Song, The (Margot Bonvalet)
    26
Florida Girl (Daphne) 25
Three Musketeers, The (Constance
    Bonacieux) 28
Untitled Benefit 21
Vaudeville [Palace] 23
Yankee Princess (Odette Darimonde)
    22
Ziegfeld Follies (a principal) 24

5437
SEGAR, Lucia*
Knockout Reilly

5438
SEICKARD, Joseph--see: Joseph
    Swickard

5439
SEIGMANN, George (1884-1928)
Anna Christie
Big Punch, The
Born to the West
California Romance, A
Carnival Girl
Cat and the Canary, The (Hendricks)
Connecticut Yankee in King Arthur's
    Court, A (Sir Sagamore)
Desperate Trails
Fools First
Guilty One, The
Hawk's Trail, The [serial]
Hotel Imperial (Russian General)
Hungry Hearts
Janice Meredith (Col. Rahl)
King of Kings, The (Barabbas)
Little Miss Rebellion
Little Yank, The
Lost and Found
Love Me and the World Is Mine
Man Who Laughs, The (Dr. Hard-
    quanonne)
Manhattan
Merry-Go-Round (Shani Huber--re-
    placed by Wallace Berry)
Midnight Sun, The
Monte Cristo (Luigi Vampa)
Mother Love and the Law
My Old Dutch
Never the Twain Shall Meet
Oliver Twist (Bill Sikes)
Poker Faces
Queen of Sheba, The (King Armud)
Recompense
Red Mill, The (William)
Revelation
Sainted Devil, A (El Tigre)
Scaramouche (Georges Jacques Dan-
    ton)
Shame
Shooting of Dan McGrew, The (John
    Hubbel)
Singer Jim McKee
Slander the Woman
Stop that Man!
Three Musketeers, The (Porthos)
Thirteenth Juror, The
Truthful Liar, The
Uncle Tom's Cabin (Simon Legree)
Zander the Great (Black Bart)

5439a
SEITZ, George B. (1888-1944)
Rogues and Romance
Sky Ranger, The [serial]
Velvet Fingers, The [serial]

5440
SELANDER, Concordia*
Thy Soul Shall Bear Witness

5441
SELBIE, Evelyn*
Broken Gates, The
Broken Wing, The
Cafe in Cairo, A
Camille
Devil to Pay, The
Eternal Love (Pia's mother)
Half-Breed, The (Mary)
Hell Bent for Heaven
Into Her Kingdom
Mademoiselle Midnight
Mysterious Dr. Fu Manchu, The
   /aka/ The Insidious Dr. Fu
   Manchu (Fai Lee)
Name the Man
Poisoned Paradise (Madame Tran-
   quille)
Romance Ranch
Seeds of Vengeance
Silken Shackles
Wild Geese
Without Benefit of Clergy

5442
SELBY, Norman /aka/ "Kid Mc-
   Coy"*
Painted Angel, The

5443
SELIG ZOO, The
Jungle Tragedy, A

5444
SELL, Henry G. *
East Lynne (Francis Levinson)
Woman in Gray, A (Tom Thurston)
Stage:
Virtue (?) (Richard W. Greene) 22

5445
SELLON, Charles A. (1878-   )
Alias Jimmy Valentine
Bad Man, The
Big News (editor)
Big Scoop, The
Bulldog Drummond (Travers)
Butter and Egg Man, The

Count of Ten, The
Easy Come, Easy Go (Jim Bailey)
Easy Pickings
Feel My Pulse (sanitarium caretaker)
Flowing Gold
Gamblers, The
Girl in the Glass Cage, The (Dan
   Jackson)
Happiness Ahead
Hot Stuff
Love Me and the World Is Mine
Lucky Devil, The
Man and the Moment, The
Men Are Like That
Merton of the Movies
Mighty, The (manager)
Monster, The (Constable)
Mysterious Rider, The
Number Please
Old Home Week
Painted Ponies
Prairie King, The
Roughneck, The
Saturday Night Kid, The (Leon Wood-
   ruff)
Something Always Happens
Sweetie (Dr. Oglethorpe)
Tracked in the Snow Country
Under a Texas Moon
Vagabond Lover
Valley of the Giants, The
What a Night!
Woman Proof

5446
SELWYN, Clarissa*
Baby Cyclone
Beau Brummel (Mrs. Wertham)
Black Gate, The
Black Oxen (Dora Dwight)
Brass Bottle, The
Broadway Daddies
Broadway Lady
Come Across
Confessions of a Wife
Crystal Cup, The
Cup of Fury, The
Dangerous Days
Devil Dancer, The
Fast Worker, The
Glorious Betsy
Hard to Get
Heart of a Follies Girl, The
Infatuation
Isle of Lost Ships, The
Jazz Mad
Last Man on Earth, The
Love Trap

Lucky Horseshoe, The
Lure of Jade, The
Mademoiselle Midnight
Marriage of William Ashe, The
  (Lady Mary Lyster)
My Man
Naughty but Nice (Miss Perkins)
Quarantined Rivals
Resurrection
Sackcloth and Scarlet
Sacred and Profane Love
Secrets (Audrey Carlton)
Sinners Paradise
Straight from Paris
We Moderns

5447
SELZICK, Stephen*
Condemned (prison inmate)

5448
SEMELE, Harry*
America /aka/ Love and Sacrifice
  (Hikatoo, Seneca Chief)
Into the Net [serial]
Last Command, The (soldier)
Plunder [serial]
Royal Rider

5449
SEMMLER, Gustav*
Eleven Who Were Loyal 29

5450
SEMON, Larry (1889-1928)
Bakery, The
Barnyard, The
Bell Hop, The
Clodhopper, The
Counter Jumper, The
Dome Doctor, The
Dummies
Fall Guy, The
Fly Cop, The
Girl in the Limousine, The
Golf
Gown Shop, The
Grocery Clerk, The
Her Boy Friend
Hick, The
Horsehoes
Kid Speed
Lightning Love
Midnight Cabaret
No Wedding Bells
Oh, What a Man!
Pair of Kings, A
Perfect Clown, The

Rent Collector, The
Sawmill, The
School Days
Show, The
Simple Sap, A
Sleuth, The
Solid Concrete
Sportsman, The
Spuds
Stagehand, The
Stop, Look and Listen
Stuntman, The
Suitor, The
Trouble Brewing
Underworld ("Slippy" Lewis)
Wizard of Oz, The (scarecrow)

5451
SENNETT, Mack (Michael Sinnott)
  (1880-1960) King of Comedy,
  Sennett produced countless slap-
  stick comedies, discovered talent
  and turned them into stars, created the famous Keystone Kops and
  glamorous Bathing Beauties. Sen-
  nett acted in, directed, and pro-
  duced many hours of humor. [See
  Volume I for his earlier credits
  as an actor.] In 1937, he received
  a special Academy Award for
  "...his lasting contribution to the
  comedy technique of the screen."
  Listed below are most of his
  greatest laughs.
Alice Be Good 26
All Night Long 24
Asleep at the Switch 23
Astray from the Steerage 21
Bachelor Butt-In, A 26
Bashful Jim 25
Be Reasonable 21
Beach Club, The 28
Bee's Buzz, The 29
Beloved Bozo, The 25
Best Man, The 28
Bicycle Flirt, The 28
Big Palooka, The 29
Black Oxfords 24
Bloggie's Vacation 20
Blonde's Revenge, A 26
Boobs in the Woods 25
Bow Wow 22
Breaking the Ice 25
Bride's Relations, The 29
Bright Eyes 22
Broadway Blues 29
Broke in China 27
Bull Fighter, The 27

Taxi Dolls 29
Taxi for Two 28
Taxi Scandal, A   28
Taxi Spooks 28
Tee for Two 25
Ten Dollars or Ten Days 20
There He Goes 25
Three Foolish Weeks 24
Trimmed in Gold 26
Unhappy Finish, The   21
Uppercut O'Brien 29
Wall Street Blues 24
Wandering Waist Line 28
Wandering Willies 26
Water Wagons 25
Wedding Bells Out of Tune 21
When a Man's a Man 26
When Summer Comes 22
Where Is My Wandering Boy Tonight?
  23
Whirls and Girls 29
Whispering Whiskers 26
White Wing's Bride 25
Wide Open Faces 26
Wife's Relations 28
Wild Goose Chaser, The   25
Window Dummy 25
Yankee Doodle Duke, A   26
You Wouldn't Believe It 20
Yukon Jake 24

5452
SERDA, Julia*
Atlantic [German] (Clara von Schroe-
  der)
Eine Du Barry von Heute [A Modern
  Du Barry] (Aunt Julie)
Der Juxbaron [The Imaginary Baron]
  (Zerline Windisch)

5453
SERENA, Sigmund*
White Sister, The (Prof. Ugo Severi)

5454
SERGEANT, Lewis*
Oliver Twist

5455
SERGYL, Yvonne*
Miracle of the Wolves, The

5456
SERIALS
Remember those wonderful Saturday
  afternoons when you were hooked
  on a world of serials? Each
  week a chapter ended with an

impossible situation for the hero
or heroine, created by an insidi-
ous, diabolical villain. The first
sound serial, Ace of Scotland
Yard, 1929, from Universal Stu-
dios followed a series of great
silent cliff hangers. All that re-
mains today are memories of dime
matinees and the thrill of cinema
serials.
Ace of Scotland Yard 29
Ace of Spades 25
Adventures of Robinson Crusoe, The
  /aka/ Robinson Crusoe 22
Adventures of Tarzan 21
Around the World in 18 Days 23
Avenging Arrow, The   21
Bar C Mystery, The   26
Battling Brewster 24
Beasts of Paradise 23
Black Book, The   29
Blake of Scotland Yard 27
Blue Fox, The   21
Branded Four, The   20
Branded H, The   20
Breaking Through 20
Bride 13-20
Captain Kidd 22
Casey of the Coast Guard 26
Charlatan Mystery, The   25
Chinatown Mystery, The   28
Crimson Flash, The   27
Crimson Lash, The   21
Count of Monte Cristo, The   22
Crooked Dagger, The   20
Dangerous Adventure 22
Daredevil Jack 20
Days of Daniel Boone 23
Days of '49, The   24
Diamond Master, The   29
Diamond Queen, The   21
Do or Die 21
Double Adventure 21
Dragon's Net, The   20
Eagle of the Night 28
Eagle's Talons, The   23
Elmo the Fearless 20
Evil Eye, The   20
Fantomas 20
Fast Express, The   24
Fatal Sign, The   20
Fatal Thirty, The   20
Fatal Warning, The   29
Fighting Blood 29
Fighting Coward, The   24
Fighting Fate 21
Fighting for Fame 27
Fighting Marine, The   26

Trunk Mystery, The /aka/ The
  Shamrock and the Rose 27
Undersea Kingdom 28
Vanishing Dagger, The 20
Vanishing Millions 26
Vanishing Rider, The 28
Vanishing Trails 20
Vanishing West, The 28
Veiled Mystery, The 20
Velvet Fingers 20
Vultures of the Sea 28
Way of a Man, The 24
What Would You Do? 20
When Danger Smiles 22
Where Men Are Men 21
Whirlwind, The 20
Whispering Smith Rides 27
White Eagle 22
White Horseman, The 21
Who Pays? 23
Winking Idol, The 26
Winners of the West 21
Winsome Winnie
With Stanley in Africa 22
Wolf Face 23
Wolves of the North 24
Woman in Gray, A 20
Yellow Cameo, The 28

5457
SEROFF, George*
Volga-Volga (Filka)

5458
SERRANO, Vincent*
Branded Woman, The
Convoy
Stage:
Alarm Clock, The (Reggie Wynn) 23
Fools Errant (John Pritchard) 22
Rio Rita (Gen. Enrique Joselito Este-
  ban) 27
Werewolf, The (Vincente) 24

5459
SERVAES, Dagny*
Das Weib des Pharao [The Wife of
  the Pharaoh] /aka/ The Loves of
  the Pharaoh (Theonis)
Fortune's Fool
Peter the Great
Stage:
Dantons Tod (Julie) 27
Jedermann [Everyman] (Lechery) 27
Midsummer Night's Dream, A (Hip-
  polyta) 27
Peripherie (Anna) 28

5460
SERVANTI, Luigi*
President, The

5461
SEVERIN-MARS*
J'Accuse

5462
SEWELL, Audrey*
Night Life (profiteer's daughter)

5463
SEXTON, Carter*
Happy Days (chorus)

5464
SEYLER, Athene*
This Freedom (Miss Keggs)

5465
SEYMOUR, Clarine (1900-1920)
Idol Dancer, The (White Almond
  Flower)
Scarlet Days

5466
SEYMOUR, Harry*
East Lynne (Mr. Dill)
Stage:
Vaudeville [Palace] 28

5467
SEYMOUR, Madeline*
Blinkeyes (Sophie Clay)
Evidence
His Glorious Night
Last of Mrs. Cheney, The (Mrs.
  Winton)

5467a
SEZBIE, Evelyn--see: Evelyn Selbie

5468
SHAEFER, Anna*
Chorus Girl's Romance, A (Aunt
  Emma)

5469
SHAHDOODAKIAN, Tatiezam*
Honor

5469
SHAKESPEARE IN SILENT FILMS
  1889-1929
Beerbohm Tree, Sarah Bernhardt,
  Buster Keaton, Theda Bara, Will
  Rogers, Norma Shearer, even the

westerns brought Shakespeare's
plays to the screen.
Whether the actual work, a take-off,
or inspired by characters of the
Bard, films presented Shakespeare
to wide audiences. Romeo be-
came synonymous with male lover,
from Bumptious as Romeo to the
real Romeo.
Adventures of Henry IV of France
  11 (Cines)
Alas! Poor Yoriek! 13 (Selig)
Alias Julius Caesar 22 (FN)
All's Well that Ends Well 09 (Pathé);
  11 (Brockliss); 12 (Urban-Eclipse-
  Radios); 12 (Cines); 12 (Eclair);
  13 (Mutual Educational); 13 (Cricks
  and Martin); 14 (Tyler); 14 (Prin-
  cess)
Das Alte Gesetz 23 (Comedia)
'Amlet 19 (Hepworth)
Amleto I il suo Clown 19 (D'Ambro)
Anne Boleyn 13 (Eclipse); 20 (UFA)
Anthony and Cleopatra 08 (V); 13
  (Cines); 24 (Un)
Arizona Romeo, The 25 (Fox)
As You Like It 08 (Kalem); 12 (V)
Barbe Russe 17 (Film d'Art)
Barnyard Hamlet, The 17 (Powers)
Bianco Contro Negro 13 (Pasquali)
Bluebeard's Seven Wives 25 (FN)
Bromo and Juliet 26 (Pathé)
Bruto I and Bruto II 10 (Milano)
Brutus 10 (Cines)
Bumptious as Romeo 11 (Edison)
Burlesque on Romeo and Juliet 02
  (Edison)
Cardinal Wolsey 12 (V)
Carnival 21 (Alliance)
Cleo to Cleopatra 28 (V)
Cleopatra 03 (Pathé); 10 (Pathé); 12
  (Gardner); 13 (Pathé); 17 (Fox);
  20 (Fox); 28 (MGM)
Cleopatra and Her Easy Mark 25
  (Pinellas)
Cleopatre 99 (Mélies)
Cleopatsy 18 (Pathé-Rolin)
Colonel Heeza Liar Plays Hamlet
  (Cartoon) 16 (Bray)
Comedy of Errors, A 08 (V); 12
  (Solax); 12 (Cines); 15 (Yorkshire
  Cine Co.)
Court Intrigue in the Reign of Henry
  VIII 11 (Pathé)
Cymbeline 13 (Thanhauser)
Daughters of Shylock 09 (Gaumont)
Day Dreams 22 (FN)
Dente per Dente 13 (Latium)

Depot Romeo, A 17 (Essany)
Desdemona 11 (Nordick)
Le Diable et la Statue 01 (Mélies)
Don Q, Son of Zorro 25 (UA)
Doubling for Romeo 21 (Goldwyn)
Un Drame Judiciare à Venise 08
  (Cines)
Duel Scene from Macbeth 05 (Bio-
  graph)
Elfenszene aus dem Sommeracht-
  straum 17 (Harmonie-Film)
Enchantment 21 (Cosmopolitan)
Les Enfants d'Edouard 10 (Film
  d'Art); 14 (Cosmograph)
Ethel's Romeo 15 (Casino)
Falstaff 11 (Eclipse)
Der Fliegentuten 18 (Paul Beckers
  Film)
Flying Romeos 28 (FN)
Footlight Parade, A 17 (Fox)
Freddy vs Hamlet 16 (V)
Galloping Romeo, The 13 (Selig)
Ham og Hun og Hamlet 22 (Palladi-
  um)
Hamlet 99 (Bernhardt); 07 (Mélies);
  08 (Cines); 08 (Milano); 10 (Lux);
  10 (Cines); 19 (Eclipse); 10
  (Mounet-Sully); 10 (Nordisk); 12
  (Nazimova); 13 (Gaumont); 14
  (Ambrosio); 15 (Cricks and Mar-
  tin); 17 (Rudolfi); 20 (Art-Film)
Hamlet Made Over /aka/ Hamlet
  Up-To-Date 16 (Lubin)
Henry IV 09 (Eclipse)
Henry IV et le Bucheron 11 (Pathé)
Henry V 13 (Stratford); 13 (Eric
  Williams)
Henry VIII 11 (Barker)
Her Rustic Romeo 18 (Strand)
Hero Romeo 15 (Lubin)
Horse, a Horse!, A 16 (Clarendon)
Hubert and Arthur 13 (Gaumont/Eric
  Williams)
Iago's Inheritance 13 (Savoia)
Indian Romeo and Juliet 12 (V)
Iron Strain, The 15 (Triangle)
Jewish King Lear, The 12
John Falstaff 23 (British and Colo-
  nial)
Juliet and Her Romeo 23 (Butcher)
Julius Caesar /aka/ Brutus 09
  (Italia)
Julius Caesar 08 (V); 08 (Lubin); 10
  (Kineto); 11 (Co-operative); 13
  (Edison-Kintophone); 13 (Gloria);
  14 (Cines); 15 (Weston)
Katherine Howard and Henry VIII 10
  (Urban)

Kean 22 (Albatross-Sequana)
King Lear 99 (Tree); 05; 09 (V); 10
(Film d'Art Italiana); 10 (Milano)
16 (Thanhauser)
Lady Killer, The 16 (Metro)
Lady Macbeth 17 (Palatino-Film)
Last Moment, The 28 (Zakoro)
Der Leibgardest 25 (Pan-Phoebus)
Leonce Plays Othello 14 (Gaumont)
Life of William Shakespeare, The
14 (British and Colonial)
Love in a Wood 16 (London)
Love's Labor's Lost 12 (Lubin); 13
(Gaumont); 14 (United); 16 (Edison)
Love's Labor's Won 22 (British Ex-
hibitors)
Macbeth 08 (V); 09 (Cines); 10 (Film
d'Art); 11 (Co-operative); 13
(Film Industrie); 16 (Triangle-
Reliance); 16 (Eclair); 22 (Elel-
Film)
Mad Lover, The 17 (Rapf-Pathé)
Martha's Romeo 15 (Edison)
Martin as Hamlet 14 (Neue)
La Maschera che Sanguia 14 (Pas-
quali)
Masks and Faces 17 (Ideal)
Measure for Measure 09 (Lubin)
Merchant of Venice, The 01 (Hor-
bach); 08 (V); 11 (Film d'Art-
Italiana); 12 (Thanhauser); 14 (Un);
19 (Hepworth); 16 (Bosworth); 22
(Masters); 23 (Peter Paul Films)
Merry Wives of Windsor, The 10
(Selig); 17 (Beck Film)
Midsummer Night's Dream, A 06
(V); 09 (V); 09 (Le Lion); 12 (Lu-
bin); 13 (Tommaisi-Hubner); 13
(Deutsche Bioscop); 25 (Neumann)
Mile-A-Minute Romeo 23 (Fox)
Le Miroir de Venise 05 (Mélies)
Modern Othello, A 14 (American
Beauty)
Modern Portia, A 12 (Lubin); 13
(Pathé)
Modern Romeo, A 14 (American
Kinema)
Modern Shylock, A 11 (Urban-
Eclipse)
Monkey Romeo, A 24 (Fox)
Much Ado About Nothing 09 (Es-
sanay); 13 (Crystal); 13 (Cricks
and Martin)
Nina of the Theatre 14 (Kalem)
Othello 02 (V); 07 (Cines); 07 (Mas-
ters); 08 (V); 08 (Pathé); 08 Nor-
disk); 09 (Cines); 09 (Pineschi);
09 (Film d'Art); 14 (Ambrosio);

18 (Max Mack Film); 20 (Hep-
worth); 20 (Caesar); 22 (Worner
Film)
Othello in Jonesville 13 (Edison)
Passing of the Third Floor Back 18
(Walturdow)
Perfect Flapper 24 (FN)
Picture of Dorian Gray, The 15
(Thiemann and Reinhardt)
Pimple as Hamlet 16 (Piccadilly)
Polly of the Follies 22 (FN)
Prairie Romeo, A 17 (Un)
Princess in the Tower 14 (Hepworth)
Queenie of the Nile 15 (Lubin)
Racing Romeo, A 27 (FBO)
Real Thing at Last, The 16 (British
Actors Film Co.)
Reckless Romeo, A 17 (Par)
La Reine Elisabeth 12 (L'Historionis
Film)
Richard III 08 (V); 11 (Co-operative);
13 (Sterling)
Ridin' Romeo, A 21 (Fox)
Rival Romeos 28 (Un)
Roameo (Cartoon) 27 (Educational)
Roaming Romeo, A 16 (Victor)
Romeo and Julia im Schnee 20 (Max-
im/UFA)
Romeo and Julia 08 (Gaumont); 08
(V); 08 (Cines); 03; 11 (Film
d'Art); 11 (Thanhauser); 14 (Bio-
graph); 15 (Pathé); 15 (Cricks and
Martin); 16 (Fox); 16 (Metro); 17
(Savoia); 17 (Educational); 18
(Crystal); 19 (Hepworth); 20 (Un);
20 (Christie); 24 (Sennett)
Romeo and Juliet at the Seaside 10
(Messter)
Romeo and Juliet in Town 10 (Selig)
Romeo Geht im Kino 14 (Comica)
Romeo in Pajamas 13 (Solax); 22; 29
Romeo in the Stone Age 28 (Pathé)
Romeo Mixup 24 (Arrow)
Romeo of the Coal Wagon 16 (Kalem)
Romeo Turns Bandit 10 (Pathé)
Romeo und Julia 09 (Deutsche Vita-
scope)
Romeo's Dad 20 (Un)
Roping Her Romeo 17 (Par)
Rural Hamlet, A 17 (L-KO)
Rural Romeo, A 10 (Imp)
Rural Romeos 14 (Luna)
Sage Brush Hamlet, A 19 (Exhibitors
Mutual)
Schatten eine Nachtliche Halluzintion
22 (Dafu)
Seashore Romeo, A 15 (Rex)
Seaside Romeos 17 (Kalem)

Seven Ages 05 (Edison)
Seven Ages of Man, The 14 (Planet)
Shades of Shakespeare 19 (Christie)
Shakespeare Writing Julius Caesar
    07 (Mélies)
Shylock 13 (Eclipse)
Shylock of Wall Street 22 (Burton
    King)
Der Shylock von Krakau /aka/
    The Jew 13 (Projections-A. G.
    Union)
Something Rotten in Havana 13 (Es-
    sanay)
Spanish Romeo, A 25 (Fox)
Lo Spettro de Iago 12 (Aeguila)
Taming Mrs. Shrew 12 (Rex)
Taming of the Shrew, The 08 (Bio-
    graph); 08 (Pineschi); 11 (Co-op-
    erative); 11 (Nordisk); 11 (Eclipse);
    13 (Ambrosio); 14 (Nordisk); 15
    (Davidson); 15 (British and Colo-
    nial); 16 (Unicorn Film Service)
Taming of the Shrewd, The 12
    (Knickerbocker)
Tempest, The 05 (Urban); 08 (Cla-
    rendon); 11 (Thanhauser); 12
    (Eclair); 14 (Prieur); 27 (UA); 29
    (Wukfu); 21 (Pathé)
To Be Or Not to Be 16 (Beauty)
Triumph 24 (Famous Players/Lasky)
Tropical Romeo, A 23 (Fox)
Trouper, The 22 (Un)
Tugboat Romeo, A 16 (Triangle/
    Keystone)
Twelfth Night 10 (V)
Two Little Dromios 14 (Thanhauser)
Two Small Town Romeos 17 (Nestor)
Wet Paint 26 (Famous Players/Lasky)
When Macbeth Came to Snakeville 14
    (Essanay)
When Two Hearts Are Won 11 (Ka-
    lem)
Wie Einst im Mai 26 (Richter)
Winter's Tale, A 09 (Edison); 10
    (Thanhauser); 10 (Cines); 13 (Mi-
    lano); 14 (Belle Alliance)
Would Be Romeo, A 13 (Punch)

5470
SHANNAW, Phyllis*
Fifth Form at St. Dominic's (Nancy
    Sevios)

5471
SHANNON, Effie (1867-1954)
Blazing Barriers
Mama's Affair
Man Who Played God, The

New Commandment, The
Roulette
Sally of the Sawdust (Mrs. Foster)
Secrets of Paris
Side Show of Life, The
Sinners in Heaven
Soul Fire
Sure-Fire Flint
Three Weeks
Tie That Binds, The
Wandering Fires (Mrs. Satorius)
Stage:
L'Aiglon (Empress Maria Louisa) 27
Detour, The (Helen) 21
Good Boy (Ma Meakin) 28
Heartbreak House (Hesione Hushabye)
    20
Her Unborn Child (Mrs. Kennedy) 28
House of Fear, The (Madame Zita)
    29
In His Arms (Mrs. Arthur Fairleigh)
    24
Mama's Affair (Mrs. Orrin) 20
Merry Andrew (Ernestine Aiken) 29
Other Rose, The (Mrs. Mason) 23
Pearl of Great Price, The (pilgrim's
    mother) 26
She Stoops to Conquer (Mrs. Hard-
    castle) 24
Trelawney of the Wells (Miss Trafal-
    gar Gower) 27

5472
SHANNON, Ethel*
Babe Comes Home
Beware of the Bride
Birth of the Gods
Buckaroo Kid, The
Charley's Aunt (Ela Delahay)
Daughters of the Rich
Great Hope, The
High Flyer, The
Master Stroke, A
Maytime (Ottilie Van Zandt)
Oh, Baby!
Old-Fashioned Boy, An
Sign of the Claw, The
Silent Power
Stop Flirting
Texas Trail, The

5473
SHANNON, Frank*
Icebound
Monsieur Beaucaire (Badger)
Stage:
Anna Christie (Mat Burke) 21
Brass Buttons (Dan Flynn) 27

Common Sin, The (Donlin) 28
Elmer Gantry (Father Harvey) 28
Hangman's House (John D'Arcy) 26
Patriot, The (Stephan) 28
Twelve Miles Out (Michael McCue)
 25
Undercurrent, The (Tom Flanagan)
 25
White Desert (Michael Kane) 23

5474
SHANOR, Peggy*
Mystery Mind, The [serial]

5475
SHARKEY, Sailor*
Capital Punishment (convict)
Good Morning, Judge

5476
SHARLAND, Reginald*
Show of Shows, The
Woman to Woman

5477
SHARTELS, Wally*
Bath Between, The

5478
SHATERNIKOVA, Nina*
Khveska /aka/ Bolnichny Starozh
 Khveska; Hospital Guard

5479
SHATTUCK, Truly*
Beauty's Worth (Mrs. Garrison)
Rubber Heels

5480
SHAVROVA, Tamaia*
Love of Zero, The

5481
SHAW, Brinsley*
Four Horsemen of the Apocalypse,
 The (Celendonic)
Prince of Pep, The
Stage:
Sherlock Holmes (John Forman) 29

5482
SHAW, George Bernard (1856-1950)
Shaw Talks for Movietone News

5483
SHAW, Lewis*
Two Little Vagabonds (Dick)

5484
SHAW, Montague (1884-1968)
Behind that Curtain (Hilary Gatt)
Morgan's Raiders /aka/ Morgan's
 Last Raid
Water Hole, The (Mr. Endicott)
Stage:
Sherlock Holmes (James Larrabee) 29
Soldiers and Women (Col. John Rit-
 chie) 29

5485
SHAW, Oscar*
Cocoanuts, The
Great White Way, The
King on Main Street, The
Subway Sadie
Upstage
Stage:
Dear Sir (Laddie Munn) 24
Five O'Clock Girl, The (Gerald
 Brooks) 27
Good Morning, Dearie (Billy Van
 Cortlandt) 21
Half-Moon, The (Bradford Adams) 20
Lambs Gambol
Music Box Revue (a principal)
Oh, Kay! (Jimmy Winter) 26
One Kiss (Bastien) 23
Two Little Girls in Blue (Robert
 Barker) 21

5486
SHAW, Peggy*
Ballyhoo Buster, The
In Hollywood with Potash and Perl-
 mutter
Little Child Shall Lead Them, A
Skid Proof
Subway Sadie
Winner Take All

5487
SHAY, William E. *
Telephone Girl

5488
SHEA, Olive*
Glorifying the American Girl

5489
SHEAN, Al (Alfred Schoenberg)
 (1868-1949)
Around the Town
Record:
Mr. Gallagher and Mr. Shean
 (B-26728-2) (LPV560)

Stage:
Betsy (Stonewall Moskowitz) 26
Vaudeville [Palace] 27; 28; 29

5490
SHEARER, Norma (Edith Norma
Shearer) (1900-) Born in
Montreal, Canada on August 10,
1900. Has brown hair, blue-
grey eyes and is 5'1" tall.
Married Irving Thalberg 1927,
widowed 1936. Two children:
Irving, Jr. and Katharine. Mar-
ried Martin Arouge in 1942.
Academy Award nominations:
The Divorcee 1929-30 (Won); A
Free Soul 1930-31; The Barretts
of Wimpole Street 1934; Romeo
and Juliet 1936; and Marie An-
toinette 1938.
Actress, The
After Midnight
Blue Waters (Squaw)
Bootleggers, The
Broadway after Dark
Broken Barriers
Channing of the Northwest
Clouded Name, A
Demi-Bride, The
Devil's Circus, The
Devil's Partner, The
Divorcee, The
Empty Hands
End of the World, The
Excuse Me
Flapper, The (debut as an extra)
He Who Gets Slapped (Consuelo)
His Secretary
Hollywood Revue of 1929 (Juliet)
Lady of Chance, A
Lady of the Night (dual role)
Last of Mrs. Cheyney, The (Mrs.
Cheyney)
Latest from Paris, The
Leather Pushers, The [series]
Lucretia Lombard
Man and Wife
Man Who Paid, The
Married Flirts
Metro player 23
Pleasure Mad
Pretty Ladies
Restless Sex, The
Sign on the Door, The
Slave of Fashion, A
Snob, The
Stealers, The
Student Prince, The (Katchen)

Their Own Desire
Tower of Lies, The (Goldie)
Trail of the Law
Trelawney of the Wells (Rose Tre-
lawney)
Trial of Mary Dugan, The (Mary
Dugan)
Upstage
Waking Up the Town
Waning Sex, The
Wanters, The
Way Down East (extra)
Wolf Man, The

5491
SHEFFIELD, Reginald (1901-1957)
Adorable Cheat, The
Classmates
Green Goddess, The (Lt. Carew)
Interference
Pinch Hitter, The (Alexis Thompson)
Sweet Sixteen
White Mice (Peter de Peyster)
Winning Through (Bert Stafford)
Stage:
Hay Fever (Sandy Tyrell) 25
Helena's Boys (Henry) 24
Pearl of Great Price, The (Love) 26
Slaves All (George Squitch) 26
Soldiers and Women (Lt. Mason) 29
Way Things Happen, The (Chussie
Hare) 24
Youth (Stephen Hartwig) 20

5492
SHELBY, Margaret*
Jenny, Be Good

5493
SHELDON, James*
Over the Hill (Charles, the boy)

5494
SHELLY, Maxine*
Win that Girl

5495
SHELTON, Eleanor
Little French Girl, The

5496
SHELTON, Maria*
Manhandled (model)
Society Scandal, A (Marjorie's friend)

5497
SHEPLEY, Ruth (1889-)
When Knighthood Was In Flower
(Lady Jane Bobingbroke)

Stage:
Cape Smoke (Catherine Bradbroke) 25
Her Salary Man (Emily Sladen) 21
New York (Madeline Conway) 27
Squealer, The (Dora Deane) 28

5498
SHERART, Georgia*
Vanity Fair (Miss Briggs)

5499
SHERIDAN, Ann*
Wedding Bells

5500
SHERIDAN, Frank*
Daughter of Two Worlds, A
Fast Life, The (the warden)
Man Next Door, The
One Exciting Night (detective)
Side Street
Stage:
Everyday (Judge Nolan) 21
Law Breaker, The (Father Spalding)
     22
Madeleine and the Movies (Callahan)
     22
Virtue (Robert Duncan) 22

5501
SHERMAN, Evelyn*
Blonde or Brunette?
Proud Flesh
Suzanna

5502
SHERMAN, Jane*
Hunchback of Notre Dame, The
Merry-Go-Round, The (Marie)

5503
SHERMAN, Lois*
Reckless Lady, The

5504
SHERMAN, Lowell (1885-1934)
Angel Face
Convoy
Divine Woman, The (Legrande)
Evidence
Face in the Fog, The
First National player 23
Garden of Eden
General Crack (Leopold II of Austria)
Gilded Lily, The (Creighton Howard)
Girl from Gay Paree, The
Grand Larceny
Heart of a Follies Girl, The

Lady of Chance, A
Lost at Sea
Love Toy, The
Mad Hour, The
Midnight Mystery, The
Molly-O
Monsieur Beaucaire (Louis XV)
Nearly Divorced
New York Idea, The
Reckless Lady, The
Satan in Sables
Scarlet Dove, The
Way Down East (Lennox Sanderson)
Whip, The (Baron)
Whip Woman
Wilderness Woman, The
What No Man Knows
Yes or No?
You Never Know Women
Stage:
Casanova (Chevalier de Seingalt Gia-
     como Casanova) 23
Fool, The ("Jerry" Goodkind) 22
High Stakes (Joe Lennon) 24
Lawful Larceny (Guy Tarlow) 22
Leah Kleschna (Raul Berton) 24
Man's Name, The (Hal Marvin) 21
Masked Woman, The (Baron Tolento)
     22
Morphis (Julian Wade) 23
Vaudeville [Palace] 27
Woman Disputed, A (Capt. Freidrich
     Von Hartmann) 26

5505
SHERMAN SISTERS, The
Daring Years, The (Moran girls)

5506
SHERON, André*
Love Parade, The (LeMaré)

5507
SHERRY, Craighall*
Spione [Spies]

5508
SHERRY, J. Barney (1874-)
Barbarian, The
Born Rich
Breath of the Gods
Broadway Scandals
Brown Derby, The
Crackerjack, The
Dinty
Forged Bride, The
Forgotten Faces
Go and Get It

Jazz Heaven
Lying Wives
Man-Woman-Marriage
Miami
Occasionally Yours
Play Ball [serial]
Prince of Tempters, The
River's End, The
Spider Web, The
Victorious Defeat
Warrens of Virginia (General Lee)
White Sister, The (Monsignor Sara-
  cinesca)

5509
SHERWOOD, C. L. *
Sporting Youth
Two Girls Wanted

5510
SHERWOOD, Henry*
Broadway Nights
Stage:
Broadway (Dolph) 26
City Haul (Tony Scaranza) 29
Elmer Gantry (Oscar Dowling) 28

5511
SHERWOOD, Yorke*
Gentlemen Prefer Blondes (Mr. Jen-
  nings)

5512
SHIELDS, Ernest*
Chinatown Mystery, The [serial]
Detectives Wanted
Hired and Fired
Ladder Jinx, The
Purple Riders, The [serial] (General
  March)

5513
SHIELS, Una*
Irish Destiny

5514
SHINE, Billy*
Under the Greenwood Tree (Leaf)

5515
SHINE, Wilfred E. *
Under the Greenwood Tree (Parson
  Maybold)

5516
SHIPMAN, Nell (1892-1970)
Back to God's Country
Girl from God's Country, The

Golden Yukon
Grub Stake, The

5517
SHIRLEY, Anne (Dawn Evelyeen
  Paris) /aka/ Dawn O'Day (1918-)
As: Dawn O'Day
Callahans and the Murphys, The
  (Mary Callahan)
Fast Set, The (Little Margaret Sones)
Four Devils (Marion as a child)
Hidden Woman, The (debut as a girl)
Man Who Fights Alone, The (Dorothy)
Moonshine Valley (Nancy as a child)
Mother Knows Best (Sally as a child)
Night Life (war profiteer's daughter)
Riders of the Purple Sage (Fay Lar-
  kin)
Rustle of Silk, The (girl)
Sins of the Father (Mary as a girl)
Spanish Dancer, The (Don Balthazar
  Carlos)

5518
SHIRLEY, Dorinea*
Calude Duval (Moll Crisp)
Nell Gwyn (Maid of Honor)

5519
SHORES, Lynn*
Sally of the Scandals
Sally's Shoulder
Skinner's Big Idea
Stolen Love

5520
SHORT, Antrim*
Beauty's Worth (Tommy)
Black Beauty
Classmates
Cressy
Married? (Chuck English)
O'Malley of the Mounted
Pinch Hitter, The (Jimmy Slater)
Right of Way, The
Son of Wallingford ("Toad" Edward
  Jessup)
Wildfire
Winning Through (Jones)
Stage:
Carnival (Fred Spalding) 29

5521
SHORT, Florence*
Idol Dancer, The (Pansy)
Lessons in Love
Love Flower, The (Mrs. Bevan)
Way Down East (eccentric aunt)

Stage:
Drifting (Mrs. Polly VonFrances) 22
Romance (Signora Vanucci) 21
Starlight (Mama Bourgevin) 25
To-Night at 12 (Ellen) 28

5522
SHORT, Gertrude (1902-1968)
Adam and Evil
Beggar on Horseback
Cinderella's Twin
Code of the West (Mollie Thurman)
Cowboy and the Lady, The
Gold Diggers (Topsy St. John)
Gold Diggers of Broadway (Topsy)
Ladies at Ease
Masked Woman
My Lady's Lips (Crook girl)
Narrow Street, The
None but the Brave
Polly of the Movies
Prisoner, The
Rent Free
She Couldn't Help It
Show, The
Sweet Adeline
Sweet Lavender
Talker, The
Tessie
Tillie the Toiler (Bubbles)
Trial Marriage
Women's Wares
You Never Can Tell
Youth to Youth

5523
SHORT, Harry*
Just Suppose
Stage:
China Rose (Hi) 25
It's Up to You (Jim Duke) 21
Kid Boots (Peter Pillsbury) 24
Nic-Nax of 1926 (a principal) 26
Sidewalks of New York (governor) 27
Ziegfeld Follies (a principal) 23

5524
SHORT, Hassard*
Woman's Place, A

5525
SHORT, Lou (1875-   )
Big City, The (O'Hara)
Blue Eagle, The (Capt. McCarthy)
Blue Pearl, The
Girl in the Show, A
Last of the Mohicans, The
Leatherstocking [serial]

5526
SHOTWELL, Marie*
Blackbirds
Chains of Evidence
Civilian Clothes (Mrs. Smythe)
Evil Eyes, The [serial]
Harvest Moon, The
Her Lord and Master
Lovers in Quarantine
Manicure Girl, The
Master Mind, The
One Woman to Another
Running Wild (Mrs. Finch)
Sally of the Sawdust (society leader)
Shackles of Gold
Shore Leave

5527
SHRAM, Violet*
Riders of the Dawn

5528
SHTRAUKH, Maxim*
Stachka /aka/ Strike

5529
SHU-HU*
Veil of Happiness, The

5530
SHULTZ, Harry*
One Stolen Night

5531
SHUMAN, Harry*
Red Raiders, The

5532
SHUMLEY, Walter*
Greater Glory, The

5533
SHUMWAY, Lee C. /aka/ L. C.
   Shumway (1884-   )
Air Mail, The
Alarm, The
Bat, The (the unknown)
Beggar in Purple
Big Adventure, The
Brawn of the North
Catch as Catch Can
Checkered Flag
Conflict
Evangeline
Gamesters, The
Great Mail Robbery, The
Handsome Brute, The
Hearts Aflame

His Foreign Wife
Hit of the Show
House of Scandal, The
Introduce Me
Last Trail, The
Leatherneck, The
Let It Rain
Lure of the Jade
Million for Love, A
Night Parade
One Minute to Play
Over the Border
Price of Success
Queen of the Nightclubs
Sign of the Claw, The
So This Is College
Society Secrets
Son of the Golden West
South Sea Love
Speed Maniac, The
Step on It
To Please One Woman
Torrent, The
Valley of Hunted Men
When Dawn Came
Whispering Canyon
Yankee Consul, The

5534
SHUMWAY, Walter*
Pretty Ladies
Wine (Revenue Officer)

5535
SIBERSKAIA, Nadia*
Blighty
Menilmontant

5536
SIDMAN, Sam*
Daring Years, The (Curly)
Stage:
Antonia (a profiteer) 25
Humoresque (Abraham Kantor) 23
Just a Minute (Louis Schultz) 28

5537
SIDNEY, George (Sammy Greenfield)
  (1878-1945)
Auctioneer, The
Clancy's Kosher Wedding
Classified
Cohens and the Kellys, The
Cohens and the Kellys in Atlantic
  City, The
Cohens and the Kellys in Paris, The
Flying Romeos
For the Love of Mike (Abraham Katz)

Give and Take
In Hollywood with Potash and Perl-
  mutter
Latest from Paris, The
Life of Riley, The
Lost at the Front
Millionaires
Partners Again /aka/ Partners
  Again with Potash and Perlmutter
Potash and Perlmutter
Prince of Pilson, The
Sweet Daddies
Universal player 24
We Americans
Stage:
Give and Take (Albert Kruger) 23
Vaudeville [Palace] 28
Welcome Stranger (Isidor Solomon) 20

5538
SIDNEY, Sylvia (Sophia Kosow)
  (1910-)
Broadway Nights (herself)
Through Different Eyes (dual role,
  Valerie Briand/Elsie Smith)
Stage:
Bad Girl (Dot) 29
Breaks, The (Amy) 28
Challenge of Youth, The (Washington)
  26
Crime (Annabelle Porter) 27
Cross Roads (Patricia) 29
Denver Colorado Stock Company 28
George Cukor Stock Company 28
Gods of the Lightning (Rosalie) 28
Many-A-Ship (Patsy Coster) 29
Mirrors (Mary Norton) 28
Nice Women (Elizabeth Gerard) 29
Prunella 26
Squall, The (Anita)
Stock in Rochester New York 29

5539
SIEGEL, Bernard*
Beau Geste (Schawartz)
Crimson Runner, The
Dead Men Tell No Tales
Desert Gold (Goat Herder)
Divine Sinner, The (Johann Ludwig)
Heart of Maryland, The
Land of Hope, The
Laugh, Clown, Laugh (Simon)
Next Corner, The (the stranger)
Phantom of the Opera, The (Joseph
  Buquet)
Redskin, The (Chahi)
Rescue, The
Romance Ranch

Sea Fury
Stand and Deliver (blind operator)
Vanishing American, The /aka/ The
    Vanishing Race
Wild Horse Mesa

5540
SIEGMANN, George--see: George
    Seigmann

5541
SIGNORET, Gabriel*
Two Little Vagabonds (Bill Mullins
    alias "The Gaffer")

5542
SIKLA, Ferry*
Tragödie der Liebe [Tragedy of
    Love]

5543
SILBERT, Liza /aka/ Lisa*
Broken Hearts
Stage:
Mendel, Inc. (Zelde) 29

5544
SILBERT, Theodore*
Broken Hearts

5545
SILLS, Milton (1882-1930)
Adam's Rib (Michael Ramsay)
As Man Desires
At the End of the World
Barker, The
Behold My Wife
Borderland
Burning Daylight
Burning Sands
Circus Life
Crash, The
Dangerous Men
Environment, The
Faith Healer, The
Fire Patrol, The
Flaming Youth
Flowing Gold
Framed
Furnace
Great Moment, The (Bayard Delavel)
Hard Boiled Haggerty
Hawk's Nest
Heart Bandit, The
His Captive Woman
I Want My Man
Isle of Lost Ships (Frank Howard)
Knockout, The

Lady of Quality, A
Last Hour, The
Legally Dead
Little Fool
Love and the Devil
Madonna of the Streets, A (John Mor-
    ton)
Making of O'Malley, The
Marriage Chance, The
Marriage Gamble, The
Men of Steel
Miss Lulu Bett (Neil Cornish)
One Clear Call
Paradise
Puppets
Salvage (Fred Martin)
Sea Hawk, The (dual role, Sir Oliver
    Tressilion/Sakr-el-Bahr)
Sea Tiger, The
Silent Lover, The
Single Wives
Skin Deep
Spoilers, The (Roy Glennister)
Sweet Lavender
Unguarded Hour, The
Valley of the Giants, The
Weekend, The
What a Wife Learned
Why Women Remarry
Woman Who Walked Alone, The

5546
SILLY SYMPHONIES (Cartoons)
Hell's Bells
Jungle Rhythm
Merry Dwarfs, The
Skeleton Dance
Springtime

5547
SILVAIN, Falconetti*
Passion of Joan of Arc, The

5548
SILVERMAN, Dave*
Show of Shows, The

5549
SILVERS, Lou*
Show of Shows, The

5550
SILVERS, Sid (1908-   )
Show of Shows, The
Stage:
Artists and Models 25
Night in Spain, A (a principal) 27
Vaudeville [Palace] 28

5551
SIMA, Oskar*
Die Frau, Nach du Man Sich Sehnt
 [The Woman One Longs For]
 /aka/ Three Loves (Charles
 Leblanc)
Gefahren der Brautzeit [Dangers of
 the Engagement Period] /aka/
 Aus dem Tagebuch eines Verführ-
 rers; Eine Nacht der Liebe;
 Liebesnächte; Liebersbriefe (bit)

5552
SIMMONS, H. C.*
Into Her Kingdom

5553
SIMON, Michel (Francois Simon)*
Feu Mathias Pascal
Passion of Joan of Arc, The

5554
SIMON, S. S.*
Barker, The
Greed

5555
SIMON-GIRARD, Aimé*
Milady
Three Musketeers, The (D'Artagnan)

5556
SIMONX, S. S.--see: S. S. Simon

5557
SIMPSON, Allan*
Bertha, the Sewing Machine Girl
Exciters, The
Padlocked
School for Wives
Sea Horses (Harvey)
Society Scandal, A (Hector Colbert)
Wages of Virtue, The

5558
SIMPSON, Dr.*
Cupid, Cowpuncher

5559
SIMPSON, Ivan F. (1875-)
Disraeli (Hugh Myers)
Evidence
Green Goddess, The (Watkins)
Kiss for Cinderella, A (Mr. Cutaway)
Lovers in Quarantine
Man Who Played God, The
Miss Bluebeard
Twenty Dollars a Week

Twenty-One
Wild, Wild Susan
Womanhandled
Stage:
Charm School, The (David MacKen-
 zie) 20
Command Performance, The (Paul
 Mascoch) 28
Garden of Eden, The (Uncle Herbert)
 27
Green Goddess, The (Watkins) 21
Julius Caesar (a soothsayer) 27
Old English (Joseph Pillin) 24
Perfect Alibi, The (Edward Laverick)
 28
Rollo's Wild Oat (Hewston) 20
Way Things Happen, The (Bennett
 Lomax) 24

5560
SIMPSON, Russell (1880-1959)
Across the Deadline
Annie Laurie /aka/ Ladies from
 Hell (Sandy)
Barrier, The
Branding Iron, The (John Carver)
Bunty Pulls the Strings
Bush Ranger, The
Circus Days
Deadlier Sex, The
Faint Perfume (Grandpa Crumb)
First Alto, The
Fools of Fortune
Girl of the Golden West, The
Godless Men
God's Great Wilderness
Hand Me Down, The
Heart of the Yukon
Hearts Aflame
Human Hearts
Innocents of Paris (Emile Leval)
Kid's Clever, The
Kingdom Within, The
Lahoma
Life's Mockery
Lovey Mary
My Lady's Past
Narrow Street, The
Noisy Neighbors
Old Shoes
Out of the Dust
Painted People
Peg O' My Heart (Jim O'Connell)
Rags to Riches
Rip Tide
Rustlin' for Cupid
Sap, The
Shadows of Conscience, The

Sinclair   490

Ship of Souls
Snow Blind
Social Highwayman
Splendid Road, The
Trail of '98, The (Old Swede)
Tropical Midnights
Under the Lash (Simeon Krillet)
Virginian, The
We're in the Air Now
Wild Geese

5561
SINCLAIR, Eleanor*
Under the Red Robe

5562
SINCLAIR, Jerry*
Get Rich Quick Wallingford (Judge
    Lampton)
So's Your Old Man (Al)

5563
SINCLAIR, Johnny*
Royal Rider

5564
SINCLAIR, Maud*
Restless Wives
Stage:
Advertising of Kate, The (Miss Wan-
    da) 22
Other Rose, The (Etty Doolittle) 23
Salvation (Third Woman) 28
Six Characters in Search of an
    Author (the character woman) 22

5565
SINCLAIR, Ruth*
Masquerader, The

5566
SINDING, Ellen*
Syv Dager for Elisabeth

5567
SINGER, Jack*
Applause (producer)

5568
SINGH, Ram*
Beau Geste

5569
SINGLETON, Joe E. *
Great Redeemer, The
Mad Whirl, The
Skin Deep
Toll Gate, The (Jordan)
Treasure Island (Israel Hands)

5570
SIPPERLY, Ralph*
Blue Eagle, The (Slats Mulligan)
Sunrise (the barber)

5571
SISCART, Solango*
Living Dead Man, The

5572
SISSON, Vera (1895-)
Bolted Door, The
Love 'em and Leave 'em
Man from Nowhere, The
Married Virgin, The /aka/ Frivolous
    Wives

5573
SJÖSTRON, Victor (1879-1960)
Ardet (the Word)
Man There Was, A
Stroke of Midnight, The
Thy Soul Shall Bear Witness

5574
SKELLY, Hal (1891-1934)
Dance of Life, The (Skid Johnson)
Woman Trap
Stage:
Betty Lee (Wallingford Speed) 24
Burlesque (Skid) 27
Girl in the Spotlight, The (Watchen
    Tripp) 20
Lambs Gambol
Mary Jane McKane (Joe McGillicudy)
    23
Night Boat, The (Freddie Ides) 20
Orange Blossoms (Jimmy Flynn) 22
Vaudeville [Palace] 25; 26

5575
SKETCHLEY, Leslie*
Tiger Rose (mounted police officer)

5576
SKINNER, Marion*
Stranger, The

5577
SKINNER, Otis (1858-1942)
First National player 29
Kismet
Mr. Antonio
Romance
Stage:
Blood and Sand (Juan Gallardo) 21
Henry IV, Part I (Sir John Falstaff)
    26
Honor of the Family, The (Col.

Philippe Bridau) 26
Hundred Years Old, A (Papa Juan)
29
Pietro (dual role, Pietro Barbano/
Peter Barban) 20
Sancho Panza (Title role) 23

5578
SKIPWORTH, Alison (1875-1952)
Circle, The
Handcuffs or Kisses
Strictly Unconventional
Stage:
Angela (Queen Ferdinande) 28
Ashes of Love (Mrs. Headfort
Blythe) 26
Button, Button (Rita Weed) 29
Buy, Buy, Baby (Esmeralda Pottle)
26
Cafe de Danse (Tomasa) 29
Enchanted April, The (Mrs. Fisher)
25
Garden of Eden, The (Rosa) 27
Grand Duchess and the Waiter, The
(Countess Avaloff) 25
Julie (Maman) 27
Lilies of the Field (Florette Ellwood)
21
Los Angeles (Mrs. Jones) 27
New York Exchange (Mrs. Ella May
Morton) 26
Port O' London (Harriet Pook) 26
Primer for Lovers, A (Jessica
Featherston) 29
Say When (Countess Scaracchi) 28
Spellbound (Mrs. Bateson) 27
Swan, The (Princess Maria Domini-
ca) 23
Torch Bearers, The (Mrs. J. Duro
Pampinelli) 22

5579
SKURKOY, Mary*
Greatest Love of All, The

5580
SLATER, Bob*
Brown Derby, The

5581
SLATER BROTHERS, The
Happy Days (principals)

5582
SLATER, Frank*
Fifth Form At St. Dominic's (Raleigh
of the Sixth)

5583
SLATTER, Charles*
White Moll, The

5584
SLATTERY, Charles*
Dangerous Money (O'Hara)
Dream Street (Police Inspector)
Lunatic at Large, A
Ragged Edge, The
Rapids, The
Stage:
Black Velvet (Smith) 27
Chicago (Sgt. Murdock) 26
City Haul (Mark Moore) 29
Clutching Claw, The (Patrolman
Cairnes) 28
Crooks' Convention, The (Smith) 29
Mr. Moneypenny (triple role, Murphy/
Mr. Rich/The End) 28
Piker, The (Broderick) 25

5585
SLEEMAN, Philip*
After Midnight
Cop, The
So This Is Marriage

5586
SLEEPER, Martha (1901-)
Air Legion, The
Crazy Like a Fox
Danger Street
Little Yellow House, The
Long Live the King
Mail Man, The
Should Tall Men Marry?
Skinner's Big Idea
Taxi Thirteen
Voice of the Storm
Stage:
Stepping Out (Madge Horton) 29

5587
SLEZAK, Walter (1902-)
Chained
Queen of Sin and the Spectacle of
Sodom and Gomorrah
Stage:
Viennese musical comedy 29

5588
SLIPPERY, Ralph*
Six Cylinder Love

5589
SLOAN, Ted*
Hot Heels
When Romance Rides

5590
SMALLEY, Phillips (1870-   )
Awful Truth, The
Blindfolded
Border Patrol
Broadway Daddies
Broken Gates
Case of Mary Brown, The
Charley's Aunt (Sir Francis Clesney)
Daughters of Today
Fatal Warning, The [serial]
Flaming Youth
For Sale (Mr. Winslow)
High Voltage (J. Milton Hendrickson)
Honeymoon Flats
Irresistible Love
Man Crazy
Money Talks
Peacock Alley
Queen of Diamonds
Sensation Seekers
Single Wives
Soul Mates
Stage Kisses
Taxi Mystery, The
Tea for Three
Too Many Crooks
True Heaven

5591
SMIAH, C. C. *
Ranson's Folly

5592
SMIDD, Gorm*
David Copperfield

5593
SMILES, Finch*
Behind that Curtain (Gatt's clerk)
For Sale (the butler)
Last of Mrs. Cheney, The (William)
Lost World, The (Austin)
Love Thrill, The
Teaser, The

5594
SMILEY, Joseph W. *
Aloma of the South Seas (Andrew
    Taylor)
Old Home Week
Potters, The (Rankin)
Show-Off, The
Untamed Lady (Uncle George)
Wild, Wild Susan
Stage:
Talk About Girls (George V. Grubble)
    27

5595
SMIRNOVA, Dina*
Coffin Maker, The
She Goes to War

5596
SMITH, Anderson*
Darling of New York, The

5597
SMITH, Buddy*
Only Thing, The
Roughneck, The

5598
SMITH, C. Aubrey (Charles Aubrey
    Smith) (1863-1948)
Bohemian Girl, The (Devilshoof)
Bump, The
Castles in Spain
Face at the Window, The (detective)
Flame of Passion
Rejected Woman, The
Temptation of Carlton Earle, The
Unwanted
Stage:
Bachelor Father, The (Sir Basil Win-
    terton) 28

5599
SMITH, Charles*
General, The (Mr. Lee)

5600
SMITH, Cyril (1892-1963)
British films 20's

5601
SMITH, D. A. Clarke*
Atlantic [English] (Tate Hughes)

5602
SMITH, Donald*
Marriage Playground, The (Chip)

5603
SMITH, Dudley*
Circus Ace, The

5604
SMITH, Gerald Oliver*
School for Wives
Stage:
Lady Be Good (Bertie Bassett) 24
Mike Angelo (Tommy Sloane) 23
Oh, Kay! (the Duke) 26
Silent House, The (Philip Barty) 28
Wait Till We're Married (Marshall) 21

5605
SMITH, "Gunboat"*
Great Gatsby, The (Bert)
Let's Get Married
Lucky Devil, The
Manhattan
Say It Again
Shock Punch, The
We're All Gamblers
Wings (a sergeant)

5606
SMITH, H. Reeves*
Return of Sherlock Holmes (Dr. Watson)
Stage:
Sporting Thing to Do, The (Jim
    Loundsbury) 23

5607
SMITH, Jay R.*
Moan and Groan, Inc.

5608
SMITH, Joe (Joe Seltzer)*
Paramount player 29
Warner Brothers player 29
Stage:
Mendel, Inc. (Bernard Shnaps) 29
Sidewalks of New York (Moe Zimmer-
    mann) 27
Synthetic Sin (stage doorman) 27
Vaudeville [Palace] 29
Whirl of New York, The (I. Ketchum)
    21

5609
SMITH, L.*
Mademoiselle from Armentieres (the
    sergeant)

5610
SMITH, Leigh R.*
Down to the Sea in Ships ("Scuff"
    Smith)

5611
SMITH, Nayland*
Coughing Horror, The

5612
SMITH, Oscar*
At Yale
Beau Sabreur (Djikki)
Canary Murder Case, The (stuttering
    bellboy)
Close Harmony
Dangerous Curves (bartender)

Man Power
Marriage Clause, The
Wizard, The

5613
SMITH, Sid*
Hallroom Boys Comedies (Percy)
His First Flat Tire
Lizzies of the Field
Ne'r Do-Well, The
Water Wagons

5614
SMITH, Stanley*
Sophomore, The
Sweetie (Biff Bentley)

5615
SMITH, Ted*
Happy Days (chorus)

5616
SMITH, Vivian*
Hearts in Dixie

5617
SMITH, Whispering Jack*
Happy Days (a principal)

5618
SNEGOFF, Leonid*
Broken Hearts
Forbidden Woman, The
Stage:
First Law, The (Vladimir) 29

5619
SNOW, Marguerite (1888-1958)
Felix O'Day
Lavender and Old Lace
Veiled Woman, The
Woman in Room 13, The

5620
SNOW, Mortimer*
When Knighthood Was in Flower (bit)

5621
SNOWDEN, Carolynne*
First Year, The
In Old Kentucky
Marriage Clause, The
Movietone Follies of 1929
Orchids and Ermine

5622
SOAMES, Arthur*
Tale of Two Worlds, A (Dr. New-
    comb)

5623
SOBOLEVSKY, Pyotr*
New Babylon

5624
SOJIN, Kamiyama (1891-1954)
Across the Pacific
All Aboard
Bat, The (Billy)
Careers
China Slaver
Chinatown Charlie
Chinese Parrot, The (Charlie Chan)
City of Sin
Devil Dancer, The
Diplomacy
East of Suez
Eve's Leaves
Foreign Devils
Haunted Ship, The
Hawk's Nest, The
King of Kings, The (Prince of Per-
   sia)
Lady of the Harem
Lucky Lady, The
Man Without a Face, The [serial]
My Lady's Lips (Oriental)
Old San Francisco
Out with the Tide
Proud Flesh
Rescue, The
Road to Mandalay, The
Sea Beast, The (Fedallah)
Seven Footprints to Satan
Ships of the Night
Show of Shows, The
Soft Shoes
Something Always Happens
Streets of Shanghai
Telling the World
Thief of Bagdad, The (Mongol Prince)
Tropic Madness
Unholy Night, The (the Mystic)
Wanderer, The

5625
SOKOLOFF, Vladimir /aka/ Wladi-
   mir (1890-1962)
Loves of Jeanne Ney, The /aka/
   Die Liebe der Jeanne Ney
Das Schiff der Verlorenen Menschen
   [The Ship of Lost Souls] /aka/ La
   Navire des Hommes Perdue [The
   Ship of Lost Men] (Grischa)
Stage:
Dantons Tod (Robespierre) 27
Jedermann [Everyman] (Death) 27
Midsummer Night's Dream, A (Puck)
   27

Peripherie (a Judge) 28

5626
SOLM, Fred*
U-Boat 9

5627
SOLVEG, Maria*
Meistersinger
Stage:
Dantons Tod (a lady) 27
Jedermann [Everyman] (Good Deeds)
   27
Midsummer Night's Dream, A (Her-
   mia) 27

5628
SOMERS, Bud*
Condemned (prison inmate)

5629
SOMERSALONI, Urho*
Johan

5630
SOMERSET, Pat*
Black Watch, The
From Headquarters
King of the Khyber Rifles (Highland
   Officer)
Mother Machree
Stage:
Dancers, The (Evan Carruthers) 23
Orange Blossoms (Lawyer Brassac)
   22
Outsider, The (Basil Owen) 24

5631
SON OF MAN HAMMER*
Vanishing American, The /aka/ The
   Vanishing Race (Masja)

5632
SONJA, Magda*
Maria Stuart
Mata Hari: The Red Dancer
That Murder in Berlin

5633
SORIN, Louis*
Mother's Boy (Mr. Bumber)
Stage:
Animal Crackers (Roscoe W. Chand-
   ler) 28
Constant Nymph, The (Jacob Birn-
   baum) 26
Footlights (Jacob Perlstein) 27
Humoresque (Isador Kantor, grown)
   23

Los Angeles (Mr. Rosebud) 27
Money Lender, The (Solomon Levi)
  28

5634
SORINA, Alexandra*
Hands of Orlac, The
Peter the Great

5635
SORLEY, Edward*
Nell Gwyn (soldier)

5636
SOTHERN, Ann (Harriette Lake)
  (1909-)
Hearts in Exile
Show of Shows, The (billed as Har-
  riet Lake)

5637
SOTHERN, Harry*
Tragedy of the East Side, A
Stage:
Constant Nymph, The (Roberto) 26
First Stone, The (Fred Bliss) 28
Good Hope, The (Kaps) 27
Two Plus Two Equals Five (Paul
  Abel) 27

5638
SOULTEN, Graham*
Hindle Wakes /aka/ Fanny Haw-
  thorne (Mr. Hollis)

5639
SOUSSANIN, Nicholas*
Adoration
Gentleman of Paris, A
Hotel Imperial (Adjutant)
Last Command, The (Adjutant)
Midnight Sun, The
Night Watch, The
Spotlight, The
Squall, The (El Moro)
Swan, The
Woman Disputed (the Count)
Yellow Lily, The
Stage:
Vaudeville [Palace] 29

5640
SOUTHERN, Eve (1898-)
After the Show
Clothes Make the Woman
Gaucho, The (Girl of the Shrine)
Girl in His Room
Girl Who Came Back, The

Golden Gallows
Haunted House, The
Lilies of the Field
Nice People
Rage of Paris, The
Remembrance
Resurrection
Souls for Sale (Velma Slade)
Stormy Waters
Trimmed in Scarlet
Voice Within, The
Whispering Winds
Wild Geese

5641
SOUTHERN, Sam*
Dream Cheater, The
Silk Husbands and Calico Wives
Whispering Devils

5642
SOUTHERN, Virginia*
Greater Glory, The

5643
SPADE, Marcello*
Kif Tebbi

5644
SPAGNOLI, Genaro*
Honeymoon Hate
Lost, a Wife

5645
SPARKS, Martha Lee*
Happy Days (Nancy Lee)

5646
SPARKS, Ned A. (1883-1957)
Alias the Deacon
Alias the Lone Wolf
Auction Block, The (Nat Salnson)
Big Noise, The
Bond Boy, The
Boomerang, The
Bright Lights
Canary Murder Case, The (Tony
  Skeel)
Faint Perfume (Orrin Clumb)
Good References (Peter Stearns)
His Supreme Moment
In Search of a Sinner
Leathernicking
Magnificent Flirt, The (Tim)
Mike
Money Talks
Nothing but the Truth
On to Reno

Only Thing, The
Perfect Woman, The
Secret Studio, The
Seven Keys to Baldpate (Bland)
Soul Mates
Strange Cargo
Street Girl
Wide Open Town, A
Stage:
Jim Jam Jems (Archie Spotter) 29
My Golden Girl (Mr. Hanks) 20

5647
SPAULDING, Nellie Parker*
Good References (Caroline Marshall)
Time, the Comedian
Twenty-One

5648
SPEAR, Harry (1921-)
Bouncing Babies
Boxing Gloves
Lazy Days
Railroadin'
Small Talk
Wiggle Your Ears

5649
SPELVIN, George S. *
Just Suppose
Stage:
Ashes (Brewl) 24
Big Boy ("Silent" Ransom) 25
Broken Wing (Marco) 20
Chicken Feed (Harry Taylor) 23
Command Performance, The (Police
  Sgt.) 28
Dear Me (Robert Jackson) 21
Deep Tangled Wildwood, The
  (Schwartz) 23
Gorilla, The (Dr. Wilner) 25
Gossipy Sex, The (Richard Foster)
  27
Hearts Are Trumps! (M. Palette) 27
Hell's Bells! (Mahoney) 25
Holy Terror, A (Schwartz) 25
Houses of Sand (Jepson) 25
Lady of the Rose (Doctor) 25
Love's Call (donkey driver) 25
Merry Merry (subway passenger) 25
Merton of the Movies (a sheik) 22
Ringside (referee) 28
Shannons of Broadway, The (Charley
  Dill) 27
Sitting Pretty (Prof. Appleby) 24
Thank You (Alfred Watrous) 21
What's Your Wife Doing? (Detective
  Magee) 23
Wheel, The (Jake) 21

5650
SPENCER, James*
Adventure

5651
SPENCER, Norman*
Show of Shows, The

5652
SPENCER, Robert*
Sea Hawk, The
Stage:
How's Your Health? (a pirate) 29
Present Arms (Gadget) 28

5653
SPERLING, Hazel*
Happy Days (chorus)

5654
SPEYER, Eve*
Women Without Men

5655
SPIRA, Camilla*
Aftermath

5656
SPITZER, Marian*
Through Different Eyes (2nd reporter)

5657
SPIVEY, Victoria*
Hallelujah! (Missy Rose)

5658
SPLETTSTÖBER, Erwin*
Menschen am Sonntag [People on Sun-
  day]

5659
SPOTTSWOOD, James (1882-1940)
Thunderbolt
Stage:
Close Harmony (Ed Graham) 24
Deluge (Charlie, a waiter) 22
New Toys (Tom Lawrence) 24
Out of the Night (Tom Holland) 27
Partners Again (Mozard Rabiner) 22
Robert E. Lee (Duff Penner) 23
Wait Till We're Married (Tom Hatch)
  21

5660
SPROTTE, Bert*
Confessions of a Queen
His Hour
Jes' Call Me Jim
Little Robinson Crusoe

Married in Hollywood
O'Malley of the Mounted
Private Life of Helen of Troy, The
    (Achilles)
Rosita (Jaibo)
Shooting of Dan McGrew, The
    (beachcomber)
Singer Jim McKee
Soul of the Beast, The
Wild Bill Hickok

5661
STAHL-NACHBAUER, Ernst*
Gefahren der Brautzeit [Dangers of
    the Engagement Period] /aka/
    Aus dem Tagebuch eines Verführ-
    rens; Eine Nacht der Liebe;
    Liebesnächte [Nights of Love];
    Liebesbriefe (McClure)

5662
STALENIN, Evan*
Scandal

5663
STAMBAUGH, Jack*
Married in Hollywood

5664
STAMP-TAYLOR, Enid (1904-1946)
Broken Melody
Cocktails
Easy Virtue (Sarah)
Land of Hope and Glory
Little Bit of Fluff, A
Rememberance
Yellow Stockings

5665
STANDING, Gordon*
Married? (Clark Jessup)
Stage:
Hamlet (Marcellus) 25

5666
STANDING, Herbert*
Brown Derby, The
Impossible Mrs. Bellew, The (Rev.
    Dr. Helstan)
Judy of Rogues Harbor
Mansquerader, The
Trap, The (the priest)
Stage:
Napoleon (Gourgaud) 28
Outrageous Mrs. Palmer, The (Hon.
    Charles Cardigan North) 20
Queen Victoria (Lord Conyngham) 23

5667
STANDING, Joan (1903-)
Beau Sabreur (Maudie)
Branding Iron, The (Maude Upper)
Campus Flirt, The
College Hero, The
Dancers, The
Empty Hearts (Hilda, the maid)
Faint Perfume (hired girl)
Fashions in Love
Greed (Cousin Selina)
Happiness
Home James
Marriage Playground, The (Miss
    Scapey)
Memory Lane
Oliver Twist
Pleasure Mad
Romance of a Queen, The (Isabella)
Three Weeks
Women Who Give

5668
STANDING, Percy Darnell*
Gypsy Cavalier, The (Stirrett)

5669
STANDING, Wyndham (1880-)
Bride's Play, The
Canadian, The
City Gone Wild, A
Dark Angel, The (Capt. Gerald Shan-
    nan)
Earthbound
Gold Diggers (Stephen Lee)
Inner Man, The
Iron Trail, The
Isle of Doubt, The
Journey's End
Lion's Mouse, The
Little Johnny Jones
Marriage of William Ashe, The (Wil-
    liam Ashe)
My Lady's Garter
Port of Missing Girls, The
Rejected Woman, The
Secrets
Smilin' Through (John Carteret)
Teaser, The
Thumbs Down
Unchastened Woman, The (Hubert
    Knolys)
Vanity's Price
Widdecombe Affair (the Squire)
Women Who Give

5670
STANFORD, Stanley*
Circus, The

5671
STANLEY, Forest (1889-   )
Bare Knees
Beauty's Worth (Cheyne Rovlin)
Breath of Scandal, The
Cat and the Canary, The (Charles
   Wilder)
Climbers, The (Duke Cordova "El
   Blanco")
Dancing Days
Enchantment
Fate of a Flirt, The
Forbidden Fruit (Nelson Rogers)
Forest Havoc
Her Accidental Husband
House that Jazz Built, The
Into the Night
Jazzland
Phantom of the Turf
Pride of Palomar, The
Sacred and Profane Love
Shadow of the Law, The (James Rey-
   nolds)
Through the Dark
Tiger Rose
Triflers
Up the Ladder
Virgin Queen, The
Wheel of Destiny, The
When Knighthood Was in Flower
   (Charles Brandon)
Wine (Carl Graham)
Young Diana, The

5672
STANMORE, Frank (1877-   )
Blinkeyes (Flowerpots)
Chamber of Horrors
Mumsie ("Nobby" Clark)
Only Way, The (Jarvis Lorry)

5673
STANTON, Fred R.*
Find Your Man
Trifling with Honor
When a Man's a Man

5674
STANTON, Will*
Sadie Thompson (Quartermaster
   Bates)
Sugar Daddies
True Heaven

5675
STANWYCK, Barbara (Ruby Stevens)
   (1907-   )
Broadway Nights (fan dancer)

Locked Door, The
Mexicali Rose
Stage:
Burlesque (Bonny) 27
Dancer in speakeasies 22
Noose, The (Dot) 26
Vaudeville [Palace] 29

5676
STAR, Frederick*
Riders of the Dawn

5677
STARK-GSTETTENBAUR, Gustl*
Frau im Mond [Woman in the Moon]
Volga-Volga (Kolka)

5678
STARKE, Pauline (1900-   )
Adventure
Adventurer, The
Bright Lights
Captain Salvation
Connecticut Yankee in King Arthur's
   Court, A (Sandy)
Courage of Marge O'Doone, The
Dance Magic
Dante's Inferno
Devil's Cargo, The
Fallen Angels
Flower of the North
Forbidden Paradise (Anna)
Forgotten Woman, The
Goldwyn player 23
Hearts of Oak
Honesty Is the Best Policy
If You Believe It, It's So
In the Palace of the King
Kingdom Within, The
Little Church Around the Corner, The
Little Girl Next Door, The
Lost and Found
Love's Blindness
Man Without a Country, The /aka/
   As No Man Has Loved
Man, Woman and Wife
My Wild Irish Rose
Perfect Sap, The
Salvation Nell
Seeds of Vengeance
Silent Years
Snow Blind
Streets of Shanghai
Sun Up
Viking, The
War Paint
Women Love Diamonds

5679
STARKEY, Bert*
Wild Geese

5680
STARR, Fred*
Daredevil Jack [serial]

5681
STARR, Jane*
Fighting American, The

5682
STARR, Sally*
So This Is College
Stage:
Optimists, The (a principal) 28
Rufus Le Maire's Affairs (a prin-
    cipal) 27

5683
STARRETT, Charles (1904-)
Quarter Back, The (himself)
Stage:
Claire Adams (Gene Adams) 29

5684
STEADE, Douglas*
Happy Days (chorus)

5685
STEADMAN, Vera (1900-1966)
Are Waitresses Safe?
Bedroom Blunder, A
Campus Cuties
Chased Bride, The
Exit Quietly
Fit to Fight
Gallant Gob, A
Gobs of Love
Happy Heels
Hula Hula Land
License Applied For
Marry Me
Nervous Wreck, The
Oh, Doctor, Oh!
Oriental Hugs
Papa by Proxy
Pullman Bride, A
Sand Witches
Scrap Iron
Sea Food
She-Going Sailor, A
Stop Flirting
That Night
Tugboat Romeo, A
Watch Your Step, Mother
Wedding Blues
Why Men Go Wild

5686
STEDMAN, Lincoln (1900-1941)
Be My Wife
Black Oxen (Donnie Ferris)
Captain January
Charm School, The
Dangerous Age, The
Devil's Cage, The
Farmer's Daughter, The
Freshie, The
Green Grass Widows
Harold Teen
Homespun Vamp, A
Let It Rain
Little Firebrand
Meanest Man in the World, The
Nineteen and Phyllis
Ole Swimmin' Hole, The
One Minute to Play
Out of the Storm
Peaceful Valley
Perch of the Devil
Prince of Headwaiters
Prisoner, The
Red Hot Tires
Rookies
Student Prince, The
Tanned Legs
Two Minutes to Go
Under the Lash (Jan Vanderberg)
White Shoulders
Why Be Good?
Wife of the Centaur, The
Wild Party
Youth to Youth

5687
STEDMAN, Myrtle (1888-1938)
Alias the Deacon
Ashes
Black Diamond Express
Black Roses
Bread
Breath of Scandal, The
Bucko McAllister
Chickie
Concert, The
Crashing Through
Dangerous Age, The
Don Juan's Three Nights
Famous Mrs. Fair, The
Far Cry, The
Flaming Youth
Goose Hangs High, The (Eunice In-
    gals)
Hands of Nara, The
Harriet and the Piper
If I Marry Again
Irresistible Lover

5694
STEIN, Lotte*
Der Mensch am Wege [Man by the
  Roadside]

5695
STEINRUCK, Albert /aka/ Albert
  Steinrisck
At the Edge of the World (the mil-
  ler)
Decameron Nights
Eleven Who Were Loyal
Der Golem
Jew of Mestri, The (Tubal)

5696
STEN, Anna (Anjuschka Stenski
  Suijakevitch) (1910-)
Bomber auf Monte Carlo
Captain Craddoc
Girl with the Hatbox, The
Lash of the Czar, The
Der Morder Dmitri Roramazoo (Gru-
  shenka)
When Moscow Laughs
Stage:
Hennelei Himmelfahrt [In Russia] 25

5697
STENERMANN, Salka*
Seven Faces

5698
STENGEL, Leni*
Royal Box, The
Stage:
Princess Turnadot (Adelma) 26
These Few Ashes (Olga Bukarov) 28

5699
STEPHENSON, Henry (1871-1956)
Men and Women
Wild, Wild Susan
Stage:
Adorable Liar, The (Rupert Barry)
  26
Command to Love, The (French Am-
  bassador to Spain) 27
Crown Prince, The (the Emperor)
  27
Dancing Mothers (Hugh Westcourt)
  24
Fool, The (George F. Goodkind)
  22
Love Duel, The (Herr Professor) 29
Magda (Hefterdingt) 25
Pelican, The (Charles Cheriton) 25
Spanish Love (Domingo) 20

5700
STEPIN FETCHIT (Lincoln Theodore
  Perry) (1896-)
Big Time
Cameo Kirby
Galloping Ghost, The
Ghost Talks, The
Hearts in Dixie
In Old Kentucky
Kid's Clever, The
Movietone Follies of 1929
Salute
Show Boat
Through Different Eyes

5701
STEPPLING, John*
Black Beauty
Cafe in Cairo, A
California Straight Ahead
Dramatic Life of Abraham Lincoln,
  The /aka/ Abraham Lincoln
Eve's Lover (Burton Gregg)
Fast Worker, The
Going Up
Husband Hunter, The (Kelly)
Man Next Door, The
Memory Lane
Reckless Age, The
Sin Flood, The
Wedding Bills

5702
STERLER, Hermine*
Strauss, the Waltz King

5703
STERLING, Bruce*
In the Palace of the King

5704
STERLING, Edythe*
Two reelers (5)

5705
STERLING, Ford (George Ford Stitch)
  (1885-1939)
American Venus, The
Among Those Present
Brass Bottle, The
Casey at the Bat
Chicken a la King (Horace Trundle)
Daddy's Gone-A-Hunting
Day of Faith, The
Don't Weaken
Drums of the Desert
Everybody's Acting
Fall of Eve, The

For the Love of Mike (Herman
 Schultz)
Gentlemen Prefer Blondes (Gus Eis-
 man)
Girl in the Show, A
Good and Naughty
Guardian Angel
He Who Gets Slapped (Tricaud)
Hearts and Flowers
His Last False Step
His Youthful Fancy
Hollywood
Lady's Tailor, A
Little Widow, The
Love and Glory
Love, Honor and Behave
Married Life
Mike
Miss Brewster's Millions
Mr. Romeo
My Lady's Lips (Smike)
Oh, Kay!
Road to Glory, The (James Allen)
Sally ("Pops" Shendorff)
Shamrock and the Rose, The /aka/
 The Trunk Mystery [serial]
Show-Off, The
So Big (Jakob Hoogandunk)
Spoilers, The ("Slapjack" Simms)
Sporting Goods
Stage Struck (Buck)
Stranded in Paris
Stranger's Banquet
That's My Daddy
Trouble with Wives, The
Uncle Tom Without the Cabin
Unhappy Finish, The
Wife Savers
Wild Oranges
Woman on the Jury, The

5706
STERLING, Harriet*
Soul Fire
Wilderness Woman, The
Stage:
Great Music (Tihuti) 24
Woman of Bronze, The (Mrs. Douglas
 Graham) 20; 27

5707
STERLING, Merta*
Paid to Love (maid)

5708
STERN, Louis*
I Want My Man
Wedding Bills
Where East Is East (Father Angelo)

5709
STERRALL, Gertrude*
Glorious Adventure, The (Duchess of
 Morelane)

5710
STEVENS, Charles (1893-1964)
Black Pirate, The (powder man)
Captain-Fly-By-Night
Diamond Handcuffs
Don Q, Son of Zorro (Robledo)
Doomsday
Empty Hands
Experience
Gaucho, The (Gaucho's first lieu-
 tenant)
Grandman's Boy
Her Gilded Cage (Gaston Ornoff)
Iron Mask, The (Planchet)
Mantrap (Jackfish)
Mark of Zorro, The (a peon)
Mollycoddle, The
Mysterious Dr. Fu Manchu, The
 /aka/ The Insidious Dr. Fu
 Manchu (General Petrie)
Recompense
Robin Hood
Rustle of Silk, The (Henry DeBreze)
Son of His Father, A
Spanish Dancer, The (Cardinal's Am-
 bassador)
Stand and Deliver (Krim)
Thief of Bagdad, The (Persian
 Prince's awaker)
Three Musketeers, The (Planchet)
Vanishing American, The /aka/ The
 Vanishing Race
Virginian, The
Where the North Begins
Woman's Law, A

5711
STEVENS, Charlotte*
Mother
Tornado

5712
STEVENS, Clancey*
Vanishing American, The /aka/ The
 Vanishing Race

5713
STEVENS, Edwin*
Charm School
Dollar a Year Man, The
Her First Elopement
Lover's Oath, A /aka/ Rubaiyat of
 Omar Khayyam
Man Unconquerable, The

Passions Playground
Snob, The
Sting of the Lash (Daniel Keith)
Voice from the Minaret, The (Lord
  Leslie Carlyle)
What's Worth While?

5714
STEVENS, George (1905-1975)
Dr. Jekyll and Mr. Hyde

5715
STEVENS, Landers*
Temple of Dawn, The (Richard Wil-
  loughby)
Trial of Mary Dugan, The

5716
STEVENS, Lester*
Show of Shows, The

5717
STEVENSON, Charles*
Cheat, The
Doomsday
Garrison's Finish
Hot Water
Man Who Found Himself, The
Pied Piper Malone
Rustle of Silk, The
Spanish Dancer, The
Woman with Four Faces, The

5718
STEVENSON, Douglas*
Janice Meredith (Capt. Charles
  Mowbray)
Stage:
Blue Kitten, The (Armand Duvelin)
  22
Hitchy-Koo 1920 (a principal) 20
Sun Showers (Bobby Brown) 23

5719
STEVENSON, Hayden*
Abysmal Brute, The (Sam Stubener)
Acquital, The (Sam)
Behind the Front
Blake of Scotland Yard [serial] (An-
  gus Blake)
Bookworm Hero
College Love
Collegiates, The
Diamond Master, The [serial]
Fourflusher, The
I'll Show You the Town
King of the Campus
Leather Pushers, The [series]

Man, Woman and Sin
On Your Toes
Reckless Age, The
Red Lips
Trifling with Honor
Whole Town's Talking, The

5720
STEVER, Hans*
Pawns of Passion

5721
STEWARD, Leslie*
Squibs (Jim Wall)

5722
STEWART, Anita (Anna May Stewart)
  (1895-1961)
Baree, Son of Kazan
Boomerang, The
Fighting Shepherdess, The
Great White Way, The
Harriet and the Piper
Her Kingdom of Dreams
Her Mad Bargain
Hollywood
Human Desire
In Old Kentucky
Invisible Fear, The
Isle of Sunken Gold, The [serial]
Lodge in the Wilderness
Love Piker, The
Morganson's Finish
Name the Woman
Never the Twin Shall Meet
Playthings of Destiny
Prince of Pilsen, The
Question of Honor, A
Romance of a Rogue
Rose O' the Sea
Rustlin' for Cupid
Sisters of Eve
Smudge
Sowing the Wind
Whispering Wires
Wild Geese
Woman He Married, The
Yellow Typhoon (dual role)

5723
STEWART, George*
Abysmal Brute, The (Wilfred Sang-
  ster)
Mollycoddle, The (college boy)

5724
STEWART, Lucille Lee (1894-   )
Bad Company

Eastward Ho!
Ninety and Nine, The
Woman Gives, The
Woman's Business, A

5725
STEWART, Roy (1884-1933)
Back to the Yellow Jacket
Burning Words, The
Candy Kid, The
Devil to Pay, The
Great Divide, The
Heart of the North (dual role)
Hearts of Oak
In Old Arizona (Commandant)
Innocent Cheat, The
Just a Wife
Lady from Hell, The
Life's Greatest Question
Lone Hand, The
Love Brand, The
Lumberjack, The [series]
Midnight Watch
Mistress of Shenstone
Motion to Adjourn, A
One Eighth Apache
One Woman to Another
Prisoners of Love
Protection
Radio King, The [serial]
Riders of the Dawn
Ridin' Wild
Roarin' Fires
Sagebrush Trail, The
Sagebrusher, The
Snowshoe Trail, The
Social Value
Sparrows /aka/ Human Sparrows
   (Richard Wayne)
Stormy Waters
Sundown
Tall Timber
Timber Tales
Timberland Treachery
Time, the Comedian
Trimmed in Scarlet
U. P. Trail, The
Under Secret Orders
Viking, The
With Buffalo Bill on the U. P. Trail
With Daniel Boone Through the Wilder-
   ness
With General Custer at Little Big
   Horn
With Kit Carson over the Great Di-
   vide
Woman on the Jury, The
You Never Know Women

Stage:
Guns (Hokey Pokey Kid) 28

5726
STEWART, Ted*
Courtship of Miles Standish, The

5727
STEWART, Virginia Lee*
Friendly Enemies

5728
STIEDA, Heinz*
Hamlet (Horatio)

5729
STIFTER, Magnus*
Othello /aka/ The Moor (Montano)

5730
STIVERS, Duskal*
Son of Wallingford, The (Manks)

5731
STOCK, Valeska*
Weavers, The

5732
STOCKBRIDGE, Fanny*
Old Nest, The

5733
STOCKBRIDGE, Henry*
Dynamite (a wise fool)
No, No, Nanette (Brady)

5734
STOCKDALE, Carlton (1874-1942)
After Hours
Black Pearl, The
Brass Buttons
Bride of the Colorado
Broken Barriers
Cafe in Cairo, A
Carnation Kid, The
China Bound
Coast of Opportunity, The
Darling of New York, The
Double Adventure [serial]
Extra Girl, The
Half Breed, The (John Spavinaw)
Jazzland
King of Kings, The (bit)
Love Parade, The (Admiral)
Meanest Man in the World, The
Money, Money, Money
My Home Town
Oliver Twist (Mr. Monks)

Red Hot Romance
Regular Fellow, A
See You in Jail
Shepherd of the Hills
Sisters
Society Secrets
Son of His Father, A
Spirit of the U. S. A.
Suzanna
Terror, The
Thorns and Orange Blossoms
Try and Get It
While London Sleeps

5735
STOCKTON, Edith*
Keep to the Right
Out of the Chorus
Through the Storm

5736
STODDARD, Belle*
Hangman's House

5737
STOKES, Dorothy*
Butterflies in the Rain
Society Scandal, A (Marjorie's
  friend)
Stage:
Camel's Back, The (Annie) 23

5738
STONE, Arthur (1897-   )
Affair of the Follies, An
Babe Comes Home
Burning Daylight
Captain Lash
Chicken a la King (Oscar)
Far Call, The
Farmer's Daughter, The
Frozen Justice
Fugitives
Girl of the Golden West
Hard Boiled Haggerty
Husbands Are Liars
It Must Be Love
Me, Gangster (Dan the Dude)
Movietone Follies of 1929 (Al
  Leaton)
New Year's Eve
Patent Leather Kid, The
Red Wine
Sea Tiger, The
Silent Lover, The
Through Different Eyes (Crane)
Valley of the Giants, The

5739
STONE, Doc*
Circus, The

5740
STONE, Fred (1873-1959)
Billy Jim
Duke of Chimney Butte
Stage:
Criss Cross (Christopher Cross) 26
Stepping Stones (Peter Plug) 23
Tip-Top (a principal) 20

5741
STONE, Gene*
Fair Co-Ed, The (Herbert)

5742
STONE, George E. (George Stein)
  (1903-1967)
Beautiful but Dumb
Brass Knuckles
Clothes Make the Woman
Desperate Trails
Fourth Musketeer, The
Girl in the Glass Cage, The (Carlos)
Jackie
Just Pals
Melody Lane
Naughty Baby
Penny of Hilltop Trail
Racket, The
Redeeming Sin, The
San Francisco Nights
Scoffer, The
Seventh Heaven (Sewer Rat)
Skin Deep
State Street Sadie
Tenderloin
Turn Back the Hours
Two Men and a Maid
Under a Texas Moon
Walking Back
Weary River
Whistle, The
White and Unmarried

5743
STONE, Helen*
Salvage (Ruth Martin)

5744
STONE, Jack*
Lilac Time

5745
STONE, Lewis (Lewis S. Stone)
  (1879-1953)
Affair of the Follies, An

Beau Revel
Blonde Saint, The
Cheaper to Marry
Child Thou Gavest Me, The
Concert, The
Confessions of a Queen
Cytheria (Lee Randon)
Dangerous Age, The
Don Juan's Three Nights
Don't Neglect Your Wife
Eternal City, The
Fine Clothes
Fool There Was, A
Foreign Legion, The
Freedom of the Press
Girl from Montmartre, The
Golden Snare, The
Held by the Enemy
Husbands and Lovers
Inez from Hollywood
Lady Who Lied, The
Lonesome Ladies
Lost World, The (Sir John Paxton)
Madame X (Floriot)
Midnight Lovers
Milestones (John Rhead)
Muffled Drum, The
Nomads of the North (Corp. O'Con-
ner)
Northern Trail, The
Notorious Lady
Old Loves and New /aka/ The
Desert Healer
Patriot, The (Count Pahlen)
Pilgrims of the Night
Prince of Headwaiters
Prisoner of Zenda, The (King Ru-
dolf Rassendyll)
Private Life of Helen of Troy, The
(Mehelaus)
River's End, The
Rosary, The
Scaramouche (Marquis de la Tour
d'Azyr)
Stranger, The
Talker, The
Their Own Desire
Too Much Money
Trial of Mary Dugan (Edward West)
Trifling Women
What Fools Men
White Mouse, The
Why Men Leave Home
Wild Orchids (John Sterling)
Woman of Affairs, A
Wonder of Women
World's Applause, The
You Can't Fool Your Wife

5746
STONEHOUSE, Ruth (1894-1941)
Are All Men Alike?
Broken Barriers
Cleanup, The
Devil's Cage, The
Ermine and Rhinestones
Fifth Avenue Models
Flame of Passion
Hope
I Am Guilty
Lady Bird
Lights Out
Love Never Dies
Parlor, Bedroom and Bath
Satin Woman
Scarlet West, The (Mrs. Custer)

5747
STOREY, Edith (1892-)
Beach of Dreams
Golden Hope, The
Greater Profit
Metro player 20
Moon Madness

5748
STOREY, Rex*
Idle Class, The

5749
STORM, Olaf*
Last Laugh, The (young guest)

5750
STORMONT, Leo*
Sonia (Sir Adolph Erckmann)

5751
STOWE, Leslie*
Mother's Boy (Evangelist)
Second Fiddle
Tongues of Flame

5752
STOWE, Lester*
Copperhead, The

5753
STOWITZ*
Magician, The

5754
STRAIN, Thayer*
Which Shall It Be?

5755
STRANG, Harry*
Greene Murder Case, The (cop)

5756
STRANGE, Philip*
Ace of Cads, The
Behind that Curtain (Eric Durand)
Broadway Nights (Bronson)
Loves of an Actress
Man Power
Nevada (Ben Ide)
Popular Sin, The
Rescue, The
Sporting Goods
Unholy Night, The (Lt. Williams)
Wall Street

5757
STRASSBERG, Morris*
Broken Hearts
Stage:
Merchant of Venice, The (Chus) 22
We Americans (Mr. Horowitz) 26

5758
STRASSNY, Fritz*
Hands of Orlac, The

5759
STRATTON, Gene*
Keeper of the Bees, The (little
  scout)

5760
STRAUCH, I.*
Prisoners of the Sea

5761
STRAUCH, Maxim*
Battleship Potemkin
Stachka /aka/ Strike

5762
STRAUSS, William H. (1885-)
Abie's Irish Rose
Ankles Preferred
Barracade, The
Do Your Duty
For Ladies Only
Ghetto, The
Lucky Boy
Magic Cup, The
North Wind's Malice
Private Izzy Murphy
Rawhide Kid, The
Rubber Tires
Sally in Our Alley
Shamrock and the Rose, The
  /aka/ The Trunk Mystery
  [serial]
Skinner's Dress Suit
So This Is Love

5763
STRIBOLT, Oscar*
Han og Hun og Hamlet [He and She
  and Hamlet]
Witchcraft Through the Ages /aka/
  Häxan

5764
STRIKER, Joseph*
Annie Laurie /aka/ Ladies from
  Hell (Alastair)
Best People
Climbers, The (Ensign Carlos)
Cradle Snatchers
I Am the Man
King of Kings, The (John)
Painted People
Silver Wings
Steadfast Heart, The
Wise Wife
Wrecker, The
Stage:
Mendel, Inc. (Milton Kahn) 29

5765
STRONG, Eugene*
Coney Island
Crooks Can't Win
Drop Kick, The

5766
STRONG, Porter*
Dream Street (Samuel Jones)
Idol Dancer, The (Peter)
One Exciting Night (Romeo Washing-
  ton)
Way Down East (Seth Holcomb)
White Rose, The (Apollo)

5767
STRONGHEART (Dog)
Brawn of the North
Flapper Wives
Love Master, The
North Star
Return of Boston Blackie, The
Silent Call, The
Warning, The

5768
STRONGHEART, Nipo (George Strong-
  heart) (1891-1967)
Brave Heart
Last Frontier, The
Road to Yesterday

5769
STROTHERS, Bill*
Safety Last (the pal)

5770
STRUEWE, Hans*
Prince of Rogues, The

5771
STRUM, Hans*
Monna Vanna

5772
STRUMWAY, Lee*
Bat, The

5773
STRYKER, Joseph*
Broadway Peacock, The

5774
STUART, Donald*
Beau Geste (Buddy)
Bride of the Storm
Interference (Freddie)
Lone Eagle, The
Silver King, The

5775
STUART, Henry*
Die Freudlase Gasse [The Joyless
  Street] /aka/ The Street of Sor-
  rows (Egon Stirner)
Sajenko, the Soviet
When Duty Calls
When Fleet Meets Fleet (British
  Commander)
Wrath of the Sea

5776
STUART, Iris*
Casey at the Bat
Children of Divorce (Mousey)
Stranded in Paris
Wedding Bills

5777
STUART, John (John Alfred Louden
  Croall) (1898-)
Alley of Golden Hearts
Atlantic (Lawrence)
Bachelor Husbands
Back to the Trees
Baddesley Manor
Brat, The
Children of Chance
Claude Duval
Constant Hot Water
Curfew Must Not Ring Tonight
Daughter of Love
Eileen Allanah
Eve's Fall

Extra Knot, The
Film Song Album [series]
Flight Commander, The
Gayest of the Gay, The
Glad Eye, The
Great Gay Road, The
Her Redemption
Her Son (debut)
High Seas
Hindle Wakes /aka/ Fanny Hawth-
  orne
His Grace Gives Notice
If Four Walls Told
Kenilworth Castle
Kitty
Land of My Fathers
Leaves from My Life [series]
Lights of Home, The
Little Miss Nobody
Little Mother
London Love (Allan Jeffcote)
Loves of Mary Queen of Scots,
  The
Mademoiselle from Armentieres
  (John)
Mademoiselle Parlez-Voos (John)
Memories
Mistletoe Bough, The
No Exit
Parted
Pleasure Garden, The
Reverse of the Medal
Roses of Picardy (Lt. Skene)
Sailors Don't Care
Sally in Our Alley
School for Scandal, The
Sinister Street
Smashing Through
Sporting Double, The
Taxi for Two
This Freedom (Huggo)
Tower of London
Venetian Lovers
We Women
Woman in Pawn, A
Woman Juror, The
Yacht of Seven Sins
Stage:
Chinese Puzzle, The (on tour) 20
Our Betters (Globe Theatre) 23
Sumurun (Coliseum) 25

5778
STUART, Madge*
Beloved Vagabond, The (Blan-
  quette)
Only Way, The (Mimi)
Women and Diamonds

5779
STUART, Nick (Nicholas Pratza)
(1904-1973)
Chasing Through Europe
Cradle Snatchers
Girls Gone Wild
Gold Diggers of Broadway
Happy Days (a principal)
High School Hero
Joy Street
News Parade, The
River Pirate, The
Why Leave Home?
Why Sailors Go Wrong

5780
STUART, Simeon*
Gypsy Cavalier, The (Sir Julian
   Carew)
Paddy the Next Best Thing (General
   Adair)
Vortex, The (David Lancaster)

5781
STUBBS, Harry*
Alibi /aka/ The Perfect Alibi
   (Buck Bachman)
Locked Door, The
Night Ride (Bob O'Leary)
Three Live Ghosts
Stage:
Big Fight, The (Dr. Driggs) 28
Butter and Egg Man, The (Bernie
   Sampson) 25
Dice of the Gods, The (Roger Canby)
   23
Endless Chain, The (Billy Dens-
   more) 22
Listening In (Harry Van Sloan) 22
Nightstick (Buck Bachman) 27

5782
STUDAKEVICH, Anna*
Storm over Asia

5783
STUDDIFORD, Grace*
Branded Woman, The

5784
STURGIS, Eddie*
After Midnight
Big City, The (Blinkie)
Fazil (Rice)

5785
STURGIS, Edwin*
Seven Keys to Baldpate

5786
STURM, Erna*
Constant Nymph, The (Susan)

5787
STURM, Hannes*
Lost Shadow, The

5788
STURT, Lois*
Glorious Adventure, The (Nell Gwyn)

5789
SUDAKEVICH, Annel*
Yellow Ticket, The

5790
SUEDO, Julie*
Rat, The (Mou-Mou)
Triumph of the Rat, The (Mou-Mou)
Vortex, The (the dancer)
White Sheik, The

5791
SUL-TE-WAN, Mme.*
Narrow Street, The

5792
SULLIVAN, Billy*
Leather Pushers, The
Universal player 28

5793
SULLIVAN, Charles*
Detectives Wanted
Cock-Eyed World, The (brawler)
Hit the Deck
Rookies
Waltzing Around

5794
SULLIVAN, Fred*
Beggar on Horseback
Winds of Chance

5795
SULLIVAN, Helene*
Claw, The (Judy Saurin)
Hell's Highroad
Steel Preferred

5796
SULLIVAN, James E.
Pinch Hitter, The (college dean)
Stage:
Chiffon Girl, The (Mortimer Stevens)
   24
Love Birds (Bronson Charteris) 21

5797
SULLIVAN, William*
Courtship of Miles Standish, The

5798
SUMMERVILLE, Amelia (1862-1934)
April Folly (Olive Connal)
Great Deception, The
Romola (Brigida)
Stage:
Gingham Girl, The (Sophia Trask) 22

5799
SUMMERVILLE, Slim (George J.
  Summerville) (1892-1946)
Beloved Rogue, The (Jehen)
Chinese Parrot, The
Hey, Hey, Cowboy
King of the Rodeo
Last Warning, The
One Hysterical Night
Painted Ponies
Riding for Fame
Shannons of Broadway, The /aka/
  Goodbye Broadway
Spoilers, The
Strong Boy, The
Tiger Rose (Heine)
Wreck of the Hesperus, The

5800
SUMNER, Kathryn*
Son of Wallingford, The (Flora Dora)

5801
SUNDIN, Jerre*
Chorus Girl's Romance, A (Betty
  Darrell)

5802
SUSANDS, Cecil*
Fifth Form at St. Dominic's (Bul-
  linger of the Sixth)

5803
SUSSIN, Mathilde*
It's Easy to Become a Father
U-Boat 9
Waltz Dream, The (Countess Cocker-
  tiz)

5804
SUTCH, Herbert*
One Exciting Night (Clary Johnson)
White Rose, The (the Bishop)

5805
SUTHERLAND, Dick*
Beloved Rogue, The (executioner)

Claw, The (Chief Logenbuela)
Hoose Gow, The
Masters of Men
Red Lily, The (the Toad)
Secrets
Shriek of Araby, The
Tornado

5806
SUTHERLAND, Eddie (Albert Eddie
  Sutherland) (1897-1973)
All of a Sudden Peggy
Conrad in Quest of His Youth (Con-
  rad at 17)
Dollar-A-Year Man
Dramatic Life of Abraham Lincoln,
  The /aka/ Abraham Lincoln (Wil-
  liam Scott)
Just Outside the Door
Roundup, The
Witching Hour, The

5807
SUTHERLAND, Hope*
Potash and Perlmutter
Stage:
Bronx Express (Leah Hungerstoltz)
  22
Two Block Away (Molly Finnegan) 21
Wild Oats Lane (Rose O'Connell) 22

5808
SUTTON, Charles*
Beyond Price
Democracy, the Vision Restored
Virgin Paradise, A

5809
SUTTON, Gertrude*
Big News (Helen)

5810
SUTTON, Grady (1908-)
Boy Friend, The
Freshman, The
Hit the Deck
Mad Whirl, The
Skinner's Dress Suit
Sophomore, The
Tanned Legs

5811
SVASHENKO, Semyon*
Arsenal

5812
SVENDSEN, Olga*
Han og Hun og Hamlet [He and She
  and Hamlet]

5813
SVENNBERG, Tore*
Dream Waltz, The
Stroke of Midnight, The
Thy Soul Shall Bear Witness

5814
SWAIN, Mack (1876-1935)
Becky
Beloved Rogue, The (Micholas)
Caught in the Fog
Cohens and the Kellys in Atlantic
  City, The
Finnegan's Ball
Footloose Widows
Gentlemen Prefer Blondes (Francis
  Beekman)
Girl from Everywhere, The
Girl from Nowhere, The
Gold Rush, The (Big Jim McKay)
Hands Up! (Silas Woodstock)
Her Big Night
Idle Class, The
Kiki
Last Warning, The
Locked Door, The
Marianne
Mockery (Mr. Gaidaroff)
My Best Girl
Nervous Wreck, The
Pay Day
Pilgrim, The (the deacon)
Redemption
Sea Bat, The
Sea Horses (Bimbo-Bomba)
See You in Jail
Shamrock and the Rose, The /aka/
  The Trunk Mystery [serial]
Texas Steer, A
Tillie's Punctured Romance (Tillie's
  father)
Torrent, The
Whispering Wires
Stage:
Vaudeville [Palace] 26

5815
SWANSON, Gloria (Gloria Josephine
  May Swanson) (1898-)
Affairs of Anatol, The (Vivian Spen-
  cer)
Beyond the Rocks (Theodosa Fitz-
  gerald)
Bluebeard's Eighth Wife (Mona de-
  Briac)
Coast of Folly, The (Nadine and
  Joyce Gathway)
Don't Tell Everything (Marian West-
  over)

Fine Manners (Orchid Murphy)
Great Moment, The (Nadine Pelham)
Her Gilded Cage (Suzanne Ornoff)
Her Husband's Trademark (Lois Mil-
  ler)
Her Love Story (Princess Marie)
Humming Bird, The (Toinette)
Impossible Mrs. Bellew, The (Betty
  Bellew)
Loves of Sunya, The (Sunya Ashling)
Madame Sans-Gene (Catherine
  Hubscher)
Manhandled (Tessie McGuire)
My American Wife (Natalie Chester)
Prodigal Daughters (Swiftie Forbes)
Queen Kelly (Patricia Kelly)
Sadie Thompson (Title role)
Society Scandal, A (Marjorie Colbert)
Something to Think About (Ruth An-
  derson)
Stage Struck (Jennie Hagen)
Trespasser, The (Marion Donnell)
Under the Lash (Deborah Krillet)
Untamed Lady (St. Clair Van Tassel)
Wages of Virtue (Carmelita)
Why Change Your Wife? (Beth Gordon)
Zaza (Title role)
Records:
Love (Your Spell Is Everywhere)
  RCA-LPV538

5816
SWANSTRAM, Karin*
Doctor's Women, The
Story of Gösta Berling, The (Gustafva
  Sinclaire)

5817
SWEENEY, Augustin*
Sandra

5818
SWEET, Blanche (Sarah Blanche
  Sweet) (1896-)
Always Faithful
Anna Christie (Title role)
Bluebeard's Seven Wives /aka/ Pur-
  ple Passions
Deadlier Sex, The
Diplomacy
Far Cry, The
For Those Unborn
Girl in the Web, The
Help Wanted: Male
Her Unwilling Husband
His Supreme Moment
Human Mill, The
In the Palace of the King
Lady from Hell, The

Meanest Man in the World, The
New Commandment, The
Night Hostess
Quincy Adams Sawyer (Alice Petten-
    gill)
Simple Souls
Singed
Souls for Sale
Sporting Venus, The
Tess of the D'Ubervilles (Title role)
That Girl Montana
Those Who Dare
Why Women Love /aka/ Barriers
    Aflame
Woman in White, The

5819
SWEET, Harry*
Fascinating Youth
Hit the Deck

5820
SWICKARD, Joseph (1867-1940)
Across the Deadline
Another Man's Shoes
Bachelor's Club, The
Blind Youth
Boy of Flanders, A
Comrades
Cricket on the Hearth, The
Dante's Inferno
Dark Skies
Daughters of the Rich
Desert Gold (Sebastian Castanada)
Devil's Chaplain, The
Don Juan (Duke Della Varnese)
Eagle of the Night [serial]
Eternal Struggle, The
Eternal Woman, The
Fifth Avenue Models
Four Horsemen of the Apocalypse
    (Marcelo Desnoyers)
Frozen River
Get Your Man (Duc de Bellecontre)
Golden Gift
Golden Stallion, The [serial]
Hotel Imperial (Austrian General)
John of the Woods
Keeper of the Bees, The (bee mas-
    ter)
King of Kings, The (bit)
Maytime (Col. VanZandt)
Men
Mr. Billings Spends His Dime
Moon Madness
Mothers-In-Law
My American Wife (Don Fernando
    DeContas)

No Woman Knows
Old San Francisco
One Increasing Purpose
Open Shutters
Pawned
Phantoms of the North
Playing with Souls
Poisoned Paradise (Prof. Durand)
Robinson Crusoe [serial]
Senor Daredevil
Senorita (Don Francisco Hernandez)
Serenade
Sharp Shooters
Sowing the Wind
Storm, The
Street Corners
Time to Love (Elvire's father)
Times Square
Trumpet Island
Turn Back the Hours
Veiled Woman, The
Whispering Canyon
Wizard of Oz, The

5821
SWICKARD, Josie*
Don Juan

5822
SWINBURNE, Nora (Elinore Johnson)
    (1902-)
Alf's Button (Lady Isabel FizPeter)
Autumn of Pride
Branded
Fortune of Christina McNab, The
Girl of London, A
His Grace Gives Notice
Hornet's Nest
One Colombo Night
Saved from the Sea
Unwanted
Wee McGreegor's Sweetheart (Jessie
    Mary)
Stage:
Mary, Mary Quite Contrary (Sheila)
    23
Mountebank, The (Evadne) 23

5823
SWINLEY, Ion*
Unwritten Law, The

5824
SWOR, Bert*
Golfers, The
Hollywood Star, A
New Halfback, The
Uppercut O'Brien
Why Bring That Up?

5825
SWOR, Bert, Jr.*
Carnation Kid, The

5826
SWOR, Mabel*
For the Love of Mike (Evelyn Joyce)

5827
SYDNEY, Basil (1897-1968)
Red Hot Romance
Romance (debut)
Stage:
Becky Sharp (Rawdon Crawley) 29
Crown Prince, The (Title role) 27
Devil's Disciple, The (Richard Dud-
    geon) 23
Hamlet (Title role) 25
Henry IV, Part I (Henry, Prince of
    Wales) 26
Humble, The (Rodion Rasholnikoff)
    26
Jest, The (Giannette Malespini) 26
Meet the Prince (Prince Michael) 29
Romance (Thomas Armstrong) 21
Romeo and Juliet (Mercutio) 22
RUR (Harry Domin) 22
Sandro Botticelli (Title role) 23
She Stoops to Conquer (young Marlow)
Taming of the Shrew, The (Petruchio)
    27
12,000 (Piderit) 28

5827a
SYLVA, Vesta*
Son of David, A
Stage:
Bitter Sweet (Effie) 29

5828
SYLVAIN, M.*
Passion of Joan of Arc, The

5829
SYLVESTER, Charles*
Thief of Bagdad, The (eunnuch)

5830
SYLVESTER, Lillian*
Merry-Go-Round, The (Aurora Ross-
    reiter)

5831
SYM, Igo*
Cafe Electric (Max Stöger)

5832
SYMONDS, Augustine*
Four Feathers, The (Col. Sutch)

5833
SZOREGHI, Julius V.*
Eine Du Barry von Heute (A Modern
    DuBarry)

- T -

5834
TABER, Richard*
At Bay
Kick In
Lucky in Love
Stage:
Blue Bonnet (Terry Mack) 20
Mrs. Jimmie Thompson (Richard
    Ford) 20
Nigger Rich (The Big Shot) (Gunny
    Jones) 29
Ringside (Bobby Murray) 28

5835
TABLER, P. Dempsey (Perce Demp-
    sey Tabler (1880-1953)
Son of Tarzan, The [serial] (Tarzan)

5836
TAFT, Billy*
College Coquette, The

5837
TAIT, Walter*
Hallelujah! (a Johnson kid)

5838
TALAMO, Gino*
Messalina

5839
TALIAFERRO, Edith (1892-)
Who Is Your Brother?
Stage:
Fashions of 1924 (a principal) 23
Kissing Time (Clairce) 20
Love Scandal, A (Bettina Tilton) 23

5840
TALIAFERRO, Hal--see: Wally
    Wales

5841
TALIAFERRO, Mabel (1887-)
Sentimental Tommy
Stage:
Piper, The (Barbara) 20

5842
TALLI, Carloni*
White Sister, The (Mother Superior)

5843
TALMADGE, Constance (1900-1973)
Breakfast at Sunrise
Dangerous Business (Nancy Flavell)
Dangerous Maid
Divorce
Duchess of Buffalo, The
Dulcy
East Is West (Ming Toy)
Goldfish, The
Good References (Mary Wayne)
Heart Trouble
Her Night of Romance
Her Sister from Paris (dual role)
In Search of a Sinner
Learning to Love
Lessons in Love
Love Expert, The
Mama's Affair
Perfect Woman
Polly of the Follies
Primitive Lover, The
Sybil
Two Weeks
Venus
Venus of Venice
Wedding Bells
Woman's Place

5844
TALMADGE, Joseph Keaton*
Our Hospitality

5845
TALMADGE, Natalie (1898-1969)
Blacksmith, The
Electric House, The
First National player 21
Love Expert, The
Our Hospitality
Passion Flower, The
Yes or No?

5846
TALMADGE, Norma (1896-1957)
Ashes of Vengeance (Yeoland de
   Breux)
Branded Woman, The
Camille (Title role)
Daughter of Two Worlds, A
Dove, The
Eternal Flame, The (Duchess de
   Langeais)
Foolish Wives
Girl of Gold
Graustark (Princess Yetive)
Kiki
Lady, The

Love's Redemption
New York Nights
Only Woman, The
Passion Flower, The
Secrets (Mary Carlton)
She Loves and Lies
Show People (cameo)
Sign on the Door, The
Smilin' Through (dual role, Kathleen/
   Moonyen)
Song of Love /aka/ Dust of Desire
Voice from the Minaret, The (Lady
   Adrienne Carlyle)
Within the Law (Mary Turner)
Woman Disputed, A (Mary Ann Wag-
   ner)
Woman Gives, The
Wonderful Thing, The
Yes or No?

5847
TALMADGE, Richard (Sylvester
   Ricardo Metzetti) (1896-)
American Manners
Bachelor's Club, The
Better Man, The
Blue Streak, The
Broadway Gallant, The
Cavalier, The
Cub Reporter, The
Danger Ahead
Double for Douglas Fairbanks and
   Harold Lloyd
Fighting Demon
Hail the Hero
In Fast Company
Isle of Hope, The
Jimmie's Millions
K-the Unknown /aka/ The Unknown
Laughing at Danger
Lawless Legion, The
Let's Go
Lucky Dan
Night Patrol
Pioneer Studio stunt man
Poor Millionaires
Prince of Pep, The
Putting It Over
Speed King, The
Taking Chances
Tearing Through
Through the Flames
Wall Street Whizz, The
Watch Your Step
Wildcat Jordan
Youth and Adventure

5848
TALMAN, Lloyd*
Robin Hood (Alan-A-Dale)

5849
TAMARA*
Die Freudlose Gasse [The Joyless
Street] /aka/ The Street of Sor-
rows (Lia Leid)
Midsummer Night's Dream, A (Ober-
on)

5850
TAMARIN, B. P.*
Station Master, The

5851
TANSEY, Sheridan /aka/ Sherry*
Over the Hill (Isaac, the boy)
Steadfast Heart, The

5852
TANTOR (Elephant)
Adventures of Tarzan [serial] (him-
self)
Son of Tarzan, The [serial] (him-
self)

5853
TAPLEY, Rose (1883-)
Charlatan, The
It (welfare worker)
Java Head
Man Who Fights Alone, The (Aunt
Louise)
Memories that Haunt
Pony Express
Redeeming Sin, The
Rip Van Winkle
Vanity Fair

5854
TARRON, Elsie*
Extra Girl, The

5855
TASHMAN, Lilyan (1899-1934)
Black Swan
Bright Lights
Bulldog Drummond (Irma)
Camille (Olympe)
Craig's Wife
Declassee
Don't Tell the Wife
Evening Clothes
Experience
For Alimony Only
French Dressing

Garden of Weeds, The
Gold Diggers of Broadway (Eleanor)
Happiness Ahead
Hardboiled
I'll Show You the Town
Lady Raffles [series]
Leathernecking
Lone Wolf's Daughter, The
Love's Blindness
Manhandled (Pinkie Doran)
Manhattan Cocktail (Renov's wife)
Marriage Playground, The (Joyce
Wheater)
Nellie, the Beautiful Cloak Model
New York Nights
No, No, Nanette (Lucille)
Paramount player 22
Parasite, The
Phyllis of the Follies
Playing Around
Ports of Call
Pretty Ladies (Selma Larson)
Prince of Headwaiters
Rocking Moon
Seven Days
Siberia
Skyrocket
So This Is Paris (Georgette Lalle)
Stolen Bride, The
Take Me Home
Texas Steer, A
Trial of Mary Dugan, The (Dagmar
Lorne)
Whispering Smith
Woman Who Did Not Care, The
Stage:
Barnum Was Right (Phoebe O'Dare)
23
Garden of Weeds, The (Hazel Har-
bury) 24
Lady Bug (Pauline Manning) 22

5856
TASKU, V. *
In Old Siberia

5857
TAUBE, Mathias*
Johan

5858
TAVERNIER, Albert*
Tiger's Club, The
Too Many Kisses

5859
TAYLOR, Al*
Dangerous Dub, The
Rawhide

5860
TAYLOR, Alma (1896-   )
Alf's Button
Anna the Adventuress
Comin' Thro' the Rye (Helen Adair)
Dollars in Surrey
Helen of Four Gates
House of Marney, The
Mist in the Valley
Mrs. Erricker's Reputation
Narrow Valley, The
Pipes of Pan, The
Quinneys
Shadow of Egypt
South Sea Bubble, A
Strangling Threads
Tansy
Tinted Venus, The
Two Little Drummer Boys

5861
TAYLOR, Avonne*
My Best Girl

5862
TAYLOR, Estelle (Estelle Boylan)
    (1899-1958)
Adventurer, The
Alaskan, The
Bavu
Bayou, The
Blind Wives
California Romance, A
Desire
Don Juan (Lucretia Borgia)
Dorothy Vernon of Haddon Hall
    (Mary Queen of Scots)
Double for Dorothy Dalton
Fool There Was, A
Footfalls
Happiness
Honor Bound
Lady Raffles [series]
Lights of New York
Manhattan Madness
Monte Cristo (Mercedes)
New York (Angie Miller)
One Night in Rome
Only a Shop Girl
Peg O' My Heart
Pusher-In-the-Face, The
Revenge of Tarzan, The /aka/ The
    Return of Tarzan (Countess de
    Caude)
Show People (cameo)
Singapore Mutiny
Ten Commandments, The (Miriam)
Thorns and Orange Blossoms

Tiger Love
Tragedy of the East Side, A
Where East Is East (Mme. DeSilva)
While New York Sleeps
Whip Woman (Sari)
Stage:
Big Fight, The (Shirley) 28
Vaudeville [Palace] 29

5863
TAYLOR, Laurette (Laurette Cooney)
    (1884-1946)
Happiness
One Night in Rome
Peg O' My Heart (Peg O'Connell)
Stage:
Furies (Fifi Sands) 28
Humoresque (Sarah Kantor) 23
In a Garden (Lissa Terry) 25
National Anthem (Marian Hale) 22
Peg O' My Heart (Peg O'Connell) 21
Pierrot the Prodigal (young Pierrot)
    25
Sweet Nell of Old Drury (Nell Gwynne)
    23
Trelawney of the Wells (Rose Tre-
    lawney) 25
Untitled Benefit 21
Vaudeville [Palace] 26

5864
TAYLOR, Ruth*
College Coquette, The
Gentlemen Prefer Blondes (Lorelei Lee)
Just Married
This Thing Called Love (Dolly)
Stage:
Taboo (Sadie) 22

5865
TAYLOR, Sidney*
Light of the Western Stars, The

5866
TAYLOR, Stanley*
Ancient Highway, The
Glad Rag Doll
Guilty One, The
Home Towners, The
Hottentot, The
Kosher Kitty Kelly
Pacemakers, The [serial]
Red Lips
Romantic Age, The

5867
TAYLOR, William--see: Wilton
    Taylor

5868
TAYLOR, Wilton*
Alias Jimmy Valentine
Cave Girl, The
Drivin' Fool, The
Outside the Law (inspector)
Treasure Island (Black Dog)

5869
TAYO, Lyle*
Bouncing Babies
Perfect Day
Small Talk

5870
TCHUVELEV, Ivan*
Lash of the Czar, The

5871
TCHVERVIAKOF*
Czar and Poet

5872
TEAD, Phillips*
Fighting Blade, The (Lord Trevor)
She Loves and Lies
Stage:
Children's Tragedy, The (elder
  brother) 21
Tavern, The (tavern keeper's son) 20

5873
TEAGUE, Frances*
Iron Horse, The (Polka Dot)
Last Edition, The

5874
TEARLE, Constance*
Just a Woman

5875
TEARLE, Conway (Frederick Levy)
  (1882-1938)
After Midnight
Altars of Desire
April Folly (Kerry Sarle)
Ashes of Vengeance (Rupert deVrieac)
Bad Company
Bella Donna
Black Oxen (Lee Clavering)
Bucking the Tiger
Common Law, The
Dancer of Paris, The
Dancing Mothers (Jerry Naughton)
Dangerous Maid
Eternal Flame, The (Gen. de Mon-
  treveau)
Evidence

Fighter, The
Flirting with Love
Forbidden Woman, The
Gold Diggers of Broadway (Stephen
  Lee)
Great Divide, The
Greater Glory, The
Heart of a Siren, The
Her Game
Isle of Forgotten Women
Just a Woman
Learning to Love
Lilies of the Field
Love's Masquerade
Man of Stone, The
Marooned Hearts
Moulders of Men
My Official Wife
Mystic, The
Next Corner, The (Robert Maury)
Oath, The
One Week of Love
Referee, The
Road of Ambition
Rustle of Silk, The (Arthur Fallaray)
School for Wives
Selznick player 20
Shadows of the Sea
She Loves and Lies
Smoke Bellew
Sporting Lover, The
Two Weeks
Venus of Venice
Viennese Melody, The
Virtuous Vamp, The
Whispering Devils
White Moth, The
Wide Open Town, A
Woman of Bronze
Stage:
Mad Dog, The (Rab Mobley) 21
Mid-Channel [Pasadena, Calif.] 28

5876
TEARLE, David*
Green Goddess, The (High Priest)
Stage:
Scotch Mist (Freddie Lansing) 26
Still Waters (Lumsley Panhaven) 26

5877
TEARLE, Sir Godfrey (1884-1953)
If Youth but Knew
Kenilworth Castle
One Colombo Night
Salome of the Tenements
Stage:
Fake, The (Geoffrey Sands) 24

5878
TEARLE, Noah*
Over the Hill

5879
TEASDALE, Veree (1897-)
Syncopation
Stage:
Buy, Buy, Baby (Pauline Lunt) 26
By Request (Claudia Wynn) 28
Constant Wife, The (Marie-Louise
  Durham)
Master of the Inn, The (Harriet
  Norton)
Morning After, The (Mrs. Madera)
  25
Nice Women (Dorothy Drew) 29
Precious (Sonia) 29
Soldiers and Women (Helen Arnold)
  29
Youngest, The (Augusta Winslow
  Martin) 24

5880
"TEDDY"*
Manslaughter (Gloomy Gus)

5881
TEDDY (the Keystone dog)
Boy of Flanders, A

5882
TEDDY (Lion)
Extra Girl, The

5883
TEJE, Tora*
Witchcraft Through the Ages /aka/
  Häxan

5884
TELL, Alma (1892-1937)
Broadway Rose
Iron Trail, The
On with the Dance
Paying the Piper
Right to Love, The
San Francisco Nights
Saturday's Children
Stage:
Aren't We All (Margot Tatham) 23
It Is the Law (Ruth) 22
Lass O' Laughter (Lady Ailsa Wey-
  man) 25
Main Street (Carol) 21
Odd Man Out (Julie Bancroft) 25
These Charming People (Julia Ber-
  ridge) 25

When We Are Young (Annie Laurie
  Brown) 20

5885
TELL, Olive (1894-1951)
Chickie
Clothes
Good Medicine
Hearts in Exile
Love Without Question
Nothing a Year
Prince of Tempters, The
Sailors' Wives
Slaves of Beauty
Soft Living
Summer Bachelors
Trial of Mary Dugan, The (Mrs. Ed-
  gar Rice)
Very Idea, The
Wings of Pride
Womanhandled
Woman's Business, A
Worlds Apart
Wrong Woman, The
Stage:
Morphia (Nurse Margaret) 23
Nemesis (Marcia Kallan) 21

5886
TELLEGEN, Lou (Isador Louis
  Bernard van Dameler) (1881-1934)
After Business Hours
Between Friends
Blind Youth
Breath of Scandal, The
East Lynne (Sir Francis Levison)
Greater than Marriage
Let Not Man Put Asunder
Little Firebrand, The
Married Alive
Outsider, The
Parisian Love (Pierre Marcel)
Parisian Nights
Princess from Hoboken
Redeeming Sin, The
Siberia
Silver Treasure, The
Single Wives
Sporting Chance, The
Stage Madness
Three Bad Men
Vitagraph player 24
Woman and the Puppet, The
Womanpower
Stage:
Anna (Peter Torrelli) 28
Cortez (Don Hernando Cortez y
  Romero) 29

Don Juan (Title role) 21
Vaudeville [Palace] 27

5887
TEMARY, Elza*
Gefahren der Brautzeit [Dangers of
the Engagement Period]
Aus dem Tagebuch eines Verführers;
Eine Nacht der Liebe; Liebes-
nächte [Nights of Love]; Liebes-
briefe (Florence)

5888
TEMPLE, Lorraine*
Pink Gods

5889
TEN EYCK, Lillian*
Sandra

5890
TEN EYCK, Melissa*
Happy Days (chorus)

5891
TENBROOK, Harry*
Blue Eagle, The (Bascom)
Capital Punishment (executioner)
Danger Street
Seven Footprints to Satan

5892
TENBROOK, James*
If Winter Comes

5893
TENENHOLTZ, Nettie*
Salome of the Tenements

5894
TENNANT, Barbara*
Captain January
Circus Days
Dollar Mark, The
King of Kings, The (bit)
Masked Woman, The
Poisoned Paradise (Mrs. Kildair)
Wolves of the North [serial]

5895
TENNYSON, Gladys*
Broadway after Dark
Last Man on Earth, The

5896
TENNYSON, Walter*
Bride of the Storm
Dress Parade

Virgin Queen, The (Viscount Heres-
ford)

5897
TERALE, Noel*
Disraeli (Flojambe)

5898
TERRIBILL, Giovanni*
Messalina

5899
TERRIS, Norma*
Cameo Kirby
Married in Hollywood
Stage:
Night in Paris, A (a principal)
Queen O' Hearts (Grace) 22
Show Boat (Magnolia) 27
Vaudeville [Palace] 27

5900
TERRISS, Ellaine (1871-)
Atlantic (English) (Mrs. Rool)
Blighty

5901
TERRY, Alice (Alice Taafe) (1896-)
Any Woman
Arab, The (Mary Hilbert)
Confessions of a Queen
Conquering Power, The (Eugenie
Grandet)
Four Horsemen of the Apocalypse,
The (Marguerite Laurier)
Garden of Allah, The
Great Divide, The
Hearts Are Trumps
Lovers
Magician, The
Maré Nostrum [Our Sea] (Freya Tal-
berg)
Metro player 23
Prisoner of Zenda, The (Princess
Flavia)
Sackcloth and Scarlet
Scaramouche (Aline de Kercadiou)
Three Passions, The
Turn to the Right
Where the Pavement Ends (Matilda
Spencer)

5902
TERRY, Don*
Me, Gangster (Jimmy Williams)
Untamed
Valiant, The

5903
TERRY, Ellen (1848-1928)
Bohemian Girl, The (nurse)

5904
TERRY, Ethel Grey (1898-)
Brass
Breaking Point, The (Lucia Deeping)
Canceled Debts
Confessions of a Wife
Cross Roads of New York
Dumb Waiter, A
Fast Worker, The
Food for Scandal
Garrison's Finish
Going Some
Greater than Love
Habit
Hardboiled
Kick Back, The
Love Toy, The
Metro player 23
Modern Mothers
Oath Bound
Object Alimony
Old Shoes
Peg O' My Heart (Ethel Chichester)
Penalty, The (Rose)
Self Made Wife, The
Shattered Idols
Skinner's Big Idea
Too Much Business
Under Two Flags (Princess Corona)
Unknown Purple, The
What Fools Men
What Wives Want
White Mouse, The
Why Women Remarry
Wild Bill Hickok
Stage:
Honor Be Damned (Agnes Delrae) 27

5905
TERRY, Francis*
Screaming Shadow, The

5906
TERRY, Harry*
American Prisoner, The (Boatswain
  Knapps)
Return of the Rat, The (Alf)

5907
TERRY, Jack*
Old Home Week
West of the Water Tower
Stage:
What Every Woman Knows (James
  Wylie) 26

5908
TETZLAFF, Toni /aka/ Tony*
Kopf Hoch, Charly! [Heads Up,
  Charly!] (Frau Zangenberg)
Sein Grösster Bluff [Her Greatest
  Bluff] (Madame Andersson)

5909
THALASSO, Arthur*
Strong Man, The (Zandow the Great)
Venus of Venice
Wine (Amoti)

5910
THANE, Gibson*
Lady from Paris, The /aka/ Das
  Schone Abenteuer

5911
THATCHER, Heather*
Express Love
Flag Lieutenant, The
Little House of Peter Wells, The
Plaything
Will O' the Wisp [series]

5912
THAW, Russell*
Hidden Woman, The (Johnny Randolph)

5913
THAYER, Merewyn*
Merry Widow, The (Ambassador's
  wife)

5914
THEBURN, Robert--see: Robert
  Thorne

5915
THEBY, Rosemary (1885-)
Across the Divide
As No Man Desires
Behold This Woman
Bowery Cinderella, A
Chinatown Mystery, The [serial]
Connecticut Yankee in King Arthur's
  Court, A (Queen Morgan la Fay)
Dice of Destiny
Dream Melody
Eternal Flame, The (Madame de
  Serizy)
Fifth Avenue Models
Fightin' Mad
Girl of the Golden West, The
Girls Who Dare
Good Women
Long Live the King
Lost and Found

Midnight Daddies
Mill of the Gods
Montmartre Rose
More to Be Pitied than Scorned
One Year to Live
Partners of Fate
Peacock Fan, The
Port of Missing Girls
Red Lily, The (Nana)
Rich Men's Wives
Rio Grande
Rip Tide
Secrets of the Night
Shame
Slander the Woman
So Big (Pauline Storm)
Son of the Sahara, A
Splendid Hazard, A
Trial Marriage
Truthful Sex, The
Weight of a Crown
Woman Against the World
Yellow Men and Gold
Your Friend and Mine

5916
THEADORE, Ralph*
Dance of Life, The (Harvey Howell)
Stage:
Burlesque (Harvey Howell) 27
Devil Within, The (Murdock) 25
Gossipy Sex, The (Chief Mason) 27
Sweet Land of Liberty (Jack Richards)
  29

5917
THESIGER, Ernest (1879-1961)
West End Wives

5918
THIMIG, Hermann*
Die Bergkatze /aka/ The Mountain
  Cat; The Wildcat (Pepo)
Die Flamme [The Flame] /aka/
  Montmartre (Leduc)
Stage:
Dantons Tod (dual role, Herault-
  Sechelles/Deputy from Lyon) 27
Jedermann [Everyman] (Fellowship-
  Guttergesell) 27
Midsummer Night's Dream, A
  (Demetrius) 27
Peripherie (Franzie) 28

5919
THIRWELL, George*
Chinese Bungalow, The (Harold
  Marquis)

5920
THOMAS, Edward*
Tea for Three

5921
THOMAS, Frank (1889-)
Deadline at Eleven

5922
THOMAS, Helga*
Cinderella
Richthofhen: The Red Knight of the
  Air
When Duty Calls

5923
THOMAS, Jameson (1892-1939)
Afraid to Love
Apache, The
As We Lie
Blighty
Brotherhood, The
Cavern Spider, The
Chester Forgets Himself
Chu-Chin Chow (Omar)
Daughter of Love, A
Decameron Nights
Drum, The
Farmer's Wife, The
Feather, The
Gold Cure, The
Hate Ship
High Treason (Michael Deane)
Jungle Woman
Memories
Pearl of the South Seas
Piccadilly (Valentine Wilmot)
Poppies of Flanders
Power over Men
Rising Generation
Roses of Picardy (Georges D'Arche-
  ville)
Sins Ye Do, The
Tesha
Weekend Wives
White Sheik, The
Woman in the Night, A

5924
THOMAS, Jane*
Heedless Moths
Hoosier Schoolmaster, The
North Wind's Malice, The
Silver Wings
Town that Forgot God, The
White Rose, The (cigar stand girl)
Stage:
Gambling (Miss Daly) 29

5925
THOMAS, John Charles (1887-1960)
Under the Red Robe (Gil de Berault)
Stage:
Love Letter, The (Philip Delma) 21
Vaudeville [Palace] 29

5926
THOMAS, Olive (Olive Duffy) (1898-
   1920)
Darling Mine
Everybody's Sweetheart
Flapper, The
Footlights and Shadows
Glorious Lady, The
Jennie
Out Yonder
Youthful Folly

5927
THOMAS, Peter Evan*
Constant Nymph, The (Ike)

5928
THOMAS, Queenie (1900-)
Alley of Golden Hearts, The
Gayest of the Gay, The
Gold Cure, The
Her Redemption
Juliet and Her Romeo
Last Witness, The
Rainbow comedies
Safety First
School for Scandal, The
Straws in the Wind
Syncopated Picture Plays [series]
Trousers
Warned Off

5929
THOMAS, Virginia*
Private Life of Helen of Troy, The
   (Hera)
Wild Party, The (Tess)

5930
THOMAS, Yvonne*
Constant Nymph, The (Kate)

5931
THOMPSOM, Lotus--see: Lotus
   Thompson

5932
THOMPSON, Al*
Golf

5933
THOMPSON, Clarence*
Butterflies in the Rain
Sensation Seekers, The

5934
THOMPSON, Denton*
Wee MacGreegor's Sweetheart (Wullie
   Thomson)

5935
THOMPSON, Duane (1905-)
Born to the Saddle
Beauty and Bullets
Eyes of the Underworld
Fighting Redhead, The
Flying Buckaroo
Frozen River
Her Summer Hero
Kiss Doctor, The
Phantom Fingers
Phantom of the Range
Phyllis of the Follies
Price of Fear, The
Silent Avenger, The
Slim Fingers
Sweet Rosie O'Grady
Tip Off, The
Voice of the City
Wireless Lizzie

5936
THOMPSON, Fred (1890-1928) [Horse:
   Silver King]
All Around the Frying Pan
Bandit's Baby, The
Dangerous Coward, The
Don Mike
Eagle's Talons, The [serial]
Fighting Sap, The
Galloping Gallagher
Hands Across the Border
Into No Man's Land
Jessie James
Kit Carson
Lone Hand Saunders
Love Light, The (Joseph)
Mask of Lopez, The
North of Nevada
Pioneer Scout, The
Quemado, that Devil
Regular Scout, A
Ridin' the Wind
Sheriff of Tombstone, The
Silent Stranger
Silver Comes Through
Sunset Legion, The
Thundering Hoofs

Tough Guy
Two Gun Man
Wild Bull's Lair, The

5937
THOMPSON, George*
Why Bring That Up?
Stage:
Brook (Mooney Blackburn) 23
Devil Within, The (Officer Dugan) 25
Great Adventure, The (Albert Shawn)
   26
Holy Terror, A (Uncle Tod Yancey)
   25
Noose, The (Hughes) 26

5938
THOMPSON, Hugh*
Half-Breed, The (Ross Kennion)
Stage:
Guns (Jimmy Plankey, The "Colora-
   do Special")

5939
THOMPSON, J. Denton*
Christie Johnstone (Wully)

5940
THOMPSON, Johnny*
In the Name of the Law

5941
THOMPSON, Kenneth--see: Kenneth
   Thomson

5942
THOMPSON, Leonard*
Wrecker, The

5943
THOMPSON, Lotus*
Dangerous Dude, The
Folly of Vanity
Freckled Rascal, The

5944
THOMPSON, Nick*
General Crack (Gypsy Chiefton)
Married? (Joe Pinto)
Puppets
Snow Bride, The
Tongues of Flame

5945
THOMPSON, Roy*
Enchanted Hill, The
When a Man's a Man

5946
THOMPSON, William*
Enemies of Women (Col. Marcos)
Stage:
Czarina, The (Malakoff) 22
Guest of Honor, The (Mr. Warner)
   20
Sonya (Prince Michael) 21

5947
THOMSON, Kenneth (1889-1967)
Bellamy Trial, The (Stephen Bellamy)
Broadway Melody, The (Jack Warri-
   ner)
Careless Age, The
Corporal Kate
Girl from Havana, The
King of Kings, The (Lazarus)
Letter, The
Man Bait
Pathê player 28
Risky Business
Say It with Songs
Secret Hour, The
Song Writer, The
Veiled Woman, The
White Gold (Alec Carson)
Stage:
Czarina, The (Nicholas Jaschikoff) 22
Great Broxopp, The (Ronny Derwent)
   21
Hush Money (Harry Bentley) 26

5948
THORNDIKE, Lucille*
Garden of Weeds, The

5949
THORNDIKE, Russell*
School for Scandal, The

5950
THORNDIKE, Dame Sybil (1882-1975)
Dawn (Edith Cavell)
Esmeralda (Title role)
Merchant of Venice, The (Portia)
Moth and Rust (debut)
To What Red Hell?

5951
THORNE, Robert*
Janice Meredith (Patrick Henry)
Stage:
Distant Drum, A (Carl Franken) 28
Extra (R. H. Osgood) 23
In the Night Watch (Chief Engineer
   Birodat)
Othello (Lodovico) 25

Taps (a doctor) 25
Virgin, The (Dr. Hall) 26

5952
THORNE, William L. *
Drake Case, The
Thunderbolt
Stage:
Big Boy ("Bully" John Bagby) 25
Love Call, The (Henry Canby) 27
Thrills (Horace Benson) 25
Try It with Alice (Harry Mattox) 24

5953
THORNTON, Edith*
Fair Play
Lightning Hutch [serial]
Little Firebrand, The
Was It Bigamy?
Whirlwind, The [serial]

5954
THORNWALL, Francis*
Cradle of Courage, The (Jim Kelly)

5955
THORPE, Gordon*
Bridge of San Luis Rey, The (Jaime)
Iron Mask, The (dual role, young
    Price Louis/his twin

5956
THORPE, Richard*
Restless Wives
Three O'Clock in the Morning
Stage:
Bitter Sweet (Lord Edgar James) 29

5957
THUNDER (Dog)
Black Lightning (himself)

5958
THURMAN, Mary (1894-) [Death
date 1925 in error in Vol. I]
Bare Knuckles
Bond Boy, The
Fool, The
Green Temptation
In the Heart of a Fool
Lady from Longacre, The
Primal Law
Prince and Betty, The
Sand!
Scoffer, The
Should a Man Marry?
Sin of Martha Queed, The
Tents of Allah

That Night
Valley of Yesterday
Wife in Name Only
Wildfire
Zaza (Florianne)
Stage:
Babes in Toyland (Jack) 29
Merry Widow, The (Margot) 29
Sweethearts (Clairette) 29

5959
THURSTON, Charles*
Chaser, The
Rolling Home

5960
TIBBETT, Lawrence (1896-1960)
Rogue Song, The (Yegor)
Stage:
King Lear (Edgar) 23

5961
TICHENOR, Edna*
Drifting
Gold Diggers (Dolly Baxter)
London after Midnight (bat girl)
Merry Widow, The (Dopey Marie)
Silent Accuser, The

5962
TIDEN, Zelma /aka/ Selma*
Old Home Week
Stage:
Baby Mine (Maggie O'Flarety) 27
Steam Roller, The (Dora Worthing-
    ton) 24

5963
TIEDTKE, Jakob /aka/ Jacob*
Die Flamme [The Flame] /aka/
    Montmartre
Jew of Mestri, The (Beppo)
Der Kleine Napoleon [The Little Na-
    poleon] /aka/ So Sind die Männer
    [Men Are Like That]; Napoleons
    Kleiner Bruder [Napoleon's Little
    Brother] (Jeremias von Katzenel-
    lenbogen)
Kölhiessel Töchter (Mathias Kolhies-
    sel)
Luther
Romeo and Julia im Schnee [Romeo
    and Juliet in the Snow]
Sumurun /aka/ One Arabian Night
    (head eunuch)
Waltz Dream, The (Eberhard XXIII,
    Duke of Flausenburg)

5964
TIGE (Dog)
Buster Brown

5965
TILBURY, Zeffie (1863-1945)
Clothes
Marriage of William Ashe, The
  (Lady Tranmore)
Mothers of Men
Single Standard, The
Stage:
Breaking Point, The (Lucy) 23
Just Beyond (Mrs. Towers) 25
Letter of the Law, The (Madame
  Vagret) 20
My Aunt from Ypsilanti (Mrs. Har-
  per) 23

5966
TILDEN, William T. *
Music Master, The

5967
TILTON, Edwin Booth*
Love Chance, The
Midnight Express, The

5968
TILTON, James A.
Down to the Sea in Ships (Captain of
  the "Morgan")

5969
TIMBROOKE, Harry*
Play Girl, The

5970
TIMONTAYEV, A. *
Tanka-Trakitirschitsa /aka/ Portin
  Otsa; Against Her Father; Tanka,
  the Innkeeper

5971
TINCHER, Fay*
Gumps, The (Min Gump) [series]

5972
TING-LIANG-TCHAO*
Veil of Happiness, The

5973
TISSOT, Alice*
La Cousin Bette
Un Chapeau de Paille d'Italie [The
  Italian Straw Hat]

5974
TITMUSS, Phyllis*
Beloved Vagabond, The (Joana Rush-
  worth)

5975
TITUS, Lydia Yeamans (1874-1929)
All Dolled Up
Beau Revel
Beauty's Worth (Jane)
Boy of Flanders, A
Concert, The
Cytherea (laundress)
Deep Waters
Famous Mrs. Fair, The
Freeze Out
God's Desire, A
High Speed
His Nibs
Invisible Power, The
Irene
Limited Mail, The
Mad Marriage
Marriage of William Ashe, The (Lady
  Parham)
Married Flapper, The
Night Life (landlady)
Nobody's Fool
Nurse Marjorie
Prince of Avenue A, The
Queenie
Scaramouche (Madame Binet)
Shanghai Lady
Sweet Sixteen
Talker, The
Tarnish
Two Lovers (innkeeper's wife)
Up the Ladder
Upstream
Voice of the Storm
Wanters, The
Water Hole, The
While the City Sleeps (Mrs. Sullivan)
Winter Has Come

5976
TOBEY, Dan*
Waltzing Around

5977
TOD, Malcolm*
Daughter of Israel, A
Dick Turpin's Ride to New York (Earl
  of Weston)
Woman Tempted, The

5978
TODD, Dana*
Wall Flower, The

5979
TODD, Harry*
Flaming Frontier, The
Jack-Knife Man, The
One Stolen Night
Sky Pilot, The
Third Degree, The
White Pebbles

5980
TODD, Lola*
Bells, The
Count of Luxembourg, The
Fifty-Fifty Girl, The
Harvester, The
Iron Man, The [serial] (Mimi)
Return of the Riddle Rider [serial]
Scarlet Streak, The [serial]
Taking a Chance

5981
TODD, Thelma (Alison Lloyd)
   (1905-1935)
Arizona Bound
Bachelor Girl
Careers
Crash, The
Crazy Feet
Fascinating Youth
Fighting Parson, The
Flaming Youth
Gay Defender, The
God Gave Me Twenty Cents
Haunted House, The
Heart to Heart
Her Private Life
Hotter than Hot
House of Horror, The
It's All Greek to Me
King, The
Look Out Below
Naughty Baby
Nevada (Hettie Ide)
Noose, The
Popular Sin, The
Rubber Heels
Seven Footprints to Satan
Shield of Honor
Sky Boy
Snappy Sneezer
Sport Girl, The
Stepping Out
Trial Marriage
Unaccustomed As We Are
Vamping Venus
Wrecking Boss, The

5982
TOKONAGA, Frank*
Willow Tree, The

5983
TOLER, Sidney (1874-1947)
Madame X (debut as Merivel)
Stage:
Canary Dutch ("Biff" Schultz) 25
Deburau (the "Barker") 20
Dove, The (Mike Morowich) 25
49er's, The (a principal) 22
It's a Wise Child (Cool Kelly) 29
Kiki (Joly) 21
Laugh, Clown, Laugh! (Flok) 23
Mrs. Bumpstead-Leigh (Peter Swal-
   low) 29
Poldekin (Welch) 20
Sophie (Sophie's First Lackey) 20
Tommy (David Tuttle) 27

5984
TOLLAIRE, August*
Four Sons
His Captive Woman
Hot for Paris
Monkey Talks, The
Plastered in Paris
What Price Glory? (French Major)
Wife Savers

5985
TOLLEY, Jean*
Take It from Me

5986
TOLSTOY, Countess Tamara*
Die Freudlöse Gasse [The Joyless
   Street] /aka/ The Street of Sor-
   row (Henriette)

5987
TOLSTOY, Count Illya*
Resurrection

5989
TOMLINSON, Daniel G. *
Bardley's the Magnificent
Crowd, The (Jim)

5990
TOMLINSON, Leslie*
Luck of the Navy, The (Wing, as a
   boy)

5991
TOMMY, Chief Tony*
Winning Through (Indian guide)

5992
TONCRAY, Kate*
Bing, Bang, Boom!
Charm School, The
Country Kid, The
Daddy's Gone a-Hunting
Failure, The
Mam'selle, Jo
Match Breaker, The
Narrow Street, The
Prisoners of Love
Silent Years

5993
TONGE, Lillian Bernard*
Laughing Lady, The
Stage:
Becky Sharp (Marchioness of Steyne)
  29
Meet the Prince (Emily) 29

5994
TOOKER, William (1875-)
Bellamy Trial, The
Beyond the Rainbow (Dr. Ramsey)
Birds of Prey
Cradle Buster, The
Devil Dancer, The
Fashion Madness
God's Country and the Law
Greatest Love, The
Heliotrope
Ladies Must Dress
Lone Wolf, The
Lookout Girl, The
Lotus Eaters, The
Love in the Desert
Night Watch
No Defense
Peacock Alley (Joseph Carleton)
Power Within, The
Protection
Proxies
Romance of a Rogue
Romance of the Underworld, A
Scarlet Letter, The (the Governor)
Stealers, The
Sweet Sixteen
Tell It to Sweeney
Two Girls Wanted (William Moody)
Virgin Lips
Whip, The
White Black Sheep
Why Girls Go Wrong
Woman Against the World, A
Worlds Apart

5995
TOOMEY, Regis (1902-)
Alibi /aka/ Perfect Alibi (Danny
  McGann)
Framed
Illusion (Eric Schmittlap)
Rich People (Jeff MacLeon)
Wheel of Life, The
Stage:
Little Nelly Kelly (British tour) 25

5996
TORF, Silva*
Die Freudlöse Gasse [The Joyless
  Street] /aka/ The Street of Sor-
  row (Mrs. Lechner)

5997
TORNBECH, Svend*
Story of Gösta Berling, The

5998
TORNING, Alice*
Wie Einst im Mai

5999
TORRENCE, David (1880-1942)
Abysmal Brute, The (Mortimer Sang-
  ster)
Annie Laurie /aka/ Ladies from
  Hell (Robert Laurie)
Auction Block, The (Robert Wharton)
Big Noise
Black Watch
Brown of Harvard
Cavalier, The
City of Purple Dreams, The (Syming-
  ton Otis)
Dawn of Tomorrow, The
Devil to Pay, The
Disraeli (Sir Michael, Lord Probert)
Drums of Jeopardy, The
Forever After
Hazardous Valleys
Hearts in Exile
Her Husband's Secret
Inside of the Cup, The
Isle of Retribution
Kentucky Courage
King of the Khyber Rifles (field
  marshall)
Laddie
Light that Failed, The
Little Shepherd of Kingdom Come,
  The
Love's Wilderness
Man in the Shadow
Man Next Door, The

Midnight Watch
Mysterious Rider, The
Mystic, The
Oh, What a Nurse!
On the Stroke of Twelve
Other Woman's Story, The
Paramount player 24
Power of a Lie, The
Race Wild
Rolled Stockings
Sherlock Holmes /aka/ Moriarty
Silks and Saddles
Steamboat Bill, Jr.
Strong Boy, The
Tess of the Storm Country (Elias
  Graves)
Third Degree, The
Tiger Love
Tower of Lies, The (Erik)
Trimmed in Scarlet
Undressed
Untamed Justice
What Fools Men
When Knighthood Was in Flower
  (Count von Stalburg)
Which Shall It Be?
World at Her Feet, The

6000
TORRENCE, Ernest (1878-1933)
Across to Singapore (Mark)
American Venus, The
Blind Goddess, The
Brass Bottle, The
Bridge of San Luis Rey, The (Uncle
  Pio)
Broken Chains
Captain Salvation
Circle, The
Cossacks, The (Ivan)
Covered Wagon, The (Jackson)
Desert Nights
Dressmaker from Paris, The
Fighting Coward, The [serial]
Heritage of the Desert, The
Hunchback of Notre Dame, The
  (Clopin)
King of Kings, The (Peter)
Lady of the Harem
Mantrap (Joe Astor)
Night Life in New York
North of '36
Officer O'Brien
Paramount player 26
Peter Pan (Captain Hook)
Pony Express
Prodigal Judge, The
Rainmaker, The

Ruggles of Red Gap
Side Show of Life, The
Silks and Saddles
Singer of Seville
Speedway
Steamboat Bill, Jr.
Tol'able David (Luke Hatburn)
Trail of the Lonesome Pine, The
Twelve Miles Out (Red McCue)
Unholy Night, The (Dr. Ballou)
Untamed (Ben Murchison)
Wanderer, The
West of the Water Tower
Stage:
Night Boat, The (Captain Robert
  White) 20

6001
TORRES, Raquel (Marie Osterman)
  (1908-)
Bridge of San Luis Rey, The (Pepita)
Desert Rider, The
Sea Bat, The
Under a Texas Moon
White Shadows of the South Seas
  (Fayaway)

6002
TOTO (Dog)
Bringing Up Father

6003
TOUCHAGUES*
Entr'acte

6004
TOUGHEY, John*
Steele of the Royal Mounted

6005
TOULOUT, Jean*
Chantelouve
Les Miserables (Javert)
Trois Masques, The [The Three
  Masques]

6006
TOURNEUR, Andree*
Actress, The
Trelawney of the Wells (Clara De-
  foenix)

6007
TOWNE, Rosella (1919-)
Blockade
Blondes at Work
Cowboy from Brooklyn, The
Patient in Room 18, The
Sergeant Murphy

6008
TOWNSEND, Anna*
Grandma's Boy
Safety Last (the grandma)

6009
TOWNSEND, Genevieve*
Chinese Bungalow, The (Charlotte)

6010
TRACY, Helen*
Twenty-One
Stage:
Romance (Mrs. Frothingham) 21

6011
TRACY, Lee (1898-1968)
Big Time (debut)
Stage:
Book of Charm, The (Rudolph Klein)
    25
Broadway (Roy Lane) 26
Front Page, The (Hildy Johnson) 28
Glory Hallelujah (clerk) 26
Show-Off, The (Joe) 24

6012
TRAUBERG, Leonid*
Shinel /aka/ The Clock

6013
TRAUX, Maude*
Hula (Margaret Haldane)
Midnight Adventure, A
No Camping
No Picnic
"No Sale" (Smitty)
No Vacation
Ten Modern Commandments, The
Up in Mabel's Room

6014
TRAVERNIER, Albert*
Democracy, the Vision Restored
Too Many Kisses (Manuel Hurja)

6015
TRAVERS, George*
Sonia (Lord Loring)

6016
TRAVERS, Madalaine (1875-1964)
Hell Ship, The
Iron Heart, The
Lost Money
Penalty, The
Snares of Paris, The
Spirit of Good, The

Tattlers, The
What Would You Do? [serial]

6017
TRAVERS, Richard C. (1890-   )
Acquittal, The
Among Those Present
Black Watch, The
Broad Road, The
Dangerous Dude, The
Dawn of Revenge
Egg, The
Hoodooed
In the Palace of the King
Lightnin'
Mountain Woman, The
Notoriety
Rendezvous, The
Rider of the King, Log
Unholy Night, The (Major McDougal)
White Moll, The

6018
TRAVERS, Roy*
Q Ships

6019
TREACHER, Arthur (Arthur Veary)
    (1894-1975)
Battle of Paris, The /aka/ The Gay
    Lady
Stage:
Madcap, The (Sir Bertram Hawley) 28

6020
TREBAOL, Children*
Honest Hutch

6021
TREBAOL, Edouard*
Oliver Twist (the Artful Dodger)
Penalty, The (Bubble)

6022
TRENKER, Luis (1896-   )
Fight for the Matterhorn, The
Peak of Fate
Peaks of Destiny

6023
TRENT, Bob*
Dangerous Coward, The

6024
TRENT, John*
Chinese Parrot, The

6025
TRENTO, Guido*
Shepherd King, The
Street Angel (Neri)

6026
TRENTON, Pell*
Willow Tree, The

6027
TREVELYAN, Una*
Devil's Passkey, The (Mrs. Good-
   right)

6028
TREVOR, Ann*
Daniel Deronda (Mirah Lapidoth)
Stage:
Captive, The (Gisele DeMontcel) 26

6029
TREVOR, Hugh (1903-1933)
Beau Broadway
Cream of the Earth
Dry Martini
FBO player 29
Hey, Rube!
Love in the Desert
Man About Town
Midnight Mystery
Night Parade
Red Lips
Skinner's Big Idea
String
Taxi Thirteen
Very Idea, The

6930
TREVOR, Jack*
Geheimisse Seele [Secrets of the
   Soul]
Der Oberkellner
Rasputin: The Holy Sinner

6031
TREVOR, Norman (1877-1929)
Ace of Cads, The
Afraid to Love
Beau Geste (Major deBeaujolais)
Black Panther's Cub, The
Children of Divorce (Duke De Gond-
   reville)
Coward, The
Dancing Mothers (Hugh Westcourt)
Daughter Pays, The
Jane Eyre
Love Trap
Mad Hour, The

Man Who Found Himself, The
Music Master, The
New York (Randolph Church)
Restless Youth
Romance
Roulette
Siren, The
Song and Dance Man
Sorrell and Son (Thomas Roland)
Tonight at Twelve
Wages of Virtue (John Boule)
Warning, The
Wizard, The
Stage:
All Dressed Up (Raymond Stevens) 25
Captive, The (De Montcel) 26
Desert Sands (Hugh Berndon) 22
Enter Madame (Gerald Fitzgerald) 20
Foot Loose (Sir Horace Welby) 20
It All Depends (Julian Lane) 25
Lilies of the Field (Lewis Welling) 21
Love Scandal, A (Dr. Besson/Arthur
   Presby) 23
Manhattan (Duncan Van Norman) 22
Married Woman, The (Hugh Dellamy)
   21
Mountebank, The (Horatio Bakkus)
Young Blood (Alan Dana) 25

6032
TREVOR, Spencer*
Alf's Button (Lord Dunwater)

6033
TRIMBLE, Arthur*
Buster Brown (Title role)

6034
TRIPOD, Irene*
Beloved Vagabond, The (Madame
   Boin)

6035
TRUAX, Maude--see: Maude Traux

6036
TRUBETZSKOY, Youcca (1905-)
Beautiful Cheat, The
Flower of Night
Four Devils
His Glorious Night
Peacock Feathers
Road Show

6037
TRUE, Bess*
Sailors' Wives

6038
TRUESDALE, Howard (1870-)
Ashes of Vengeance (Vicomte de
   Briege)
Burning Daylight
French Heels
Go West
Lawless Legion, The
Mating Call
No Thoroughfare
Reno
Three-Ring-Marriage
Tigress, The
Van Bibber comedies
Whisper Market, The
Why Men Leave Home
Youthful Folly

6039
TRUESDELL, Frederick C. /aka/
   Fred*
Love Piker, The
Pleasure Mad
Stage:
Crashing Through (Peter Poole) 28
Gorilla, The (Cyrus Stevens) 25
Our Betters (Arthur Fenwick) 28
That Day (Sylvester Carhart) 22
Voltaire (Aristide Freron) 22

6040
TRUEX, Ernest (1890-1973)
Night of the Pub, The
Six Cylinder Love
Stage:
Annie Dear (George Wimbledon) 24
Blue Bonnet (Billy Burleson) 20
Fall Guy, The (Johnnie Quinan) 25
Lambs Gambol
Many Waters (James Barcaldine) 29
New Toys (Will Webb) 24
No More Blondes (James Howells) 20
Pomeroy's Past (Pomeroy Chilton) 26
Six-Cylinder Love (Gilbert Sterling)
   21

6041
TRUMPS (Dog)
My Rural Relations
Western Ways
Winter's Tale, A

6042
TRYON, Glenn (1897-)
Barnum Was Right
Battling Orioles, The
Broadway (Roy Lane)
Forty-Five Minutes from Hollywood

Gate Crasher, The
Half Marriage
Hero for a Night, A
Hot Heels
How to Handle Women
It Can Be Done
Kid's Clever, The
Leave It to Me
Lonesome
Painting the Town
Poor Nut, The
Skinner Steps Out
Thanks for the Buggy Ride
Two Girls Wanted (Dexter Wright)
White Sheep, The

6043
TSAPPI, V. *
Storm over Asia

6044
TSCHEKOWA, Olga*
Aftermath
Un Chapeau de Paille d'Italie [The
   Italian Straw Hat]
Haunted Castle, The
Tatjana
When Duty Calls

6045
TSESSARSKAYA, Emma*
Village of Sin, The

6046
TUCKER, Harlan*
Dragon's Net, The [serial]

6047
TUCKER, Richard (1869-1942)
Air Mail, The
Beau Brummel (Lord Stanhope)
Beware of Married Men
Bit of Heaven, A
Blind Goddess, The
Border Patrol
Branding Iron (Prosper Gael)
Bridge of Sighs, The
Broken Wing, The
Brothers
Bush Leaguer, The
Cameo Kirby
Captain Swagger
Crimson City
Dangerous Age, The
Daughters of Desire
Dearie
Desired Woman, The
Devil's Island

Dollars and Sense
Don't Neglect Your Wife
Dummy, The (Blackie Baker)
Everything for Sale
Fast Worker, The
Ghetto, The
Girl from Rio, The
Golden Cocoon, The
Goldwyn player 21
Grain of Dust, A
Grand Larceny
Great Lover, The
Half Marriage
Hearts Aflame
Helen's Babies (Tom Lawrence)
Her Accidental Husband
Is Divorce a Failure?
Jazz Singer, The (Harry Lee)
King of the Congo [serial]
Kiss in a Taxi, A
Lily, The
Love over Night
Loves of an Actress
Lucky Boy /aka/ My Mother's
   Eyes
Lure of the Wild
Man Without a Country, The /aka/
   As No Man Has Loved
Matinee Ladies
My Man
Night Rose, The
Old Nest, The
On Trial (Prosecutor Gray)
Peacock Alley
Poor Men's Wives
Rags to Riches
Rememberance
Roads of Destiny
Self Made Man, A
Shameful Behavior
Show Folks
Show Girl, The
Squall, The (Josef Lajos)
Strange Idols
Thanks for the Buggy Ride
That's My Baby
This Is Heaven
Tornado
Unholy Night, The (Col. Davidson)
Virginia Courtship, A
Voice in the Dark, A
What Love Will Do
When the Desire Drives
Wings (Air Commander)
Woman in Room 13, The
Women's Wares
World at Her Feet, The
Worldly Madonna, The
Yellow Men and Gold

6048
TUCKER, Sophie (Sophia Abuza)
   (1884-1966)
Honky Tonk (Sophie Leonard)
Record:
He's Tall, Dark and Handsome (Col.
   492) (MES/7031)
Stage:
Earl Carroll's Vanities (a principal)
   24
Vaudeville [Palace] 23; 26; 28; 29

6049
TUCKER, William H.*
Purple Highway, The
Wife in Name Only
Stage:
Nightingale, The (Otto Goldschmidt)
   27

6050
TUNNEY, Gene (James Joseph Tun-
   ney) (1898-)
Fighting Marine, The [serial]

6051
TUPPER, Pearl*
Hunchback of Notre Dame, The

6052
TURFLER, James*
Down to the Sea in Ships (cabin boy)

6053
TURNBULL, Stanley*
Amazing Quest of Mr. Ernest Bliss,
   The (Willie Mott)

6054
TURNER, Baby*
Singer Jim McKee

6055
TURNER, Bowditch*
Four Horsemen of the Apocalypse,
   The ("Smoke" Argensola)
Scaramouche (Le Chapelier)

6056
TURNER, Doreen*
Rosita (Rosita's sister)
Through the Back Door (Constant)

6057
TURNER, Florence (1887-1946)
Broken Gates
Canceled Debts
Chinese Parrot
College

Dark Angel, The (Roma)
Gilded Highway, The
Hornet's Nest
Janice Meredith
Jazzland
Jean and the Calico Dog
Kid's Clever, The
Law and the Man, The
Little Mother, The
Marry the Girl
Never the Twain Shall Meet
Old Wive's Tale, The
Padlocked
Passion Fruit
Road to Ruin, The
Sally Bishop (Janet)
Sally in Our Alley
Stranded
Tiffany player 27
Ugly Duckling, The
Walking Back
Was She Justified?
Women and Diamonds
Stage:
Sign of the Leopard (Taylor) 28

6058
TURNER, Fred A. *
Jack-Knife Man, The
Uncharted Seas

6059
TURNER, George*
Sally Bishop (Arthur)

6060
TURNER, Maidel*
Eligible Mr. Bangs, The
Stage:
Book of Charm, The (Mrs. Wilson)
  25
Egotist, The (Sally Jenkins) 22
Martinique (Azaline) 20
Spring Is Here (Emily Braley) 29
Tommy (Mrs. Thurber) 27
Varying Shore, The (Mrs. Venable)
  21

6061
TURNER, Maude*
Last of Mrs. Cheney, The (Mrs.
  Webley)
Wizard, The

6062
TURNER, Raymond*
Detectives Wanted
Little Johnny Jones

Love Mart, The
Naughty Baby
Synthetic Sin
Weary River
Young Nowheres

6063
TURNER, William*
Darling of New York, The
Enemy Sex, The
Garden of Weeds, The
Last Performance, The
Pony Express

6064
TURPIN, Ben (1874-1940)
Asleep at the Switch
Bloggie's Vacation
Blonde's Revenge, A
Bright Eyes
Broke in China
College Kiddo
Countess Bloggie
Daddy's Boy
Daredevil, The
Down on the Farm
Eyes Have It, The
Harem Night, A
Hogan's Alley
Hollywood
Hollywood Hero, A
Hollywood Kid, The
Home Made Movies
Idle Eyes
Jolly Jilter, The
Love and Doughnuts
Love Parade, The (Cross-eyed
  Lackey)
Love's Languid Lure
Love's Outcast
Married Life
Pitfalls of a Big City
Pride of Pikeville
Prodigal Bridegroom, The
Raspberry Romance
Reel Virginian, The
Romeo and Juliet (Romeo)
Show of Shows, The
Shriek of Araby, The
Small Town Idol, A
Snakeville Debutantes
Snakeville Hen Medic
Snakeville's Champion
Star Boarder, The
Steel Preferred
Step Forward
Ten Dollars or Ten Days
Three Foolish Weeks

When a Man's a Prince
Where Is My Wandering Boy Tonight?
Wife's Relations, The
Wild Goose Chaser
Woman's Way, A
Yukon Jake

6065
TUSTAIN, George*
Romance of a Queen, The (Captain
    of the Guard)
Three Weeks

6066
TUTTLE, Eugenia*
Boy of Flanders, A

6067
TWEED, Frank*
Puritan Passions
Stage:
Saint Joan (Bertrand de Pulengy) 23
Windows (Mr. Barnabas) 23

6068
TWELVETREES, Helen (Helen Marie
    Jurgens) (1908-1958)
Blue Skies
Ghost Talks, The
Paris to Bagdad
True Heart
Words and Music

6069
TYLER, Harry (1888-1961)
Shannons of Broadway, The /aka/
    Goodbye Broadway
Stage:
Shannons on Broadway, The (Eddie
    Allen) 27

6070
TYLER, Tom (William Burns)
    (1903-1954)
Arizona Streak, The
Avenging Rider
Battling Buckaroo
Born to Battle
Canyon of Missing Men
Cherokee Kid, The
Cowboy Cop, The
Cyclone of the Range
Desperate Pirate
Eagle's Talons, The [serial]
FBO player 24
Flying-U Ranch, The
Gun Law
Hearts and Hoofs

Idaho Red
Let 'er Go Gallagher
Lightning Lariats
Lone Horseman
Man from Nevada, The
Masquerade Bandit, The
Mystery Valley
Neath Western Skies
Only Thing, The
Out of the West
Phantom of the Range
Phantom Rider
Red Hot Hoofs
Road to Eldorado
Sonora Kid, The
Sorcerer, The
Splitting the Breeze
Terror Mountain
Texas Tornado
Tom and His Pals
Trail of Horse Thieves
Tyrant of Red Gulch
When the Law Rides
Wild to Go
Wyoming Wildcat

6071
TYNAN, Brandon (1879-)
Success
Stage:
Human Nature (Mr. Hale) 25
Lambs Gambol 25
Mandarin, The (the Baron) 20
Purple Mask, The (Brisquet) 20
That French Lady (Michael Maloney)
    27
Tyranny of Love (Paul Cartier) 21
Ziegfeld Follies 22; 23; 24

6072
TYROLER, William*
Phantom of the Opera, The

6073
TYRON, Max*
Greed (Uncle Oelberman)

- U -

6074
UCCELLINI, Ugo*
Romola

6075
UKIL, Sarada*
Light of Asia, The

6076
ULMER, Fritz*
Waterloo

6077
ULRIC, Lenore (1892-1970)
Frozen Justice
South Sea Rose
Tiger Love
Stage:
Harem, The (Carla) 24
Kiki (Title role) 21
Lulu Belle (Title role) 26
Mima (Title role) 28
Vaudeville [Palace] 27; 28

6078
ULRICH, Florence*
Galloping Cowboy, The

6079
UNDA, Emilie*
Der Mensch am Wege [Man by the
   Roadside]

6080
UNDERWOOD, Franklin (1877-1963)
News Parade, The

6081
UNDERWOOD, Lawrence*
Old Lady 31
Passionate Youth

6082
UNDERWOOD, Loyal*
Dixie Handicap, The
Idle Class, The
My American Wife (Danny O'Hare)
Pay Day
Pilgrim, The

6083
UNGER, Gunnar*
Youth

6084
UNTERKIRCHEN, Hans*
Last Laugh, The /aka/ Der Letze
   Mann (hotel manager)

6085
UNTERSHIAK, J. *
Seeds of Freedom

6086
URANEFF, Vadim*
Fazil (Ahmed)

Magic Flame, The (the visitor)
Sea Beast, The (Pip)
Sea Hunt, The

6087
URIBE, Justa*
Arab, The (Myrza)

- V -

6088
VACHON, Jean*
For Sale (the flapper)

6089
VALDEMAR, Thais*
Bluebeard's Eighth Wife (bit)

6090
VALE, Viola /aka/ Vola*
Alias Jimmy Valentine
Alimony
Crashing Through
Daughters of the Rich
Iron Rider, The
Little Annie Rooney
Man Between, The
Master Stroke, A
Mothers-in-Law
Someone in the House
Soul of the Beast, The
Two Can Play (Mimi)
White Oak, The

6091
VALENE, Nanette*
Lost Lady, A

6092
VALENTINE, Grace (1890-)
Man's Home, A
Stage:
Cave Girl, The (Margot Merrill) 20
Chivalry (Tottie Lanier) 25
Kidding Kidders (Betty Kidder) 28
Trial Marriage (Peggy Hall) 27

6093
VALENTINE, John*
American Prisoner, The (Commander
   Miller)
Lost Patrol, The

6094
VALENTINE, Leila*
Passers By

6095
VALENTINO, Rudolph (Rodolpho Al-
fonzo Raffaelo Pierre Filibert
Guglielmi di Valentino d'Anton-
quolla) (1895-1926)
Adventuress, An /aka/ The Isle of
Love
Beyond the Rocks (Lord Bracondale)
Blood and Sand (Juan Gallardo)
Camille (Armand)
Cheater, The
Cobra (Count Rodrigo Torriani)
Conquering Power, The (Charles
Grandet)
Eagle, The (Vladimir Dubrovsky)
Equity player 20
Fog, The
Four Horsemen of the Apocalypse,
The (Julio Desmayers)
Lady of Quality, A
Married Virgin, The /aka/ Frivo-
lous Wives
Monsieur Beaucaire (Duke de Char-
tres)
Moran of the Lady Letty
Once to Every Woman /aka/ The
Scarlet Power (Jullantimo)
Passion's Playground
Rudolph Valentino and His 88 Ameri-
can Beauties
Sainted Devil, A (Don Alonzo de
Castro)
Sheik, The (Sheik Ahmed Ben Has-
san)
Son of the Sheik, The (dual role,
Ahmed/Ahmed Ben Hassan)
Stolen Moments
Uncharted Seas
Wonderful Chance, The
Young Rajah, The (Title role)
Record:
Kashmiri Song (Pelican LP130)

6096
VALERIE, Gladys*
Live Wire, The

6097
VALERIE, Olive*
Red Hot Romance

6098
VALERO, Albano*
Loves of Ricardo, The

6099
VALIA, Mdlle. *
Fruitful Vine, The

Romance of a Wastdale, A (Kate Nugent)
Sally Bishop (Miss Standish Rowe)

6100
VALLE, Felix*
Girl in Every Port, A
Plastic Age, The (Merton Billings)

6101
VALLÉE, Marcel*
L'Affaire de la Rue de Laurcine
Three Musketeers, The (Mousqueton)

6102
VALLEE, Rudy (1901-)
Campus Sweethearts
Glorifying the American Girl
Radio Rhythm
Rudy Vallee and His Connecticut
Yankees
Vagabond Love, The
Radio:
Fleischmann Hour, The (Host) 29
Stage:
Vaudeville [Palace] 29

6103
VALLÉE, Yvonne (Mrs. Maurice
Chevalier)*
Bonjour New York! (herself)

6104
VALLENTIN, Hermann*
Atlantic [German] (Dr. Holtz)
Madame Wüncht Keine Kinder [Mad-
ame Doesn't Want Children] /aka/
Madame Wants No Children (Paul's
uncle)
Strange Case of Captain Ramper, The
Tragödie der Liebe [Tragedy of Love]
Trial of Donald Westhof, The

6105
VALLES, Dave*
Hot for Paris

6106
VALLI, Virginia (Virginia McSweeney)
(1898-1968)
Behind Closed Doors
Black Bag, The
Confidence Man, The
East Side, West Side
Escape /aka/ The Exquisite Sinner
Evening Clothes
Family Upstairs, The
Flames

For Your Daughter's Sake
Fox player 27
Idle Rich, The
In Every Woman's Life
In the Palace of the King
Isle of Lost Ships, The
Judgment of the Hills
K-the Unknown
Ladies Must Dress (Eve)
Lady of Quality, A
Lady Who Lied, The
Love's Penalty
Man Who, The
Man Who Found Himself, The
Marriage
Mr. Antonio
Paid to Love (Gabby)
Pleasure Garden
Plunger, The
Price of Pleasure, The
Sentimental Tommy
Shock, The (Gertrude Hadley)
Siege
Signal Tower, The
Stage Madness
Storm, The
Street of Illusion
Trip to Paradise, A
Universal player 23
Up the Ladder
Very Idea, The
Village Blacksmith, The
Watch Your Wife
Wild Oranges

6107
VALLIS, Robert*
Son of David, A

6108
VALRAY, Maria*
Bandolero, The

6109
VALVERDA, Rafael*
Loves of Carmen

6110
VAN, Wally*
Barriers Burned Away
Common Law, The
Drivin' Fool, The
Slave of Desire

6111
van AAITERN, Truus*
Sajenko, the Soviet

6111a
VANAIRE, Jacques*
Fashions in Love

6112
van ANTWERP, Albert*
Chechahcos, The

6113
VAN BOUSEN, H.*
America /aka/ Love and Sacrifice
   (Capt. John Parker)

6114
VAN BUREN, Mabel*
Beyond the Rocks (Mrs. McBride)
Conrad in Quest of His Youth (Nina)
Craig's Wife
Dawn of Tomorrow, The
Four Horsemen of the Apocalypse
   (Elena)
His Secretary
King of Kings, The (bit)
Light that Failed, The
Manslaughter (a prisoner)
Miss Lulu Bett (Mrs. Deacon)
Ramona
Smooth as Satin
Top of the World, The

6115
VANBURGH, Irene (1872-1949)
Gay Lord Quex, The

6116
VANCE, Clarice*
Down to the Sea in Ships (Nahoma)

6117
VANCE, Virginia*
His Private Life
New Year's Eve
Weak Knees

6118
van DEELE, Edmond*
Napoleon
6 1/2 x 11

6119
VANDIVERE, Elinor*
Hoose Gow, The
Into Her Kingdom

6119a
VAN DOBENECK, Baron*--see:
   Baron von Dobeneck

6120
van DOMMELEN, Caroline (1874-
1957)
De Dood Van Pierrot [The Death of
Pierrot]

6121
VAN DORN, Mildred*
Hold Your Man
Son of the Gods (Eileen)
Stage:
Get Me in the Movies (Dorothy
Gray) 28

6122
VAN DYKE, Truman (1897-)
Betty Reforms
Daughters of Today
Mad Marriage

6123
VANE, Charles*
This Freedom (Uncle Pyke)

6124
VANE, Myrtle*
K-the Unknown

6125
VANEL, Charles*
Iceland Fisherman, The
Waterloo
Stage:
Le Bourgeois Gentilhomme 24
L'Homme Qui Assassina 24
Le Procureur Hallers 24
Taming of the Shrew, The   24

6126
VAN LENT, Lucille*
Merry Widow, The

6127
VANN, Polly*
Wedding Bells

6128
VANNA, Nina*
Cafe Electric /aka/ Wenn ein Weib
den Weg Verliert [When a Woman
Loses Her Way]
Man Without Desire, The
Triumph of the Rat, The (Comtese
Madeleine de l'Orme)
Woman Tempted, The
Youth Astray

6129
VAN RIEL, Raimondo*
Quo Vadis
Strange Case of Captain Ramper, The

6130
VAN VLIET, Jean*
Ladies at Ease

6131
VANWALLY--see: Wally Van

6132
VAN WINTERSTEIN, Edward--see:
Eduard von Winterstein

6133
VANYA, Elsie*
Last Waltz, The

6134
VARCONI, Victor (1896-1958)
Angel of Broadway, The
Changing Husbands
Chicago
Dance Fever
Dancers, The
Divine Lady, The (Lord Nelson)
Eternal Love (Lorenz Gruber)
Feet of Clay (the bookkeeper)
Fighting Love
For Wives Only
Forbidden Woman
King of Kings (Pontius Pilot)
King of the Bernina /aka/ King of
the Mountain
Last Days of Pompeii, The (Glaucus)
Paramount player 25
Poisoned Paradise
Silken Shackles
Sinner's Paradise
Sodom and Gomorrah
Tenth Avenue
Triumph (William Silver)
Volga Boatman, The (Prince Dimitri
Orlaff)
Worldly Goods

6135
VARNA, Victo*--see: Victo Vina

6136
VARTIAN, Thomas*
Happy Days (chorus)

6137
VARVAROW, Feodor*
End of St. Petersberg, The

6138
VASAROFF, Michael*
Paris

6139
VASSELI, Judith*
Dance Magic

6140
VAUGHAN, Bernard*
First Born, The (butler)
Paddy the Next Best Thing (Dr.
  Adair)

6141
VAUGHN, Ada Mae*
Courtship of Miles Standish, The
Show of Shows, The

6142
VAUGHN, Alberta (1908-)
Adorable Deceiver
Adventures of Mazie [serial]
Age of Old Handicap
Ain't Love Funny?
Arabian Fights, The
Back Stage
Broadway Ladies
Broadway Sap, The
Drop Kick, The
Fighting Blood
Flip Flops
Forbidden Hours, The
Jessie's James
Mild, but She Satisfied
Molly and Me
Naughty Forties, The
Noisy Neighbors
Pacemakers, The [serial]
Picking Peaches
Points West
Queen of Burlesque
Romantic Age, The
Ruth Is Stranger than Fiction
Show of Shows, The
Sinews of Steel
Skyscraper
Smile Please
Son of Wallingford, The (Lottie Mc-
  Cabe)
Sweet Buy and Buy
Telephone Girl [serial]
That Wild Irish Pose
Uneasy Payments
Wages of Synthetic
Watch Your Pep!
You Just Know She Dares 'em

6143
VAUGHN, Hilda (1898-1957)
Three Live Ghosts
Stage:
Glory Hallelujah (Ida) 26
Lady Bug (Julia) 22
Prisoner, The (Irene Polosova) 27
Seed of the Brute (Lizzie Saunders)
  26

6144
VAUGHN, William*
Condemned (Vidal's Orderly)

6145
VAUSDEN, Val*
Irish Destiny

6146
VAUTIER, Elmire*
Vivre

6147
VAVERKA, Anton*
Love Parade, The (a Cabinet Minis-
  ter)
Merry-Go-Round, The (Emperor
  Franz Joseph)
Phantom of the Opera, The (the
  prompter)
Rolling Home

6148
VAVITCH, Michael (Mikhail Vavitch)*
Bridge of San Luis Rey, The (Vice-
  roy)
Crown of Lies
Devil Dancer, The
Divine Lady, The (King of Naples)
Dove, The
Gaucho, The (Ruiz's 1st lieutenant)
Glorious Betsy
Graustark (Capt. Quinnox)
His Hour
Hotel Imperial (Petroff)
Midnight Sun, The
My Official Wife
Mysterious Island
Swan, The
Thief in the Dark, A
Third Degree, The
Two Arabian Nights
Valencia
Venus of Venice
Wolf Song (Don Solomon Salazar)
Woman Disputed (Father Roche)

6149
VEGA, Rose*
Loves of Ricardo, The

6150
VEIDT, Conrad (1893-1943)
Affairs of Lady Hamilton (Nelson)
Beloved Rogue (Louis XI)
Black Hussar, The
Brothers Schellenberg
Carlos and Elizabeth (Don Carlos)
Le Conte Costia /aka/ Graf Costia
Denton
Die Flucht im die Nacht
Dürfen wir Schweigen?
Enrico IV
Erick the Great
Der Geiger von Florenz /aka/ The
    Violinist of Florence
Hands of Orlac
Husbands or Lovers
Impetuous Youth
In Dalarna and Jerusalem
Das Indische Grabmal
Janus Faced
Jerusalem
Der Jonuskopf /aka/ Love's Mockery
    (dual role, Dr. Warren/Mr.
    O'Connor)
Lady Hamilton
Last Performance, The
Life's Mockery
Love Makes Us Blind /aka/ Lieb
    Macht Blind
Lucrecia Borgia
Magic Flame, The
Man Who Cheated Life, The
Man Who Laughs, The (Gwymplaine)
Man's Past, A
Les Maudits
Mystic Mirror, The
NJU
Orlac's Hände (Title role)
Prince Cuckoo
Prinz Kuckuck
Der Student von Prag (Title role)
Three Wax Men
Three Way Works, The
Two Brothers, The
Universal player 28
Unwelcome Children
Das Wachsfigurenkabinet /aka/ The
    Waxworks (Ivan the Terrible)

6151
VEJAR, Harry*
Mexicali Rose

6152
VELEZ, Lupe (Guadeloupe Velez de
    Villa Lobos) (1909-1944)
Gaucho, The (the mountain girl)
Lady of the Pavements (Nanon del
    Rayon)
Love Song, The
Masquerade
Sailors Beware (extra)
Stand and Deliver (Jania)
Tiger Rose (Rose)
Where East Is East (Toyo)
Wolf Song (Lola Salazar)
Stage:
Rataplan - (Mexico City)

6153
VENABLE, Evelyn (1913-)
Cradle Song

6154
VENUTA, Benay (1912-)
Trail of '98

6155
VENZUELLA, Peter*
Bad Man, The

6156
VEREBES, Ernest*
Ghost Train, The (Richard Winthrop)
Paul Street Boys, The

6157
VERLY, Michele*
Legion of Honor, The
Soul of France, The

6158
VERMOYAL, Paul*
Arab, The (Iphraim)
Terror /aka/ The Perils of Paris

6159
VERNE, M. *
Soul of France, The

6160
VERNON, Agnes*
Universal player 22

6161
VERNON, Bobby (1895-1939)
Air Tight
All Jazzed Up
Bright Lights
Broken China
Busy My Dear

Christie Comedies 23; (8) 27-28
Dead Easy
Don't Pinch!
Dummy Love
Footloose Widows
French Pastry
Great Guns
Hey, Rube!
Hold 'er Cowboy
Hoot Mon!
Hot Sparks
Jail Birdies
Page Me
Slippery Feet
Sock Exchange, The
Stop Kidding
Sure Fire
Sweeties
Watch Out!
Wife Shy
Yes, Yes, Nabette

6162
VERNON, Dorothy*
Christie Johnstone (Widow McKay)
Tenderloin
Wireless Lizzie

6163
VERNON, Vivian*
White Mice (La Borrachita)
Stage:
Sally (Kitty) 20

6164
VESPERMANN, Kurt*
Der Kleine Napoleon [The Little Na-
poleon] /aka/ So Sind die Männer
[Men Are Like That]; Napoleons
Kleiner Bruder [Napoleon's Little
Brother] (Florian Wunderlich)
Tragödie der Liebe [Tragedy of
Love] (Judge)

6165
VIBART, Henry*
Amazing Quest of Mr. Ernest Bliss,
The (Sir James Aldroyd, M. D.)
Bohemian Girl, The (Count Arnheim)
Comin' Thro' the Rye (Mr. Tempest)
Dancer of Paris, The
Four Feathers, The (Gen. Fever-
sham)
Just Suppose
Kiss for Cinderella, A (Richard Bo-
die)
Prince of Tempters, The
Sonia (Rev. A. A. Burgess)

Wilderness Woman, The
Woman of No Importance, A (Elsie's
father)

6166
VIBERT, Marcel*
Garden of Allah, The
Le Grillon du Foyer
Oppressed, The

6167
VICCOLA, Giovanni*
White Sister, The

6168
VICTOR, Henry (1898-1945)
After the Verdict
As God Made Her
Beloved Rogue, The (Thibault d'Aus-
signy)
Bentley's Conscience
Beyond the Dreams of Avarice
Bill of Divorcement, A
Calvary
Colleen Bawn
Crimson Circle, The
De Vrouw Van Den Minister (John
Heriot's wife)
Diana of the Crossways
Down Channel
Fourth Commandment, The
Guns of Loos, The
Hate Ship
Henry King of Navarre (Duke of
Guire)
His Grace Gives Notice
Love Story of Aliette Brunton, The
Luck of the Navy, The (Lt. Clive
Stanton)
Prodigal Son, The
Old Wives' Tale, The
Romance of Mayfair, A
Romance of Old Bagdad
Royal Oak, The
Scandal
Sheer Bluff
Sins Ye Do, The
Slaves of Destiny
Tommy Atkins
Topsy and Eva
White Monkey, The
White Shadow, The

6169
VICTRIX, Claudia*
L'Occident

6170
VIDOR, Catherine*
La Boheme (Louise)

6171
VIDOR, Florence (Florence Arto)
  (1895-)
Afraid to Love
Alice Adams
Are Parents People?
Barbara Frietchie
Beau Revel
Borrowed Husbands
Chinatown Nights
Christine of the Hungry Heart
Conquering the Woman
Doomsday
Dusk to Dawn
Eagle of the Sea
Enchanted Hill, The
Family Honor
Flaming Forties, The
Grand Duchess and the Waiter, The
Grounds for Divorce
Hail the Woman
Honeymoon Hate
Husbands and Lovers
Jack-Knife Man, The
Lying Lips
Magnificient Flirt, The (Mme. Flo-
  rence Laverne)
Main Street
Marriage Circle, The (Mrs. Braun)
Marry Me
Mirage, The
One Woman to Another
Patriot, The (Countess Anna Oster-
  mann)
Popular Sin, The
Real Adventure, The
Sea Horses (Helen Salvia)
Skin Deep
Trouble with Wives, The
Virginian, The
Welcome Stranger, The
Woman Wake Up!
World at Her Feet, The
You Never Know Woman

6172
VIDOR, King (1894-)
MGM player 25

6173
VINA, Victo*
Carmen (Le Dancaire)

6174
VINCENT, Allen*
Mother's Boy (Dinslow)
Stage:
Spread Eagle (Charles Parkman) 27
Starlight (a reporter) 25

6175
VINCENT, Mildred*
Fast Worker, The
Time, the Comedian

6176
VIOTTI, Gino*
Kif Tebbi
Quo Vadis

6177
VIRGIL, Helen*
Temple of Venus, The

6178
VISAROFF, Michael (1890-1951)
Adventurer, The
Cactus Trails
Camille
Disraeli (Count Bosrinov)
Exalted Flapper, The
Four Devils (circus director)
House of Horror, The
Hungarian Rhapsody
Illusion
Last Command, The (Serge, valet
  and bodyguard)
Marquis Preferred
Nickel Hopper, The
Night Bird, The
Paris
Plastered in Paris
Ramona (Juan Canito)
Sunset Derby
Swan, The
Tempest, The
Two Arabian Nights
Valencia
We Americans

6179
VITALIANI, Italia*
Last Days of Pompeii, The (Stratoni-
  ca)

6180
VIVIAN, Robert (1885-1944)
Restless Sex, The (Chilsmer Grismer)
Stage:
High Stakes (Murray) 24
Lady Dedlock (William) 29

Michael and Mary (Dr. Roberts) 29
Mr. Moneypenny (dual role, Gray/
  Mr. Smudge)
Mystery Square (Roland Tenby) 29
Personality (Jenkins) 21
Scotland Yard (Rudge) 29
Taming of the Shrew, The (dual
  role, valet/Pedant)
These Charming People (Minx) 25
12,000 (Treysa) 28

6181
VOKES, May*
Janice Meredith (Susie)
Stage:
Annie Dear (Lottie) 24
Bat, The (Lizzie) 20
Cold Feet (Sophie) 23
Holka Polka (Gundel) 25
Matrimonial Bed, The (Corinne) 27

6182
VÖLKER, Wilhelm*
Cafe Electric (Dr. Lehner)
Der Mensch am Wege [Man by the
  Roadside]

6183
vonALTEN, Ferdiand*
Anna Boleyn /aka/ Deception
Jew of Mestri, The (Prince of Arra-
  gon)
Man Who Cheated Life, The
Othello /aka/ The Moor (Roderigo)
Sajenko, the Soviet
Small Town Sinners

6184
vonBERNE, Eva*
Masks of the Devil

6185
vonBRINCKEN, William*
General Crack (Capt. Schmidt)
Queen Kelly (Wolfram's lieutenant)
Wedding March, The (guard)

6186
vonDOBENECK, Baron*
Tillie's Punctured Romance

6187
VON ELTZ, Theodore (1889-1964)
Awful Truth, The
Bardely's the Magnificient (Rene de
  Lesperon)
Being Respectable
Broadway Lady

Common Law, The
Divorcee, The
Fools for Fashion
Four Feathers, The (Lt. Castleton)
Fourteenth Lover, The
Glorious Fool, The
Great Mail Robbery, The
Hearts of Oak
His New York Wife
Laddie
Life's Mockery
Lights Out
Locked Doors
Love and the Law
Nickle Hopper, The
No Man's Law
Nothing to Wear
On Thin Ice
One Woman to Another
Paint and Powder
Paramount player 22
Perch of the Devil
Queen of Diamonds
Red Kimono, The
Redhead Preferred
Rescue, The
Sea Wolf, The
Should Tall Men Marry?
Speed Girl, The
Sporting Chance
Tiger Rose
Very Idea, The
Voice of the Storm
Way of the Strong
Woman with Four Faces, The (Jim
  Hartigan)

6188
VON ENGLEMAN, André*
Maré Nostrum [Our Sea] (submarine
  commander)

6189
vonESTERHAZY, Agnes, Countess*
Escaped from Hell

6190
vonGOTH, Rolf*
Berlin after Dark

6191
vonHAGEN, Egon*
Der Kleine Napoleon [The Little Na-
  poleon] /aka/ So Sind die Männer
  [Men Are Like That]; Napoleons
  Kleiner Bruder [Napoleon's Little
  Brother] (Napoleon Bonaparte)

6192
vonHARDENBURG, William*
Love Parade, The (a Cabinet Minister)
Slave of Desire

6193
vonHARTMAN, Carl*
Awakening, The
Very Confidential
Wings (German officer)
Woman Disputed

6194
VON HEASE, Baron*
Prisoners

6195
vonHOLLAY, Camilla*
At the Edge of the World (John's wife)
Madame Wünscht Keine Kinder [Madame Doesn't Want Children] /aka/ Madame Wants No Children (Louise's maid)

6196
vonLENKEFFY, Ica*
Othello /aka/ The Moor (Desdomona)

6197
VON LENT, Lucille*
Merry Widow, The (innkeeper's daughter)

6198
vonLINNENKOFF, Barbara*
Midsummer Night's Dream, A (Helena)

6199
VON METER, Harry*
Alias Miss Dodd
Beautiful Gambler, The
Cheater, The
Dangerous Love
Hunchback of Notre Dame, The (M. Neufchatel)
Judah
Kid Boots (Polly's lawyer)
Reputation

6200
vonMEYERINCK, Hubert*
Aftermath
Manon Lescaut (de Bli's son)

6201
vonRITOY, Theodore*
Bardelys the Magnificient

6202
von RITZAU, Erik*
Greed (traveling dentist)

6203
VON RUE, Greta*
Her Honor, the Governor

6204
vonSCHACHT, Count*
Isn't Life Wonderful?

6205
vonSCHLETTOW, Hans*
Aftermath
Cottage on Dartmoor, A
Dr. Mabuse, the Gambler /aka/ Dr. Mabuse, the Great Unknown
Isn't Life Wonderful? (hungry worker)
Last Waltz, The
Die Nibelungen /aka/ The Nibelungs

6206
vonSCHWINDT, Wolfgang*
Sein Grösster Bluff [Her Greatest Bluff] (gangster)

6207
vonSEYFFERTITZ, Gustav B. (1863-1943)
Bandolero, The
Barbed Wire
Bells, The
Birds of Prey
Canary Murder Case, The (Dr. Ambrose Lindquist)
Case of Lena Smith, The
Chasing Through Europe
Come Across
Danger Girl
Dead Men Tell No Tales
Diplomacy
Docks of New York, The
Don Juan (Nehri)
Face in the Fog, The
Gaucho, The (Ruiz, the Usurper)
Going Crooked
Goose Woman, The (Mr. Vogel)
His Glorious Night
Inner Man, The
It's All Greek to Me
Little Shepherd of Kingdom Come, The
Lone Wolf, The

Lone Wolf Returns, The
Magic Flame, The (the Chancellor)
Me, Gangster (factory owner)
My Best Girl
Mysterious Lady, The /aka/ War
  in the Dark (General Alexandroff)
Price of Honor, The
Private Izzy Murphy
Red Dice
Red Mark, The
Rose of the Golden West
Seven Faces
Sherlock Holmes /aka/ Moriarty
  (Prof. Moriarty)
Sparrows /aka/ Human Sparrows
  (Grimes)
Student Prince, The (King Karl VII)
Under the Red Robe (Clon)
Unknown Treasures /aka/ The House
  Behind the Hedge
Vamping Venus
When Knighthood Was in Flower
  (Soothsayer)
Wizard, The (Prof. Paul Corilos)
Woman Disputed (Otto Kreuger)
Yellow Lily, The
Yolanda (Olivier de Daim)

6208
VON STROHEIM, Erich (Hans Erich
  Maria Stroheim von Nordenwall)
  (1885-1957)
Devil's Passkey, The [directed]
Farewell to Thee
Foolish Wives (Count Sergius Karam-
  zin)
Great Gabbo, The (Title role)
Greed [directed]
Honeymoon, The [Part II of Greed;
  unreleased; directed]
Merry-Go-Round [directed]
Merry Widow, The [directed]
Queen Kelly [directed]
Universal player 25
Wedding March, The (Prince Nicki;
  also directed)

6209
vonSZÖREGHY, Julius*
Eine Du Barry von Heute [A Modern
  DuBarry] (Gen. Padilla)
Prinzessin Olala [Princess Olala]
  (strong man)
Wie Einst im Mai

6210
vonWALTHER, Hertha*
Die Freudlose Gasse [The Joyless

Street] /aka/ The Street of Sor-
  row (Else)
Geheimnisse einer Seele /aka/
  Secrets of the Soul
Loves of Jeanne Ney, The
Peak of Fate

6211
vonWANGENHEIM, Gustav*
Frau im Mond [Woman in the Moon]
Kölhiessel's Töchter (Paul)
Nosferatu
Romeo und Julia im Schnee [Romeo
  and Juliet in the Snow] (Romeo)

6212
vonWINTERSTEIN, Eduard*
Destiny /aka/ The Third Death; The
  Three Lights; Between Worlds;
  Der Mude Tod
Hamlet (Claudius)
Mystic Mirror, The
Stage:
Dantons Tod (Legendre) 27
Jedermann [Everyman] (Debtor) 27
Midsummer Night's Dream, A (Snug)
  27

6213
VORONINA, Vera*
Patriot, The (Mlle. Lapoukhine)
Time for Love (Countess Elvire)
Whirlwind of Youth, The

6214
VOSBURGH, Harold*
House of Mystery
If Women Only Knew
What Every Woman Knows

6215
VOSPER, Frank (1899-)
Blinkeyes (Seymour)

6216
VOSS, Peter*
Fight for the Matterhorn, The

6217
VOSSELLI, Judith*
Prince of Tempters, The
Rogue Song, The (Countess Tatiana)
Stage:
Back Pay (Queenie) 21
Casanova (the courtesan) 23
Crashing Through (Mrs. Harvey Rob-
  bins)
Forbidden Roads (Isabel) 28

Merry Wives of Gotham [Fanshastics]
(dual role, Mother Agnes/Hudson
Bess)
Wild Oats Lane (Mlle. Helen) 22

6218
VROOM, Frederick*
Acquittal, The
Day of Faith, The
Faith Healer, The
General, The (Southern General)
His Hour
Navigator, The
Sporting Youth

- W -

6219
WACHSMITH, Fee*
Children of No Importance

6220
WADAMS, Golden*
Hotel Imperial

6221
WADE, John P.*
White Moll, The

6222
WADSWORTH, Henry*
Applause (Tony)
Stage:
Flight (Richard "Scoofy" Scofield) 29
Lady Lies, The (Alex Huntington) 28

6223
WADSWORTH, William*
White Mice (Sylvanus Codman)
Stage:
Eva the Fifth (Leon Montrose) 28
Seeing Things (Yogi) 20
Wisdom Tooth, The (a man patient)
26
Zander the Great (Jackson Pepper) 23

6224
WAGGNER, George*
Iron Horse, The (Col. Cody-Buffalo
Bill)
Sheik, The (Youssef)

6225
WAGNER, Elsa*
Atlantic [German] (Anna Thomas)
Luther
Meistersinger

6226
WAGNER, Erika*
Queen of Sin and the Spectacle of
Sodom and Gomorrah

6227
WAGNER, George*
His Hour
Iron Horse, The

6228
WAGNER, Kid*
Abysmal Brute, The (Battling Levin-
sky)

6229
WAINWRIGHT, Marie*
Polly with a Past
Stage:
Captain Applejack (Mrs. Agatha What-
combe) 21

6230
WAITE, Malcolm*
Durand of the Badlands (Clem Allison)
Gold Rush, The (Jack Cameron)
Hill Billy, The
Kid Boots (George Fitch)
Lucky Horseshoe, The
Monkey Talks, The
Noah's Ark (dual role, Sham/the
Balkan)
Vagabond Lover, The
We're in the Air Now

6231
WAITE, Marjorie*
Red Hot Tires

6232
WALBROOK, Anton (Adolf Wohlbruck)
(1900-1967)
Der Fluch der Bösen Tat
Salto Mortale

6233
WALBURN, Raymond /aka/ Ray
(1887-)
Laughing Lady, The
Stage:
Awful Truth, The (Rufus Kempster)
22
Freddy (Freddy Hall) 29
If I Was Rich (William Dunroy) 26
Manhattan (Skiddy Stillman) 22
On Call (George Pierpont) 28
Sinner (John Pemberton, Jr.) 27
Take My Advice (Jim Thayer) 27

Triumphant Bachelor, The (Bob Farley) 27
Zepplin (Ed Totten) 29

6234
WALCAMP, Marie (1894-)
Blot, The
Dragon's Net, The [serial]

6235
WALCOTT, Arthur*
Kissing Cup's Race (John Wood)
Son of David, A

6236
WALCOTT, George*
Swan, The
Stage:
It's a Wise Child (Bill Stanton) 29
Old English (Jock) 24
Piper, The (Jan) 20
Swan, The (George) 23
Young Woodley (Cope) 25

6237
WALCOTT, William*
Down to the Sea in Ships (William
W. Morgan)
Stage:
Home Towners, The (Casey) 26
Philadelphia (Judge Densford) 29
Song and Dance Man, The (Curtis)
24
White Flame (Logan) 29

6238
WALCZ, Ethel*
Cradle Snatchers

6239
WALDRIDGE, Harold*
Ruling Passion, The

6240
WALDRON, Charles D. (1874-1946)
Thief, The
Stage:
Bill of Divorcement, A (Gray Mere-
dith) 21
Coquette (Dr. Besant) 27
Elton Case, The (Donald Hayston) 21
Guilty One, The (Ronald Short) 23
Hamlet (Claudius) 25
Heaven Trappers, The (David Calvin
alias "The Parson")
Madame X (Floriot) 27
Magda (Lt. Col. Leopold Schwartze)
25

Mary Stuart (Darnley) 21
Passion Flower, The (Estaban) 20
Pinch Hitter, A (Nigel Bellamy) 22
Pyramids (Martin Van Cott) 26
Swords (Ugolino) 21

6241
WALES, Bert*
Her Love Story (boy)

6242
WALES, Ethel*
Almost Human
Bedroom Window, The
Beggar on Horseback
Bertha, the Sewing Machine Girl
Blue Skies
Bonded Woman, The
Covered Wagon, The (Mrs. Wingate)
Cradle Snatchers
Craig's Wife
Doctor's Secret, The
Donovan Affair, The
Fog, The
Girl in the Show, A
Girl on the Pullman, The
Go Straight
Grail, The
Icebound
John of the Woods /aka/ Gigi
Ladies at Play
Loose Ankles
Made for Love
Manslaughter (a prisoner)
Marriage Maker, The
Masks of the Devil, The
Merton of the Movies
Miss Lulu Bett (Grandma Bett)
Monster, The (Mrs. Watson)
My Friend from India
Old Homestead, The
On to Reno
Perfect Crime, The
Revelation
Satin Woman
Saturday Night Kid, The (Lily Wood-
ruff)
Stage Kisses
Take It from Me
Taxi Thirteen
Tenth Avenue
Unguarded Gate
Unknown Soldier, The
Which Shall It Be?
Wreck of the Hesperus, The

6243
WALES, Wally /aka/ Hal Taliaferro
Carrying the Mail

Cyclone Cowboy, The
Desert of the Lost
Desperate Courage
Double Daring
Fighting Cheat, The
Flying Buckaroo, The
Galloping On
Hurricane Horseman, The
Meddlin' Stranger, The
Overland Bound
Riders of the Cactus
Riding Rivals
Roaring Rider
Saddle Mates
Skedaddle Gold
Soda Water Cowboy, The
Tearin' into Trouble
Tearin' Loose
Twisted Trigger
Vanishing Hoofs
Voice from the Sky, The
White Pebbles

6244
WALKER, Ben*
Tracked by the Police

6245
WALKER, Catherine*
Clothes Make the Woman
Fourth Commandment, The
Guilty One, The

6246
WALKER, Charlotte (1878-1958)
Classmates
Great Deception, The
Lightnin'
Lone Wolf, The
Manicure Girl, The
Midnight Girl
Paris Bound (Helen White)
Savage, The
Sixth Commandment, The
South Sea Rose
Winning Through (Mrs. Stafford)
Stage:
Call the Doctor (Catherine Mowbray)
    20
Comedienne (Helen Blakemore) 24
Skylark, The (Daisy) 21
Trilby (Title role) 21
Two by Two (Mrs. Cleves) 25

6247
WALKER, George*
Redskin, The

6248
WALKER, John*
Over the Hill

6249
WALKER, Johnnie (1894-1949)
Bare Knees
Boys of the Streets
Broken Hearts of Broadway
Captain Fly-by-Night
Children of Dust
Cross Breed
Earth Woman, The
Extra! Extra!
Fangs of Justice
Fantomas [serial]
Fourth Musketeer, The
Fox player 21
Galloping Hoofs [serial]
Held by the Law
Honesty is the Best Policy
In the Name of the Law
Jolt, The
Life's Greatest Game
Lightning Reporter
Lilies of the Street
Live Wires
Matinee Idol, The
Morganson's Finish
My Dad
Old Ironsides
Over the Hill (John, the man)
Play Square
Pretty Clothes
Princess Broadway
Red Lights
Scarlet West (Lt. Parkman)
Shattered Reputations
Snarl of Hate
So This Is Love
Spirit of the U. S. A.
Stepping Lively
Swelled Head, A
Third Alarm, The (Johnny McDowell)
Transcontinental Limited
Vultures of the Sea [serial]
What Love Will Do
Where Trails Begin
Wine of Youth, The
Wolves of the Air

6250
WALKER, June*
Coincidence
Stage:
Bachelor Father (Antoinette "Tony"
    Flagg)
Gentlemen Prefer Blondes (Lorelei
    Lee) 26

Glass Slipper, The (Irma Szabo) 25
Glory Hallelujah (Lilly) 26
Love Nest, The (Celia Gregg) 27
Nervous Wreck, The (Sally Morgan) 23
Processional, The (Sadie Cohen) 25
Six-Cylinder Love (Marilyn Sterling) 21
Waterloo Bridge (Myra) 29

6251
WALKER, Lillian (1888-)
Million Dollar Reward [serial]
Woman of No Importance, A (Hester Worsley)
Stage:
Banshee, The (Joan Walker) 27
Mating Season, The (Betty Stratford) 27

6252
WALKER, Nella*
Seven Keys to Baldpate
Tanned Legs
Vagabond Lover, The

6253
WALKER, Paul*
Sein Grösster Bluff [Her Greatest Bluff] (Goliath, a dwarf)

6254
WALKER, Polly*
Hit the Deck
Stage:
Billie (Title role) 28
Merry Malones (Molly Malone) 27
Ziegfeld's Revue No Foolin' (a principal) 26

6255
WALLACE, Dorothy*
Merry-Go-Round (Komtese Gisella von Steinbrueck)

6256
WALLACE, Grace*
Nix on Dames

6257
WALLACE, John*
Black Pirate, The
Donovan Affair, The

6258
WALLACE, Katherine*
Illusion

6259
WALLACE, May*
Reckless Age, The
Skirt Shy

6260
WALLACE, Morgan (1885-1953)
Dangerous Maid
Dream Street (masked violinist)
Fighting Blade, The (Lord Robert Erisey)
Flying Pat
One Exciting Night (J. Wilson Rockmaine)
Orphans of the Storm (Marquis de Praille)
Stage:
Acquittal, The (Robert Armstrong) 20
Ballyhoo (Judge of the races) 27
Gentle Grafters (Jim Merrick) 26
Law Breaker, The (Bill Dobbs) 22
Nature's Nobleman (Charles Johnson) 21
Stork, The (Theophile Surat) 25
Tavern, The (the Governor) 20
Women Go On Forever (Jake) 27

6261
WALLACE, Ramsey*
Broken Laws
Drivin' Fool, The
Empty Hands
Extra Girl, The
Voice in the Dark, A
Stage:
Clouds (Richard Adams) 25
Lost (Gerald Lansing) 27
90 Horse Power (Smith) 26
Open House (Lloyd Bellamy) 25
Valley of Content, The (John Benton) 25

6262
WALLACK, Edwin N.*
Ace of Hearts (chemist)
Hunchback of Notre Dame, The (King's Chamberlain)

6263
WALLACKS, Clara*
Merry Widow, The (a Hansen sister)

6264
WALLECK, Anna*
Humoresque

6265
WALLER, Lewis*
Monsieur Beaucaire (Francois)

Stage:
Dancing Mothers (Andrew) 24

6266
WALLING, Richard*
Dark Streets
Companionate Marriage, The
Fox player 27
Midnight Kiss, The (Thomas H. Atkins, Jr.)
Return of Peter Grimm, The (James Hartman)
Slaves of Beauty
Walking Back

6267
WALLING, Will R. /aka/ William*
Clash of Wolves, The
Harvester, The
Iron Horse, The (Thomas Marsh)
Jazz Singer, The (doctor)
Little Robinson Crusoe
Man Without a Country, The /aka/ As No Man Has Loved
Mating Call
Nellie, the Beautiful Cloak Model
Temple of Venus, The (Dennis Dean)
Village Blacksmith, The
Welcome Danger
Winners of the Wilderness (General Braddock)

6268
WALSH, Frank*
America /aka/ Love and Sacrifice (Thomas Jefferson)
Joy Girl, The
Married? (Harvey Williams)

6269
WALSH, George (1892-)
American Pluck
Back to Liberty
Ben Hur
Broadway Drifter
Count of Luxembourg, The
Deadline, The
Dynamite Allen
From Now On
Goldwyn player 24
His Rise to Fame
Inspiration
Kick-Off, The
Man of Quality, A
Manhattan Knight, A
Number Seventeen
Plunger, The
Prince of Broadway, The

Reno
Rosita (Don Diego)
Serenade
Shark, The
Slave of Desire
Striving for Fortune
Test of Donald Norton, The
Vanity Fair (Rawdon Crawley)
Winning Oar, The
With Stanley in Africa [serial]

6270
WALSH, J. B.*
Man Who Played God, The

6271
WALSH, Raoul (1889-)
Sadie Thompson (Sgt. Tim O'Hara)

6272
WALTER, Harry*
Blood Money (Mark Harper)

6273
WALTER, Rosa*
Ghost Train, The (Julia Price)

6274
WALTERS, Dorothy*
Beyond Price
Confidence Man, The
Good References (landlady)
Kiss for Cinderella, A (Mrs. Maloney)
Light in the Dark, The (Mrs. Callerty)
Man Must Live, A
Stage:
Desert Flower, The (Mrs. McQuade) 24
Devil Within, The (Nora) 25
First Mortgage (Elmer's aunt)
Judge's Husband, The (Stella) 26
Kosher Kitty Kelly (Mrs. Mary Kelly) 25
Manhattan Mary ("Ma" Brennan) 27
Whirlpool (Mrs. Schultz) 29

6275
WALTERS, Ethel*
On with the Show (Bernice from Birmingham)

6276
WALTERS, Glen*
She Goes to War

6277
WALTHAL, Anna Mae*
As Man Desires
Desert Flower, The

6278
WALTHAL, Henry B. (1880-1936)
Able-Minded Lady, The
Barrier, The (John Dale)
Black Magic
Blaze O'Glory
Boy of Mine
Bridge of San Luis Rey, The (Father
 Junipero)
Enchanted Island
Everybody's Acting
Face on the Bar Room Floor, The
Fighting Love
Flower of the North
Freedom of the Press
From Headquarters
Gimme
Golden Bed, The (Col. Peake)
Ice Flood, The
In Old California
Jazz Age, The
Kentucky Pride
Kick Back
Light in the Window, A
Little Colonel, The
London after Midnight (Sir James
 Hamlin)
Love Me and the World Is Mine
Mine with the Iron Door, The
One Clear Call
Parted Curtains
Phantom in the House, The
Plastic Age, The (Henry Carver)
Retribution
River of Romance
Road to Mandalay
Rose of Kildare
Scarlet Letter, The (Roger Prynne)
Simon the Jester
Single Wives
Speakeasy
Splendid Hazard, A
Stark Mad
Street Corners
Three Faces West
Trespasser, The (Fuller)
Unknown Purple, The (Carlos)
Unknown Soldier, The
Wings (Mr. Armstrong)
With Kit Carson over the Great Di-
 vide
Woman on the Jury, The

6279
WALTON, Fred*
Dynamite (doctor)
Fast Set, The (Simpson)
His Dog
Marriage in Transit (valet)
New Brooms
Splendid Crime, The
Wise Wife
Stage:
Song Writer, The (Joe) 28

6280
WALTON, Gladys (1904-)
All Dolled Up
Cross Wires
Dangerous Game, A
Desperate Youth
Girl Who Ran Wild, The
Gossip
Guttersnipe, The
High Heels
Lavender Bath Lady, The
Love Letter
Man Tamer, The
Near Ready
Pink Tights
Playing with Fire
Rich Girl, Poor Girl
Risky Business
Rowdy, The
Sawdust
Second Hand Rose
Secret Light, The
Short Skirts
Top O' the Morn
Town Scandal
Trouper, The
Untamable, The
Wild Party
Wise Kid, The
Stage:
June Days (Susie Rolles) 25
Lady in Ermine, The (Angelina) 22
Last Waltz, The (Petruschka) 21
Midnight Rounders, The (a principal)
 20

6281
WALTON, Henry*
Livingstone in Africa

6282
WAMPUS BABY STARS
(Western Association of Motion Pic-
 ture Advertisers)
Arlen, Betty 25
Astor, Mary 26

Avery, Pauline 27
Avon, Violet 25
Aye, Marion 22
Basquette, Lena 28
Boardman, Eleanor 23
Bonner, Priscilla 27
Borden, Olive 25
Bow, Clara 24
Bramley, Flora 28
Brent, Evelyn 23
Brian, Mary 26
Carewe, Rita 27
Carol, Sue 28
Christy, Ann 28
Collier, June 28
Compton, Joyce 26
Cornwall, Ann 25
Costello, Dolores 26
Costello, Helene 27
Crawford, Joan 26
Day, Alice 28
Day, Marceline 26
Del Rio, Dolores 26
Devore, Dorothy 23
Eilers, Sally 28
Fair, Eleanor 24
Faire, Virginia Brown 23
Ferguson, Helen 22
Ferris, Audrey 28
Francisco, Betty 23
Garon, Pauline 23
Gaynor, Janet 26
Geraghty, Carmelita 24
Gregory, Ena 25
Grey, Gloria 24
Gulliver, Dorothy 28
Hiatt, Ruth 24
Hurlock, Madeline 25
Johnston, Julianne 24
Joyce, Natalie 25
Keener, Hazel 24
Kent, Barbara 27
Key, Kathleen 23
Kingston, Natalie 27
La Plante, Laura 23
Leahy, Margaret 23
Lee, Gwen 27
Lee, Lila 22
Logan, Jacqueline 22
Long, Sally 26
Lorraine, Louise 22
Love, Bessie 22
Loy, Myrna 27
Lynch, Helen 23
McAllister, Mary 27
McConnell, Gladys 27
McGuire, Katherine 22
Mackaill, Dorothy 24

Mahaffey, Blanche 24
Marion, Edna 26
Marlowe, June 25
Meredyth, Joan 25
Miller, Patsy Ruth 22
Moore, Colleen 22
Morris, Margaret 24
Nixon, Marian 24
O'Day, Molly 28
O'Neill, Sally 26
Perdue, Derelys 23
Philbin, Mary 23
Phipps, Sally 23
Pierce, Evelyn 25
Ralston, Jobyna 23
Rand, Sally 27
Revier, Dorothy 25
Reynolds, Vera 26
Rickson, Lucille 24
Rork, Ann
Shannon, Ethel 23
Sleeper, Martha 27
Starke, Pauline 22
Stuart, Iris 27
Taylor, Ruth 28
Thompson, Duane 25
Todd, Lola 25
Vaughn, Alberta 24
Vaughn, Anamae (Adama) 27
Velez, Lupe 28
Wilson, Lois 22
Windsor, Claire 22
Wray, Fay 26

6283
WANG, James*
Fighting American, The
Singed
Yankee Clipper, The

6284
WANGEL, Hedwig*
Eine Du Barry von Heute [A Modern
  DuBarry] (Rosalie)
Rasputin, the Holy Sinner

6285
WANGENHEIM, Gustav*
Nosferatu

6286
WANGERMANN, Richard*
Idols of Clay (Old Master)

6287
WARD, Bradley*
Sinners in Silk

6288
WARD, Carrie Clarke*
Awful Truth, The
Eagle, The (Aunt Aurelia)
Golden Cocoon, The
His Hour
Old Lady 31
Only Thing, The
Rose of the World
Scaramouche (Madame Benoit)

6289
WARD, Carrie Lee*
Paliser Case, The

6290
WARD, Craig*
Our Hospitality
Stage:
Puppets of Passion (unexpected
   guest) 27

6291
WARD, Eddie*
Show of Show, The

6292
WARD, Fannie (1872-1952)
Hardest Way, The
Lure of Crooning Waters, The
Pathé player 20
She Played and Paid
Stage:
Vaudeville [Palace] 26; 27; 28

6293
WARD, George--see: George Warde

6294
WARD, Kathrin Claire*
Drag
Isle of Lost Ships, The

6295
WARD, Lucille*
California Straight Ahead
His Majesty Bunker Bean
Oh, Doctor!
Sixty Cents an Hour
Sporting Youth
Woman of the World, A

6296
WARD, Mackenzie*
Syncopation
Stage:
Happy Husbands, The ("Sosso"
   Stephens) 28

High Road, The (Ernest) 28
Red Blinds (Maurice Benn) 26
This Was a Man (Lord Romford) 27

6297
WARD, Polly (Byno Poluski) (1908-)
Alf's Button (Liz)
Shooting Stars

6298
WARD, Robert*
Fascinating Youth

6299
WARD, Roscoe*
West of Zanzibar (Tiny)

6300
WARD, Tiny*
Waning Sex, The

6301
WARD, Valerie*
Lady from Paris, The /aka/ Das
   Schöne Abenteuer

6302
WARDE, Frederick*
Lover's Oath, A /aka/ Rubaiyat of
   Omar Khayyam

6303
WARDE, George*
American Manners

6304
WARDE, Warwick (1898-1967)
After the Verdict
Belphegor, the Mountebank
Build Thy House
Bulldog Drummond
Call of the East
Call of the Road
Corinthian Jack
Dancer of Barcelona, The
Demos
Diamond Necklace, The
Eva and the Grasshopper
Golden Dawn, The
Great Turf Mystery, The
Handy Andy
Hotel Mouse, The
Human Desires
Hurricane Hutch in Navy Adventures
Informer, The
Lady Owner, The
Lilac Sunbonnet, The
Little Meg's Children

Looping the Loop
Madame Sans-Gene (Neipperg)
Manchester Man, The
Maria Marten
Mary Latimer, Nun
Mayor of Casterbridge
Money Habit, The
Petticoat Loose
Prude's Fall, The
Southern Love
Tell Your Children
Three Kings, The
Variété [Variety]
White Sheik, The
Woman He Scorned, The
Woman Tempted, The
Wuthering Heights

6305
WARDWELL, Geoffrey*
Taming of the Shrew, The (Horten-
sio)
Stage:
Broken Chain, The (Emanuel Sutro)
29
Goose Hangs High, The (Ronald Mur-
doch) 24

6306
WARE, Helen (1877-1939)
Beyond the Rainbow (Mrs. Gardner)
Colorado Pluck
Deep Purple, The
Garden of Allah, The
Half Way to Heaven
Napoleon's Barber
New Year's Eve
Speakeasy
Virginian, The (Ma Taylor)
Stage:
Montmartre (Charlotte) 22
Pagans (Mme. Moreli) 21
Vaudeville [Palace] 23; 26
Wandering Jew, The (Judith) 21
Within Four Walls (Delphine) 23

6307
WARFIELD, Natalie*
Through Different Eyes (Olive Craig)

6308
WARNER, Adele*
Sky High (Marguerite)

6309
WARNER, H. B. (Henry Byron
Charles Stewart Warner) (1876-
1958)
Argyle Case, The (Hurley)

Black Swan, The
Conquest
Dice of Destiny
Divine Lady, The (Sir William Hamil-
ton)
Doctor's Secret, The
Felix O'Day
For a Woman's Honor
French Dressing
Fugitive from Matrimony
Gamblers, The
Green Goddess, The (Major Creslin)
Gray Wolf's Ghost
Haunting Shadows
Hellion, The
King of Kings, The (Christ)
Lone Fighter, The
MGM player 26
Man-Made Woman
Maruga
Naughty Duchess, The
One Hour Before Dawn
Romance of a Rogue
Show of Shows, The (victim)
Silence
Sorrell and Son (Sorrell)
Silence
Stark Mad
Temptress, The
Tiger Rose (Dr. Crusick)
Trial of Mary Dugan, The (D.A.)
Unchartered Channels
Wedding Rings
When We Were Twenty-One
Whispering Smith
White Dove, The
Zaza (Bernard Dufresne)
Stage:
Danger (John Fitzroy Scorrier) 21
Silence (Jim Warren) 24
You and I (Maitland White) 23

6310
WARNER, James B. (1895-1924)
Behind Two Guns
Crimson Gold
Danger
Flaming Hearts
Lone Fighter, The
Treasure Canyon

6311
WARREN, E. Alyn*
Born to the West
Courtship of Miles Standish, The
Hungry Hearts
Outside the Law (Chang Lo)
Son of the Gods (Lee Ying)
Sweet Rosie O'Grady

Tale of Two Worlds, A (Ah Wing)
Trail of '98 The (engineer's boy)
Unholy Three, The (Prosecuting Atty)

6312
WARREN, Frank*
Tale of Two Worlds, A

6313
WARREN, Fred*
Bells, The
Capital Punishment (pawnbroker)
Desert Flower, The
In Old Arizona (piano player)
Masked Bride, The
Shooting of Dan McGrew, The (the
  Ragtime Kid)
Spieler, The
Stephen Steps Out
Winds of Chance
Woman on the Jury, The

6314
WARREN, Mary*
Voices of the City (Mary Rodman)

6315
WARRENTON, Lule*
Ladies Must Live
Sin That Was His, The
Stage:
Heaven Tappers, The (Mrs. Ketcham)
  27

6316
WARWICK, Robert (Robert Taylor
  Bien) (1881-1964)
Adventure in Hearts, An
City of Masks
Fourteenth Man, The
Hunting Trouble
Jack Straw
Mad Lover, The
Modern Othello, A
Paramount player 21
Thou Art the Man
Tree of Knowledge
Unmasked
Stage:
Cheaper to Marry (Jim Knight) 24
Drifting (Badlands McKinney) 22
His Queen (Thales) 25
In the Night Watch (Capt. de Corlaix)
  21
Lady's Virtue, A (Harry Holstead) 25
Mrs. Dane's Defense (Sir Daniel Car-
  teret) 28
Nice Women (Mark Chandler) 29

Primer for Lovers, A (Elkin Beech-
  more) 29
Rivals (Capt. Absolute) 22
Sherlock Holmes (Title role) 28
To Love (Challange) 22
Two Orphans, The (Jacques Frochard)
  26
Vaudeville [Palace] 27

6317
WARWICK, Virginia*
Four Horsemen of the Apocalypse,
  The (Chicki)
My Own Pal

6318
WASCHER, Aribert*
Prinzessin Olala [Princess Olala]
  (Police Superintendent)

6319
WASHBURN, Bryant (1889-1963)
Amateur Devil, The
Beware of Widows
Bit of Heaven, A
Black Tears
Breakfast at Sunrise
Burglar Proof
Chorus Kid, The
Common Law, The
Flames
Full House, A
Her Sacrifice
Honeymoon Flats
Hungry Hearts
In the First Degree
Jazzland
June Madness
King of Kings, The (a young Roman)
Love Thrill, The
Meanest Man in the World, The
Meet the Prince
Mine to Keep
Mrs. Temple's Telegram
Night Life in Hollywood
Nothing to Wear
Parasite, The
Passionate Youth
Road to London, The (Rex Rowlands,
  Jr.)
Rupert of Hentzau (Fritz von Tarlen-
  heim)
Selznick player 22
Sick Abed
Sins of St. Anthony
Six Best Cellars, The
Skinner's Big Idea
Sky Pirate, The

Temptation
Too Much Johnson
Try and Get It
Undressed
Watered Stock
Wet Paint
What Happened to Jones?
With Sitting Bull at Spirit Lake Massacre
Wizard of Oz, The
Woman Conquers, A
Young April

6320
WASHBURN, Ralph*
Passionate Youth

6321
WASHINGTON, Blue*
Black Magic
Beggars of Life
Blood Ship, The
By Whose Hand?
Do Your Duty
Haunted Ship, The
Phantom City
Ransom
There It Is
Wyoming

6322
WASHINGTON, Mildred*
Hearts in Dixie
Shopworn Angel, The

6323
WASSMANN, Hans*
Eine Du Barry von Heute [A Modern
  DuBarry] (theatre director)
Meistersinger
Tragödie der Liebe [Tragedy of
  Love]

6324
WATA, Sussie*
Veil of Happiness

6325
WATERMAN, Ida*
Enchanted Cottage, The
Lady Rose's Daughter
Lotus Eater, The
Love's Redemption
Say It Again
Social Celebrity, A
Society Scandal, A (Mrs. Maturin
  Colbert)
Swan, The

That Royle Girl (Mrs. Clarke)
Stage:
Lawful Larceny (Mrs. French) 22
Martinique (Madame DeChauvalons) 20

6326
WATERS, Ethel (1900-   )
On with the Show
Stage:
Vaudeville [Palace] 27; 28

6327
WATERS, Ted*
Happy Days (chorus)

6328
WATSON, Adele*
Jazz Heaven
Rolling Home
This Thing Called Love (secretary)
Welcome Home

6329
WATSON, Bobby*
Song and Dance Man, The
Syncopation
That Royle Girl (Hofer)
Stage:
Allez-Opp! (a principal) 27
American Born (Stephen Clark) 25
Annie Dear (Twilly) 24
Cross My Heart (Charles Graham) 28
Greenwich Village Follies (a principal) 28
Optimists, The (a principal) 28
Vaudeville [Palace] 29

6330
WATSON, Coy*
Restless Youth
Smart Set, The

6331
WATSON, Harry*
Great White Way, The
Little Old New York (Bully Boy Brewster)
Zander the Great (Good News)
Stage:
Passing Show of 1921, The (a principal) 20
Tip-Toes (Hen Kaye) 25
Vaudeville [Hippodrome] 24

6332
WATSON, Roy*
Elmo, the Fearless [serial]
Flaming Disc, The [serial]

6333
WATTS, James*
Lost Patrol, The
Stage:
Passing Show of 1923, The (a prin-
    cipal) 23
Patience (Reginald Bunthorne) 27
Spice of 1922 (a principal) 22
Vaudeville [Winter Garden] 22

6334
WAWERKA, Anton*
Merry-Go Round, The (Emperor
    Franz Joseph)
Wedding March, The (Emperor
    Franz Joseph)

6335
WAYBURN, Ned*
Great White Way, The
Stage:
Vaudeville [Palace] 24
Vaudeville [Proctor's] 27

6336
WAYNE, John (Marion Michael Mor-
    rison) (1907-)
Four Sons (bit)
Hangman's House (bit)
Mother Machree (extra)
Salute (Annapolis cadet)
Words and Music (bit, billed as Duke
    Morrison)
Stage:
Glendale High School

6337
WAYNE, Mabel*
Song of Love /aka/ Dust of Desire

6338
WAYNE, Maude*
Behold My Wife!
Fashions for Women
Prodigal Daughters (Connie)
Song of Love /aka/ Dust of Desire

6339
WAYNE, Richard*
Broadway Gold
Cheaper to Marry
Cheat, The
Her Husband's Trademark (Allan
    Franklin)
Impossible Mrs. Bellew, The (Jerry
    Woodruff)
Reno
Unknown Purple, The

6340
WAYNE, Robert*
Fashions in Love
Stage:
Lily Sue (Uncle Johnny Hines) 26
19th Hole, The (Col. Hammer) 27
That Awful Mrs. Eaton! (Martin Van
    Buren, Secty of State) 24

6341
WEBB, Clifton (Webb Parmelee Hol-
    lenbeck) (1890-1966)
First National player 26
Heart of a Siren, The
New Toys
Polly with a Past
Stage:
As You Were (Louis, Comte de Bela-
    my) 20
Jack and Jill (Jimmy Eustace) 23
Little Show, The (a principal) 29
Meet the Wife (Victor Staunton) 23
Parasites (Eliot Phelps, 3rd) 23
She's My Baby (Clyde Parker) 28
Sunny (Harold Harcourt Wendell-
    Wendell)
Treasure Girl ("Nat" McNally) 28
Vaudeville [Palace] 29

6342
WEBB, Dick*
Faust

6343
WEBB, George*
Alarm Clock Andy
Below the Surface
Black Beauty
Homespun Folks
Little Johnny Jones
Luck Devil, The
My Man
Son of Wallingford, The (Blackie Daw)

6344
WEBB, Louis K.*
Foolish Wives (Dr. Judd)

6345
WEBER, Jean*
Figaro

6346
WEBER, Joe (1867-1942)
Friendly Enemies
Stage:
Friar's Club Frolic 22
Vaudeville [Central] 22

6347
WEBSTER, Ben (1864-1947)
Call of Youth, The
Downhill (Dr. Dawson)
In the Blood
Miriam Rozella
Only Way, The (Marquis St. Evre-
   monde)

6348
WEBSTER, Howard*
Chechahcos, The

6349
WEGENER, Paul (1874-1948)
Daughter of Destiny, A /aka/ Al-
   raune
Golem, The (Title role)
Lost Shadow, The
Lucrezia Borgia
Magician, The (Title role)
Monna Vanna
Strange Case of Captain Ramper,
   The
Sumurun /aka/ One Arabian Night
   (old Sheik)
Survival
Svengali
Vanina
Weavers, The
Das Weib des Pharao [The Wife of
   the Pharaoh] /aka/ The Loves of
   the Pharaoh (Smlak, King of Ethi-
   opia)

6350
WEIDMAN, Charles*
Arabian Duet

6351
WEIGEL, Paul*
Blonde or Brunette
Bluebeard's Eighth Wife (Marquis de
   Briac)
Breath of the Gods
Broadway after Midnight
Bullets of Jussice
Déclassée
Excuse Me
Folly of Vanity
For Heaven's Sake
Hidden Aces [serial]
Leatherneck, The
Mademoiselle Midnight
Marry the Girl
Master Stroke, A
Merely Mary Ann
Red Lane, The

Right or Wrong
Silent Accuser, The
Wagon Show

6352
WELJDEN, Tor*
Thy Soul Shall Bear Witness

6353
WEINBERG, Gus*
Coming Through
Frontier of the Stars, The (Ganz)
Homeward Bound
Ne'er Do-Well, The
Soul Fire

6354
WEISSE, A.*
Moon of Israel

6355
WEISSE, Hanni*
Berlin after Dark

6356
WEISSMULLER, Johnny (Peter John
   Weissmuller) (1904-   )
Glorifying the American Girl (bit)
Grantland Rice short

6357
WELCH, James*
Dramatic Life of Abraham Lincoln,
   The /aka/ Abraham Lincoln (Gen.
   Robert E. Lee)
Iron Horse, The (Pvt. Schultz)
Tornado, The

6358
WELCH, Niles (1888-   )
Courage of Marge O'Doone, The
Ermine and Rhinestones
Evidence (Phillip Rowland)
From Rags to Riches
In Borrowed Plumes
Little Child Shall Lead Them, A
Luck of Geraldine Laird, The
Lying Wives
My Man
Realart player 22
Reckless Youth (John Carmen)
Remorseless Love
Reputation
Sawdust
Sin of Martha Queed
Spenders, The
Spider Web, The
What Wives Want

Who Am I?
Why Do We Live?
Wine of Youth
Stage:
Donovan Affair, The (David Cornish)
26

6359
WELCH, William*
Over the Hill (Dad Benton)
Price She Paid, The

6360
WELCKER, Gertrude*
Dr. Mabuse, the Gambler /aka/ Dr.
  Mabuse, the Great Unknown
  (Countess Tolst)

6361
WELDON, Bunny*
Broadway Nights (night club producer)

6362
WELDON, Jess*
Thief of Bagdad, The (eunuch)

6363
WELFORD, Dallas (1874-)
Wedding Bells
Stage:
Blue Kitten, The (Popinet) 22
French Leave (Corporal Sykes) 20
Girl with Carmine Lips, The
  (Mathews) 20
Mary Jane McKane (Martin Frost)
  23
Mrs. Bumpstead-Leigh (Kitson) 29
No More Blondes (Tanner) 20
Oh! Henry! (Henry Boswell) 20
Shadow, The (Willes Gay) 22

6364
WELFORD, Nancy*
Gold Diggers of Broadway (Jerry)
Stage:
Cinders (Title role) 23
Lady Do (Dorothy Walthal) 27
Orange Blossoms (Ninetta) 22
Rain or Shine (Mary Wheeler) 28

6365
WELLES, Jada*
Betrayal, The

6366
WELLES, Ralph*
Night Ride (Blondie)

6367
WELLESLEY, Charles*
Acquittal, The
Cytherea (William Grove)
Don't Marry for Money
Lost World, The (Major Hibbard)
Outcast (John Moreland)
Perfect Flapper, The
Rapids, The
Skinner's Big Idea
Unholy Three, The (John Arlington)

6368
WELLESLEY, William*
Goldfish, The

6369
WELLS, Jacqueline*
Classified
Golden Bed, The
Home Maker, The

6370
WELLS, Marie*
Desert Song, The (Clementina)
Song of the West (Lotta)
Stage:
Floradora (Marquita) 20
Merry Widow, The (Olga) 21

6371
WELLS, May*
Excuse Me
Pilgrim, The (the mother)

6372
WELLS, Raymond*
Death Valley
Oh! What a Nurse!
Tony Runs Wild
Yankee Senor, The

6373
WELLS, Ted*
Across the Plains
Arizona Speed
Border Wildcat
Born to the Saddle
Bravery and Bullets
Crimson Canyon, The
Forbidden Trails
Greased Lightning
Gun Grit
Mystery Rider, The [serial]
Pawnee Bill, Jr. [series]
Riding Demon, The
Smiling Terror, The
Straight Shootin'

Texas Flash, The
Thrill Chaser, The
Thunder Riders, The
Where the West Begins

6374
WELLS, William K.*
Cock-Eyed World, The (bit)

6375
WELSH, Niles--see: Niles Welch

6376
WELSH, Betty*
Come and Get It
Stage:
Dove, The (cigarette girl) 25

6377
WELSH, William*
Mississippi Gambler
Shock, The (Mischa Hadley)
Skinner Steps Out

6378
WENGREN, David*
Soft Living

6379
WENMAN, Henry (1875-)
Silver King, The
Stage:
Journey's End (2nd Lt. Trotter) 29

6380
WENN, Clifton*
Let Not Man Put Asunder

6381
WERCKMEISTER, Vicky*
Sein Grösster Bluff [Her Greatest
  Bluff] (Suzanne)

6382
WERRENRATH, Reinald*
Vitaphone

6383
WERTH, Barbara*
Fast and Furious

6384
WERTZ, Clarence*
Three-Must-Get-Theirs, The

6385
WEST, Billie*
Billy West Comedy [series]

Ship Ahoy
Sweethearts

6386
WEST, Charles (1886-)
Black Roses
Bob Hampton of Placer
Eternal Three, The
From Headquarters
Handcuffed
King of Kings, The (bit)
Manslaughter
Nobody's Widow
Not Guilty
One in a Thousand
Page Tim O'Brien
Phantom Melody, The
Red Lights
Road to Yesterday, The (Watt Earn-
  shaw)
Talker, The
Things Have Changed
Witching Hour, The

6387
WEST, Claire*
Sainted Devil, A (Dona Encarnacion)

6388
WEST, Edna*
Half Way to Heaven
Stage:
Jack in the Pulpit (Maude Hoxie) 25

6389
WEST, Ford*
Half Way to Heaven
Sherlock Junior

6390
WEST, George*
Alias the Deacon
On Your Toes

6391
WEST, H. St. Barbe*
Balaclava (prosecutor)

6392
WEST, Henry*
Crackerjack, The
Girl on the Barge, The
Men of Steel
Speed Spook, The

6393
WEST, Isabel*
Old Home Week

Sainted Devil, A
Stage:
Paddy the Next Best Thing (Mary
    O'Hara) 20
Romance (Miss Armstrong) 21
Seventh Heaven (Aunt Valentine) 22

6394
WEST, Lillian*
Seventh Heaven (Arlette)

6395
WEST, William H. /aka/ Billy
    (1888-)
Orderly, The

6396
WESTAYER, Harry*
Unguarded Women

6397
WESTCOTT, Gordon*
Queen Kelly (Lackey)
Stage:
House of Fear, The (Craig Kendall)
    29

6398
WESTERFELT, John*
Happy Days (chorus)

6399
WESTMAN, Theodore*
Get Rich Quick Wallingford (bellboy)
Stage:
Brook (Norman Tracey) 23
Family Upstairs, The (Willie Heller)
    25
Houses of Sand (Eric Ford) 25
Not So Fast (Sylvester Vane) 23
Romancin' Round (gunner's mate
    James Dade) 27
Thank You (Monte Jones) 21

6400
WESTON, William*
Blackbird, The (Red)

6401
WESTOVER, Winifred (1890-)
All the World to Nothing
Anne of Little Smoky
Bucking the Tiger
Firebrand Trevision
Forbidden Trails
Love's Masquerade
Paramount player 20
Village Sleuth, The

6402
WESTWOOD, John*
Shepherd of the Hills, The
Varsity

6403
WETHERELL, M. A.*
Livingstone in Africa
Wee MacGreegor's Sweetheart (John
    Robinson)

6404
WEYHER, Ruth*
Apaches of Paris
Appassionata
Doctor's Women, The
Geheimnisse Seele [Secrets of the
    Soul]
Midsummer Night's Dream, A (Hip-
    polyta)
Schatten eine Nachtliche Halluzination

6405
WHALLEY, Norma*
Gypsy Cavalier, The (Lady Forrest)
Luck of the Navy, The (Mrs. Peel)
Virgin Queen, The (Countess of Len-
    nox)

6406
WHEAT, Laurence*
Back Home and Broke
Coming Through
Confidence Man, The
Inez from Hollywood
Irene
Ne'er-Do-Well, The
Not So Long Ago
Old Home Week
Song of Love, The /aka/ Dust of
    Desire

6407
WHEATCROFT, Stanhope (1888-)
Beggar in Purple, A
Blood and Sand
Blow Your Own Horn
Breath of the Gods
Cold Steel
Dr. Jim
Harmony Ranch
Hottentot, The
House of Toys
Iron Horse, The (John Hay)
King of Kings, The (bit)
Madame Behave
Manslaughter
Their Mutual Child

Way Down East
Women's Wares
Yankee Consul, The

6408
WHEELER, Bert (Albert Jerome
   Wheeler) (1895-1968)
Rio Rita (Chick Bean)
Stage:
Rio Rita (Chick Bean) 27
Vaudeville [Hippodrome] 24
Vaudeville [Palace] 25; 26; 29
Ziegfeld Follies 23; 29

6409
WHEEZER--see: Bobby Hutchins

6410
WHITAKER, Charles*
Cheyenne

6411
WHITAL, Russ*
Argentine Love

6412
WHITE, Alice (Alva White) (1907-)
American Beauty
Big Noise, The
Breakfast at Sunrise
Broadway Babies
Dove, The
Gentlemen Prefer Blondes (Dorothy
   Shaw)
Girl from Woolworths, The
Harold Teen
Hot Stuff
Lingerie
Mad Hour
Naughty Baby
Private Life of Helen of Troy, The
   (Adraste)
Satin Woman
Sea Tiger, The
Show Girl
Show of Shows, The
Widow from Chicago

6413
WHITE, Chrissie (1895-)
Amazing Quest of Mr. Ernest Bliss,
   The (Frances Clayton)
Aylwin
Bargain, The
Boden's Boy
John Forrest Finds Himself
Lilly of the Alley
Lunatic at Large, The

Naked Man, The
Simple Simon
Temporary Vagabond, A
Tit for Tat
Wild Heather
Wonderful World of Reality, The

6414
WHITE, J. Fisher*
Balaclava (Lord Raglan)
Blinkeyes (Uncle Dick)
Only Way, The (Dr. Manette)
Stage:
Thunder in the Air (Major Vexted) 29

6415
WHITE, Leo (1887-1948)
Adventuress, An /aka/ The Isle of
   Love
Beauty Shoppers
Ben Hur (Samballat)
Blonde Saint, The
Blood and Sand (Antoine)
Born to the Saddle
Bowery Cinderella, A
Campus Knights
Devil's Island
Devil's Passkey, The (Monsieur
   Malot)
Girl from Gay Paree
Goldfish, The
How to Handle Women
Keeping up with Lizzie
Lady Bird
Lady of Quality, A
McFadden Flats
Manhattan Knights
Masked Bride, The
One Year to Live
Rookies' Return, The
Rustle of Silk, The (Emil)
See You in Jail
Silks and Saddles
Slaver, The
Smilin' Guns
Sporting Youth
Thunder Riders, The
Truthful Sex, The
Vanity Fair (Isadore)
What Price Beauty?
Why Worry?
Wine (the Duke)
Wolves of the North [serial]
Woman on the Jury, The
You Never Can Tell

6416
WHITE, Malcom*
Gold Rush, The (Jack Cameron)

6417
WHITE, Marjorie (1910-)
Happy Days (Margie)
Sunny Side Up (Bee Nichols)
Stage:
Hello, Lola! (Jane Baxter) 26
Lady Fingers (Molly Maloney) 29

6418
WHITE, Pearl (Pearl Fay White)
  (1889-1938)
Any Wife
Beyond Price
Broadway Peacock, The
Hands of the Strangler [serial]
Know Your Men
Mountain Woman, The
Parisian Nights
Plunder [serial]
Terror /aka/ The Perils of Paris
Thief, The
Tiger's Club, The
Virgin Paradise, A
White Moll, The
Without Fear

6419
WHITE, Thomas*
Down to the Sea in Ships (Tommy,
  as a child)

6420
WHITE, Victoria*
Heart of Maryland, The (Nancy
  McNair)
Stage:
Clinging Vine, The (Victoria) 22
My Golden Girl (Mildred Ray) 20

6421
WHITE SPEAR, Chief*
Iron Horse, The (Sioux Chief)

6422
WHITEFORD, Blackie*
Hoose Gow, The

6423
WHITEHEAD, Omar*
Captain Blood

6424
WHITESPEAR, Greg*
Water Hole, The

6425
WHITLOCK, Lloyd (1900-1962)
Air Mail, The

Ancient Highway, The
Courage
Cowpuncher, The
Fatal Warning, The [serial]
From Headquarters
Hero for a Night
Home Maker, The
Hot Heels
House of Shame, The
Kid's Clever, The
Leatherneck, The
Love Special, The
Man in the Saddle, The
Michigan Kid, The
Midnight Express, The
New Champion, The
One Man in a Million
Paradise
Perfect Sap, The
Pretty Clothes
Price She Paid, The
Private Scandal, A
Queen of the Chorus
Scratch My Back
See My Lawyer
Skinner Steps Out
Slippy McGee
Sparrows /aka/ Human Sparrows
  (Bailey)
Too Much Money
Trespasser, The (member of Board
  of Directors)
War Horse
White and Unmarried

6426
WHITMAN, Alfred (Alfred Vosburgh)
  (1890-)
Vitagraph player 20

6427
WHITMAN, Gayne*
Adventurer, The
Back Stage
Exclusive Rights
Ghetto, The
Hell Bent for Heaven
His Jazz Bride
His Majesty Bunker Bean
Love Hour, The
Love Toy, The
Lucky Boy /aka/ My Mother's Eyes
Night Cry, The
Oh, What a Nurse!
Sailors' Wives
Stolen Pleasures
Sunshine of Paradise Alley
Too Many Crooks

Wife Who Wasn't Wanted, The
Wolves of the Air
Woman on Trial
Woman's Heart, A

6428
WHITMAN, Walt*
Dangerous Hours
Long Live the King
Mark of Zorro, The (Frey Felipe)
Three Musketeers, The (D'Artagan's
   father)

6429
WHITNEY, Claire*
Fine Feathers
Great Gatsby, The (Catherine)
Leech, The
Love, Honor and Obey
Mothers of Men
Neglected Wives
Passionate Pilgrim, The
Stage:
Innocent Idea, An (Bonnie Wing) 20
Vaudeville [Palace] 24

6430
WHITNEY, Renee*
Wild Party, The (Janice)

6431
WHITSON, Frank*
Adventures of Tarzan [serial] (Rokoff)
Captain Blood

6432
WHITTAKER, Charles*
Bandit Buster, The
Open Switch, The [serial chapter]
Phantom Buster, The
Rawhide
Ridin' Wild

6433
WHITTEN, Delbert Emery, Jr.*
Tin Gods (Billy)

6434
WHITTINGTON, Margery*
Stage Struck (Soubrette)

6435
WIARD, Joyce*
Mother Machree

6436
WICHELOW, Walter*
First Born, The (Impett)

6437
WICKS, Florence*
Enticement

6438
WIEMAN, Matthias*
Jolly Peasant, The

6439
WILBUR, Crane (1889-   )
Heart of Maryland, The (Alan Ken-
   drick)
Something Different
Stage:
Bride of the Lamb (Rev. Albough) 26
Celebrity ("Circus" Snyder) 27
Easy Terms (Dr. Alexander G. Tor-
   rance) 25
Fast Life (Bradford Palmer) 28
Fountain, The (Diego Mendez) 25
Nirvana (Dr. Alonzo Weed) 26
Ouija Board, The (Barney McClare)
   20
Vaudeville [Palace] 27
Woman Disputed, A (Father Rocham-
   beau) 26

6440
WILKE, Hubert (1855-1940)
Great Deception, The
Stage:
Humoresque (Max Elsass) 23
L'Aiglon (Emperor Francis of Austria)
   27
Poldekin (Krimoff) 20
Queen Victoria (Baron Stockmar) 23
Sophie (Christoph Willibald Ritter
   Von Gluck) 20

6441
WILKINSON, Sam*
Lost Patrol, The

6442
WILKINSON, Walter*
Man Who Came Back, The
Sea Hawk, The

6443
WILLARD, Charles Mrs.*
Get Rich Quick Wallingford (Mrs.
   Dempsey)
Stage:
Puppets of Passion (maid) 27

6444
WILLARD, John*
Fantomas [serial]

Sherlock Holmes /aka/ Moriarty
   (Inspector Gregson)
Stage:
Cat and the Canary, The (Harry
   Blythe) 22
Helena's Boys (Richard) 24
Lambs Gambol 25
Love in a Mist (Colin) 26
Mikado, The (a noble) 25
Natja (Ali) 25

6445
WILLARD, Leigh*
Fourth Commandment, The
Last Edition, The

6446
WILLIAM, Warren (Warren William
   Krech) (1895-1948)
Pearl White serial
Perils from Plunder [serial chapter]
Stage:
Blue Peter, The (David Hunter) 25
Fanny (Joe White) 26
Golden Age, The (the stranger) 28
Let Us Be Gay (Bob Brown) 29
Mrs. Jimmie Thompson (debut as
   Edgar Blodgett) 20
Nocturne (Keith Reddington) 25
Paradise (Dr. Achilles Swain) 27
Rosmersholm (Johannes Rosmer) 25
Sign of the Leopard (Capt. Leslie)
   28
Twelve Miles Out (Gerald Fay) 25

6447
WILLIAMS, Albert*
Jack and the Beanstalk

6448
WILLIAMS, Bransby (1870-1964)
Gold Cure, The
Jungle Woman
Troublesome Wives

6449
WILLIAMS, Cora*
Sensation Seekers
Womanhandled

6450
WILLIAMS, Earle (1880-1927)
Adventurous Sex, The (the adventurer)
Ancient Mariner, The (Victor Brandt)
Black Gate, The
Borrowed Husbands
Bring Him In
Captain Swift

Diamonds Adrift
Diplomacy
Eternal Struggle, The
Fortune Hunter, The
Fortune's Mask
Hillman, The
It Can't Be Done
Jealous Fools
Jealous Husbands
Man from Downing Street, The
Master Stroke, A
Masters of Men
My Official Wife
Painted Lady, The
Purple Cipher, The
Red Signals
Restless Souls
Romance Promoters
Say It with Diamonds
Silver Case, The
Skyrocket, The
When a Man Loves
You Never Know
You'd Be Surprised

6451
WILLIAMS, Eric Bransby*
Easy Virtue (the co-respondent)

6452
WILLIAMS, George B. *
Captain Blood
Cradle of Courage, The (Lt. Riley)
Dancin' Fool (McGammon)
Flaming Disc, The [serial]
Fifth Avenue Models
Midnight Sun, The
Phantom of the Opera, The (M. Ri-
   chard, Mgr.)
Stage:
Bewitched (Another) 24
Up She Goes (bus driver) 22

6453
WILLIAMS, Guinn "Big Boy" (1907-
   1962)
Across the Border
Back Stage
Black Cyclone
Blaze Away
Brown of Harvard
Burning Daylight
College Widow, The
Cyclone Jones
Down Grade, The
End of the Rope
Forward Pass, The (Honey Smith)
Freshie, The

From Headquarters
It's All Greek to Me
Jack Riders, The
King of the Wild Horses
Ladies' Night in a Turkish Bath
Lightning
Lucky Star (Martin Wrenn)
My Man
Noah's Ark (dual role, Ham/Al)
Quarantined Rivals
Red Blood and Blue
Rounding Up the Law
Slide, Kelly, Slide
Snowbound
Trail of Fate
Vamping Venus
Warner Brothers player 29
Western Firebrands
Whistling Jim

6454
WILLIAMS, Gwen*
Four Feathers, The (Mrs. Adi)

6455
WILLIAMS, Jeffrey*
Saphead, The

6456
WILLIAMS, Kathlyn (1888-1960)
Best People
Broadway Gold
City that Never Sleeps, The
Clarence
Conrad in Quest of His Youth (Mrs.
    Adaile)
Everything for Sale
Forbidden Fruit (Mrs. Mallory)
Girl Named Mary, A
Honeymoon Flats
Hush Money
Just a Wife
Locked Doors
Man's Home, A
Morals
Our Dancing Daughters (Ann's mother)
Paramount player 25
Prince Chap, The
Private Scandal, A
Sally in Our Alley
Single Man, A
Single Standard, The
Single Wives
Spanish Dancer, The (Queen Isabel
    of Bourbon)
Tree of Knowledge, The
Trimmed in Scarlet
U. P. Trail, The

Virginia Courtship, A
Wanderer, The
Wanderer of the Wasteland (Magdalene
    Virey)
We Americans
Wedding Rings
World's Applause, The

6457
WILLIAMS, Kid*
Waltzing Around

6458
WILLIAMS, Lottie*
Twin Beds

6459
WILLIAMS, Lucille*
Half Way to Heaven

6460
WILLIAMS, Malcolm*
First Kiss, The
Stage:
Beyond the Horizon (James Mayo) 26
Breaks, The (Manson) 28
Comic, The (the manager) 27
God Loves Us (George W. Dawson)
    26
Little Accident (J. J. Overbeck) 28
Mirage, The (Henry M. Galt) 20
Magnolia (Gen. Orlando Jackson) 23
Wisdom Tooth, The (Mr. Porter) 26

6461
WILLIAMS, Marie*
Eternal Struggle, The

6462
WILLIAMS, Percy*
Black Oxen
Children of Divorce (Manning)
Goldfish, The
Learning to Love
London after Midnight (butler)
Oh, Kay!
Unholy Three, The (butler)

6463
WILLIAMS, Ted Adagio Dancers
Show of Shows, The

6464
WILLIAMS, Zack*
Easy Pickings
Four Feathers, The (Idris)
Hearts in Dixie
Merry Widow, The (George Washing-
    ton White)

Yankee Clipper, The

6465
WILLIAMSON, Robert*
Bond Boy, The
Stage:
Castles in the Air (Amos) 26
Champion, The (Simmons) 21
Jack in the Pulpit (Jim Opie) 25
Shipwrecked (Steward Chumly) 24

6466
WILLIANS, Ann*
Broadway Melody, The

6467
WILLIS, Herbert, Mrs. *
Beloved Vagabond, The (Mrs. Du-
  bose)
Every Mother's Son (Mrs. Brent)

6468
WILLIS, Hubert*
Hound of the Baskervilles, The

6469
WILLIS, Leo*
All the Brothers Were Valiant (Tom)
Flying Elephants
Hoose Gow, The
Kid Brother, The
Looking for Sally
O'Malley of the Mounted
Their Purple Moment
Way of a Girl, The
Wild Bill Hickok

6470
WILLIS, Paul*
Thunderclap

6471
WILLS, Norma*
Deadwood Coach, The
Golden Princess

6472
WILSE, Lulee*
Wedding March, The (servant)

6473
WILSEY, Jay /aka/ Buffalo Bill,
  Jr. *
Ballyhoo Buster, The
Bonanza Buckaroo
Fast and Furious
Final Reckoning, A [serial]
Hard-Hittin' Hamilton

Interferin' Gent
Pals in Peril
Pirate of Panama [serial]
Rawhide
Roarin' Broncos
Roarin' to Go

6474
WILSON, Alice*
Passion's Playground

6475
WILSON, Anne M. *
Winds of Chance

6476
WILSON, Ben (1885-   )
Baited Trap, The
Branded Four, The [serial]
Bye, Bye, Buddy
China Slaver
Girls Who Dare
Man from Nowhere, The
Mystery Brand, The
Officer 444 [serial]
Range Riders
Riders of the West
Screaming Shadow, The [serial]
Sheriff's Girl, The
Tonio, Son of the Sierras
West of the Law
Wolves in the Desert

6477
WILSON, Charles (Charles Cahill
  Wilson)*
Broadway Scandals
Stage:
Adrienne (Sid Darrel alias Nadir
  Sidarah) 23
Donovan Affair, The (Ben Holt) 26
Lazybones (Elmer Ballister) 24
War Song, The (Capt. Conroy) 28

6478
WILSON, Clarence H. *
Big News (coroner)
Little Robinson Crusoe

6479
WILSON, Cronin*
Squibs (Bully Dawson)

6480
WILSON, Ed*
Flaming Frontier, The

6481
WILSON, F. Vaux*
White Mice (Vincenti)

6482
WILSON, Hal*
Love Master, The

6483
WILSON, Henry*
Magician, The

6484
WILSON, Janice*
White Circle, The

6485
WILSON, Katherine*
New Toys
Stage:
American Tragedy, An (Roberta Al-
    den) 26
Among the Married (Ethel Mills) 29
Chicken Feed (Miss Johnson) 23
Cock O' the Roost (Phyllis Dawn) 24
Devil's Disciple, The (Mrs. William
    Dudgeon) 23
Distant Drum, A (Edith Reed) 28
Guardsman, The (an usher) 24
He Who Gets Slapped (wardrobe lady)
    22
Love 'em and Leave 'em (Janie
    Walsh) 26
Paid (Agnes Baxter) 25
Play Without a Name, A (Billy Neu-
    man) 28
Top O' the Hill (Ann Leicester) 29

6486
WILSON, Lois (1896-)
Advice to Husbands
Alias the Lone Wolf
Bella Donna
Bird in the Hand, A
Bluebeard's Seven Wives /aka/ Pur-
    ple Passion
Border Legion, The
Broad Daylight
Broadway Nights (Fannie Franchette)
Call of the Canyon, The
City of Masks, The
City of Silent Men, The
Coney Island
Conquest
Contraband
Covered Wagon, The (Molly Wingate)
French Dressing
Full House, A

Gamblers, The
Gingham Girl
Great Gatsby, The (Daisy Buchanan)
Hell Diggers
Her Husband's Women
Icebound
Irish Luck
Is Matrimony a Failure?
Kid Gloves
Let's Get Married
Lost Romance
Man Who Fights Alone, The (Marion)
Manslaughter (Evans, the maid)
Midsummer Madness
Miss Information
Miss Lulu Bett (Title role)
Monsieur Beaucaire (Queen Marie of
    France)
New York (Marjorie Church)
North of '36
Object Alimony
On Trial (Mary Strickland)
Only 38
Our Leading Citizens
Paramount player 25
Pied Piper Malone
Pony Express
Ransom
Ruggles of Red Gap
Sally's Shoulder
Show of Shows, The
Show-Off, The
Thou Art the Man
Thundering Herd, The (Milly Fayre)
To the Last Man
Too Much Johnson
Vanishing American, The /aka/ The
    Vanishing Race (Marion Warner)
Wedding Rings
Welcome Home
What Every Woman Knows
What's Your Hurry?
Without Compromise
World's Champion, The

6487
WILSON, Lola*
On Trial

6488
WILSON, Margery*
Blooming Angel, The
Finger Prints
Insinuation
Marked Cards
Offenders, The
Old Loves and New /aka/ The
    Desert Healer
That Something

6489
WILSON, Tom (1880-1965)
Alias Julius Caesar
Battling Butler
Best Bad Man, The (Sam)
California Straight Ahead
Courtship of Miles Standish, The
Dinty
Don't Ever Marry
Fools in the Dark
Ham and Eggs at the Front
His Lady /aka/ When a Man Loves
    (convict in boat)
Isobel
Kid, The
Minnie
My Wife's Relations
Quicksands
Rainmaker, The
Remittance Woman, The
Reported Missing
Riley, the Cop
Scrap Iron
Strong Boy, The
Two Minutes to Go
What Fools Men

6490
WILSON, Toni*
Red Hot Romance

6491
WIMAN, Dwight Deere (1894-1951)
Puritan Passions

6492
WINCHESTER (Horse)
When Knighthood Was in Flower

6493
WINDSOR, Adele*
Girl from Havana, The
Stage:
Naughty Cinderella (Chouchou Rous-
    selle) 25
Sh! The Octopus (Polly) 28

6494
WINDSOR, Claire (Claire Viola
    Cronk) (1897-1972)
Acquittal, The
Blondes by Choice
Blot, The
Born Rich
Broken Chains
Brothers under the Skin
Bugle Call, The
Captain Lash

Clash, The
Claw, The (Disdre Saurin)
Dance Madness
Denial, The
Dixie Handicap, The
Domestic Meddlers
Eternal Three
Family Row, The
Fashion Madness
First National player 24
Fools First
For Sale (Eleanor Bates)
Foreign Devils
Frontiersman, The
Grain of Dust, A
Grand Larceny
Just a Woman
Lady Who Lied, The
Little Church Around the Corner,
    The
Little Journey, A
MGM player 26
Midstream
Money Talks
Nameless Man
Nellie, the Beautiful Cloak Model
One Clear Call
Opening Night
Rich Men's Wives
Rupert of Hentzau (Helga von Tarlen-
    heim)
Satan and the Woman
Show People (cameo)
Son of the Sahara, A
Souls for Sables
Stranger's Banquet
Tin Hats
To Please a Woman
Too Wise Wives
What Do Men Want?
What's Worth While?
White Desert, The

6495
WING, Ah*
Tale of Two Worlds, A (servant spy)

6496
WING, Ward*
Conquering Power, The (Adolph)

6497
WING, Wong, Mrs.*
Chinatown Nights
East of Suez
Mr. Wu (Ah Wong)
Where East Is East (Ming)

6498
WINN, Godfrey*
Blighty

6499
WINN, Jack*
Blood and Sand (Potaje)

6500
WINNMAN, Dwight--see: Dwight
Deere Wiman

6501
WINNINGER, Charles (1884-1969)
Canadian, The
Pied Piper Malone
Summer Bachelors
Stage:
Broadway Whirl, The (a principal) 21
No, No, Nanette (Jimmy Smith) 25
Oh, Please! (Nicodemus Bliss) 26
Show Boat (Cap'n Andy) 27
Vaudeville [Hippodrome] 24
Vaudeville [Palace] 24
Yes, Yes, Yvette (S. M. Ralston) 27
Ziegfeld Follies (a principal) 20

6502
WINSLOW, Dick*
Avalanche
Marianne
Sweetie
Virginian, The
Which Shall It Be?

6503
WINTER, David*
Percy

6504
WINTER, Laska /aka/ Laska Win-
ters*
Fashion Madness
Frozen Justice
Marriage Cheat, The
Mysterious Dr. Fu Manchu, The /aka/
The Insidious Dr. Fu Manchu
Night of Love, The (gypsy bride)
Rescue, The
Rocking Moon
Satin Woman
Seven Footprints to Satan
Tender Hour, The
Tides of Passion

6505
WINTHER, Karen*
David Copperfield

Witchcraft Through the Ages /aka/
Häxan

6506
WINTON, Bruce*
Alf's Button (Mustapha)

6507
WINTON, Jane (1905-1959)
Across the Pacific
Bare Knees
Beloved Rogue, The (the Abbess)
Bride of San Luis Rey, The (Donna
Clara)
Burning Daylight
Captain Lash
Crystal Cup, The
Don Juan (Beatrice)
Fair Co-Ed, The (Betty)
Footloose Widows
Gay Old Birds
His Supreme Moment
Honeymoon Express, The
Honeymoon Flats
Lonesome Ladies
Melody of Love
Monkey Talks, The
Nothing to Wear
Paramount player 25
Passionate Quest, The
Patsy, The (Grace Harrington)
Perch of the Devil
Poor Nut, The
Scandal
Sunrise (manicurist)
Tomorrow's Love
Upstream
Why Girls Go Back Home
Yellow Lily, The

6508
WISE, Jack*
Lawful Cheaters (Graveyard Lazardi)

6509
WISE, Tom (1865-)
Great White Way, The
Romeo's Dad

6510
WITHERS, Grant (1904-1959)
Bringing Up Father
College
FBO player 27
Final Extra, The
Golden Shackles
Greyhound Limited, The
Hearts in Exile

In the Headlines
Life's Like That
Madonna of Avenue A
Nothing to Wear
Road to Ruin, The
Saturday's Children
Show of Shows, The
So Long Letty
Tiger Rose (Bruce)
Tillie's Punctured Romance (hero)
Time, the Place and the Girl, The
Upstream

6511
WITLOCK, Lloyd*--see: Lloyd
   Whitlock

6512
WITWER, H. C.*
Great White Way, The

6513
WIX, Florence*
Enticement
Secrets (Lady Lossington)

6514
WOJZIK, Anna*
Flames on the Volga

6515
WOLBERT, Burton*
Guilty One, The

6516
WOLBERT, Clarence*
Guilty One, The

6517
WOLBERT, Dorothy /aka/ Dorothea*
Abysmal Brute, The (Mrs. Mac-
   Tavish)
Guilty One, The
Love and Learn
Romeo and Juliet
Woman of the World, A

6518
WOLFE, Harry*
Broadway Melody, The

6519
WOLFE, Jane*
Behold My Wife!
Why Change Your Wife? (woman
   client)

6520
WOLFF, Jan*
Why Change Your Wife?

6521
WOLHEIM, Dan*
Across to Singapore
East Side, West Side
Fleet's In, The (Double Duty Duffy)
Sal of Singapore
Tenderloin

6522
WOLHEIM, Louis R. (1880-1931)
America /aka/ Love and Sacrifice
   (Capt. Hare)
Awakening, The
Condemned (Jacques Duval)
Dr. Jekyll and Mr. Hyde (Music Hall
   owner)
Enemies of Women
Face in the Fog, The
Frozen Justice
Little Old New York (Hoboken Terror)
Lover's Island
Manhattan Knight, A
Number Seventeen
Orphans of the Storm (executioner)
Racket, The
Shady Lady, The
Sherlock Holmes /aka/ Moriarty
   (Craigin)
Ship from Shanghai, The
Sorrell and Son (Sgt. Major Buck)
Square Shoulders
Story Without a Name, The
Tempest, The
Two Arabian Nights
Unseeing Eyes
Wolf Song (Guillion)
Stage:
Broken Wing, The (Gen. Panfilo
   Aguilar) 20
Catskill Dutch (Cobby) 24
Fair Circassian, The (the Prince
   Regent) 21
Hairy Ape, The (Robert "Yank"
   Smith) 22
Idle Inn, The (Bendet) 21
Lambs Gambol 25
Letter of the Law, The (Bridet) 20
Macbeth (Porter) 24
What Price Glory? (Capt. Flagg) 24

6523
WOLOSHIN, Alex*
Case of Lena Smith, The
His Private Life

6524
WÖMER, Hilda*
Die Flamme [The Flame] /aka/
  Montmartre (Louise)

6525
WONDERLY, Frank*
Great White Way, The

6526
WONG, Anna May (Wong Liu Tsong)
  (1907-1960)
Across to Singapore
Alaskan, The
Bits of Life
Chinatown Charlie
Chinese Parrot, The
Crimson City
Desert's Toll, The
Devil Dancer, The
Dinty
Driven from Home
Fifth Avenue
Fortieth Door, The [serial]
Forty Winks
His Supreme Moment
Mr. Wu (Loo Song)
My Souvenirs
Old San Francisco
Paramount player 24; 28
Peter Pan (Tiger Lily)
Piccadilly (Shosho)
Shame
Show Life
Song a Minute, A
Streets of Shanghai
Tale of the Sea
Thief of Bagdad, The (princess'
  slave)
Trip to Chinatown, A
Wasted Love

6527
WONTNER, Arthur (1875-1960)
Bonnie Prince Charlie
Diamond Man, The
Eugene Aram
Infamous Lady, The
Jose Collins [series]
Stage:
Captive, The (D'Aeguines) 26
Interference (Sir John Marlay, M.D.)
  27
Mariners (Rev. Benjamin Cobb) 27

6528
WOOD, Dorothy*
Daughters of Today

6529
WOOD, Ernest*
Certain Young Man, A
Passionate Youth
Take Me Home
Stage:
Marriage Bed, The (Clyde Saunders)
  29

6530
WOOD, Freeman*
Chinatown Nights
Dancers, The
Divorce
Fashion Row
Female, The
Garden of Eden, The
Half a Bride
Hearts and Spurs (Oscar Estabrook)
Legion of the Condemned (bored man)
Lilies of the Field
Mannequinn
Price She Paid, The
Raffles
Social Celebrity, A
Taxi! Taxi!
Why Bring That Up?
Wings of Youth
Stage:
Ruined Lady, The (Jack Torrence) 20

6531
WOOD, Gloria (Baby)
Don't Tell Everything (Cullen's niece)

6532
WOOD, Peggy (1892-)
Almost a Husband
Wonder of Women, The
Stage:
Bride, The (Marie Duquesne) 24
Clinging Vine, The (Antoinette Allen)
  22
Henry IV (Lady Percy) 26
Lady in Love, A (Clarissa) 27
Marjolaine (Mlle. Marjolaine Laches-
  nais) 22
Merchant of Venice, The (Portia) 28
Play Without a Name, A (Anne Rus-
  sell) 28
Untitled Benefit 21

6533
WOODFORD, John*
Get Rich Quick Wallingford (Mr.
  Wells)
Tiger's Club, The
White Moll, The

6534
WOODRUFF, Bert (1856-   )
Awakening, The
Barrier, The ("No Cheek" Lee)
Children of Dust
Eighty Dollars
Fighting Heart, The
Fire Brigade, The
Flowing Gold
For Those We Love (Dr. Bailee)
Grim Comedian, The
Homer Comes Home
Isle of Lost Ships
Jailbird, The
Life of Riley, The
Making of a Man, The
Manhattan Cocktail
Marked Money
Noise in Newboro, A
Paris Green
Paths to Paradise
River, The /aka/ La Femme au
   Corbeau
Rosary, The
Sea Hawk, The
See My Lawyer
Siren of Seville, The
Speedy
Spring Fever
Two Minutes to Go
Vanishing American, The /aka/ The
   Vanishing Race (Bart Wilson)
Veteran Sinners
Watch Your Step
Worldly Goods

6535
WOODS, Alfred*
Beloved Vagabond, The (Simon Rush-
   wood)

6536
WOODS, Arthur*
Lost Patrol, The

6537
WOODS, Dorothy*
In the Days of Buffalo Bill [serial]

6538
WOODS, Franker*
Hit the Deck
Stage:
Hit the Deck! ("Battling" Smith) 27
Present Arms (Frank Derryberry) 28
Queen O' Hearts (Ferdinand Budd) 22

6539
WOODS, Harry (1889-1968)
Battling Buckaroo
Cafe in Cairo, A
Candy Kid, The
China Bound
Desert Rider, The
Gun Law
Jesse James
Love and the Law
Mystery Valley
Neath Western Skies
Phantom Rider
Red Riders of Canada
Silver Comes Through
Sunset Legion
Viking, The
When the Law Rides

6540
WOODTHORPE, Georgia*
Four Horsemen of the Apocalypse,
   The (lodgekeeper's wife)

6541
WOODWARD, Henry*
Deep Waters
Last of the Mohicans, The

6542
WOOLSEY, Robert (1889-1944)
Rio Rita (Ed Lovett)
Stage:
Blue Kitten, The (Octave) 22
Honest Liars (Dickie Chambers) 26
Lady in Ermine, The (Suitangi) 22
My Princess (Augustus Tonks) 27
Poppy (Mortimer Pottle) 23; 26
Right Girl, The (Henry Watkins) 21
Rio Rita (Ed Lovett) 27

6543
WORNE, Duke*
Chinatown Mystery, The [serial]
Secret Service Saunders [serial]

6544
WORNER, Hilda
Alles für Geld [All for Money]

6545
WORTH, Barbara*
Bachelor's Club, The
Below the Deadline
Fast and Furious
Fearless Rider, The
Fury of the Wild
On Your Toes

Plunging Hoofs
Prairie King, The
Universal player 27

6546
WORTH, Harry*
Four Feathers, The (Major Willough-
by)
His House in Order (butler)
Stage:
House of Fear, The (Dr. Jack Ladd)
29

6547
WORTH, Lillian*
Adventures of Tarzan [serial] (Queen
La of Opar)
Docks of New York, The
In Search of a Sinner
Tarzan the Tiger [serial] (Queen La
of Opar)

6548
WORTH, Richard*
Dawn (Jean Pilou)

6549
WORTHIN, Helen Lee*
Crowded Hour, The
Flower of the Night
Janice Meredith (Mrs. Loring)
Night Life in New York
Other Woman's Story, The
Swan, The
Thumbs Down
Vanity
Watch Your Wife
Stage:
Greenwich Village Follies 20
Ziegfeld Follies 23

6550
WORTHINGTON, William (-1941)
Grand to Fight
Good Morning, Judge
Green Goddess, The (High Priest)
Half a Bride
Happiness Ahead
Her Honor, the Governor
Kid Boots (Polly's father)
Out of the Silent North
Red Lights
Stage:
Mrs. Partridge Presents (Pete) 25
Shanghai Gesture, The (M. Le Comp-
te de Michot) 26
Treasure, The (another man) 20
Will Shakespeare (secretary) 23

6551
WRANEFF, Vadim*
Blonde Saint, The

6552
WRAY, Fay (1907-)
Border Legion, The
Coast Patrol, The
First Kiss, The
Four Feathers, The (Ethne Eustace)
Gasoline Love
Honeymoon
Lazy Lightning
Legion of the Condemned, The
(Christine)
Loco Luck
Man in the Saddle, The
No Father to Guide Him
One Man Game, A
Pointed Heels (Lora Nixon)
Spurs and Saddles
Street of Sin, The
Thunderbolt
Wedding March, The (Mitzi)
What Price Goofy?
Wild Horse Stampede

6553
WRAY, Jane*
Broken Laws
Playing with Souls

6554
WRAY, John*
New York Nights
Stage:
Broadway ("Scar" Edwards)
Enemy, The (Fritz Winckelman) 25
Nightcap, The (policeman) 21
Nightstick (Charles "Chick" Williams)
27
Ouija Board, The (Bartlett) 20
Silence (Harry Silvers) 24
Tin Pan Alley (Joe Prividi) 28

6555
WRIGHT, Ethel*
Enchanted Cottage, The
Stage:
Enchanted Cottage, The (Mrs. Corsel-
lis) 23
White Desert (Annie Peterson) 23

6556
WRIGHT, Fred*
Glorious Adventure, The (Bunny)
Stage:
Iolanthe (Lord Chancellor) 27
Mikado, The (Ko-Ko) 27

6557
WRIGHT, Haidee*
Glorious Adventure, The (Mrs. Bul-
  finch)
Paddy the Next Best Thing (an aunt)
Stage:
Mariners (Anne Shepperley) 27
Royal Family, The (Fanny Caven-
  dish) 27
What Never Dies? (Rosina Von Dal-
  lereder) 26
Will Shakespeare (Queen Elizabeth) 23

6558
WRIGHT, Hugh E. (1879-)
Silver King, The
Squibs (Sam Hopkins)

6559
WRIGHT, H. Humberstone*
Alf's Button (Eustace)
Fifth Form at St. Dominic's (Dr.
  Senior Headmaster)
Flag Lieutenant, The (Stiffy Steele)
Garden of Allah, The
Henry, King of Navarre (Charles IX)
High Treason (Dr. Seymour)
Hindle Wakes /aka/ Fanny Hawthorne
  (Chris Hawthorne)
Mademoiselle from Armentieres (the
  old soldier)
Mademoiselle Parley Voo (the old
  soldier)
Roses of Picardy (Jerome Vanderlyn-
  den)
Sally Bishop (Judge)
Waterloo

6560
WRIGHT, Mack*
Open Switch, The (serial chapter)

6561
WRIGHT, Marbeth*
Happy Days (chorus)

6562
WRIGHT, Marie*
Paddy the Next Best Thing (an aunt)

6563
WRIGHT, Tenny*
Panthers of the Night

6564
WUEST, Ida*
Last Waltz, The
Tragödie der Lieb [Tragedy of Love]

6565
WUNDERLEE, Frank*
One Exciting Night (Samuel Jones)
Sunken Silver [serial]

6566
WUST, Ida--see: Ida Wuest

6567
WYCHERLY, Margaret (1881-1956)
Thirteenth Chair, The (Madame Ro-
  salie Le Grange)
Stage:
Adding Machine, The (Daisy Diana
  Dorothea Devore) 23
Back to Methuselah (dual role, voice
  of the Serpent/the parlor maid) 22
Blue Peter, The (Mrs. Hunter) 25
Devil to Pay, The (Eva Bonheur) 25
Eyvind of the Hills (Halla) 21
Jade God, The (Perkins) 29
Jane Clegg (Title role) 20
Mr. Moneypenny (Carie Jones) 28
Mixed Marriage (Mrs. Rainey) 20
Proud Woman, A (Mrs. Merritt) 26
Rosmersholm (Rebecca West) 25
Set a Thief (Mrs. Dowling) 27
Six Characters in Search of an
  Author (the mother) 22
Taboo (Mrs. Gaylord) 22
Verge, The (Claire Archer) 21

6568
WYLIE, Constance*
Only Thing, The

6569
WYNDHAM, Poppy*
Son of David, A

6570
WYNN, Ed (Isaiah Edwin Leopold)
  (1886-1966)
Rubber Heels
Stage:
Ed Wynn's Carnival (a principal) 20
Grab Bag, The (a principal) 24
Lambs Gambol 22
Manhattan Mary (Crickets) 27
Perfect Fool, The (a principal) 21

6571
WYTALL, Russ, Mrs.*
Tarnish

- Y -

6572
YACONELLI, Frank*
Senor Americano

6573
YAKOVLEVA, K.*
Scandal

6574
YAKOVLEVA, S.*
Yellow Ticket, The

6575
YAMMAMOTO, Togo*
Flesh and Blood (the prince)
Something to Think About (servant)
Tale of Two Worlds, A (One Eye)

6576
YARDE, Margaret (1878-)
Only Way, The (vengeance woman)
Stage:
Many Waters (Doris Rosel) 29

6577
YASTREBITSKY, A.*
Village of Sin, The

6578
YASTREBITSKY, K.*
Tanka-Trakitirschitsa /aka/ Protin
Osta; Against Her Father; Tanka,
the Innkeeper

6579
YEAGER, Irene*
Breaking Point, The (Camilla)

6580
YEARSLEY, Ralph*
Desert Gold (Halfwit)
Hill Billy, The
Kid Brother, The
Rose-Marie
Show Boat (the killer)
Tol'able David (Saul Hatburn)
Village Blacksmith, The

6581
YELINA, Y.*
Khveska /aka/ Bolnichny Starozh
Khevska (hospital guard)

6582
YERRARD, Charles*
Better 'Ole, The

6583
YOLTZ, Gretel*
Girl in Every Port, A (Dutch girl)
Hot Heels

6584
YORK, Powell*
Disraeli (Flookes)
Stage:
Wall Street (Peter Breckenridge) 27

6585
YORKE, Edith (1872-)
Belle of Broadway
Below the Line
Below the Surface
Born to the West
Capital Punishment (condemned boy's
mother)
Chickens
Daughter of Luxury, A
Don't Marry for Money
Excuse Me
False Road, The
Fourth Musketeer, The
Fugitives
Happiness
Heart of a Coward, The
His New York Wife
Homespun Folks
Husbands and Lovers
Lying Lips
Making the Varsity
Merry-Go Round, The (Ursala Urban)
My Man
Oh, What a Nurse!
One Clear Call
Passing Through
Phantom of the Opera, The (Mama
Valerius)
Port of Missing Girls
Red Dice
Rustlers Ranch
Satan and the Woman
Sensation Seekers
Seven Keys to Baldpate
Silent Sanderson
Slippy McGee
Souls for Sale (Mrs. Steddon)
Step on It
Timid Terror
Valiant, The
Wild Horse Mesa

6586
YORKE, Oswald*
Monsieur Beaucaire (Miropax)
Stage:
Happy-Go-Lucky (Lucius Welwyn) 20

Sophie (the Abbee de Voisenon) 20
Talking Parrot, The (Felix Barlow)
    23

6587
YOSHIWARA, Tomaki*
Letter, The

6588
YOUNG, Art*
Alaskan Adventures

6589
YOUNG, Chow*
Tale of Two Worlds, A (slave girl)

6590
YOUNG, Clara Kimball (1890-1960)
Charge It
Cordelia the Magnificent
Enter Madame
For the Soul of Rafael
Forbidden Woman, The
Hush Money
Lying Wives
Metro player 21; 24
Mid-Channel
My Official Wife
Straight from Paris
What No Man Knows
Wife's Romance, A
Woman of Bronze, The
Young Diana, The

6591
YOUNG, John Royal (1915-)
Sheik, The (extra)

6592
YOUNG, Joseph*
Spanking Breezes

6593
YOUNG, Loretta (Gretchen Michaela
    Young) (1913-)
Careless Age, The (Muriel
Devil to Pay, The
Fast Life, The (Patricia Mason)
Forward Pass, The (Patricia Car-
    lyle)
Girl in the Glass Cage, The (Gladys
    Cosgrove)
Head Man, The (Carol Watts)
Laugh, Clown, Laugh (Simonette)
Loose Ankles (bit)
MGM player 27
Magnificent Flirt (Denise Laverne)
Naughty but Nice (bit)

Scarlet Seas (Margaret Barbour)
Sheik, The (debut as extra)
Show of Shows, The
Squall, The (Irma)
Whip Woman (bit)

6594
YOUNG, Ming*
Toll of the Sea, The

6595
YOUNG, Noah*
Battling Orioles, The
Before the Public
Do Detectives Think?
Dumb-Bell, The
For Heaven's Sake
Kill or Cure
Looking for Sally
Safety Last (the Law)
Sharp Shooters
Sugar Daddies
Welcome Danger

6596
YOUNG, Polly Ann (1908-)
Bellamy Trial, The
Masks of the Devil
Rich People (Sally Vanderwater)
Sheik, The (extra)
Tanned Legs

6597
YOUNG, Roland (1887-1953)
Bishop Murder Case, The
Grit (Houdini Hart)
Her Private Life
Sherlock Holmes /aka/ Moriarty
    (debut as Dr. Watson)
Unholy Night, The (Lord Montague)
Stage:
Anything Might Happen (Richard
    Keating) 23
Devil's Disciple, The (General Bur-
    goyne) 23
49ers, The (a principal) 22
Hedda Gabler (Judge Brack) 24
Madame Pierre (Pierre Cottrel) 22
Queen's Husband, The (King Eric
    VIII)
Rollo's Wild Oat (Rollo Webster) 20
Scrambled Wives (John Chiverick) 20
Tale of the Wolf, The (Dr. Eugene
    Kelemen) 25

6598
YOUNG, Silvia*
This Freedom

6599
YOUNG, Tammany (-1935)
Bits of Life
Imp, The
John Smith
New Toys
Our Gray Brothers
Rainbow
Right Way, The
Roadhouse Nights
Seventh Day, The
Till We Meet Again
When the Desert Calls
White Monkey, The
Stage:
Front Page, The (Schwartz) 28
Lulu Belle (Shorty Noyes) 26
Spring 3100 ("Spark") 28
Wasp, The (Gaynor) 23
White Lights (Teddy Harlow) 27

6600
YOUNG, Tex*
Virginian, The (Shorty)
Water Hole, The

6601
YOUREE, Charles*
Thief in Paradise, A

6602
YOWLACHE, Chief*
Red Raiders, The
Scarlet Letter, The (Indian)
Tiger Rose

6603
YURTSEV, Boris*
Stachka /aka/ Strike

6604
YVES, Christiane*
Slightly Scarlet
They Had to See Paris (Fleurie)

6605
YVONNECK*
Un Chapeau de Paille d'Italie [The
  Italian Straw Hat]

6506
YZARDUY, Mme. /aka/ Mme. De
  Yzarduy*
Michael Strogoff

- Z -

6607
ZAMISSI, Lucia*
Messalina

6608
ZANGRILLI, O.*
Greatest Love of All, The

6609
ZANN, Nancy*
Sea Hawk, The

6610
ZANY, King*
Garden of Weeds, The

6611
ZARANA, Zalla*
Merry Widow, The (Frenchie Chris-
  tine)

6612
ZELLIF, Seymour*
Uncle Tom's Cabin ("Skipper" Mr.
  Harris)

6613
ZEMINA, Valentina--see: Valentina
  Zimina

6614
ZEMTZOVA, Anna*
Mother

6615
ZESSARSKAYA, Emma*
Her Way of Love

6616
ZHILLINSKY, A.*
In Old Siberia

6617
ZHUKOV, A.*
Her Way of Love

6618
ZIBOLD, Carlos*
Royal Box, The

6619
ZIEGER, Bruno*
Midsummer Night's Dream, A (Milon)

6620
ZIENER, Bruno*
Die Frau Nach der Man Sich Selnt
    [The Woman One Longs For]
    (Philipp)
Gefahren der Brautzeit [Dangers of
    the Engagement Period] /aka/
    Aus dem Tagebuch eines Verftlh-
    rers; Eine Nacht der Liebe;
    Liebesnächte [Nights of Love];
    Liebesbriefe

6621
ZIER, Jerry*
Dynamite (a good mixer)

6622
ZILZER, Wolfgang*
Mata Hari: The Red Dancer
Primanerliebe
Shadows of Fear

6623
ZIMBO (Dog)
Man Who Laughs, The

6624
ZIMINA, Valentina*
La Boheme (Phemie)
Scarlet Lady, The
Son of His Father, A
Woman on Trial, The

6625
ZIMMER, Toni*
Monna Vanna

INDEX

This index covers films referred to in the first section. Research for The Flaming Years uncovered many deficiencies in titles such as article omissions, inconsistencies of articles, and word and name misspellings and/or omissions.

Dates following titles refer to either release or production dates. A great many inconsistencies also exist in this area of reference. Wherever reliable, release date is given in preference to production date. Films bearing identical titles are listed according to date. Following the date is the production and/or releasing company. Numbers after company refer to players in the first section, enabling the researcher to locate players in a specific film. In as many instances as possible, complete casts may be determined. Where obtainable, chapter titles of serials are listed under the film.

This volume covers the period 1920-1929, although it may be that some of the films listed were produced in 1919 or 1929 and not released until 1920 or 1930; however, the date used is the one this author found most reliable. Therefore, should you not find a film you feel, or know, was produced in 1919, check Volume I. Should a film you know to have been released in 1929 not be listed here, please check Volume III.

British and other foreign films are included either because of their importance to the industry or because the player later became an American artist.

To use this index simply look up the film title, then refer to the numbers for cast list:

Our Dancing Daughters 1928 (Cos/MGM) 149, 612, 1206, 1238, 1407, 2283, 2482, 2928, 3298, 3445, 4531, 4650, 4910, 5425, 6456

Produced by Cosmopolitan, released by Metro Goldwyn Mayer

149-Nils Asther	Norman
612-Johnny Mack Brown	Ben Black
1206-Joan Crawford	Diana
1238-Dorothy Cummings	Diana's Mother
1407-Sam DeGrasse	Freddie's Father
2283-Huntley Gordon	Diana's Father
2482-Evelyn Hall	Freddie's Mother
2928-Lelia Hyams	
3298-Lydia Knott	
3445-Rod LaRocque	
4531-Edward Nugent	Freddie
4560-Anita Page	Anne
4910-Eddie Quillan	
5425-Dorothy Sebastian	Beatrice
6456-Kathlyn Williams	Anne's Mother

It is understandably impossible to list every film made from 1920 to 1929 and the roles portrayed by the players. The author will appreciate corrections and/or additions for a revised edition. Write care of publisher.

PRODUCTION AND RELEASING COMPANY ABBREVIATIONS

AE	Associated Exhibitors
AP	Associated Producers
Art	Artcraft
BIP	British International Pictures
Br	British - Company unknown
Bw	Broadwest
CFC	Capital Film Co.
Ch	Chadwick
Col	Columbia Pictures
Cos	Cosmopolitan
CTC	Coronet Talking Comedy
D	Davis Distribution Division
DB	David Belasco Productions
EFA	Europäische Film Allianz
F	Douglas Fairbanks Productions
FA	Fine Arts
FBO	Film Booking Office of America
FdA	Film d'Art
FFE	Federated Film Exchange
FN	First National
FPL	Famous Players Lasky
Fr	French - Company unknown
G	Samuel Goldwyn
Ga	Gainsborough
GB	Gaumont British
Gr	German - Company unknown
H	Hodkinson
HB	Hugo Ballin Productions
Hep	Hepworth
IP	Inspiration Pictures
It	Italian - Company unknown
K	Kleine
Kal	Kalem
Key	Keystone
Las	Lasky
LFC	London Film Co.
L-KO	Lehrman-Knock Out
M	Metro
MG	Metro-Goldwyn
MGM	Metro-Goldwyn-Mayer
Mon	Monogram
Mu	Mutual
P	Pathé
Par	Paramount Pictures
PDC	Producer's Distributing Co.
PFC	Pioneer Film Corp.
Pic	Mary Pickford Productions
Pre	Preferred

R	Hal Roach
RC	Robertson-Cole
RDC	Republic Distributing Co.
Rep	Republic Pictures
RKO	Radio and RKO
S	Selznick
Sen	Sennett
So	Société Général de Films
Sv	Svenska
T	Tiffany
Th	Thanhouser
Tri	Triangle
UA	United Artists
Un	Universal
V	Vitagraph
Wa	Wardour
WB	Warner Brothers and Warner
Wo	World
WP	Welsh-Pearson

Black Butterflies 28 ( ) 315, 688, 2054, 2497, 3514, 4755, 4942

Black Cargo of the South Seas 29 ( ) 673, 3648, 5145

Black Circle, The 20 ( ) 2471

Black Cyclone 25 (R) 1041, 2044, 3239, 3370, 5059, 6453

Black Diamond Express, The 27 (WB) 434, 3795, 4380, 5687

Black Feather 28 ( ) 1150, 1861, 2003, 4539, 4952

Black Gate, The 20 ( ) 988, 5446, 6450

Black Hills 29 ( ) 876

Black Husar, The 29 ( ) 6150

Black Is White 20 ( ) 1222, 2714

Black Jack 27 ( ) 3067

Black Lightning 24 (Gotham) 171, 508, 706, 1898, 2790, 4062, 4791, 4887, 5957

Black Magic 29 ( ) 1665, 1891, 2025, 3076, 3579, 3607, 6278, 6321

Black Oxen 24 (FN) 157, 508, 1080, 2120, 2175, 2398, 2433, 2470, 3497, 3556, 3795, 4111, 4158, 4459, 4549, 5097, 5446, 5686, 5875, 6462

Black Panther's Cub, The 21 ( ) 2025, 4865, 5002, 6031

Black Paradise 26 ( ) 311, 1897, 3067, 3684

Black Pearl, The 28 ( ) 2068, 2414, 3514, 5734

Black Pirate, The 26 (F/UA) 289, 305, 1214, 1407, 1588, 1844, 4803, 4814, 4954, 4971, 5710, 6257

Black Roses 21 ( ) 2650, 5687, 6386

Black Shadows 20 ( ) 2929

Black Sheep, A 21 ( ) 2565, 3583

Black Spider, The 20 (Br) 666, 947, 1046, 2652, 3364, 3615

Black Swan, The 24 (WB) 434, 867, 3582, 3875, 4194, 4698, 4881, 4957, 5855, 6309

Black Tears 27 ( ) 2836, 6319

Black Watch, The 29 (Fox) 866, 1294, 1989, 2556, 3098, 3244, 3577, 3648, 3690, 3870, 5191, 5630, 5999, 6017

Black Waters 29 (World Wide) 90, 563, 1101, 2512, 3050, 3274, 3632, 5018

Blackbird, The 26 (MGM) 22, 28, 519, 879, 3623, 3882, 4111, 4278, 6400

Blackbirds 20 ( ) 2185, 2497, 3062, 5526

Blackguard 26 ( ) 4524

Blackie's Redemption 28 ( ) 1631

Blackmail 20 ( ) 1276, 3188, 3298

Blackmail 29 (BIP) (First British Talkie) 81, 101, 215, 245, 393, 518, 702, 737, 2777, 3070, 3649, 4253, 4599, 4696, 5130

Blacksmith, The 22 (Fn) 2023, 3155, 5845

Blake of Scotland Yard--serial 27 (Un) 1241, 2386, 5719

Blanky 23 ( ) 2065

Blarney 26 ( ) 28, 2349

Blasted Hopes 24 ( ) 1009

Blaze Away 22 (Herbst) 6453

Blaze o' Glory 29 ( ) 1057, 1077, 1308, 1334, 1593, 5290, 5400, 6278

Blazing Arrows 22 (Doubleday) 1243, 4118, 4601

Blazing Away 21 ( ) 3948

Blazing Barriers 23 ( ) 2696, 5471

Blazing Days 26 (Un) 2276, 2379

Blazing Trail, The 21 ( ) 4113, 4787, 5077

Bleak House 20 ( ) 1037

Le Bled 29 (Fr) 4254

Bleeders, The 20 ( ) 2490

Blessed Miracle, A 20 ( ) 975

Blighty 27 (Br) 2491, 5535, 5900, 5923, 6498

Blind Alleys 27 ( ) 560, 871, 4124, 4198, 4495

Blind Bargain, The 22 (G) 440, 879, 2730, 3450, 3638, 3857, 3918

Blind Chance 20 ( ) 4562

Blind Goddess, The 26 (Par) 970, 1070, 1200, 1606, 2824, 3411, 4587, 4722, 4940, 6000, 6047

Blind Hearts 21 (FN) 311, 498, 3857

Blind Love 20 ( ) 1155

Blind Wives 21 (Fox) 3776, 5862

Blind Youth 20 ( ) 2840, 5820, 5886

Blindfolded 28 ( ) 1001, 1891, 2025 2827, 3209, 4290, 4547, 5590

Blinkeyes 27 (WP) 34, 201, 821, 1506, 1586, 2148, 5416, 5467, 5672, 6215, 6414

Blinky 23 (Un) 2200, 3017

Blizzard, The 21 (V) 160, 2553

Block Signal, The 26 ( ) 141, 3578

Blockade 28 ( ) 521, 3781, 3789, 3815, 4493, 6007

Bloggie's Vacation 20 (Sen) 6064

Blonde for a Night 28 ( ) 231, 1990, 3613, 4670, 4881

5452, 5833, 6209, 6284, 6323
Du Barry, Woman of Passion 28
( ) 2995
Duchess of Buffalo, The 26 (FN)
783, 1063, 1382, 1533, 2048,
2342, 4048, 5843
Duck Hunter, The 22 (Sen) 363
Duck In ( ) 2512
Duck Soup 27 (R/P) 2553, 3458
Ducks and Drakes 20 ( ) 499, 1282,
2824, 3190, 4048
Dude Cowboy, The 26 ( ) 1256
Dude Ranch, The 29 (FBO) 4239
Duds 20 ( ) 921
Dugan of the Dugout 28 ( ) 2771,
3814
Duke of Chimney Butte 21 ( ) 5429,
5740
Duke Steps Out, The 29 (MGM)
1142, 1206, 1279, 1328, 2467,
2569, 2825, 3510, 4157, 4531,
4891, 5205
Duke's Son, The 20 (Br) 1639, 4148,
4476
Dulcy 23 (FN) 343, 1127, 1327, 1810,
2220, 2593, 3603, 4362, 4830,
5843
Dumb-Bell, The 22 (R) 4354, 4838,
6595
Dumb Daddies 28 ( ) 1333, 4568,
5080
Dumb Waiter, A 29 ( ) 1457, 5904
Dummies 28 (Ch/Educational) 5450
Dummy, The 29 (Par) 339, 906,
1221, 1307, 3310, 3993, 4536,
4661, 4820, 6047
Dummy Love 26 ( ) 6161
Durand of the Badlands 25 (Fox) 395,
1132, 1142, 1473, 1866, 3037,
3067, 3555, 3640, 4496, 6230
Dürfen wir Schweigen? 26 (Gr) 3330,
6150
Dusk to Dawn 22 ( ) 4362, 6171
Dust 20 ( ) 2112
Dust Flower, The 22 ( ) 867, 2220,
4734, 5047
Dust of Desire see The Song of
Love
Duty's Reward 27 ( ) 1882, 4523,
5212
Dwelling Place of Light 21 ( ) 21,
189, 1384, 2730, 3298, 3862
Dynamite 29 (MGM) 370, 592, 684,
1179, 1589, 1731, 1746, 1862,
1886, 1897, 2146, 2287, 2466,
2512, 2709, 2771, 2794, 3045,
3157, 3318, 3446, 3549, 3640,
3759, 3771, 4418, 4433, 5408,
5415, 5733, 6279, 6621

Dynamite Allen 21 ( ) 2696, 4380,
6269
Dynamite Dan 24 (Sunset) 3137, 3787,
5075
Dynamite Doggie 25 ( ) 5301
Dynamite Smith 24 (P) 300, 3298,
3638, 3680, 4982
Dynamite Special, The 28 ( ) 2199

- E -

Eager Lips 27 ( ) 438, 2137, 2980,
5086
Eagle, The 25 (UA) 210, 1083, 1108,
1606, 1711, 3996, 4486, 6095,
6288
Eagle of the Night--serial 28 ( )
1150, 4160, 5820
Eagle of the Sea, The 26 (Par) 343,
1139, 2954, 3137, 3577, 3579,
3996, 4587, 5037, 6171
Eagle's Feather, The 23 (M) 51,
1243, 1841, 3274
Eagles of the Fleet 28 ( ) 3140
Eagle's Talons, The--serial 23 (Un)
2232, 3612, 5936
Eagle's Talons, The--serial 28 ( )
1309, 6070
Early Bird, The 25 ( ) 2775
Early to Bed 28 (R/MGM) 2553,
3458
Early to Wed 26 ( ) 2850, 4275,
4820
Earth Woman 26 ( ) 51, 470, 6249
Earthbound 20 ( ) 703, 921, 2033,
2513, 3556, 4889, 5053, 5669
East Is West 22 (FN) 236, 673,
2490, 4579, 5843
East Is West 29 ( ) 1985, 2733,
3319, 3321, 5157
East Is Worst 22 ( ) 2705
East Lynn 21 (H) 1712
East Lynne 22 (HB) 205, 1012, 5201,
5444
East Lynne 26 (Fox) 329, 1351,
1897, 2665, 3165, 3298, 3684,
4034, 4084, 4111, 4671, 5254,
5466, 5886
East Lynne with Variations 20 ( )
1062
East of Broadway 24 ( ) 799, 1421,
2392, 3578, 3781, 4278, 4486
East of Suez 25 (Par) 299, 739,
1894, 3120, 3684, 4447, 4965,
5013, 5624, 6497
East Side Sadie 29 ( ) 2495

- **F** -

Gigolette 20 ( ) 1466

Gigolo 26 (PDC) 866, 1606, 3445, 4486, 4942

Gilded Butterfly, The 26 ( ) 2283, 3165, 3582, 3740, 4978, 5254

Gilded Dream, A 20 ( ) 2957, 4407

Gilded Highway, The 26 (WB) 116, 1493, 2593, 3579, 3690, 6057

Gilded Lies 21 ( ) 3983, 4546

Gilded Lily, The 21 (Robert Leonard Prod) 2185, 4396, 4628, 5138, 5504

Gimme 23 ( ) 439, 867, 2235, 3556, 6278

Gingham Girl 27 ( ) 140, 467, 2039, 2096, 6486

Ginsberg the Great 28 (WB) 152, 2186, 3025

Girl and the Goose, The 20 ( ) 3968

Girl Crazy 29 (Sen) 327, 1001, 1457, 2766

Girl from Chicago, The 27 (WB) 3690, 4418, 4533, 4671, 5276

Girl from Coney Island see Just Another Blonde

Girl from Everywhere, The 27 (Sen/P) 185, 1861, 1919, 3640, 4836, 5814

Girl from Frisco, The ( ) 5305

Girl from Gay Paree, The 27 ( ) 293, 438, 3617, 3819, 5504, 6415

Girl from God's Country, The 21 ( ) 2957, 3529, 5516

Girl from Havana, The 29 ( ) 605, 890, 2232, 2932, 3415, 3656, 4287, 4654, 5431, 5947, 6493

Girl from Montmartre, The 26 (FN) 739, 767, 1055, 1781, 1817, 3388, 3836, 4734, 5745

Girl from Nowhere, The 21 ( ) 3916

Girl from Nowhere, The 28 (Sen/P) 1861, 1919, 2283, 2517, 2807, 3640, 5814

Girl from Porcupine, The 22 ( ) 3550

Girl from Rio, The 27 (Gotham) 2586, 4407, 4804, 6047

Girl from Rocky Point, The 22 ( ) 760

Girl from Woolworths, The 29 (FN) 788, 1327, 1422, 1978, 2476, 2981, 4285, 4539, 4613, 6412

Girl He Didn't Buy, The 28 ( ) 160, 2137

Girl He Left Behind, The 20 ( ) 3050

Girl I Loved, The 23 (UA) 888, 1167, 3539, 4009, 4203, 4830, 4982

Girl in Bohemia 20 ( ) 2929

Girl in Every Port, A 28 (Fox) 132, 595, 831, 838, 1444, 3094, 3106, 3263, 3596, 3684, 3781, 3820, 4074, 4313, 4952, 6100, 6583

Girl in His Room 22 ( ) 272, 730, 5640

Girl in London, A 25 (Br) 2909

Girl in Number 29, The 20 ( ) 1841, 2772, 4257

Girl in the Glass Cage, The 29 (FN) 362, 980, 1034, 2286, 2466, 2467, 3578, 3613, 4533, 5445, 5742, 6593

Girl in the Limousine, The 24 (Ch/FN) 2553, 5450

Girl in the Rain, The 20 (Par) 1127, 1862

Girl in the Show, A 29 ( ) 280, 779, 1568, 2454, 3243, 3680, 4531, 5525, 5705, 6242

Girl in the Taxi, The 22 (FN) 189, 1411, 1412, 2565

Girl in the Web, The 20 ( ) 236, 5818

Girl in 29, The 20 ( ) 4113 see also The Girl in Number 29

Girl Named Mary, A 20 ( ) 961, 6456

Girl o' My Heart 20 ( ) 3857, 4066, 4084

Girl of Gold 23 (FN) 2065, 4883, 5846

Girl of London, A 25 (Br) 5822

Girl of the Golden West 29 ( ) 2232, 2549, 2850, 5738

Girl of the Golden West, The 23 (FN) 548, 763, 2536, 3226, 3701, 3797, 3825, 5560, 5915

Girl of the South 25 ( ) 1390

Girl on the Barge, The 29 (Un) 2733, 3184, 3819, 3830, 4572, 4603, 5059, 5153, 6392

Girl on the Pullman, The 27 ( ) 1990, 3821, 4408, 4670, 4881, 6242

Girl Overboard 29 ( ) 51, 552, 2565, 3781

Girl Shy 24 (R/P) 1284, 2395, 3625, 4942

Girl Shy Cowboy 28 ( ) 310, 4120, 4470

Girl Troubles 29 ( ) 2336

Girl Who Came Back, The 28 ( ) 3795, 3819, 4203, 4820, 5640

Girl Who Dared, The 20 ( ) 2237

Girl Who Knew All About Men, The
21 ( ) 189
Girl Who Ran Wild, The 21 ( )
1594, 6280
Girl Who Wouldn't Work, The 25
(Schulberg) 250
Girl with the Hatbox, The 27 (Russian) 5696
Girl with the Jazz Heart, The 21
( ) 3201
Girl's Decision, A 21 ( ) 2199,
2730
Girl's Desire, A 22 ( ) 272, 730
Girl's Diary, A 26 ( ) 728
Girls Gone Wild 29 ( ) 362, 552,
786, 1294, 1309, 1897, 1911,
2556, 2836, 3888, 4437, 5276,
5779
Girls Who Dare 29 ( ) 470, 3490,
5915, 6476
Give and Take 28 (Un) 1226, 2554,
2733, 3571, 3732, 3930, 5537
Give Me My Son 22 ( ) 634
Glad Eye, The 27 (Br) 582, 3649,
4856, 5777
Glad Rag Doll 29 (WB) 283, 343,
1147, 1910, 2092, 2185, 2186,
2220, 2288, 2331, 2349, 3204,
4289, 4957, 5097, 5866
Glad Rags 21 ( ) 2115, 4257
Glamis Castle 26 (Br) 1787
Glass Houses 22 ( ) 1276, 1623
Glean O'Dawn 22 (Fox) 293, 1862,
2212, 2314, 2897
Glenister of the Royal Mounted 26
( ) 1972, 1977
Glimpses of the Moon 23 (Par) 1150,
1282, 1463, 2185, 4421
Glorifying the American Girl 29
(Par) 661, 756, 1193, 1723, 1747,
2666, 4304, 5038, 5488, 6102,
6356
Glorious Adventure, The (Britain's
first color film) 22 (Stuart Blackton) 297, 995, 1204, 1332, 1361,
1391, 2672, 2741, 2901, 3431,
3477, 3494, 3710, 3870, 3976,
4716, 5709, 5788, 6556, 6557
Glorious Betsy 28 (WB) 438, 1147,
1471, 3776, 4190, 4418, 4671,
4974, 5446, 6148
Glorious Fool, The 22 (G) 867, 1535,
2787, 3556, 3582, 6187
Glorious Lady, The 20 ( ) 5926
Glorious Trail, The 28 (FN) 520,
2459, 3758, 4108
Glory of Clementina, The 22 ( )
1606, 2061, 2667, 4048

Glory of Love, The 23 (Tourneur)
879, 2212, 3783, 3979
Die Glückliche Mutter (The Happy
Mother) (Home movie released as
a short) 25-28 (Gr) 1517
Go and Get It 20 (Nelian/FN) 175,
247, 299, 3648, 3930, 4257,
4596, 5508
Go as You Please 20 (R) 4838
Go Get 'em 20 ( ) 2112
Go Get 'em, Kid 28 ( ) 876
Go Get 'em Hutch--serial 22 ( )
977, 2459, 2923
Go Getter, The 23 ( ) 231, 1251,
3581, 4510, 4637
Go Straight 25 ( ) 799, 1731, 1882,
2889, 3017, 3529, 3781, 4113,
4278, 5077, 6242
Go West 25 (MGM) 607, 3155, 4171,
4409, 6038
Goat, The 21 (M) 3155
Gobs of Love 28 ( ) 5685
God Gave Me Twenty Cents 26 (Par)
1038, 1460, 4290, 4362, 5981
God in the Garden, The 21 (Br)
4856
Godless Girl, The 28 (P) 55, 248,
259, 299, 684, 1680, 1699, 1886,
2954, 2955, 3676, 4881, 4883,
4907, 4910, 5019, 5335
Godless Men 21 ( ) 319, 509, 867,
2033, 4062, 5076, 5560
God's Country and the Law 22 ( )
2351, 3550, 5994
God's Crucible 21 ( ) 3509
God's Desire, A 22 ( ) 5975
God's Gold 20 ( ) 2599
God's Great Wilderness 27 ( ) 337,
799, 5077, 5560
God's Prodigal 23 (Br) 88, 3494
Going Crooked 26 ( ) 1897, 3680,
6207
Going Some 20 (G) 1748, 1904, 1977,
2753, 3405, 3425, 3677, 5904
Going Straight 22 ( ) 4803
Going to Congress 24 ( ) 5182
Going Up 23 ( ) 499, 1101, 1351,
2402, 2890, 3425, 3547, 3781,
3841, 3880, 4380, 5701
Gold 28 ( ) 5, 5400
Gold and Grit 25 ( ) 5204
Gold and the Girls 25 ( ) 3067
Gold Braid 26 (MGM) 499, 2349,
3795, 4525, 4531, 4533, 4650
Gold Cure, The 25 (Br) 5923, 5928,
6448
Gold Digger of Weepah, The 27 (Sen)
363

Gold Diggers 24 (DB/WB) 199, 278, 616, 1127, 1887, 2033, 2221, 2525, 2593, 2871, 4871, 4897, 5076, 5223, 5427, 5522, 5669, 5961, 6364

Gold Diggers of Broadway 29 (WB) 199, 283, 1746, 1887, 2014, 2286, 2331, 3117, 3592, 3699, 4289, 4747, 5522, 5779, 5855, 5875

Gold Grabbers 22 ( ) 1867, 1989

Gold Hunters, The 25 ( ) 2917

Gold Madness 23 ( ) 4853

Gold Nut, The 27 (Sen) 363

Gold Rush, The 25 (UA) 346, 885, 2473, 4319, 4343, 4397, 5814, 6230, 6416

Gold Widows 28 ( ) 1457, 1990, 3232, 5066

Golden Bed, The 25 (Par) 272, 725, 970, 1731, 1886, 2955, 3333, 3445, 4005, 4575, 5066, 6077, 6278, 6369

Golden Bridle, The 29 ( ) 3814

Golden Cocoon, The 25 (WB) 751, 867, 2283, 3131, 3825, 5427, 6047, 6288

Golden Dawn, The 21 (Br) 6304

Golden Dreams 22 (G) 2733, 3528

Golden Dreams 28 ( ) 3642

Golden Gallows, The 22 ( ) 1669, 5640

Golden Gift, The 21 ( ) 509, 3382, 5820

Golden Girl, The 28 ( ) 3168

Golden Hope, The 21 ( ) 5305, 5747

Golden Princess, The 25 ( ) 585, 1594, 1894, 2515, 2642, 2954, 3197, 4005, 5382, 6471

Golden Shackles 28 ( ) 470, 4063, 6510

Golden Shower 20 ( ) 3550

Golden Snare, The 21 (FN) 300, 3796, 4825, 5046, 5745

Golden Stallion, The--serial 27 ( ) 1977, 3829, 3948, 5820

Golden Strain, The 25 ( ) 4747

Golden Trail, The 21 (Arrow) 2733, 4524

Golden Web, The 20 (Br) 5218

Golden Web, The 26 (Gotham) 2283, 3137, 5077

Golden Youth see Soul Fire

Golden Yukon 28 ( ) 5516

Der Goldene Schmetterling 26 (Gr) 149

Goldfish, The 24 (FN) 1064, 1069, 1769, 2104, 2733, 3556, 4111, 4362, 4698, 4820, 5843, 6368, 6415, 6462

Golem, The 20 ( ) 1891, 6349

Der Golem 20 (Gr) 1480, 4404, 5311, 5695

Golf 22 (V) 1457, 2289, 2553, 2638, 3399, 5450, 5932

Golf Widows 28 ( ) 4952

Golfers, The 29 (Sen) 1001, 2393, 2426, 2766, 4583, 5824

Gone to the Country 21 (R) 4838

Gonzague 23 (Fr) 918, 4299, 4877

Good and Naughty 26 (Par) 1669, 2819, 4282, 4354, 4447, 5091, 5705

Good as Gold 27 (Fox) 2065, 3067, 3508

Good Bad Girl, The 24 ( ) 153, 4493

Good-Bye Kiss, The 28 (Sen/FN) 319, 327, 663, 1001, 1756, 2175, 3194, 3466, 4539, 4661

Good Intentions 29 ( ) 3319

Good Medicine 29 (CTC) 333, 2841, 5885

Good Men and True 22 ( ) 299, 766, 4033

Good Morning, Judge 28 ( ) 1030, 1333, 1334, 1456, 2437, 2565, 4257, 4503, 5320, 5475, 6550

Good Provider 22 ( ) 268, 1038, 2293, 4620, 5165

Good References 22 (FN) 362, 1036, 1882, 3618, 3704, 5646, 5647, 5843, 6274

Good Time Charley 27 (WB) 63, 1091, 1148, 3059, 3682, 4579

Good Women 21 ( ) 358, 3125, 4234, 5915

Goodbye Broadway see The Shannons of Broadway

Goodbye Girls 23 ( ) 4407, 5276

Goodwin Sands 29 (Wa) 4191

Goose Hangs High, The 25 (Par) 332, 944, 1171, 1821, 2954, 3996, 4626, 4735, 4940, 5359, 5687

Goose Woman, The 25 (Un) 240, 332, 1109, 1606, 3776, 4486, 4801, 6207

Gorilla, The 27 (WB) 324, 1227, 1358, 2220, 2235, 2730, 3188, 4033, 4100, 4388, 4804, 4876

Gossip 23 ( ) 189, 6280

Governor's Lady, The 23 ( ) 2466

Gown Shop, The 23 (V) 5450

Grab That Ghost 20 (R) 4838

Grail, The 23 ( ) 327, 1866, 2451, 2665, 6242

Grain of Dust, A 28 ( ) 327, 1139, 2787, 4897, 5297, 6047, 6494

- H -

Habeas Corpus 28 (R/MGM) 772,
2553, 3458
Habit 21 ( ) 2586, 3245, 3815, 5904
Hail the Hero 24 ( ) 5847
Hail the Woman 22 (FN) 311, 944,
2884, 4033, 4048, 4142, 5150,
6171
Hair Trigger Baxter 26 ( ) 1256
Hair Trigger Burke 21 ( ) 766
Hairbreath Harry (FBO)
Hairpins 20 ( ) 333, 1064, 2730,
4275
Haldane of the Secret Service 23
( ) 2848, 3550
Hale and Hearty 22 (R) 4838
Half a Bride 29 (Par) 1108, 1568,
2112, 4587, 4940, 6530, 6550
Half a Chance 20 ( ) 1231, 2314,
2513, 3746, 5077
Half a Dollar Bill 24 ( ) 4493
Half a Man 25 (Standard Cinema/S)
3458, 4723
Half a Truth 22 (Br) 3955
Half an Hour 20 ( ) 1269, 3673,
5088
Half an Hour 29 ( ) 3632
Half-Breed, The 23 (FN) 99, 1371,
1409, 1468, 1594, 1833, 2210,
2613, 3361, 3413, 3621, 4101,
4539, 4891, 5441, 5734, 5938
Half Marriage 29 ( ) 416, 481,
1863, 2373, 2836, 4394, 6042,
6047
Half-Way Girl, The 25 (FN) 498,
2554, 2884, 3215, 4033
Half Way to Heaven 29 (Par) 112,
141, 184, 2066, 2760, 3713, 4587,
5176, 6306, 6388, 6389, 6459
Halfback Hannah 28 ( ) 1127, 1631,
2591
Hallelujah! 29 (MGM) 314, 1074,
1157, 1418, 1507, 1536, 2017,
2142, 2360, 2660, 3807, 3864,
5657, 5937
Hallroom Boys Comedies 20-21 (FFE)
24, 1061, 1746, 3767, 4251, 4496,
5613
Ham and Eggs at the Front 27 (WB)
1062, 1063, 1148, 2220, 3204,
3690, 4190, 6489
Hamlet 20 (Art-Film) 10, 540, 1078,
1483, 2974, 3105, 5728, 6212
Hamlet 21 (Asta) 4451
Han og Hun og Hamlet (He and She
and Hamlet) 22 (Palladium) 322,

1896, 2308, 3714, 3919, 4591,
5367, 5763, 5812
Hand Me Down, The 23 ( ) 5560
Handcuffed 29 (Rayart) 1850, 2976,
4539, 6386
Handcuffs and Kisses 21 (S) 892,
1046, 1781, 2286, 2517, 5578
Handle with Care 22 ( ) 4203, 4408
Hands Across the Border 26 ( )
1972, 5334, 5936
Hands of Nara, The 22 ( ) 358,
1500, 4084, 5687
Hands of Orlac, The 28 ( ) 817,
3330, 5634, 5758, 6150
Hands of the Strangler--serial 23
( ) 6418
Hands Off! 21 (Fox) 4239
Hands Off! 27 ( ) 2276
Hands Up! (Par) 382, 1119, 2065,
2402, 3050, 3682, 4496, 5814
Handsome Brute, The 26 ( ) 1119,
1847, 5533
Handy Andy 21 (Br) 6304
Handy Man, The 21 (Br) 1997
Handy Man, The 23 (Quality/M)
3458
Hangman's House 28 (Fox) 498, 662,
1045, 1992, 2025, 3211, 3870,
4111, 5736, 6336
Hank Mann Comedies ( ) 1457
Hansel and Gretel 22 ( ) 4262
Hanson Cabman, The 24 (Sen) 3424
Happiness 24 ( ) 866, 1504, 2342,
2836, 4221, 4596, 5667, 5862,
5863, 6585
Happiness Ahead 28 (FN) 888, 1774,
1775, 2850, 3684, 4271, 5445,
5855, 6550
Happy Days 29 (Fox) 272, 1448,
1808, 1822, 1871, 2157, 2269a,
2274a, 2286a, 2321a, 2499, 2505,
2531, 2534, 2557, 2685, 2688,
2800, 3025, 3096, 3136, 3154
3164, 3313, 3349, 3390, 3422,
3436, 3456, 3462, 3503, 3541,
3567, 3630, 3665, 3684, 3732,
3783, 3806, 3854, 3855, 3870,
3892, 3966, 4064, 4090, 4391,
4439, 4440, 4505, 4590, 4654,
4700, 4739, 4747, 5009, 5064,
5085, 5166, 5168, 5182, 5191,
5251, 5365, 5463, 5581, 5615,
5617, 5645, 5653, 5684, 5779,
5890, 6136, 6327, 6398, 6417,
6561
Happy Daze 28 ( ) 1652
Happy Ending, The 25 (Br) 245, 642,
1058, 2784, 2893, 3018

Headin for Danger 28 (RKO) 1901,
2002, 4135, 5075, 5689
Headin' Home 20 ( ) 581, 5277
Headin' Through 24 ( ) 3949
Headin' West--serial 22 ( ) 3670
Headin' Westward 29 ( ) 1256,
3814
Headless Horseman, The 22 (H)
2700, 2980, 4143, 5182
Headlines 25 (AE) 1119, 1774, 3092,
3140, 3783, 3819, 4300, 4531,
4569
Heads Up 26 ( ) 5176
Heads Up, Charly! see Kopf Hoch,
Charly!
Heart Bandit, The 24 ( ) 1276, 5545
Heart Line 21 ( ) 54, 192, 3299
Heart of a Child, The 20 ( ) 636,
1622, 4442, 4855
Heart of a Clown 28 ( ) 308a, 1757,
1900
Heart of a Coward, The 26 ( ) 6585
Heart of a Follies Girl, The 28 (FN)
1588, 1665, 2586, 3211, 5446,
5504
Heart of a Fool, The 20 ( ) 1200
Heart of a Siren, The 25 (FN) 1301,
3388, 4300, 5073, 5875, 6341
Heart of a Texan, The 21 ( ) 2599,
2917
Heart of a Woman, The 21 ( ) 2470
Heart of Broadway 28 ( ) 31, 2137,
4539
Heart of Jennifer, The 21 ( ) 1353
Heart of Lincoln, The 21 ( ) 1989
Heart of Maryland, The 21 (V) 738,
1038, 3347, 3734, 5091, 5325,
5539, 6420, 6439
Heart of Maryland, The 28 (WB)
1147, 1148, 1989, 3690, 4533,
5138
Heart of New York, The 26 ( ) 2466
Heart of Salome, The 27 (Fox) 31,
1637, 2714, 3365, 3918, 4513,
4804, 5254
Heart of the North 21 (Quality) 3683,
5725
Heart of the Yukon 27 ( ) 751, 1127,
5560
Heart of Twenty, The 20 ( ) 2115,
4820
Heart Raider, The 23 (Par) 175, 665,
1159, 2513, 5108, 5263
Heart Specialist, The 22 (Realart)
4223, 4789
Heart Strings 20 ( ) 1869, 2171
Heart Thief, The 27 ( ) 1460, 1731,
1841, 2185, 3022, 5006, 5368

Heart to Heart 28 (FN) 153, 1887,
2391, 2884, 3613, 3857, 3975,
5981
Heart to Let, A 21 (Realart) 1526,
1990, 2591, 3062
Heart Trouble 24 (FN) 319, 888,
1046, 1355, 2988, 3424, 5843
Heartbalm 21 ( ) 2392
Heartbuster, The 24 (Fox) 4239
Hearts Aflame 22 (M) 2665, 3165,
4084, 4493, 5533, 5560, 6047
Hearts and Fists 26 ( ) 509, 1421
Hearts and Flowers 21 ( ) 1887,
2642, 5705
Hearts and Hoofs 28 ( ) 1308, 1901,
6070
Hearts and Masks 21 ( ) 3781,
5387
Hearts and Spangles 26 ( ) 1308,
2646
Hearts and Spurs 25 (Fox) 1335,
1760, 3067, 3397, 3640, 5141,
5273, 6530
Hearts and Trumps 20 ( ) 3237,
4257, 5901
Heart's Haven, The 22 (H) 2730,
2733, 3795
Hearts in Dixie 29 ( ) 379, 779,
1912, 2857, 2947, 2948, 2966,
4335, 4402, 4815, 5616, 5700,
6322, 6464
Hearts in Exile 29 (WB) 811, 1147,
1533, 1636, 1882, 2956, 3274,
5636, 5885, 5999, 6510
Hearts of Men 28 ( ) 2286, 2586,
3159, 3767, 4362, 5091
Hearts of Oak 24 ( ) 498, 1989,
5066, 5678, 5725, 6187
Hearts of the West ( ) 1009, 1847
Hearts of the Yukon 27 ( ) 509
Hearts Up 21 ( ) 766
Heartstrings 23 (Br) 3870
Heaven on Earth 27 ( ) 28, 2286,
3510, 4418
Hedda Gabler 24 ( ) 4451
Hedi 21 (Prizma) 1828
Heedless Moths 21 ( ) 2714, 2836,
5924
Heir to Genghis Khan, The 28 (Rus-
sian) 2949
Held by Law 27 ( ) 1421, 3578,
4971, 6249
Held by the Enemy 20 (Par) 175,
602, 1231, 2646, 2824, 5745
Held in Trust 20 ( ) 82, 2342, 3648
Held to Answer 23 (M) 560, 4772,
5297
Helen and Warren--series 20-24 ( )
1101

Ladies to Board 24 (Fox) 4239

Lady, The 25 (FN) 1685, 1958, 2019, 2318, 2450, 2720, 2877, 2916, 3623, 3648, 3757, 3776, 3789, 5427, 5846

Lady Be Good 28 (FN) 974, 1350, 1722, 1861, 1942, 2730, 3849, 4038, 4190, 4362

Lady Bird 27 ( ) 1057, 2232, 3579, 3819, 3964, 4190, 5746, 6415

Lady from Hell, The 26 ( ) 3578, 5725, 5818

Lady from Longacre, The 22 ( ) 1989, 5276, 5958

Lady from Paris, The /aka/ Das Schone Abenteuer) 24 (Gr) 210, 5017, 5910, 6301

Lady from the Sea, The 29 (Par) 4024, 4191

Lady Godiva 28 (Br) 3018

Lady in Ermine, The 27 (FN) 694, 1200, 2398, 2539, 3157

Lady in Furs, The 25 (Br) 3955

Lady in Love, A 20 ( ) 975, 1837, 1990, 2957

Lady in the Wilderness 26 (Fox) 673

Lady Hamilton 28 ( ) 6150

Lady Lies, The 29 (Par) 440, 617, 1027, 1375, 1399, 1538, 2129, 2920, 4748, 5263

Lady Noggs 20 (Br) 4308

Lady of Chance, A 28 (MG) 358, 612, 3510, 4156, 5490, 5504

Lady of Leisure, A 28 ( ) 4881

Lady of Quality, A 23 (Un) 2025, 5135, 5545, 6095, 6106, 6415

Lady of Shalott, The 25 ( ) 4883

Lady of the Harem 24 ( ) 343, 1038, 1887, 4495, 5624, 6000

Lady of the Lake, The 28 (Br) 2893, 4021

Lady of the Night 25 (MG) 515, 1206, 1810, 2092, 2313, 2613, 3819, 4343, 5490

Lady of the Pavements 29 (UA) 128, 199, 515, 1083, 1882, 2313, 4670, 6152

Lady of Victory 29 ( ) 175

Lady Owner, The 23 (Br) 2837, 3291, 6304

Lady Raffles--series 28 ( ) 450, 1612, 2771, 5855, 5862

Lady Robin Hood 25 (FBO) 560, 1781, 3137

Lady Rose's Daughter 20 ( ) 1092, 1903, 2714, 3673, 4859, 6325

Lady Violette 23 ( ) 3713

Lady Who Lied, The (FN) 763, 1535, 1712, 4421, 4585, 4940, 5184, 5745, 6494

Lady Windermere's Fan 25 (WB) 330, 1046, 1317, 1651, 3740, 3753, 4048, 5076

Lady's Tailor, A 21 ( ) 5705

Ladyfingers 21 ( ) 760, 3017, 3740

Lafayette, Where Are We? see Hello, Lafayette

Laffin' Fool 27 ( ) 4759

Lahoma 20 ( ) 499, 2968, 4759, 5560

La, La, Lucille 20 (Par) 1127, 3737, 4289

Lamp in the Desert 22 (Br) 140, 3018

Lamplighter, The 21 ( ) 3857, 4066

Land Beyond the Law 27 (FN) 1352, 4108, 5334

Land of Hope, The 21 ( ) 528, 5539

Land of Hope and Glory 27 (Br) 5664

Land of Jazz, The 21 ( ) 4752

Land of Missing Men ( ) 5689

Land of My Fathers 22 (Br) 5777

Land of Opportunity, The 20 ( ) 2942

Land of the Lawless, The 23 ( ) 2910

Land of the Silver Fox 28 (WB) 2928, 4190, 4533, 5120, 5334

Lane that Has No Turning Point, The 22 ( ) 751, 2513, 3333

Lariat Kid, The 28 (Un) 256, 337, 558, 1009, 1989, 2200, 4619, 4705, 5075

Lash of the Czar, The 29 ( ) 3145, 4170, 4780, 5696, 5870

Last Adventure of Sherlock Holmes, The--series 23 (Br) 4518

Last Chance 22 (Canyon) 1867, 4705

Last Command, The 28 (FPL/Par) 560, 2995, 3310, 4863, 4993, 5348, 5448, 5639, 6178

Last Crusade, The 22 (Br) 3650

Last Days of Pompeii, The 26 (Societ Italiana Grandi Films) 443, 1120, 1430, 1681, 1820, 2195, 2257, 3323, 4013, 6134, 6179

Last Door, The 21 ( ) 4546

Last Edition 25 ( ) 199, 499, 2047, 2687, 3265, 3490, 3552, 3578, 4722, 5873, 6445

Last Flight, The 29 ( ) 1357, 1433

Last Frontier, The 26 ( ) 515, 578, 1022, 1421, 2873, 3783, 5768

Last Hour, The 23 ( ) 3648, 4407, 4596, 5545

Liebesnächte (Nights of Love) see
Gefahren der Brautzeit

Lt. Daring R. N. and the Water Rats
(Br) 4291

Life 20 ( ) 1729, 3612, 4421, 4880

Life and Death of 9413-A Hollywood
Extra 28 ( )

Life of an Actress, The 27 ( )
3579

Life of Beethoven, The 29 ( ) 2363,
3330, 5375

Life of Riley, The 27 (FN) 804,
1339, 2554, 4020, 4388, 5537,
5687, 6534

Life of the Party, The 20 ( ) 118,
704, 751, 1280, 1886, 2375, 3140

Life Sparks 20 ( ) 1594

Life's Crossroads 28 ( ) 1064, 2513,
2889

Life's Darn Funny 21 ( ) 1276,
2883

Life's Greatest Game 25 (FBO) 5334,
6249

Life's Greatest Question 22 ( )
3683, 5725

Life's Like That 28 ( ) 499, 6510

Life's Mockery 28 ( ) 1057, 1238,
2033, 2137, 2276, 5560, 6187

Life's Twist 20 ( ) 189, 237, 1623,
3815, 4755

Lifting Shadows 20 ( ) 2286

Light Fingers 29 ( ) 2185, 3174,
4533, 5056, 5097

Light in the Clearing, A 21 ( )
358, 529, 2450, 3528

Light in the Dark, The 22 (FN) 879,
1075, 1330, 2525, 3597, 4403,
4514, 6274

Light in the Window, A 27 ( ) 3159,
6278

Light of Asia, The 28 ( ) 1487,
1693, 3356, 4930, 6075

Light of the Western Stars, The 25
( ) 299, 327, 876, 1588, 2514,
2824, 4486, 4587, 4661, 4761,
5413, 5865

Light Showers 22 (R) 4838

Light that Failed, The 23 ( ) 1142,
1333, 2821, 2955, 3017, 3638,
3740, 4021, 4206, 4661, 5362,
5999, 6114

Light Woman, A 20 ( ) 1101, 1623,
1729

Light Woman, A 28 (Br) 88, 2893

Lighter that Failed, The 28 (R/
MGM) 2553

Lighthouse by the Sea, The 24 (WB)
362, 1038, 1887, 2186, 3930, 5120

Lightnin' 25 (Fox) 888, 975, 2054,
2565, 3783, 3789, 6017

Lightnin' 29 (Fox) 311, 751, 1142,
2905, 3225, 3732, 3771, 5138,
5182, 6246

Lightnin' Bull 26 ( ) 141

Lightnin' Shot, The 28 ( ) 3814

Lightnin' Wins 26 ( ) 1108

Lightning 27 ( ) 3617, 4942, 6453

Lightning Hutch--serial 26 ( )
3579, 4726, 5953

Lightning Justice 25 ( ) 1108

Lightning Lariats 27 ( ) 1308, 6070

Lightning Love 23 (V) 5450

Lightning Reporter 26 ( ) 548, 6249

Lightning Rider 24 ( ) 766

Lightning Shot 29 (Rayart) 5204

Lightning Speed 28 ( ) 5689

Lightning Warrior 29 (WB) 5120

Lights o' London, The 22 (Br) 3291

Lights of Home, The 20 (Br) 5777

Lights of New York 23 ( ) 2185,
3776, 5862

Lights of New York 28 (WB) 578,
799, 1148, 1424, 1451, 1636,
1774, 2715, 3405, 3823, 3901,
4539, 4661, 4750

Lights of Old Broadway 25 (Cos/MG)
140, 362, 652, 1251, 1336, 1482,
2245, 2286, 2579, 2754, 3482,
4250, 4418, 5216

Lights of the Desert 22 ( ) 4066

Lights Out 23 ( ) 3815, 5746, 6187

Lilac Sunbonnet, The 22 (Br) 4308,
6304

Lilac Time 28 (FN) 358, 907, 1108,
1109, 1526, 3383, 3821, 3829,
4269, 4271, 5744

Lilies of the Field 24 (FN) 327,
548, 576, 1956, 2185, 2398,
2642, 3209, 4388, 4774, 4961,
5687, 5875

Lilies of the Field 29 ( ) 343, 631,
692, 1986, 3446, 3632, 3633,
5640, 6530

Lilies of the Street 25 ( ) 6249

Lilly of Bloomsbury see Tilly of
Bloomsbury

Lilly of the Alley 23 (Br) 1743, 6413

Lily, The 26 ( ) 329, 4513, 5297,
6047

Lily of the Dust 24 (Par) 299, 1314,
2402, 3734, 4447

Limited Mail, The 25 (WB) 434,
2115, 2392, 2565, 2880, 3677,
5066, 5975

Limousine Love 28 ( ) 903, 3197,
4006, 4257, 5080

Mile a Minute Romeo 23 (Fox) 4239
Milestones 22 (G) 51, 319, 958,
1557, 1963, 2015, 2804, 2957,
3270, 4888, 5745
Milestones 28 (Br) 4429
Milk White Flag, A ( ) 2565
Milky Way, The 22 ( ) 697
Mill of the Gods 23 ( ) 5915
Million Bid, A 27 (WB) 438, 1147,
1444, 2186, 2281, 3819, 4579
Million Dollar Collar 29 (WB) 849,
1636, 2067, 3194, 3591, 3773,
5120
Million Dollar Handicap 26 ( ) 673,
1200, 3578, 5066
Million Dollar Mystery, The 27 ( )
3274, 3514
Million Dollar Reward--serial 20 ( )
6251
Million for Love, A 28 ( ) 799,
1665, 2870, 5335, 5533
Million in Jewels, A 22 ( ) 2812
Millionaire, The 21 ( ) 4978, 5077,
5135
Millionaire Baby, The 20 ( ) 4158
Millionaire Policeman, The 26 ( )
4523, 4978
Millionaires 26 (WB) 1887, 2293,
5537
Millions to Burn 23 ( ) 4978
Mills of the Gods 28 ( ) 1109
Mind over Matter 24 ( ) 2077, 2349
Mind Your Business 26 ( ) 1493
Mine to Keep 23 ( ) 6319
Mine with the Iron Door, The 24 ( )
2637, 6278
Minister's Wife, The 26 ( ) 4703
Minnie 22 (FN) 2402, 3091, 3726,
4275, 6489
Miracle Baby, The 23 ( ) 766
Miracle Girl, The 28 ( ) 1057,
4539
Miracle of Life, The 26 ( ) 688,
4021, 4421
Miracle of Manhattan, The 21 ( )
2517
Miracle of the Jungle 21 ( ) 1901
Miracle of the Wolves 25 (Fr) 349a,
1640, 2721, 3085, 3995, 4092,
4241, 5455
Mirage, The 20 (Br) 4476
Mirage, The 24 ( ) 587, 6171
Miriam Rozella 24 (Br) 4429, 6347
Mirror, The 23 ( ) 1846
Miser, The 23 ( ) 3613
Les Miserables 26 (European) 187,
769, 1291, 2102, 2428, 3081,
3932, 4216, 5164, 5186, 5252,
5295, 5296, 6005

Miser's Revenge, The 22 ( ) 519
Misfit Wife, The 20 ( ) 3382, 4048
Misfits and Matrimony 28 ( ) 1631
Misleading Lady 21 ( ) 866, 1155,
1251, 3740
Mismates 26 (FN) 82, 272, 3215,
3773, 4388, 5343
Miss Bluebeard 25 ( ) 381, 1282,
2054, 2402, 3123, 3917, 5559
Miss Brewster's Millions 26 ( )
272, 343, 344a, 1282, 5705
Miss Gingersnaps 20 ( ) 4617
Miss Hobbs 20 ( ) 1990, 2646,
3059
Miss Information 28 (WB) 2841,
5420, 6486
Miss Lulu Bett 21 (Par) 684, 1904,
2230, 2231, 2350, 4575, 5150,
5545, 6114, 6242, 6486 .
Miss Nobody 26 (FN) 1091, 3577,
4493, 4804
Miss 139 20 ( ) 4971
Missing Link, The 27 (WB) 887,
2748, 3209, 3823
Missing Man, The 28 ( ) 4076,
5091
Missing Millions 22 ( ) 528, 3673,
4859
Mississippi Gambler 29 (Un) 336,
2033, 2175, 2565, 5368, 6377
Mist in the Valley 23 (Br) 5860
Mistaken Orders 26 ( ) 2812
Mr. Antonio 29 (T) 358, 809, 2883,
5018, 5577, 6106
Mr. Barnes of New York 22 (G) 921,
2787, 3525, 4282, 4525
Mr. Billings Spends His Dime 23
( ) 684, 1882, 2753, 3638, 3862,
4587, 5820
Mr. Bingle 22 ( ) 116
Mr. Gilfil's Love Story 20 (Br) 4568
Mr. Justice Raffles 21 (Br) 88
Mr. Logan, U.S.A. 20 (Fox) 4239
Mr. Nobody 27 (Br) 3291
Mr. Oddy 22 (Br) 2909
Mr. Parol and Company 23 ( ) 3948
Mr. Potter of Texas 22 ( ) 116
Mr. Prim Passes By 21 (Br) 2929,
3195
Mr. Romeo 28 ( ) 814, 3507, 4120,
5705
Mr. Smith Wakes Up 29 (Br) 3400
Mr. Wu 21 ( ) 3420
Mr. Wu 27 (MGM) 28, 879, 1606,
1986, 2714, 3244, 3691, 4589,
6497, 6526
Mistletoe Bough, The 23 (Br) 3018,
3494, 5777

1623, 3677, 4033, 4338, 5862
Only a Shop Girl 27 ( ) 688
Only Me 29 ( ) 3416
Only Saps Work 29 ( ) 2343, 2954,
3188, 3474, 5086
Only the Brave 29 ( ) 1108, 1863,
4546
Only Thing, The 25 (MGM) 439, 534,
762, 767, 1069, 1206, 2092, 2249,
2644, 3575, 3582, 4224, 4418,
4722, 4827, 5597, 5646, 6070,
6288, 6568
Only 38 23 ( ) 31, 1127, 1500,
1882, 3529, 3753, 6486
Only Way, The 26 (FN) 599, 684,
824, 1087, 1107, 1849, 2370,
2612, 2615, 2936, 3004, 3876,
3884, 4931, 4993, 5672, 5778,
6347, 6414, 6576
Only Woman, The 24 (FN) 324, 338,
362, 739, 1339, 1521, 1542, 2490,
3900, 4546, 4595, 5846
Open All Night 24 (Par) 1276, 1977,
2313, 2402, 2705, 4137, 4901
Open Another Bottle 21 (R) 4838
Open Country 22 (Br) 3955
Open Range 27 (Par) 585, 878, 3310,
4587
Open Shutters 21 ( ) 5145, 5820
Open Switch, The--serial 26 ( )
2812, 4207, 4759, 5206, 6432,
6560
Open Trail, The 25 ( ) 2873
Opening Night 27 ( ) 509, 6494
Oppressed, The 29 ( ) 368, 4131,
5137, 5399, 6166
Opry House, The 29 (Disney) 4356
Oranges and Lemons 23 (R/P) 2341,
3458, 5244
Orchids and Ermine 27 (FN) 324,
327, 1350, 1958, 2554, 2836,
3510, 4271, 4362, 4883, 4897,
5202, 5621
Ordeal, The 22 ( ) 175, 684, 1623,
4380
Orderly, The 21 ( ) 6395
Orderly Room, The 28 (Br) 3675
Oregon Trail, The--serial 23 (Un)
14, 3670
Oriental Hugs 28 ( ) 5685
Orlac's Hände 24 ( ) 6150
Orphan, The 20 ( ) 1869, 3683
Orphan of the Sage 28 ( ) 256,
4705, 5075
Orphans of the Storm 21 (Griffith/
UA) 434, 628, 781, 1796, 1937,
2233, 2234, 2471, 2718, 3252,
3320, 3465, 3557, 3579, 3673,
4902, 5368, 6260, 6522

L'Orpheline 21 (Fr) 941, 1969, 3277
Oscillation 26 (Br) 4856
Oswald the Lucky Rabbit Cartoons
27-28 (Disney) 4624
Othello /aka/ The Moor 22 (Wörmer
Film) 1460, 1465, 2995, 3344,
3354, 3532, 3654, 5729, 6183,
6196
Other Men's Shoes 20 ( ) 3209
Other Men's Wives 26 ( ) 434,
4881
Other Side, The 22 ( ) 3726
Other Woman, The 21 ( ) 1064,
1594, 1729, 3509, 4524, 4883
Other Woman's Story, The 26 ( )
730, 2054, 2513, 5999, 6549
Other Women's Clothes 22 ( ) 205
Other Women's Husbands 26 (WB)
434, 2283, 2642, 4698, 4881
Our Blushing Brides 29 ( ) 2454
Our Congressman 24 ( ) 5182
Our Dancing Daughters 28 (Cos/MGM)
149, 612, 1206, 1238, 1407,
2283, 2482, 2928, 3298, 3445,
4531, 4650, 5910, 5425, 6456
Our Gang 22 (R) 4838
Our Gang Comedies (R) 1010, 1061,
1112, 1283, 1302, 1343, 1597,
1839, 3326, 4336, 4361, 4767,
5648
Our Gang Kids (R) 4632
Our Gray Brothers 20 ( ) 6599
Our Hospitality 23 (M) 522, 693,
889, 1044, 1177, 1632, 1643,
3155, 3156, 3643, 5148, 5844,
5845, 6290
Our Leading Citizens 22 ( ) 3204,
3613, 4124, 4575, 4587, 5150,
6486
Our Modern Daughter 27 ( ) 4380
Our Modern Maidens 29 (MGM) 475,
1206, 1564, 1665, 1843, 2331,
3445, 4531, 4532, 4650
Our Sea see Maré Nostrum
Out All Night 27 ( ) 1456, 1710,
2032, 2700, 4060, 4496
Out for Game 27 ( ) 3613
Out of Luck 23 (Par) 2200, 2233,
2349, 3017
Out of Place 22 ( ) 5301
Out of the Chorus 21 ( ) 528, 779,
2185, 5735
Out of the Darkness 21 ( ) 3766,
5386
Out of the Depths 21 ( ) 1009
Out of the Dust 20 ( ) 5560, 5693
Out of the Night 27 ( ) 4539
Out of the Past 27 ( ) 2586, 3098
Out of the Ruins 28 (FN) 253, 907,

- Q -

1069, 1119, 1669, 1688, 1765, 1769, 2210, 2733, 2836, 3723, 4137, 4418, 4698, 6287
Sinners' Paradise 29 ( ) 4006, 4357, 5056, 5446, 6134
Sins of Rosanne, The 20 ( ) 975, 2002, 3450, 3942, 4587
Sins of St. Anthony 20 ( ) 3652, 6319
Sins of the Father 28 (Par) 141, 362, 906, 1123, 1327, 2461, 2850, 2995, 3706, 4513, 4820, 5018, 5517
Sins of the World 20 ( ) 5097
Sins Ye Do, The 24 (Br) 5923, 6168
Sioux Blood 29 ( ) 519, 2054, 2165, 2379, 3769
Sir Lumberjack 26 ( ) 1977, 3204
Sir or Madame 28 (Br) 342, 2924, 4021
Sir Rupert's Wife 22 (Br) 587
Siren, The 28 ( ) 1325, 2787, 4282, 4897, 5056, 6031
Siren Call, The 22 ( ) 529, 1276, 3577, 4859
Siren of Seville, The 24 ( ) 362, 1372, 1436, 2004, 2819, 6534
Sister Against Sister 23 ( ) 4726
Sister to Salome 20 ( ) 578
Sisters 22 ( ) 3550, 4275, 4637
Sisters 29 ( ) 2241, 2349, 4564, 4603, 5138, 5734
Sisters of Eve 28 ( ) 438, 688, 1989, 2471, 3243, 5722
Sitting on the World 20 ( ) 358, 3059
6 1/2 x 11 29 ( ) see 16 1/2 x 11
Six Best Cellars, The 20 (Art/Par) 684, 1231, 1886, 2646, 3299, 6319
Six Best Fellows, The 28 ( ) 1093, 6142
Six Cylinder Love 23 (Fox) 990, 1761, 4119, 4235, 5588, 6040
Six Days 23 ( ) 2092, 2171, 2398, 3244, 4113, 5687
Six Fifty 23 ( ) 28
Six Fellows see Six Best Fellows, The
600,000 Francs Per Month 22 ( ) 3491
Six Shootin' Justice 21 ( ) 766
Six Shootin' Romance, A 26 ( ) 2873
Sixth Commandment, The 24 ( ) 6246
16 1/2 x 11 29 ( ) 1081, 2009, 4813

Sixty Cents an Hour 23 ( ) 1139, 1629, 2753, 3638, 4575, 6295
Skating Home 28 ( ) 3507
Skedaddle Gold 27 ( ) 6243
Skeleton Dance 29 (Disney) 5546
Skid Proof 23 (Fox) 3067, 5486
Skin Deep 22 (FN) 3981, 5545, 5569, 6171
Skin Deep 29 (WB) 434, 509, 751, 1057, 1331, 1358, 2490, 3501, 4033, 4761, 5742
Skin Game, The 22 (Granger) 43, 57, 225, 947, 1107, 1541, 2144, 2446, 2653, 2784, 3163, 4220, 5147
Skinner Steps Out 29 (Un) 3203, 3829, 4971, 6042, 6377, 6425
Skinner's Big Idea 28 (Un) 521, 1629, 4467, 4613, 4614, 5519, 5586, 5904, 6029, 6319, 6367
Skinners' Dress Suit 26 (Un) 239, 532, 1456, 2700, 2836, 3383, 3438, 4343, 4971, 5762, 5810
Skinners in Silk 25 (Sen) 363
Skipper's Scheme, The 21 ( )
Skirt Shy 29 (R/MGM) 1589, 2478, 3424, 5097, 6259
Skirts 28 ( ) 887
Skirts, The 21 ( ) 237, 2502, 3204, 3767, 4292
Sky Boy 29 (R/MGM) 1663, 3424, 5981
Sky Hawk, The 29 (Fox) 363, 870, 877, 1059, 1794, 2139, 2556, 4716, 4836
Sky High 22 (Fox) 645, 924, 3079, 3783, 3798, 4239, 4523, 6308
Sky High Corral 26 ( ) 14
Sky Pilot 21 (FN) 509, 697, 1132, 3271, 3779, 3780, 4271, 5979
Sky Pirate, The 26 ( ) 1422, 3579, 6319
Sky Ranger, The 29 ( ) 2870
Sky Rangers, The--serial 21 (P) 758, 1247, 5000, 5439a
Sky Rider, The 28 ( ) 2883, 3579
Sky Skidder 29 ( ) 2014
Skyfire 20 (Pinnacle) 2599
Skyrocket 26 (AE) 1022, 1025, 1526, 1685, 2377, 2476, 2889, 3095, 3964, 4257, 4278, 4953, 5855, 6450
Skyscraper 28 ( ) 515, 786, 2470, 6142
Skyscraper Symphony 28 ( )
Skyway Man, The 20 ( ) 3683
Slam Bang Jim 20 ( ) 5276
Slam the Law 20 ( ) 5276
Slander 21 ( ) 438

Souls for Sale 23 (MG) 148, 158,
439, 688, 1015, 1535, 1748,
2092, 2467, 2875, 2886, 2939,
3388, 3698, 4113, 4302, 4613,
4889, 5086, 5158, 5640, 5818,
6585
Sound Your A's 27 ( ) 2600
Sour Milk 28 ( ) 1652
Sous Les Toits de Paris (Under the
Roofs of Paris) 29 (Fr) 941,
2937, 4241, 4588, 4877
South of Panama 28 ( ) 2175, 3773,
5335
South of Suva 22 ( ) 509, 639,
3648, 4223, 5693
South of the Northern Lights 21
(Steiner) 1373, 2599
South Sea Bubble, A 28 (Br) 342,
2893, 2924, 4527, 5860
South Sea Love 23 ( ) 4066
South Sea Love 28 ( ) 594, 1217,
2223, 4203, 5533
South Sea Rose 29 (Fox) 154, 370,
905, 907, 2476, 3783, 3806,
3859, 4700, 4703, 4836, 6077,
6246
Southern Love 24 (Br) 438, 6304
Souvenir 28 ( ) 3098
Sowing and Reaping 20 ( ) 2276
Sowing the Wind 20 (FN) 3578, 4250,
4338, 4339, 5687, 5722, 5820
Spangles 26 (Un) 192, 578, 4496,
4596
Spaniard, The 25 (Par) 299, 1139
Spanish Dancer, The 23 (Par) 31,
300, 2327, 2883, 3267, 4137,
4298, 4447, 5517, 5710, 5717,
6456
Spanish Jade 22 ( ) 560, 1466,
3776
Spanish Love 25 ( ) 2313
Spanish Romeo, A 25 ( ) 2025
Spanking Breezes 26 (Sen/P) 1358,
2600, 2689, 2967, 6592
Sparrows /aka/ Human Sparrows 26
(UA) 348, 354, 707, 2514, 3037,
3038, 3053, 3066, 3467, 3565,
3759, 3873, 4202, 4221, 4569,
4576, 4803, 5175, 5359, 5361,
5725, 6207, 6425
Spawn of the Desert 23 (Arrow) 1847
Speak Easy, The 21 ( ) 2392
Speakeasy 29 (Fox) 294, 858, 1808,
2431, 2932, 3415, 3607, 3726,
3732, 4654, 6278, 6306
Special Delivery 22 (Fox) 5301
Special Delivery 27 (Par) 118, 756,
799, 1581, 3172, 3185, 4855,
4863, 4942

Speed--serial 22 ( ) 2923, 5301
Speed Classic 28 ( ) 1729, 2565,
2586, 3490, 3577, 5086
Speed Girl, The 21 ( ) 1282, 6187
Speed King, The 23 ( ) 5847
Speed Limit 26 ( ) 3857
Speed Mad 25 ( ) 1847, 5145
Speed Maniac, The 21 ( ) 5533
Speed Spook, The 24 ( ) 387, 552,
2775, 3673, 5091, 6392
Speed to Spare 20 (R) 4838
Speed Wild 25 ( ) 1977
Speeder, The 26 ( ) 2512
Speeding Through 26 ( ) 2471
Speeding Venus 26 ( ) 1372, 2054,
2092
Speedway 29 ( ) 358, 1279, 2467,
4190, 4292, 4650, 6000
Speedy 28 (Par) 324, 936, 3625,
6534
Speedy Spurs 26 ( ) 376
Spellbinder, The 28 (Fox) 320
Spenders, The 21 ( ) 21, 152, 1594,
3011, 5097, 6358
Spider, The 28 ( ) 3310
Spider and the Rose, The 23 ( )
751, 1594, 2235, 2565, 2665,
3382, 3862
Spider Web, The 26 ( ) 1150, 3382,
5508, 6358
Spieler, The 29 ( ) 28, 1091, 2470,
3310, 3453, 4309, 4914, 6313
Spies see Spione
Spiker and the Rose, The 23 ( ) 299
Spione (Spies) 28 (UFA) 1501, 1696,
1856, 2079, 2838, 3283, 4093,
4800, 4939, 4970, 5507
Spirit of Good, The 20 ( ) 6016
Spirit of the Lake 22 ( ) 3680
Spirit of the U.S.A. 24 ( ) 538,
799, 1114, 1898, 2386, 2831,
2849, 3268, 5734, 6249
Spirit of Youth, The 29 ( ) 1261,
2039, 3211, 5425, 5689
Spirits 29 (Br) 3675
Spite Marriage 29 ( ) 284b, 715,
1712, 2928, 3155, 5210, 5425
Splendid Crime, The 25 ( ) 1121,
1127, 1133, 1231, 1282, 2515,
3087, 3754, 6279
Splendid Hazard, A 20 (FN) 2005,
3011, 3228, 5915, 6278
Splendid Road, The 26 (FN) 250,
578, 1339, 1360, 1712, 1748,
2054, 2137, 2955, 3017, 3379,
3754, 4493, 5560
Splinters 29 (Br) 2863
Spliting the Breeze 27 ( ) 6070
Spoilers, The 23 (MG) 293, 299,

- V -

- W -